Study Guide

to accompany

KATHLEEN STASSEN BERGER

The Developing Person Through the Life Span

Third Edition

RICHARD O. STRAUB

University of Michigan, Dearborn

JOAN WINER BROWN

WORTH PUBLISHERS

Study Guide by Richard O. Straub and Joan Winer Brown
to accompany
Berger: **The Developing Person Through the Life Span,** Third Edition

Printed in the United States of America.

ISBN: 0–87901–680–9

Printing: 4 5 Year: 98 97 96

Cover: Maurice Prendergast, *Yacht Race* (detail), 1900, watercolor, 33.3 x 52.1 cm, Watson F. Blair Purchase Prize, 1932.175. © 1988 The Art Institute of Chicago

Worth Publishers
33 Irving Place
New York, New York 10003

Contents

Preface

This Study Guide is designed for use with *The Developing Person Through the Life Span*, Third Edition, by Kathleen Stassen Berger. It is intended to help you evaluate your understanding of the text material, and then to review any problem areas. "How to Manage Your Time Efficiently, Study More Effectively, and Think Critically" provides detailed instructions on how to use the textbook and this Study Guide for maximum benefit. It also offers additional study suggestions based on principles of time management, effective note-taking, evaluation of exam performance, and an effective program for improving your comprehension while studying from textbooks. Another useful feature of this essay is a critical thinking exercise that can help you to improve your ability to evaluate the arguments presented by the author and others, as well as to more effectively formulate your own.

Each chapter of the Study Guide includes a Chapter Overview, a set of Guided Study questions to pace your reading of the text chapter, a Chapter Review section to be completed after you have read the text chapter, and three review tests. The review tests are of two types: Progress Tests that consist of questions focusing on facts and definitions, and a Challenge Test that evaluates your understanding of the text chapter's broader conceptual material and its application to real-world situations. For all three review tests, the correct answers are given, followed by textbook page references (so you can easily go back and reread the material), and complete explanations not only of why the answer is correct but also of why the other choices are incorrect.

I would like to thank Joan Winer Brown for use of some of her excellent material from the first two editions of this Study Guide. Thanks, too, to Laura Rubin for keeping us all on schedule, and especially to Betty and Don Probert of The Special Projects Group for their exceptional work in all phases of this project.

Those at Worth Publishers who assisted in the preparation of this Study Guide join me in hoping that our work will help you to achieve your highest level of academic performance in this course and to acquire a keen appreciation of human development.

Richard O. Straub
May 1993

How to Manage Your Time Efficiently, Study More Effectively, and Think Critically

How effectively do you study? Good study habits make the job of being a college student much easier. Many students, who *could* succeed in college, fail or drop out because they have never learned to manage their time efficiently. Even the best students can usually benefit from an in-depth evaluation of their current study habits.

There are many ways to achieve academic success, of course, but your approach may not be the most effective or efficient. Are you sacrificing your social life or your physical or mental health in order to get A's on your exams? Good study habits result in better grades *and* more time for other activities.

Evaluate Your Current Study Habits

To improve your study habits, you must first have an accurate picture of how you currently spend your time. Begin by putting together a profile of your present living and studying habits. Answer the following questions by writing *yes* or *no* on each line.

______ **1.** Do you usually set up a schedule to budget your time for studying, recreation, and other activities?

______ **2.** Do you often put off studying until time pressures force you to cram?

______ **3.** Do other students seem to study less than you do, but get better grades?

______ **4.** Do you usually spend hours at a time studying one subject, rather than dividing that time between several subjects?

______ **5.** Do you often have trouble remembering what you have just read in a textbook?

______ **6.** Before reading a chapter in a textbook, do you skim through it and read the section headings?

______ **7.** Do you try to predict exam questions from your lecture notes and reading?

______ **8.** Do you usually attempt to paraphrase or summarize what you have just finished reading?

______ **9.** Do you find it difficult to concentrate very long when you study?

______ **10.** Do you often feel that you studied the wrong material for an exam?

Thousands of college students have participated in similar surveys. Students who are fully realizing their academic potential usually respond as follows: (1) yes, (2) no, (3) no, (4) no, (5) no, (6) yes, (7) yes, (8) yes, (9) no, (10) no.

Compare your responses to those of successful students. The greater the discrepancy, the more you could benefit from a program to improve your study habits. The questions are designed to identify areas of weakness. Once you have identified your weaknesses, you will be able to set specific goals for improvement and implement a program for reaching them.

Manage Your Time

Do you often feel frustrated because there isn't enough time to do all the things you must and want to do? Take heart. Even the most productive and successful people feel this way at times. But they establish priorities for their activities and they learn to budget time for each of them. There's much in the saying "If you want something done, ask a busy person to do it." A busy person knows how to get things done.

If you don't now have a system for budgeting your time, develop one. Not only will your academic accomplishments increase, but you will actually find more time in your schedule for other activities. And you won't have to feel guilty about "taking time off," because all your obligations will be covered.

Establish a Baseline

As a first step in preparing to budget your time, keep a diary for a few days to establish a summary, or baseline, of the time you spend in studying, socializing, working, and so on. If you are like many students, much of your "study" time is nonproductive; you may sit at your desk and leaf through a book, but the time is actually wasted. Or you may procrastinate. You are always getting ready to study, but you rarely do.

Besides revealing where you waste time, your diary will give you a realistic picture of how much time you need to allot for meals, commuting, and other fixed activities. In addition, careful records should indicate the times of the day when you are consistently most productive. A sample time-management diary is shown in Table 1.

Table 1 Sample Time-Management Diary

Monday		
Behavior	Time Completed	Duration Hours: Minutes
Sleep	7:00	7:30
Dressing	7:25	:25
Breakfast	7:45	:20
Commute	8:20	:35
Coffee	9:00	:40
French	10:00	1:00
Socialize	10:15	:15
Videogame	10:35	:20
Coffee	11:00	:25
Psychology	12:00	1:00
Lunch	12:25	:25
Study Lab	1:00	:35
Psych. Lab	4:00	3:00
Work	5:30	1:30
Commute	6:10	:40
Dinner	6:45	:35
TV	7:30	:45
Study Psych.	10:00	2:30
Socialize	11:30	1:30
Sleep		

Prepare a similar chart for each day of the week. When you finish an activity, note it on the chart and write down the time it was completed. Then determine its duration by subtracting the time the previous activity was finished from the newly entered time.

Plan the Term

Having established and evaluated your baseline, you are ready to devise a more efficient schedule. Buy a calendar that covers the entire school term and has ample space for each day. Using the course outlines provided by your instructors, enter the dates of all exams, term paper deadlines, and other important academic obligations. If you have any long-range personal plans (concerts, weekend trips, etc.), enter the dates on the calendar as well. Keep your calendar up to date and refer to it often. I recommend carrying it with you at all times.

Develop a Weekly Calendar

Now that you have a general picture of the school term, develop a weekly schedule that includes all of your activities. Aim for a schedule that you can live with for the entire school term. A sample weekly schedule, incorporating the following guidelines, is shown in Table 2.

1. Enter your class times, work hours, and any other fixed obligations first. *Be thorough.* Using information from your time-management diary, allow plenty of time for such things as commuting, meals, laundry, and the like.

2. Set up a study schedule for each of your courses. The study habits survey and your time-management diary will direct you. The following guidelines should also be useful.

(a) Establish regular study times for each course. The 4 hours needed to study one subject, for example, are most profitable when divided into shorter periods spaced over several days. If you cram your studying into one 4-hour block, what you attempt to learn in the third or fourth hour will interfere with what you studied in the first 2 hours. Newly acquired knowledge is like wet cement. It needs some time to "harden" to become memory.

(b) Alternate subjects. The type of interference just mentioned is greatest between similar topics. Set up a schedule in which you spend time on several *different* courses during each study session. Besides reducing the potential for interference, alternating subjects will help to prevent mental fatigue with one topic.

(c) Set weekly goals to determine the amount of study time you need to do well in each course. This will

Table 2 Sample Weekly Schedule

Time	Mon.	Tues.	Wed.	Thurs.	Fri.	Sat.
7–8	Dress Eat	Dress Eat	Dress Eat	Dress Eat	Dress Eat	
8–9	Psych.	Study Psych.	Psych.	Study Psych.	Psych.	Dress Eat
9–10	Eng.	Study Eng.	Eng.	Study Eng.	Eng.	Study Eng.
10–11	Study French	Free	Study French	Open Study	Study French	Study Stats.
11–12	French	Study Psych. Lab	French	Open Study	French	Study Stats.
12–1	Lunch	Lunch	Lunch	Lunch	Lunch	Lunch
1–2	Stats.	Psych. Lab	Stats.	Study or Free	Stats.	Free
2–3	Bio.	Psych. Lab	Bio.	Free	Bio.	Free
3–4	Free	Psych.	Free	Free	Free	Free
4–5	Job	Job	Job	Job	Job	Free
5–6	Job	Job	Job	Job	Job	Free
6–7	Dinner	Dinner	Dinner	Dinner	Dinner	Dinner
7–8	Study Bio.	Study Bio.	Study Bio.	Study Bio.	Free	Free
8–9	Study Eng.	Study Stats.	Study Psych.	Open Study	Open Study	Free
9–10	Open Study	Open Study	Open Study	Open Study	Free	Free

This is a sample schedule for a student with a 16-credit load and a 10-hour-per-week part-time job. Using this chart as an illustration, make up a weekly schedule, following the guidelines outlined here.

depend on, among other things, the difficulty of your courses and the effectiveness of your methods. Many professors recommend studying at least 1 to 2 hours for each hour in class. If your time-management diary indicates that you presently study less time than that, do not plan to jump immediately to a much higher level. Increase study time from your baseline by setting weekly goals [see (4)] that will gradually bring you up to the desired level. As an initial schedule, for example, you might set aside an amount of study time for each course that matches class time.

(d) Schedule for maximum effectiveness. Tailor your schedule to meet the demands of each course. For the course that emphasizes lecture notes, schedule time for a daily review soon after the class. This will give you a chance to revise your notes and clean up any hard-to-decipher shorthand while the material is still fresh in your mind. If you are evaluated for class participation (for example, in a language course), allow time for a review just before the class meets. Schedule study time for your most difficult (or least motivating) courses during hours when you are the most alert and distractions are fewest.

(e) Schedule open study time. Emergencies, additional obligations, and the like could throw off your schedule. And you may simply need some extra time periodically for a project or for review in one of your courses. Schedule several hours each week for such purposes.

3. After you have budgeted time for studying, fill in slots for recreation, hobbies, relaxation, household errands, and the like.

4. Set specific goals. Before each study session, make a list of specific goals. The simple note "7–8 PM: study psychology" is too broad to ensure the most effective use of the time. Formulate your daily goals according to what you know you must accomplish during the term. If you have course outlines with advance assignments, set systematic daily goals that will allow you, for example, to cover fifteen chapters before the exam. And be realistic: Can you actually expect to cover a 78-page chapter in one session? Divide large tasks into smaller units; stop at the most logical resting points. When you complete a specific goal, take a 5- or 10-minute break before tackling the next goal.

5. Evaluate how successful or unsuccessful your studying has been on a daily or weekly basis. Did you reach most of your goals? If so, reward yourself immediately. You might even make a list of five to ten rewards to choose from. If you have trouble studying regularly, you may be able to motivate yourself by making such rewards contingent on completing specific goals.

6. Finally, until you have lived with your schedule for several weeks, don't hesitate to revise it. You may need to allow more time for chemistry, for example, and less for some other course. If you are trying to study regularly for the first time and are feeling burned out, you probably have set your initial goals too high. Don't let failure cause you to despair and abandon the program. Accept your limitations and revise your schedule so that you are studying only 15 to 20 minutes more each evening than you are used to. The point is to identify a regular schedule with which you can achieve some success. Time management, like any skill, must be practiced to become effective.

Techniques for Effective Study

Knowing how to put study time to best use is, of course, as important as finding a place for it in your schedule. Here are some suggestions that should enable you to increase your reading comprehension and improve your note-taking. A few study tips are included as well.

Using SQ3R to Increase Reading Comprehension

How do you study from a textbook? If you are like many students, you simply read and reread in a *passive* manner. Studies have shown, however, that most students who simply read a textbook cannot remember more than half the material ten minutes after they have finished. Often, what is retained is the unessential material rather than the important points upon which exam questions will be based.

This *Study Guide* employs a program known as SQ3R (Survey, Question, Read, Recite, and Review) to facilitate, and allow you to assess, your comprehension of the important facts and concepts in *The Developing Person Through the Life Span,* Third Edition, by Kathleen Stassen Berger.

Research has shown that students using SQ3R achieve significantly greater comprehension of textbooks than students reading in the more traditional passive manner. Once you have learned this program, you can improve your comprehension of any textbook.

Survey Before reading a chapter, determine whether the text or the study guide has an outline or list of objectives. Read this material and the summary at the end of the chapter. Next, read the textbook chapter fairly quickly, paying special attention to the major headings and subheadings. This survey will give you an idea of the chapter's contents and organization. You will then be able to divide the chapter into logical sections in order to formulate specific goals for a more careful reading of the chapter.

In this Study Guide, the *Chapter Overview* summarizes the major topics of the textbook chapter. This section also provides a few suggestions for approaching topics you may find difficult.

Question You will retain material longer when you have a use for it. If you look up a word's definition in order to solve a crossword puzzle, for example, you will remember it longer than if you merely fill in the letters as a result of putting other words in. Surveying the chapter will allow you to generate important questions that the chapter will proceed to answer. These question correspond to "mental files" into which knowledge will be sorted for easy access.

As you survey, jot down several questions for each chapter section. One simple technique is to generate questions by rephrasing a section heading. For example, the "Preoperational Thought" head could be turned into "What is preoperational thought?" Good questions will allow you to focus on the important points in the text. Examples of good questions are those that begin as follows: "List two examples of . . .." "What is the function of . . .?" "What is the significance of . . .?" Such questions give a purpose to your reading. Similarly, you can formulate questions based on the chapter outline.

The *Guided Study* section of this Study Guide provides the types of questions you might formulate while surveying each chapter. This section is a detailed set of objectives covering the points made in the text.

Read When you have established "files" for each section of the chapter, review your first question, begin reading, and continue until you have discovered its answer. If you come to material that seems to answer an important question you don't have a file for, stop and write down the question.

Using this Study Guide, read the chapter one section at a time. First, preview the section by skimming it, noting headings and boldface items. Next, study the appropriate section objectives in the *Guided Study.* Then, as you read the chapter section, search for the answer to each objective.

Be sure to read everything. Don't skip photo or art captions, graphs, marginal notes. In some cases, what may seem vague in reading will be made clear by a simple graph. Keep in mind that test questions are sometimes drawn from illustrations and charts.

Recite When you have found the answer to a question, close your eyes and mentally recite the question and its answer. Then write the answer next to the question. It is important that you recite an answer in your own words rather than the author's. Don't rely on your short-term memory to repeat the author's words verbatim.

In responding to the objectives, pay close attention to what is called for. If you are asked to identify or list, do just that. If asked to compare, contrast, or do both, you should focus on the similarities (compare) and differences (contrast) between the concepts or theories. Answering the objectives carefully will not only help you to focus your attention on the important concepts of the text, but it will also provide excellent practice for essay exams.

Recitation is an extremely effective study technique, recommended by many learning experts. In addition to increasing reading comprehension, it is useful for review. Trying to explain something in your own words clarifies your knowledge, often by revealing aspects of your answer that are vague or incomplete. If you repeatedly rely upon "I know" in recitation, you really may not know.

Recitation has the additional advantage of simulating an exam, especially an essay exam; the same skills are required in both cases. Too often students study without ever putting the book and notes aside, which makes it easy for them to develop false confidence in their knowledge. When the material is in front of you, you may be able to recognize an answer, but will you be able to recall it later, when you take an exam that does not provide these retrieval cues?

After you have recited and written your answer, continue with your next question. Read, recite, and so on.

Review When you have answered the last question on the material you have designated as a study goal, go back and review. Read over each question and your written answer to it. Your review might also include a brief written summary that integrates all of your questions and answers. This review need not take longer than a few minutes, but it is important. It will help you retain the material longer and will greatly facilitate a final review of each chapter before the exam.

In this Study Guide, the *Chapter Review* section contains fill-in and one- or two-sentence essay questions for you to complete after you have finished reading the text and have written answers to the objectives. The correct answers are given at the end of the chapter. Generally, your answer to a fill-in question should match exactly (as in the case of important terms, theories, or people). In some cases, the answer is not a term or name, so a word close in meaning will suffice. You should go through the Chapter Review several times before taking an exam, so it is a good idea to mentally fill in the answers until you are ready for a final pretest review. Textbook page references are provided with each section title, in case you need to reread any of the material.

Also provided to facilitate your review are two *Progress Tests* that include multiple-choice questions and, where appropriate, matching or true–false questions. These tests are not to be taken until you have read the chapter, written answers to the objectives, and completed the *Chapter Review.* Correct answers, along with explanations of why each alternative is correct or incorrect, are provided at the end of the chapter. The relevant text page numbers for each question are also given. If you miss a question, read these explanations and, if necessary, review the text pages to further understand why. The *Progress Tests* do not test every aspect of a concept, so you should treat an incorrect answer as an indication that you need to review the concept.

Following the two Progress Tests is a *Challenge Test,* which should be taken just prior to an exam. It includes questions that test your ability to analyze, integrate, and apply the concepts in the chapter. As with the *Progress Tests,* answers for the *Challenge Test* are provided at the end of each chapter, along with relevant page numbers.

The chapter concludes with a list of *Key Terms;* definitions are to be written on a separate piece of paper. As with the *Guided Study* objectives, it is important that these answers be written from memory, and in your own words. The *Answers* section at the end of the chapter gives a definition of each term, sometimes along with an example of its usage and/or a tip to help you remember its meaning.

One final suggestion: Incorporate SQ3R into your time-management calendar. Set specific goals for completing SQ3R with each assigned chapter. Keep a record of chapters completed, and reward yourself for being conscientious. Initially, it takes more time and effort to "read" using SQ3R, but with practice, the steps will become automatic. More important, you will comprehend significantly more material and retain what you have learned longer than passive readers do.

Taking Lecture Notes

Are your class notes as useful as they might be? One way to determine their worth is to compare them with those taken by other good students. Are yours as thorough? Do they provide you with a comprehensible outline of each lecture? If not, then the following suggestions might increase the effectiveness of your note-taking.

1. Keep a separate notebook for each course. Use $8\frac{1}{2} \times 11$-inch pages. Consider using a ring binder, which would allow you to revise and insert notes while still preserving lecture order.

2. Take notes in the format of a lecture outline. Use roman numerals for major points, letters for supporting arguments, and so on. Some instructors will make this easy by delivering organized lectures and, in some cases, by outlining their lectures on the board. If a lecture is disorganized, you will probably want to reorganize your notes soon after the class.

3. As you take notes in class, leave a wide margin on one side of each page. After the lecture, expand or clarify any shorthand notes while the material is fresh in your mind. Use this time to write important questions in the margin next to notes that answer them. This will facilitate later review and will allow you to anticipate similar exam questions.

Evaluate Your Exam Performance

How often have you received a grade on an exam that did not do justice to the effort you spent preparing for the exam? This is a common experience that can leave one feeling bewildered and abused. "What do I have to do to get an A?" "The test was unfair!" "I studied the wrong material!"

The chances of this happening are greatly reduced if you have an effective time-management schedule and use the study techniques described here. But it can happen to the best-prepared student and is most likely to occur on your first exam with a new professor.

Remember that there are two main reasons for studying. One is to learn for your own general academic development. Many people believe that such knowledge is all that really matters. Of course, it is possible, though unlikely, to be an expert on a topic without achieving commensurate grades, just as one can, occasionally, earn an excellent grade without truly mastering the course material. During a job interview or in the workplace, however, your A in Cobol won't mean much if you can't actually program a computer.

In order to keep career options open after you graduate, you must know the material and maintain competitive grades. In the short run, this means performing well on exams, which is the second main objective in studying.

Probably the single best piece of advice to keep in mind when studying for exams is to *try to predict exam questions.* This means ignoring the trivia and focusing on the important questions and their answers (with your instructor's emphasis in mind).

A second point is obvious. How well you do on exams is determined by your mastery of both lecture and textbook material. Many students (partly because of poor time management) concentrate too much on one at the expense of the other.

To evaluate how well you are learning lecture and textbook material, analyze the questions you missed on the first exam. If your instructor does not review exams during class, you can easily do it yourself. Divide the questions into two categories: those drawn primarily from lectures and those drawn primarily from the textbook. Determine the percentage of questions you missed in each category. If your errors are evenly distributed and you are satisfied with your grade, you have no problem. If you are weaker in one area, you will need to set future goals for increasing and/or improving your study of that area.

Similarly, note the percentage of test questions drawn from each category. Although exams in most courses cover both lecture notes and the textbook, the relative emphasis of each may vary from instructor to instructor. While your instructors may not be entirely consistent in making up future exams, you may be able to tailor your studying for each course by placing additional emphasis on the appropriate area.

Exam evaluation will also point out the types of questions your instructor prefers. Does the exam consist primarily of multiple-choice, true–false, or essay questions? You may also discover that an instructor is fond of wording questions in certain ways. For example, an instructor may rely heavily on questions that require you to draw an analogy between a theory or concept and a real-world example. Evaluate both your instructor's style and how well you do with each format. Use this information to guide your future exam preparation.

Important aids, not only in studying for exams but also in determining how well prepared you are, are the Progress and Challenge Tests provided in this Study Guide. If these tests don't include all of the types of questions your instructor typically writes, make up your own practice exam questions. Spend extra time testing yourself with question formats that are most difficult for you. There is no better way to evaluate your preparation for an upcoming exam than by testing yourself under the conditions most likely to be in effect during the actual test.

A Few Practical Tips

Even the best intentions for studying sometimes fail. Some of these failures occur because students attempt to work under conditions that are simply not conducive to concentrated study. To help ensure the success of your time-management program, here are a few suggestions that should assist you in reducing the possibility of procrastination or distraction.

1. If you have set up a schedule for studying, make your roommate, family, and friends aware of this commitment, and ask them to honor your quiet study time. Close your door and post a "Do Not Disturb" sign.

2. Set up a place to study that minimizes potential distractions. Use a desk or table, not your bed or an extremely comfortable chair. Keep your desk and the walls around it free from clutter. If you need a place other than your room, find one that meets as many of the above requirements as possible—for example, in the library stacks.

3. Do nothing but study in this place. It should become associated with studying so that it "triggers" this activity, just as a mouth-watering aroma elicits an appetite.

4. Never study with the television on or with other distracting noises present. If you must have music in the background in order to mask outside noise, for example, play soft instrumental music. Don't pick vocal selections; your mind will be drawn to the lyrics.

5. Study by yourself. Other students can be distracting or can break the pace at which your learning is most efficient. In addition, there is always the possibility that group studying will become a social gathering. Reserve that for its own place in your schedule.

If you continue to have difficulty concentrating for very long, try the following suggestions.

6. Study your most difficult or most challenging subjects first, when you are most alert.

7. Start with relatively short periods of concentrated study, with breaks in between. If your attention starts to wander, get up immediately and take a break. It is better to study effectively for 15 minutes and then take a break than to fritter away 45 minutes out of an hour. Gradually increase the length of study periods, using your attention span as an indicator of successful pacing.

Critical Thinking

Having discussed a number of specific techniques for managing your time efficiently and studying effectively, let us now turn to a much broader topic: What exactly should you expect to learn as a student of developmental psychology?

Most developmental psychology courses have two major goals: (1) to help you acquire a basic understanding of the discipline's knowledge base, and (2) to help you learn to think like a psychologist. Many students devote all of their efforts to the first of these goals, concentrating on memorizing as much of the course's material as possible.

The second goal—learning to think like a psychologist—has to do with critical thinking. Critical thinking has many meanings. On one level, it refers to an attitude of healthy skepticism that should guide your study of psychology. As a critical thinker, you learn not to acept any explanation or conclusion about behavior as true until you have evaluated the evidence. On another level, critical thinking refers to a systematic process for examining the conclusions and arguments presented by others. In this regard, many of the features of the SQ3R technique for improving reading comprehension can be incorporated into an effective critical thinking system.

To learn to think critically, you must first recognize that psychological information is transmitted through the construction of persuasive arguments. An argument consists of three parts: an assertion, evidence, and an explanation (Mayer and Goodchild, 1990).

An assertion is a statement of relationship between some aspect of behavior, such as intelligence, and another factor, such as age. Learn to identify and evaluate the assertions about behavior and mental processes that you encounter as you read your textbook, listen to lectures, and engage in discussions with classmates. A good test of your understanding of an assertion is to try to restate it in your own words. As you do so, pay close attention to how important terms and concepts are defined. When a researcher asserts that "intelligence declines with age," for example, what does he or she mean by "intelligence"? Assertions such as this one may be true when a critical term ("intelligence") is defined one way (for example, "speed of thinking"), but not when defined in another way (for example, "general knowledge"). One of the strengths of psychology is the use of *operational* definitions that specify how key terms and concepts are measured, thus eliminating any ambiguity about their meaning. "Intelligence," for example, is often operationally defined as performance on a test measuring various cognitive skills. Whenever you encounter an assertion that is ambiguous, be skeptical of its accuracy.

When you have a clear understanding of an argument's assertion, evaluate its supporting evidence, the second component of an argument. Is it *empirical*? Does it, in fact, support the assertion? Psychologists accept only *empirical (observable) evidence* that is based on direct measurement of behavior. Hearsay, intuition, and personal experiences are not acceptable evidence. Chapter 1 discusses the various research methods used by developmental psychologists to gather empirical evidence. Some examples include surveys, observations of behavior in natural settings, and experiments.

As you study developmental psychology, you will become aware of another important issue in evaluating evidence—determining whether or not the research on which it is based is faulty. Research can be faulty for many reasons, including the use of an unrepresentative sample of subjects, experimenter bias, and inadequate control of unanticipated factors that might influence results. Evidence based on faulty research should be discounted.

The third component of an argument is the explanation provided for an assertion, which is based on the evidence that has been presented. While the argument's assertion merely *describes* how two things (such as intelligence and age) are related, the explanation tells *why*, often by proposing some theoretical mechanism that causes the relationship. Empirical evidence that thinking speed slows with age (the assertion), for example, may be explained as being caused by age-related changes in the activity of brain cells (a physiological explanation).

Be cautious in accepting explanations. In order to think critically about an argument's explanation, ask yourself three questions: (1) Can I restate the explanation in my own words?; (2) Does the explanation make sense based on the stated evidence?; and (3) Are there alternative explanations that adequately explain the assertion? Consider this last point in relation to our sample assertion: It is possible that the slower thinking speed of older adults is due to their having less recent experience than younger people with tasks that require quick thinking (a disuse explanation).

Because psychology is a relatively young science, its theoretical explanations are still emerging, and often change. For this reason, not all psychological arguments will offer explanations. Many arguments will only raise additional questions for further research to address.

Some Suggestions for Becoming a Critical Thinker

1. Adopt an attitude of healthy skepticism in evaluating psychological arguments.

2. Insist on unambiguous operational definitions of an argument's important concepts and terms.

3. Be cautious in accepting supporting evidence for an argument's assertion.

4. Refuse to accept evidence for an argument if it is based on faulty research.

5. Ask yourself if the theoretical explanation provided for an argument "makes sense" based on the empirical evidence.

6. Determine whether there are alternative explanations that adequately explain an assertion.

7. Use critical thinking to construct your own effective arguments when writing term papers, answering essay questions, and speaking.

8. Polish your critical-thinking skills by applying them to each of your college courses, and to other areas of life as well. Learn to think critically about advertising, political speeches, and the material presented in popular periodicals.

A Critical-Thinking Exercise

You should now be ready to test your understanding of critical thinking by evaluating an actual psychological argument from your textbook (pp. 540–541). Carefully read the following passage regarding the decline in adult IQ. Next, answer the questions about the argument. Finally, compare your answers with those given on page xv.

> For most of the twentieth century, psychologists were convinced that intelligence reaches a peak in adolescence, and then gradually declines during adulthood. This belief was based on what seemed to be solid evidence. For instance, all literate American draftees in World War I were given an intelligence test, called Alpha, that tested a variety of cognitive skills. When the scores of men of various ages were compared, one conclu-

sion seemed obvious: the average American male reached an intellectual peak at about age 18, stayed at that level until his mid-20s, and then began to show a decline (Yerkes, 1923). . . .

As we saw in Chapter 1, developmentalists now recognize that cross-sectional research can sometimes yield a misleading picture of adult development, not only because it is impossible to select adults who are similar to each other in every important aspect except age, but also because of the cohort effects created by each group's own uique history of life experiences. Cohort effects, in particular, complicate the interpretation of adult differences in intellectual performance. Adults who grew up during the Great Depression, for example, or during World War II, might have acquired different cognitive skills than younger cohorts who grew up during the 1950s or 1960s. Among other influences, the quality of public education, the variety of cultural opportunities, and the dissemination of information in the popular media, have provided advantages to later-born cohorts. Even more significant, elderly adults who grew up before every 16-year-old was expected to be in high school rather than in the work force are likely to differ intellectually from those who grew up later, when a high school education was more normative.

From Berger, K. (1993). *The Developing Person Through the Life Span* (3rd ed.) New York: Worth Publishers.

Evaluate the Argument

1. State the assertion of psychologists regarding developmental changes in intelligence, giving operational definitions of all important concepts and terms. Use your own words.

2. State the evidence for this assertion, noting whether or not it is empirical, and whether or not it is based on faulty research.

3. State an adequate alternative explanation for this assertion.

Sample Answers to the Critical Thinking Exercise

1. State the assertion of psychologists regarding developmental changes in intelligence, giving operational definitions of all important concepts and terms. Use your own words.

Until recently most psychologists asserted that intelligence, operationally defined as performance on a test measuring various cognitive skills, reaches a peak in adolescence, and then declines with age.

2. State the evidence for this assertion, noting whether or not it is empirical, and whether or not it is based on faulty research.

The evidence is based on empirical cross-sectional research comparing intelligence-test scores of people of various ages. It was later discovered that cross-sectional research can sometimes create a misleading picture of adult development, because the comparison groups typically differ not only in their ages, but also in their history of life experiences. Research that does not control for factors other than the one under study is faulty.

3. State an adequate alternative explanation for this assertion.

Because cross-sectional research compares groups that differ not only in age, but also in life experiences that may have fostered different cognitive skills, it is possible that age alone does not cause a decline in mental ability, or that age is not even a factor in differing cognitive abilities. Factors such as the quality of public education or the format of the test have provided advantages to later-born adults. These factors cannot be ruled out as an explanation for the typical pattern found in cross-sectional studies of mental ability.

If you would like more information on critical thinking, consult the following source.

Mayer, R., & Goodchild, F. (1990). *The critical thinker: Thinking and learning strategies for psychology students.* Dubuque, IA: Wm. C. Brown Publishers.

Some Closing Thoughts

I hope that these suggestions help make you more successful academically, and that they enhance the quality of your college life in general. Having the necessary skills makes any job a lot easier and more pleasant. Let me repeat my warning not to attempt to make too drastic a change in your life-style immediately. Good habits require time and self-discipline to develop. Once established they can last a lifetime.

CHAPTER 1 Introduction

Chapter Overview

The first chapter introduces the study of human development. In the first section, a definition of development is provided and the three domains into which it is often divided are described. The story of David illustrates the interaction of the biosocial, cognitive, and psychosocial domains in an individual's life. Furthermore, according to the ecological perspective, the individual is affected by, and affects, many other individuals, groups of individuals, and larger systems in the environment.

The second section of the chapter focuses on three important controversies that have evolved among developmentalists: (1) how much of any given characteristic or behavior is due to nature, or heredity, and how much is due to nurture, or environmental influences; (2) whether development is best described as a gradual, continuous process, or as occurring in identifiable stages; and (3) whether there is one universal pattern of normal development.

The third section discusses the ways in which developmentalists work, beginning with a description of the scientific method. Several specific techniques for testing hypotheses are discussed, including naturalistic observation, experiments, surveys, and case studies. Also described are the research designs that developmentalists have created to study people over time: cross-sectional research (the comparison of people of different ages) and longitudinal research (the study of the same people over a period of time).

The chapter concludes by noting that the study of human development involves values and goals—including those of you, the student.

NOTE: Answer guidelines for all Chapter 1 questions begin on page 10.

Guided Study

The text chapter should be studied one section at a time. Before you read, preview each section by skimming it, noting headings and boldface items. Then read the appropriate section objectives from the following outline. Keep these objectives in mind and, as you read the chapter section, search for the information that will enable you to meet each objective. Once you have finished a section, write out answers for its objectives.

The Study of Human Development (pp. 4–15)

1. Define the study of human development.

2. Identify and describe the three domains into which human development is often separated.

3. Describe the ecological approach to human development and explain how this approach leads to the need for understanding cultural-historical influences.

Three Controversies (pp. 15–20)

4. Explain and discuss the nature-nurture controversy.

5. Explain and discuss the continuity-discontinuity controversy.

6. Explain and discuss the deficit-difference controversy.

The Scientific Method (pp. 20–31)

7. List the basic steps of the scientific method.

8. Describe four methods psychologists commonly use to test hypotheses, noting at least one advantage (or strength) and one disadvantage (or weakness) for each.

9. (Research Report) List five steps scientists often take to ensure that their research is as valid as possible.

10. (Text and A Closer Look) Define correlation and give at least one example of a positive correlation, a negative correlation, and a correlation of zero.

11. Describe the two basic research designs used by developmental psychologists.

Ethics and Values (pp. 31–32)

12. Discuss the most important ethical concerns of psychologists.

Chapter Review

When you have finished reading the chapter, work through the material that follows to review it. Complete the sentences and answer the questions. As you proceed, evaluate your performance for each section by consulting the answers on page 10. Do not continue with the next section until you understand each answer. If you need to, review or reread the appropriate section in the textbook before continuing.

The Study of Human Development (pp. 4–15)

1. The study of human development can be defined as the study of ________________ ________________.

2. The study of human development involves many academic disciplines, especially ____________, ____________, and ____________.

3. The study of human development can be separated into three domains: ____________, ____________, and ____________.

4. The study of brain and body changes and the social influences that guide them falls within the ____________ domain.

5. Thinking, perception, and language learning fall mainly in the ____________ domain of development.

6. The study of emotions, personality, and interpersonal relationships fall within the ____________ domain.

7. Each of the domains ____________ (is/is not) affected by the other two.

8. The approach that emphasizes the influence of the ecosystem that supports the developing person is called the ____________ approach to development.

9. The family, the peer group, and other aspects of the immediate social setting constitute the ____________ in an individual's life.

10. Systems that link one microsystem to another constitute the ____________.

11. The neighborhood and community structures make up the ____________.

12. The overarching patterns of culture, politics, the economy, and so forth make up the ____________.

13. The ecological perspective emphasizes the ____________ (unidirectional/multidirectional) nature of social influences.

Give an example of how the ecological approach provides a larger perspective on development.

14. The ecological approach emphasizes that human development must be understood in both its ____________ context and its ____________ context.

15. A group of people born roughly at the same historical time is called a(n) ____________.

16. A collection of people who share certain attributes, such as national origin, religion, culture, and language, and, as a result, have similar values and experiences is called a(n) ____________ ____________.

17. A contextual influence that is determined by a person's income, education, residence, and occupation, is called ____________ ____________, which is often abbreviated ____________.

18. As an influence on development, SES is believed by many social scientists to be ____________ (more/less) important than either cohort or ethnicity.

19. Because his mother contracted the disease ____________ during her pregnancy, David was born with a heart defect and cataracts over both eyes. Thus, his immediate problems centered on the ____________ domain.

20. In David's case, the ____________ of communication between home and school worked very effectively.

21. David is fortunate in that the macrosystem —such as the laws of the land—is becoming increasingly sensitive to the needs of handicapped people.

Three Controversies (pp. 15–20)

22. In the nature-nurture controversy, traits inherited at conception give evidence of the influence of Nature; those that emerge in response to learning and environmental influences give evidence of the effect of Nurture.

23. Developmentalists agree that, at every point, the interaction between nature and nurture is the crucial influence on any particular aspect of development.

24. Proving whether nature or nurture is more responsible for a particular developmental change is (is/is not) very difficult.

25. Theorists who see a slow, steady, and gradual progression from the beginning of life to the end emphasize the Continuity of development.

26. Theorists who see growth as occurring in identifiable stages emphasize the Discontinuity of development.

27. In the twentieth century, the Stage (Discontinuity) view of development has been dominant. Recently, developmentalists such as Flavell have cautioned against overemphasizing this viewpoint.

28. How rapidly a person matures and ages is reflected in the concept of the Biological Clock.

29. The behaviors and attitudes a particular culture deems appropriate for a given age are reflected in the concept of the Sociological Clock.

30. Many of the earliest developmentalists believed that there is (is/is not) one universal pattern of human development. One such developmentalist was Gesell, who identified norms for various behaviors and abilities in young children.

31. Today developmentalists are more likely to view children who do not follow the usual path of development as displaying an alternative (inferior/abnormal/alternative) path of development.

32. A criticism of early developmental research is that most of it involved researchers and children who were White, middle-class, and American.

The Scientific Method (pp. 20–31)

33. In order, the basic steps of the scientific method are:

a. Formulate a Research Question
b. Develop a Hypothesis
c. Test the Hypothesis
d. Draw Conclusions
e. Make the Findings Available

34. To repeat an experimental test procedure and obtain the same results is to Replicate the test of the hypothesis.

35. The observation of people in their everyday environment for the purpose of testing a scientific hypothesis is called Naturalistic observation.

Identify the chief limitation of naturalistic observation.

36. (Research Report) The researcher who carefully selects a sample population that is large enough to prevent his or her results from being unduly affected by extreme individual cases is aware of the importance of sample Size.

37. (Research Report) When a sample population is typical of the group under study—in gender, ethnic background, and other important variables, the sample is called a(n) Representative sample.

38. (Research Report) When the person carrying out research is unaware of the purpose of the research, that person is said to be a(n) ________________ ________________.

39. (Research Report) To test a hypothesis, researchers often compare a(n) ________________ group, which receives some special treatment, with a(n) ________________ group, which does not.

40. (Research Report) To determine whether or not experimental results are merely the result of chance, researchers use a statistical test, called a test of ________________.

41. (text and A Closer Look) A statistic that indicates whether two variables are related to each other is ________________.

42. (text and A Closer Look) To say that two variables are correlated ________________ (does/does not) necessarily imply that one caused the other.

43. (A Closer Look) When one variable changes in the same direction as another variable, the correlation is said to be ________________. When one variable increases while the other decreases, the correlation is said to be ________________.

44. (A Closer Look) Correlations range from ________________, the highest positive correlation, to ________________, the most negative correlation. A value of ________________ indicates no correlation between two variables.

45. The method that allows a scientist to test a hypothesis in a controlled environment, in which the variables may be manipulated, is the ________________.

46. Experiments are sometimes criticized for studying behavior in a situation that is ________________.

47. In a(n) ________________, scientists ask people for information through personal interviews or questionnaires.

48. An intensive study of one individual is called a(n) ________________ ________________.

49. Research that involves the comparison of people of different ages is called a(n) ________________-________________ research design.

50. Research that follows the same people over a relatively long period of time is called a(n) ________________ research design.

Ethics and Values (pp. 31–32)

51. The most difficult ethical question raised by the study of human development is not ________________ the participants, but attending to larger ________________ of the research.

Progress Test 1

Multiple-Choice Questions

Circle your answers to the following questions and check them against the answers on page 11. If your answer is incorrect, read the explanation for why it is incorrect and then consult the appropriate pages of the text (in parentheses following the correct answer).

1. The study of human development is defined as the study of:
   a. how and why people change over time.
   b. psychosocial influences on aging.
   c. individual differences in learning over the life span.
   d. all of the above.

2. The cognitive domain of development includes:
   a. perception.
   b. memory.
   c. imagination.
   d. all of the above.

3. Changes in height, weight, and bone thickness are part of:
   a. cognitive development.
   b. biosocial development.
   c. the psychosocial domain.
   d. the physical domain.

4. Psychosocial development focuses primarily on personality, emotions, and:
   a. intellectual development.
   b. sexual maturation.
   c. relationships with others.
   d. perception.

5. The ecological approach in developmental psychology focuses on the:
   a. biochemistry of the body systems.
   b. cognitive domain only.
   c. nature-nurture controversy.
   d. overall environment of development.

6. The nature-nurture controversy considers how much traits, characteristics, and behaviors are the result of:
   a. continuity or discontinuity.
   b. genes or heredity.
   c. heredity or experience.
   d. different historical concepts of childhood.

7. The stage view of development emphasizes:
   a. the continuity of development.
   b. the discontinuity of development.
   c. enduring personality characteristics.
   d. the effects of ecosystems.

8. A hypothesis is a:
   a. conclusion.
   b. prediction to be tested.
   c. statistical test.
   d. correlation.

9. A scientist can manipulate the environment to provide a precise test of a hypothesis:
   a. by using statistics.
   b. in an experiment.
   c. in interviews with representative population samples.
   d. in naturalistic observation.

10. A disadvantage of experiments is that:
    a. people may behave differently in the artificial environment of the laboratory.
    b. control groups are too large to be accommodated in most laboratories.
    c. it is the method most vulnerable to bias on the part of the researcher.
    d. proponents of the ecological approach overuse them.

11. For a psychologist's generalization to be valid, the population sample must be both representative of the group under study and:
    a. significant.
    b. large enough.
    c. all the same age.
    d. none of the above.

12. The correlation of two variables that are entirely unrelated is:
    a. positive.
    b. negative.
    c. inverse.
    d. zero.

13. To study how behavior changes over time, scientists:
    a. study more than one control group.
    b. use longitudinal studies.
    c. present their interpretations before reporting on the behavior studied.
    d. employ only the case study.

14. A developmentalist who is interested in studying the influences of a person's immediate environment on his or her behavior is focusing on which system?
    a. mesosystem
    b. macrosystem
    c. microsystem
    d. exosystem

15. Socioeconomic status is determined by a combination of variables, including:
    a. age, education, and wealth.
    b. wealth, ethnicity, and occupation.
    c. wealth, education, and occupation.
    d. age, ethnicity, and occupation.

True or False Items

Write *true* or *false* on the line in front of each statement.

_____ 1. Psychologists separate human development into three domains, or areas of study.

_____ 2. The case study of David clearly demonstrates that for some children only nature (or heredity) is important.

_____ 3. "Nurture" can refer to environmental influences that come into play before a person is born.

_____ 4. Theorists who emphasize the discontinuity of development maintain that growth occurs in distinct stages.

_____ 5. Some researchers see development as a continuous gradual progression without identifiable stages.

_____ 6. A study of history suggests that particular well-defined periods of child and adult development have always existed.

_____ 7. Naturalistic observation usually indicates a clear relationship between cause and effect.

_____ 8. The case-study method of research involves interviewing a number of people.

_____ 9. A "blind" experimenter is one who is not sufficiently objective.

I 10. To eliminate the possibility that their results are due to chance, scientists test for significance.

Progress Test 2

Progress Test 2 should be completed during a final chapter review. Answer the following questions after you thoroughly understand the correct answers for the Chapter Review and Progress Test 1.

Multiple-Choice Questions

1. Psychologists study development:
   a. in order to identify factors that foster healthy development.
   b. in order to identify factors that impair development.
   c. in order to help people reach their full potential.
   d. for all of the above reasons.

2. The three domains of developmental psychology are:
   a. physical, cognitive, psychosocial.
   b. physical, biosocial, cognitive.
   c. biosocial, cognitive, psychosocial.
   d. biosocial, cognitive, emotional.

3. Which of the following is true of the three domains of development?
   a. They are important at every age.
   b. They interact in influencing development.
   c. They are more influential in some cultures than in others.
   d. a and b are true.

4. Early developmentalists emphasized biological, cognitive, and psychological changes:
   a. that occurred within each individual.
   b. as taking place in a larger social context.
   c. that could be quantified.
   d. that were common to all people.

5. According to the ecological perspective, the macrosystem would include:
   a. the peer group.
   b. the neighborhood.
   c. politics.
   d. the family.

6. The effects of a person's family life on his or her development would be classified as part of the:
   a. microsystem.
   b. mesosystem.
   c. exosystem.
   d. macrosystem.

7. According to the systems perspective:
   a. developmental influences are multidirectional.
   b. actions in any one part of the system affect all the other parts.
   c. human development must be understood in terms of both its cross-cultural and historical context.
   d. all of the above are true.

8. A cohort is defined as a group of people:
   a. of similar national origin.
   b. who share a common language.
   c. born roughly at the same historical time.
   d. who share the same cultural background.

9. According to developmentalists who believe in continuity, development proceeds:
   a. in a gradual progression from the beginning of life to the end.
   b. in identifiable stages.
   c. in a series of abrupt transitions.
   d. according to a biologically determined timetable.

10. According to the text:
    a. many social scientists believe that SES is a more potent influence on development than either cohort or ethnicity.
    b. SES is a particularly potent factor among the very poor.
    c. no one is exactly like the typical person of his or her SES.
    d. all of the above are true.

11. Nature is to nurture as ________________ is to ________________ .
    a. environment; heredity
    b. heredity; environment
    c. gradual development; sudden development
    d. sudden development; gradual development

12. The dominant view of developmental psychologists in the present century has been that development is:
    a. continuous.
    b. discontinuous.
    c. more a product of nurture than nature.
    d. a. and c.

13. (Research Report) In order to ensure that their research is as valid as possible, researchers:
    a. study a large sample population.
    b. select a representative sample population.

c. remain "blind" to the hypothesis being tested.
d. take all of the above steps.

14. (Research Report) The control group in an experiment:
    a. receives the treatment of interest.
    b. does not receive the treatment of interest.
    c. is always drawn from a different population than the experimental group.
    d. must be larger in size than the experimental group.

15. (A Closer Look) To say that two variables are positively correlated means that:
    a. one causes the other.
    b. as one increases, the other decreases.
    c. as one increases, the other increases.
    d. a. and c.

Matching Items

Match each definition or description with its corresponding term.

Terms

_____ 1. biological clock
_____ 2. social clock
_____ 3. norm
_____ 4. replicate
_____ 5. survey
_____ 6. case study
_____ 7. cross-sectional research
_____ 8. longitudinal research
_____ 9. cohort
_____ 10. ethnic group

Definitions or Descriptions

a. group of people born at the same time
b. following one group of people over a long time
c. questionnaire
d. studying one person in great detail
e. group of people who share certain attributes, such as national origin
f. comparing people of different ages at the same time
g. metaphor for how rapidly the body matures
h. culturally acceptable ages for certain behaviors
i. the age at which a behavior typically occurs
j. to repeat a study and obtain the same findings

Challenge Test

Answer these questions the day before an exam as a final check on your understanding of the chapter's terms and concepts.

1. A developmental psychologist interviews a large sample of young people to learn about their sexual experiences and values. The psychologist is using:
   a. an unrepresentative population sample.
   b. the case study.
   c. the survey.
   d. naturalistic observation.

2. A team of psychologists observes the play patterns of groups of 12-month-old, 18-month-old, and 24-month-old infants. The team is conducting:
   a. a longitudinal study.
   b. research of questionable ethics and worth.
   c. research concerning only one of the three domains.
   d. a cross-sectional study.

3. Snow and summer:
   a. are negatively correlated.
   b. have zero correlation.
   c. are positively correlated.
   d. are unrelated.

4. Dr. Ramirez looks at human development in terms of the individual's supporting ecosystems. Evidently, Dr. Ramirez subscribes to the _______________ perspective.
   a. psychosocial
   b. ecological
   c. biosocial
   d. cognitive

5. For her class project, Shelly decides to write a paper on how neighborhood and community structures influence development. She cleverly titles her paper:
   a. "The Microsystem in Action."
   b. "The Mesosystem in Action."
   c. "The Exosystem in Action."
   d. "The Macrosystem in Action."

6. In concluding his presentation, "The Nature-Nurture Controversy Today," Enrique states that:
   a. "Developmentalists increasingly acknowledge the greater influence of heredity in directing the course of development."
   b. "Developmentalists today agree that nurture, rather than nature, is the more potent influence on development."
   c. "The debate has been abandoned as unproductive."
   d. "Developmentalists agree that the interaction between nature and nurture is the crucial influence on any particular aspect of development."

7. Dr. Jenkins' class on life-span development was organized around the concept of age-related crises, such as the "midlife crisis." Evidently, Dr. Jenkins is working from the ________________ perspective on development.
   a. nature
   b. nurture
   c. continuity
   d. discontinuity

8. A psychologist who watches the behaviors of people in their usual surroundings is engaged in which type of research?
   a. survey
   b. experiment
   c. naturalistic observation
   d. case study

9. In explaining why psychologists prefer the experiment to other research methods, Dr. Nash notes that:
   a. its results are usually more applicable to everyday life.
   b. it may uncover cause-and-effect relationships.
   c. it eliminates the need for statistical analysis.
   d. all of the above are true.

10. Which of the following is an example of longitudinal research?
   a. An investigator compares the performance of several different age groups on a test of memory.
   b. The performance of the same group of people on a test of memory is compared at several different ages.
   c. The performance of an experimental group and a control group of subjects on a test of memory is compared.
   d. The performance of several different age groups of subjects on a test of memory is compared as each group is tested repeatedly over a period of years.

11. In explaining the concept of the social clock to her roommate, Allison notes that it represents:
   a. a person's inner timetable for development.
   b. the body's mechanisms for timing development.
   c. that point in each individual's life when the need to be accepted by others is especially strong.
   d. society's standards, or age norms, for when certain life events should occur.

12. Compared to earlier scientists, contemporary developmentalists are more likely to view a child whose development differs from age norms as:
   a. in need of psychological intervention.
   b. abnormal.
   c. deficient.
   d. following an alternative path of development.

13. If height and body weight are positively correlated, which of the following is true?
   a. There is a cause-and-effect relationship between height and weight.
   b. Knowing a person's height, one can predict his or her weight.
   c. As height increases, weight decreases.
   d. All of the above are true.

14. "It is difficult to get valid data with this research method because it is particularly vulnerable to bias on the part of the researcher and the subjects." The person who uttered this statement is *most likely* referring to which research method?
   a. case study
   b. experiment
   c. naturalistic observation
   d. survey

15. When researchers find that the results of a study are significant, this means that:
   a. they may have been caused purely by chance.
   b. it is unlikely they could be replicated.
   c. it is unlikely they could have occurred by chance.
   d. the sample population was representative of the general population.

Key Terms

Using your own words, write a brief definition or explanation of each of the following terms on a separate piece of paper.

1. biosocial domain
2. cognitive domain

3. psychosocial domain
4. ecological approach
5. microsystem
6. mesosystem
7. exosystem
8. macrosystem
9. cohort
10. ethnic group
11. socioeconomic status (SES)
12. nature
13. nurture
14. continuity
15. discontinuity
16. biological clock
17. social clock
18. norm
19. scientific method
20. replicate
21. naturalistic observation
22. sample size
23. representative sample
24. blind experimenter
25. experimental group
26. control group
27. significance
28. correlation
29. experiment
30. survey
31. case study
32. cross-sectional research
33. longitudinal research

ANSWERS

CHAPTER REVIEW

1. how and why people change over time, as well as how and why they remain the same
2. biology; education; psychology
3. biosocial; cognitive; psychosocial
4. biosocial
5. cognitive
6. psychosocial
7. is
8. ecological
9. microsystem
10. mesosystem
11. exosystem
12. macrosystem
13. multidirectional

Until recently, parental employment was believed to have an impact on child development only indirectly. Ecological research has demonstrated, however, that the stresses of parents' work directly affect the quality of their parenting.

14. cultural; historical
15. cohort
16. ethnic group
17. socioeconomic status; SES
18. more
19. rubella; biosocial
20. mesosystem
21. macrosystem
22. nature; nurture
23. interaction
24. is
25. continuity
26. discontinuity
27. stage (or discontinuity); Flavell
28. biological clock
29. social clock
30. is; Gesell
31. alternative
32. white; middle; American
33. a. formulate a research question;
    b. develop a hypothesis;
    c. test the hypothesis;
    d. draw conclusions;
    e. make the findings available
34. replicate
35. naturalistic

Naturalistic observation does not pinpoint the direct cause of the behaviors being observed.

36. size
37. representative
38. blind experimenter
39. experimental; control
40. significance

41. correlation
42. does not
43. positive; negative
44. +1.0; -1.0; 0
45. experiment
46. artificial
47. survey
48. case study
49. cross-sectional
50. longitudinal
51. safeguarding; implications

PROGRESS TEST 1

Multiple-Choice Questions

1. **a.** is the answer. (p. 4)

   b. & c. The study of development is concerned with a broader range of phenomena, including biosocial aspects of development, than these answers specify.

2. **d.** is the answer. (p. 5)
3. **b.** is the answer. (p. 5)

   a. This domain is concerned with thought processes.

   c. This domain is concerned with emotions, personality, and interpersonal relationships.

   d. This is not a domain of development.

4. **c.** is the answer. (p. 5)

   a. This falls within the cognitive and biosocial domains.

   b. This falls within the biosocial domain.

   d. This falls within the cognitive domain.

5. **d.** is the answer. This approach sees development as occurring within four interacting levels, or environments. (p. 6)
6. **c.** is the answer. (p. 15)

   a. This controversy is concerned with the issue of whether development is gradual and continuous, or abrupt and stage-like.

   b. Genes and heredity refer to the same thing.

   d. This is not an aspect of the nature-nurture controversy.

7. **b.** is the answer. (p. 17)

   a. Researchers who emphasize this view see development as occurring in gradual increments rather than abrupt transitions.

   c. & d. The stage view of development is not concerned with either of these issues.

8. **b.** is the answer. (p. 20)
9. **b.** is the answer. (p. 25)

   a. Statistics are used *after* research has been conducted, in order to summarize data and determine whether results are significant or due to chance.

   c. & d. Only in experiments can researchers directly manipulate environmental variables.

10. **a.** is the answer. (p. 27)
11. **b.** is the answer. (p. 22)

    a. Significance refers to whether or not research results are due to chance factors.

    c. This is not a requirement of a valid population sample.

12. **d.** is the answer. (p. 26)
13. **b.** is the answer. (p. 30)

    a. & c. These are irrelevant in studying how behavior changes over time.

    d. The case study *can* be used to study how behavior changes over time; it is not the only method that serves this purpose, however.

14. **c.** is the answer. (p. 6)

    a. This refers to systems that link one microsystem to another.

    b. This refers to the overarching patterns of culture, politics, the economy, and so forth.

    d. This refers to the community structures that affect the functioning of smaller systems.

15. **c.** is the answer. (p. 9)

True or False Items

1. T (p. 5)
2. F The case study of David shows that both nature and nurture are important in affecting outcome. (pp. 10–14)
3. T (p. 15)
4. T (p. 17)
5. T (p. 17)
6. F Our ideas about the stages of childhood and adulthood are cultural creations that have varied over the centuries. (p. 17)
7. F A disadvantage of naturalistic observation is that the variables are numerous and uncontrolled, and therefore cause-and-effect relationships are difficult to pinpoint. (p. 21)

8. F The case-study method is an intensive study of one individual. (p. 28)
9. F A "blind" experimenter is one who is unaware of the purpose of an experiment, and can therefore be objective in reporting results. (p. 23)
10. T (p. 23)

PROGRESS TEST 2

Multiple-Choice Questions

1. **d.** is the answer. (p. 4)
2. **c.** is the answer. (p. 5)
3. **d.** is the answer. (p. 5)

   c. Research has not revealed cultural variations in the overall developmental influence of the three domains.
4. **a.** is the answer. (p. 6)

   b. This is the emphasis of the newer, ecological perspective.

   c. & d. These do not distinguish early developmentalists from more contemporary researchers.
5. **c.** is the answer. (p. 6)

   a. & d. These are part of the microsystem.

   b. This is part of the exosystem.
6. **a.** is the answer. (p. 6)

   b. This refers to systems that link one microsystem to another.

   c. This refers to the community structures that affect the functioning of smaller systems.

   d. This refers to the overarching patterns of culture, politics, the economy, and so forth.
7. **d.** is the answer. (p. 7)
8. **c.** is the answer. (p. 8)

   a., b., & d. These are attributes of an ethnic group.
9. **a.** is the answer. (p. 17)

   b., c., & d. These are viewpoints of developmentalists who believe in discontinuity.
10. **d.** is the answer. (p. 9)
11. **b.** is the answer. (p. 15)

    c. & d. These are concerned with the continuity-discontinuity issue.
12. **b.** is the answer. (pp. 17–18)
13. **d.** is the answer. (pp. 22–23)
14. **b.** is the answer. (p. 23)

    a. This is true of the experimental group.

    c. The control group must be similar to the experimental group (and therefore drawn from the same population).

    d. The control group is usually the same size as the experimental group.
15. **c.** is the answer. (p. 26)

    a. Correlation does not imply cause and effect.

    b. This describes a negative correlation.

Matching Items

1. g (p. 17)
2. h (p. 17)
3. i (p. 18)
4. j (p. 20)
5. c (p. 28)
6. d (p. 28)
7. f (p. 29)
8. b (p. 30)
9. a (p. 8)
10. e (p. 8)

CHALLENGE TEST

1. **c.** is the answer. (p. 28)

   a. It is impossible to determine whether the population sample is representative or unrepresentative from the information provided.

   b. In this method one person is studied for a long time.

   d. In this method people are observed in their natural environments.
2. **d.** is the answer. (p. 29)

   a. In such a study a single group is studied for a long time.

   b. & c. Whether or not these are true of the study described cannot be determined from the information provided.
3. **a.** is the answer. As temperatures warm (summer), snow becomes unlikely. (p. 26)

   b. & d. When the correlation between two events is zero, the events are unrelated. In such an instance, it is impossible to predict one from the other. In this example, it *is* possible to predict that snow will not occur during summer.

   c. When two events are positively correlated, increases in one are accompanied by increases in the other. In this example, increases in temperature are accompanied by decreases in the likelihood of snow.
4. **b.** is the answer. (p. 6)

   a., c., & d. These are the three domains of development.
5. **c.** is the answer. (p. 6)
6. **d.** is the answer. (p. 15)
7. **d.** is the answer. (p. 17)

   a. & b. The nature-nurture issue is separate from the continuity-discontinuity issue.

   c. Continuity theorists see development as gradual, rather than as occurring in abrupt transitions.

8. **c.** is the answer. (p. 21)

   a. Survey researchers conduct interviews or distribute questionnaires.

   b. Experimenters test hypotheses in a controlled situation.

   d. The case study is an intensive study of one person.

9. **b.** is the answer. (p. 27)

   a. In fact, experiments are often criticized because they occur in artificial settings.

   c. Statistical analysis is needed in virtually every type of research, including the experiment.

10. **b.** is the answer. (p. 30)

    a. This is an example of cross-sectional research.

    c. This is an example of an experiment.

    d. This type of study is not described in the text.

11. **d.** is the answer. (p. 17)

12. **d.** is the answer. (p. 18)

13. **b.** is the answer. (pp. 25, 26)

    a. Correlation does not imply causality.

    c. This would be true if height and body weight were *negatively* correlated.

14. **d.** is the answer. (p. 28)

15. **c.** is the answer. (p. 23)

KEY TERMS

1. The **biosocial domain** is concerned with brain and body changes and the social influences that guide them. (p. 5)
2. The **cognitive domain** is concerned with thought processes, perceptual abilities, language, and the educational institutions that influence these aspects of development. (p. 5)
3. The **psychosocial domain** is concerned with emotions, personality, interpersonal relationships, and the complex social contexts in which they occur. (p. 5)
4. Developmentalists who take the **ecological approach** study the ways in which the individual affects, and is affected by, other individuals, groups of individuals, and larger systems in his or her environment. (p. 6)
5. The **microsystem** refers to the immediate social settings, such as the family and peer group, that directly affect each person. (p. 6)
6. The **mesosystem** refers to the systems that link one microsystem to another. (p. 6)
7. The **exosystem** refers to the neighborhood and community structures that directly affect the functioning of smaller systems. (p. 6)
8. The **macrosystem** refers to the overarching patterns of culture, politics, the economy, and so forth. (p. 6)

   Memory aid: To help remember the four systems within the ecological approach, pay attention to the distinct meanings of the prefixes: *micro* means "small," and in this context refers to the smallest of the individual's environments—the family or peer group; *meso* means "middle," or "intermediate," as in systems that are intermediate between aspects of the microsystem; *exo* means "outside," and in this context refers to external systems, such as the neighborhood and community; and *macro* means "large," which in this context refers to the larger influences of culture and society.
9. A **cohort** is a group of people born roughly at the same historical time. (p. 8)
10. An **ethnic group** is a collection of people who share certain attributes, such as national origin, religion, culture, and language, and, as a result, tend to have similar values and experiences. (p. 8)
11. An individual's **socioeconomic status (SES)** is determined by his or her wealth, education, residence, and occupation. (p. 9)
12. **Nature** refers to the range of traits, capacities, and limitations that each person inherits genetically. (p. 15)
13. **Nurture** refers to all the environmental influences that come into play after conception, including the mother's health during pregnancy, and all of one's experiences in the outside world. (p. 15)
14. Researchers who emphasize the **continuity** of development believe that there is a continual, gradual progression from the beginning of life to the end. (p. 17)
15. Researchers who emphasize the **discontinuity** of development see growth as occurring in identifiable stages. (p. 17)
16. The **biological clock** is a metaphor for how rapidly the body matures and ages. (p. 17)
17. The **social clock** reflects what behaviors and attitudes a particular culture deems appropriate for a given age. (p. 17)
18. **Norms** are ages at which specific behaviors and abilities typically occur. (p. 18)
19. The **scientific method** is a procedural model that helps researchers remain objective as they study behavior. The five basic steps of the scientific method are: (1) formulate a research question;

(2) develop a hypothesis; (3) test the hypothesis; (4) draw conclusions; and (5) make the findings available. (p. 20)

20. To **replicate** a test of a research hypothesis is to repeat it and obtain the same results using a different but related set of subjects or procedures. (p. 20)

21. In **naturalistic observation** scientists observe people in their natural environments. (p. 21)

22. In order to make research more valid, scientists ensure that **sample size** is sufficiently large so that a few extreme cases will not distort the picture of the group as a whole. (p. 22)

23. A **representative sample** is a group of subjects who are typical of the general population the researchers wish to learn about. (p. 22)

24. A **blind experimenter** is one who is unaware of the purpose of the research and can therefore remain objective in gathering data. (p. 23)

25. In an experiment, the **experimental group** receives some special treatment. (p. 23)

    Example: In a study of the effects of a new drug on reaction time, subjects in the **experimental group** would actually receive the drug being tested.

26. The **control group** of an experiment is the one in which the treatment of interest is withheld so that comparison to the experimental group can be made. (p. 23)

27. **Significance** means that an obtained result, such as a difference between two groups, very likely reflects a real difference rather than chance factors. (p. 23)

28. **Correlation** is a statistic that merely indicates whether two variables are related to each other. (p. 25)

    Example: If there is a *positive correlation* between air temperature and ice cream sales, the warmer (higher) it is, the more ice cream is sold. If there is a *negative correlation* between air temperature and sales of cocoa, the cooler (lower) it is, the more cocoa is sold.

29. The **experiment** is the research method in which an investigator tests a hypothesis in a controlled situation in which the relevant variables are limited and can be manipulated by the experiment. (p. 25)

30. The **survey** is the research method in which a sample of people are questioned about their attitudes or behavior. (p. 28)

31. The **case study** is the research method involving the intensive study of one person. (p. 28)

32. In **cross-sectional research** groups of people of various ages are compared on a characteristic of interest. (p. 29)

33. In **longitudinal research** the same group of individuals is studied over a long period of time. (p. 30)

CHAPTER 2 Theories

Chapter Overview

Developmental theories are systematic statements of principles that explain behavior and development. Many such theories have influenced our understanding of human development. This chapter describes and evaluates the four kinds of theories—psychoanalytic, learning, cognitive, and humanistic—that will be used throughout the book to present information and to provide a framework for interpreting events and issues in human development. Each of the theories has developed a unique vocabulary with which to describe and explain events as well as to organize ideas into a cohesive system of thought.

Two of the theories presented—psychoanalytic theory and Piaget's cognitive theory—are clearly stage theories. Details of each particular stage will be amplified in subsequent chapters; this chapter provides an overview of the stages and a sense of the theories' perspectives on development. The learning, information-processing, and humanistic theories, on the other hand, are not stage theories; each, in varying degrees, offers principles of behavior that can be applied to people of all ages.

As you study the chapter, consider what each of the theories has to say about your own development, as well as that of friends and relatives in other age groups. It is also a good idea to keep the following questions in mind as you study each theory: Which of the theory's principles are generally accepted by contemporary developmentalists? How has the theory been criticized? In what ways does this theory agree with the other theories? In what ways does it disagree?

NOTE: Answer guidelines for all Chapter 2 questions begin on page 26.

Guided Study

The text chapter should be studied one section at a time. Before you read, preview each section by skimming it, noting headings and boldface items. Then read the appropriate section objectives from the following outline. Keep these objectives in mind and, as you read the chapter section, search for the information that will enable you to meet each objective. Once you have finished a section, write out answers for its objectives.

What Theories Do (pp. 35–36)

1. Define developmental theory and explain how developmental theories are used to understand human behavior and development.

Psychoanalytic Theories (pp. 37–42)

2. Discuss the major focus of psychoanalytic theories and explain Freud's views on childhood sexuality and psychological development.

3. Contrast Erikson's theory of psychosocial development with Freud's theory.

4. Evaluate the psychoanalytic perspective on development.

Learning Theories (pp. 43–50)

5. Discuss the major focus of learning theories and explain the basic principles of classical and operant conditioning.

6. Discuss the social learning theory and evaluate the contributions of learning theory in general to the understanding of development.

Cognitive Theories (pp. 50–58)

7. Discuss the prime focus of cognitive theories and explain Piaget's theory of cognitive development.

8. Explain how information-processing theorists portray the human mind and describe the steps of the information-processing system.

9. Evaluate the contributions of cognitive theories to developmental psychology.

Humanistic Theories (pp. 59–61)

10. Discuss the basic ideas of Maslow and Rogers and evaluate the humanistic perspective on development.

The Theories Compared (pp. 61–64)

11. Summarize the contributions and criticisms of the major developmental theories and explain the eclectic perspective of contemporary developmentalists.

Chapter Review

When you have finished reading the chapter, work through the material that follows to review it. Complete the sentences and answer the questions. As you proceed, evaluate your performance for each section by consulting the answers on page 26. Do not continue with the next section until you understand each answer. If you need to, review or reread the appropriate section in the textbook before continuing.

What Theories Do (pp. 35–36)

1. A systematic statement of principles that explain behavior and development is called a(n) _______ _______.

2. Developmental theories form the basis for educated guesses, or _______, about behavior.

Psychoanalytic Theories (pp. 37–42)

3. Psychoanalytic theories interpret human development in terms of intrinsic _______ and _______, many of which are _______ (conscious/unconscious).

4. The psychoanalytic theory, which was formulated by _______, challenged many of the ideas that prevailed in Europe in the late 1800s, including that _______ _______.

5. The medical establishment _______ (supported/did not support) Freud's "talking cure," which was based on the assumption that the origin of many physical disorders was in the _______.

6. According to Freud's theory of _______ _______, children experience sexual pleasures and desires long before adolescence as they pass through three _______ _______. From infancy to early childhood to the preschool years, these stages are the _______ stage, the _______ stage, and the _______ stage. Finally, after a period of sexual _______, which lasts for about _______ years, the individual enters the _______ stage, which begins during _______ and lasts throughout adulthood.

Specify the focus of sexual pleasure and the major developmental need associated with each psychosexual stage.

oral _______

anal _______

phallic _______

genital _______

7. According to Freud, personality consists of three components: the _______, the _______, and the _______.

8. The source of unconscious impulses toward gratification of needs is the _______, which operates according to the _______ _______.

9. The ego, which develops _______ (before/after) the id and attempts to satisfy the id's demands in realistic ways, operates according to the _______ _______.

10. The superego starts to develop at about age _______, as children begin to

identify with their parents' ________________ standards and develop their own conscience.

11. According to psychoanalytic theory, the growth of new skills, understanding, and competence is largely an outgrowth of the functioning of the ________________.

12. In order to cope with internal conflict or challenging environmental demands, the ego may resort to using a ________________ ________________, such as ________________, in which a disturbing memory or impulse is blocked from consciousness.

13. The theorists who developed their own, modified versions of Freud's psychoanalytic theory are called ________________.

14. Erik Erikson's theory of development, which focuses on social and cultural influences, is called a(n) ________________ theory. In this theory, there are ________________ (number) developmental stages, each characterized by a particular developmental ________________ related to the person's relationship to the social environment. Unlike Freud, Erikson proposed stages of development that ________________ (span/do not span) a person's lifetime. Central to Erikson's theory is the conviction that different cultures ________________ (promote/do not promote) different paths of development.

15. Identify three psychoanalytic ideas that are widely accepted.

a. ________________

b. ________________

c. ________________

16. Identify two psychoanalytic ideas that are not widely accepted by contemporary developmentalists.

a. ________________

b. ________________

Learning Theories (pp. 43–50)

17. A major theory in American psychology is ________________, which is now more commonly called ________________ ________________ because of its emphasis on how we learn specific behaviors. This theory emerged early in the present century under the influence of ________________.

18. Learning theorists have formulated laws of behavior that are believed to apply ________________ (only at certain ages/at all ages). The basic principles of learning theory explore the relationship between a behavior or event (called the ________________) and the behavioral reaction associated with it (called the ________________). The learning process, which is called ________________, takes two forms: ________________ ________________ and ________________ ________________.

19. In classical conditioning, which was discovered by the Russian scientist ________________ and is also called ________________ conditioning, a person or an animal learns to associate a(n) ________________ stimulus with a more meaningful one. Many human ________________ responses are susceptible to classical conditioning, particularly in childhood.

20. According to ________________, the learning of more complex responses is the result of ________________ conditioning, in which a person learns that a particular behavior produces a particular ________________, such as a reward. This type of learning is also called ________________ conditioning.

21. A stimulus that increases the likelihood that a behavior will be repeated is called a(n) ________________. A stimulus that strengthens the behavior that leads to its presentation is a(n) ________________ ________________. A stimulus that strengthens the behavior that leads to its removal is called a(n) ________________ ________________, whereas a stimulus that makes behavior less likely to be repeated is referred to as ________________.

22. Reinforcers that come from the environment are ______________ ; those that come from within are ______________ .

23. The extension of learning theory that emphasizes the ways that people learn new behaviors by observing others is called ______________ ______________ ______________ .

The process whereby a child patterns his or her behavior after a parent or teacher, for example, is called ______________ .

24. Children's susceptibility to modeling ______________ (does/does not) change as they mature. This indicates that cognitive and motivational processes ______________ (are/are not) important factors in modeling.

25. Also important in social learning is a person's sense of his or her own talents, standards, and goals, or the person's perceptions of ______________ .

26. Social learning theorists find that behavior is the outcome of the mutual interaction of the person's internal characteristics, the environment, and the behavior itself; this interaction is called ______________ ______________ .

Identify two ways in which the study of human development has benefited from learning theory.

Identify one common criticism of learning theories.

Cognitive Theories (pp. 50–58)

27. Theorists who focus on the structure and development of the individual's thought processes and the way those thought processes affect the person's understanding of the world are called ______________ theorists. The most famous such theorist is ______________ .

28. In Piaget's first stage of development, the ______________ stage, children experience the world through their senses and motor abilities. This stage occurs between infancy and age ______________ .

29. According to Piaget, during the preschool years (up to age ______________), children are in the ______________ stage. A hallmark of this stage is that children begin to think ______________ .

30. Piaget believed that children begin to think logically in a consistent way at about ______________ years of age. At this time, they enter the ______________ ______________ stage.

31. In Piaget's final stage, the ______________ ______________ stage, reasoning expands from the purely concrete to encompass ______________ thinking. Piaget believed most children enter this stage by age ______________ .

32. According to Piaget, cognitive development is guided by the need to maintain a state of mental balance, called ______________ .

33. A mental concept that helps one think about or interact with ideas and objects in the environment is a(n) ______________ . When new experiences challenge existing schemas, creating a kind of imbalance, the individual experiences ______________ , which eventually leads to mental growth.

34. According to Piaget, this mental growth is achieved through two innate, interrelated processes: ______________ and ______________ .

35. People adapt their thinking to include new ideas by simply adding new information to existing schemas (a process called ______________) and by changing schemas to adjust to the new information (a process called ______________).

An example of these processes at work is mastery of the principle that the amount of a liquid does not change even when the appearance of its container changes; this is called ______________ of liquids.

36. The recent view of cognitive development that takes the computer as a model for the human mind is the ______________ - ______________ theory.

37. In the information-processing system, incoming sensory information is first stored, for a split second, in the ______________ ______________. Meaningful material that is currently receiving attention is held in short-term memory, which is also called ______________ memory. Some of that information is transferred to long-term memory, or the ______________ ______________, where it is stored for months, weeks, or years.

38. According to information-processing theory, a person's reactions to the environment are organized by the ______________ ______________.

39. Throughout childhood and adolescence, the ______________ ______________ expands. In late adulthood, limitations in the speed and efficiency of ______________ memory may restrict how easily complex information can be recalled. The most significant developmental changes occur in the person's ______________ ______________, as the child acquires more sophisticated memory, attention, and retrieval strategies. These processes regulate the analysis and flow of ______________.

40. Unlike Piaget, information-processing theorists view cognitive development as a ______________ (more/less) gradual process that ______________ (continues/does not continue) over the entire life span.

Cite several contributions, and several criticisms, of cognitive theories of development.

Humanistic Theories (pp. 59–61)

41. Two influential humanistic theories were proposed by ______________ and ______________. These theories take a(n) ______________ view of development that seeks to encompass all the diverse aspects of human experience. According to this view, development is guided by a variety of needs, including the need to achieve one's full potential, which is called ______________.

List some of the characteristics of the people Maslow described as self-actualized.

42. According to Maslow, if a person's basic survival needs are not satisfied, that person's capacity for self-actualization is ______________ (restricted/increased). When a person identifies with universal values and has frequent peak experiences, that person has attained ______________.

43. Rogers believed that all people strive to fulfill their potential and to become ______________ ______________ human beings, and that healthy people have an ______________ ______________ that they strive to become.

44. According to Rogers, significant others nurture a person's growth by being accepting and offering ______________ ______________ ______________.

State several contributions, and several criticisms, of humanistic theories.

The Theories Compared (pp. 61–64)

45. Which theory of development emphasizes:
   a. individual goals in development? ______________
   b. the ways in which thought processes affect actions? ______________
   c. environmental influences? ______________
   d. the impact of "hidden dramas" on development? ______________

46. Which theory of development has been criticized for:
   a. being too mechanistic? ______________
   b. being too idealistic? ______________
   c. being too subjective? ______________
   d. overemphasizing rational, logical thought? ______________

47. Because no one theory can encompass all of human behavior, most developmentalists have a(n) ______________ perspective, which capitalizes on the strengths of all the theories.

Progress Test 1

Multiple-Choice Questions

Circle your answers to the following questions and check them with the answers on page 27. If your answer is incorrect, read the explanation for why it is incorrect and then consult the appropriate pages of the text (in parentheses following the correct answer).

1. Which of the following describes the purpose of a developmental theory?
   a. to provide a broad and coherent view of the complex influences on human development
   b. to offer guidance for practical issues encountered by parents, teachers, and therapists
   c. to generate testable hypotheses about development
   d. all of the above

2. Which developmental theory emphasizes the influence of unconscious drives and motives on behavior?
   a. psychoanalytic
   b. learning
   c. cognitive
   d. humanistic

3. Which of the following is the correct order of the psychosexual stages proposed by Freud?
   a. oral stage; anal stage; phallic stage; latency period; genital stage
   b. anal stage; oral stage; phallic stage; latency period; genital stage
   c. oral stage; anal stage; genital stage; latency period; phallic stage
   d. anal stage; oral stage; genital stage; latency period; phallic stage

4. Erikson's psychosocial theory of human development describes:
   a. eight psychosocial crises all people are thought to face.
   b. four psychosocial stages and a period of latency.
   c. the same number of stages as Freud's, but with different names.
   d. a stage theory that is not psychoanalytic.

5. The learning process whereby new behaviors emerge in response to new stimuli, while old, unproductive responses fade away is called:
   a. negative reinforcement.
   b. conditioning.
   c. stimulation.
   d. social modeling.

6. An American psychologist who explained complex human behaviors in terms of operant conditioning was:
   a. Carl Rogers.
   b. Ivan Pavlov.
   c. B. F. Skinner.
   d. Jean Piaget.

7. Pavlov's dogs learned to salivate at the sound of a bell because they associated the bell with food. This experiment was an early demonstration of:
   a. classical conditioning.
   b. operant conditioning.
   c. positive reinforcement.
   d. social learning.

8. A reinforcer can be the removal of something unpleasant when a person or animal responds in a particular way. Such a reinforcer is called:
   a. punishment.
   b. a negative reinforcer.
   c. a positive reinforcer.
   d. a physiological response.

9. Social learning is sometimes called modeling because it:
   a. follows the scientific model of learning.
   b. molds character.
   c. follows the immediate reinforcement model.
   d. involves people's patterning their behavior after that of others.

10. Cognitive theories focus most closely on the individual's:
    a. observable behaviors.
    b. correct answers and perceptions.
    c. emotional development.
    d. thought processes.

11. Working memory includes current, conscious mental activity—such as your reading of this question. Another name for working memory is:
    a. the sensory register.
    b. the response generator.
    c. short-term memory.
    d. the knowledge base.

12. Which is the correct sequence of stages in Piaget's theory of cognitive development?
    a. sensorimotor, preoperational, concrete operational, formal operational
    b. sensorimotor, preoperational, formal operational, concrete operational
    c. preoperational, sensorimotor, concrete operational, formal operational
    d. preoperational, sensorimotor, formal operational, concrete operational

13. When an individual's existing schema no longer satisfies abilities to perceive and remember new experiences, the result is called:
    a. assimilation. c. disequilibrium.
    b. equilibrium. d. repression.

14. Intelligence, in Piaget's view, consists of two interrelated processes: organization and:
    a. cognition. c. assimilation.
    b. adaptation. d. accommodation.

15. The humanistic perspective on development:
    a. emphasizes the driving force of unconscious motives.
    b. emphasizes the effect of conditioning on behavior.
    c. has been criticized for being "reductionistic."
    d. takes a holistic view of human development.

True or False Items

Write *true* or *false* on the line in front of each statement.

_______ 1. Learning theorists study what people actually do, not what they might be thinking.

_______ 2. Erikson's eight developmental stages are centered not on a body part but on each person's relationship to the social environment.

_______ 3. A stage view of human development is held by most learning theorists.

_______ 4. A reinforcer is always pleasant and takes the form of a reward, such as candy or a pat on the back.

_______ 5. The term *reciprocal determinism* describes behavior that is determined mostly by the environment.

_______ 6. The finding that some adults never attain the capacity for abstract thinking has led some researchers to conclude that Piaget's stages are not universal.

_______ 7. The sensory register stores incoming stimulus information for approximately three minutes.

_______ 8. In part, cognitive theories examine how an individual's understandings and expectations affect his or her behavior.

_______ 9. According to Piaget, children begin to think only when they reach preschool age.

_______ 10. Most contemporary researchers have adopted an eclectic perspective on development.

Progress Test 2

Progress Test 2 should be completed during a final chapter review. Answer the following questions after you thoroughly understand the correct answers for the Chapter Review and Progress Test 1.

Multiple-Choice Questions

1. Sigmund Freud began his career as a(n):
   a. medical doctor working in Europe during the 1870s.
   b. widely traveled American psychologist.
   c. student of Erik Erikson in the 1950s.
   d. advocate of extrinsic reinforcement.

2. Of the following terms, the one that does *not* describe a stage of Freud's theory of childhood sexuality is:
   a. phallic.
   b. oral.
   c. anal.
   d. sensorimotor.

3. We are more likely to imitate the behavior of others if we particularly admire and identify with them. This belief finds expression in:
   a. stage theory.
   b. humanistic theory.
   c. social learning theory.
   d. Pavlov's experiments.

4. The id can best be described as:
   a. a relentless moral conscience.
   b. one of Erikson's stages of psychosocial development.
   c. a defense mechanism that entails banishing a threatening impulse from consciousness.
   d. the source of unconscious impulses toward gratification of needs.

5. Children and adults are drawn to certain models more than to others, based in part on their perceptions of self-efficacy. *Self-efficacy* is best defined as:
   a. a kind of reciprocal determinism.
   b. a person's sense of his or her own goals and capabilities.
   c. a person's expectancies about the likely responses to a given behavior.
   d. an individual's academic or athletic potential.

6. Defense mechanisms are best described as:
   a. evidence of mental illness.
   b. infantile sexual behavior.
   c. a means of avoiding unbearable inner conflict.
   d. smoking and other ways of gaining oral gratification.

7. When a disturbing idea is blocked from consciousness, the defense mechanism that is operating is:
   a. assimilation.
   b. repression.
   c. accommodation.
   d. adaptation.

8. Learning theorists have found that they can often solve a person's seemingly complex psychological problem by:
   a. analyzing the patient.
   b. admitting the existence of the unconscious.
   c. altering the environment.
   d. administering well-designed punishments.

9. According to Piaget, an infant first comes to know the world through:
   a. sucking and grasping schemas.
   b. naming and counting schemas.
   c. preoperational thought.
   d. instruction from parents.

10. According to Piaget, the stage of cognitive development that generally characterizes preschool children (2 to 6 years old) is the:
    a. preoperational stage.
    b. sensorimotor stage.
    c. oral stage.
    d. psychosocial stage.

11. People organize their thoughts so that they make sense. When they encounter new ideas and experiences, they adapt their thinking by means of assimilation and:
    a. equilibrium.
    b. organization.
    c. conservation.
    d. accommodation.

12. Information-processing theory is an example of a:
    a. learning theory.
    b. social learning theory.
    c. cognitive theory.
    d. psychoanalytic theory.

13. Selective attention, rehearsal, rules of thumb, and other strategies for regulating and retrieving information are called:
    a. control processes.
    b. sensory registers.
    c. working memory.
    d. knowledge bases.

14. Which of the following is a common criticism of humanistic theory?
    a. It places too great an emphasis on unconscious motives and childhood sexuality.
    b. Its mechanistic approach fails to explain many complex human behaviors.
    c. Development is more gradual than its stages imply.
    d. Its view of development is overly idealistic.

15. According to Maslow's theory:
    a. the most basic needs are related to survival.
    b. needs are satisfied in a specified order.
    c. the highest needs relate to self-actualization.
    d. all of the above are true.

Matching Items

Match each theory or term with its corresponding description or definition.

Theories or Terms

_______ 1. psychoanalytic theory
_______ 2. psychosocial theory
_______ 3. learning theories
_______ 4. social learning theory
_______ 5. cognitive theories
_______ 6. information-processing theory
_______ 7. humanistic theories
_______ 8. negative reinforcer
_______ 9. punishment
_______ 10. self-efficacy
_______ 11. reciprocal determinism

Descriptions or Definitions

a. emphasize the impact of the immediate environment on behavior
b. a stimulus that makes behavior less likely to be repeated
c. emphasize each person's potential for growth and self-actualization
d. the removal of an unpleasant stimulus as the result of a particular behavior
e. a person's sense of his or her own capabilities
f. emphasizes the "hidden dramas" that influence behavior
g. emphasizes social and cultural factors in development
h. emphasize how our thoughts shape our actions
i. the mutual interaction of a person's characteristics, the environment, and the behavior
j. uses the computer as a metaphor for the human mind
k. emphasizes that people learn by observing others

Challenge Test

Answer these questions the day before an exam as a final check on your understanding of the chapter's terms and concepts.

1. Psychoanalytic theories are difficult to test in a laboratory, under controlled conditions, because:
   a. attempting to manipulate the id, ego, and superego could cause permanent psychological damage.
   b. the sexual emphasis of its perspective would make testing unethical.
   c. its concepts are subjective and cannot be experimentally manipulated.
   d. the variables cannot be introduced before a child reaches the phallic stage.

2. When a pigeon is rewarded for producing a particular response, and so learns to produce that response to obtain rewards, psychologists describe this chain of events as:
   a. operant conditioning.
   b. classical conditioning.
   c. modeling.
   d. reflexive actions.

3. At every age, a word of praise can have a powerful effect. Praise is a(n):
   a. negative reinforcer.
   b. extrinsic reinforcer.
   c. intrinsic reinforcer.
   d. modeling device.

4. A reinforcer is something that makes it more likely that a behavior will be repeated. Which of the following would *not* be considered a reinforcer?
   a. a reward such as a piece of candy
   b. a kind word or a pat on the back
   c. a spanking or a slap
   d. a smile

5. A child who thinks that only old people die is forced to acknowledge the death of a young friend. The child must therefore rearrange his or her thinking, a kind of adaptation called:
   a. accommodation.
   b. assimilation.
   c. organization.
   d. equilibrium.

6. Piaget's four major stages of cognitive development describe:
   a. different bodies of knowledge.
   b. different ways of thinking.
   c. conservation of intelligence.
   d. conservation of liquids.

7. Which of Freud's ideas would *not* be accepted by most psychologists today?
   a. Sexuality is a potent drive in humans.
   b. People are often unaware of their deep needs, wishes, and fears.
   c. The child's experiences during the first three psychosexual stages form the basis for character structure and personality problems in adulthood.
   d. Human thoughts and actions are probably far more complicated than is at first apparent.

8. After watching several older children climbing around a new junglegym, 5-year-old Jennie decides to try it herself. Which of the following best accounts for her behavior?
   a. classical conditioning
   b. modeling
   c. information-processing theory
   d. working memory

9. Carl cannot remember the details of the torture he experienced as a prisoner of war. According to Freud, Carl's failure to remember these painful memories is an example of:
   a. a peak experience.
   b. the reality principle.
   c. the pleasure principle.
   d. a defense mechanism.

10. Two-year-old Jamail has a simple schema for "dad," and so each time he encounters a man with a child, he calls him "dad." Jamail is demonstrating Piaget's process of:
    a. conservation.
    b. cognition.
    c. accommodation.
    d. assimilation.

11. Sixty-five-year-old Betty can't memorize new information as quickly as she could when she was younger. Evidently, Betty's ______________ has declined.
    a. sensory register
    b. working memory
    c. knowledge base
    d. response generator

12. The school psychologist believes that having a clear concept of an ideal self is necessary before students can achieve their potential. Evidently, the school psychologist is working within the ______________ perspective.
    a. psychoanalytic
    b. humanistic
    c. learning
    d. cognitive

13. Nadine wishes to encourage her children to fulfill their potential as human beings. Maslow and Rogers would probably recommend that she:
    a. use discipline sparingly.
    b. be affectionate with her children only when they behave as she wishes.
    c. help her children perceive that they are loved and respected no matter what they do.
    d. encourage her children to develop lofty goals, no matter how unrealistic they may be.

14. Dr. Cleaver's developmental research draws upon insights from several theoretical perspectives, including learning, cognitive, and humanistic theories. Evidently, Dr. Cleaver is working from a(n) ______________ perspective.
    a. holistic
    b. reductionistic
    c. eclectic
    d. reciprocal determinism

15. Professor Bazzi believes that development is a lifelong process of gradual and continous growth. Based on this information, with which of the following theories would Professor Bazzi most likely agree?
    a. Piaget's cognitive theory
    b. Erikson's psychosocial theory
    c. Freud's psychoanalytic theory
    d. learning theory

Key Terms

Using your own words, write a brief definition or explanation of each of the following terms on a separate piece of paper.

1. developmental theory
2. psychoanalytic theory
3. childhood sexuality
4. psychosexual stages
5. oral stage
6. anal stage
7. phallic stage
8. latency
9. genital stage
10. id
11. ego
12. superego
13. repression
14. psychosocial theory
15. learning theory (behaviorism)
16. stimulus and response
17. conditioning
18. classical conditioning

19. operant conditioning
20. reinforcement/reinforcer
21. positive reinforcer
22. negative reinforcer
23. punishment
24. extrinsic reinforcers
25. intrinsic reinforcers
26. social learning theory
27. modeling
28. self-efficacy
29. reciprocal determinism
30. cognitive theory
31. sensorimotor stage
32. preoperational stage
33. concrete operational stage
34. formal operational stage
35. equilibrium
36. schema
37. disequilibrium
38. organization and adaptation
39. assimilation
40. accommodation
41. conservation of liquids
42. information-processing theory
43. sensory register
44. working memory
45. knowledge base
46. response generator
47. control processes
48. holistic
49. humanistic theory
50. self-actualization
51. unconditional positive regard
52. phenomenological
53. eclectic perspective

ANSWERS

CHAPTER REVIEW

1. developmental theory
2. hypotheses
3. motives; drives; unconscious
4. Sigmund Freud; behavior is governed by rational thought and mature judgment, and that children are "innocent" and devoid of sexual feelings
5. did not support; mind (unconscious)
6. childhood sexuality; psychosexual stages; oral; anal; phallic; latency; 5 or 6; genital; adolescence

Oral stage: The mouth is the focus of pleasurable sensations as the baby becomes emotionally attached to the person who provides the oral gratifications derived from sucking and biting.

Anal stage: Pleasures related to control and self-control, initially in connection with defecation and toilet training, are paramount.

Phallic stage: Pleasure is derived from genital stimulation; interest in physical differences between the sexes leads to the development of gender identity and to the child's identification with the moral standards of the same-sex parent.

Genital stage: Mature sexual interests that last throughout adulthood emerge.

7. id; ego; superego
8. id; pleasure principle
9. after; reality principle
10. 4 or 5; moral
11. ego
12. defense mechanism; repression
13. neo-Freudians
14. psychosocial; 8; crisis, or challenge; span; promote
15. a. development occurs in a series of stages
    b. unconscious motives affect behavior
    c. the early years are a formative period of personality development
16. a. Freud's emphasis on experiences during the earliest psychosexual stages as the basis for character structure and personality problems in adulthood
    b. Freud's depiction of the struggle between the impulsiveness of the id and the relentless morality of the superego
17. behaviorism; learning; John B. Watson
18. at all ages; stimulus; response; conditioning; classical conditioning; operant conditioning
19. Ivan Pavlov; respondent; neutral; emotional
20. B. F. Skinner; operant; consequence; instrumental
21. reinforcer; positive reinforcer; negative reinforcer; punishment
22. extrinsic; intrinsic
23. social learning theory; modeling
24. does; are
25. self-efficacy

26. reciprocal determinism

First, learning theory's emphasis on the causes and consequences of behavior has led researchers to see that many seemingly inborn problem behaviors may be the result of the environment. Second, learning theory's emphasis on scientific rigor has challenged researchers to define terms precisely and to avoid reliance on theoretical concepts that cannot be tested.

Learning theorists are criticized for providing an incomplete explanation for complex behaviors and developmental changes that ignores biological and maturational influences.

27. cognitive; Jean Piaget

28. sensorimotor; 2

29. 6; preoperational; symbolically

30. 7; concrete operational

31. formal operational; abstract, or hypothetical; 12

32. equilibrium

33. schema; disequilibrium

34. organization; adaptation

35. assimilation; accommodation; conservation

36. information-processing

37. sensory register; working; knowledge base

38. response generator

39. knowledge base; working; control processes; information

40. more; continues

By focusing attention on active mental processes, cognitive theory has given developmentalists a greater appreciation of the different ways in which each age knows the world and of the ways these capacities affect behavior. Critics have found fault with Piaget's depiction of cognitive stages as universal, with his lack of emphaiss on the role of culture and education in development, and with information-processing theory's use of the computer as a metaphor for the mind.

41. Abraham Maslow; Carl Rogers; holistic; self-actualization

Maslow found that such people were realistic, creative, spontaneous, spiritual, independent, purposeful, and deeply concerned for their fellow human beings. Furthermore, they accepted themselves, enjoyed their lives, and experienced moments of happiness and insight that he called peak experiences.

42. restricted; self-transcendence

43. fully functioning; ideal self

44. unconditional positive regard

Humanistic theory has advanced an optimistic view that development is lifelong. This view has helped researchers integrate the whole of development, including physical, cognitive, psychosocial, and spiritual growth. Critics maintain the theory is overly idealistic and ignores the many ways that personal growth may be stunted by social processes.

45. **a.** humanistic
b. cognitive
c. learning
d. psychoanalytic

46. **a.** learning
b. humanistic
c. psychoanalytic
d. cognitive

47. eclectic

PROGRESS TEST 1

Multiple-Choice Questions

1. **d.** is the answer (p. 35)

2. **a.** is the answer. (p. 37)

b. Learning theory emphasizes the influence of the immediate environment on behavior.

c. Cognitive theory emphasizes the impact of *conscious* thought processes on behavior.

d. The humanistic perspective reacts against the explanation of behavior in terms of unconscious drives, emphasizing instead how individual goals and self-actualizing tendencies direct development.

3. **a.** is the answer. (p. 38)

4. **a.** is the answer. (pp. 40–41)

b. & c. Whereas Freud identified five stages of psychosexual development, Erikson proposed eight psychosocial stages.

d. Although his theory places greater emphasis on social and cultural forces than Freud's, Erikson's theory is nevertheless classified as a psychoanalytic theory.

5. **b.** is the answer. (p. 43)

a. Negative reinforcement is the response-strengthening influence of the removal of an unpleasant stimulus. Although negative reinforcement is one means by which new behaviors are conditioned, it does not account for the elimination of unproductive responses.

c. Although stimulation was not presented as a term in the text, a stimulus refers to an event, rather than a learning process.

d. Social modeling refers to learning that results from the imitation of other people's behavior.

6. **c.** is the answer. (p. 44)
7. **a.** is the answer. In classical conditioning, a neutral stimulus—in this case, the bell—is paired with a meaningful stimulus—in this case, food. (p. 43)

   b. In operant conditioning, the consequences of a voluntary response determine the likelihood of its being repeated. Salivation is an involuntary response.

   c. & d. Positive reinforcement and social learning pertain to voluntary, or operant, responses.
8. **b.** is the answer. (p. 45)

   a. Punishment is an unpleasant event that makes behavior *less* likely to be repeated.

   c. Positive reinforcement is the *presentation* of a *pleasant* stimulus following a desired response.

   d. Reinforcers are stimuli, not responses.
9. **d.** is the answer. (p. 46)

   a. & c. These are true of all types of learning.

   b. This was not discussed as an aspect of developmental theory.
10. **d.** is the answer. (p. 50)

    a. This describes learning theory.

    b. & c. Neither of these was discussed in association with any particular developmental theory.
11. **c.** is the answer. (p. 55)

    a. & d. We are not directly conscious of material in either of these storage mechanisms.

    b. The response generator is a network of mental processes that organize behavior.
12. **a.** is the answer. (p. 51)
13. **c.** is the answer. (p. 52)

    a. & b. Assimilation and equilibrium occur when existing schema *do* satisfy a person's abilities to perceive new experiences.

    d. Repression is a Freudian defense mechanism.
14. **b.** is the answer. (p. 53)

    a. Cognition refers to all ongoing thought processes.

    c. In the process of assimilation, new information is incorporated into an existing schema.

    d. In the process of accommodation, existing schema are modified to incorporate new experiences.
15. **d.** is the answer. (p. 59)

    a. This describes psychoanalytic theory.

    b. This describes learning theory.

    c. This is what the humanists charge the other theories are.

True or False Items

1. T (p. 43)
2. T (p. 40)
3. F Learning theorists see development as a gradual and continuous process based on principles of conditioning that operate throughout the life span. (p. 43)
4. F Reinforcement can entail the removal of an unpleasant stimulus (negative reinforcement). (pp. 44–45)
5. F Reciprocal determinism refers to the mutual interaction of the individual's internal characteristics, the environment, and the behavior itself. (p. 47)
6. T (p. 42)
7. F This describes working memory; the sensory register lasts for only a split second. (p. 55)
8. T (p. 50)
9. F The hallmark of Piaget's theory is that, at every age, individuals think about the world in unique ways. (p. 51)
10. T (pp. 63–64)

PROGRESS TEST 2

Multiple-Choice Questions

1. **a.** is the answer. (p. 37)
2. **d.** is the answer. This is one of Piaget's stages of cognitive development. (p. 38)
3. **c.** is the answer. (p. 46)
4. **d.** is the answer. (pp. 38–39)

   a. This describes the superego.

   b. The id is a concept described by Freud; it is not a stage.

   c. This describes repression.
5. **b.** is the answer. (p. 47)

   a. Reciprocal determinism refers to the mutual interaction of a person's internal characteristics, the environment, and the behavior.

   c. This aspect of social learning theory addresses a different cognitive issue in learning; it does not pertain to self-efficacy.

   d. These were not discussed in association with any developmental theory.
6. **c.** is the answer. (p. 39)
7. **b.** is the answer. (p. 39)

   a., c., & d. These are aspects of Piaget's theory of cognitive development, not defense mechanisms.

8. **c.** is the answer. (p. 43)

   a. & b. These are psychoanalytic approaches to treating psychological problems.

   d. Learning theorists generally do not recommend the use of punishment.

9. **a.** is the answer. These behaviors are typical of infants in the sensorimotor stage. (p. 51)

   b., c., & d. These are typical of older children.

10. **a.** is the answer. (p. 51)

    b. The sensorimotor stage describes development from birth until 2 years of age.

    c. This is a psychoanalytic stage described by Freud.

    d. This is not the name of a stage; "psychosocial" refers to Erikson theory of stages.

11. **d.** is the answer. (p. 53)

    a. Equilibrium refers to a state of mental balance between a person's schemas and experiences.

    b. Organization refers to the general cognitive process by which people integrate their knowledge in systematic and cohesive ways.

    c. Conservation is the awareness that a substance does not change simply because its appearance changes.

12. **c.** is the answer. (p. 55)

    a. & b. These theories are concerned with the impact of environmental factors on behavior and development.

    d. Unlike information-processing theory, which is concerned with the processing of conscious experiences, psychoanalytic theory emphasizes unconscious thought processes.

13. **a.** is the answer. (p. 56)

    b. The sensory register is a memory stage that stores incoming stimulus information for a split second.

    c. Working memory, which is also called short-term memory, refers to a person's current, conscious memory.

    d. The knowledge base, or long-term memory, stores information for days, months, or years.

14. **d.** is the answer. (p. 61)

    a. This is a common criticism of psychoanalytic theory.

    b. This is a common criticism of learning theory.

    c. This is a common criticism of psychoanalytic and cognitive theories that describe development as occurring in a sequence of stages.

15. **d.** is the answer. (p. 59)

Matching Items

1. f (p. 37)
2. g (p. 41)
3. a (p. 43)
4. k (p. 46)
5. h (p. 50)
6. j (p. 55)
7. c (p. 59)
8. d (p. 45)
9. b (p. 45)
10. e (p. 47)
11. i (p. 47)

CHALLENGE TEST

1. **c.** is the answer. (p. 42)

2. **a.** is the answer. This is an example of operant conditioning because (a) a voluntary, rather than involuntary, response is involved, and (b) positive reinforcement is described. (p. 44)

   b. & d. Classical conditioning, which entails reflexive responses, is a form of learning in which the individual learns to associate a neutral stimulus with a meaningful stimulus.

   c. In modeling, learning occurs through the observation of others, rather than through direct exposure to reinforcing or punishing consequences, as in this example.

3. **b.** is the answer. (p. 45)

   a. Negative reinforcement is the removal of an unpleasant stimulus following a desired behavior.

   c. Intrinsic reinforcers, such as a feeling of satisfaction in a job well done, come from within the individual.

   d. This concept was not introduced in the text.

4. **c.** is the answer. These are examples of punishment. (pp. 44–45)

5. **a.** is the answer. (p. 53)

   b. Assimilation entails incorporating new experiences *without* modifying existing schemas.

   c. Organization refers to the general process by which individuals integrate their thought processes; it is not a kind of adaptation.

   d. Equilibrium is a state of mental balance in which new experiences are fully consistent with existing schemas.

6. **b.** is the answer. (pp. 50–51)

   a. Piaget's theory does not concern specific bodies of knowledge.

   c. No such phenomenon is described in Piaget's theory.

   d. Conservation of liquids is a cognitive *concept* that children acquire during the stage of concrete operations.

7. **c.** is the answer. Although the early years are an important formative age, most developmentalists agree that development is lifelong. (p. 42)

8. **b.** is the answer. Evidently, Jennie has learned by observing the other children at play. (p. 46)

   a. Classical conditioning is concerned with reflexive responses and the association of stimuli, not with complex, voluntary responses, as in this example.

   c. Information-processing theory is concerned with the ways in which the mind analyzes and processes information.

   d. Working memory is a stage in information processing.

9. **d.** is the answer. Carl has evidently banished his painful memories from conscious awareness; this is an example of the defense mechanism called repression. (p. 39)

   a. According to Maslow, peak experiences are moments of great happiness and insight.

   b. & c. According to Freud, the reality and pleasure principles are the bases by which the ego and id, respectively, operate.

10. **d.** is the answer. Jamail is assimilating each encounter with a new man into his existing schema. (p. 53)

    a. Conservation is the ability to recognize that objects do not change when their appearances change.

    b. Cognition refers to all mental activities associated with thinking.

    c. Jamail is not accommodating because he does not have to adjust his schema to fit his new experiences.

11. **b.** is the answer. In late adulthood, limitations in the speed and efficiency of working memory may restrict how easily adults can recall information. (p. 55)

    a., c., & d. These components of the information-processing system do not usually decline with advancing age.

12. **b.** is the answer. (p. 59)

    a., c., & d. The self-concept is not relevant to the psychoanalytic, learning, or cognitive theories of development.

13. **c.** is the answer. (pp. 59–60)

    a. The text does not discuss the impact of discipline on development.

    b. This would constitute *conditional*, rather than unconditional, positive regard and would likely restrict, rather than promote, her children's development.

    d. Humanistic theorists encourage people to develop honest and *realistic* self-concepts.

14. **c.** is the answer. (pp. 63–64)

    a. & b. In contrast to a holistic approach, which focuses on the individual as a whole entity, a reductionistic approach breaks behavior into its separate components, including drives, cognitive processes, and prior conditioning. Neither of these approaches necessarily draws insights from more than one theoretical perspective.

    d. Reciprocal determinism is a social learning process that refers to the mutual interaction among an individual's internal characteristics, the environment, and the behavior.

15. **d.** is the answer. (p. 43)

    a., b., & c. Each of these theories emphasizes that development is a discontinuous process that occurs in stages.

KEY TERMS

1. A **developmental theory** is a systematic statement of principles that explain behavior and development. (p. 35)
2. **Psychoanalytic theory** interprets human development in terms of intrinsic drives and motives, many of which are hidden from awareness. (p. 37)
3. Freud's theory of **childhood sexuality** views development in the first six years as occurring in three psychosexual stages. (p. 38)
4. In each of Freud's five **psychosexual stages**, sexual urges and pleasures are focused in a particular part of the body. (p. 38)
5. In the **oral stage**, which occurs during infancy, the mouth is the focus of pleasurable sensations as the baby becomes emotionally attached to the person who provides oral gratification of its needs. (p. 38)
6. In the **anal stage**, which occurs during early childhood, pleasures related to control and self-control, initially in connection with defecation and toilet training, are paramount. (p. 38)
7. In the **phallic stage**, which occurs during the preschool years, pleasure is derived from genital stimulation and interest in physical differences between the sexes leads to the development of gender identity and to the child's identification with the moral standards of the same-sex parent. (p. 38)
8. During **latency**, which occurs in children from 7 to 11 years of age, sexual needs are quiet and psychic energy is invested in other activities. (p. 38)

   Memory aid: Something that is *latent* exists but is not manifesting itself.

9. During the **genital stage**, which begins during adolescence, mature sexual interests that last throughout adulthood emerge. (p. 38)
10. In Freud's theory, the **id** is the source of our unconscious impulses toward fulfillment of our needs. (p. 38)
11. According to Freud, the **ego** is the rational component of personality that develops in order to mediate between the unbridled demands of the id and the limits imposed by the real world. (p. 39)
12. The **superego** is the third component of personality according to Freud's theory. At age 4 or 5, the superego, which is like a relentless conscience that distinguishes right from wrong in unrealistically moral terms, begins to emerge as children identify with their parents' moral standards. (p. 39)
13. **Repression** is a Freudian defense mechanism in which a disturbing memory or impulse is blocked from consciousness. (p. 39)
14. In his **psychosocial theory**, Erikson proposed that development follows a sequence of eight stages, or crises, that are are centered on each person's relationship to the social environment. (p. 41)

    Memory aid: To help remember the difference between the theories of Freud and Erikson, remember that the former proposed a sequence of psycho*sexual* stages and the latter a sequence of psycho*social* stages.
15. According to **learning theory (behaviorism)**, development is a process of learning. Learning theorists have formulated laws of behavior that emphasize how environmental influences shape development. (p. 43)
16. Learning theorists explore the relationship between a particular experience or event (**stimulus**) and the behavioral reaction (**response**) associated with it. (p. 43)
17. **Conditioning** is the process of learning that occurs either through the association of two stimuli (classical conditioning) or through the use of positive or negative reinforcement (operant conditioning). (p. 43)
18. In **classical conditioning**, a person or an animal learns to associate a neutral stimulus with a meaningful one. Human emotional responses are susceptible to this type of learning. (p. 43)

    Memory aid: Classical conditioning is also called *respondent* conditioning because, in this case, learning involves involuntary *responses* elicited by specific stimuli.
19. In **operant conditioning**, a person or an animal learns to perform or to refrain from performing particular behaviors because of their consequences. According to B. F. Skinner, this type of learning plays a role in the acquisition of more complex responses. (p. 44)

    Memory aid: In operant, or *instrumental*, conditioning, voluntary behavior operates on the environment and is *instrumental* in obtaining rewards.
20. **Reinforcement** is the process that makes it more likely that a behavior will recur, and a **reinforcer** is the stumulus that strengthens a behavior or makes it occur more often. (p. 44)
21. A **positive reinforcer** is a pleasant stimulus, such as praise, presented following a desired behavior that increases the likelihood that the behavior will recur. (p. 44)
22. A **negative reinforcer** is the removal of an unpleasant stimulus following a desired behavior that increases the likelihood that the behavior will recur. (p. 45)

    Memory aid: In operant conditioning, "positive" and "negative" do not mean good and bad, but to present or withdraw a stimulus, respectively.
23. **Punishment** is the presentation of an unpleasant stimulus that makes a behavior less likely to be repeated. (p. 45)
24. **Extrinsic reinforcers** are reinforcers that come from the environment and other people—for example, money, praise, and privileges. (p. 45)
25. **Intrinsic reinforcers** are reinforcers that come from within the individual, such as pride in completing a difficult assignment. (p. 45)

    Memory aid: Extrinsic means "from the outside"; *intrinsic* means "from within."
26. An extension of learning theory, **social learning theory** emphasizes that people often learn new behaviors merely by observing others. (p. 46)
27. **Modeling** refers to the process by which we observe other people's behavior and then pattern our own after it. (p. 46)
28. Social learning is affected by perceptions of **self-efficacy**, that is, by a person's sense of his or her own goals and capabilities. (p. 47)
29. **Reciprocal determinism** is a social learning developmental concept that refers to the mutual interaction of a person's internal characteristics, the environment, and his or her behavior. (p. 47)
30. **Cognitive theory** emphasizes that individuals think and choose, and that these mental activities have a powerful influence on behavior. (p. 50)

31. According to Piaget, during the **sensorimotor stage** (birth–2 years) infants think exclusively through their senses and motor abilities. (p. 51)

32. According to Piaget, during the **preoperational stage** (2–6 years) children begin to think symbolically. (p. 51)

33. According to Piaget, during the **concrete operational stage** (7–11 years) children begin to think logically in a consistent way—but only about real and concrete features of their world. (p. 51)

    Memory aid: To help differentiate Piaget's stages, remember that "operations" are mental processes, such as conservation of liquids, that form the basis of logical thinking. *Pre*operational children, who lack these operations, are "before" this developmental milestone. Concrete operational children can operate on real, or concrete, objects.

34. In Piaget's final stage of cognitive development, the **formal operational stage** (from 12 years on), adolescents and adults are able, in varying degrees, to think hypothetically and abstractly. (p. 51)

35. In Piaget's theory, **equilibrium** refers to a universal need for mental balance between current experiences and a person's mental concepts (p. 51)

36. In Piaget's theory, a **schema** is a general way of thinking about, or interacting with, ideas and objects in the environment. (p. 52)

37. According to Piaget, **disequilibrium** is a state of mental imbalance that occurs when existing schemas do not fit present experiences. This imbalance eventually leads to cognitive growth. (p. 52)

    Memory aid: The prefix *dis* means "to cause to be the opposite of." *Disequilibrium* is the opposite of equilibrium.

38. In Piaget's view, cognitive understanding is achieved through two innate, interrelated processes: **organization** and **adaptation**. People organize their thoughts so that they make sense, separating important thoughts from those that are less important and connecting one idea to another. People adapt their thinking to include new experiences and maintain mental equilibrium. (p. 53)

39. **Assimilation** refers to the addition of new information to existing schemas. (p. 53)

40. **Accommodation** refers to the modification of existing schemas in order to incorporate new, conflicting experiences. (p. 53)

41. **Conservation of liquids** is the realization that the amount of liquid in a container does not change despite changes in the container's appearance. (p. 54)

42. Using the computer as a model for the human mind, **information-processing theory** studies the flow of information within the mind and the way information is handled by different cognitive processes. (p. 55)

43. The first step in the information-processing system occurs in the **sensory register**, where information is stored for a split second after it is received. (p. 55)

43. **Working memory**, also called short-term memory, is the information-processing stage in which current conscious mental activity occurs. (p. 55)

45. The **knowledge base**, or long-term memory, stores information for days, months, or even years. (p. 55)

46. In the information-processing theory, the **response generator** is a network of mental processes that organize behavior. (p. 55)

47. In the information-processing theory, **control processes**, such as memorization strategies, regulate the analysis and flow of information. (p. 56)

48. In contrast to a "reductionistic" approach, which breaks behavior into component drives, learned responses, and cognitive processes, a **holistic** view seeks to encompass all the diverse aspects of human experience. (p. 59)

49. In **humanistic theory**'s holistic view of human development, people are seen as unique, self-determined, and worthy of respect. (p. 59)

50. In humanistic theory, **self-actualization** refers to the human need to achieve one's full potential. (p. 59)

51. In Rogers' humanistic theory, **unconditional positive regard** refers to the feeling of unqualified respect and understanding that one person can have toward another. (p. 60)

52. According to Rogers, a **phenomenological** approach to others is an empathic openness to viewing the world from the other person's point of view. (p. 61)

53. Most contemporary developmentalists have an **eclectic perspective**: Rather than adopting any single theory exclusively, they incorporate insights from several perspectives. (p. 64)

CHAPTER 3 Heredity and Environment

Chapter Overview

Conception occurs when the male and female reproductive cells—the sperm and ovum, respectively—come together to create a new, one-celled organism with its own unique combination of genetic material. The genetic material furnishes the instructions for development—not only for obvious physical characteristics, such as sex, coloring, and body shape, but also for certain psychological characteristics, such as moodiness, intelligence, and verbal fluency.

Every year scientists make new discoveries and reach new understandings about genes and their effects on the development of individuals. This chapter presents some of their findings, including that most human characteristics are polygenic and multifactorial, the result of the interaction of many genetic and environmental influences. Perhaps the most important findings have come from research into the causes of genetic and chromosomal abnormalities. The chapter discusses the most common of these abnormalities and concludes with a discussion of genetic counseling. Genetic testing before and after conception can help predict whether a couple will have a child with a genetic problem.

Many students find the technical material in this chapter difficult to master, but it can be done with a great deal of rehearsal. Working the chapter review several times and mentally reciting terms are both useful techniques for rehearsing this type of material.

NOTE: Answer guidelines for all Chapter 3 questions begin on page 43.

Guided Study

The text chapter should be studied one section at a time. Before you read, preview each section by skimming it, noting headings and boldface items. Then read the appropriate section objectives from the following outline. Keep these objectives in mind and, as you read the chapter section, search for the information that will enable you to meet each objective. Once you have finished a section, write out answers for its objectives.

The Beginning of Development (pp. 68–69)

1. Describe the process of conception and the first hours of development of the zygote.

Genes and Chromosomes (pp. 69–74)

2. Identify the mechanisms of heredity and explain how sex is determined.

3. Discuss genetic uniqueness and distinguish between monozygotic and dizygotic twins.

4. Differentiate genotype from phenotype and explain the polygenic and multifactorial nature of human traits.

5. Explain the additive and dominant-recessive patterns of genetic interaction. Give examples of the traits that result from each type of interaction.

Identifying Genetic Influences (pp. 74–80)

6. Explain how scientists distinguish the effects of genes and environment on development.

7. Identify some environmental variables that affect genetic inheritance and describe how a particular trait, such as susceptibility to alcoholism or shyness, might be affected.

Genetic and Chromosomal Abnormalities (pp. 81–84)

8. Describe the most common chromosomal abnormalities.

9. Identify several common genetic disorders and discuss reasons for their relatively low incidence of occurrence.

Genetic Counseling (pp. 84–90)

10. Describe six situations in which couples should seek genetic testing and counseling.

Chapter Review

When you have finished reading the chapter, work through the material that follows to review it. Complete the sentences and answer the questions. As you proceed, evaluate your performance for each section by consulting the answers on page 43. Do not continue with the next section until you understand each answer. If you need to, review or reread the appropriate section in the textbook before continuing.

The Beginning of Development (pp. 68–69)

1. The human reproductive cells, which are called ____________, include the female's ____________ and the male's ____________.
2. When the gametes' genetic material combine, a one-celled organism referred to as a(n) ____________ is formed.
3. Before the zygote begins the process of cellular division that starts human development, the combined genetic material from both gametes is ____________ to form two complete sets of genetic instructions.
4. A complete copy of the genetic instructions inherited by the zygote at the moment of conception is found in ____________ (every/most/only a few) cell(s) of the body.

Genes and Chromosomes (pp. 69–74)

5. The body's genetic plans are stored within the ____________, which are segments of ____________ molecules, each arranged in particular ____________ sequences that direct the form and function of every body cell. The genes are organized in precise sequences on structures called ____________. Each person inherits ____________ of these structures, ____________ from each parent.
6. Scientists can create a picture of a person's chromosomes, called a(n) ____________, by removing, chemically treating, and photographing a cell taken from the person's body.
7. The developing person's sex is determined by the ____________ pair of chromosomes. In the female, this pair is composed of two ____________-shaped chromosomes and is designated ____________. In the male, this pair includes one ____________ and one ____________ chromosome and is therefore designated ____________.
8. During cell division, the gametes each receive ____________ (one/both) member(s) of each chromosome pair. Thus, in number each gamete has ____________ chromosomes.
9. The critical factor in the determination of a zygote's sex is which ____________ (sperm/ovum) reaches the other gamete first.
10. A ____________ (vast/slight) ____________ (majority/minority) of each person's genes are identical to those of any unrelated person of the same sex.
11. When the twenty-three chromosome pairs divide up during the formation of gametes, which of the two pair members will end up in a particular gamete is determined by ____________. Genetic variability is also affected by the exchange of segments of chromosome pairs, a process called ____________ ____________, and by the interaction of genetic instructions in ways unique to the individual. This means that any given mother and father can form approximately ____________ genetically different offspring.
12. Identical twins, which occur about once in every ____________ pregnancies, are called ____________ twins because they come from one zygote. Such twins ____________ (are/are not) genetically identical.
13. Twins who begin life as two separate zygotes created by the fertilization of two ova, are called ____________ twins. Such twins share approximately ____________ percent of their genes in common.
14. Most human characteristics are affected by many genes, and so are ____________; and by many factors, and so are ____________.

15. The total of all the genes a person inherits for a given trait is called the ______________________. The actual expression of traits is called the ______________________.

16. For any given trait, the phenotype arises from the interaction of the specific ______________________ that make up the genotype, and from the interaction between the genotype and the ______________________.

17. A phenotype that reflects the sum of all the genes involved in its determination illustrates the ______________________ pattern of genetic interaction. Genes that affect ______________________, most ______________ ______________________, and ______________ ______________________ are of this type.

18. In another pattern of genetic interaction, some genes are more influential than others; this is called the ______________________-______________________ pattern. In this pattern, the more influential gene is called ______________________, and the weaker gene is called ______________________. Hundreds of ______________________ characteristics follow this pattern.

19. A person who has a recessive gene paired with a dominant gene is said to be a(n) ______________________ of the recessive gene.

Explain how it is possible for two brown-eyed parents to have a blue-eyed child.

20. Some recessive genes are called ______________________ because they are located only on the *X* chromosome. Examples of such genes are the ones that determine ______________________ ______________________. Because they have only one X chromosome, ______________________ (females/males) are more likely to have these characteristics on their phenotype.

21. Recessive genes ______________________ (are/are not) always completely suppressed by dominant genes.

22. The complexity of genetic interaction is particularly apparent in ______________________ characteristics.

Identifying Genetic Influences (pp. 74–80)

23. To identify genetic influences on development, researchers must distinguish genetic effects from ______________________ effects. To this end, researchers study ______________________ and ______________________ children.

24. If ______________________ (monozygotic/dizygotic) twins are found to be much more similar on a particular trait than ______________________ (monozygotic/dizygotic) twins are, it is likely that genes play a significant role in the appearance of that trait.

25. Traits that show a strong correlation between adopted children and their ______________________ (adoptive/biological) parents suggest a genetic basis for those characteristics.

26. The best way to try to separate the effects of genes and environments is to study ______________________ twins who have been raised in ______________________ (the same/different) environments.

Explain how social scientists define environment.

27. Environment, as broadly defined in the textbook, affects ______________________ (most/every/few) human characteristic(s).

28. During the first half of the twentieth century, as ______ and ______ ______ improved, each generation grew slightly taller than the previous one. Over the past few decades, this trend has ______ (continued/stopped).

Briefly explain how shyness, which is influenced by genes, is also affected by the social environment.

29. Genes are ______ (often/rarely/never) the exclusive determinant of any psychological characteristic.

30. If one monozygotic twin becomes schizophrenic, the chances are about ______ percent that the other will too. Environmental influences ______ (do/do not) play an important role in the appearance of schizophrenia.

31. Alcoholism ______ (is/is not) strongly genetic; furthermore, its expression ______ (is/is not) affected by the environment. Certain temperamental traits correlate with abusive drinking, including ______ ______.

Genetic and Chromosomal Abnormalities (pp. 81–84)

32. Chromosomal abnormalities occur during the formation of the ______, producing a sperm or ovum that does not have the normal complement of chromosomes.

Give three reasons that researchers study genetic and chromosomal abnormalities.

33. An estimated ______ of all zygotes have too few or too many chromosomes. Most of these ______ (do/do not) begin to develop. Nevertheless, about 1 in every ______ newborns has one chromosome too few or one too many.

34. In most cases, the presence of an extra chromosome ______ (is/is not) lethal. Two exceptions are when the extra chromosome is at the ______ pair, or at the ______ pair. These cases lead to a recognizable ______.

35. The most common extra-chromosome syndrome is ______ ______, which is also called ______.

List several of the physical and psychological characteristics of Down-syndrome individuals.

36. About 1 in every 500 infants has a missing ______ chromosome, or three or more such chromosomes.

Look at Table 3.1 on page 83, which lists the most common sex-linked chromosomal abnormalities. List at least two characteristics associated with each of the following syndromes:

Kleinfelter syndrome: ______

XYY: ______

XXX: ______

Turner syndrome: ______

37. Genetic diseases that may be the result of extra genetic material on a particular chromosome include ______ ______.

38. When genetic material is missing, problems are usually ______ (more/less) severe than when additional genetic material is

present. The syndrome in which the newborn's cry resembles that of a cat, called ______ syndrome, is caused by missing material on chromosome ______.

39. In some individuals, part of the *X* chromosome is attached by such a thin string of molecules that it seems about to break off; this abnormality is called the ______ syndrome.

40. Chromosomal abnormalities such as Down and Kleinfelter syndromes ______ (occur/do not occur) more frequently when the parents are middle-aged, possibly because of ______.

41. It is much ______ (more/less) likely that a person is a carrier of one or more harmful genes than that he or she has abnormal chromosomes.

42. Although all of us carry some of the destructive genes of our parents, most babies have no apparent genetic problems because many genetic problems are ______, others are ______, and many are ______. About one in every ______ babies is born with a serious genetic problem.

Study Table 3.2 (pp. 86–87). Name two common genetic diseases or conditions that are multifactorial.

______

______

Name two genetic diseases or conditions that are carried by a recessive gene.

______

______

Genetic Counseling (pp. 84–90)

43. Through ______ ______, couples today can learn more about their genes, and about their chances of conceiving a child with chromosomal or other genetic abnormalities.

44. List six situations in which genetic counseling is strongly recommended.
   - **a.** ______
   - **b.** ______ ______
   - **c.** ______
   - **d.** ______
   - **e.** ______
   - **f.** ______

45. A simple blood test is all that is needed for carrier detection of the genes for ______ ______.

For disorders for which the harmful genes have yet to be located, screening involves identifying the presence of ______ in the person's phenotype or genotype.

46. The worldwide effort to map all the codes of the 100,000 human genes is called the ______ ______ ______.

47. When two carriers of the same recessive gene for a particular disorder procreate, each of their children has one chance in ______ of having the disease. When genetic diseases are carried by the dominant rather than the recessive gene, the chances are about ______ that a child will inherit the condition.

48. Once pregnancy has begun, further tests, such as testing the level of ______, the ______, ______, and ______ ______ ______, can often reveal if the fetus has an abnormality.

49. It is estimated that, within the next decade, researchers will be able to detect elevated genetic vulnerability for many conditions, including ______.

Progress Test 1

Circle your answers to the following questions and check them against the answers on page 45. If your answer is incorrect, read the explanation for why it is incorrect and then consult the appropriate pages of the text (in parentheses following the correct answer).

Multiple-Choice Questions

1. When a sperm and an ovum merge, the new cell is called a:
   a. zygote.
   b. reproductive cell.
   c. gamete.
   d. monozygote.

2. Genes are segments of DNA molecules that provide the biochemical instructions a cell needs to become:
   a. a zygote.
   b. a chromosome.
   c. a specific part of a functioning human body.
   d. deoxyribonucleic acid.

3. In the male, the twenty-third pair of chromosomes is designated ________________ ; in the female, this pair is designated ________________ .
   a. *XX*; *XY*
   b. *XY*; *XX*
   c. *XO*; *XXY*
   d. *XXY*; *XO*

4. Since the twenty-third pair of chromosomes in females is *XX*, each ovum carries an:
   a. *XX* zygote.
   b. *X* zygote.
   c. *XY* zygote.
   d. *X* chromosome.

5. When a zygote splits, the two identical, independent clusters that develop become:
   a. dizygotic twins.
   b. monozygotic twins.
   c. fraternal twins.
   d. trizygotic twins.

6. In scientific research, the *best* way to separate the effects of genes and the environment is to study:
   a. dizygotic twins.
   b. adopted children and their biological parents.
   c. adopted children and their adoptive parents.
   d. monozygotic twins raised in different environments.

7. Genes are organized in a precise sequence on threadlike structures called:
   a. DNA.
   b. dizygotes.
   c. monozygotes.
   d. chromosomes.

8. When we say that a characteristic is multifactorial, we mean that:
   a. many genes are involved.
   b. many environmental factors are involved.
   c. many genetic and environmental factors are involved.
   d. the characteristic is polygenic.

9. Genes are composed of molecules of:
   a. genotype.
   b. deoxyribonucleic acid (DNA).
   c. karyotype.
   d. chromosome.

10. The potential for genetic diversity in humans is so great because:
    a. there are approximately 8 million possible combinations of chromosomes.
    b. when the sperm and ovum unite, genetic combinations not present in either parent can be formed.
    c. just before a chromosome pair divides during the formation of gametes, genes cross over and create new recombinations.
    d. of all the above reasons.

11. A chromosomal abnormality that affects males only involves an:
    a. *XO* chromosomal pattern.
    b. *XXX* chromosomal pattern.
    c. *YY* chromosonal pattern.
    d. *XXY* or *XYY* chromosomal pattern.

12. Polygenic complexity is most apparent for ________________ characteristics.
    a. physical
    b. psychological
    c. recessive gene
    d. dominant gene

13. Babies born with trisomy-21 (Down syndrome) are often:
    a. born to older parents.
    b. unusually aggressive.
    c. abnormally tall by adolescence.
    d. blind.

14. Some serious diseases or handicaps are polygenic. This means that:
    a. many genes make it more likely that the individual will inherit the disease or handicap.
    b. several genes must be present in order for the individual to inherit the disease or handicap.
    c. the condition is multifactorial.
    d. most people carry some destructive genes for the disease or handicap.

15. Many genetic diseases are recessive, so the child cannot inherit the condition unless both parents:
    a. have Kleinfelter syndrome.
    b. carry the same recessive gene.
    c. have *XO* chromosomes.
    d. have the disease.

Matching Items

Match each term with its corresponding description or definition.

Terms

_______ 1. gametes
_______ 2. chromosome
_______ 3. genotype
_______ 4. phenotype
_______ 5. markers
_______ 6. monozygotic
_______ 7. dizygotic
_______ 8. additive
_______ 9. fragile-X syndrome
_______ 10. carrier
_______ 11. zygote

Descriptions or Definitions

a. a person's genetic potential for a particular characteristic
b. identical twins
c. sperm and ovum
d. the first cell of the developing person
e. a person who has a recessive gene paired with a dominant gene
f. fraternal twins
g. a pattern in which each gene in question makes an active contribution to the final outcome
h. a threadlike structure of DNA
i. the behavioral or physical expression of genetic potential
j. indicators of harmful genes
k. a chromosomal abnormality

Progress Test 2

Progress Test 2 should be completed during a final chapter review. Answer the following questions after you thoroughly understand the correct answers for the Chapter Review and Progress Test 1.

1. Which of the following provides the best broad description of the relationship between heredity and environment in determining development?
   a. Heredity is the primary influence, with environment affecting development only in severe situations.
   b. Heredity and environment contribute equally to development.
   c. Environment is the major influence on physical characteristics.
   d. Heredity determines the individual's potential and environment determines whether and to what degree the individual reaches that potential.

2. Research studies of monozygotic twins who were raised apart suggest that:
   a. virtually every human trait is affected by both genes and environment.
   b. only a few psychological traits, such as emotional reactivity, are affected by genes.
   c. most traits are determined by environmental influences.
   d. most traits are determined by genes.

3. Males with the "fragile-X syndrome" are:
   a. feminine in appearance.
   b. less severely affected than females.
   c. frequently retarded intellectually.
   d. unusually tall and aggressive.

4. Which of the following is true regarding genetic diseases that are caused by dominant or recessive genes?
   a. There are twice as many known recessive-gene disorders.
   b. There are twice as many known dominant-gene disorders.
   c. There are an equal number of dominant- and recessive-gene disorders.
   d. Research has not shown either type of disorder to be more common than the other.

5. The incidence of sickle-cell anemia, phenylketonuria, thalassemia, and Tay-Sachs disease indicate that:
   a. these disorders are more common today than 50 years ago.
   b. these disorders are less common today than 50 years ago.
   c. certain genetic disorders are more common in certain ethnic groups.
   d. a. and c. are true.

6. Dizygotic twins result when:
   a. a single egg is fertilized by a sperm and then splits.
   b. a single egg is fertilized by two sperm.
   c. two eggs are fertilized by different sperm.
   d. either a single egg is fertilized by one sperm or two eggs are fertilized by different sperm.

7. The threadlike structures of DNA that in humans are organized into twenty-three distinct pairs are called:
   a. zygotes.
   b. genes.
   c. chromosomes.
   d. ova.

8. Shortly after the zygote is formed, it begins a process of duplication and division. Each resulting new cell has:
   a. the same number of chromosomes that was contained in the zygote.
   b. half the number of chromosomes that was contained in the zygote.
   c. twice, then four times, then eight times the number of chromosomes that was contained in the zygote.
   d. all the chromosomes except those that determine sex.

9. If an ovum is fertilized by a sperm bearing a *Y* chromosome:
   a. a female will develop.
   b. cell division will result.
   c. a male will develop.
   d. spontaneous abortion will take place.

10. When the male cells in the testes and the female cells in the ovaries divide to produce gametes, they do so in a way that is different from that of body cells. The difference is that the resulting gametes have:
    a. one rather than both members of each chromosome pair.
    b. twenty-three chromosome pairs.
    c. *X* but not *Y* chromosomes.
    d. chromosomes from both parents.

11. Most human traits are:
    a. polygenic.
    b. multifactorial.
    c. determined by dominant-recessive patterns.
    d. a. and b.
    e. all of the above.

12. Genotype is to phenotype as ______________ is to ______________.
    a. genetic potential; physical expression
    b. physical expression; genetic potential
    c. sperm; ovum
    d. gamete; zygote

13. The genes that influence height, most intellectual abilities, and temperamental traits interact according to the ______________ pattern.
    a. dominant-recessive
    b. *X*-linked
    c. additive
    d. subtractive

14. *X*-linked recessive genes explain why some traits seem to be passed:
    a. from father to son.
    b. from father to daughter.
    c. from mother to daughter.
    d. from mother to son.

15. According to the text, the effects of environment on genetic inheritance include:
    a. direct effects, such as nutrition, climate, and medical care.
    b. indirect effects, such as the individual's broad economic, political, and cultural context.
    c. irreversible effects, such as those due to brain injury.
    d. everything that can interact with the person's genetic inheritance at every point of life.

True or False Items

Write *true* or *false* on the line in front of each statement.

______ 1. Most human characteristics are multifactorial, caused by the interaction of genetic and environmental factors.

______ 2. Less than 10 percent of all zygotes have harmful genes or abnormal chromosomal makeup.

______ 3. Research suggests that susceptibility to alcoholism is at least partly the result of genetic inheritance.

______ 4. The human reproductive cells (ova and sperm) are called gametes.

______ 5. Only a very few human traits are polygenic.

______ 6. The zygote contains all the biologically inherited information—the genes and chromosomes—that a person will have during his or her life.

______ 7. A couple should probably seek genetic counseling if several earlier pregnancies ended in spontaneous abortion.

_______ 8. Many genetic conditions are recessive, so a child will have the condition even if only the mother carries the gene.

_______ 9. Two people who have the same phenotype may have a different genotype for a trait such as eye color.

_______ 10. When cells divide to produce reproductive cells (gametes), each sperm or ovum receives only twenty-three chromosomes, half as many as the original cell.

Challenge Test

Answer these questions the day before an exam as a final check on your understanding of the chapter's terms and concepts.

1. Each person has two eye-color genes, one from each parent. If one gene is for brown eyes and the other for blue, the person's eye color is:
   a. blue.
   b. recessively produced.
   c. brown.
   d. impossible to predict.

2. If two people have brown eyes, they have the same phenotype with regard to eye color. Their brown eyes may be caused by:
   a. different genotypes.
   b. one brown-eye gene and one blue-eye gene.
   c. two brown-eye genes.
   d. all of the above.

3. Eye color can be hundreds of shades and tones, depending on the genes inherited. This is a result of:
   a. sex-linked chromosomal inheritance.
   b. the influence of the dominant genes only.
   c. the action of the twenty-third chromosome pair.
   d. polygenic inheritance.

4. Some men are color-blind because they inherit a particular recessive gene from their mother. That recessive gene is carried on:
   a. the *X* chromosome.
   b. the *XX* chromosome pair.
   c. the *Y* chromosome.
   d. the *X* or *Y* chromosome.

5. If your parents are much taller than your grandparents, the explanation probably lies in:
   a. genetics.
   b. environmental factors.
   c. better family planning.
   d. good genetic counseling.

6. If a dizygotic twin becomes schizophrenic, the likelihood of the other twin experiencing serious mental illness is much lower than with monozygotic twins. This suggests that:
   a. schizophrenia is caused by genes.
   b. schizophrenia is influenced by genes.
   c. environment is unimportant in the development of schizophrenia.
   d. monozygotic twins are especially vulnerable to schizophrenia.

7. A person's skin turns yellow-orange as result of a carrot-juice diet regimen. This is an example of:
   a. an environmental influence.
   b. an alteration in genotype.
   c. polygenic inheritance.
   d. a secular trend.

8. The personality trait of shyness seems to be partly genetic. A child who inherits the genes for shyness will be shy:
   a. under most circumstances.
   b. only if shyness is the dominant gene.
   c. if the environment does not encourage greater sociability.
   d. if he or she is raised by biological rather than adoptive parents.

9. If a man carries the recessive gene for Tay-Sachs disease and his wife does not, the chances of their having a child with Tay-Sachs disease is:
   a. one in four.
   b. fifty-fifty.
   c. zero.
   d. dependent upon the wife's ethnic background.

10. One of the best ways to distinguish how much genetic and environmental factors affect behavior is to compare children who have:
    a. the same genes and environments.
    b. different genes and environments.
    c. similar genes and environments.
    d. the same genes but different environments.

11. Even when identical twins have been reared apart, researchers have generally found strong similarities because:
    a. identical twins tend to evoke similar degrees of warmth and encouragement.
    b. they are usually raised in families that have a great deal in common culturally.
    c. most identical twins reared apart have quite similar home experiences.
    d. of all of the above reasons.

12. Laurie and Brad, who both have a history of alcoholism in their families, are concerned that the child they hope to have will inherit a genetic predisposition to alcoholism. Based on information presented in the text, what advice should you offer them?
    a. "Stop worrying, alcoholism is only weakly genetic."
    b. "It is almost certain that your child will become alcoholic."
    c. "Social influences, such as the family and peer environment, play a critical role in determining whether alcoholism is expressed."
    d. "Wait to have children until you are both middle-aged, in order to see if the two of you become alcoholic."
13. Sixteen-year-old Joey experiences some mental slowness and hearing and heart problems, yet he is able to care for himself and is unusually sweet-tempered. Joey probably:
    a. is mentally retarded.
    b. has Alzheimer's disease.
    c. has Kleinfelter syndrome.
    d. has Down syndrome.
14. Genetically, Claude's potential height is 6'0. Because he did not receive a balanced diet, however, he grew to only 5'9". Claude's actual height is an example of a:
    a. recessive gene.
    b. dominant gene.
    c. genotype.
    d. phenotype.
15. Winona inherited a gene from her mother that, regardless of her father's contribution to her genotype, will be expressed in her phenotype. Evidently the gene Winona received from her mother is a(n) ________________ gene.
    a. polygenic
    b. recessive
    c. dominant
    d. *X*-linked

Key Terms

Using your own words, write on a separate piece of paper a brief definition or explanation of each of the following terms.

1. gametes
2. ovum
3. sperm
4. zygote
5. genes
6. DNA (deoxyribonucleic acid)
7. chromosomes
8. twenty-third pair
9. *XX*
10. *XY*
11. monozygotic twins
12. dizygotic twins
13. polygenic
14. multifactorial
15. genotype
16. phenotype
17. additive pattern
18. dominant-recessive pattern
19. carrier
20. *X*-linked gene
21. environment
22. syndrome
23. Down syndrome (trisomy-21)
24. fragile-*X* syndrome
25. genetic counseling
26. markers
27. Human Genome Project
28. alphafetoprotein (AFP)
29. sonogram
30. amniocentesis
31. chorionic villi sampling

ANSWERS

CHAPTER REVIEW

1. gametes; ova; sperm
2. zygote
3. duplicated
4. every
5. genes; DNA; coded; 100,000; chromosomes; 46; 23
6. karyotype
7. twenty-third; *X*; *XX*; *X*; *Y*; *XY*
8. one; 23
9. sperm
10. vast; majority
11. chance; crossing over; 64 trillion
12. 200; monozygotic; are
13. dizygotic; 50

14. polygenic; multifactorial
15. genotype; phenotype
16. genes; environment
17. additive; height, intellectual abilities; temperamental traits
18. dominant-recessive; dominant; recessive; physical
19. carrier

Eye color follows the dominant-recessive pattern of genetic interaction. Thus, a person with brown eyes (phenotype) may have two dominant genes for brown eyes (genotype)—or one dominant gene for brown eyes and a recessive gene for blue eyes (genotype). In order for a child to inherit blue eyes from brown-eyed parents, both parents have to be carriers, with each contributing the recessive gene for blue eyes.

20. X-linked; color blindness, certain allergies and diseases, some learning disabilities; males
21. are not
22. psychological
23. environmental; twins; adopted
24. monozygotic; dizygotic
25. biological
26. identical (monozygotic); different

Social scientists define *environment* broadly to refer to the multitude of variables that can interact with the person's genetic inheritance at every point of life. These variables include direct effects, such as nutrition, climate, medical care, and family interaction; indirect effects, such as the broad economic, political, and cultural context; irreversible effects, such as the impact of brain injury; and less permanent effects, such as the impact of the immediate social environment on temper.

27. every
28. nutrition; medical care; stopped

A genetically shy child whose parents are outgoing would have many contacts with other people and would observe his or her parents socializing more freely than if this same child's parents were also shy. The child will probably grow up less timid socially than he or she would have with more introverted parents, despite the genetic predisposition toward shyness.

29. never
30. 50; do
31. is; is; a quick temper, willingness to take risks, and a high level of anxiety
32. gametes

By studying genetic disruptions of normal development, researchers (a) gain a fuller appreciation of the complexities of genetic interaction, (b) reduce misinformation and prejudice directed toward those afflicted by such disórders, and (c) help individuals understand the likelihood of occurrence and to become better prepared to limit their harmful effects.

33. half; do not; 200
34. is; twenty-first; twenty-third; syndrome
35. Down syndrome; trisomy-21

Most Down syndrome people have certain facial characteristics—a thick tongue, round face, slanted eyes—as well as distinctive hands, feet, and fingerprints. Many also have hearing problems, heart abnormalities, muscle weakness, and short stature. Almost all experience some mental slowness.

36. sex

Kleinfelter syndrome (*XXY*): undeveloped secondary sex characteristics; learning disabled

XYY: prone to acne, unusually tall, aggressive, and mildly retarded

XXX: retarded in most intellectual skills; normal female appearance

Turner syndrome (*XO*): short in stature, undeveloped secondary sex characteristics, learning disabled

37. Charcot-Marie Tooth syndrome, some forms of Alzheimer's disease, and schizophrenia
38. more; cri du chat; 4 or 5
39. fragile-X
40. occur; degeneration of the aging gametes
41. more
42. recessive; polygenic; multifactorial; thirty

Multifactorial diseases: cleft palate, cleft lip, club foot, hydrocephalus, pyloric stenosis, muscular dystrophy, neural tube defects

Recessive gene diseases: thalassemia, Tay-Sachs, sickle-cell anemia, PKU, cystic fibrosis

43. genetic counseling
44. Genetic counseling is recommended for (a) those who already have a child with a genetic disease; (b) those who have relatives with genetic problems; (c) those who have had previous pregnancies that ended in spontaneous abortions; (d) those who have a history of infertility; (e) those in which the woman is over 34 or the man is over 44; and (f) those whose ancestors came from particular regions of the world where matings usually occurred between members of the same group.

45. sickle-cell anemia, Tay-Sachs, PKU, hemophilia, thalassemia; markers
46. Human Genome Project
47. four; 50-50
48. AFP; sonogram; amniocentesis; chorionic villi sampling (CVS)
49. cancer, heart disease, diabetes, many types of retardation and psychopathology

PROGRESS TEST 1

Multiple-Choice Questions

1. **a.** is the answer. (p. 68)

   b. & c. The reproductive cells (sperm and ova), which are also called gametes, are individual entities.

   d. *Monozygote* refers to one member of a pair of identical twins.

2. **c.** is the answer. (p. 69)

   a. The zygote is the first cell of the developing person.

   b. Like genes, chromosomes are units of heredity that are found *within* cells.

   d. DNA is deoxyribonucleic acid.

3. **b.** is the answer. (p. 70)

4. **d.** is the answer. When the gametes are formed, one member of each chromosome pair splits off; since in females both are *X* chromosomes, each ovum must carry an *X* chromosome. (p. 70)

   a., b., & c. The zygote refers to the merged sperm and ovum that is the first new cell of the developing individual.

5. **b.** is the answer. *Mono* means "one." Thus, monozygotic twins develop from one zygote. (p. 71)

   a. & c. Dizygotic, or fraternal, twins develop from two (*di*) fertilized ova.

   d. A trizygotic birth would result in triplets (*tri*), rather than twins.

6. **d.** is the answer. This is so because, in this situation, one factor (genetic similarity) is held constant while the other factor (environment) is varied. Therefore, any similarity in traits is strong evidence of genetic inheritance. (pp. 74–75)

7. **d.** is the answer. (p. 69)

   a. Genes are segments of DNA.

   b. Dizygotes are fraternal twins.

   c. Monozygotes are identical twins.

8. **c.** is the answer. (p. 72)

   a., b., & d. *Polygenic* means "many genes"; *multifactorial* means "many factors," which are not limited to either genetic or environmental ones.

9. **b.** is the answer. (p. 69)

   a. Genotype is a person's genetic potential.

   c. A karyotype is a picture of a person's chromosomes.

   d. Genes are organized into sequences on chromosomes.

10. **d.** is the answer. (pp. 70–71)

11. **d.** is the answer. (p. 83)

    a. & b. These chromosomal abnormalities affect females.

    c. There is no such abnormality.

12. **b.** is the answer. (p. 74)

    c. & d. The text does not equate polygenic complexity with either recessive or dominant genes.

13. **a.** is the answer. (pp. 83–84)

14. **b.** is the answer. (p. 72)

    a. It is the combination of several specific genes that makes polygenic diseases somewhat uncommon.

    c. Multifactorial diseases are those that are manifest only if several influences, both genetic and environmental, are present.

    d. Although this is true, it is not the definition of *polygenic.*

15. **b.** is the answer. (p. 84)

    a. & c. These abnormalities involve the sex chromosomes, not genes.

    d. In order for an offspring to inherit a recessive condition, the parents need only be carriers of the recessive gene in their genotypes; they need not actually have the disease.

Matching Items

1. c (p. 68)	5. j (p. 88)	9. k (p. 83)
2. h (p. 69)	6. b (p. 71)	10. e (p. 73)
3. a (p. 72)	7. f (p. 71)	11. d (p. 68)
4. i (p. 72)	8. g (p. 72)	

PROGRESS TEST 2

Multiple-Choice Questions

1. **d.** is the answer. (p. 78)
2. **a.** is the answer. (p. 75)
3. **c.** is the answer. (p. 83)

   a. Physical appearance is usually normal in this syndrome.

b. Males are more frequently and more severely affected.

d. This is true of the *XXY* chromosomal abnormality, but not the fragile-X syndrome.

4. **b.** is the answer. (p. 89)
5. **c.** is the answer. Sickle-cell anemia is more common among African-Americans; phenylketonuria, among those of Scandinavian ancestry; thalassemia, among Greek, Italian, Thai, and Indian-Americans; and Tay-Sachs, among Jews of Polish descent as well as certain French-Canadians. (pp. 86–87)

   a. & b. The text does not present evidence indicating that the incidence of these disorders has changed.
6. **c.** is the answer. (p. 71)

   a. This would result in monozygotic twins.

   b. Only one sperm can fertilize an ovum.

   d. A single egg fertilized by one sperm would produce a single offspring or monozygotic twins.
7. **c.** is the answer. (p. 69)

   a. Zygotes are fertilized ova.

   b. Genes are the smaller units of heredity that are organized into sequences on chromosomes.

   d. Ova are female reproductive cells.
8. **a.** is the answer. (p. 68)
9. **c.** is the answer. The ovum will contain an *X* chromosome, and with the sperm's *Y* chromosome, will produce the male *XY* pattern. (p. 70)

   a. Only if the ovum is fertilized by an *X* chromosome from the sperm will a female develop.

   b. Cell division will occur regardless of whether the sperm contributes an *X* or a *Y* chromosome.

   d. Spontaneous abortions are likely to occur when there are chromosomal or genetic abnormalities; the situation described is perfectly normal.
10. **a.** is the answer. (p. 70)

    b. & d. These are true of all body cells *except* the gametes.

    c. Gametes have either *X* or *Y* chromosomes.
11. **d.** is the answer. (p. 72)
12. **a.** is the answer. Genotype refers to the total of all the genes a person inherits for a given characteristic; phenotype refers to the actual expression of that characteristic. (p. 72)
13. **c.** is the answer. (p. 72)
14. **d.** is the answer. *X*-linked genes are located only on the *X* chromosome. Since males inherit only one *X* chromosome, they are more likely than females to have these characteristics on their phenotype. (p. 73)
15. **d.** is the answer. (p. 75)

True or False Items

1. T (p. 73)
2. F An estimated half of all zygotes have an odd number of chromosomes. (p. 81)
3. T (p. 80)
4. T (p. 68)
5. F Most traits are polygenic. (p. 72)
6. T (p. 69)
7. T (p. 85)
8. F A trait from a recessive gene will be part of the phenotype only when the person has two recessive genes for that trait. (p. 84)
9. T (p. 72)
10. T (p. 70)

CHALLENGE TEST

1. **c.** is the answer. If one gene is for brown eyes and the other for blue, the person's eyes will be brown, since the brown-eye gene is dominant. (p. 73)

   b. In this eye-color example, the dominant gene will determine the phenotype.
2. **d.** is the answer. (pp. 72–73)
3. **d.** is the answer. (p. 72)

   a. & c. Eye color is not a sex-linked trait.

   b. Recessive genes are not always completely suppressed by dominant genes.
4. **a.** is the answer. (p. 73)

   b. The male genotype is *XY*, not *XX*.

   c. & d. The mother contributes only an *X* chromosome.
5. **b.** is the answer. This trend in increased height has been attributed to improved nutrition and medical care. (p. 78)

   a., c., & d. It is unlikely that these factors account for height differences from one generation to the next.
6. **b.** is the answer. Since monozygotic twins are genetically identical, while dizygotic twins share only 50 percent of their genes in common, greater similarity of traits between monozygotic twins suggests that genes play an important role. (p. 79)

   a. & c. Even though schizophrenia has a strong genetic component, it is not the case that if one twin is schizophrenic the other is also automatically. Therefore, the environment also is an important influence.

d. This does not necessarily follow.

7. **a.** is the answer. (p. 75)

   b. Genotype is a person's genetic potential, established at conception.

   c. Polygenic inheritance refers to the influence of many genes on a particular trait.

   d. The secular trend refers to the increase in average height that occurred from one generation to the next during the first part of the twentieth century.

8. **c.** is the answer. (p. 78)

   a. & b. Research on adopted children shows that shyness is affected both by genetic inheritance and the social environment. Therefore, if a child's environment promotes socializing outside the immediate family, a genetically shy child might grow up much less timid socially than he or she would have with less outgoing parents.

   d. Either biological or adoptive parents are capable of nurturing, or not nurturing, shyness in their children.

9. **c.** is the answer. Tay-Sachs is a recessive-gene disorder; therefore, in order for a child to inherit this disease, he or she must receive the recessive gene from both parents. (p. 84)

10. **d.** is the answer. To separate the influences of genes and environment, one of the two must be held constant. (p. 75)

    a., b., & c. These situations would not allow a researcher to separate the contributions of heredity and environment.

11. **d.** is the answer. (p. 77)

12. **c.** is the answer. (pp. 79–80)

    a. Some people's inherited biochemistry makes them highly susceptible to alcoholism.

    b. Despite a strong genetic influence, the environment plays a critical role in the expression of alcoholism.

    d. Not only is this advice unreasonable, but it might increase the likelihood of chromosomal abnormalities in the parent's sperm and ova.

13. **d.** is the answer. (pp. 81–82)

14. **d.** is the answer. (p. 72)

    a. & b. Genes are segments of DNA.

    c. Genotype refers to genetic potential.

15. **c.** is the answer. (p. 73)

    a. There is no such thing as a "polygenic gene." *Polygenic* means "many genes."

    b. A recessive gene paired with a dominant gene will not be expressed in the phenotype.

    d. *X*-linked genes are recessive genes.

KEY TERMS

1. **Gametes** are the human reproductive cells. (p. 68)
2. **Ovum** (the Latin word for "egg") refers to the female reproductive cell, which, if united with a sperm, develops into a new individual. (p. 68)
3. Male gametes are called **sperm**. (p. 68)
4. The **zygote** (a term derived from the Greek word for "joint") is the fertilized egg, that is, the one-celled organism formed during conception by the union of sperm and egg. (p. 68)
5. **Genes** are segments of DNA molecules that are the basic units of heredity. (p. 69)
6. **DNA (deoxyribonucleic acid)** is a complex molecule containing genetic information that makes up the chromosomes. (p. 69)
7. **Chromosomes** are threadlike structures of DNA, which contain the genes organized in precise sequences. (p. 69)
8. The **twenty-third pair** of chromosomes determines the individual's sex. (p. 70)
9. In the female, the twenty-third pair of chromosomes is composed of two large, *X*-shaped chromosomes, accordingly designated *XX*. (p. 70)
10. In the male, the twenty-third pair of chromosomes is composed of one large *X*-shaped chromosome and one, much smaller *Y*-shaped chromosome, accordingly designated *XY*. (p. 70)
11. **Monozygotic**, or identical, **twins** develop from a single fertilized ovum that splits in two, producing two genetically identical zygotes. (p. 71)

    Memory aid: Mono means "one"; **monozygotic twins** develop from one fertilized ovum.

12. **Dizygotic**, or fraternal, **twins** develop from two separate ova fertilized by different sperm and therefore are no more genetically similar than ordinary siblings. (p. 71)

    Memory aid: A fraternity is a group of two (*di*) or more nonidentical individuals.

13. Most human traits, especially psychological traits, are **polygenic**, that is, affected by many genes. (p. 72)
14. Most human traits are also **multifactorial**—that is, influenced by many factors, including genetic and environmental factors. (p. 72)

    Memory aid: The roots of the words *polygenic* and *multifactorial* give their meaning: *poly* means "many" and *genic* means "of the genes"; *multi* means "several" and *factorial* is obviously factors.

15. The total of all the genes a person inherits for a given characteristic—his or her genetic potential—is called the **genotype.** (p. 72)
16. The actual physical or behavioral expression of a genotype, the result of the interaction of the genes with each other and with the environment, is called the **phenotype.** (p. 72)
17. In the **additive pattern** of genetic interaction, the phenotype reflects the sum of all the genes involved. The genes affecting height, for example, interact in this fashion. (p. 72)
18. In the **dominant-recessive pattern**, some genes are dominant and act in a controlling dominant manner as they hide the influence of the weaker (recessive) genes. (p. 73)
19. A person who has a recessive gene in his or her genotype is called a **carrier** of that gene. (p. 73)
20. **X-linked genes** are recessive genes that are located only on the *X* chromosome. Since males have only one *X* chromosome, they are more likely to have these characteristics determined by these genes in their phenotype than are females. (p. 73)
21. When social scientists discuss the effects of the **environment** on genes, they are referring to everything—from the impact of the immediate cell environment on the genes to the multitude of ways elements in the outside world, such as nutrition, climate, and family interactions—that might impinge on the individual. (p. 75)
22. A **syndrome** is a cluster of distinct characteristics that tend to occur together. (p. 81)
23. **Down syndrome (trisomy-21)** is a chromosomal disorder in which there is an extra chromosome at site 21. Most Down syndrome people have distinctive physical and psychological characteristics, including rounded face, short stature, and mental slowness. (p. 81)
24. The **fragile-*X* syndrome** is a single gene disorder in which part of the *X* chromosome is attached by such a thin string of molecules that it seems about to break off. Although the characteristics associated with this syndrome are quite varied, mental deficiency is relatively common. (p. 83)
25. **Genetic counseling** involves a variety of tests through which couples can learn more about their genes, and can thus make informed decisions about their childbearing future. (p. 84)
26. **Markers** are harmless physical, behavioral, or sometimes genetic characteristics that suggest that an individual is a carrier of harmful genes. (p. 88)
27. The **Human Genome Project** is a worldwide effort to map all 3 billion codes of the 100,000 human genes. (p. 88)
28. Testing the level of **alphafetoprotein (AFP)** in the mother's blood indicates the possibility that a fetus has a neural tube defect or Down syndrome. (p. 89)
29. A **sonogram** uses high frequency sound waves to outline the shape of the fetus, allowing the detection of abnormalities in body shape or rate of growth. (p. 89)
30. **Amniocentesis** is a genetic test in which amniotic fluid is withdrawn and analyzed for chromosomal abnormalities, as well as other genetic and prenatal problems.
31. In **chorionic villi sampling (CVS)**, a tiny piece of the placental membrane is obtained and analyzed, providing much the same information as in amniocentesis, only sooner. (p. 89)

CHAPTER 4 Prenatal Development and Birth

Chapter Overview

Chapter 4 discusses prenatal development, the prevention of problems that can occur during the prenatal period or at birth, the birth process and the newborn's first few minutes, and, finally, the impact of the birth on the family.

Prenatal development is complex and startlingly rapid—more rapid than any other period of the life span. During the prenatal period, the individual develops from a one-celled zygote to a complex human baby. Whether that baby is born without defects depends on the complex web of both destructive and protective factors to which the mother-to-be may be exposed. Birth marks the most radical transition of the entire life span—that is, the biggest change or adjustment. The developing person moves from the protective environment of the uterus to the outside world, and becomes a separate and named member of the family and the community.

The way in which birth occurs can significantly affect the developing person, as can various environmental hazards that can result in low-birth-weight, preterm, and SGA infants. The last section discusses birth as it affects family members and aspects of the attachment that forms between parents and their children during the first few hours and weeks of life, and throughout childhood.

NOTE: Answer guidelines for all Chapter 4 questions begin on page 60.

Guided Study

The text chapter should be studied one section at a time. Before you read, preview each section by skimming it, noting headings and boldface items. Then read the appropriate section objectives from the following outline. Keep these objectives in mind and, as you read the chapter section, search for the information that will enable you to meet each objective. Once you have finished a section, write out answers for its objectives.

From Zygote to Newborn (pp. 94–98)

1. Describe the significant developments that occur during the germinal period.

2. Describe the significant developments that occur during the period of the embryo.

3. Describe the significant developments that occur during the period of the fetus.

Potential Complications (pp. 98–107)

4. Identify the most common causes of major congenital malformations, define teratology, and discuss several factors that determine whether a specific teratogen will be harmful.

5. (Text and Research Report) Identify at least five teratogens and describe their effects on the developing embryo or fetus, focusing on the effects of social drugs.

6. Discuss several factors that may moderate the risk of teratogenic exposure.

Birth (pp. 107–113)

7. Describe the birth process, as well as how the newborn's condition is assessed at birth.

8. Distinguish among low-birth-weight, preterm, and small-for-gestational-age infants and discuss the possible causes, challenges, and consequences of these conditions.

Birth as a Family Event (pp. 113–118)

9. Discuss the advantages of prepared childbirth for both the baby and the new parents, and characterize the experience of siblings in the birth event.

10. Explain the concept of parent-infant bonding and the current view of most developmentalists on bonding in humans.

Chapter Review

When you have finished reading the chapter, work through the material that follows to review it. Complete the sentences and answer the questions. As you proceed, evaluate your performance for each section by consulting the answers on page 60. Do not continue with the next section until you understand each answer. If you need to, review or reread the appropriate section in the textbook before continuing.

From Zygote to Newborn (pp. 94–98)

1. Prenatal development is divided into ______________ main periods. The first ______________ weeks of development are called the ______________ period;

between ____________ and ____________ weeks is known as the period of the ____________; and from this point until birth is the period of the ____________.

2. Within hours after conception, the multiplying cells form ____________ distinct masses. The outer layers of cells will become the ____________ and other membranes that protect the inner cells, which will become the ____________ and then the ____________.

3. After conception, the next significant event is the burrowing of the many-celled organism into the lining of the uterus, a process called ____________. This process, which usually occurs by the ____________ day following conception, ____________ (is/is not) automatic.

4. At this point in development, the ____________ (outer/inner) cells of the developing individual divide into three layers: the outer layer will become the ____________; the middle layer will become the ____________; and the inner layer becomes the ____________.

5. An important early development is the appearance of a fold down the middle of the cell mass that becomes the ____________ ____________, the precursor of the ____________ ____________ ____________. Once this structure is fully formed, the mass of cells is referred to as the ____________.

6. Growth then proceeds from the head downward, referred to as ____________-____________ ____________, and from the center outward, referred to as ____________-____________ ____________. Following these patterns, the ____________ system is the first organ system to begin to function.

7. The life-giving organ that enables the fetus to obtain nourishment from the mother's blood and to excrete waste into her blood is the ____________.

Briefly describe the major features of development during the second month.

8. Eight weeks after conception, the embryo weighs about ____________ and is about ____________ in length. The organism now becomes known as the ____________, a term that denotes ____________ ____________.

9. All the major organs, including the ____________, ____________, ____________, and ____________, complete their formation during the ____________ month.

10. The first stage of development of the sex organs is the appearance in the ____________ week of the ____________ ____________, a cluster of cells that can develop into male or female sex organs.

11. If the fetus has a ____________ (*X*/*Y*) chromosome, one gene sends a biochemical signal to the developing organism, triggering the development of the ____________ (male/female) sex organs at about seven weeks. Without that chromosome, no signal is sent, and the fetus begins to develop (male/female) sex organs at about the ____________ week. Not until the ____________ week are the external male or female genital organs fully formed.

12. By the end of the ____________ month, the fetus is fully formed, weighs approximately ____________, and is about ____________ long.

13. Each three-month period of pregnancy is referred to as a(n) ____________.

14. During the second trimester, weight increases by a factor of ____________, while the brain increases in size by a factor of ____________.

Briefly describe some of the other major developments during the second trimester.

15. The age at which a fetus has at least some chance of surviving outside the uterus is called the ____________ ____________ ____________, which occurs between ____________ and ____________ weeks after conception.

16. Two important developments during the third trimester are the strengthening of the muscles that enable ____________ and a final maturation of the ____________ system. Measurement of the brain's electrical activity during this trimester reveals distinct patterns of ____________ and ____________.

17. An important part of the fetus's weight gain is the formation of body____________, which will provide a layer of insulation to keep the newborn warm, along with nourishment and vitamins in the early days after birth.

18. The normal due date is calculated at ____________ weeks after conception.

Potential Complications (pp. 98–107)

19. Fewer than ____________ of all conceptions survive to birth. Approximately ____________ percent of newborns have major malformations, and another ____________ percent have severe problems that become apparent within the first year. It is estimated that as many as ____________ percent are born susceptible to various learning problems.

20. The possible causes of major congenital malformations include ____________ ____________.

21. The scientific study of birth defects is called ____________. Harmful agents that can cause birth defects, called ____________, include ____________.

22. Because predicting birth defects is complicated and imprecise, teratology is considered a science of ____________ ____________, which attempts to evaluate what factors make prenatal harm more, or less, likely to occur.

23. When contracted during the critical period, German measles, also called ____________, is known to cause structural damage to the heart, eyes, ears, and brain.

24. Another highly teratogenic virus, for which there is no immunization, is ____________. About one in every four infants born to women with this virus will die of ____________, usually before age ____________.

25. Prescription drugs that can be teratogenic include ____________.

26. Environmental pollutants that can be teratogenic include ____________, ____________, ____________, and ____________.

27. Exposure before pregnancy to ____________, ____________, and ____________ results in an increased risk of slow growth during prenatal development, a higher miscarriage rate, and learning disabilities.

28. The prenatal period of the embryo is often called the ____________ ____________, because teratogenic exposure during this time can produce malformations of basic body organs and structures.

29. The entire prenatal period is critical for some teratogens, especially those that damage the ____________, impairing the future child's ____________ and ____________ functioning. Such sub-

stances are called ____________________

____________________.

30. Another factor in potential teratogenic damage is ____________________ ____________________ ____________________. For some drugs, such as nicotine, the effect of exposure is cumulative; for other drugs there is a ____________________ effect, meaning that the substance is harmless until the mother's use of it reaches a certain frequency or dosage level.

31. Teratogenic agents ____________________ (can/cannot) interact with other potentially harmful substances.

32. Spina bifida and anencephaly are caused by ____________________ ____________________ ____________________, which occur in about 1 in every 500 embryos. Genes ____________________ (do/do not) play an important role in these defects, possibly in conjunction with a deficiency of ____________________ ____________________ in the mother's diet.

33. (Research Report) Social drugs, such as ____, are also suspected teratogens.

34. (Research Report) The teratogenic effects of social drugs are ____________________ (more/less) variable than those of other teratogens; these effects usually show up in ____________________, rather than structural problems.

State some of the effects of fetal exposure to tobacco.

35. (Research Report) Average consumption of ____________________ or more drinks daily is teratogenic.

36. (Research Report) Prenatal exposure to alcohol may lead to ____________________ ____________________ ____________________, which includes abnormal facial characteristics, slowed physical growth, behavior problems, and mental retardation. Likely victims of this syndrome are those who are genetically vulnerable and whose mothers drink more than ____________________ drinks on several occasions during the first ____________________ months of pregnancy.

37. (Research Report) Less pronounced symptoms due to exposure to alcohol, such as an estimated intellectual deficit of 5 IQ points, occur in ____________________ ____________________ ____________________, which is believed to occur in children whose mothers consume a daily average of ____________________ or more drinks in the first month of pregnancy.

38. (Research Report) Infants born to heavy users of marijuana often show impairment to their ____________________ ____________________ systems.

39. (Research Report) Exposure to cocaine early in pregnancy increases the risk of structural damage, especially to the ____________________ ____________________. Cocaine consumption also ____________________ (shortens/lengthens) the birth process and increases the risk of birth complications and seizures that can cause lasting ____________________ damage.

Describe two defenses against teratogenic hazards that are "built into" the developmental process.

40. Three important categories of factors that protect the developing individual against teratogenic hazards are adequate ____________________, ____________________ ____________________, and ____________________ ____________________.

41. As long as a woman is well-nourished at the start of her pregnancy and gains at least ____________________ pounds, she is likely to have a healthy, full-term baby.

42. China has achieved a lower rate of birth defects and complications than many wealthier nations,

largely due to efforts of a network of workers in basic medicine, called ______________ ______________, who provide prenatal care even in the most remote areas.

43. Objective measures of social networks ______________ (are/are not) as accurate as subjective indices, such as how helpful the woman feels her friends and relatives are.

Birth (pp. 107–113)

44. Birth is triggered by biochemical signals that originate in the ______________ and cause strong contractions of the ______________. This causes the ______________ to dilate to about ______________ in diameter, allowing the fetus to move through the vagina into the outside world.

45. The average length of time for the birth process is ______________ for a first birth and ______________ for subsequent births.

46. The newborn is usually rated on the ______________ scale, which assigns a score of 0, 1, or 2 to each of the following five characteristics: ______________ ______________.

A score below ______________ indicates that the newborn is in critical condition and requires immediate attention; if the score is ______________ or better, all is well. This rating is made twice, at ______________ after birth and again ______________ minutes later.

47. The final stage of labor is delivery of the ______________.

48. Most newborns weigh about ______________ pounds and are born full-term about ______________ weeks after conception.

49. One newborn in every seven weighs less than ______________ and is classified as a ______________-______________-______________ infant. Infants are called ______________ if they are born ______________ or more weeks early.

Infants who weigh substantially less than they should, given how much time has passed since conception, are called ______________-______________-______________-______________.

Describe the most common immediate difficulties facing low- birth-weight infants.

50. The leading cause of preterm death is ______________ ______________ ______________.

51. In developed countries, most low-birth-weight infants ______________ (do/do not) survive.

52. Since 1970, infant mortality in the United States has ______________ (increased/decreased/not changed); seventeen other countries have even lower infant-death rates, primarily because of ______________ (prenatal/postnatal) care.

53. Being small-for-gestational-age is generally a sign of prenatal ______________.

54. The most common causes of low birth weight are ______________.

55. Compared to a single fetus, twins tend to weigh ______________ (more/less) and to be born ______________ (earlier/later).

56. Poverty is related to low birth weight, perhaps because poverty is linked to ______________ ______________.

Give some statistical evidence that low birth weight is more common among infants from impoverished areas than among others.

57. Many low-birth-weight infants experience ______________ damage as a result of episodes of ______________, a temporary lack of oxygen, or of cerebral hemorrhaging, called ______________ ______________.

58. Hospitals recognize that providing substitute stimulation for low-birth-weight infants in the form of special massages enhances ______________ ______________.

59. Low-birth-weight infants born into families of lower socioeconomic status ______________ (are/are not) more likely to continue to have learning problems than are children raised in middle-class families.

60. The deficits related to low birth weight usually ______________ (can/cannot) be overcome.

Birth as a Family Event (pp. 113–118)

State two psychological factors that are important in determining the parents' overall birth experience.

61. A delivery technique that stresses active control in the birth process through breathing, concentration, and the father's assistance as a labor "coach" is the ______________ method.

62. The less ______________ and ______________ women have, the more likely they are to experience pain, loneliness, and confusion during childbirth.

63. Before 1970, fathers usually ______________ (were/were not) permitted in the delivery room.

Describe how parents can prepare a child for the presence of a new baby in the family.

64. The term used to describe the close parent-child relationship that begins within the first hours after birth is ______________.

65. Bonding, insofar as it exists in humans, is ______________ (less/more) biologically determined than in other animal species. In certain cases, such as when mothers are ______________, ______________, or under ______________ ______________, immediate contact with the infant seems to be especially important.

Progress Test 1

Multiple-Choice Questions

Circle your answers to the following questions and check them with the answers on page 62. If your answer is incorrect, read the explanation for why it is incorrect and then consult the appropriate pages of the text (in parentheses following the correct answer).

1. The fourth through the eighth week after conception is called the:
   a. period of the embryo.
   b. period of the ovum.
   c. period of the fetus.
   d. germinal period.

2. Marijuana is a behavioral teratogen whose damage is:
   a. related to the timing of exposure.
   b. dose related.
   c. related to the socioeconomic status of the mother-to-be.
   d. related to both the timing and the amount of exposure.

3. The neural tube develops into the:
   a. respiratory system.
   b. umbilical cord.
   c. brain and spinal cord.
   d. circulatory system.

4. The embryo's growth from the head downward is called:
   a. cephalo-caudal development.
   b. fetal development.
   c. proximo-distal development.
   d. teratogenic development.

5. By the eighth week after conception, the embryo has almost all of the basic organs except the:
   a. skeleton.
   b. elbows and knees.
   c. sex organs.
   d. fingers and toes.

6. The idea of a parent-infant bond in humans—a bond that might have to be formed a short time after birth—arose from:
   a. observations in the delivery room.
   b. data on adopted infants.
   c. animal studies.
   d. studies of disturbed mother-infant pairs.

7. The most critical factor in attaining the age of viability is development of the:
   a. placenta.
   b. eyes.
   c. brain.
   d. skeleton.

8. During the last trimester, the:
   a. fetus gains about 1 pound in weight.
   b. lungs and heart become able to sustain life without the placenta.
   c. brain's activity reveals distinctive patterns of sleeping and waking.
   d. the indifferent gonad appears.

9. The birth process begins:
   a. when the fetal monitor records the fetus's heartbeat.
   b. when the uterus begins to contract at regular intervals to push the fetus out.
   c. when the Apgar score reaches 7.
   d. when the baby's head begins to emerge through the vaginal opening.

10. The neonate's heart rate, breathing, muscle tone, circulation, and reflexes are usually measured on a ten-point system known as the:
    a. fetal monitor.
    b. critical period.
    c. Apgar scale.
    d. Lamaze scale.

11. A teratogen:
    a. cannot cross the placenta during the first trimester.
    b. is usually inherited from the mother.
    c. can be counteracted by good nutrition most of the time.
    d. may be a virus, drug, chemical, or radiation.

12. Because most body organs form during the first two months of pregnancy, the period of the embryo is sometimes called the:
    a. period of teratology.
    b. genetically dangerous period.
    c. proximo-distal period.
    d. critical period.

13. Maternal cigarette smoking is most often associated with:
    a. nicotine addiction in the newborn.
    b. low birth weight and prematurity.
    c. serious brain damage.
    d. physical deformities of the head and face.

14. Among the characteristics of babies born with fetal alcohol syndrome are:
    a. slowed physical growth and behavior problems.
    b. addiction to alcohol and methadone.
    c. deformed arms and legs.
    d. blindness.

15. Several pollutants, when ingested in large doses, have been proven to be teratogenic. Among them are:
    a. dust and silver chloride.
    b. mercury, lead, and PCBs.
    c. carbon dioxide.
    d. salt water.

Matching Items

Match each definition or description with its corresponding term.

Definitions or Descriptions

_______ 1. a deficiency of oxygen
_______ 2. the scientific study of birth defects
_______ 3. when the age of viability is attained
_______ 4. the precursor of the central nervous system
_______ 5. also called German measles
_______ 6. a disease characterized by abnormal facial characteristics, slowed growth, behavior problems, and mental retardation
_______ 7. a virus that gradually overwhelms the body's immune responses
_______ 8. the life-giving organ that nourishes the embryo and fetus
_______ 9. when implantation occurs
_______ 10. the prenatal period when all major body structures begin to form
_______ 11. a 3-month-long segment of pregnancy

Terms

a. period of the embryo
b. period of the fetus
c. placenta
d. trimester
e. teratology
f. rubella
g. HIV
h. anoxia
i. neural tube
j. fetal alcohol syndrome
k. germinal period

Progress Test 2

Progress Test 2 should be completed during a final chapter review. Answer the following questions after you thoroughly understand the correct answers for the Chapter Review and Progress Test 1.

Multiple-Choice Questions

1. During which period does cocaine use affect the fetus and/or newborn?
   a. throughout pregnancy
   b. before birth
   c. after birth
   d. during all of the above periods

2. In order, the correct sequence of prenatal stages of development is:
   a. embryo; germinal; fetus
   b. germinal; fetus; embryo
   c. germinal; embryo; fetus
   d. ovum; fetus; embryo

3. Risk analysis attempts to evaluate what factors make prenatal harm more, or less, likely to occur. The most influential factors are:
   a. genetic vulnerability and health care.
   b. timing and amount of exposure.
   c. nutrition and social support.
   d. all of the above.

4. Low-birth-weight babies who are born three or more weeks early:
   a. frequently have a waxy coating on their feet.
   b. are called small-for-dates.
   c. usually have no sex organs.
   d. are designated preterm infants.

5. Studies of fathers present during delivery found:
   a. that 50 percent were emotionally disoriented.
   b. that most were glad they had been there.
   c. that the fathers introduced infection into the delivery room.
   d. that most would not repeat the experience.

6. The 3-month-old fetus is an active, fully formed organism that weighs:
   a. less than 1 ounce.
   b. approximately 3 ounces.
   c. approximately 3 pounds.
   d. slightly more than 3 pounds.

7. Extra early mother-infant contact seems to be most beneficial to mothers of preterms and to:
   a. low-income, first-time mothers.
   b. Canadian and Guatemalan mothers.
   c. mothers of female infants.
   d. mothers who have had only routine contact with infants.

8. Among the characteristics rated on the Apgar scale is (are):
   a. the shape of the newborn's head and nose.
   b. the presence of body hair.
   c. birth-related bruises.
   d. muscle tone and color.

9. Minimal medical assistance, psychological support, and preparation are factors in:
   a. Lamaze childbirth.
   b. the Apgar.
   c. the mother-infant bond.
   d. birth trauma.

10. Many of the factors that contribute to low birth weight are related to poverty; for example, women of lower socioeconomic status tend to:
    a. be less well nourished.
    b. have less education.
    c. be subjected to stressful living conditions.
    d. be all of the above.

11. Spina bifida and anencephaly are classified as:
    a. behavioral teratogens.
    b. neural tube defects.
    c. teratogenic diseases.
    d. disorders caused by low birth weight.

12. One of the most devastating teratogens, possibly causing deafness, blindness, and brain damage if the fetus is exposed during the first trimester, is:
    a. rubella (German measles).
    b. anoxia.
    c. acquired immune deficiency syndrome (AIDS).
    d. neural tube defect.

13. Nourishment is carried to, and waste is removed from, the embryo or fetus through the:
    a. uterus.
    b. placenta.
    c. neural cord.
    d. Fallopian tubes.

14. A pollutant that is teratogenic if a woman is exposed to an unusually high amount is:
    a. rubella.
    b. lithium.
    c. mercury.
    d. HIV

15. In the case of very-very-low-birth-weight infants, the medical interventions that save their lives may cause blindness as a result of:
    a. the administration of high concentrations of oxygen to enhance breathing.
    b. the brain damage that occurred during the emergency birth.
    c. hemorrhaging during surgery.
    d. all of the above.

True or False Items

Write *true* or *false* on the line in front of each statement.

_______ 1. The Apgar is used to measure vital signs such as heart rate and breathing.

_______ 2. For siblings, the birth of a new baby typically results in a loss of parental attention, leading to intellectual or learning difficulties that persist into adulthood.

_______ 3. Research shows that immediate mother-infant contact at birth is necessary for the normal emotional development of the child.

_______ 4. Once the zygote reaches the uterus, implantation is almost assured.

_______ 5. Eight weeks after conception, the embryo has formed almost all the basic organs.

_______ 6. The embryo develops from the head downward, and from the center outward.

_______ 7. Unless a woman is severely malnourished, the adequacy of her diet is most important in the last months of pregnancy.

_______ 8. In general, behavioral teratogens have the greatest affect during the first trimester.

_______ 9. The effects of cigarette smoking during pregnancy remain highly controversial.

_______ 10. Low-birth-weight babies are more likely than other children to experience developmental difficulties in early childhood.

Challenge Test

Answer these questions the day before an exam as a final check on your understanding of the chapter's terms and concepts.

1. A mother gives birth in a crowded, understaffed hospital and it is several hours before her newborn is brought to her. The most likely effect of this separation is that:
   a. the mother will initially reject the infant.
   b. the mother will have difficulty bonding with the infant, especially if it is a female.
   c. the infant will experience difficulties in interacting with the mother during the first year or so.
   d. the mother will develop a normal attachment to her infant, and vice versa.

2. A newborn whose mother has used cocaine during pregnancy is most likely to be described as:
   a. shorter than normal.
   b. brain damaged.
   c. sleepy and inattentive.
   d. abnormal in facial appearance.

3. Babies born to mothers who are powerfully addicted to a social drug are most likely to suffer from:
   a. structural problems. c. both a. and b.
   b. behavioral problems. d. neither a. nor b.

4. Your sister and brother-in-law, who are about to adopt a 1-year-old, are worried that the child will never "bond" to them. What advice should you offer?
   a. Tell them that, unfortunately, this is true; they would be better off waiting for a younger child who has not yet "bonded."
   b. Tell them that, although the first year is a biologically determined critical period for attachment, there is a fifty-fifty chance the child will "bond" with them.
   c. Tell them that "bonding" is a long-term process between parent and child that is determined by the nature of interaction throughout infancy, childhood, and beyond.
   d. Tell them that if the child is female, there is a good chance that she will "bond" to them, even at this late stage.

5. At Carla's first prenatal checkup her doctor cautions her regarding the use of alcohol because of:
   a. the potential for FAS.
   b. the potential for HIV.
   c. the danger of preterm birth.
   d. the danger of brain damage from anoxia.

6. Nadia was treated for rubella during the eighth month of her pregnancy. Her doctor is not overly worried about her child-to-be because this disease has its greatest effect:
   a. during the second trimester of pregnancy..
   b. during the first trimester of pregnancy.
   c. during the last trimester of pregnancy.
   d. in women in developing countries.

7. Antonia and Fernando wanted very much to have natural childbirth, so they attended Lamaze classes. Because she received no medication during childbirth, Antonia probably:
   a. felt mostly negative about the whole event and the baby.
   b. had a short labor and a positive reaction to birth and the baby.
   c. felt positive about the baby, but negative about the birth process itself.
   d. felt generally positive or neutral about birth and the baby.

8. I am about 1 inch long and 1 gram in weight. I have all of the basic organs (except sex organs) and features of a human being. What am I?
   a. a zygote
   b. an embryo
   c. a fetus
   d. an indifferent gonad

9. Karen and Brad are thrilled to report to their neighbors that, 5 weeks after conception, a sonogram of their child-to-be revealed female sex organs. The neighbors are skeptical because:
   a. sonograms are never administered before the third trimester.
   b. sonograms only reveal the presence or absence of male sex organs.
   c. the fetus does not begin to develop female sex organs until about the ninth week.
   d. it is impossible to determine that a woman is pregnant until at least six weeks after conception.

10. Concern about a fetus's health would be greatest if the mother contracted rubella during the __________ week of her pregnancy.
    a. fourth
    b. ninth
    c. sixteenth
    d. thirty-second

11. Five-year-old Benjamin can't sit quietly and concentrate on a task for more than a minute. Dr. Simmons, who is a teratologist, suspects that Benjamin may have been exposed to __________ during prenatal development.
    a. human immunodeficiency virus
    b. a behavioral teratogen
    c. rubella
    d. lead

12. Sylvia and Stan, who are of British descent, are hoping to have a child. Doctor Caruthers asks for a complete nutritional history and is particularly concerned when she discovers that Sylvia may have a deficiency of folic acid. Doctor Caruthers is probably worried about the risk of __________ in their offspring.
    a. FAS
    b. brain damage
    c. neural tube defects
    d. ectopic pregnancy

13. Three-year-old Kenny was born underweight, premature, and with respiratory difficulties. Today, he is small for his age and has learning disabilities in reading and spelling. His doctor suspects that:
    a. Kenny was a victim of fetal alcohol syndrome.
    b. Kenny was a victim of fetal alcohol effects.
    c. Kenny's mother smoked heavily during her pregnancy.
    d. Kenny's mother used cocaine during her pregnancy.

14. Which of the following newborns would be most likely to have problems in body structure and functioning?
    a. Anton, whose Apgar score is 6
    b. Debora, whose Apgar score is 7
    c. Sheila, whose Apgar score is 3
    d. Simon, whose Apgar score is 4

15. Fetal alcohol syndrome is much more common in newborns whose mothers were heavy drinkers than in those whose mothers were moderate drinkers during pregnancy. This finding shows that to assess and understand risk we must know:
    a. the kind of alcoholic beverage (for example, beer, wine, or whiskey).
    b. the level of exposure to the teratogen.
    c. whether the substance really is teratogenic.
    d. the timing of exposure to the teratogen.

Key Terms

Using your own words, on a separate piece of paper write a brief definition or explanation of each of the following terms.

1. germinal period
2. period of the embryo
3. period of the fetus
4. implantation
5. neural tube
6. central nervous system
7. embryo
8. cephalo-caudal development
9. proximo-distal development
10. placenta
11. fetus
12. trimester
13. age of viability
14. teratology
15. teratogens
16. risk analysis
17. critical period
18. behavioral teratogens
19. fetal alcohol syndrome (FAS)
20. fetal alcohol effects (FAE)
21. threshold effect
22. neural tube defects
23. Apgar
24. low-birth-weight infant
25. preterm
26. small-for-gestational-age (SGA)
27. respiratory distress syndrome
28. anoxia
29. Lamaze method
30. parent-infant bond

ANSWERS

CHAPTER REVIEW

1. three; three; germinal (ovum); four; eight; embryo; fetus
2. two; placenta; embryo; fetus
3. implantation; tenth; is not
4. inner; skin and nervous system; circulatory, excretory, and reproductive systems, and muscles and bones; digestive and respiratory systems
5. neural tube; central nervous system; embryo
6. cephalo-caudal; proximo-distal; cardiovascular
7. placenta

Following the proximo-distal sequence, the upper arms, then the forearms, hands, and fingers appear. Legs, feet, and toes follow. At eight weeks, the embryo's head is more rounded and the facial features are fully formed. The tail is no longer visible.

8. 1/30 of an ounce (1 gram); 1 inch (2.5 centimeters); fetus; that the basic body parts have been formed but that the developing organism is still dependent upon its mother's body
9. stomach, heart, lungs, and kidneys; third
10. sixth; indifferent gonad

11. *Y*; male; female; ninth; twelfth
12. third; 3 ounces (90 grams); 3 inches (7.5 centimeters)
13. trimester
14. ten; six

The heartbeat is stronger and can be heard. The digestive and excretory systems develop as the fetus begins to suck, swallow, and urinate. Occasional bursts of electrical activity reveal that the brain is becoming functional.

15. age of viability; 20; 26
16. breathing; circulatory; sleeping; waking
17. fat
18. thirty-eight
19. one-third; 3; 3; 15
20. chromosomal abnormalities, single-gene defects, environmental factors, and multifactorial inheritance
21. teratology; teratogens; viruses, bacteria, drugs, chemicals, and types of radiation
22. risk analysis
23. rubella; can
24. HIV; AIDS; 3
25. tetracycline, Retinoic acid, lithium, valium, and hormones
26. lead; mercury; PCBs; radiation
27. pesticides; herbicides; fungicides
28. critical period
29. brain; intellectual; emotional; behavioral teratogens
30. amount of exposure; threshold
31. can
32. neural tube defects; 1; do; folic acid
33. alcohol, tobacco, marijuana, and cocaine
34. more; behavioral

Smoking increases risk of ectopic pregnancy, stillbirth, prematurity, and premature separation of the placenta from the uterus. Babies born to regular smokers weigh less and are shorter. In addition, they are more likely to have respiratory difficulties and learning disabilities.

35. three
36. fetal alcohol syndrome; five; two
37. fetal alcohol effects; three
38. central nervous
39. sex organs; lengthens; brain

Spontaneous abortions when severe fetal damage is likely tend to ensure normal development. The lengthy growth process, especially of the brain, means that harm to the fetus at one point can generally be overcome if the rest of the pregnancy is healthy.

40. nutrition, prenatal care, social support
41. 15
42. barefoot doctors
43. are not
44. placenta; uterus; cervix; 10 centimeters
45. 12 hours; 7 hours
46. Apgar; heart rate, breathing, muscle tone, color, reflex irritability; 4; 7; one minute; four
47. placenta
48. 7 1/2; thirty-eight
49. 5 1/2; low-birth-weight; preterm; three; small-for-gestational-age

Low-birth-weight infants may have difficulty maintaining body heat, digesting food, resisting infection, and getting sufficient oxygen.

50. respiratory distress syndrome
51. do
52. decreased; prenatal
53. malnutrition
54. maternal malnutrition, poor maternal health or health habits, drug use, prenatal infections, genetic handicaps
55. less; earlier
56. malnutrition, less education, more stressful living conditions, greater exposure to teratogens

The vast majority of low-birth-weight infants born each year are from developing countries. In the United States, the rate of low birth weight in inner cities is more than double that in the more affluent suburbs. Ethnic group variations in low-birth-weight births tend to follow socioeconomic, rather than genetic, patterns.

57. brain; anoxia; brain bleeds
58. weight gain
59. are
60. can

Preparation for childbirth and the father's direct involvement are two important factors in determining the quality of the parents' overall birth experience.

61. Lamaze

62. education; income
63. were not

Parents can help an older child prepare for the arrival of a new child by telling him or her what to expect in the days surrounding the birth and reassuring them that becoming a big brother or sister will have its benefits. Parents can also relieve the anxiety the child feels when the mother goes to the hospital by showing him or her photographs of his or her early days at the hospital, and making plans for a special outing with the father when mother is away.

64. bonding
65. less; young, poor, or under special stress

PROGRESS TEST 1

Multiple-Choice Questions

1. **a.** is the answer. (p. 95)

   b. & d. The germinal, or ovum, period occurs during the first three weeks.

   c. The period of the fetus is from the ninth week until birth.

2. **b.** is the answer. (p. 102)
3. **c.** is the answer. (p. 95)
4. **a.** is the answer. (p. 95)

   b. This term refers to all development that occurs from the ninth week after conception until birth.

   c. This describes development from the center outward.

   d. There is no such thing as "teratogenic development"; teratogens are substances that harm the developing embryo or fetus.

5. **c.** is the answer. The sex organs do not begin to take shape until the period of the fetus. (p. 95)
6. **c.** is the answer. (p. 117)
7. **c.** is the answer. (p. 97)
8. **c.** is the answer. (p. 98)

   a. During the final trimester the fetus actually gains about 5 1/2 pounds in weight.

   b. This occurs during the second trimester.

   d. This occurs during the first trimester.

9. **b.** is the answer. (p. 107)
10. **c.** is the answer. (p. 108)

    a. This device monitors the fetus's heart beat and the strength of labor contractions.

    b. This is the period of the embryo, when exposure to teratogens is particularly hazardous.

    d. There is no such thing; Lamaze is a childbirth method that emphasizes concentration, breathing, and the father's involvement.

11. **d.** is the answer. (pp. 98–99)

    a. Teratogens can cross the placenta at any time.

    b. Teratogens are agents in the environment, not heritable genes (although *susceptibility* to individual teratogens has a genetic component).

    c. Although nutrition is an important factor in healthy prenatal development, the text does not suggest that nutrition alone can usually counteract the harmful effects of teratogens.

12. **d.** is the answer. (p. 95)

    a., b., & c. There are no such periods; development proceeds proximo-distally *throughout* prenatal development.

13. **b.** is the answer. (p. 103)
14. **a.** is the answer. (p. 101)
15. **b.** is the answer. (p. 99)

Matching Items

1. h (p. 111)
2. e (p. 96)
3. b (p. 95)
4. i (p. 95)
5. f (p. 99)
6. j (p. 101)
7. g (p. 99)
8. c (p. 95)
9. k (p. 94)
10. a (p. 95)
11. d (p. 97)

PROGRESS TEST 2

Multiple-Choice Questions

1. **a.** is the answer. (p. 102)
2. **c.** is the answer. (pp. 94–96)
3. **b.** is the answer. (pp. 99–100, 103)

   a. These were not mentioned in the text.

   c. Nutrition and social support are two of the protective factors that moderate the risk of teratogenic exposure.

4. **d.** is the answer. (p. 109)
5. **b.** is the answer. (p. 115)
6. **b.** is the answer. (p. 96)
7. **a.** is the answer. (p. 117)

   b. & c. There is no evidence that bonding varies with the mother's cultural background or the gender of her offspring.

   d. On the contrary, early mother-infant contact seems to be most beneficial when the frail health of low-birth-weight or preterm babies has restricted mother-infant contact.

8. **d.** is the answer. (p. 108)
9. **a.** is the answer. (p. 114)
10. **a.** is the answer. (p. 100)
11. **b.** is the answer. (pp. 100, 104)

    a. Behavioral teratogens are substances that cause intellectual or emotional impairment in the child-to-be; spina bifida and anencephaly are *structural defects.*

    c. & d. Spina bifida and anencephaly have been attributed to genetic vulnerability in conjunction with a teratogenic insufficiency of folic acid in the mother's diet, rather than to disease or low birth weight.
12. **a.** is the answer. (p. 99)
13. **b.** is the answer. (p. 95)

    a. This is the part of the woman to which the zygote implants itself.

    c. This is the precursor of the central nervous system.

    d. Fertilization normally takes place in these tubes, which link the mother's ovaries with her uterus.
14. **c.** is the answer. (p. 99)
15. **a.** is the answer. (p. 112)

True or False Items

1. T (p. 108)
2. F Although the birth of a younger sibling is often stressful, the text does not suggest that it leads to persistent intellectual or learning difficulties. (pp. 115–116)
3. F Though highly desirable, mother-infant contact at birth is not necessary for the child's normal development, or for a good parent-child relationship. Many opportunities for bonding occur throughout childhood. (p. 117)
4. F It is estimated that 58 percent of all conceptions never achieve implantation. (p. 94)
5. T (p. 95)
6. T (p. 95)
7. T (p. 110)
8. F Behavioral teratogens can affect the fetus at any time during the prenatal period. (p. 100)
9. F There is no controversy about the damaging effects of smoking during pregnancy. (p. 103)
10. T (p. 111)

CHALLENGE TEST

1. **d.** is the answer. (p. 117)

   a., b., & c. Most developmentalists now believe that the importance of early contact between mother and child has been overly popularized and that the strength of their bond is determined by the nature of their interaction throughout infancy, childhood, and beyond.
2. **c.** is the answer. These behaviors are the result of instability of the central nervous system, caused by cocaine in the newborn's bloodstream. (p. 102)
3. **b.** is the answer. (p. 101)
4. **c.** is the answer. (p. 117)

   b. Bonding in humans is not a biologically determined event limited to a critical period, as it is in many other animal species.

   d. There is no evidence of any gender differences in the formation of the parent-infant bond.
5. **a.** is the answer. (pp. 101–102)

   b. HIV is a teratogenic virus.

   c. Although it has other harmful effects, alcohol is not linked to preterm births.

   d. Anoxia is a temporary lack of oxygen, usually experienced by low-birth-weight infants.
6. **b.** is the answer. (p. 99)
7. **b.** is the answer. (pp. 114–115)
8. **b.** is the answer. (p. 95)

   a. The zygote is the fertilized ovum.

   d. The indifferent gonad is the mass of cells that will eventually develop into female or male sex organs.
9. **c.** is the answer. (p. 96)
10. **a.** is the answer. The fourth through the eighth weeks of pregnancy (period of the embryo) are a critical period in prenatal development; exposure to teratogens at this time is particularly hazardous. (p. 99)
11. **b.** is the answer. (p. 100)

    a. This is the virus that causes AIDS.

    c. Rubella may cause blindness, deafness, and brain damage.

    d. The text does not discuss the effects of exposure to lead.
12. **c.** is the answer. (p. 104)

    a. FAS is caused in genetically vulnerable infants by the mother-to-be drinking five or more drinks several times during the first two months of pregnancy.

b. Brain damage is caused by episodes of anoxia or by cerebral hemorrhaging, or "brain bleeding."

d. Risk of ectopic (tubal) pregnancy is increased when the mother smokes, but is not linked to folic acid deficiency.

13. **c.** is the answer. (p. 102)

14. **c.** is the answer. (p. 108)

15. **b.** is the answer. (p. 101)

KEY TERMS

1. The first three weeks of development are called the **germinal period** (also called the period of the ovum). (p. 94)

   Memory aid: A *germ cell* is one from which a new organism can develop. The *germ*inal **period** is the first stage in the development of the new organism.

2. The **period of the embryo** is the fourth through the eighth week of prenatal development. (p. 94)
3. From the ninth week until birth is the **period of the fetus.** (p. 94)
4. **Implantation** is the process by which the mass of developing cells burrows into the uterine lining and ruptures its blood vessels to obtain nourishment and trigger the bodily changes that signify the beginning of pregnancy. (p. 94)
5. The **neural tube** is a fold that develops in the middle of the cell mass during the germinal period; it is the precursor of the central nervous system. (p. 95)

   Memory aid: Neural means "of the nervous system." The **neural tube** is the precursor of the central nervous system.

6. The **central nervous system** is the network of nerve cells that includes the brain and the spinal cord. (p. 95)
7. **Embryo** is the name given to the mass of developing cells once the neural tube has been formed at about four weeks following conception. (p. 95)
8. **Cephalo-caudal development** refers to growth that proceeds from the head downward. (p. 95)

   Memory aid: Cephalo-caudal literally means "of the head-of the tail." Think of *cephalic*, an adjective which also means "of the head."

9. **Proximo-distal development** refers to growth that proceeds from "near to far." According to this process the most vital organs and body parts form first, before the extremities. (p. 95)

   Memory aid: Something that is *proximal* is situated very near. ***Proximo*-distal development** begins with the very near organs at the center of the body.

10. The **placenta** is the life-giving organ that makes it possible for the developing person to have its own blood supply, and at the same time to receive oxygen and nourishment from the mothers's blood and to rid itself of body wastes. (p. 95)
11. Between nine weeks after conception and birth, the developing organism is known as the **fetus,** a term that denotes that although the developing organism has all the basic organs (except the sex organs) and features of a human being, it is still dependent on the mother for survival. (p. 96)
12. Pregnancy is often referred to in terms of three-month-long segments called **trimesters.** (p. 97)

    Memory aid: A semester is one of two terms during an academic year; a **trimester** is one of three, three-month-long periods during pregnancy.

13. Sometime between the twentieth and twenty-sixth week after conception the fetus attains the **age of viability,** at which time it has at least some slight chance of survival outside the uterus. (p. 97)
14. **Teratology** is the study of birth defects. (p. 98)
15. **Teratogens** are harmful agents, such as viruses, bacteria, drugs, chemicals, and radiation, that can cause damage to the embryo and fetus. (p. 99)
16. The science of teratology is a science of **risk analysis,** meaning that it attempts to evaluate what factors make prenatal harm more, or less, likely to occur. (p. 99)
17. The period of the embryo is often called the **critical period** because teratogenic exposure between the third and ninth week can produce malformations of basic body organs and structure. (p. 100)
18. **Behavioral teratogens** damage the neural networks of the brain, impairing the future child's intellectual and emotional functioning. (p. 100)
19. Prenatal alcohol exposure may cause **fetal alcohol syndrome (FAS),** which includes abnormal facial characteristics, slowed growth, behavior problems, and mental retardation. Likely victims are those who are genetically vulnerable and whose mothers drink more than five drinks on several occasions during the first two months of pregnancy. (p. 101)
20. Children whose mothers consume a daily average of three or more drinks in the first month of pregnancy are likely to experience **fetal alcohol**

effects (FAE). FAE consists of less pronounced symptoms than occur in FAS, including a small decline in IQ. (p. 101)

21. For some teratogens there is a **threshold effect;** that is, the substance is virtually harmless until fetal exposure reaches a certain frequency or dosage level. (p. 103)

22. **Neural tube defects** occur when an embryo's neural tube does not grow properly: either the lower spine does not close, causing spina bifida, or the upper part of the central nervous system does not develop, causing anencephaly. (p. 104)

23. Newborns are rated at one and then at five minutes after birth according to the **Apgar.** This scale assigns a score of 0, 1, or 2 to each of five characteristics—heart rate, breathing, muscle tone, color, and reflex irritability. A score of 7 or better indicates that all is well. (p. 108)

24. Newborns that weigh less than 2,500 grams (5 1/2 pounds) are called **low-birth-weight** infants. Such infants are at risk for many immediate and long-term problems. (p. 109)

25. Infants who are born three or more weeks early are called **preterm.** (p. 109)

26. Infants who weigh substantially less than they should, given how much time has passed since conception, are called **small-for-gestational-age (SGA),** or small-for-dates. (p. 109)

27. **Respiratory distress syndrome** is the leading cause of preterm death. It is especially common in infants who are more than a month preterm because their immature reflexes often do not regulate breathing properly. (p. 109)

28. **Anoxia** is a temporary lack of oxygen during prenatal development that can cause brain damage. (p. 111)

29. The **Lamaze method** of childbirth emphasizes breathing and concentration techniques and the father's involvement as a labor coach. This method often results in a less painful and more rapid delivery with less anesthesia. (p. 114)

30. The term **parent-infant bond** describes the tangible and metaphorical fastening of parent to child in the early moments of their relationship together. Insofar as bonding exists in humans, it is much less biologically determined than in other animal species. (p. 117)

CHAPTER 5 The First Two Years: Biosocial Development

Chapter Overview

Chapter 5 is the first of a three-chapter unit that describes the developing person from birth to age 2 in terms of biosocial, cognitive, and psychosocial development. Physical development is the first to be examined.

The chapter begins with observations on the size and shape of infants, and their rapid rate of growth during the first two years. Following is a discussion of brain growth and maturation and the role of the brain in regulating the infant's physiological states. Vision and hearing and the development of these and other sensory abilities are discussed next, along with recent research on infant perception and the role of sensory experience in normal development. The chapter then turns to a discussion of motor abilities, and the ages at which the average infant acquires them. The final section discusses the importance of nutrition during the first two years, and the consequences of severe malnutrition and undernutrition.

NOTE: Answer guidelines for all Chapter 5 questions begin on page 76.

Guided Study

The text chapter should be studied one section at a time. Before you read, preview each section by skimming it, noting headings and boldface items. Then read the appropriate section objectives from the following outline. Keep these objectives in mind and, as you read the chapter section, search for the information that will enable you to meet each objective. Once you have finished a section, write out answers for its objectives.

Size and Shape (p. 124)

1. Describe overall physical growth during the first two years.

2. Describe the size and proportions of an infant's body, including how they change during the first two years and how they compare with those of an adult.

Brain Growth and Maturation (pp. 125–126)

3. Describe the ways in which the brain changes or matures during infancy.

4. Discuss the role of the brain in regulating the infant's physiological states and name three normal physiological states of the infant.

Sensory Development (pp. 127–130)

5. Distinguish between sensation and perception and describe how and why habituation is used in research on infant perception.

6. Describe the extent and development of an infant's perceptual abilities in terms of the senses of vision, hearing, taste, and smell.

7. Discuss the role of sensory experience in brain development.

Motor Skills (pp. 130–135)

8. Describe the basic reflexes of the newborn and distinguish between gross motor skills and fine motor skills.

9. Describe the basic pattern of motor-skill development and discuss variations in the timing of motor-skill acquisition.

Nutrition (pp. 135–140)

10. Describe the nutritional needs of infants and discuss the causes and results of malnutrition and undernutrition in the first years.

Chapter Review

When you have finished reading the chapter, work through the material that follows to review it. Complete the sentences and answer the questions. As you proceed, evaluate your performance for each section by consulting the answers on page 76. Do not continue with the next section until you understand each answer. If you need to, review or reread the appropriate section in the textbook before continuing.

Size and Shape (p. 124)

1. The average North American newborn measures ____________ inches and weighs ____________.

2. In the first days of life, most newborns ____________ (gain/lose) between 5 and 10 percent of their body weight.

3. By age 1, the typical baby weighs about ____________ pounds and measures almost ____________.

4. Newborns often seem top-heavy because their heads are equivalent to about ____________ (what proportion) of their total length, compared to about ____________ at one year and ____________ in adulthood.

5. Newborns' legs represent about ______________ (what proportion) of their total length, whereas an adult's legs represent about ______________ of it.

6. Proportionally, the smallest part of a newborn's body is ______________.

Brain Growth and Maturation (pp. 125–126)

7. At birth the brain has attained about ______________ percent of its adult weight; by age 2 the brain is about ______________ percent of its adult weight. In comparison, body weight at age 2 is about ______________ percent of what it will be in adulthood.

8. The nervous system is made up of long, thin, nerve cells called ______________. Most of these cells ______________ (are/are not) present at birth.

9. During the first months of life, brain development is most noticeable in its outer layer, which is called the ______________. This area of the brain controls ______________ and ______________.

10. From birth until age 2, the communication networks of the cortex, which are called ______________, show an estimated five-fold increase in density. These networks also become coated with the insulating substance called ______________, which makes neural transmission more efficient. This coating process continues until ______________.

11. The various conditions of sleep and waking in an infant are referred to as physiological ______________.

List and briefly describe the most distinctive of these conditions in the infant.

12. Patterns of electrical activity in the brain, which are called ______________ ______________, can be measured by the device called a(n) ______________.

13. While the infant's total daily sleep ______________ (does/does not) change much between birth and age 1, the length and ______________ of sleep episodes more closely match the family pattern. Approximately ______________ of all 3-month-olds and ______________ percent of all 1-year-olds sleep through the night. In comparison, preterm infants sleep ______________ (more/less) with ______________ (greater/lesser) regularity than full-term infants.

Compare and contrast the reactions of full-term and preterm infants to startling sensory stimuli.

Sensory Development (pp. 127–130)

14. The process by which the visual, auditory, and other sensory systems respond to stimuli is called ______________; ______________ occurs when the brain recognizes that response so that the individual becomes aware of it. At birth, both of these processes ______________ (are/are not) apparent.

Briefly describe the sensory abilities of the newborn.

15. An infant presented with an unfamiliar stimulus will respond with intensified sucking on a pacifier, or concentrated gazing. When the stimulus becomes so familiar that these responses no longer occur, ______________ is said to have occurred. If the infant reacts to a new stimulus, researchers conclude that the infant can ______________ between the stimuli.

16. Newborns' visual focusing is best for objects between ____________ and ____________ inches away, giving them distance vision of about 20/____________. Distance vision improves rapidly, reaching 20/20 by ____________ of age. This improvement is due mostly to changes that have taken place in the newborn's ____________.

17. The ability to use both eyes together to focus on one object, which is called ____________ ____________, develops at about ____________ of age.

18. By ____________ of age, infants can use both eyes to track a moving object and can use both hands to grab a stationary object. The ability to catch a moving object is not attained until sometime during the ____________ year.

19. Generally speaking, newborns' hearing is ____________ (more/less) sensitive than their vision. By ____________ of age, infants can perceive differences between very similar sounds. Infants' hearing for low-frequency sounds is ____________ (more/less) acute than their hearing for high-frequency sounds.

20. Newborns' sense of taste is ____________ (more/less) developed than their other senses. Newborns only 2 hours old display sensitivity to all the basic taste qualities except ____________.

21. Newborns' sense of smell is ____________ (more/less) acute than their sense of taste.

22. By late infancy, the senses of ____________ and ____________ are more sensitive than at any other time in the entire life span.

23. Sensory experience is an important factor in the development of ____________ ____________, as well as in the development of the ____________ and other brain structures that make seeing, hearing, and motor skills possible.

Briefly describe the results of animal studies of sensory restriction.

Motor Skills (pp. 130–135)

24. Large movements such as running and climbing are called ____________ ____________ skills; abilities that require more precise, small movements, such as picking up a coin, are called ____________ ____________ skills.

25. An involuntary physical response to a stimulus is called a(n) ____________.

26. The involuntary response of breathing, which causes the newborn to take the first breath even before the umbilical cord is cut, is called the ____________ ____________.

Because breathing is irregular during the first few days, other reflexive behaviors, such as ____________, ____________, and ____________, are common.

27. Shivering, crying, and tucking the legs close to the body are examples of reflexes that help to maintain ____________ ____________.

28. A third set of reflexes fosters ____________. One of these is the tendency of the newborn to suck anything that touches the lips; this is the ____________ reflex. Another is the tendency of newborns to turn their heads and start to suck when something brushes against their cheek; this is the ____________ reflex.

29. The tendency of a baby's toes to fan upward when the feet are stroked is called the ____________ reflex.

30. The tendency of babies to move their feet as if to walk when the feet touch a flat surface is called the ____________ reflex.

31. The tendency of a baby's arms and legs to stretch out when he or she is held horizontally on the stomach is called the ______________________ reflex.

32. The tendency of a baby's hands to close tightly when something touches the palm is called the ______________________ reflex.

33. The tendency of newborns to fling their arms outward and then bring them together on the chest when someone bangs the table on which they are lying is called the ______________________ reflex.

34. A measure used to assess the newborn's physical condition and brain development is the ______________________ ______________________ ______________________ ______________________ Scale; the scale's underlying premise is that the newborn's simple reflexes form the basis for ______________________, ______________________, and motor skills.

35. Most infants are able to crawl on all fours (sometimes called creeping) between ______________ and ______________________ months of age.

List the major landmarks in children's mastery of walking.

36. Babies who have just begun to walk are given the name ______________________ for the characteristic way they move their bodies from side to side.

37. By ______________________ of age, most babies can reach for, grab, and hold on to almost any object of the right size.

Briefly describe the development of the ability to pick up and manipulate small objects.

38. Although the ______________________ in which motor skills are mastered is the same in all healthy infants, the ______________________ of acquisition of skills varies greatly.

39. The average ages at which most infants master major motor skills are known as ______________________. These averages are based on a large sample of infants drawn from ______________________ (a single/many) ethnic group(s).

40. Motor skill norms vary from one ______________________ group to another.

List several factors that account for the variation in the acquisition of motor skills.

41. Motor skill acquisition in identical twins ______________________ (is/is not) more similar than in fraternal twins, suggesting that genes ______________________ (do/do not) play an important role.

42. Most developmentalists would say that the age at which a particular baby first displays a particular skill depends on the interaction between ______________________ and ______________________ factors.

43. A child who is a little late in acquiring a particular motor skill ______________________ (should/should not) be cause for parental concern.

Nutrition (pp. 135–140)

44. More important than an infant's feeding schedule in fostering development is the overall ______________________ and ______________________ of the infant's nutritional intake.

State several advantages of breast milk over cow's milk for the developing infant.

45. Severe protein-calorie deficiency in early infancy causes a disease called ______________.
In toddlers, protein-calorie deficiency is more likely to cause a disease called ______________, which involves swelling or bloating of the face, legs, and abdomen.

46. The primary cause of malnutrition in developing countries is ______________ ______________.

Briefly explain why, in developing countries, bottle-fed babies have a higher risk of death and disease than breast-fed babies.

List some of the deficits of infants who are chronically malnourished.

47. In both developing and developed countries ______________ is more prevalent than severe malnutrition. Worldwide, approximately ______________ of young children in developing countries are undernourished.

Identify several possible causes of infant undernutrition.

48. Children who were undernourished as infants show impaired learning, especially in ______________ and in ______________ skills. Recovery from undernourishment is influenced by several factors, including ______________ ______________.

Progress Test 1

Multiple-Choice Questions

Circle your answers to the following questions and check them with the answers on page 77. If your answer is incorrect, read the explanation for why it is incorrect and then consult the appropriate pages of the text (in parentheses following the correct answer).

1. The average North American newborn:
  a. weighs approximately 6 pounds.
  b. weighs approximately 7 pounds.
  c. is "overweight" because of the mother's diet.
  d. weighs 10 percent less than is desirable.

2. Compared to the first year, growth during the second year:
  a. proceeds at a slower rate.
  b. continues at about the same rate.
  c. includes more insulating fat.
  d. includes more bone and muscle.

3. In the United States, the major motor skill most likely to be mastered by an infant before the age of 6 months is:
  a. rolling over.
  b. sitting without support.
  c. turning the head in search of a nipple.
  d. grabbing an object with thumb and forefinger.

4. Norms suggest that the earliest walkers in the world are infants from:
  a. western Europe.
  b. the United States.
  c. Central Africa.
  d. Denver.

5. The interaction between inherited and environmental factors is responsible for:
  a. variation in the age at which infants master specific motor skills.
  b. physical growth, but not the development of motor skills.
  c. the fact that babies in the United States walk earlier than Ugandan babies.
  d. the fact that infants master motor skills more slowly today than they did fifty years ago.

6. The development of binocular vision at about 14 months:
  a. results in a dramatic improvement in depth and motion perception.
  b. results in the rapid development of distance vision.
  c. results in the refinement of the ability to discriminate colors.
  d. results in both a. and b.

7. Proportionately, the head of the infant is about ________ of total body length; the head of an adult is about ________ of total body length.
   a. one-fourth; one-third
   b. one-eighth; one-fourth
   c. one-fourth; one-eighth
   d. one-third; one-fourth

8. Research has shown that young animals prevented from moving or using their senses in a normal way experience:
   a. no significant impairment.
   b. harmful overstimulation.
   c. deficits in behavior only.
   d. permanent impairment.

9. Compared with formula-fed infants, breast-fed infants tend to have:
   a. greater weight gain.
   b. fewer allergies and digestive upsets.
   c. less frequent feedings during the first few months.
   d. more social approval.

10. Marasmus and kwashiorkor are caused by:
   a. bloating.
   b. protein-calorie deficiency.
   c. living in a developing country.
   d. poor family food habits.

11. The infant's first motor skills are:
   a. fine motor skills. c. reflexes.
   b. gross motor skills. d. unpredictable.

12. The Brazelton Neonatal Behavioral Assessment Scale measures:
   a. infant reflexes and other behaviors.
   b. fine motor skills.
   c. gross motor skills.
   d. infant IQ.

13. Babies are referred to as toddlers when:
   a. their newborn reflexes have disappeared.
   b. they can walk well unassisted.
   c. they begin to creep or crawl.
   d. they speak their first word.

14. Which of the following is true of motor skill development in healthy infants?
   a. It follows the same basic sequence the world over.
   b. It occurs at different rates from individual to individual.
   c. It follows norms that vary from one ethnic group to another.
   d. All of the above are true.

15. Most of the nerve cells a human brain will ever possess are present:
   a. at conception.
   b. about 1 month following conception.
   c. at birth.
   d. at age 5 or 6.

Matching Items

Match each definition or description with its corresponding term.

Definitions or Descriptions

______ 1. nerve cells
______ 2. protein deficiency during the first year
______ 3. picking up an object
______ 4. newborn takes his or her first breath even before the umbilical cord is cut
______ 5. protein deficiency during toddlerhood
______ 6. newborns suck anything touching their lips
______ 7. communication networks among nerve cells
______ 8. declining physiological response to a familiar stimulus
______ 9. running or climbing
______ 10. insulating substance for nerve cells
______ 11. an involuntary response

Terms

a. neurons
b. dendrites
c. myelin
d. kwashiorkor
e. marasmus
f. habituation
g. gross motor skill
h. fine motor skill
i. reflex
j. sucking reflex
k. breathing reflex

Progress Test 2

Progress Test 2 should be completed during a final chapter review. Answer the following questions after you thoroughly understand the correct answers for the Chapter Review and Progress Test 1.

Multiple-Choice Questions

1. As a percentage of total body length, the head at birth comprises about ______________ percent.
   a. 6 c. 40
   b. 25 d. 50

2. A reflex is best defined as:
   a. a fine motor skill.
   b. a motor ability mastered at a specific age.
   c. an involuntary physical response to a given stimulus.
   d. a gross motor skill.

3. Habituation describes the:
   a. increased physiological arousal of the newborn to unfamiliar or interesting stimuli.
   b. decreased physiological arousal of the newborn to stimuli that are familiar or no longer interesting.
   c. preterm infant's immature brain wave patterns.
   d. universal sequence of motor skill development in children.

4. Most babies can reach for, grasp, and hold on to an object by about the ______________ month.
   a. second c. ninth
   b. sixth d. fourteenth

5. Activity level, rate of physical maturation, and body type affect the age at which an infant walks and acquires other motor skills. They are examples of:
   a. norms.
   b. environmental factors.
   c. inherited factors.
   d. the interaction of environment and heredity.

6. During the first weeks of life, babies seem to focus reasonably well on:
   a. little in their environment.
   b. objects at a distance of 4 to 30 inches.
   c. objects at a distance of 1 to 3 inches.
   d. objects several feet away.

7. At 12 months, the infant's senses of taste and smell are:
   a. relatively undeveloped.
   b. beginning a period of rapid development.
   c. more limited than those of an older child or adult.
   d. more sensitive than at any other age.

8. An EEG is best described as:
   a. a device that picks up and records electrical impulses from the nerve cells.
   b. a device that measures the physical growth of the skull and brain.
   c. a means of treating brain immaturity in preterm infants.
   d. a brain wave pattern that is known as electrical silence.

9. An advantage of breast milk over formula is that:
   a. it is always sterile and at body temperature.
   b. it contains traces of medications ingested by the mother.
   c. it can be given without involving the father.
   d. it contains more protein and vitamin D than does formula.

10. The primary cause of malnutrition in developing countries is:
    a. formula feeding.
    b. inadequate food supply.
    c. disease.
    d. early cessation of breast-feeding.

11. Severe and long-lasting malnutrition during infancy is most likely to result in:
    a. compensatory obesity in later life.
    b. shorter stature and reduced cognitive ability.
    c. kwashiorkor in later childhood.
    d. no predictable physical or intellectual deficits.

12. Climbing is to using a crayon as ______________ is to ______________.
    a. fine motor skill; gross motor skill
    b. gross motor skill; fine motor skill
    c. reflex; fine motor skill
    d. reflex; gross motor skill

13. Some infant reflexes:
    a. are essential to life.
    b. disappear in the months after birth.
    c. provide the foundation for later motor skills.
    d. do all of the above.

14. When they are startled by a noise, newborns will fling their arms outward and then bring them together as if to hold on to something. This is an example of:
    a. a fine motor skill.
    b. a gross motor skill.
    c. the Babinski reflex.
    d. the Moro reflex.

15. A common cause of undernutrition in young children is:
    a. ignorance of the infant's nutritional needs.
    b. the absence of socioeconomic policies that reflect the importance of infant nutrition.
    c. family problems, such as maternal depression.
    d. all of the above.

True or False Items

Write *true* or *false* on the line in front of each statement.

_______ 1. By age 2, boys are slightly taller than girls, but girls are slightly heavier.
_______ 2. Studies show that the preterm infant is more easily aroused by a given stimulus than is the normal full-term infant.
_______ 3. Reflexive hiccups, sneezes, and spit-ups are signs that the infant's reflexes are not functioning properly.
_______ 4. Infants of all ethnic backgrounds develop the same motor skills at approximately the same age.
_______ 5. Studies have shown that in the first few days of life, infants are unable to taste anything but sweet solutions.
_______ 6. Vision is better developed than hearing in most newborns.
_______ 7. Myelination and other processes of brain maturation are completed within the first few years of childhood.
_______ 8. Certain basic sensory experiences seem necessary to ensure full brain development in the human infant.
_______ 9. Breast-feeding is by far the most common method of infant feeding in the United States.
_______ 10. Severe malnutrition is rare among young children in the United States.

Challenge Test

Answer these questions the day before an exam as a final check on your understanding of the chapter's terms and concepts.

1. Newborns cry, shiver, and tuck their legs close to their bodies. This set of reflexes helps them:
   a. ensure proper muscle tone.
   b. learn how to signal distress.
   c. maintain constant body temperature.
   d. communicate serious hunger pangs.

2. If a baby sucks harder on a nipple, evidences a change in heart rate, or stares longer at one image than at another when presented with a change of stimulus, the indication is that the baby:
   a. is annoyed by the change.
   b. is both hungry and angry.
   c. has become habituated to the new stimulus.
   d. perceives some differences between stimuli.

3. A classic experiment on hearing in infants (Eimas et al., 1971) showed that 1-month-olds can detect:
   a. the father's voice more quickly than the mother's.
   b. sounds they won't be able to hear at age 2.
   c. differences between very similar sounds.
   d. the correct location of auditory stimuli about 80 percent of the time.

4. Mrs. Bartholomew opens the door to her infant's room to be sure everything is alright. She notices that her son's facial muscles are moving and his breathing is irregular and rapid. The infant is in which which physiological state?
   a. quiet sleep
   b. active sleep
   c. alert wakefulness
   d. somewhere between b. and c.

5. The brain development that permits seeing and hearing in human infants appears to be:
   a. totally dependent on genetic programming, present at birth.
   b. totally dependent on visual and auditory experiences in the first few months.
   c. "fine-tuned" by visual and auditory experiences in the first few months.
   d. independent of both genetic and environmental influences.

6. A child who endures a period of serious undernutrition in infancy or early childhood is best described as:
   a. cognitively impaired.
   b. suffering from "failure to thrive."
   c. at risk for learning difficulties and other problems.
   d. small compared to other children in his or her age range.

7. Michael has 20/600 vision, is able to discriminate subtle sound differences, as well as sweet, sour, and bitter tastes. Michael most likely:
   a. is a preterm infant.
   b. has brain damage in the visual processing areas of the cortex.
   c. is a newborn.
   d. is slow-to-mature.

8. A baby turns her head and starts to suck when her receiving blanket is brushed against her cheek. The baby is displaying:
   a. the sucking reflex.
   b. the rooting reflex.
   c. the Babinski reflex.
   d. the Moro reflex.

9. Toddlers whose parents give them a bottle of milk before every nap and with every meal:
   a. may be at increased risk of undernutrition, because the milk reduces the child's appetite for other foods.
   b. are ensured of receiving a sufficient amount of iron in their diets.
   c. are more likely to develop lactose intolerance.
   d. are likely to be overweight throughout life.

10. Sensation is to perception as ______________ is to ______________.
   a. hearing; seeing
   b. responding to a stimulus; recognizing a stimulus
   c. recognizing a stimulus; responding to a stimulus
   d. tasting; smelling

11. Adults often speak to infants in a high-pitched voice. This is because they discover from experience that:
   a. low-pitched sounds are more frightening to infants.
   b. infants are more sensitive to high-pitched sounds.
   c. high-pitched sounds are more soothing to infants.
   d. all of the above are true.

12. Kittens who are blindfolded for the first several weeks of life:
   a. do not develop the visual pathways in their brains to allow normal vision.
   b. recover fully if visual stimulation is normal thereafter.
   c. develop only binocular vision.
   d. can see clearly, but lack sensitivity to color.

13. Your friend Isadore is a stockbroker in Chicago. She is also the mother of a 3-month-old. Isadora is concerned that her busy schedule prevents her from breast-feeding her infant. What should you tell Isadora?
   a. "Spend as much time as possible cuddling your daughter to simulate the closeness you would have had with breast-feeding."
   b. "Obtain a formula that simulates breast milk, because it's vital to your child's development."
   c. "Don't worry. Children in developed countries who have not been breast-fed develop as well as those who have."
   d. "It's never too late to breast-feed, and you should do so, because it's important to your child's development."

14. Three-week-old Nathan should have the least difficulty focusing on the sight of:
   a. stuffed animals on a bookshelf across the room from his crib.
   b. his mother's face as she holds him in her arms.
   c. the checkerboard pattern in the wallpaper covering the ceiling of his room.
   d. the family dog as it dashes into the nursery.

15. Geneva has been undernourished throughout childhood. It is likely that she will be:
   a. smaller and shorter than her genetic potential.
   b. slow in intellectual development.
   c. less resistant to disease.
   d. all of the above.

Key Terms

Using your own words, write a brief definition or explanation of each of the following terms on a separate piece of paper.

1. neurons
2. dendrites
3. myelin
4. physiological states
5. brain waves
6. sensation
7. perception
8. habituation
9. binocular vision
10. gross motor skills
11. fine motor skills
12. reflexes
13. breathing reflex
14. sucking reflex
15. rooting reflex
16. Brazelton Neonatal Behavioral Assessment Scale (NBAS)

17. toddler
18. norms
19. marasmus
20. kwashiorkor

ANSWERS

CHAPTER REVIEW

1. 20 inches (51 centimeters); 7 pounds (3.1 kilograms)
2. lose
3. 22 pounds (10 kilograms); 30 inches (75 centimeters)
4. one-fourth; one-fifth; one-eighth
5. one-fourth; one-half
6. the feet
7. 25; 75; 20
8. neurons; are
9. cortex; perception; thinking
10. dendrites; myelin; adolescence
11. states

Quiet sleep: breathing is regular and slow and muscles are relaxed.

Active sleep: facial muscles move and breathing is less regular and more rapid.

Alert wakefulness: eyes are bright and breathing is relatively regular and rapid.

12. brain waves; electroencephalogram (EEG)
13. does not; timing; one-third; 80; more; lesser

A sudden loud noise makes a normal baby startle, cry, and then "self-soothe." The preterm infant, whose nervous system is less mature, takes longer and requires more intense stimuli to be aroused; once crying occurs, the preterm infant takes longer to settle down again.

14. sensation; perception; are

Although their sensory abilities are selective, newborns see, hear, smell, taste, and respond to pressure, motion, temperature, and pain.

15. habituation; discriminate
16. 4; 30; 600; 6 months; brain
17. binocular vision; 14 weeks
18. 6 months; second
19. more; 1 month; less
20. less; salty
21. more
22. taste; smell
23. perceptual abilities; dendrites

Animals that were prevented from using their senses or moving their bodies in infancy became permanently handicapped. For example, kittens blindfolded for the first several weeks did not develop brain pathways to allow normal vision.

24. gross motor; fine motor
25. reflex
26. breathing reflex; hiccups, sneezes, spit-ups
27. body temperature
28. feeding; sucking; rooting
29. Babinski
30. stepping
31. swimming
32. grasping
33. Moro
34. Brazelton Neonatal Behavioral Assessment; cognitive; social
35. eight; ten

On average, a child can walk while holding a hand at 9 months, can stand alone momentarily at 10 months, and can walk well unassisted at 12 months.

36. toddler
37. 6 months

At first, infants use their whole hand, especially the palm and the fourth and fifth fingers to grasp. Then they use the middle fingers and the center of the palm, or the index finger and the side of the palm. Finally, they use thumb and forefinger together.

38. sequence; age
39. norms; many
40. ethnic

Of primary importance in variations in the acquisition of motor skills are inherited factors, such as activity level, rate of physical maturation, and body type. Particular patterns of infant care may also be influential.

41. is; do
42. inherited; environmental
43. should not
44. quality; quantity

Breast milk is always sterile and at body temperature; it is more digestible and contains more iron, vitamin C, and vitamin A; and it also contains antibodies that provide the infant some protection against disease.

45. marasmus; kwashiorkor

46. early cessation of breast-feeding

For many people in the developing world, the hygienic conditions for the proper use of infant formula do not exist. The water and bottles are unclean and the formula is often diluted to make it last longer.

Malnourished infants who survive are physically shorter and intellectually less able than their peers. Other deficits are particularly likely to involve visual and auditory skills.

47. undernutrition; one-fifth

Undernutrition is caused by the interaction of many factors, with insufficient food as the immediate cause, and problems in the family and/or society as underlying causes. For example, depressed mothers tend to feed their infants erratically, and emotional stresses in a child's life are sometimes reflected in less healthy eating habits.

48. concentration; language; the duration of the undernutrition and the quality of intellectual stimulation experienced after infancy

PROGRESS TEST 1

Multiple-Choice Questions

1. b. is the answer. (p. 124)

2. a. is the answer. (p. 124)

3. a. is the answer. (p. 134)

b. The age norm for this skill is 7.8 months.

c. This is a reflex, rather than an acquired motor skill.

d. This skill is acquired between 9 and 14 months.

4. c. is the answer. (pp. 134–135)

5. a. is the answer. (p. 135)

b. Inherited factors and environmental factors are important for both physical growth *and* the development of motor skills.

c. On average, Ugandan babies walk earlier than babies in the United States.

d. In fact, just the opposite is true.

6. a. is the answer. (p. 128)

7. c. is the answer. (p. 124)

8. d. is the answer. (p. 129)

a. & c. Research has shown that deprivation of normal sensory experiences prevents the development of normal neural pathways that transmit sensory information.

b. On the contrary, these studies demonstrate harmful sensory *restriction.*

9. b. is the answer. This is because breast milk is more digestible than cow's milk or formula. (pp. 135–136)

a., c., & d. Breast- and bottle-fed babies do not differ in these attributes.

10. b. is the answer. (p. 136)

11. c. is the answer. (p. 131)

a. & b. These motor skills do not emerge until somewhat later; reflexes are present at birth.

d. On the contrary, reflexes are quite predictable; this is the basis for the Brazelton Neonatal Behavioral Assessment Scale.

12. a. is the answer. (p. 131)

b., c., & d. The nonreflexive behaviors measured by the Brazelton Neonatal Behavioral Assessment Scale focus on responsiveness to social stimuli, rather than on fine or gross motor skills or on IQ.

13. b. is the answer. (p. 132)

14. d. is the answer. (pp. 134–135)

15. c. is the answer. (p. 126)

Matching Items

1. a (p. 125)	**5.** d (p. 136)	**9.** g (pp. 130–131)
2. e (p. 136)	**6.** j (p. 131)	**10.** c (p. 126)
3. h (p. 131)	**7.** b (p. 126)	**11.** i (p. 131)
4. k (p. 131)	**8.** f (p. 127)	

PROGRESS TEST 2

Multiple-Choice Questions

1. b. is the answer. (p. 124)

2. c. is the answer. (p. 131)

a., b., & d. Each of these refers to voluntary responses that are acquired only after a certain amount of practice; reflexes are involuntary responses that are present at birth and require no practice.

3. b. is the answer. (p. 127)

4. b. is the answer. (p. 133)

5. c. is the answer. (p. 135)

a. Norms are average ages at which certain motor skills are acquired.

6. b. is the answer. (p. 127)

a. Although focusing ability seems to be limited to a certain range, babies do focus on many objects in this range.

c. This is not within the range that babies *can* focus on.

d. Babies have very poor distance vision.

7. **d.** is the answer. (p. 129)
8. **a.** is the answer. (p. 126)
9. **a.** is the answer. (p. 135)

   b. If anything, this is a potential *disadvantage* of breast milk over formula.

   c. So can formula.

   d. Breast milk contains more iron, vitamin C, and vitamin A than cow's milk; it does not contain more protein and vitamin D, however.
10. **d.** is the answer. (p. 138)
11. **b.** is the answer. (p. 138)

    a. There is no evidence to support this.

    c. Kwashiorkor is caused by protein-calorie deficiency during toddlerhood.
12. **b.** is the answer. (pp. 130–131)

    c. & d. Reflexes are involuntary responses; climbing and using a crayon are both voluntary responses.
13. **d.** is the answer. (p. 131)
14. **d.** is the answer. (p. 131)

    a. & b. Fine and gross motor skills are voluntary responses; the response described is clearly reflexive.

    c. The Babinski reflex is the response that infants make when their feet are stroked.
15. **d.** is the answer. (p. 139)

True or False Items

1. F Boys are both slightly heavier and taller than girls at two years. (p. 124)
2. F The preterm infant takes longer to become aroused and longer to settle down again than does the full-term infant. (p. 126)
3. F Hiccups, sneezes, and spit-ups are common during the first few days, and they are entirely normal reflexes. (p. 131)
4. F Although all healthy infants develop the same motor skills in the same sequence, the age at which these skills are acquired can vary greatly from infant to infant and from place to place. (pp. 134–135)
5. F Researchers have compiled evidence that even 2-hour-old infants react to sweet, sour, and bitter solutions. (p. 129)
6. F Vision is relatively poorly developed at birth, whereas hearing is well developed. (p. 128)
7. F Myelination is not complete until adolescence. (p. 126)
8. T (p. 129)
9. F Although there is a trend toward increased breast-feeding, bottle- or formula-feeding is more common in this country. (p. 136)
10. T (p. 138)

CHALLENGE TEST

1. **c.** is the answer. (p. 131)
2. **d.** is the answer. (p. 127)

   a. & b. These changes in behavior indicate that the newborn has perceived an unfamiliar stimulus, not that he or she is hungry, annoyed, or angry.

   c. Habituation refers to a *decrease* in physiological responsiveness to a familiar stimulus.
3. **c.** is the answer. (pp. 128–129)

   a. & b. There is no evidence that infants can detect one parent's voice more easily than the other, or that sounds perceived at 1 month can not be discriminated later.

   d. This experiment was not concerned with sound localization.
4. **b.** is the answer. (p. 126)

   a. This state is characterized by slow and regular breathing and relaxed muscles.

   c. This state is characterized by bright eyes and regular and rapid breathing.
5. **c.** is the answer. The evidence for this comes from studies in which animals were prevented from using their senses in infancy; such animals became permanently handicapped. (p. 129)

   a. If this were true, sensory restriction studies would show that restriction had no effect on sensory abilities.

   b. If this were true, sensory restriction would cause much more serious impairment than it does.

   d. Sensory restriction research demonstrates that both genetic and environmental factors are important in the development of sensory abilities.
6. **c.** is the answer. The long-term consequences of undernutrition depend on its duration and the quality of intellectual stimulation experienced after infancy. (p. 140)

   a. Even when undernourishment occurs during the brain's most rapid growth period, children's intellectual abilities can recover.

   b. No such concept is introduced in the text.

   d. Smaller stature is linked to chronic malnutrition during infancy, rather than undernutrition.

7. **c.** is the answer. (pp. 127–129)
8. **b.** is the answer. (p. 131)

   a. This is the reflexive sucking of newborns in response to anything that touches their *lips.*

   c. This is the response that infants make when their feet are stroked.

   d. In this response to startling noises, newborns fling their arms outward and then bring them together on their chests as if to hold on to something.
9. **a.** is the answer. (p. 140)
10. **b.** is the answer. (p. 127)

    a. & d. Sensation and perception operate in all of these sensory modalities.
11. **b.** is the answer. (p. 129)

    a. & c. The text does not suggest that whether a sound is soothing or frightening is determined by its pitch.
12. **a.** is the answer. (pp. 129–130)
13. **c.** is the answer. (pp. 135–136)
14. **b.** is the answer. This is true because, at birth, focusing is best for objects between 4 and 30 inches. (p. 127)

    a., c., & d. Newborns have very poor distance vision; each of these situations involves a distance greater than the optimal focus range.
15. **d.** is the answer. (p. 139)

KEY TERMS

1. **Neurons**, or nerve cells, are the basic building blocks of the nervous system. (p. 125)
2. **Dendrites** are the extensions of neurons that comprise the communication networks among the billions of neurons in the cortex. (p. 126)
3. **Myelin** is the fatty insulating substance coating neurons and dendrites that helps transmit neural impulses faster and more efficiently. (p. 126)
4. The **physiological states** of the infant include quiet sleep, active sleep, and alert wakefulness. (p. 126)
5. **Brain waves** are patterns of electrical activity in the brain, recorded by an electroencephalogram (EEG), a device that picks up the electrical impulses from neurons. (p. 126)
6. **Sensation** is the process by which a sensory system responds to a particular stimulus. (p. 127)
7. **Perception** is the process by which the brain recognizes that a stimulus has been responded to so that the individual becomes aware of it. (p. 127)
8. **Habituation** refers to the decline in physiological responsiveness that occurs when a stimulus becomes familiar. Habituation to stimuli is used by researchers to assess infants' ability to perceive by testing their ability to discriminate between very similar stimuli. (p. 127)
9. **Binocular vision** is the ability to use both eyes together to focus on one object. (p. 128)

   Memory aid: Bi- indicates "two"; *ocular* means something pertaining to the eye. **Binocular vision** refers to vision using two eyes.
10. **Gross motor skills** are abilities that demand large movements, such as climbing, jumping, or running. (pp. 130–131)
11. **Fine motor skills** are abilities that require precise, small movements, such as picking up a coin. (p. 131)
12. **Reflexes** are involuntary responses to specific stimuli. (p. 131)
13. The **breathing reflex** is an involuntary response that ensures that the infant has an adequate supply of oxygen. (p. 131)
14. The **sucking reflex** is the involuntary tendency of newborns to suck anything that touches their lips. This reflex fosters feeding. (p. 131)
15. The **rooting reflex**, which helps babies find a nipple, causes them to turn their heads and start to suck when something brushes against their cheek. (p. 131)
16. The **Brazelton Neonatal Behavioral Assessment Scale (NBAS)**, which measures twenty simple reflexes and twenty-eight other items of infant behavior, is a test of the infant's overall readiness to respond to the world. (p. 131)
17. When babies can walk well without assistance (usually at about 12 months), they are given the name **toddler** because of the characteristic way they move their bodies from side to side. (p. 132)
18. **Norms** are age averages for the acquisition of particular motor skills. (p. 134)
19. **Marasmus** is a disease caused by severe protein-calorie deficiency during the first year of life. Growth stops, body tissues waste away, and the infant dies. (p. 136)
20. **Kwashiorkor** is a disease caused by protein-calorie deficiency during toddlerhood. The child's face, legs, and abdomen swell with water, sometimes making the child appear well fed. Other body parts are degraded, including the hair, which becomes thin, brittle, and colorless. (p. 136)

CHAPTER 6 The First Two Years: Cognitive Development

Chapter Overview

Chapter 6 explores the ways in which the infant comes to learn about, think about, and adapt to his or her surroundings. It focuses on three ways in which infant intelligence is revealed: through sensorimotor intelligence, perception, and language development.

The chapter begins with Jean Piaget's theory of sensorimotor intelligence, which maintains that infants think exclusively with their senses and motor skills. Piaget's six stages of sensorimotor intelligence are described.

The second part of the chapter describes infant perception as it looks at the way the infant selects, sorts, organizes, and integrates information from different sensory systems. The influential theory of Eleanor and James Gibson is explained.

Finally, the chapter turns to the most remarkable cognitive achievement of the first two years, the acquisition of language. Beginning with a description of the infant's first attempts at language, the chapter follows the sequence of events that lead to the child's ability to utter two-word sentences. The chapter concludes with an examination of language learning as teamwork involving babies and adults, who, in a sense, teach each other the unique human process of verbal communication.

NOTE: Answer guidelines for all Chapter 6 questions begin on page 90.

Guided Study

The text chapter should be studied one section at a time. Before you read, preview each section by skimming it, noting headings and boldface items. Then read the appropriate section objectives from the following outline. Keep these objectives in mind and, as you read the chapter section, search for the information that will enable you to meet each objective. Once you have finished a section, write out answers for its objectives.

Sensorimotor Intelligence (pp. 144–150)

1. Identify and describe the first three of Piaget's stages of sensorimotor intelligence.

2. Identify and describe stages 4 through 6 of Piaget's theory of sensorimotor intelligence.

Piaget Reconsidered (pp. 150–155)

3. Review recent research findings on object permanence and cite two criticisms of Piaget's theory of sensorimotor intelligence.

4. (Research Report) Discuss recent research findings on infant memory.

Perception (pp. 156–161)

5. Explain the Gibsons's ecological view of perception and discuss the idea of affordances, giving examples of affordances perceived by infants.

6. Discuss the infant's ability to integrate perceptual information from different sensory systems, giving examples of intermodal and cross-modal perception.

7. Discuss the infant's innate ability to categorize and explain how it develops.

Language Development (pp. 162–168)

8. Describe language development during infancy and identify its major landmarks.

9. Contrast the theories of Skinner and Chomsky regarding early language development and explain current views on language learning.

10. Explain the importance of baby talk and describe its main features.

Chapter Review

When you have finished reading the chapter, work through the material that follows to review it. Complete the sentences and answer the questions. As you proceed, evaluate your performance for each section by consulting the answers on page 90. Do not continue with the next section until you understand each answer. If you need to, review or reread the appropriate section in the textbook before continuing.

Sensorimotor Intelligence (p. 144–150)

1. The interaction of all the perceptual, intellectual, and linguistic abilities that are involved in thinking and learning describes ______________ .
2. Prior to Piaget, psychologists ______________ (overestimated/underestimated) infant intelligence.
3. When infants begin to explore the environment through sucking and grasping, they are displaying what Piaget called ______________ intelligence. In number, Piaget described ______________ stages of development of this type of intelligence.
4. According to Piaget, a(n) ______________ is a general way of thinking about, and interacting with, the environment. One of the most powerful inborn abilities of this type is the ______________ reflex.

5. The first stage of sensorimotor intelligence lasts from birth to ________________ of age.

Write a sentence describing a typical stage-one behavior.

6. The second stage of sensorimotor intelligence, which occurs between ________________ and ________________ months of age, begins when infants ________________ their reflexes to the environment.

Describe a typical stage-two behavior.

7. Piaget referred to stage three, which occurs between ________________ and ________________ months of age, as ________________.

Describe a typical stage-three behavior.

8. In stage four, which lasts from ________________ to ________________ months of age, infants learn to ________________ events. At this stage babies also engage in purposeful actions, or ________________-________________ behaviors.

9. A major development at this stage is the infant's growing understanding that objects continue to exist even when they are out of sight. Piaget called this awareness ________________ ________________.

10. At 8 months, with object permanence ________________ (fully/partially) established, many babies make what Piaget called the ________________ error.

Give a behavioral example of this error.

11. Piaget referred to stage five, which lasts from ________________ to ________________ months, as the stage of ________________ ________________. One hallmark of this stage is the ________________ (reappearance/disappearance) of the AB error.

Explain what Piaget meant when he described the stage-five infant as a "little scientist."

12. Stage six, which lasts from ________________ to ________________ months, is the stage of achieving new means through ________________ ________________.

13. Piaget's term for the ability to create mental images of things and actions that are not actually in view is ________________ ________________; the ability to imitate actions seen in the past is referred to as ________________ ________________.

14. Perhaps the strongest sign that children have reached stage six is their newfound ability to ________________.

Piaget Reconsidered (pp. 150–155)

15. Piaget's analysis of infant cognition ________________ (is/is not) widely accepted today.

Identify two problems with Piaget's theory that have been revealed by recent research.

16. Researchers have found that the schema of object permanence appears ______ (more/less) gradually than Piaget believed. Furthermore, the age at which object permanence is demonstrated varies with ______ ______. Infants as young as ______ months have been found to demonstrate at least rudimentary object permanence.

Identify two factors not related to cognitive maturity that can effect the age at which object permanence is demonstrated.

17. Cognitive development seems to occur ______ (less/more) evenly and with ______ (less/greater) variability among infants than Piaget depicted.

18. Two factors that contribute to the diversity of cognitive development are individual differences in ______ ______ and ______ ______, as well as cultural differences in the specific customs and goals of ______ ______.

19. Two areas of cognition that Piaget ignored because of his emphasis on practical, skill-related cognition are ______ and ______.

Perception (pp. 156–161)

20. Infant cognitive development is demonstrated on three related fronts: ______, ______ ______, and ______ ______.

21. Much of the current research in perception and cognition has been inspired by the work of the Gibsons, who stress that perception is a(n) ______ (active/passive/automatic) cognitive phenomenon.

22. According to the Gibsons, any object in the environment offers diverse opportunities for interaction; this property of objects is called ______.

23. The object affordances an individual perceives depend on the individual's ______ ______, his or her ______ ______, and on his or her ______ ______ of what the object might afford.

24. Infants perceive the affordance of ______ long before their manual dexterity has matured.

List other affordances perceived by infants from a very early age.

25. The ability to associate information from one sensory modality with information from another is called ______ ______. This ability ______ (is/is not) demonstrated by newborns.

26. The ability to use information from one sensory modality to imagine something in another is called ______-______ ______. Infants as young as ______ have demonstrated this ability, at least in rudimentary form.

Explain the significance of research demonstrating cross-modal perception in very young infants.

27. Research indicates that, even with training or particular experiences, infants may be ______ predisposed to perceive certain characteristics of objects. This suggests that some aspects of categorization are ______, as well as dependent on experience.

28. Research indicates that infants as young as 4 months are able to perceive differences in ______ ______, ______, and ______. Infants younger than ______ months have shown that they can distinguish sets of stimuli that differ in density, angularity, shape, and number.

Language Development (pp. 162–168)

29. Everywhere, in every language, children usually talk by age ______, with a basic grasp of ______ and a suitable ______.

30. Children all over the world follow the same ______ and approximately the same ______ for early language development.

31. Children first become competent in the area of language ______; within two years this ability evolves into an impressive command of language ______.

32. By 5 months of age, most babies' verbal repertoire consists of ______ ______.

33. At ______ months of age, babies begin to repeat certain syllables, a phenomenon referred to as ______. At the same time, ______ become part of the baby's efforts to communicate.

34. Deaf babies tend to show superiority over hearing babies in communicating with ______ and ______ ______.

35. At every stage of development, children understand ______ (more/less) than they express.

36. Deaf babies begin oral babbling ______ (earlier/later than) hearing babies. Deaf babies may also babble ______, with this behavior emerging ______ (earlier than/at the same time as/later than) hearing infants begin babbling orally.

37. The average baby speaks one or two words at about ______ of age. At this time vocabulary increases at a rate of ______ words a month. When vocabulary reaches approximately 50 words, it suddenly begins to build rapidly, at a rate of ______ or more words a month.

38. One characteristic of infant speech is ______, or overgeneralization, in which the infant applies a known word to a variety of objects and contexts. Another is the use of the ______, in which a single word expresses a complete thought.

39. Vocabulary size ______ (is/is not) the best measure of early language learning. Rather, the crux of early language is ______.

40. Children begin to produce their first two-word sentences at about ______ months.

41. Reinforcement and other conditioning processes account for language development, according to the learning theory of ______.

42. The theorist who stressed the infant's innate language abilities is ______, who maintained that all children are born with a LAD, or ______ ______ ______.

What evidence led Chomsky to conclude that infants have innate language abilities?

Summarize the conclusions of recent research regarding the theories of Skinner and Chomsky.

43. Adults talk to infants using a special form of language called ______________ ______________, which is nicknamed ______________.

Briefly describe the type of speech adults use with infants.

44. The conversational aspect of parent-child communication tends to become stronger between ______________ and ______________ months of age.

45. Two important factors in language development are ______________ processes and the infant's ______________ context.

Progress Test 1

Multiple-Choice Questions

Circle your answers to the following questions and check them with the answers on page 91. If your answer is incorrect, read the explanation for why it is incorrect and then consult the appropriate pages of the text (in parentheses following the correct answer).

1. Piagetian theory holds that young babies think with:
   a. their senses and movements.
   b. patient help from their parents.
   c. the secondary motor area of the cortex.
   d. simple symbols.

2. In Piaget's terms, a schema is:
   a. an opportunity for interaction with the environment.
   b. a general way of thinking about, and interacting with, the environment.
   c. a mental combination.
   d. goal-directed behavior.

3. Sensorimotor intelligence begins with a baby's first:
   a. attempt to crawl.
   b. reflex actions.
   c. auditory perception.
   d. adaptation of a reflex.

4. Between 1 and 4 months (sensorimotor stage two), babies begin to:
   a. grasp object permanence.
   b. look for toys that fall out of the crib.
   c. engage in goal-directed behavior.
   d. adapt their reflexes to the environment.

5. By the end of the first year, infants usually learn how to:
   a. accomplish simple goals.
   b. manipulate various symbols.
   c. solve complex problems.
   d. pretend.

6. When an infant begins to understand that objects exist even when they are out of sight, she or he has begun to understand the concept of object:
   a. displacement. c. permanence.
   b. importance. d. location.

7. In general terms, the Gibsons' concept of affordances emphasizes the idea that the individual perceives an object in terms of its:
   a. economic importance.
   b. physical qualities.
   c. function or use to the individual.
   d. role in the larger culture or environment.

8. Today, most cognitive psychologists view language acquisition as:
   a. primarily the result of imitation of adult speech.
   b. determined primarily by biological maturation.
   c. a behavior that is entirely determined by learning.
   d. determined by both biological maturation and learning.

9. Despite cultural differences, children all over the world attain very similar language skills:
   a. according to ethnically specific timetables.
   b. at about the same age.
   c. according to culturally specific timetables.
   d. according to timetables that vary from child to child.

10. The average baby speaks one or two words at about:
    a. 6 months. c. 12 months.
    b. 9 months. d. 24 months.

11. A single word, used by toddlers to express a complete thought, is:
    a. a holophrase. c. an overextension.
    b. baby talk. d. a deferred imitation.

12. Compared to the child's rate of speech development, his or her comprehension of language develops:
    a. more slowly.
    b. at about the same pace.
    c. more rapidly.
    d. more rapidly in certain cultures than it does in other cultures.

13. A distinctive form of language, with a particular pitch, structure, etc., that adults use in talking to infants is called:
    a. the holophrase.
    b. the LAD.
    c. baby talk.
    d. conversation.

14. The AB error is best understood as:
    a. a stage-six behavior, involving mental combinations.
    b. a normal mistake of infants who are beginning to achieve object permanence.
    c. symbol-manipulating activity, usually associated with language learning.
    d. a repudiation or criticism of Piaget's theory.

15. With regard to object permanence, researchers have found that performance is affected by:
    a. the testing conditions.
    b. his or her prior experience in searching.
    c. the nature or memorability of the hiding place.
    d. all of the above.

Matching Items

Match each definition or description with its corresponding term.

Definitions or Descriptions

_______ 1. overgeneralization of a word to inappropriate objects
_______ 2. repetitive utterance of certain syllables
_______ 3. the interaction of perceptual, intellectual, and linguistic abilities
_______ 4. thinking through the senses and motor skills
_______ 5. the realization that something that is out of sight continues to exist
_______ 6. being able to try out actions mentally
_______ 7. opportunities for interaction with an object
_______ 8. associating information from one sensory modality with information from another
_______ 9. using a single word to express a complete thought
_______ 10. using information from one sensory modality to imagine something in another

Terms

a. mental combinations
b. affordances
c. object permanence
d. intermodal perception
e. cross-modal perception
f. cognition
g. sensorimotor intelligence
h. babbling
i. holophrase
j. overextension

Progress Test 2

Progress Test 2 should be completed during a final chapter review. Answer the following questions after you thoroughly understand the correct answers for the Chapter Review and Progress Test 1.

Multiple-Choice Questions

1. Stage five (12 to 18 months) of sensorimotor intelligence is best described as:
   a. first acquired adaptations.
   b. new means through active experimentation.
   c. procedures for making interesting sights last.
   d. new means through symbolization.

2. The child's ability to create mental images of things and actions that are not actually in view is called:
   a. mental representation.
   b. deferred gratification
   c. mental combination.
   d. object memory.

3. Recent research suggests that the concept of object permanence:
   a. fades after a few months.
   b. is a skill some children never acquire.
   c. may occur earlier and more gradually than Piaget recognized.
   d. involves pretending as well as mental combinations.

4. According to Eleanor and James Gibson, graspability is:
   a. an opportunity perceived by a baby.
   b. a quality that resides in toys and other objects.
   c. an ability that emerges at about six months.
   d. evidence of manual dexterity in the young infant.

5. Both intermodal and cross-modal perception necessarily involve:
   a. matching of sight and sound.
   b. hand-eye coordination.
   c. mental representation of a hidden object.
   d. the ability to integrate perceptual information.

6. The best and most accurate measure of early language learning is:
   a. the size of a child's vocabulary.
   b. the number of grammatical errors made by a child.
   c. the nature of the grammatical errors made by the child.
   d. the child's ability and willingness to communicate.

7. For Noam Chomsky, the "language acquisition device" refers to:
   a. the human predisposition to acquire language.
   b. the portion of the human brain that processes speech.
   c. the vocabulary of the language the child is exposed to.
   d. all of the above.

8. The first stage of sensorimotor intelligence lasts until:
   a. infants can anticipate events that will fulfill their needs.
   b. infants begin to adapt their reflexes to the environment.
   c. object permanence has been achieved.
   d. infants are capable of deferred imitation.

9. Experiments demonstrate that intermodal and cross-modal perceptual abilities begin to develop in infants:
   a. less than 6 months old.
   b. between 6 and 12 months old.
   c. between 12 and 18 months old.
   d. more than 18 months old.

10. Whether or not an infant perceives certain characteristics of objects, such as "suckability" or "graspability," seems to depend on:
    a. his or her prior experiences.
    b. the size of the object.
    c. the behaviors his or her caregivers have reinforced.
    d. none of the above.

11. The interaction of all the perceptual, intellectual, and linguistic abilities that go into learning and thinking are referred to as:
    a. sensorimotor intelligence.
    b. cognition.
    c. intermodal perception.
    d. cross-modal perception.

12. The purposeful actions that begin to develop in sensorimotor stage four ("new adaptation and anticipation") are called:
    a. reflexes.
    b. affordances.
    c. goal-directed behaviors.
    d. mental combinations.

13. What is the correct sequence of stages of language development?
    a. crying, babbling, cooing, first word
    b. crying, cooing, babbling, first word

c. crying, babbling, first word, cooing
d. crying, cooing, first word, babbling

14. Compared to hearing babies, deaf babies:
a. are less likely to babble.
b. are more likely to babble.
c. begin to babble vocally at about the same age.
d. begin to babble manually at about the same age hearing babies begin to babble vocally.

15. According to Skinner, children acquire language:
a. as a result of an inborn ability to use the basic structure of language.
b. through reinforcement and conditioning.
c. mostly because of biological maturation.
d. in a fixed sequence of predictable stages.

True or False Items

Write *true* or *false* on the line in front of each statement.

_______ 1. Cognition is the interaction of all perceptual, intellectual, and linguistic abilities.

_______ 2. Sensorimotor intelligence must be present before cognitive development can occur.

_______ 3. Piaget described cognitive development as a series of stages or periods, the first of which occurs between birth and two years of age.

_______ 4. Recent research suggests that Piaget's stages are not universal, but rather are typical of a particular culture.

_______ 5. Children all over the world learn to speak at approximately the same age.

_______ 6. B. F. Skinner maintained that infants learn to talk through conditioning.

_______ 7. The function of baby talk remains unknown and unclear.

_______ 8. After the first few words, vocabulary expands very rapidly, typically resulting in overextension.

_______ 9. Deaf babies do not babble, but are better than hearing babies at communicating with gestures and facial expressions.

_______ 10. Cooing and babbling usually begin when the infant is about 6 months old.

Challenge Test

Answer these questions the day before an exam as a final check on your understanding of the chapter's terms and concepts.

1. A baby of 9 months repeatedly reaches for his sister's doll, even though he has been told "No" many times. This is an example of:
a. the AB error.
b. an overextension.
c. deferred imitation.
d. goal-directed behavior.

2. An infant who comes to expect the sound of music to emanate from a revolving turntable is exhibiting:
a. cross-modal perception.
b. goal-directed behavior.
c. intermodal perception.
d. object permanence.

3. Experiments reveal that infants can "recognize" by sight an object that they have previously touched but not seen. This is an example of:
a. deferred imitation.
b. two related affordances.
c. categorization.
d. cross-modal perception.

4. According to Skinner's theory, an infant who learns to delight his father by saying "da-da" is probably benefiting from:
a. social reinforcers, such as smiles and hugs.
b. modeling.
c. learning by imitation.
d. a biological predisposition to use language.

5. The child's tendency to call every animal "doggie" is an example of:
a. using the holophrase.
b. babbling.
c. Motherese.
d. overextension.

6. About six months after speaking his or her first words, the typical child will:
a. have a vocabulary of between 250 and 350 words.
b. begin to speak in holophrases.
c. put words together to form rudimentary sentences.
d. do all of the above.

7. A 20-month-old girl who is able to try out various actions mentally without having to actually perform them is learning to solve simple problems by using:
a. the AB error.
b. schemas.
c. intermodal perception.
d. mental combinations.

8. A toddler who re-creates an action he or she has seen someone else perform in the past is demonstrating an ability that Piaget called:
   a. cross-modal perception.
   b. deferred imitation.
   c. intermodal perception.
   d. mental representation.

9. (Research Report) In one experiment (reported by Bower, 1989), infants were found to look more intently at films that showed someone of their own sex, no matter how that person was dressed, or what kind of toy he or she played with. Boys who watched the films seem to be puzzled by the sight of:
   a. girls who played with guns and drums.
   b. boys who played with dolls.
   c. boys who were dressed in frilly, feminine clothes.
   d. girls who were dressed in boyish pants.

10. (Research Report) Studies show that 6-month-old infants look longer at a photo of a male face when they are listening to a tape of a male voice, and longer at a female face when listening to a female voice. This is an example of:
    a. deferred imitation.
    b. a gender expectancy.
    c. cross-modal perception.
    d. intermodal perception.

11. A baby who realizes that a rubber duck has fallen out of the tub must be somewhere on the floor has achieved what Piaget called:
    a. object permanence.
    b. intermodal perception.
    c. mental combinations.
    d. cross-modal perception.

12. As soon as her babysitter arrives, 21-month-old Christine holds on to her mother's legs and, in a questioning manner, says "bye bye." Because Christine clearly is "asking" her mother not to leave, her utterance can be classified as:
    a. babbling.
    b. an overextension.
    c. a holophrase.
    d. telegraphic speech.

13. The 6-month-old infant's continual repetition of sound combinations such as "ba-ba-ba" is called:
    a. cooing.
    b. babbling.
    c. the holophrase.
    d. an overextension.

14. Which of the following is an example of a linguistic overextension that a 2-year-old might make?
    a. saying "bye-bye" to indicate that he or she wants to go out
    b. pointing to a cat and saying "doggie"
    c. repeating certain syllables, such as "ma-ma-ma"
    d. reversing word order, such as "want it, paper"

15. Many researchers believe that the infant's ability to detect the similarities and differences between shapes and colors marks the beginning of:
    a. cross-modal perception.
    b. intermodal perception.
    c. category or concept formation.
    d. full object permanence.

Key Terms

Using your own words, write a brief definition or explanation of each of the following terms on a separate piece of paper.

1. cognition
2. sensorimotor intelligence
3. goal-directed behavior
4. object permanence
5. AB error
6. mental combinations
7. mental representation
8. deferred imitation
9. affordances
10. intermodal perception
11. cross-modal perception
12. babbling
13. overextension
14. holophrase
15. baby talk

ANSWERS

CHAPTER REVIEW

1. cognition
2. underestimated
3. sensorimotor; 6
4. schema; sucking
5. 1 month

Stage-one infants suck everything that touches their lips, grasp at everything that touches the center of their palms, stare at everything that comes within focus, and so forth.

6. 1; 4; adapt

During this stage infants adapt their sucking to specific objects. For example, they learn that efficient breast-sucking requires a squeezing sucking, whereas efficient pacifier-sucking does not.

7. 4; 8; procedures for making interesting sights last

Stage-three infants often will repeat a specific action that has just elicited a pleasing response.

8. 8; 12; anticipate; goal-directed
9. object permanence
10. partially; AB

Having found an object that was hidden in one place, and then observing it being hidden in a second place, the infant will look for the object in the first place, and then give up looking.

11. 12; 18; new means through active experimentation; disappearance

Having discovered some action or set of actions that is possible with a given object, stage-five "little scientists" seem to ask, "What else can I do with this?"

12. 18; 24; mental combinations
13. mental representation; deferred imitation
14. pretend
15. is

Recent research suggests that Piaget's timetable for development may have been too strict, and that the ages Piaget assigned to various stages must be regarded as approximate. It also suggests that development is more gradual or continuous, with each new stage being arrived at, ability by ability, rather than all at once, as Piaget described.

16. more; the conditions of testing; 4

The age at which object permanence is demonstrated varies with the relative "memorability" of the hiding places and the time interval between the hiding and the searching.

17. less; greater
18. inherited characteristics; early experiences; child care
19. perception; memory
20. language; sensorimotor intelligence; perceptual organization
21. active
22. affordance
23. past experiences; present needs; cognitive awareness
24. graspability

From a very early age, infants understand which objects afford suckability, which afford noise-making, which afford movability, and so forth.

25. intermodal perception; is
26. cross-modal perception; 1 month

To some researchers it suggests that, from a very early age, infants are coordinating and organizing their perceptions into categories, such as soft, hard, flat, round, and so forth.

27. neurologically; innate
28. geometric form; color; size; 8
29. 2; grammar; vocabulary
30. sequence; timetable
31. function; structure
32. squeals, growls, grunts, croons, and yells
33. 6 or 7; babbling; gestures
34. gestures; facial expressions
35. more
36. later; manually; at the same time as
37. 1 year; a few; one hundred
38. overextension; holophrase
39. is not; communication
40. 16 to 21
41. B. F. Skinner
42. Noam Chomsky; language acquisition device

For Chomsky, the fact that all children learn to communicate so rapidly, beginning at the same age, implies that infants have innate language abilities.

Recent research has offered some support for both Skinner's and Chomsky's theories. Developmentalists today believe that language acquisition is an interactional process between the infant's biological predisposition and the communication that occurs in the caregiver-child relationship.

43. baby talk; Motherese

Baby talk is higher in pitch, has a characteristically low-to-high intonation pattern, uses simpler and more concrete vocabulary, shorter sentence length, and employs more questions, commands, and repetitions, and fewer past tenses, pronouns, and complex sentences.

44. 5; 7

45. innate; social

PROGRESS TEST 1

Multiple-Choice Questions

1. **a.** is the answer. This is what is meant by sensorimotor intelligence. (p. 144)

b. This is needed by children of all ages, not merely young babies.

c. Piaget's theory is not concerned with cortical areas involved in thinking.

d. The use of symbols—an example of mental representation—comes at a later stage.

2. **b.** is the answer. (p. 145)

a. Affordances, as described by the Gibsons, are opportunities for interaction provided by objects in the environment.

c. Mental combinations are behaviors or actions that are carried out mentally; the reflexes of the stage-one infant are not mental combinations, but they are schemas nonetheless.

d. Schemas are not limited to goal-directed behaviors; they can also be the reflexive responses of the very young infant.

3. **b.** is the answer. This was Piaget's most basic contribution to the study of infant cognition—that intelligence is revealed in behavior at every age. (p. 145)

4. **d.** is the answer. (p. 146)

a., b., & c. These behaviors are typical of stage-four infants.

5. **a.** is the answer. (p. 147)

b. & c. These abilities are not acquired until children are much older.

d. Pretending emerges in stage six (18 to 24 months).

6. **c.** is the answer. (p. 147)

7. **c.** is the answer. (p. 156)

8. **d.** is the answer. (pp. 165–166)

9. **b.** is the answer. (p. 162)

a., c., & d. Children the world over, and in every Piagetian stage, follow the same sequence and approximately the same timetable for early language development.

10. **c.** is the answer. (p. 164)

11. **a.** is the answer. (p. 164)

b. Baby talk is the speech adults use with infants.

c. An overextension is a grammatical error in which a word is generalized to an inappropriate context.

d. Deferred imitation is the ability to imitate actions seen in the past.

12. **c.** is the answer. At every age, children understand more speech than they can produce. (pp. 163–164)

13. **c.** is the answer. (p. 166)

a. A holophrase is a single word uttered by a toddler to express a complete thought.

b. According to Noam Chomsky, the LAD, or "language acquisition device," is a biological predisposition in humans to acquire language.

d. These characteristic differences in pitch and structure are precisely what distinguish baby talk from regular conversation.

14. **b.** is the answer. (p. 147)

a. The AB error is typically a stage 4 behavior.

c. & d. The AB error occurs when an infant, having found an object that was hidden in one place and then observing it being hidden in a second place, searches for the object in the first place and then gives up looking.

15. **d.** is the answer. (pp. 151–152)

Matching Items

1. j (p. 164)	**5.** c (p. 147)	**8.** d (p. 157)
2. h (p. 163)	**6.** a (p. 149)	**9.** i (p. 164)
3. f (p. 144)	**7.** b (p. 156)	**10.** e (p. 158)
4. g (p. 144)		

PROGRESS TEST 2

Multiple-Choice Questions

1. **b.** is the answer. (p. 148)

a. This is stage two.

c. This is stage three.

d. This is not a stage of sensorimotor intelligence.

2. **a.** is the answer. (p. 149)

3. **c.** is the answer. (p. 151)

4. **a.** is the answer. (p. 157)

   b. Affordances are perceptual phenomena.

   c. & **d.** Infants perceive graspability at an earlier age, and long before their manual dexterity enables them to actually grasp successfully.

5. **d.** is the answer. (pp. 157–158)

   a. Intermodal and cross-modal perception are not limited to vision and hearing.

   b. Intermodal and cross-modal perception are *perceptual* abilities and do not involve motor responses, as hand-eye coordination does.

   c. This ability is called object permanence.

6. **d.** is the answer. (p. 164)

7. **a.** is the answer. Chomsky believed this device was innate. (p. 165)

8. **b.** is the answer. (p. 145)

   a. & **c.** These are hallmarks of stage four.

   d. This is a hallmark of stage six.

9. **a.** is the answer. (p. 157)

10. **d.** is the answer. Infants seem to be "prewired," or neurologically primed, to perceive characteristics of objects, for example, their suckability or graspability. (p. 159)

11. **b.** is the answer. (p. 144)

    a. This is intelligence revealed by infants' sensory and motor abilities.

    c. & **d.** These are perceptual abilities involving coordination between sensory systems.

12. **c.** is the answer. (p. 147)

    a. Reflexes are involuntary (and therefore unintentional) responses.

    b. Affordances are perceived opportunities for interaction with objects.

    d. Mental combinations are actions that are carried out mentally, rather than behaviorally. Moreover, mental combinations do not begin until a later age, during sensorimotor stage six.

13. **b.** is the answer. (pp. 163–164)

14. **d.** is the answer. (p. 163)

    a. & **b.** Hearing and deaf babies do not differ in the overall likelihood they will babble.

    c. Deaf babies begin to babble vocally several months later than hearing babies do.

15. **b.** is the answer. (p. 165)

    a., **c.**, & **d.** These views on language acquisition describe the theory offered by Noam Chomsky.

True or False Items

1. T (p. 144)
2. F Sensorimotor intelligence describes the first period of cognitive development. (p. 144)
3. T (p. 145)
4. F Piaget's stages are universal; children all over the world pass through them in sequence, though the age at which they reach the stages may vary from culture to culture. (p. 153)
5. T (p. 162)
6. T (p. 165)
7. F The function of baby talk is to facilitate language learning. (p. 166)
8. F Vocabulary growth is at first very slow. Overextension refers to a characteristic of toddler speech that enables the child to use one word to refer to many different things. (p. 164)
9. F Deaf babies do babble, several months later than hearing babies. Between 6 and 12 months, they are also better than hearing babies at communicating with gestures and facial expressions. (p. 163)
10. F Babbling begins at about six months; but cooing begins much earlier—at about two months. (p. 163)

CHALLENGE TEST

1. **d.** is the answer. The baby is clearly behaving purposefully, the hallmark of goal-directed behavior. (p. 147)

   a. The AB error occurs when the infant, having found an object that was hidden in one place and then observing it being hidden in a second place, searches for the object in the first place and then gives up looking.

   b. An overextension occurs when the infant overgeneralizes the use of a word to an inappropriate object or context.

   c. Deferred imitation is the ability to imitate actions seen in the past.

2. **c.** is the answer. Intermodal perception is the ability to associate information from one sensory modality with information from another. In the example, the infant is associating visual information (the sight of the revolving turntable) with auditory information (the sound of a record album). (p. 157)

a. Cross-modal perception is the ability to use information from one sensory modality to imagine something in another.

b. Goal-directed behavior is purposeful action.

d. Object permanence is the awareness that objects do not cease to exist when they are out of sight.

3. **d.** is the answer. (p. 158)

a. Deferred imitation is the ability to imitate actions seen in the past.

b. Affordances are perceived opportunities for interacting with objects.

c. Categorization refers to cognitively classifying objects according to certain features.

4. **a.** is the answer. The father's expression of delight is clearly a reinforcer in that it has increased the likelihood of the infant's vocalization. (p. 165)

b. & c. Modeling, or learning by imitation, would be implicated if the father attempted to increase the infant's vocalizations by repeatedly saying "da-da" himself, in the infant's presence.

d. This is Chomsky's viewpoint; Skinner maintained that language is acquired through learning.

5. **d.** is the answer. The child is clearly overgeneralizing the word "dog" by applying it to other animals. (p. 164)

a. The holophrase is a single word that is used to express a complete thought.

b. Babbling is the repetitious uttering of certain syllables, such as "ma-ma," or "da-da."

c. Motherese, or baby talk, is the characteristic manner in which adults change the structure and pitch of their speech when conversing with infants.

6. **c.** is the answer. (p. 165)

a. At 18 months of age, most children have much smaller vocabularies.

b. Speaking in holophrases is typical of younger infants.

7. **d.** is the answer. (p. 149)

a. The AB error occurs when the infant, having found an object that was hidden in one place and then observing it being hidden in a second place, searches for the object in the first place and then gives up looking.

b. Schemas are general ways of thinking about, and interacting with, the environment. In this example, the child is *mentally* exercising a particular schema, not interacting with the environment.

c. Intermodal perception is the ability to associate information from one sensory modality with information from another.

8. **b.** is the answer. (p. 150)

a. Cross-modal perception is the ability to use information from one sensory modality to imagine something in another.

c. Intermodal perception is the ability to associate information from one sensory modality with information from another.

d. Mental representation is the ability to imagine things and actions that are not actually in view.

9. **c.** is the answer (p. 160)

10. **d.** is the answer. In this experiment the infants are associating the visual information from the photograph with the auditory information from the tape recording (p. 160)

11. **a.** is the answer. Before object permanence is attained, an object that disappears from sight ceases to exist for the infant. (p. 147)

b. Intermodal perception, which is not a Piagetian concept, is the ability to associate information from one sensory modality with information from another.

c. Mental combinations are actions that are carried out mentally.

d. Cross-modal perception, which also is not a Piagetian concept, is the ability to use information from one sensory modality to imagine something in another.

12. **c.** is the answer. (p. 164)

a. Because Christine is expressing a complete thought, her speech is much more than babbling.

b. An overextension is the application of a word the child knows to an inappropriate context, such as "doggie" to all animals the child sees.

d. Telegraphic speech emerges later, when children begin forming 2- and 3-word sentences.

13. **b.** is the answer. (p. 163)

a. Cooing is the pleasant-sounding utterances of the infant at about 2 months.

c. The holophrase occurs later, and refers to the infant's use of a single word to express a complete thought.

d. An overextension, or overgeneralization, is the application of a word to an inappropriate context, such as "doed" for the past tense of "do."

14. **b.** is the answer. In this example, the 2-year-old has overgeneralized the concept "doggie" to all four-legged animals. (p. 164)

15. **c.** is the answer. (pp. 159, 161)

    a. & b. These perceptual abilities are based on the integration of perceptual information from different sensory systems.

    d. Object permanence, or the awareness that objects do not cease to exist simply because they are not in view, is not based on perceiving similarities among objects.

KEY TERMS

1. **Cognition** is the interaction of all the perceptual, intellectual, and linguistic abilities that comprise thinking and learning. (p. 144)
2. Piaget's stages of **sensorimotor intelligence** are based on his theory that infants think exclusively with their senses and motor skills. (p. 144)
3. **Goal-directed behavior** is purposeful responding in order to meet a certain objective, which emerges during Piaget's stage four, "new adaptation and anticipation." (p. 147)
4. In Piaget's theory, **object permanence** refers to the understanding that objects continue to exist even when they are out of sight. This development occurs during sensorimotor stage four. (p. 147)
5. In Piaget's theory, the **AB error** is made by stage-four infants in whom object permanence is only partially established. The AB error occurs when an infant, having found an object that was hidden in one place and then observing it being hidden in a second place, searches for the object in the first place and then gives up looking. (p. 147)
6. In Piaget's theory, **mental combinations** are actions that are carried out mentally. Mental combinations enable stage-six toddlers to begin to anticipate and solve problems without resorting to trial-and-error experiments. (p. 149)
7. In Piaget's theory, mental combinations are made possible by **mental representation**, the ability to create mental images of things and actions that are not actually in view. (p. 149)
8. **Deferred imitation** is the ability to imitate actions seen in the past. According to Piaget, this ability emerges in sensorimotor stage six. (p. 150)
9. **Affordances** are perceived opportunities for interacting with objects in the environment. Infants perceive sucking, grasping, noise-making, and many other affordances of objects at an early age. (p. 156)

   Memory aid: According to Eleanor and James Gibson, all objects have many **affordances** in that they offer or "afford" diverse opportunities for interaction.
10. **Intermodal perception** is the ability to associate information from one sensory modality with information from another. (p. 157)
11. **Cross-modal perception** is the ability to use information from one sensory modality to imagine something in another. (p. 158)
12. The **babbling** stage of language development, which begins at 6 or 7 months, is characterized by the spontaneous repetition of certain syllables (such as "ma-ma.") (p. 163)
13. **Overextension** is a characteristic of infant speech in which the infant overgeneralizes a known word by applying it to a large variety of objects or contexts. (p. 164)

    Memory aid: In this behavior the infant *extends* a word or grammatical rule beyond, or *over* and above, its normal boundaries.
14. Another characteristic of infant speech is the use of the **holophrase**, in which a single word is used to convey a complete thought. (p. 164)
15. **Baby talk**, or Motherese, is a form of speech used by adults when talking to infants. Its hallmark is exaggerated expressiveness; it employs more questions, commands, and repetitions; it uses simpler vocabulary and grammar; it has a higher pitch and more low-to-high fluctuations. (p. 166)

CHAPTER 7 The First Two Years: Psychosocial Development

Chapter Overview

Chapter 7 describes the emotional and social life of the developing person during the first two years. It begins with a sequential description of the infant's emerging emotions and how they reflect increasing cognitive abilities. A second section presents the theories of Freud, Erikson, and Mahler that help us understand how the infant's emotional and behavioral responses begin to take on the various patterns that form personality. Important research on the nature and origins of temperament, which informs virtually every characteristic of the person's developing personality, is also considered.

In the next section, emotions and relationships are examined from a different perspective—that of parent-infant interaction. Videotaped studies of parents and infants, combined with laboratory studies of attachment, have greatly expanded our understanding of psychosocial development. The chapter concludes with a life-span perspective on the most destructive of parent-child interactions: child maltreatment.

NOTE: Answer guidelines for all Chapter 7 questions begin on page 107.

Guided Study

The text chapter should be studied one section at a time. Before you read, preview each section by skimming it, noting headings and boldface items. Then read the appropriate section objectives from the following outline. Keep these objectives in mind and, as you read the chapter section, search for the information that will enable you to meet each objective. Once you have finished a section, write out answers for its objectives.

Emotional Development (pp. 172–175)

1. Name three emotions that are expressed by infants during the first days and months and describe the main developments in the emotional life of the child between 8 months and 2 years.

2. Discuss the effects of cognitive development on emotional development between 8 months and two years, including the effects of the infant's emerging self-awareness.

The Origins of Personality (pp. 175–182)

3. Describe Freud's psychosexual stages of infant development.

4. Describe Erikson's psychosocial stages of infant development and Mahler's separation-individuation period of infant development.

5. Discuss the origins and development of temperament as an interaction of nature and nurture, and explain the significance of research on temperament for parents and caregivers.

Parent-Infant Interaction (pp. 183–190)

6. Describe the synchrony of parent-infant interaction during the first year and discuss its significance to the developing person.

7. Define attachment, tell how it is measured, and discuss the long-term consequences of secure and insecure attachment.

8. (Research Report) Discuss contemporary views on the role of the father in infant psychosocial development.

Child Maltreatment (pp. 190–205)

9. (A Life-Span Perspective) Identify the various categories of child maltreatment and discuss several factors that contribute to the relatively high incidence of maltreatment in the United States.

10. (A Life-Span Perspective) Discuss the consequences of child maltreatment, and identify several approaches to its treatment or prevention in terms of the four categories of mistreating families.

Chapter Review

When you have finished reading the chapter, work through the material that follows to review it. Complete the sentences and answer the questions. As you proceed, evaluate your performance for each section by consulting the answers on page 107. Do not continue with the next section until you understand each answer. If you need to, review or reread the appropriate section in the textbook before continuing.

Emotional Development (pp. 172–175)

1. Even very young infants express many emotions, including: ______________________________

______________________________.

2. Infants' capacity for specific emotions emerge according to a developmental schedule, which is related to ______ maturation.

3. The infant's smile in response to seeing another person, which is called a(n) ______ ______, begins to appear at about ______ of age. The development of smiling ______ (is/is not) universal in infants.

4. Stranger anxiety, which is called ______ ______ ______, is first noticeable at about ______ of age and becomes full-blown by ______ of age. All infants ______ (do/do not) experience this fear. How a baby responds to a stranger depends on aspects of the infant, such as ______.

5. An infant's fear of being left by the mother or other caregiver, called ______ ______, peaks at about ______ of age and then gradually subsides. Whether separation distresses an infant depends on such factors as ______ ______.

6. As infants become older, emotions such as anger ______ (intensify/weaken) and smiling and laughing become ______ (more/less) selective. These emotional changes may be the result of ______ maturation.

7. By 10 months infants look to trusted adults for emotional cues in uncertain situations; this is called ______ ______.

8. The emerging sense of "me and mine" is part of what psychologists call ______-______. This makes possible many new self-conscious emotions, including ______, ______, ______, and ______.

9. In the first few months infants ______ (do/do not) have a sense of self and/or an awareness of their bodies as their own.

Briefly describe the nature and findings of the classic rouge-and-mirror experiment on self-awareness in infants.

10. The development of self-awareness seems ______ (universal/to vary from culture to culture); its onset changes the ______ and ______ of the toddler's reactions to others.

The Origins of Personality (pp. 175–182)

11. An early prevailing view among psychologists was that the individual's personality was permanently molded by the actions of his or her ______. Two versions of this theory were the ______ and ______.

12. According to the behaviorist perspective, personality is molded through the processes of ______ and ______ of the child's various behaviors. A strong proponent of this position was ______.

13. According to Freud, the experiences of the first ______ years of life and the child's relationship with his or her ______ were decisive in personality formation.

14. In Freud's theory, development begins with the ______ stage, so named because the ______ is the infant's prime source of gratification and pleasure.

15. According to Freud, in the ______ year the prime focus of gratification comes from stimulation and control of the bowels. Freud referred to this period as the ______ stage. This stage represents a shift in the way the infant interacts with others, from the more ______ mode of orality to the more ______ mode of anality.

Describe Freud's ideas on the importance of early oral and anal experiences to later personality development.

16. Research has shown that the parents' overall pattern of ______________________ is more important to the child's emotional development than the particulars of feeding and weaning or toilet-training.

17. The theorist who believes that development occurs through a series of crises is ______________________. According to his theory, the crisis of infancy is one of ______________________, while the crisis of toddlerhood is one of ______________________. He maintained that experiences later in life ______________________ (can alter/have little impact on) the effects of infant experiences on personality development.

18. The need for a proper balance between protection and freedom is also central to the theory proposed by ______________________. According to this view, the period from 5 months to 3 years, during which the infant gains a sense of self apart from the mother, is the period of ______________-______________.

19. A person's inherent, relatively consistent, basic dispositions define his or her ______________________. This characteristic, which ______________________ (is/is not) evident at birth, begins in the ______________________ codes that guide the development of the brain, and is affected by many prenatal experiences, including: ______________________.

20. List the nine temperamental characteristics measured in the NYLS study: ______________________ ______________________

21. Most young infants can be described as one of three types: ______________________, ______________-______________-______________-______________, or ______________________.

22. Two aspects of temperament that are quite variable are ______________________ and ______________________ ______________________.

Describe two ways in which the environment can influence a child's temperamental characteristics.

23. (Research Report) Every ethnic and racial group ______________________ (has/does not have) a portion of individuals who are very outgoing and another portion who are unusually shy. Among Caucasians, shyness seems to be genetically linked with certain physical characteristics, including ______________________ ______________________.

24. (Research Report) The personality trait of extroversion/shyness is readily observable by age ______________________. A recent study found that infants who were high or low in both ______________________ ______________________ and ______________________ at 4 months were, respectively, high or low in fear at 9 and 14 months. Results such as these suggest that extroversion/shyness is a(n) ______________________ (inherited/learned) trait. They further suggest that shyness is one manifestation of a more general physiological pattern of ______________________ to new stimuli and a trait that ______________________ (is/is not) inherited in an additive fashion.

Parent-Infant Interaction (pp. 183–190)

25. The intricate dialogue, or coordinated interaction, of response between infant and caregiver is called ______________. Partly through this interaction, infants learn to ______________ and ______________ emotions.

26. The signs of synchrony include ______________; the signs of dyssynchrony include ______________.

27. The ease of synchrony is affected not only by the caregiver's personality, but also by the infant's ______________ and ______________.

28. The emotional bond that develops between parents and young infants is called ______________. An infant who derives comfort and confidence from the secure base provided by the caregiver is displaying ______________ ______________. By contrast, ______________ ______________ is characterized by an infant's fear, anger, or seeming indifference to the caregiver.

29. The procedure developed by Ainsworth to measure attachment is called the ______________ ______________. Approximately ______________ of American infants tested with this procedure demonstrate secure attachment.

Briefly describe three types of insecure attachment.

30. Among the features of caregiving that affect the quality of attachment are:

a. ______________

b. ______________

c. ______________

31. Cross-cultural comparisons of the Strange Situation reveal that children from ______________ and ______________ show a higher rate of resistance and anxiety than American infants do, while infants from some western European countries show higher rates of ______________. Overall, such studies demonstrate ______________ (an essential similarity/great differences) in the behavior of infants of various nationalities in the Strange Situation.

32. Most infants ______________ (do/do not) show signs of attachment to other caregivers, such as fathers, siblings, and day-care workers.

33. According to Jay Belsky, high-quality day care ______________ (is/is not) likely to result in negative developmental outcomes.

34. List several characteristics of 3- and 4-year-olds who, at age 1, were rated as:

securely attached: ______________

insecurely attached: ______________

35. Some contemporary researchers have found evidence that insecure attachment may ______________ (never be overcome by the developing individual/disappear eventually, especially if the caregiver becomes more attentive). This issue remains controversial, however.

36. (Research Report) Traditional views of infant development focused ______________ (exclusively on mothers/on both mothers and fathers). Overall, researchers ______________ (have/have not) found evidence that women are biologically predisposed to be better parents than men are.

37. (Research Report) In contemporary marriages, with both parents working outside the home, most child caregiving is ______________ (shared equally by mothers and fathers/done by the mother).

38. (Research Report) Although fathers provide less basic child care, they spend more time ______________ with their children.

Describe several differences in how mothers and fathers typically play with their children.

39. (Research Report) In one study, an infant's reaction to a stranger was found to correlate with attachment to the ________________, but not with attachment to the other parent. In another study, the ________________ (mother's/ father's) presence made toddlers more likely to smile and play with a stranger than did the presence of the other parent.

Child Maltreatment (pp. 190–205)

40. The most common form of child maltreatment is a persistent pattern of abuse or neglect that, over the years, affects the child's ________________-________________ and personality.

41. (A Life-Span Perspective) Forty years ago, the concept of child maltreatment was mostly limited to gross ________________ abuse, which was thought to be the outburst of a mentally disturbed person. Today, it is known that most perpetrators of maltreatment ________________ (are/are not) mentally ill.

42. (A Life-Span Perspective) Intentional harm to, or avoidable endangerment of, someone under age 18 defines child ________________. Actions that are deliberately harmful to a child's well-being are classified as ________________. A failure to act appropriately to meet a child's basic needs is classified as ________________.

43. (A Life-Span Perspective) Child abuse and neglect can be divided into six subcategories:

a. ________________ ________________

b. ________________ ________________

c. ________________ ________________

d. ________________ ________________

e. ________________ ________________

f. ________________ ________________

44. (Research Report) It is estimated that about one out of every ________________ American children under age 18 has experienced some form of severe maltreatment within the past year.

45. (Research Report) The four methods commonly used to estimate the prevalence of child maltreatment are:

a. ________________

b. ________________

c. ________________

d. ________________

The method that leads to the highest reported abuse rate is ________________.

46. (A Closer Look) An important factor in understanding the context of child maltreatment is ________________ ________________.

47. (A Closer Look) The acceptability of physical punishment for children ________________ (varies/does not vary) from culture to culture.

48. (A Closer Look) The seriousness of an act of maltreatment depends partly on a particular child's ________________, ________________, and ________________.

49. (A Closer Look) Putting a child at risk for serious harm, which is called ________________, is now accepted as a criterion for child abuse.

List four community values that protect children from abuse.

Give four reasons for the prevalence of child maltreatment in the United States.

50. (A Life-Span Perspective) The daily routines of maltreating families typically are either very rigid in their ______________ so that no one can measure up, or they are so ______________ that no one can be certain of what is expected.

51. (A Life-Span Perspective) Maltreatment is more likely if the family is ______________ and distrusting of others. Also, maltreatment may result when there are ______________ ______________ among other family members. In families where there are more than ______________ young children, maltreatment is more common. Low-income single mothers are ______________ (no more/more) abusive than their married counterparts. No matter what their income, single fathers are ______________ (no more/more) abusive than married fathers.

52. (A Life-Span Perspective) Serious and intentional harm to a child by a brother or sister is called ______________ ______________.

53. (A Life-Span Perspective) It is estimated that only about ______________ percent or fewer of maltreating parents are pathological.

List several personality traits of maltreating parents.

54. (A Life-Span Perspective) Abusive parents are more likely to misread their child's ______________ as displays of anger.

55. (A Life-Span Perspective) Drug dependency ______________ (increases/does not increase) the likelihood of child maltreatment.

List several characteristics of children who are more likely to be maltreated.

56. (A Life-Span Perspective) The difficult nature of some abused and neglected children is almost always a ______________ (result/cause) of their maltreatment.

Describe some of the deficits of children who have been maltreated.

57. (A Life-Span Perspective) The phenomenon of mistreated children growing up to become abusive or neglectful parents themselves is called ______________ ______________.

A widely held misconception is that this phenomenon ______________ (is/is not) avoidable.

58. (A Life-Span Perspective) Approximately ______________ percent of abused children actually become abusive parents. This rate is about ______________ times that of the general population.

59. (A Life-Span Perspective) There have been recent signs that the rate of violent punishment reported by parents is ______________ (rising/falling).

60. (A Life-Span Perspective) Mistreating families who are experiencing unusual problems, such as divorce or the loss of a job, are classified as ______________ ______________ ______________. It is relatively ______________ (easy/difficult) to help these families overcome their mistreating ways.

61. (A Life-Span Perspective) Mistreating families that have many problems caused by their immediate situation, past history, and their temperament, that seriously impair their parenting abilities are classified as ______________. Treatment of these families is ______________ (more/less) difficult.

62. (A Life-Span Perspective) Mistreating families who will probably never be able to function adequately and independently of the help of social workers, therapists, and others until the children are grown are classified as ______________.

63. (A Life-Span Perspective) Mistreating families that are so impaired by deep emotional problems or serious cognitive deficiencies that they may never be able to meet the needs of their children are classified as ______________. For children born into these families, long-term ______________ ______________ is the best solution.

64. (A Life-Span Perspective) The most promising strategy for preventing child maltreatment focuses on mothers, especially ______________ ______________.

65. (A Life-Span Perspective) Other measures needed to reduce the rate of child abuse include ______________ ______________.

Progress Test 1

Multiple-Choice Questions

Circle your answers to the following questions and check them with the answers on page 109. If your answer is incorrect, read the explanation for why it is incorrect and then consult the appropriate pages of the text (in parentheses following the correct answer).

1. One of the first emotions that can be discerned in infancy is:
   a. shame.
   b. distress.
   c. guilt.
   d. pride.

2. The social smile begins to appear:
   a. at about 6 weeks.
   b. at about 8 months.
   c. after stranger anxiety has been overcome.
   d. after the infant has achieved a sense of self.

3. An infant's fear of being left by the mother or other caregiver, called ______________, peaks at about ______________.
   a. separation anxiety; 14 months
   b. fear of strangers; 8 months
   c. separation anxiety; 8 months
   d. fear of strangers; 14 months

4. Social referencing refers to:
   a. parenting skills that change over time.
   b. changes in community values regarding, for example, the acceptability of using physical punishment on children.
   c. the support network for new parents provided by extended family members.
   d. the infant response of looking to trusted adults for emotional cues in uncertain situations.

5. According to Margaret Mahler, separation-individuation is the period during which:
   a. dependence on the mother is strongest.
   b. infants feel as though they are part of their mother.
   c. the mother exclusively emphasizes toilet training.
   d. the infant gradually develops a sense of self.

6. Psychologists who favored the ______________ perspective believed that the personality of the child was virtually "created" through reinforcement and punishment.
   a. psychoanalytic
   b. behaviorist
   c. psychosocial
   d. separation-individuation

7. Freud's oral stage corresponds to Erikson's crisis of:
   a. orality versus anality.
   b. trust versus mistrust.
   c. autonomy versus shame and doubt.
   d. secure versus insecure attachment.

8. Erikson feels that the development of a sense of trust in early infancy depends on the quality of the:
   a. infant's food.
   b. child's genetic inheritance.
   c. maternal relationship.
   d. introduction of toilet training.

9. Like Freud, Margaret Mahler believes that:
   a. the social environment of the infant overshadows the effects that heredity has on development.
   b. the personality of the child is created through reinforcement and punishment.
   c. each stage of development is important for later psychological health.
   d. development occurs through a series of basic crises.

10. "Easy," "slow-to-warm-up," and "difficult" are descriptions of different:
    a. forms of attachment.
    b. types of temperament.
    c. types of parenting.
    d. toddler responses to the "Strange Situation."

11. (Research Report) Most developmentalists believe that social shyness:
    a. is an inherited trait.
    b. is one manifestation of a more general, physiological pattern of inhibition to new stimuli.
    c. can be modified by the reaction of parents, caregivers, and others in the environment.
    d. is all of the above.

12. Synchrony is a term that describes:
    a. the carefully coordinated play of parent and infant.
    b. a mismatch of the temperaments of parent and infant.
    c. a research technique involving videotapes.
    d. separation-individuation.

13. The emotional tie that develops between an infant and his or her primary caregiver is called:
    a. self-awareness.
    b. synchrony.
    c. affiliation.
    d. attachment.

14. An important effect of secure attachment is the promotion of:
    a. self-awareness.
    b. curiosity and self-directed behavior.
    c. dependency.
    d. all of the above.

15. (A Closer Look) A factor that may contribute to a higher incidence of child abuse in the United States is the common acceptance of:
    a. spankings and other physical punishments.
    b. mental illness.
    c. the economic value of children.
    d. dual-career families.

True or False Items

Write *true* or *false* on the line in front of each statement.

_______ 1. Emotions in infancy emerge according to a developmental schedule.

_______ 2. Happiness and sadness are emotions present by about age 1; but fear and anger do not appear for another 6 months, at about age $1\frac{1}{2}$.

_______ 3. A baby at 11 months is likely to display both stranger anxiety and separation anxiety.

_______ 4. Emotional development affects cognitive development, and vice versa.

_______ 5. A securely attached toddler is most likely to stay close to his or her mother even in a familiar environment.

_______ 6. Current research shows that the majority of infants in day care are insecurely attached.

_______ 7. Serious physical injuries are the most common form of child abuse.

_______ 8. (A Life-Span Perspective) Many parents who abuse their children have much in common with average parents.

_______ 9. (A Life-Span Perspective) Drug dependency in the parents is often associated with child maltreatment.

_______ 10. (A Life-Span Perspective) A social intervention that raised the income levels of the poorest families would probably lower the rate of child abuse.

Progress Test 2

Progress Test 2 should be completed during a final chapter review. Answer the following questions after you thoroughly understand the correct answers for the Chapter Review and Progress Test 1.

Multiple-Choice Questions

1. Infants give their first real smiles, called _______________, when they are about _______________ of age.
    a. play smiles; 3 months
    b. play smiles; 4 to 6 weeks
    c. social smiles; 3 months
    d. social smiles; 4 to 6 weeks

2. Freud's anal stage corresponds to Erikson's crisis of:
    a. autonomy versus shame and doubt.
    b. trust versus mistrust.
    c. orality versus anality.
    d. identity versus role confusion.

3. Not until the sense of self begins to emerge do babies realize that they are seeing their own faces in the mirror. This realization usually occurs:
    a. shortly before 3 months.
    b. at about 6 months.
    c. between 12 and 24 months.
    d. after 24 months.

4. (A Life-Span Perspective) Intergenerational transmission refers to the:
   a. coordinated interaction between infant and caregiver.
   b. abuse of a child by a brother or sister.
   c. phenomenon of mistreated children growing up to become abusive or neglectful parents.
   d. emotional tie between infant and caregiver.

5. Emotions such as shame, guilt, jealousy, and pride emerge at the same time that:
   a. the social smile appears.
   b. aspects of the infant's temperament can first be discerned.
   c. self-awareness begins to emerge.
   d. parents initiate toilet training.

6. According to the research, the NYLS temperamental characteristics that are not particularly stable are quality of mood and:
   a. rhythmicity.
   b. activity level.
   c. self-awareness.
   d. sociability (or shyness).

7. In the second six months, fear of strangers is a:
   a. result of insecure attachment.
   b. result of social isolation.
   c. normal emotional response.
   d. setback in emotional development.

8. The caregiving environment can affect a child's temperament through:
   a. the child's temperamental pattern and the demands of the home environment.
   b. parenting style.
   c. both a. and b.
   d. neither a. nor b.

9. Compared to children who are insecurely attached, those who are securely attached are:
   a. more independent.
   b. more cooperative.
   c. more sociable.
   d. characterized by all of the above.

10. The later consequences of secure attachment and insecure attachment for children are:
    a. balanced by the child's current rearing circumstances.
    b. irreversible, regardless of the child's current rearing circumstances.
    c. more significant in girls than in boys.
    d. more significant in boys than in girls.

11. (A Life-Span Perspective) Which of the following *best* describes parents who abuse their children?
    a. They are older and unintelligent.
    b. They are older and reclusive.
    c. They are younger and poorly educated.
    d. There are no predictable traits of abusive parents.

12. (Research Report) Compared to mothers, fathers are more likely to:
    a. engage in noisier, more boisterous play.
    b. encourage intellectual development in their children.
    c. encourage social development in their children.
    d. read to their toddlers.

13. (A Life-Span Perspective) A form of maltreatment in which parents or caregivers do not provide adequate food, shelter, attention, or supervision is referred to as:
    a. physical abuse.
    b. physical neglect.
    c. endangering.
    d. emotional abuse.

14. (A Life-Span Perspective) Which of the following is *not* typical of nonabusive cultures?
    a. Children are valued, as a psychological joy and an economic asset.
    b. Child care is considered the responsibility of the community.
    c. Children are expected to be responsible for their actions.
    d. Violence in any context is disapproved.

15. (A Life-Span Perspective) Most families involved in maltreatment of children are classified as ________________, which means that while they have the potential to provide adequate care, they have many problems that seriously impair their parenting abilities.
    a. vulnerable to crisis
    b. restorable
    c. supportable
    d. inadequate

Matching Items

Match each theorist, term, or concept with its corresponding description or definition.

Theorists, Terms, or Concepts

_______ 1. temperament
_______ 2. Erikson
_______ 3. the Strange Situation
_______ 4. restorable
_______ 5. vulnerable to crisis
_______ 6. Freud
_______ 7. supportable
_______ 8. inadequate
_______ 9. Mahler
_______ 10. Ainsworth

Descriptions or Definitions

a. maltreating family for which foster care of children is the best solution
b. maltreating family that needs temporary help to resolve unusual problems
c. maltreating family that requires a variety of helping services until the children are grown
d. theorist who described psychosexual stages of development
e. devised a laboratory procedure for studying attachment
f. laboratory procedure for studying attachment
g. the relatively consistent, basic dispositions inherent in a person
h. maltreating family that seems to have the potential to provide adequate care, but has serious problems that impair its parenting abilities
i. theorist who described psychosocial stages of development
j. theorist who described the period of separation-individuation

Challenge Test

Answer these questions the day before an exam as a final check on your understanding of the chapter's terms and concepts.

1. In laboratory tests of attachment, when the mother returns to the playroom after a short absence, a securely attached infant is most likely to:

a. cry and protest the mother's return.
b. climb into the mother's lap, then leave to resume play.
c. climb into the mother's lap and stay there.
d. continue playing without acknowledging the mother.

2. (A Life-Span Perspective) Child abuse seems *less* likely to occur in cultures in which:

a. mothers have full responsibility for child care.
b. most mothers remain in the home.
c. parents are not permissive.
d. child care is considered the responsibility of the community.

3. Which of the following is a clear sign of an infant's attachment to a particular person?

a. The infant turns to that person when distressed.
b. The infant protests when that person leaves a room.
c. The infant may cry when strangers appear.
d. All of the above are signs of infant attachment.

4. At about 8 months of age, babies are more likely to laugh in anticipation of happy experiences—in part, because they have developed expectations about what will happen. This infant behavior shows the:

a. effect of cognitive development on emotions.
b. infant's discovery of his or her own body parts.
c. validity of Freud's and Erikson's theories.
d. importance of attachment.

5. (A Life-Span Perspective) Therapy and help for a family at high risk for child abuse will be most effective if it is begun:
   a. during the first weeks of the child's life.
   b. at the first signs of abuse or neglect.
   c. upon referral by a physician.
   d. before either the parent or the child has learned a destructive pattern of interaction.

6. (A Life-Span Perspective) Claude, who is an abusive parent, is more likely than a nonabusive parent to:
   a. view any crying as a sign the baby is frightened.
   b. misinterpret a baby's cries as displays of anger.
   c. leave a baby who continues to fuss after his or her needs have been met.
   d. do all of the above.

7. Your grandmother, who took a developmental psychology class in the 1940s, wants to know whether contemporary views have changed regarding the influence of parents on the psychosocial development of their children. What should you tell her?
   a. Very little has changed; most contemporary psychologists believe that the individual's personality is permanently molded by the actions of his or her parents, especially the mother.
   b. Most contemporary psychologists believe that personality is acquired as parents reinforce or punish the child's various spontaneous behaviors.
   c. Most contemporary psychologists believe that the experiences of the first four years of life, especially those pertaining to gratification of oral needs and toilet training, play a decisive part in personality formation.
   d. Contemporary psychologists see basic elements of the infant's personality emerge so early that parental influence cannot be credited or blamed.

8. (Research Report) Jack, who is about to become a father and primary caregiver, is worried that he will never have the natural caregiving skills that the child's mother has. Studies on father-infant relationships show that:
   a. infants nurtured by single fathers are more likely to be insecurely attached.
   b. fathers can provide the emotional and cognitive nurturing necessary for healthy infant development.
   c. women are biologically predisposed to be better parents than men are.
   d. when the father is the primary caregiver, social development is usually slightly delayed in children.

9. Kalil's mother left him for a few minutes. When she returned, Kalil seemed indifferent to her presence. According to Mary Ainsworth's studies, Kalil is probably:
   a. a normal, independent infant.
   b. an abused child.
   c. insecurely attached.
   d. securely attached.

10. Connie and Lev, who are first-time parents, are concerned because their 1-month-old baby is difficult to care for and hard to soothe. They are worried that they are doing something wrong. You inform them that their child is probably that way because:
    a. they are reinforcing the child's tantrum behaviors.
    b. they are not meeting some biological need of the child's.
    c. of his or her inherited temperament.
    d. at 1 month of age all children are difficult to care for and hard to soothe.

11. Two-year-old Anita and her mother visit a day-care center. Seeing an interesting toy, Anita runs a few steps toward it, then stops and looks back to see if her mother is coming. Margaret Mahler would probably say that Anita is experiencing:
    a. the crisis of autonomy versus shame and doubt.
    b. synchrony.
    c. dyssynchrony.
    d. the need for greater psychological separation from her mother.

12. Felix's life is ruled by a need for cleanliness, precision, neatness, and punctuality. Freud would probably say that Felix is:
    a. anally expulsive.
    b. anally retentive.
    c. fixated in the oral stage.
    d. experiencing the crisis of trust versus mistrust.

13. A researcher at the child development center places a dot on an infant's nose and watches to see if the infant reacts to her image in a mirror by touching her nose. Evidently, the researcher is testing the child's:

a. attachment.
b. temperament.
c. self-awareness.
d. separation-individuation.

14. Six-month-old Carl and his 12-month-old sister Carla are left in the care of a babysitter. As their parents are leaving, it is to be expected that:
    a. Carl will become extremely upset, while Carla will calmly accept her parents' departure.
    b. Carla will become more upset over her parents' departure than will Carl.
    c. Carl and Carla will both become quite upset as their parents leave.
    d. Neither Carl nor Carla will become very upset over their parents' departure.

15. You have been asked to give a presentation on "Mother-Infant Attachment" to a group of expectant mothers. Basing your presentation on the research of Mary Ainsworth, you conclude your talk by stating that mother-infant attachment depends mostly on:
    a. an infant's innate temperament.
    b. the amount of time mothers spend with their infants.
    c. sensitive and responsive caregiving in the early months.
    d. whether the mother herself was securely attached as an infant.

Key Terms

Using your own words, write a brief definition or explanation of each of the following terms on a separate piece of paper.

1. social smile
2. fear of strangers
3. separation anxiety
4. social referencing
5. self-awareness
6. oral stage
7. anal stage
8. trust versus mistrust
9. autonomy versus shame and doubt
10. separation-individuation
11. temperament
12. synchrony
13. attachment
14. secure attachment
15. insecure attachment
16. Strange Situation
17. child maltreatment
18. abuse
19. neglect
20. endangerment
21. sibling abuse
22. intergenerational transmission
23. vulnerable to crisis
24. restorable families
25. supportable families
26. inadequate families

ANSWERS

CHAPTER REVIEW

1. joy, surprise, anger, fear, disgust, interest, sadness
2. brain
3. social smile; 6 weeks; is
4. fear of strangers; 6 months; 12 months; do not; temperament and the security of the mother-infant relationship
5. separation anxiety; 14 months; the baby's prior experiences with separation and the manner in which the parent departs
6. intensify; more; cognitive
7. social referencing
8. self-awareness; shame; guilt; jealousy; pride
9. do not

In the classic self-awareness experiment babies look in a mirror after a dot of rouge is put on their nose. If the babies react to the mirror image by touching their nose, it is clear they know they are seeing their own face. Most babies demonstrate this self-awareness between 12 and 24 months.

10. universal; intensity; conditions
11. parents; behaviorist; psychoanalytic
12. reinforcement; punishment; John Watson
13. four; mother
14. oral; mouth

15. second; anal; passive; active

Freud believed that the oral and anal stages are fraught with potential conflict that can have long-term consequences for the infant. If nursing is a hurried or tense event, the child may become fixed at the oral stage, excessively eating, drinking, smoking, or talking in quest of oral satisfaction. Toilet training that is overly strict or premature may produce an adult who has an "anal" personality. The person will either be anally retentive—overemphasizing neatness, precision, and punctuality—or anally expulsive—exhibiting messiness and disorganization.

16. warmth and management
17. Erikson; trust versus mistrust; autonomy versus shame and doubt; can alter
18. Mahler; separation-individuation
19. temperament; is; genetic; the nutrition and health of the mother
20. activity level; rhythmicity; approach-withdrawal; adaptability; intensity of reaction; threshold of responsiveness; quality of mood; distractibility; attention span
21. easy; slow-to-warm-up; difficult
22. rhythmicity; quality of mood

One way is through the "goodness of fit" between the child's temperament and the demands of the home environment. Parenting style also can influence temperament.

23. has; blue eyes, tall and thin bodies, and allergies
24. 1 year; motor activity; crying; inherited; inhibition; is not
25. synchrony; express; read
26. the caregiver mirrors the infant's expression or vocalization, and infants modify their social and emotional expressiveness to match or complement the caregiver's; averted eyes, stiffening or abrupt shifting of the body, an unhappy voice
27. personality; predispositions
28. attachment; secure attachment; insecure attachment
29. Strange Situation; two-thirds

Some infants are *anxious* and resistant: they cling nervously to their mother, are unwilling to explore, cry loudly when she leaves, and refuse to be comforted when she returns. Others are *avoidant*: they engage in little interaction with mothers before and after their departure. Others are *disoriented*: they show an inconsistent mixture of behavior toward the mother.

30. a. general sensitivity to the infant's needs,
    b. responsiveness to the infant's specific signals,
    c. talking and playing with the infant in ways that actively encourage growth and development
31. Israel; Japan; avoidance; an essential similarity
32. do
33. is not
34. securely attached: more competent in certain social and cognitive skills; more curious, outgoing, and self-directed

    insecurely attached: overly dependent on teachers, demanding their attention unnecessarily instead of playing or exploring; boys tend to be aggressive
35. disappear eventually
36. exclusively on mothers; have not
37. done by the mother
38. playing

Fathers' play is noisier, more boisterous, and idiosyncratic. Mothers are more likely to read to their toddlers, help them play with toys, or play conventional games.

39. father; father's
40. self-concept
41. physical; are not
42. maltreatment; abuse; neglect
43. physical abuse; emotional abuse; sexual abuse; physical neglect; emotional neglect; educational neglect
44. 40
45. counting the number of complaints; interviewing trained professionals; interviewing caregivers; asking adults if they were abused
46. community standards
47. varies
48. age; temperament; abilities
49. endangerment
    a. Children are highly valued.
    b. Child care is considered the responsibility of the community.
    c. Young children are not expected to be responsible for their actions.
    d. Violence is disapproved.
    a. Children are often considered to be a financial and personal burden.
    b. Social support for parents and young children is scarce.

c. The emphasis on the child's ability to learn may cause parents to forget that children are immature and dependent on others.

d. Violence is prevalent.

50. schedules; chaotic and disorganized
51. isolated; dysfunctional relationships; three; more; more
52. sibling abuse
53. 10

Maltreating parents are less trusting, less self-assured, less adaptable, less mature, and tend to view the world as a hostile and difficult place.

54. communications
55. increases

Babies who are unwanted, who are born too early, who were the product of an unhappy love affair or a difficult pregnancy, who are the "wrong" sex, or who have physical problems can all become victims of maltreatment.

56. result

Compared to well-cared-for children, chronically abused and neglected children are slower to talk, underweight, less able to concentrate, and behind in school. They also tend to regard others as hostile and exploitative, and are less friendly, more aggressive, and more isolated than other children. As adolescents and adults, they often engage in self-destructive and/or other-destructive behaviors.

57. intergenerational transmission; is not
58. 30; 6
59. falling
60. vulnerable to crisis; easy
61. restorable; more
62. supportable
63. inadequate; foster care
64. first-time mothers who are young and alone, and whose child is newborn
65. measures that raise the lowest incomes, discourage teenage parenthood, prevent social isolation, and increase the level of education

PROGRESS TEST 1

Multiple-Choice Questions

1. **b.** is the answer. (p. 172)

   a., c., & d. These emotions emerge later in infancy at about the same time as self-awareness emerges.

2. **a.** is the answer. (p. 172)

3. **a.** is the answer. (p. 173)

   b. & d. This fear, which is also called stranger anxiety, peaks at about 12 months.

4. **d.** is the answer. (p. 174)

5. **d.** is the answer. (p. 178)

   a. & b. According to Mahler, these describe the symbiotic mother-child relationship at an earlier age—during the first months of life.

6. **b.** is the answer. (p. 176)

   a. Reinforcement and punishment have no place in the psychoanalytic perspective.

   c. This is Erikson's theory, which sees development as occurring through a series of basic crises.

   d. This is a concept in Mahler's theory, which describes the development of the infant's sense of self, apart from the mother.

7. **b.** is the answer. (pp. 176, 177)

   a. Orality and anality refer to personality traits that result from fixation in the oral and anal stages, respectively.

   c. According to Erikson, this is the crisis of toddlerhood, which corresponds to Freud's anal stage.

   d. These are not developmental crises in Erikson's theory.

8. **c.** is the answer. (p. 177)

9. **c.** is the answer. (p. 178)

   a. This is not true of any theory.

   b. This is the behaviorist approach.

   d. This is Erikson's idea.

10. **b.** is the answer. (p. 180)

    a. "Secure" and "insecure" are different forms of attachment.

    c. The text does not describe different types of parenting.

    d. The Strange Situation is a test of attachment, rather than temperament.

11. **d.** is the answer. (p. 182)

12. **a.** is the answer. (p. 183)

13. **d.** is the answer. (p. 185)

    a. Self-awareness refers to the infant's developing sense of "me and mine."

    b. Synchrony describes the coordinated interaction between infant and caregiver.

    c. Affiliation describes the tendency of people at any age to seek the companionship of others.

14. **b.** is the answer. (p. 187)

    a. The text does not link self-awareness to secure attachment.

    c. On the contrary, secure attachment promotes independence in infants and children.

15. **a.** is the answer. (p. 194)

    b. Most maltreating parents are not mentally ill.

    c. Unfortunately, in the United States children are often viewed as an economic burden rather than an asset.

    d. The text does not link maltreatment to dual-career families.

True or False Items

1. T (p. 172)
2. F Fear, sadness, happiness, and anger are all present by age 1. (p. 172)
3. T (p. 173)
4. T (pp. 173–174)
5. F A securely attached toddler is most likely to explore the environment, the mother's presence being enough to give him or her the courage to do so. (p. 185)
6. F The effects of early and extended day care continue to be studied and debated. However, Jay Belsky believes that day care is not likely to harm the child. (p. 187)
7. F Neglect is actually much more common than physical abuse. (p. 191)
8. T (p. 198)
9. T (p. 199)
10. T (p. 205)

PROGRESS TEST 2

Multiple-Choice Questions

1. **d.** is the answer. (p. 172)
2. **a.** is the answer. (pp. 176, 177)

    b. This crisis corresponds to Freud's oral stage.

    c. These describe fixation in Freud's oral and anal stages, respectively.

    d. This is a crisis which, according to Erikson, occurs much later in development.

3. **c.** is the answer. (p. 175)
4. **c.** is the answer. (p. 201)

    a. This describes synchrony.

    b. This is sibling abuse.

    d. This defines attachment.

5. **c.** is the answer. (p. 174)

    a. & b. The social smile, and temperamental characteristics, emerge well before the first signs of self-awareness.

    d. Contemporary developmentalists link shame, guilt, and jealousy to self-consciousness, rather than any specific environmental event such as toilet training.

6. **a.** is the answer. (p. 180)

    b. & d. Activity level and sociability are much less variable than rhythmicity and quality of mood.

    c. Self-awareness is not a temperamental characteristic.

7. **c.** is the answer. (p. 173)
8. **c.** is the answer. (pp. 180–181)
9. **d.** is the answer. (p. 187)
10. **a.** is the answer. (p. 190)

    c. & d. The text does not suggest that the consequences of secure and insecure attachment differ in boys and girls.

11. **c.** is the answer. (p. 205)
12. **a.** is the answer. (p. 189)
13. **b.** is the answer. (p. 195)

    a. Physical abuse is deliberate, harsh injury to the body.

    c. Endangerment is putting a child at risk for serious harm by being rejecting or indifferent.

    d. Emotional abuse is deliberate destruction of self-esteem.

14. **c.** is the answer. In nonabusive cultures, children are *not* expected to be responsible for their actions. (pp. 195–196)
15. **b.** is the answer. (p. 202)

    a. Families that are vulnerable to crisis are experiencing unusual problems, such as divorce or loss of a job, and need temporary help to resolve them.

    c. Supportable families will probably never be able to function adequately and independently until the children are grown.

    d. Inadequate families are so impaired by problems that long-term foster care of the children is usually the best solution.

Matching Items

1. g (p. 179)
2. i (p. 177)
3. f (p. 185)
4. h (p. 202)
5. b (p. 202)
6. d (p. 176)
7. c (p. 203)
8. a (p. 203)
9. j (p. 178)
10. e (p. 185)

CHALLENGE TEST

1. **b.** is the answer. (p. 185)

   a., c., & d. These responses are more typical of insecurely attached infants.

2. **d.** is the answer. (p. 196)
3. **d.** is the answer. (p. 185)
4. **a.** is the answer. (pp. 173–174)
5. **d.** is the answer. (p. 204)
6. **b.** is the answer. (p. 199)
7. **d.** is the answer. (p. 179)

   a. This describes the prevailing view of psychologists during the first half of the twentieth century.

   b. & c. These describe two variations on the traditional view of psychosocial development: the behaviorist perspective (b), and psychoanalytic theory (c).

8. **b.** is the answer. (p. 188)
9. **c.** is the answer. (p. 185)

   a. & d. When their mothers return following an absence, securely attached infants usually reestablish social contact (with a smile or by climbing into their laps) and then resume playing.

   b. There is no evidence in this example that Kalil is an abused child.

10. **c.** is the answer. (p. 180)

    a. & b. There is no evidence in the question that the parents are reinforcing tantrum behavior, or failing to meet some biological need of the child's.

    d. On the contrary, about 40 percent of infants are "easy" in temperamental style.

11. **d.** is the answer. (p. 178)

    a. According to Erikson, this is the crisis of toddlerhood.

    b. This describes a moment of coordinated and mutually responsive interaction between a parent and a much younger infant.

    c. Dyssynchrony occurs when the coordinated pace and timing of a synchronous interaction are temporarily lost.

12. **b.** is the answer. (p. 177)

    a. In Freud's theory, a person who is anally expulsive exhibits messiness and disorganization in nearly all matters.

    d. Erikson, rather than Freud, proposed crises of development.

13. **c.** is the answer. (p. 175)
14. **b.** is the answer. The fear of being left by a caregiver (separation anxiety) emerges at about 8 or 9 months, and peaks at about 14 months. For this reason Carl can be expected to become less upset than his older sister. (p. 173)
15. **c.** is the answer. (p. 190)

KEY TERMS

1. The **social smile**—a smile that is a response to another person—appears at about 6 weeks. (p. 172)
2. A common early fear, **fear of strangers** (also called stranger anxiety), is first noticeable at about 6 months and reaches its peak by 12 months. (p. 173)
3. **Separation anxiety**, which is the infant fear of being left by the mother or other caregiver, emerges at about 8 or 9 months, peaks at about 14 months, and then gradually subsides. (p. 173)
4. By 10 months, infants engage in obvious **social referencing**—that is, they look to trusted adults for emotional cues in uncertain situations. (p. 174)
5. **Self-awareness** refers to the infant's emerging sense of "me and mine" that makes possible many new self-conscious emotions, including shame, guilt, jealousy, and pride. (p. 174)
6. In Freud's first stage of psychosexual development, the **oral stage**, the mouth is the most important source of gratification for the infant. (p. 176)
7. According to Freud, during the second year infants are in the **anal stage** of psychosexual development and derive sensual pleasure from the stimulation and control of the bowels. (p. 176)
8. In Erikson's theory, the crisis of infancy is one of **trust versus mistrust**, in which the infant learns whether the world is a secure place in which basic needs will be met. (p. 177)
9. In Erikson's theory, the crisis of toddlerhood is one of **autonomy versus shame and doubt**, in which toddlers strive to rule their own actions and bodies. (p. 177)
10. In Mahler's theory, between the ages of 5 months and 3 years the infant is in a period of **separation-individuation** as he or she gradually develops a sense of self that is separate and apart from the mother. (p. 178)
11. **Temperament** refers to the "relatively consistent, basic dispositions inherent in the person that underlie and modulate the expression of activity, reactivity, emotionality, and sociability." (p. 179)
12. **Synchrony** refers to the highly coordinated inter-

action between parent and infant that helps infants learn to express and read emotions. (p. 183)

13. **Attachment** is the enduring emotional tie that a person or animal forms with another. (p. 185)

14. A **secure attachment** is one in which the infant derives comfort and confidence from the "secure base" provided by a caregiver. (p. 185)

15. **Insecure attachment** is characterized by the infant's fear, anger, or seeming indifference to the caregiver. (p. 185)

16. The **Strange Situation** is a laboratory procedure developed by Ainsworth for assessing attachment. Infants are observed in a playroom, in successive episodes, with their mothers, with a friendly stranger, and by themselves. (p. 185)

17. **Child maltreatment** refers to the intentional harm to, or avoidable endangerment of, someone under age 18. (p. 192)

18. **Abuse** refers to all actions that are deliberately harmful to the child's well-being. (p. 192)

19. **Neglect** refers to failures to act appropriately to meet a child's basic needs. (p. 192)

20. **Endangerment**, or putting a child at risk for serious harm, is now accepted as one criterion for child abuse. (p. 194)

21. **Sibling abuse** occurs when serious and intentional harm is done to a child by a brother or sister. (p. 198)

22. **Intergenerational transmission** is the phenomenon of mistreated children growing up to become abusive or neglectful parents themselves. (p. 201)

23. Maltreating families classified as **vulnerable to crisis** are experiencing unusual problems, such as divorce, loss of a job, or the death of a family member, and need temporary help to resolve the problems. (p. 202)

24. Maltreating families that are classified as **restorable** seem to have the potential to provide adequate care, but have serious problems that impair their parenting abilities. Treatment with restorable families is more difficult and typically requires a committed case worker. (p. 202)

25. Maltreating families are classified as **supportable** if they are unlikely to be able to function independently of the support of nurses, housekeepers, day-care centers, social workers, and therapists in meeting their children's basic needs. (p. 203)

26. Approximately 10 percent of maltreating families are classified as **inadequate**—that is, so impaired by deep emotional or cognitive problems that they may never be able to meet the needs of their children. (p. 203)

CHAPTER 8

The Play Years: Biosocial Development

Chapter Overview

Chapter 8 introduces the developing person between the ages of 2 and 6. This period is called the play years, emphasizing the central importance of play to the biosocial, cognitive, and psychosocial development of preschoolers.

The chapter begins by outlining the changes in size and shape that occur from age 2 through 6. This is followed by a look at the most important physiological development during early childhood—brain maturation. The discussion focuses on hemispheric specialization and its role in the development of physical and cognitive abilities, including activity level.

A discussion of the acquisition of gross and fine motor skills precedes a description of the types of physical play that emerge during the play years, taking a closer look at accidents (the leading cause of death in young children) and the ways in which boys and girls differ in physical development and play patterns during the play years.

NOTE: Answer guidelines for all Chapter 8 questions begin on page 122.

Guided Study

The text chapter should be studied one section at a time. Before you read, preview each section by skimming it, noting headings and boldface items. Then read the appropriate section objectives from the following outline. Keep these objectives in mind and, as you read the chapter section, search for the information that will enable you to meet each objective. Once you have finished a section, write out answers for its objectives.

Size and Shape (pp. 212–213)

1. Describe normal physical growth during the play years and account for variations in height and weight.

2. Describe changes in eating habits during the preschool years.

Brain Maturation (pp. 213–217)

3. Discuss brain maturation and its effect on development during the play years.

4. Identify the specialized functions of the two halves of the brain and discuss flexibility in brain specialization.

5. Discuss trends in the activity level of children during the play years and identify factors that contribute to variation.

Mastering Motor Skills (pp. 217–226)

6. Distinguish between gross and fine motor skills and discuss the development of each during the play years.

7. Describe three kinds of play and the skills they strengthen; give examples of each.

8. (A Closer Look) Explain what is meant by "injury control" and identify several factors that contribute to variation in the risk of injury among children.

9. (A Life-Span Perspective) Outline the main similarities and differences in the physical development and play activities of boys and girls during the play years.

10. (A Life-Span Perspective) Discuss whether male-female distinctions in play patterns are gender differences or sex differences.

Chapter Review

When you have finished reading the chapter, work through the material that follows to review it. Complete the sentences and answer the questions. As you proceed, evaluate your performance for each section by consulting the answers on page 122. Do not continue with the next section until you understand each answer. If you need to, review or reread the appropriate section in the textbook before continuing.

Size and Shape (pp. 212–213)

1. During the preschool years, from age ______________ to ______________, children add almost ______________ in height and gain about ______________ in weight per year. By age 6, the average child in a developed nation weighs about ______________ and measures ______________ in height.

2. The range of normal physical development is quite ______________ (narrow/broad).

3. Of the many factors that influence height and weight, the most influential are the child's ______________ ______________, ______________ ______________ ______________, and ______________.

4. The dramatic differences between physical development in developed and developing countries are largely due to differences in the average child's ________________ .

Compare the size and shape of boys and girls during childhood.

5. In North America, children who are in the heaviest 10th percentile are likely to be ________________ (girls/boys). This is because they have a higher proportion of ________________ ________________ when they have access to ample food, and because they are generally ________________ (more/less) active than children of the opposite sex.

6. During the preschool years, annual height and weight gain is much ________________ (greater/less) than during infancy. This means that children need ________________ (fewer/more) calories per pound during this period.

7. Serious malnutrition is much ________________ (more/less) likely to occur in infancy or in adolescence than in early childhood.

8. The most prevalent nutrition problem in developed countries during the preschool years is ________________ ________________ ________________, the chief symptom of which is ________________ ________________. This problem stems from a diet deficient in ________________ ____________. This problem is ________________ (more/ less) common among poor families than among nonpoor ones.

Brain Maturation (pp. 213–217)

9. The most important physiological development during early childhood is the continued maturation of the ________________ ________________ ________________.

By age 5, the brain has attained about ________________ percent of its adult weight; in contrast, the total body weight is about ________________ percent of that of the average adult.

10. Part of the brain's increase in size during childhood is due to the continued proliferation of the ________________ network, and to the ongoing process of ________________. This latter process is important to many of the child's developing abilities, including ________________-________________ ________________, ________________ and ________________, and the ability to ________________.

11. The band of nerve fibers that connects the two halves of the brain, called the ________________ ________________, is not fully myelinated until about age ________________.

12. Each half of the brain controls the functioning of the ________________ (same/opposite) side of the body. In 95 percent of right-handed adults and about 70 percent of left-handed adults, the ________________ brain contains key areas associated with logical analysis and ________________ development. The opposite half is the location of areas associated with various visual and ________________ skills, including ________________ ________________.

13. Because advanced motor skills and higher-order cognition require both halves of the brain and body to work together effectively, the maturation of the ________________ ________________ is an important factor for the development of these skills.

14. During infancy and childhood ________________ (fewer/more) areas of the brain are dedicated to specific functions than in adulthood. Consequently, when damage occurs to one area, the functions of that area usually ________________ (can/cannot) be taken over by some other area. During adult-

hood, this type of recovery of function is _______________ (more/less) likely to occur.

15. The flexibility of brain functioning and specialization during infancy and childhood is evident in _______________. Even by age _______________, most children can learn to use their nonpreferred hand for certain skills. By the end of childhood, such learning is _______________ (more/less) difficult to accomplish.

16. At birth, the two halves of the brain _______________ (have not yet/have already) begun to specialize.

17. Some children are poor readers because they have difficulty connecting visual symbols with their sounds and meanings. This is because they _______________.

18. How much and how often a person moves his or her body defines _______________ _______________. Brain maturation _______________ (is/is not) linked to this characteristic.

19. In the first two or three years of life, activity level _______________ (increases/decreases), and then _______________ (increases/decreases) throughout childhood. This developmental trend _______________ (is universal/varies from culture to culture).

20. Three factors that contribute to individual variation in activity level are _______________, _______________, and _______________.

State the relevance of the developmental trend in activity level during childhood.

Mastering Motor Skills (pp. 217–226)

21. Large body movements such as running, climbing, jumping, and throwing are called _______________ _______________ _______________. These skills, which improve dramatically during the preschool years, require _______________, as well as a certain level of _______________ _______________.

22. Skills that involve small body movements, such as pouring liquids and cutting food, are called _______________ _______________ _______________. Preschoolers have greater difficulty with these skills primarily because they have not developed the _______________ control, patience, or _______________ needed, in part because the _______________ of the central nervous system is not complete.

23. Many educators consider the development of _______________ (fine/gross) motor skills to be an important goal of preschool education. An influential educator who designed a series of motor tasks that foster these skills is _______________.

24. Many developmentalists believe that _______________ are a form of play that is important to the development of good communication skills. This form of play also provides a testing ground for another important skill, _______________-_______________.

25. Developmentalists view children's play as _______________, that is, a major means through which physical, cognitive, and social skills are strengthened.

26. Play through which the young child captures the pleasure of touching, tasting, smelling, moving, and balancing is called _______________ play.

27. Play that involves the practice and acquisition of new skills is called _______________ play. Such play is most obvious when physical skills are involved, but as children grow older it increasingly includes activities that are more _______________.

28. (A Closer Look) In all but the most disease-ridden or war-torn countries of the world, the leading cause of childhood death is _______________.

29. (A Closer Look) The accident risk for a particular child depends on several factors, including ______________________ ______________________.

30. (A Closer Look) Injuries and accidental deaths are ______________ (more/less) frequent among boys than girls.

31. (A Closer Look) Instead of "accident prevention," many experts speak of ______________ ______________, an approach based on the belief that most accidents ______________ (are/are not) preventable.

32. (A Closer Look) The best approaches to safety education are those that ______________ ______________________.

33. (A Closer Look) New and expectant parents are ______________ (more/less) likely than experienced parents to heed safety suggestions, such as using an infant car seat.

34. (A Closer Look) Safety laws that include penalties for noncompliance seem to be ______________ (less/more) effective than educational measures in reducing injury rates.

35. (A Closer Look) The accidental death rate for American children between the ages of 1 and 5 has ______________ (increased/decreased) over the past twenty years.

36. Play in which children (and other young animals) wrestle, chase, and pummel each other for the fun of it is called ______________-______________-______________ play.

37. Aggressive rough-and-tumble play is revealed to be fun rather than serious aggression by a child's smiling expression, or ______________ ______________. This type of play, which (occurs only in certain cultures/is universal), usually occurs among children who have had considerable ______________ experience.

38. (A Life-Span Perspective) A basic question for social scientists is whether differences in the play patterns of boys and girls are ______________ ______________ that arise from the differences between male and female chromosomes and hormones, or ______________ ______________ that arise from the special customs, values, and expectations that a particular culture attaches to one sex or the other.

(A Life-Span Perspective) Describe several distinctions in the typical play patterns of girls and boys.

39. (A Life-Span Perspective) The preference for same-sex play partners, as well as the tendency for masculine play to be more aggressive and active than feminine play, ______________ (is/is not) evident during infancy. Furthermore, these trends ______________ (are/are not) found in every culture and ______________ (have/have not) changed over time.

Identify some physical differences between the sexes that may help to explain play differences.

40. Until puberty, both sexes follow very ______________ (similar/different) paths of biological development.

Briefly describe how social pressures may help to explain play differences.

Progress Test 1

Multiple-Choice Questions

Circle your answers to the following questions and check them with the answers on page 123. If your answer is incorrect, read the explanation for why it is incorrect and then consult the appropriate pages of the text (in parentheses following the correct answer).

1. During the preschool years, the most common nutritional problem in developed countries is:
   a. serious malnutrition.
   b. excessive intake of sweets.
   c. iron deficiency anemia.
   d. excessive caloric intake.

2. The brain center for speech is usually located in the:
   a. right brain.
   b. left brain.
   c. corpus callosum.
   d. space just below the right ear.

3. An indication of brain specialization in early childhood is:
   a. the clear emergence of hand preference.
   b. rapid acquisition of gross motor skills.
   c. increased bladder and bowel control.
   d. the incidence of growth problems.

4. After age 6, the child's overall activity level:
   a. increases until adolescence.
   b. continues to decline.
   c. begins to decline rapidly.
   d. remains the same until about age 10.

5. Maria Montessori was one of the first preschool educators to emphasize the importance of ________________ in the curriculum.
   a. discipline
   b. gross motor skills
   c. fine motor skills
   d. attention-span training

6. Skills that involve large body movements, such as running and jumping, are called:
   a. rough-and-tumble play.
   b. fine motor skills.
   c. gross motor skills.
   d. mastery play.

7. Differences in activity level among children have been linked to:
   a. sex differences.
   b. genetic differences.
   c. cultural differences regarding "acceptable" levels of activity.
   d. all of the above.

8. (A Closer Look) The leading cause of death in childhood is:
   a. accidents.
   b. untreated diabetes.
   c. malnutrition.
   d. iron deficiency anemia.

9. (A Life-Span Perspective) Which one of the following statements concerning sex differences in childhood is true?
   a. Boys are generally more sociable than girls.
   b. Girls lose their baby fat earlier than boys.
   c. Boys lose their baby teeth earlier than girls.
   d. Girls are likely to be better than boys at fine motor skills.

10. Which of the following factors is *most* responsible for differences in height and weight between children in developed and developing countries?
    a. the child's genetic background
    b. health care
    c. nutrition
    d. age of weaning

11. In which of the following age groups is serious malnutrition *least* likely to occur?
    a. infancy
    b. early childhood
    c. adolescence
    d. Serious malnutrition is equally likely in each of these age groups.

12. Sensorimotor play:
    a. captures the delight of activities that explore tastes, smells, and textures.
    b. leads to the mastery of new skills.
    c. is a social activity involving physical wrestling, chasing, and rough-housing.
    d. is usually accompanied by a smiling "play face."

13. Which of the following is correct about the corpus callosum?
    a. It enables short-term memory.
    b. It connects the two halves of the brain.
    c. It must be fully myelinated before gross motor skills can be acquired.
    d. All of the above are correct.

14. Hand-eye coordination and the ability to maintain focused attention improve during the play years, in part because:

a. the brain areas associated with these abilities become more fully myelinated.
b. the corpus callosum begins to function.
c. fine motor skills have matured by age 2.
d. gross motor skills have matured by age 2.

15. Building a tower with blocks is primarily an example of:
a. rough-and-tumble play.
b. sensorimotor play.
c. mastery play.
d. intellectual play.

True or False Items

Write *true* or *false* on the line in front of each statement.

_______ 1. Growth between ages 2 and 6 is more rapid than at any other period in the life span.
_______ 2. During childhood, the legs develop faster than any other part of the body.
_______ 3. For most right-handed people, the brain center for speech is located in the left brain.
_______ 4. The ability to sit quietly and maintain focused attention would be expected to improve between the ages of 4 and 7.
_______ 5. The high activity level of the American 2-year-old is directly related to the cultural values of a fast-paced society.
_______ 6. Fine motor skills are usually easier for preschoolers to master than are gross motor skills.
_______ 7. Children who know each other are more likely than strangers to engage in rough-and-tumble play.
_______ 8. (A Closer Look) Accidents cease to be a major cause of death after age 3.
_______ 9. (A Life-Span Perspective) Social pressures have been shown to be unimportant in explaining male-female differences in play activities.
_______ 10. (A Life-Span Perspective) Most preschoolers prefer to play with someone of the same sex.

Progress Test 2

Progress Test 2 should be completed during a final chapter review. Answer the following questions after you thoroughly understand the correct answers for the Chapter Review and Progress Test 1.

Multiple-Choice Questions

1. Each year from ages 2 to 6, the average child gains and grows, respectively:
a. 2 pounds and 1 inch.
b. 3 pounds and 2 inches.
c. 4 1/2 pounds and 3 inches.
d. 6 pounds and 6 inches.

2. In which area of the brain is the center for perceiving various types of spatial relations usually located?
a. the right brain
b. the left brain
c. either the right or the left brain
d. the corpus callosum

3. After brain specialization is complete, the brain is:
a. less able to compensate for loss of function if a particular area is damaged.
b. better able to compensate for loss of function if a particular area is damaged.
c. more likely to be injured.
d. less able to learn new intellectual tasks.

4. The text emphasizes that art provides an important opportunity for the child to develop the skill of:
a. realistic representation of objects.
b. reading.
c. perspective.
d. self-correction.

5. Researchers learned about the importance of facial expressions in rough-and-tumble play by observing young:
a. lions.
b. children.
c. dogs.
d. monkeys.

6. Rough-and-tumble play is:
a. most common between girls and boys.
b. restricted to boys.
c. much more common among boys than among girls.
d. most common among aggressive or frustrated boys.

7. (A Life-Span Perspective) On the average, boys are slightly better than girls at:
a. throwing and hitting.
b. skipping.
c. scribbling and fine motor skills.
d. cooperative games.

8. Developmentalists view children's play as a major means through which children are able to strengthen their ________________ skills.
   a. physical
   b. cognitive
   c. social
   d. all of the above

9. Which of the following statements about differences between boys and girls is *generally true*?
   a. Boys have more accidental deaths than girls.
   b. During the play years gender differences in play patterns diminish.
   c. The preference for same-sex play partners does not emerge until the play years.
   d. Because they mature more quickly, boys develop gross motor skills more rapidly than girls.

10. In infancy and early childhood:
    a. myelination of the central nervous system is completed.
    b. fewer areas of the brain are dedicated to specific functions than in adulthood.
    c. the legs develop faster than any other part of the body.
    d. hand preference has not yet emerged in most children.

11. The child with the highest activity level is most likely a:
    a. 2-year-old girl.
    b. 2-year-old boy.
    c. 5-year-old boy who has an extremely active identical twin.
    d. 5-year-old girl who has excellent fine motor skills.

12. Most gross motor skills can be learned by healthy children by about age:
    a. 2.
    b. 3.
    c. 5.
    d. 7.

13. (A Life-Span Perspective) Which of the following is true of gender differences in behavior?
    a. They arise from the differences between male and female chromosomes and hormones.
    b. They arise from the special customs, values, and expectations that a particular culture attaches to one sex or the other.
    c. They usually diminish during childhood.
    d. All of the above are true.

14. (A Closer Look) Over the past two decades, the accidental death rate for American children between the ages of 1 and 5 has:
    a. decreased, largely as a result of new city, state, and federal safety laws.
    b. decreased, largely because parents are more knowledgeable about safety practices.
    c. increased.
    d. remained unchanged.

15. During the play years, because growth is slow, children's appetites seem ________________ they were in the first two years of life.
    a. larger than
    b. smaller than
    c. about the same as
    d. erratic, sometimes smaller and sometimes larger than

Matching Items

Match each term or concept with its corresponding description or definition.

Terms or Concepts

_______ 1. activity level
_______ 2. gross motor skills
_______ 3. fine motor skills
_______ 4. sensorimotor play
_______ 5. mastery play
_______ 6. injury control
_______ 7. rough-and-tumble play
_______ 8. play face
_______ 9. sex differences
_______ 10. gender differences

Descriptions or Definitions

a. play that takes pleasure in exploring sights, sounds, tastes, and textures
b. male-female distinctions that arise from chromosomes and hormones
c. distinguishing characteristic of rough-and-tumble play
d. play that develops a particular skill
e. running and jumping
f. male-female distinctions that arise from cultural values and expectations
g. painting a picture or tying shoelaces
h. play involving wrestling and chasing
i. an approach emphasizing accident prevention
j. how much and how often a person moves his or her body

Challenge Test

Answer these questions the day before an exam as a final check on your understanding of the chapter's terms and concepts.

1. Two-year-old Bonnie fidgets more and has a higher activity level than her 1-year-old brother. Her parents:
   a. should not worry since preschoolers typically have a higher activity level than infants.
   b. were probably very active preschoolers themselves.
   c. should be concerned since boys typically are more active than girls.
   d. are probably feeding Bonnie too many sugary foods.

2. Four-year-old Deon is tired all the time. On questioning Deon's mother, the pediatrician learns that Deon's diet is deficient in quality meats, whole grains, and dark-green vegetables. The doctor believes that Deon may be suffering from:
   a. malnutrition.
   b. protein anemia.
   c. iron deficiency anemia.
   d. an inherited fatigue disorder.

3. Following an automobile accident, Amira developed severe problems with her speech. Her doctor believes that the accident injured the ________________ of her brain.
   a. left brain c. dendrite network
   b. right brain d. corpus callosum

4. Two-year-old Ali is quite clumsy, falls down frequently, and often bumps into stationary objects. Ali most likely:
   a. has a neuromuscular disorder.
   b. has an underdeveloped right brain.
   c. is suffering from iron deficiency anemia.
   d. is a normal 2-year-old whose gross motor skills will improve dramatically during the preschool years.

5. Three-year-old Krista loves to play with her food, delighting in the various textures as she mixes vegetables, meats, and noodles with her hands. Like all preschoolers, Krista obviously enjoys:
   a. mastery play.
   b. sensorimotor play.
   c. rough-and-tumble play.
   d. physical play.

6. (A Closer Look) To prevent accidental death in childhood, some experts urge forethought and planning for safety, and measures to limit the damage of such accidents as do occur. This approach is called:
   a. protective analysis. c. injury control.
   b. safety education. d. childproofing.

7. Recent research reveals that some children are poor readers because they have trouble connecting visual symbols, phonetic sounds, and verbal meanings. This occurs because:
   a. their sugary diets make concentration more difficult.
   b. the brain areas involved in reading have not become localized in the left brain.
   c. they use one side of the brain considerably more than the other.
   d. their underdeveloped corpus callosums limit communication between the two halves of the brain.

8. (A Life-Span Perspective) In societies in which adult gender roles are quite distinct, boys and girls:
   a. often spontaneously play together.
   b. rarely play together.
   c. often play together, but usually their games involve one sex teaming up against the other.
   d. are less likely to play at games that rehearse traditional gender roles.

9. When brain damage affects the language areas of the brain, children are likely to experience an impairment in overall cognition, whereas adults are likely to lose a specific set of verbal abilities. This demonstrates that:
   a. compared to adults, children's cognitive abilities are more dependent on their mastery of language.
   b. the incomplete myelination of the childhood brain makes it more vulnerable to global damage.
   c. adults have more extensive dendrite networks that resist global brain damage.
   d. the greater flexibility in functioning of children's brains enables the functions of a damaged area of the brain to be taken over by some other area.

10. Adults find it much harder to learn to perform a skill with their nonpreferred hand than young children do, because:
    a. their fine motor skills are more developed.
    b. they are more disciplined in practicing new skills.
    c. patterns in the brain for such skills become localized and habitual.
    d. of all the above reasons.

11. As young children grow older, they begin to play with words and ideas, an activity that would fall under the category of:
    a. sensorimotor play.
    b. mastery play.
    c. rough-and-tumble play.
    d. learning, rather than play.

12. A factor that would figure very little in the development of fine motor skills, such as drawing and writing, is:
    a. strength.
    b. muscular control.
    c. judgment.
    d. short, fat fingers.

13. (A Life-Span Perspective) In recent years, many preschool teachers have made a deliberate effort to diminish sexual stereotypes among children. Their efforts have been:
    a. successful in reducing gender distinctions in the play patterns of preschoolers.
    b. successful in reducing gender distinctions, but only among affluent children in developing countries.
    c. unsuccessful, as developmentalists have noted a recent increase in gender differences among preschoolers.
    d. unsuccessful; during the preschool years children increasingly take on "gender-specific" roles and sort themselves into same-sex friendships.

14. While jogging one day you notice several preschoolers wrestling and punching one another. As you draw closer to the children your fear that this is a serious fight subsides when you notice:
    a. most of the children are girls.
    b. the group is a mixture of both boys and girls.
    c. there are other adults nearby.
    d. most of the children are exhibiting a play face.

15. Three-year-old Kalil's parents are concerned because Kalil, who generally seems healthy, doesn't seem to have the hefty appetite or rate of growth he had as an infant. Should they be worried?
    a. Yes, since both appetite and growth rate normally increase throughout the preschool years.
    b. Yes, since appetite (but not necessarily growth rate) normally increases during the preschool years.
    c. No, since growth rate (and hence caloric need) is less during the preschool years than during infancy.
    d. There is not enough information to determine whether Kalil is developing normally.

Key Terms

Using your own words, write a brief definition or explanation of each of the following terms on a separate piece of paper.

1. corpus callosum
2. activity level
3. gross motor skills
4. fine motor skills
5. sensorimotor play
6. mastery play
7. injury control
8. rough-and-tumble play
9. play face
10. sex differences
11. gender differences

ANSWERS

CHAPTER REVIEW

1. 2; 6; 3 inches (7 centimeters); 4 1/2 pounds (2 kilograms); 46 pounds (21 kilograms); 46 inches (117 centimeters)
2. broad
3. genetic background; health care; nutrition
4. nutrition

Generally, boys are more muscular, less fat, and slightly taller and heavier than girls throughout childhood.

5. girls; body fat; less
6. less; fewer
7. more
8. iron deficiency anemia; chronic fatigue; quality meats, whole grains, and dark-green vegetables; more
9. central nervous system; 90; 30
10. dendrite; myelination; hand-eye coordination; language; intelligence; maintain focused attention
11. corpus callosum; 8
12. opposite; left; language; artistic; recognizing faces, responding to music, perceiving various types of spatial relations
13. corpus callosum

14. fewer; can; less
15. handedness; 5; more
16. have already
17. use one half of the brain considerably more than the other
18. activity level; is
19. increases; decreases; is universal
20. gender; heredity; environmental factors

It suggests that it is a mistake to expect young children to sit quietly for very long.

21. gross motor skills; practice; brain maturation
22. fine motor skills; muscular; judgment; myelination
23. fine; Maria Montessori
24. arts and crafts; self-correction
25. work
26. sensorimotor
27. mastery; intellectual
28. accidents
29. the child's own judgment, motor skills, and activity level, and community standards and cultural norms that either foster or impede safety practices
30. more
31. injury control; are
32. reach both parents and children in situations where motivation is high
33. more
34. more
35. decreased
36. rough-and-tumble
37. play face; is universal; social
38. sex differences; gender differences

Boys spend more playtime outside, engaging in gross motor activities like running, climbing, and playing ball. Many, if not most, of boys' activities involve playful aggression, competition, and rough-and-tumble play. Girls spend more time indoors, typically engaging in activities that demand fine motor coordination and a lower activity level, such as arts and crafts, sewing, or dressing dolls.

39. is; are; have not

Boys are slightly taller, are more muscular and active, and have less body fat but greater forearm strength than girls. Girls mature more quickly than boys, which gives them more dexterity and control in fine motor skills.

40. similar

Parents typically encourage children to play with peers of their own sex. They also tend to give them "gender-appropriate" toys. In all societies, children are encouraged to engage in activities that teach them traditional adult roles.

PROGRESS TEST 1

Multiple-Choice Questions

1. **c.** is the answer. (p. 213)

   a. Serious malnutrition is much more likely to occur in infancy or in adolescence than in early childhood.

   b. Although an important health problem, eating too much candy or other sweets is not as serious as iron deficiency anemia.

   d. Since growth is slower during the preschool years, children need fewer calories per pound during this period.

2. **b.** is the answer. (p. 214)

   a. & d. The right brain, which includes the space just below the right ear, is the location of areas associated with various visual and artistic skills.

   c. The corpus callosum helps integrate the functioning of the two halves of the brain; it does not contain areas specialized for particular skills.

3. **a.** is the answer. (p. 214)
4. **b.** is the answer. (p. 215)

   a., c., & d. In the first two or three years of life, activity level increases in all children, and then decreases throughout childhood.

5. **c.** is the answer. (p. 218)
6. **c.** is the answer. (p. 217)

   a. Rough-and-tumble play is the physical wrestling and chasing that children, especially boys, engage in.

   b. Fine motor skills, such as drawing or pouring, involve small body movements.

   d. Mastery play involves the practice and acquisition of new skills.

7. **d.** is the answer. (pp. 215–217)
8. **a.** is the answer. (p. 220)
9. **d.** is the answer. Girls have greater dexterity and control in fine motor skills because they mature more quickly than boys in a number of ways. (pp. 223, 224)
10. **c.** is the answer. (pp. 212–213)
11. **b.** is the answer. (p. 213)

12. **a.** is the answer. (p. 219)
    b. This describes mastery play.
    c. & **d.** These describe rough-and-tumble play.
13. **b.** is the answer. (p. 214)
    a. The corpus callosum is not directly involved in memory.
    c. Myelination of the central nervous system is an important factor in the mastery of *fine* motor skills.
14. **a.** is the answer. (p. 214)
    b. The corpus callosum begins to function long before the play years.
    c. & **d.** Neither fine nor gross motor skills have fully matured by age 2.
15. **c.** is the answer. (p. 219)
    a. Rough-and-tumble play is the physical wrestling and chasing that children, especially boys, engage in.
    b. Sensorimotor play consists of activities that allow children to explore tastes, smells, textures, and other sensory experiences and motor skills.
    d. This is not a type of play identified in the text. In fact, play that involves intellectual activities would be classified as mastery play.

True or False Items

1. F Growth actually slows down during the play years. (p. 212)
2. F During childhood, the brain develops faster than any other part of the body. (p. 213)
3. T (p. 214)
4. T (p. 215)
5. F In all cultures, activity level is highest in the first three years. (p. 215)
6. F Fine motor skills are more difficult for preschoolers to master than are gross motor skills. (p. 218)
7. T (p. 222)
8. F Accidents continue to be the leading cause of death until age 10. (p. 220)
9. F Social pressures may contribute to male-female differences in play activities. (p. 225)
10. T (p. 224)

PROGRESS TEST 2

Multiple-Choice Questions

1. **c.** is the answer. (p. 212)
2. **a.** is the answer. (p. 214)
   b. The left half of the brain contains areas associated with logical analysis and language development.
   c. In most people, including those who are left-handed, the right half of the brain processes spatial relations.
   d. The corpus callosum does not contain brain areas for specific behaviors.
3. **a.** is the answer. (pp. 214–215)
   b. *Before* brain specialization is complete the brain is better able to compensate for loss of function following an injury.
   c. & **d.** The likelihood of injury and the ease of learning new tasks, are no different once brain specialization is complete.
4. **d.** is the answer. (p. 218)
5. **d.** is the answer. (p. 222)
6. **c.** is the answer. (p. 223)
7. **a.** is the answer. (p. 224)
   b., c., & d. On the average, girls tend to be better than boys at these activities.
8. **d.** is the answer. (p. 219)
9. **a.** is true. (p. 220)
   b. Gender differences in play patterns are strong throughout childhood.
   c. The preference for same-sex play partners is evident even in infancy.
   d. Girls mature more quickly than boys in a number of ways.
10. **b.** is the answer. (p. 214)
    a. Myelination of some areas of the brain is not complete until adolescence.
    c. During childhood, the brain develops faster than any other part of the body.
    d. By age 5, more than 90 percent of all children are clearly right- or left-handed.
11. **b.** is the answer. (p. 215)
12. **c.** is the answer. (p. 217)
13. **b.** is the answer. (p. 226)
    a. This describes sex differences.
    c. Many gender differences in behavior become *more* prominent during childhood.
14. **a.** is the answer. (p. 221)
    b. Although safety education is important, the decrease in accident rate is largely the result of new safety laws.
15. **b.** is the answer. (p. 212)

Matching Items

1. j (p. 215)
2. e (p. 217)
3. g (p. 218)
4. a (p. 219)
5. d (p. 219)
6. i (p. 220)
7. h (p. 222)
8. c (p. 222)
9. b (p. 223)
10. f (p. 223)

CHALLENGE TEST

1. **a.** is the answer. (p. 215)
2. **c.** is the answer. Chronic fatigue is the major symptom of iron deficiency anemia, which is caused by a diet deficient in quality meats, whole grains, and dark-green vegetables. (p. 213)
3. **a.** is the answer. In most people, the left brain contains centers for language and speech. (p. 214)
4. **d.** is the answer. (p. 217)
5. **b.** is the answer. (p. 219)
6. **c.** is the answer. (p. 220)
7. **c.** is the answer. Analysis of the brain's electrical activity reveals that areas in both halves of the brain are involved in reading. (p. 215)
8. **b.** is the answer. (p. 226)

   a. & c. These are more typical of societies in which adult gender roles are less rigid.

   d. In fact, in such societies children are *more* likely to engage in play that prepares them for traditional gender roles.
9. **d.** is the answer. (p. 214)
10. **c.** is the answer. (p. 215)
11. **b.** is the answer. (p. 219)
12. **a.** is the answer. Strength is a more important factor in the development of gross motor skills. (p. 218)
13. **d.** is the answer. (p. 225)
14. **d.** is the answer. The smiles and laughter of the play face indicate that rough-and-tumble play is not serious aggression. (p. 222)
15. **c.** is the answer. (pp. 212–213)

KEY TERMS

1. The **corpus callosum** is the band of nerve fibers that connects the two halves of the brain. (p. 214)
2. **Activity level** refers to how much and how often a person moves his or her body. (p. 215)
3. **Gross motor skills** are large body movements, such as running, climbing, jumping, and throwing. (p. 217)
4. **Fine motor skills** are small body movements, such as the hand movements used in painting a picture or tying shoelaces. (p. 218)
5. **Sensorimotor play** is play that captures the pleasures of using the senses and motor abilities. (p. 219)
6. **Mastery play** is play that helps children to develop new physical or intellectual skills. (p. 219)
7. **Injury control** is an approach to accident prevention that focuses on broad-based safety education, stricter enforcement of safety regulations, "childproofing" homes, and related measures. (p. 220)
8. **Rough-and-tumble play** is the physical wrestling and chasing that children, especially boys, engage in. (p. 222)
9. A smiling face, called a **play face**, accompanies rough-and-tumble play, distinguishing it from real aggression. (p. 222)
10. **Sex differences** are male-female distinctions that arise from the differences between male and female chromosomes and hormones. (p. 223)
11. **Gender differences** are male-female distinctions that arise from the special customs, values, and expectations that a particular culture attaches to one sex or the other. (p. 223)

CHAPTER 9 The Play Years: Cognitive Development

Chapter Overview

Young children think and speak quite differently from older children and adults. This chapter begins with Piaget's influential explanation of the cognitive patterns typical of early childhood. Piaget's theory is then reconsidered in light of recent research suggesting that he may have underestimated the cognitive abilities of preschoolers. The recent emphasis on the importance of the social context in learning, inspired by the writings of Piaget's contemporary Lev Vygotsky, is also discussed.

The second part of the chapter deals with language development. A discussion of the relationship between language and thought is followed by descriptions of the young child's growing mastery of vocabulary, grammar, and pragmatics. The limitations of preschoolers' ability to communicate are also noted. The chapter closes with a discussion of factors that seem to promote language competence in young children and a life-span perspective on preschool education.

NOTE: Answer guidelines for all Chapter 9 questions begin on page 136.

Guided Study

The text chapter should be studied one section at a time. Before you read, preview each section by skimming it, noting headings and boldface items. Then read the appropriate section objectives from the following outline. Keep these objectives in mind and, as you read the chapter section, search for the information that will enable you to meet each objective. Once you have finished a section, write out answers for its objectives.

How Preschoolers Think (pp. 230–234)

1. Explain how the cognitive potential of young children is expanded by symbolic thought.

2. Describe and discuss the major characteristics of preoperational thought, according to Piaget.

Beyond Piaget: The Social Context (pp. 234–242)

3. Discuss recent research on conservation and perspective-taking and explain why findings have led to qualification or revision of Piaget's description of cognition during the play years.

4. Discuss evidence that preschoolers possess a theory of mind.

5. Contrast Vygotsky's views on cognitive development with those of Piaget.

Language Development (pp. 242–252)

6. Discuss the relationship between language and thought in the child's cognitive development during the play years.

7. Outline the sequence by which vocabulary and grammar develop during the play years and discuss limitations in the preschool child's language.

8. Describe pragmatic developments and difficulties associated with language acquisition during the play years.

9. Discuss possible explanations for differences in the language development of children during the play years.

10. (A Life-Span Perspective) Discuss the long-term benefits of preschool education for the child and family, and identify the characteristics of a high-quality preschool program.

Chapter Review

When you have finished reading the chapter, work through the material that follows to review it. Complete the sentences and answer the questions. As you proceed, evaluate your performance for each section by consulting the answers on page 136. Do not continue with the next section until you understand each answer. If you need to, review or reread the appropriate section in the textbook before continuing.

How Preschoolers Think (pp. 230–234)

1. During the preschool years children become able to think ________________; that is, they can think by forming ________________ ________________ of things and events that they are not immediately experiencing.

2. Each new level of the child's symbolic play is accompanied by more elaborate use of ________________, itself an indication of symbolic thought.

3. According to Piaget, between the ages of 2 and 7, thinking is characterized by ________________ thought. One example of this operational inability is the preschooler's failure to grasp the logical idea of ________________—that reversing a process will restore the original conditions from which the process began.

4. The preschooler's tendency to think about one idea at a time is called ______________. Preoperational children are particularly likely to center on their ______________ ______________.

5. The preschooler's understanding of the world tends to be ______________ (static/dynamic), which means that they tend to think in terms of ______________ (absolutes/a range of possibilities). As a result, they have trouble understanding transitions and ______________.

6. Because they center on one aspect of an event rather than on the relationship between events, preschoolers also have difficulty in understanding ______________ ______________ ______________.

7. The idea that amount is unaffected by changes in shape or placement is called ______________. In the case of ______________ ______________ ______________, preschoolers who observe one of two equal-size balls of clay being rolled out into a long thin rope will say that the rope has more clay. Similarly, in the case of ______________ ______________ ______________, preschoolers who are shown pairs of checkers in two even rows and who then observe one row being spaced out will say that the spaced-out row has more checkers.

8. Thinking that centers on the ego, or self, is called ______________. This cognitive immaturity ______________ (is/is not) the same as selfishness.

9. The idea held by many young children that everything in the world is alive is called ______________.

10. According to Piaget, children are unable to take another's point of view until at least age ______________. The basis for this assertion is Piaget's classic experiment called the ______________-______________ experiment.

Briefly describe this experiment and its typical results when children younger than 6 are tested.

Beyond Piaget: The Social Context (pp. 234–242)

11. The standard Piagetian experiments ______________ (have/have not) been replicated with children from various cultures.

12. Many contemporary developmentalists suggest that the failure of preschoolers to demonstrate conservation or perspective-taking on Piaget's tests has more to do with the ______________ of the tests than their content.

13. It is now clear that conservation develops ______________ (more/less) gradually and ______________ (more/less) evenly than Piaget believed. With special training and more playful test conditions, children as young as ______________ can succeed at some tests of conservation.

14. A preschooler who can count to 20 ______________ (does/does not) necessarily fully understand the number system.

15. Children who fail at Piaget's three-mountains task ______________ (are/are not) able to demonstrate perspective-taking in simpler experiments.

Explain why the policemen game demonstrates an earlier understanding of perspective-taking than does Piaget's three-mountains task.

16. A person's understanding of his or her own, and others', mental processes, including complex interactions among emotions, perceptions, thoughts, and actions, constitutes a(n) ________________ ________________ ________________. In Piaget's theory, the egocentric, action-oriented thinking of younger preschoolers is ________________ (consistent/inconsistent) with this understanding. Contemporary researchers have found signs of this understanding emerging as early as age ________________.

17. One of the best ways to elicit evidence of a theory of mind is through games that involve ________________.

18. By age ________________, children show that they have an understanding of deception.

19. Contemporary developmentalists believe that, in perspective-taking and conservation, Piaget ________________ (underestimated/overestimated) the preoperational child's ability.

20. Much of the new research and perspective on the young child's emerging cognition is inspired by the Russian psychologist ________________.

21. Unlike Piaget, who focused on ________________-________________ factors that he believed are at the root of cognitive development, Vygotsky believed that the structural differences in people's thinking arise primarily from ________________ ________________ in goals and experiences. In this view, learning is seen as a(n) ________________ ________________ more than as a matter of individual discovery.

22. Vygotsky suggests that each individual is surrounded by a(n) ________________ ________________ ________________ ________________, which represents the cognitive distance between the child's actual level of development and his or her developmental potential.

23. Vygotsky's emphasis on the importance of the social context of learning explains why learning varies with the context provided by a child's ________________ and ________________.

Language Development (pp. 242–252)

24. During the preschool years a dramatic increase in language occurs, with ________________, ________________, and ________________ ________________ of language showing rapid improvement.

25. Piaget believed that cognitive development ________________ (precedes/follows) language. This explains why the first words that children learn are ones that refer to ________________.

26. However, most American developmentalists also agree with Vygotsky's idea that language ________________ (is/is not) essential to the advancement of thinking in two crucial ways. The first is through the internal dialogue in which a person talks to himself or herself, called ________________ ________________. In preschoolers, this dialogue is likely to be ________________ (expressed silently/uttered aloud).

27. According to Vygotsky, another way language advances thinking is as the ________________ of social interaction.

28. Through the process called ________________ ________________ preschoolers often learn words after only one hearing.

29. The learning of new words ________________ (does/does not) follow a predictable sequence according to parts of speech.

30. In building vocabulary, preschoolers generally learn ________________ more readily than ________________, which are learned more readily than ________________ ________________.

31. Generally, children are able to map new words more quickly when words, categories, and concepts are ________________ (explained in a formal lesson/used in the course of dialogue).

32. Abstract nouns and metaphors are ______________ (more/no more) difficult for preschoolers to understand.

33. Because preschool children tend to think in absolute terms, they have difficulty with words that express ______________, as well as words expressing relativities of ______________ and ______________.

34. The structures, techniques, and rules that a language uses to communicate meaning define its ______________. By age ______________, children typically demonstrate extensive understanding of this aspect of language.

35. Preschoolers' tendency to apply rules of grammar when they should not is called ______________.

Give several examples of overregularization.

36. During the preschool years children are able to comprehend ______________ (more/less) complex grammar and vocabulary than they can produce.

37. The practical communication between one person and another in terms of the overall context in which language is used is called ______________. The major emphasis of the study of this phenomenon concerns how children learn to adjust vocabulary and grammar to the ______________ ______________.

Give an example of the pragmatic development in language use that occurs during the play years.

38. Another pragmatic development is shown in children's developing ability to relate an event ______________.

39. By the time children enter kindergarten, differences in language skills among them are ______________ (small/great).

40. In terms of the relationship between language proficiency and gender, socioeconomic class, birth order, and multiple births, ______________ (boys/girls), ______________ (middle-income/lower-income), ______________ (first-borns/later-borns), and ______________ (single-borns/twins/triplets) tend to be more proficient.

Explain how researchers explain differences in language development.

41. Group variations in language proficiency are generally ______________ (larger/smaller) than variations among individual children from the same group.

42. Measures of the overall relationship between parent and child, such as strength of attachment, ______________ (are/are not) good predictors of a child's language competence.

43. (A Life-Span Perspective) In most developed nations, most children ______________ (do/do not) enter some form of school during the "preschool" years. Two reasons for this historical change are:

a. a shift in ______________ and

b. ______________.

44. (A Life-Span Perspective) Compared to other children from the same backgrounds who stay at home, preschool children usually fare ______________ (better/no better) in their cognitive and social development.

List several characteristics of a high-quality preschool program.

45. (A Life-Span Perspective) In the 1960s, ________________ ________________ was inaugurated to give low-income children some form of compensatory education during the preschool years. Longitudinal research found that, as they made their way through elementary school, graduates of this program scored ________________ (higher/no higher) on achievement tests and had more positive school report cards.

46. (A Life-Span Perspective) Most developmentalists believe that disadvantaged children will benefit from early education beginning at age ________________ or even sooner.

Progress Test 1

Multiple-Choice Questions

Circle your answers to the following questions and check them with the answers on page 137. If your answer is incorrect, read the explanation for why it is incorrect and then consult the appropriate pages of the text (in parentheses following the correct answer).

1. Piaget believed that children are in the preoperational stage from ages:
   a. 6 months to 1 year.
   b. 1 to 3 years.
   c. 2 to 7 years.
   d. 5 to 11 years.

2. The most significant cognitive gain of the preschool years is the emergence of:
   a. egocentrism.
   b. symbolic thought.
   c. logical thought.
   d. pragmatic language.

3. Egocentrism can most accurately be described as:
   a. the emergence of a theory of mind.
   b. the central importance of the ego in language development.
   c. the child's need to have his or her own way.
   d. the way a child's ideas about the world are limited by the child's own narrow point of view.

4. Animism refers to the idea that:
   a. between ages 2 and 6, children identify with small animals.
   b. children think that inanimate objects are alive.
   c. active children learn more quickly than do passive children.
   d. playing with animals reinforces cognitive development.

5. A preschooler is most likely to succeed at a task involving perspective-taking when the task is:
   a. modeled along the lines of Piaget's three-mountains experiment.
   b. in the question-and-answer format.
   c. verbal, formal, and simple.
   d. gamelike and nonverbal.

6. The vocabulary of preschool children consists primarily of:
   a. metaphors.
   b. self-created words.
   c. abstract nouns.
   d. verbs and concrete nouns.

7. Preschoolers sometimes apply the rules of grammar even when they shouldn't. This tendency is called:
   a. overregularization.
   b. literal language.
   c. pragmatics.
   d. single-mindedness.

8. The Russian psychologist Vygotsky emphasized that:
   a. language helps children form ideas.
   b. children form concepts first, then find words to express them.
   c. language and other cognitive developments are unrelated at this stage.
   d. preschoolers learn language only for egocentric purposes.

9. Private speech can be described as:
   a. a way of formulating ideas to oneself.
   b. fantasy.
   c. an early learning difficulty.
   d. the beginnings of deception.

10. The child who has not yet grasped the principle of conservation is likely to:
    a. insist that a tall, narrow glass contains more liquid than a short, wide glass, even though both glasses actually contain the same amount.
    b. be incapable of egocentric thought.
    c. be unable to think animistically.
    d. do all of the above.

11. (A Life-Span Perspective) In later life, Headstart graduates showed:
    a. better report cards, but more behavioral problems.
    b. significantly higher IQ scores.
    c. higher scores on achievement tests and higher aspirations.
    d. alienation from their original neighborhoods and families.

12. (A Life-Span Perspective) The best preschool programs are generally those that provide the greatest amount of:
    a. behavioral control.
    b. adult-child conversation.
    c. instruction in conservation and other logical tasks.
    d. demonstration of toys by professionals.

13. Compared to their rate of speech development, children's understanding of language develops:
    a. more slowly.
    b. at about the same pace.
    c. more rapidly.
    d. more rapidly in certain cultures than others.

14. Most contemporary developmentalists believe that the concept of conservation:
    a. emerges abruptly in children at age 4 or 5.
    b. emerges abruptly in children at age 7 or 8.
    c. develops slowly and unevenly.
    d. is relevant only in certain cultures.

15. Through the process called fast mapping, children:
    a. immediately assimilate new words by connecting them through their assumed meaning to categories of words already mastered.
    b. acquire the concept of conservation at an earlier age than Piaget believed.
    c. are able to move beyond egocentric thinking.
    d. become skilled in the pragmatics of language.

True or False Items

Write *true* or *false* on the line in front of each statement.

_______ 1. Piaget's description of cognitive development in early childhood has been universally rejected by contemporary developmentalists.

_______ 2. In conservation problems, many preschoolers are unable to understand the transformation because they focus exclusively on appearances.

_______ 3. Because of egocentrism, preschoolers often have difficulty understanding thoughts and feelings that are very different from their own.

_______ 4. Whether or not a preschooler demonstrates perspective-taking abilities in an experiment depends in part on the conditions of the experiment.

_______ 5. The preschooler's ability to mislead or deceive the teacher, for example, is evidence of egocentrism.

_______ 6. Piaget believed that preschoolers' acquisition of language makes possible their cognitive development.

_______ 7. With the beginning of symbolic thought, most preschoolers can understand abstract words.

_______ 8. A preschooler who says "You comed up and hurted me" is demonstrating a lack of understanding of English grammar.

_______ 9. (A Life-Span Perspective) Successful preschool programs generally have a low teacher-to-child ratio and are expensive.

_______ 10. Children who have many older siblings are usually the most advanced in language use.

Progress Test 2

Progress Test 2 should be completed during a final chapter review. Answer the following questions after you thoroughly understand the correct answers for the Chapter Review and Progress Test 1.

Multiple-Choice Questions

1. One of the best ways to elicit evidence of a theory of mind is through games that ask the child to demonstrate some understanding of:
    a. animism.
    b. deception.
    c. centration.
    d. reversibility.

2. Critics of Piaget's three-mountains experiment argue that:
    a. the inconsistency in results from child to child negates its validity.
    b. the task does not consider cultural influences on cognitive development.
    c. most children today cannot solve the problem until a later age than Piaget believed.
    d. the task is too complex to be a valid test of the child's ability to take another's perspective.

3. A preschooler who focuses his or her attention on only one feature of a situation is demonstrating a characteristic of preoperational thought called:
   a. centration.
   b. pragmatic thinking.
   c. reversibility.
   d. egocentrism.

4. One characteristic of preoperational thought is:
   a. the ability to categorize objects.
   b. the ability to count in multiples of 5.
   c. the inability to perform logical operations.
   d. difficulty adjusting to changes in routine.

5. The zone of proximal development represents the:
   a. cognitive distance between a child's actual level of development and his or her potential development.
   b. influence of a child's peers on cognitive development.
   c. explosive period of language development during the play years.
   d. normal variations in children's language proficiency.

6. According to Vygotsky, language advances thinking through private speech, and by:
   a. helping children to privately review what they know.
   b. helping children explain events to themselves.
   c. serving as a mediator of the social interaction that is a vital part of learning.
   d. facilitating the process of fast mapping.

7. Reversibility refers to the:
   a. awareness that other people view the world from a different perspective than one's own.
   b. ability to think about more than one idea at a time.
   c. understanding that changing the arrangement of a group of objects doesn't change their number.
   d. understanding that reversing a process will restore the original conditions.

8. According to Piaget:
   a. it is impossible for preoperational children to grasp the concept of conservation, no matter how carefully it is explained.
   b. preschoolers fail to solve conservation problems because they center their attention on the transformation that has occurred and ignore the changed appearances of the objects.
   c. with special training, even preoperational children are able to grasp some aspects of conservation.
   d. preschoolers fail to solve conservation problems because they have no theory of mind.

9. Pretend play with dolls and other toys is an indication of the preschooler's:
   a. egocentric thinking.
   b. centration.
   c. symbolic thinking.
   d. understanding of reversibility.

10. Which theorist would be most likely to agree with the statement, "Learning is a social activity more than it is a matter of individual discovery"?
    a. Piaget
    b. Vygotsky
    c. both a. and b.
    d. neither a. nor b.

11. Children first demonstrate some understanding of grammar:
    a. as soon as the first words appear.
    b. once they begin to use language for pragmatic purposes.
    c. through the process called fast mapping.
    d. in their earliest two-word sentences.

12. Pragmatics refers to the:
    a. structures, techniques, and rules that languages use to communicate meaning.
    b. practical communication between one person and another in terms of the overall context in which language is used.
    c. way children sometimes use language to deceive other people.
    d. cognitive limitations of preschool children.

13. During the preschool years, the learning of new words tends to follow the sequence:
    a. verbs, followed by nouns, then adjectives, adverbs, and interrogatives.
    b. nouns, followed by verbs, then adjectives, adverbs, and interrogatives.
    c. adjectives, followed by verbs, then nouns, adverbs, and interrogatives.
    d. interrogatives, followed by nouns, then verbs, adjectives, and adverbs.

14. In general, variations in language development among different cultural, socioeconomic, and birth-order groups are:
    a. large compared with the differences among individual children from the same group.
    b. small compared with the differences among individual children from the same group.

c. a reflection of the test conditions, rather than meaningful group differences.
d. impossible to predict.

15. (A Life-Span Perspective) Regarding the value of preschool education, most developmentalists believe that:
a. most disadvantaged children will not benefit from an early preschool education.
b. most disadvantaged children will benefit from an early preschool education.
c. because of sleeper effects, the early benefits of preschool education are likely to disappear by grade 3.
d. the relatively small benefits of antipoverty measures such as Headstart do not justify their huge costs.

Matching Items

Match each term or concept with its corresponding description or definition.

Terms or Concepts

_______ 1. egocentrism
_______ 2. animism
_______ 3. theory of mind
_______ 4. zone of proximal development
_______ 5. overregularization
_______ 6. fast mapping
_______ 7. reversibility
_______ 8. centration
_______ 9. conservation
_______ 10. pragmatics
_______ 11. sleeper effect

Descriptions or Definitions

a. the idea that amount is unaffected by changes in shape or placement
b. thinking that centers on the self
c. the cognitive distance between a child's actual and potential levels of development
d. the tendency to think about one idea at a time
e. results that become apparent sometime after the precipitating event
f. our understanding of mental processes in ourselves and others
g. the process by which words are learned after only one hearing
h. the inappropriate application of rules of grammar
i. the study of the practical use of language
j. a logical operation through which original conditions are restored by the undoing of some process
k. the idea that everything in the world is alive

Challenge Test

Answer these questions the day before an exam as a final check on your understanding of the chapter's terms and concepts.

1. An experimenter first shows a child two rows of checkers that each have the same number of checkers. Then, with the child watching, the experimenter elongates one row and asks the child if each of the two rows still has an equal number of checkers. This experiment tests the child's understanding of:
a. reversibility.
b. conservation of matter.
c. conservation of number.
d. the three mountains.

2. A preschooler believes that a "party" is the one and only attribute of a birthday. She says that Daddy doesn't have a birthday because he never has a party. This thinking demonstrates the tendency Piaget called:
a. animism.
b. centration.
c. conservation of events.
d. mental representation.

3. A child that understands that 3 + 4 = 7 means that 7 – 4 = 3 has had to master the concept of:
a. reversibility.
b. number.
c. conservation.
d. animism.

4. A 4-year-old tells the teacher that a clown should not be allowed to visit the class because "Pat is 'fraid of clowns." The 4-year-old thus shows that he can anticipate how another will feel. This is evidence of the beginnings of:
a. egocentrism.
b. deception.
c. a theory of mind.
d. conservation.

5. Evidence that 6-year-old Hilary has mastered the pragmatics of language can best be seen in the fact that:
   a. her conversation consists largely of concrete nouns.
   b. she engages in overregularization.
   c. she speaks "baby talk" to toys and pets but not to adults.
   d. she believes people understand communications when they do not.

6. A nursery school teacher is given the job of selecting holiday entertainment for a group of preschool children. If the teacher agrees with the ideas of Vygotsky, she is most likely to select:
   a. a simple TV show that every child can understand.
   b. a hands-on experience that requires little adult supervision.
   c. brief, action-oriented play activities that the children and teachers will perform together.
   d. holiday puzzles for children to work on individually.

7. Based on averages, the child who is most likely to score highest on a test that measures language production is a:
   a. middle-class girl who has no siblings.
   b. later-born middle-class boy.
   c. boy from a large, economically disadvantaged family.
   d. boy who is one of twins.

8. That a child produces sentences that follow rules of word order such as "the initiator of an action precedes the verb, the receiver of an action follows it," demonstrates a knowledge of:
   a. grammar. c. pragmatics.
   b. semantics. d. phrase structure.

9. The 2-year-old child who says, "We goed to the store," is making a grammatical:
   a. centration. c. extension.
   b. overregularization. d. pragmatic.

10. An experimenter who makes two balls of clay of equal amount, then rolls one into a long skinny rope and asks the child if the amounts are still the same, is testing the child's understanding of:
    a. conservation of number.
    b. conservation of matter.
    c. perspective-taking.
    d. centration.

11. An experimenter shows a group of 4-year-olds a large three-dimensional exhibit of three mountains of different shapes, sizes, and colors. A doll is placed on the opposite side of the exhibit from the children, who are asked to choose which one of a series of photos shows the scene that the doll is viewing. Evidently, the experimenter is testing the children's understanding of:
    a. decentering. c. conservation.
    b. centration. d. perspective-taking.

12. When children between the ages of 3 and 5 were asked to hide a little boy behind a series of "walls" so that police who were looking for him could not find him, they demonstrated an understanding of perspective-taking at an earlier age than Piaget believed possible. Why?
    a. The children's direct participation in the task made it easier for them to identify with the little boy than with the character in a standard Piagetian task.
    b. The task really did not measure the same cognitive ability that Piaget's task measured.
    c. Children today are more cognitively advanced than the children tested by Piaget.
    d. All of the above have been offered as explanations of the discrepancy in results.

13. A preschooler who becomes upset when she drops her doll and claims that "Dolly is crying" is displaying ____________ in her thinking.
    a. centration c. animism
    b. egocentrism d. reversibility

14. A preschooler fails to put together a difficult puzzle on her own, so her mother encourages her to try again, this time guiding her by asking questions such as, "For this space do we need a big piece or a little piece?" With Mother's help, the child successfully completes the puzzle. Lev Vygotsky would attribute the child's success to:
    a. additional practice with the puzzle pieces.
    b. imitation of her mother's behavior.
    c. the social interaction with her mother that restructured the task to make its solution more attainable.
    d. modeling and reinforcement.

15. Mark is answering an essay question that asks him to "discuss the positions of major developmental theorists regarding the relationship between language and cognitive development." To help organize his answer, Mark jots down a reminder that ____________ believed that language is essential to the advancement of thinking, while ____________ believe that cognitive development precedes language.
    a. Piaget; Vygotsky c. Piaget; Skinner
    b. Vygotsky; Piaget d. Vygotsky; Skinner

Key Terms

Using your own words, write a brief definition or explanation of each of the following terms on a separate piece of paper.

1. preoperational thought
2. reversibility
3. centration
4. conservation
5. conservation of matter
6. conservation of number
7. egocentrism
8. animism
9. theory of mind
10. zone of proximal development
11. private speech
12. fast mapping
13. overregularization
14. pragmatics
15. Project Headstart
16. sleeper effects

ANSWERS

CHAPTER REVIEW

1. symbolically; mental representations
2. language
3. preoperational; reversibility
4. centration; visual perceptions
5. static; absolutes; transformations
6. cause and effect
7. conservation; conservation of matter; conservation of number
8. egocentrism; is not
9. animism
10. 7; three-mountains

In the three-mountains experiment, children are shown a large three-dimensional exhibit of three mountains of different shapes, sizes, and colors. After viewing the exhibit from all sides, the children are asked to choose which one of a series of photos depicts the scene being viewed by a doll seated on the opposite side of the exhibit. Children younger than 6 mistakenly choose the photo showing the mountains as they themselves are viewing them.

11. have
12. context (or conditions)
13. more; less; 4
14. does not
15. are

The policemen game makes the task, including the motives and intentions of the characters, more understandable to the child. The child is therefore able to more readily understand and identify with another's feelings. The playful, nonverbal nature of the task also makes it less difficult.

16. theory of mind; inconsistent; 2
17. deception
18. 4
19. underestimated
20. Lev Vygotsky
21. age-related; cultural variations; social activity
22. zone of proximal development
23. culture; family
24. vocabulary; grammar; practical use
25. precedes; objects that can be manipulated and explored with the senses
26. is; private speech; expressed silently
27. mediator
28. fast mapping
29. does
30. nouns; verbs; adjectives, adverbs, conjunctions, or interrogatives
31. used in the course of dialogue
32. more
33. comparisons; time; place
34. grammar; 3
35. overregularization

Many preschoolers overapply the rule of adding "s" to form the plural, as well as the rule of adding "ed" to form the past tense. Thus, preschoolers are likely to say "foots" and "snows," and that someone "broked" a toy.

36. more
37. pragmatics; social situation

Preschoolers may use high-pitched "baby talk" when talking with dolls, and deeper, more formal "adult" speech when giving commands to dogs and cats.

38. sequentially

39. great
40. girls; middle-income; first-borns; single-borns

Researchers generally explain these differences as being due to familial and cultural variations in the language children hear. In general, mothers talk more to daughters than to sons; middle-class parents provide their children with more elaborate explanations, more responsive comments, and fewer commands than lower-income parents do; and parents talk more to first-borns and single-borns than to later-borns or twins.

41. smaller
42. are not
43. do; a. maternal work patterns; b. research on child development showing that young children can learn at least as well outside the home as within it
44. better

High-quality preschools are characterized by (a) a low teacher-child ratio, (b) a staff with training and credentials in early-childhood education, (c) a curriculum geared toward cognitive development rather than behavioral control, and (d) an organization of space that facilitates creative and constructive play.

45. Project Headstart; higher
46. 3

PROGRESS TEST 1

Multiple-Choice Questions

1. **c.** is the answer. (p. 231)
2. **b.** is the answer. (p. 230)

   a. Egocentrism, or thinking that is self-centered, is generally not viewed as a cognitive gain.

   c. Because thinking is "preoperational," logical thought is not characteristic of children at this time.

   d. An emerging understanding of pragmatics does appear during the preschool years; however, this gain is not as significant as symbolic thought.
3. **d.** is the answer. (p. 233)

   a. A theory of mind is based on an understanding of our own mental processes *as well as those of others.* Egocentric thinking does not encompass others' thought processes.

   b. Egocentrism has nothing to do with language development.

   c. Egocentrism is not the same as selfishness.
4. **b.** is the answer. (p. 233)
5. **d.** is the answer. (pp. 236–237)
6. **d.** is the answer. (p. 243)

   a. & c. Preschoolers generally have great difficulty understanding, and therefore using, metaphors and abstract nouns.

   b. Other than the grammatical errors of overregularization, the text does not indicate that preschoolers use a significant number of self-created words.
7. **a.** is the answer. (p. 246)

   b. & d. These are not terms identified in the text.

   c. Pragmatics is the practical communication between one person and another in terms of the overall context in which language is used.
8. **a.** is the answer. (p. 243)

   b. This expresses the views of Piaget.

   c. Because he believed that language facilitates thinking, Vygotsky obviously felt that language and other cognitive developments are intimately related.

   d. Vygotsky did not hold this view.
9. **a.** is the answer. (p. 243)
10. **a.** is the answer. (p. 232)

    b., c., & d. Failure to conserve is the result of thinking that is centered on appearances. Egocentrism and animism are also examples of centered thinking.
11. **c.** is the answer. (p. 251)

    b. Although there was a slight early IQ advantage in Headstart graduates, the difference disappeared by grade 3.

    a. & d. There was no indication of greater behavioral problems or alienation in Headstart graduates.
12. **b.** is the answer. (p. 250)
13. **c.** is the answer. (p. 247)
14. **c.** is the answer. (p. 235)
15. **a.** is the answer. (p. 243)

True or False Items

1. F Piaget's description of cognitive development during the play years is generally accepted, but much recent research has led to revisions and modifications. (p. 234)
2. T (p. 233)
3. T (p. 233)
4. T (pp. 236–237)
5. F The ability to mislead another involves some understanding of the other person's thoughts,

and is evidence for the beginnings of a theory of mind in the preschooler. (p. 238)

6. F Piaget believed that cognitive development precedes language development. (p. 242)
7. F Preschoolers have difficulty understanding abstract words; their vocabulary consists mainly of concrete nouns and verbs. (p. 245)
8. F In adding "ed" to form a past tense, the child has indicated an understanding of the grammatical rule for making past tenses in English, even though the construction in these two cases is incorrect. (p. 246)
9. T (p. 250)
10. F Presumably because of opportunities for contact with adults, first-born children tend to be more advanced in language learning than are children who have many older siblings. (p. 248)

PROGRESS TEST 2

Multiple-Choice Questions

1. **b.** is the answer. (p. 238)

   a. This is evidence of egocentrism.

   c. This is the tendency to think about one idea at a time.

   d. According to Piaget, preschoolers are unable to grasp the idea of reversibility.
2. **d.** is the answer. (p. 236)

   a. Piaget found remarkably consistent results in testing children.

   b. The three-mountains task is generally not criticized for this reason.

   c. Simpler tests, such as the policemen game, demonstrate perspective-taking at an earlier age than Piaget believed.
3. **a.** is the answer. (p. 231)

   b. Pragmatics is the practical use of language; a child who demonstrated pragmatic thinking would vary his or her language to fit the social situation.

   c. Reversibility is the concept that reversing an operation, such as addition, will restore the original conditions.

   d. This term is used to refer to the preschool children's belief that people think as they do.
4. **c.** is the answer. This is why the stage is called pre*operational*. (p. 231)
5. **a.** is the answer. (p. 241)
6. **c.** is the answer. (p. 243)

   a. & b. These are both advantages of private speech.

   d. Fast mapping is the process by which new words are acquired, often after only one hearing.
7. **d.** is the answer. (p. 231)

   a. This describes perspective-taking.

   b. This is the opposite of centered thinking.

   c. This defines conservation of number.
8. **a.** is the answer. (pp. 232–233)

   b. According to Piaget, preschoolers fail to solve conservation problems because they focus on the *appearance* of objects and ignore the transformation that has occurred.

   d. Piaget did not relate conservation to a theory of mind.
9. **c.** is the answer. (p. 230)

   a. Egocentric thinking is self-centered thinking.

   b. Centration refers to focusing awareness on only one aspect of a situation.

   d. Reversibility is the understanding that reversing an operation will restore the original conditions.
10. **b.** is the answer. (pp. 240-241)

    a. Piaget believed that learning is a matter of individual discovery.
11. **d.** is the answer. This is so because preschoolers almost always put subject before verb in their two-word sentences. (p. 245)
12. **b.** is the answer. (p. 247)

    a. This defines grammar.
13. **b.** is the answer. (p. 243)
14. **b.** is the answer. (p. 248)

    c. & d. Group variations are both meaningful and predictable.
15. **b.** is the answer. (p. 251)

Matching Items

1. b (p. 233)	5. h (p. 246)	9. a (p. 232)
2. k (p. 233)	6. g (p. 243)	10. i (p. 247)
3. f (p. 237)	7. j (p. 231)	11. e (p. 251)
4. c (p. 241)	8. d (p. 231)	

CHALLENGE TEST

1. **c.** is the answer. (p. 233)

   a. A test of reversibility would ask a child to perform an operation, such as adding 4 to 3, and then reverse the process (subtract 3 from 7) to determine whether the child understood that the original condition (the number 4) was restored.

b. A test of conservation of matter would transform the appearance of an object, such as a ball of clay, to determine whether the child understood that the object remained the same.

d. The three-mountains task assesses a child's ability to take another's perspective.

2. **b.** is the answer. (p. 231)

   a. Animism is the idea that everything in the world is alive.

   c. This is not a concept in Piaget's theory.

   d. Mental representation is an example of symbolic thought.

3. **a.** is the answer. (p. 231)

4. **c.** is the answer. (p. 237)

   a. Egocentrism is self-centered thinking.

   b. Although deception provides evidence of a theory of mind, the child in this example is not deceiving anyone.

   d. Conservation is the understanding that the amount of a substance is unchanged by changes in its shape or placement.

5. **c.** is the answer. (p. 247)

6. **c.** is the answer. In Vygotsky's view, learning is a social activity more than a matter of individual discovery. Thus, social interaction that provides motivation and focuses attention facilitates learning. (pp. 240–241)

   a., b., & d. These situations either provide no opportunity for social interaction (b. & d.), or do not challenge the children (a.).

7. **a.** is the answer. (p. 248)

   b., c., & d. On measures of language production, girls are more proficient than boys; middle-class children, more proficient than lower-income children; first-borns, more proficient than later-borns; and single-born children more proficient than twins.

8. **a.** is the answer. (p. 245)

   b. & d. The text does not discuss these aspects of language.

   c. Pragmatics refers to the practical use of language in varying social contexts.

9. **b.** is the answer. (p. 246)

10. **b.** is the answer. (p. 232)

11. **d.** is the answer. This describes Piaget's three-mountains test of perspective-taking. (p. 234)

12. **a.** is the answer. (pp. 236–237)

13. **c.** is the answer. Animism is the idea that everything in the world, including a doll, is alive. (p. 233)

14. **c.** is the answer. (p. 241)

15. **b.** is the answer. (pp. 242–243)

    c. & d. The text does not present Skinner's views on the relationship of language to thinking.

KEY TERMS

1. According to Piaget, thinking between ages 2 and 7 is characterized by **preoperational thought**; that is, children cannot yet perform logical operations using ideas and symbols. (p. 231)

   Memory aid: Operations are mental transformations involving the manipulation of ideas and symbols. *Pre*operational children, who lack the ability to perform transformations, are "before" this developmental milestone.

2. In Piaget's theory, **reversibility** is the logical idea that reversing a process will bring about the original conditions from which the process began. (p. 231)

3. In Piaget's theory, **centration**—the tendency to think about one idea at a time—is the most notable characteristic of preoperational thought. (p. 231)

4. **Conservation** is the principle that properties such as number and mass remain constant despite changes in the appearance of objects. (p. 232)

5. **Conservation of matter** is the understanding that changing an object's appearance does not alter its mass. (p. 232)

6. **Conservation of number** is the understanding that the rearrangement of a group of objects does not change their quantity. (p. 233)

7. **Egocentrism** refers to the self-centered thinking of preschoolers that makes it difficult for them to consider another's viewpoint. (p. 233)

   Memory aid: Ego means "self," and *centrism* indicates "in the center"; the preoperational child is "self-centered."

8. **Animism** is the idea held by many young children that everything in the world is alive. Animism is one manifestation of egocentrism. (p. 233)

9. All adults have what psychologists call a **theory of mind**, that is, a personal understanding of mental processes, of the complex interaction among emotions, perceptions, thoughts, and

actions, in themselves, as well as in others. (p. 237)

10. According to Vygotsky, each individual is surrounded by a **zone of proximal development,** which represents the cognitive distance between the child's actual level of development and his or her potential development. (p. 241)

11. **Private speech** is the internal dialogue in which a person talks to himself or herself. Preschoolers' private speech, which often is uttered aloud, helps them think, review what they know, and decide what to do. (p. 243)

12. **Fast mapping** is the process by which children rapidly learn a new word by using the context in which it is being used to create a quick, partial understanding of the word. (p. 243)

13. **Overregularization** occurs when children apply rules of grammar when they should not. It is seen in English, for example, when children add "s" to form the plural even in irregular cases that form the plural in a different way. (p. 246)

14. **Pragmatics** refers to the practical communication between one person and another in terms of the overall context in which language is used. (p. 247)

15. **Project Headstart** is a preschool program that was initiated in the 1960s in response to a perceived need to improve the educational future for low-income children. (p. 251)

16. **Sleeper effects** are results that become apparent sometime after the precipitating event. (p. 251)

CHAPTER 10 The Play Years: Psychosocial Development

Chapter Overview

Chapter 10 explores the ways in which preschoolers begin to relate to others in an ever-widening social environment. The chapter begins where social understanding begins, with the emergence of the sense of self. This section describes the increasing complexity of children's interactions with others, paying special attention to the developmental importance of social play. Next, the parent-child relationship is examined in terms of different styles of parenting and how factors such as a child's temperament, the quality of the marital relationship, and the cultural and community context influence the effectiveness of parenting.

The discussion then turns to common problems arising from aggression, early fears and fantasies, and the more serious difficulties that may become apparent during the play years. A final section explores the development of gender roles and stereotypes and the alternative viewpoint of androgyny.

NOTE: Answer guidelines for all Chapter 10 questions begin on page 152.

Guided Study

The text chapter should be studied one section at a time. Before you read, preview each section by skimming it, noting headings and boldface items. Then read the appropriate section objectives from the following outline. Keep these objectives in mind and, as you read the chapter section, search for the information that will enable you to meet each objective. Once you have finished a section, write out answers for its objectives.

The Self and the Social World (pp. 256–263)

1. Describe the emergence of the sense of self during the play years, referring to ideas from psychoanalytic, cognitive, learning, and humanist theories.

2. Discuss the relationship between the child's developing sense of self and social awareness.

3. Discuss the nature and significance of social play during the play years.

4. Describe sibling relationships during the play years, noting their developmental significance.

Parenting (pp. 263–268)

5. (A Life-Span Perspective) Compare and contrast six patterns of parenting and their effect on children.

6. (A Life-Span Perspective) Discuss the impact of a child's temperament, the quality of the marital relationship, and the cultural and community context on the effectiveness of the various styles of parenting.

Possible Problems (pp. 268–272)

7. Discuss the nature of aggression and fantasy in preschool children, and describe signs of abnormal behavior in these areas, noting the effect of TV-viewing on preschoolers.

8. Identify two serious psychological disturbances of childhood and outline the best methods of treating them.

Gender Roles and Stereotypes (pp. 273–279)

9. Summarize the three theories of gender-role development during the play years, noting important contributions of each.

10. Discuss the concept of androgyny, emphasizing what research has shown regarding the impact of traditional and androgynous gender roles on children and their parents.

Chapter Review

When you have finished reading the chapter, work through the material that follows to review it. Complete the sentences and answer the questions. As you proceed, evaluate your performance for each section by consulting the answers on page 152. Do not continue with the next section until you understand each answer. If you need to, review or reread the appropriate section in the textbook before continuing.

The Self and the Social World (pp. 256–263)

1. A common theme of the major theories of development is that early childhood is a time of emerging ______________ and ______________-______________.

2. The most encompassing psychoanalytic view of this age is that offered by ____________. According to this view, preschoolers experience the crisis of ____________ ____________ ____________, which is closely tied to their developing sense of ____________ and the awareness of the larger ____________.

3. According to cognitive theory, as preschoolers develop their ____________ ____________ ____________, they can better identify and distinguish their own perceptions, emotions, thoughts, and intentions from those of others.

4. Toward the end of early childhood, praise and blame become more powerful as reinforcements and punishments; this is the view expressed by ____________ theory. Another landmark of this age, according to this theory, is that preschoolers become ____________ (more/less) self-reinforcing.

5. Humanist theory points to the child's developing drive for ____________ and ____________. The core idea of this theory is that every human being has ____________ (innate/acquired) drives to fulfill his or her potential. This is first apparent in ____________ ____________, as young children seek to develop all their skills and competencies, whether or not adults provide incentives for them to do so.

6. According to humanists, the parents' overall acceptance of the child, called ____________ ____________ ____________, provides an emotional environment in which children thrive. Children who do not have this feeling of acceptance are believed to be handicapped in their striving for ____________-____________.

7. Psychologists emphasize the importance of children developing a positive ____________-____________. Preschoolers typically form impressions of themselves that are quite ____________ (positive/negative). One manifestation of this tendency is that preschoolers regularly ____________ (overestimate/underestimate) their own abilities. Most preschoolers think of themselves as competent ____________ (in all/only in certain) areas.

8. Research demonstrates that preschoolers who have more firmly established self-understanding tend to engage in play that is ____________ (more/less) interactive. Furthermore, children who are skilled at social interaction tend to be ____________ (more/less) confident of their own ability.

9. Play is important to preschoolers' psychosocial development because of the opportunities it provides for children to develop ____________ ____________ and ____________. In ____________ play, children acquire skills of initiating and maintaining friendly interaction with peers, and the themes of their play activity enable them to explore and rehearse the ____________ ____________ they observe around them.

10. Healthy animals of ____________ (all/only certain) species play when they are young. Such play provides an opportunity for developing social skills that may be important for their ____________. Play also provides an opportunity to learn ____________ behaviors in caring for infants. This type of play occurs ____________ (only in female animals/in animals of both sexes).

11. Among humans, social play teaches ____________, ____________, and ____________ more readily than interaction with adults does.

12. In ____________ play, children explore and rehearse various social roles and examine ____________ ____________ in ways that would not be possible with adults.

13. For many children, the first lesson in social interaction comes from their ____________. For a younger child, an older sibling provides an

important ______________ and source of learning; for an older child, a younger sibling is an important benchmark of ______________ ______________.

14. Siblings ______________ (are/are not) more likely to quarrel with each other than they are with nonrelated children. Siblings are ______________ (more/less) likely to have more positive interactions with each other, and tend to show more ______________ and ______________ than with unrelated children. According to the text, ______________ may be the best description of the typical sibling relationship.

15. The home experiences of each child in a given family are ______________ (quite different from/much the same as) those of the other children. Earlier researchers incorrectly assumed that differences in personality and intelligence among children in a given family must be ______________.

Briefly discuss environmental factors that account for the experiential differences between siblings.

16. In most ways, only-children fare ______________ (as well or better/worse) than children with siblings. Only-children are particularly likely to benefit ______________, becoming more ______________ and more ______________. A potential problem of only-children is in their development of ______________ skills.

Parenting (pp. 263–268)

17. The most crucial influence on preschool children is their ______________.

18. (A Life-Span Perspective) There ______________ (is/is not) a single best style of parenting that will guarantee a child's successful upbringing. The seminal research on parenting styles, which was conducted by ______________, found that parents varied in their ______________ toward offspring, in their efforts to ______________, in how well they ______________, and in their ______________ ______________.

19. (A Life-Span Perspective) Parents who adopt the ______________ style demand unquestioning obedience from their children. In this style of parenting, nurturance tends to be ______________ (low/high), maturity demands are ______________ (low/high), and parent-child communication tends to be ______________ (low/high).

20. (A Life-Span Perspective) Parents who adopt the ______________ style make few demands on their children and are lax in discipline. Such parents ______________ (are/are not very) nurturant, communicate ______________ (well/poorly), and make ______________ (few/extensive) maturity demands.

21. (A Life-Span Perspective) Parents who adopt the ______________ style democratically set limits and enforce rules. Such parents make ______________ (high/low) maturity demands, communicate ______________ (well/poorly), and ______________ (are/are not) nurturant.

22. (A Life-Span Perspective) Follow-up studies indicate that children raised by ______________ parents are likely to be obedient but unhappy; those raised by ______________ parents are likely to lack self-control; and those raised by ______________ parents are more likely to be successful, happy with themselves, and generous with others.

23. (A Life-Span Perspective) Permissive parents who are warm and responsive are called ______________-______________.

Permissive parents who are cold and unengaged are called ____________-____________. Parents who take somewhat old-fashioned male and female roles are labeled ____________ parents.

24. (A Life-Span Perspective) Longitudinal research suggests that traditional and democratic-indulgent parenting is less successful than ____________ parenting but more successful than ____________ or ____________-____________ parenting.

25. (A Life-Span Perspective) An important factor in the effect of parenting style on children is the child's ____________. Initially, the parents' strictness or laxness is ____________ (more/less) important than their warmth toward the child in the early years.

26. (A Life-Span Perspective) The impact of parenting styles also varies with family ____________ and with the child's ____________ and ____________. Parents with many children tend to be ____________ (more/less) controlling.

27. (A Life-Span Perspective) During early and middle childhood, the offspring of ____________-____________ parents tend to be mediocre in school achievement; as teenagers, however, they often do quite well. Girls who have been raised by such parents, for example, tend to have high ____________ and ____________ scores.

28. (A Life-Span Perspective) Authoritarian parenting is likely to be ____________ (effective/ineffective) in middle childhood, but become ____________ (increasingly/less) debilitating as children grow older. This tendency is especially obvious for ____________ (boys/girls), who, as teenagers tend to be alienated from school and to blame their problems on ____________ (themselves/others).

29. (A Life-Span Perspective) When a marriage is satisfying and mutually supportive, both parents tend to be ____________. When a marriage is unhappy, parents tend to be ____________. When a marriage is falling apart, parents are particularly likely to be ____________-____________. Parental ____________ can also indirectly affect parenting practices.

30. (A Life-Span Perspective) The efficacy of various parenting styles is also influenced by the ____________ and ____________ context, especially its stability and safety.

Possible Problems (pp. 268–272)

31. At first, toddlers are ____________ (often/rarely) aggressive in playing with other children. As they grow older and become more aware of themselves as individuals, the frequency of deliberate physical aggression ____________ (increases/decreases).

32. Physical aggression peaks during the ____________ years, and then declines. This trend is especially apparent for ____________ aggression, which involves quarreling over a(n) ____________.

33. Aggression involving an attack against someone rather than a fight about something is called ____________. After peaking during the play years, this type of aggression declines ____________ (more/less) rapidly than the other type of aggression. One reason for the decline is that aggression ____________ (is/is not) a successful strategy for resolving conflict.

34. Boys are ____________ (no more/more) frequently involved in aggressive encounters than girls. This ____________ (is/is not) true at every age, and ____________ (has/has not) been found in many cultures that have been studied.

35. Preschoolers ____________ (do/do not) normally have vivid nightmares, elaborate daydreams, and imaginary friends and enemies. For

this reason, scaring preschoolers into good behavior with fantasy untruths ________________ (is/is not) likely to be harmful to them.

36. Young children generally ________________ (do/do not) have a firm enough grasp of reality to accurately report their experiences, as in eyewitness testimony. However, because preschool children ________________ (are/are not) highly suggestible, their testimony in court cases ________________ (can/cannot) easily be influenced.

37. (A Closer Look) The average amount of time preschoolers spend watching television per week ________________ (increased/decreased) from 1984 to 1990. On the average, preschoolers spend ________________ (more/about the same amount of/less) time watching television as (than) those of other ages.

38. (A Closer Look) Most psychologists ________________ (do/do not) agree that TV violence promotes physical aggression in children. One reason preschoolers are especially sensitive to violence on television is that they have difficulty ________________.
Another reason is that watching repeated violence on TV may ________________ children to the affects of violence.

(A Closer Look) Explain why some critics feel that even the best children's television "does more harm than good."

39. A preschool child who is unusually aggressive may have ________________ problems.

Identify two characteristics of the parents of very aggressive preschoolers.

40. Children who have been physically abused ________________ (are/are not) more aggressive than other children. Aggressive children tend to have deficient ________________ -________________ skills. Aggressive behavior that continues into the later years of school may be a precursor of ________________.

41. An overwhelming irrational fear that interferes with a person'snormal life is called a(n) ________________. Occasional fears such as this are ________________ (rare/fairly common) among preschoolers.

Gender Roles and Stereotypes (pp. 273–279)

42. By age ________________, children prefer to play with gender-typed toys. By age ________________, children can consistently apply gender labels and have a rudimentary understanding of the permanence of their own gender. By age ________________, most children express stereotypic ideas of each sex. Such stereotyping ________________ (does/does not) occur in children whose parents provide nontraditional gender role models.

43. Freud called the period from age 3 to 7 the ________________ ________________.
According to this view, boys in this stage develop sexual feelings about their ________________ and become jealous of their ________________.
Freud called this phenomenon the ________________ ________________.

44. In Freud's theory, preschool boys resolve their guilty feelings defensively through ________________ with their fathers.

45. According to Freud, during the phallic stage little girls may experience the ________________ ________________, in which they want to get rid of their mother and become intimate with their father. Alternatively, they may become jealous of boys because they have a penis; this emotion Freud called ________________ ________________.

46. According to learning theory, preschool children develop gender-role ideas by being ________________ for behaviors deemed appropriate for their sex, and ________________ for behaviors deemed inappropriate. This type of learning may be strongest when peer groups ________________ (are/are not) segregated by sex.

47. Social-learning theorists maintain that children learn sexual behavior by ________________ ________________. Most adults are ________________ (more/less) gender-stereotyped in their behaviors and ________________-________________ when their children are young than they are earlier or later in life.

48. In explaining gender identity and gender-role development, cognitive theorists focus on children's understanding of ________________, as well as ________________-________________ differences.

49. According to ________________-________________ theory, preschoolers' understanding of gender is limited by their belief that gender differences depend on differences in appearance rather than on biology. It is not until after age ________________ that children realize that they are permanently male or female; this realization is called ________________ ________________. Research has shown that children ________________ (do/do not) behave in gender-typed ways before they have acquired this realization.

50. According to ________________-________________ theory, children organize their ideas about people in terms of gender-based categories and evaluations that are acquired very early in life.

51. As developmentalists use the term, ________________ refers to a person's having a balance of what are commonly regarded as "male" and "female" psychological characteristics.

52. Androgynous people are generally ________________ (more/less) flexible in their gender roles. Early studies showed that androgynous individuals are generally more ________________ and have higher ________________-________________ than people who follow traditional gender-role behavior.

53. Recent research indicates that traditional gender-role values may ________________ (foster/diminish) self-esteem at certain other stages of life. Traditional parents may do a better job of child-rearing than more androgynous parents because they tend to be more ________________-________________.

54. (A Closer Look) Psychologists generally ________________ (do/do not) accept Freud's explanation of female sexual and moral development, and are particularly critical of Freud's idea of ________________ ________________.

Progress Test 1

Multiple-Choice Questions

Circle your answers to the following questions and check them with the answers on page 152. If your answer is incorrect, read the explanation for why it is incorrect and then consult the appropriate pages of the text (in parentheses following the correct answer).

1. Preschool children have a clear (but not necessarily accurate) concept of self. Typically, the preschooler believes that she or he:
   a. owns all objects in sight.
   b. is great at almost everything.
   c. is much less competent than peers and older children.
   d. is more powerful than her or his parents.

2. According to Freud, the third stage of psychosexual development, during which the penis is the focus of psychological concern and pleasure, is the ________________ stage.
   a. oral
   b. anal
   c. phallic
   d. latent

3. Because it helps children rehearse social roles, work out fears and fantasies, and learn cooperation, an important form of social play is:
   a. dramatic play.
   b. language play.
   c. associative play.
   d. watching television with other children.

4. (A Life-Span Perspective) The three *basic* patterns of parenting described by Diana Baumrind are:
   a. hostile, loving, and harsh.
   b. authoritarian, permissive, and authoritative.
   c. positive, negative, and punishing.
   d. democratic-indulgent, rejecting-neglecting, and traditional.

5. (A Life-Span Perspective) Authoritative parents are receptive and loving, but they also normally:
   a. set limits and enforce rules.
   b. have difficulty communicating.
   c. withhold praise and affection.
   d. encourage aggressive behavior.

6. Preschoolers who are unusually aggressive are frequently found to have parents who:
   a. are rejecting.
   b. are authoritative.
   c. are neglectful.
   d. overuse physical aggression themselves.

7. An attack aimed specifically against another person may be defined as:
   a. instrumental aggression.
   b. hostile aggression.
   c. preoperational dominance.
   d. modeled aggression.

8. Preschool children who make up imaginary playmates and enemies are displaying:
   a. a normal characteristic for this age.
   b. a psychological disturbance.
   c. a phobia.
   d. antisocial behavior.

9. Learning theorists emphasize the importance of ______________________ in the development of the preschool child.
   a. mastery motivation
   b. praise and blame
   c. initiative
   d. a theory of mind

10. Children apply gender labels, and have definite ideas about how boys and girls behave, as early as age:
    a. 3.
    b. 4.
    c. 5.
    d. 7.

11. A concept that counters the idea that masculinity and femininity are exact opposites is called:
    a. modeling.
    b. Freudianism.
    c. sexual stereotyping.
    d. androgyny.

12. According to some psychologists, children very early label themselves as male and female, try to conform to these schemas, and use them in interpreting others' behavior. This theory is called:
    a. cognitive-developmental theory.
    b. gender-constancy theory.
    c. gender-schema theory.
    d. social-learning theory.

13. Compared to children with siblings, only-children are likely to:
    a. be less verbal.
    b. fare as well or better in most ways.
    c. have greater competence in social skills.
    d. be less creative.

14. (A Life-Span Perspective) Which of the following was *not* identified as a factor that influences the effectiveness of various parenting styles?
    a. the child's temperament
    b. the marital relationship
    c. the stability and safety of the larger society
    d. the parents' ages

15. (A Life-Span Perspective) Research on parenting styles reveals that traditional parents:
    a. tend to be less child-centered than authoritative parents.
    b. often do a better job of child-rearing than more androgynous parents.
    c. often raise children with lower self-esteem than more androgynous parents.
    d. often raise children with more behavior problems than more androgynous parents.

True or False Items

Write *true* or *false* on the line in front of each statement.

______ 1. (A Life-Span Perspective) According to Baumrind, only authoritarian parents make maturity demands on their children.

______ 2. (A Life-Span Perspective) Children of authoritative parents tend to be successful, happy with themselves, and generous with others.

_______ 3. Because of sibling rivalry, a typical child is more likely to help a friend than to come to the aid of a brother or sister.

_______ 4. Aggression reaches a peak during the preschool years, then declines.

_______ 5. Preschoolers' phobias tend to persist into the school and adolescent years, unless treated by a psychologist or other professional.

_______ 6. Children from feminist or nontraditional homes seldom express stereotypic ideas about feminine and masculine roles.

_______ 7. The concept of androgyny suggests that people can be flexible in their gender roles, incorporating the best qualities of men and women.

_______ 8. By age 3, most children have definite ideas about what constitutes typical masculine and feminine behavior.

_______ 9. Identification was defined by Freud as a defense mechanism in which children and adults identify with others who may be stronger and more powerful than they.

_______ 10. Dramatic play is free-wheeling, creative, and fluid.

Progress Test 2

Progress Test 2 should be completed during a final chapter review. Answer the following questions after you thoroughly understand the correct answers for the Chapter Review and Progress Test 1.

Multiple-Choice Questions

1. (A Life-Span Perspective) Children of permissive parents are *most* likely to lack:
   a. social skills.
   b. self-control.
   c. initiative and guilt.
   d. care and concern.

2. Children learn reciprocity, nurturance, and cooperation most readily from their interaction with:
   a. their mothers.
   b. their fathers.
   c. friends.
   d. others of the same sex.

3. (A Closer Look) Critics of television-viewing for preschoolers are concerned about the effect of commercials, the violent content of many programs, and:
   a. television censorship by parents.
   b. the time that TV robs from valuable social and creative activities.
   c. the deprivation of deaf children.
   d. the realistic nature of cartoons.

4. (A Life-Span Perspective) Which of the following is *not* a factor affecting parenting style?
   a. the child's temperament
   b. the ages of the children
   c. the parents' relationship
   d. the influence of the culture and the community

5. Research has shown that whether androgynous values enhance self-esteem depends on the:
   a. consistency of parenting.
   b. stage of life.
   c. influence of peers on the individual.
   d. socioeconomic status of the parents.

6. According to Freud, a young boy's jealousy of his father's relationship with his mother, and his attendant guilt feelings, are part of the:
   a. Electra complex.
   b. Oedipus complex.
   c. phallic complex.
   d. penis envy complex.

7. (A Life-Span Perspective) The style of parenting in which the parents make few demands on children, the discipline is lax, and the parents are warm and responsive is:
   a. authoritarian.
   b. authoritative.
   c. democratic-indulgent.
   d. rejecting-neglecting.

8. Compared to their interactions with friends, siblings tend to:
   a. have more positive interactions.
   b. quarrel more often.
   c. be more cooperative.
   d. do all of the above.

9. (A Life-Span Perspective) In a satisfying and mutually supportive marriage, both parents tend to adopt the _______________ style of parenting; when they are unhappy with each other, they are more likely to be _______________.
   a. permissive; authoritative
   b. permissive; authoritarian
   c. authoritarian; authoritative
   d. authoritative; authoritarian

10. At an early age, children begin to organize their knowledge about people into the categories of "male" and "female"; in other words, they acquire:
    a. gender constancy.
    b. gender identity.
    c. gender schemas.
    d. androgyny.

11. A child who has such a strong fear of dogs that it prevents her from walking on the streets near her home is probably suffering from:
    a. instrumental aggression.
    b. a phobia.
    c. vivid nightmares.
    d. physical abuse.

12. According to the major theories, the preschooler's readiness to learn new tasks and play activities reflects his or her:
    a. emerging competency and self-awareness.
    b. theory of mind.
    c. becoming self-actualized.
    d. engaging in identification.

13. (A Life-Span Perspective) In which style of parenting is the parents' word law and misbehavior strictly punished?
    a. permissive
    b. authoritative
    c. authoritarian
    d. rejecting-neglecting

14. According to humanist theory, the child's natural motivation to master new skills is enhanced by the:
    a. parents' modeling the behavior in question.
    b. parents' applying praise and blame consistently.
    c. parents' showing unconditional positive regard for the child.
    d. parents' correcting the child each time he or she makes a mistake.

15. Erikson notes that preschoolers eagerly begin many new activities but are vulnerable to criticism and feelings of failure; they experience the crisis of:
    a. identity versus role confusion.
    b. initiative versus guilt.
    c. basic trust versus mistrust.
    d. efficacy versus helplessness.

Matching Items

Match each term or concept with its corresponding description or definition.

Terms or Concepts

_______ 1. instrumental aggression
_______ 2. hostile aggression
_______ 3. mastery motivation
_______ 4. rejecting-neglecting
_______ 5. democratic-indulgent
_______ 6. Electra complex
_______ 7. Oedipus complex
_______ 8. authoritative
_______ 9. authoritarian
_______ 10. identification

Descriptions or Definitions

a. uninvolved parents who are permissive and ignorant of their child's activities
b. Freudian theory that every daughter secretly wishes to replace her mother
c. parenting style associated with high maturity demands and low parent-child communication
d. quarreling over an object or privilege
e. Freudian theory that every son secretly wishes to replace his father
f. parenting style associated with high maturity demands and good parent-child communication
g. an attack against another person
h. parents who are warm and responsive, yet quite permissive
i. children spontaneously seek to develop their skills and competencies
j. a defense mechanism through which children cope with their feelings of guilt during the phallic stage

Challenge Test

Answer these questions the day before an exam as a final check on your understanding of the chapter's terms and concepts.

1. The 4-year-old's realization that she is permanently female, will never grow a penis, and will not grow up to be a "Daddy" is called:
   a. identification.
   b. gender constancy.
   c. penis envy.
   d. the Electra complex.

2. A little girl who says she wants her mother to go on vacation so that she can marry her father is voicing a fantasy consistent with the ________________ described by Freud.
   a. Oedipus complex
   b. Electra complex
   c. theory of mind
   d. crisis of initiative versus guilt

3. According to Erikson, before the preschool years children are incapable of feeling guilt because:
   a. guilt depends on a sense of self, which is not sufficiently established in preschoolers.
   b. they do not yet understand that gender is constant.
   c. this emotion is unlikely to have been reinforced at such an early age.
   d. guilt is associated with the resolution of the Oedipus complex, which occurs later in life.

4. (A Life-Span Perspective) Parents who are strict and aloof are *most* likely to make their children:
   a. cooperative and trusting.
   b. obedient but unhappy.
   c. violent.
   d. withdrawn and anxious.

5. The belief that children's love, jealousy, and fear of their parents are primary determinants in the learning of gender roles would find its strongest adherents among ________________ theorists.
   a. psychoanalytic
   b. cognitive
   c. humanist
   d. learning

6. The belief that almost all sexual patterns are learned rather than inborn would find its strongest adherents among:
   a. cognitive theorists.
   b. learning theorists.
   c. psychoanalytic theorists.
   d. humanist theorists.

7. The belief that every human being has innate drives to fulfill his or her potential would find its strongest adherents among:
   a. cognitive theorists.
   b. learning theorists.
   c. psychoanalytic theorists.
   d. humanist theorists.

8. Five-year-old Rodney has a better-developed sense of self and is more confident than Darnell. According to the text, it is likely that Rodney will also be more skilled at:
   a. tasks involving verbal reasoning.
   b. social interaction.
   c. deception.
   d. all of the above.

9. Your sister and brother-in-law are thinking of having a second child, because they are worried that only-children miss out on the benefits of social play. You tell them that:
   a. parents can compensate for this by making sure the child has regular contact with other children.
   b. only-children are likely to possess *superior* social skills because of the greater attention they receive from their parents.
   c. the style of parenting, rather than the presence of siblings, is the most important factor in the development of the child's social and intellectual skills.
   d. unfortunately, this is true and nothing can replace the opportunities for acquiring social skills that siblings provide.

10. Concerning children's concept of gender, which of the following statements is true?
    a. Before age 3 or so, children think that boys and girls can change gender as they get older.
    b. Children as young as 18 months have a clear understanding of the physical differences between girls and boys and can consistently apply gender labels.
    c. Not until age 5 or 6 do children show a clear preference for gender-typed toys.
    d. All of the above are true.

11. (A Life-Span Persepctive) Which of the following is *not* one of the features of parenting used by Baumrind to differentiate authoritarian, permissive, and authoritative parents?
    a. maturity demands for the child's conduct
    b. efforts to control the child's actions
    c. nurturance
    d. adherence to stereotypic gender roles

12. (A Life-Span Perspective) Jan recalls her mother as being nurturant and permissive, while her father was much more authoritarian. It is likely that Jan's parents would be classified as ________________ by Diana Baumrind.
    a. democratic-indulgent
    b. traditional
    c. androgynous
    d. authoritative

13. (A Closer Look) Concerning the effect that observing violence on television has on children, which of the following is *not* true?
    a. Children who watch a lot of television are likely to be more aggressive than children who do not.
    b. Children who are aggressive are likely to watch a lot of TV violence.
    c. Children who see a lot of violence on television are more likely to regard violence as a "normal" part of everyday life.
    d. The impact of TV violence on preschoolers remains a controversial issue among social scientists.

14. Dr. Rubenstein believes that young preschoolers' understanding of gender is limited by their belief that sex differences depend on differences in appearance or behavior rather than on biology. Evidently, Dr. Rubenstein is an advocate of ________________ theory.
    a. psychoanalytic
    b. learning
    c. cognitive-developmental
    d. gender-schema

15. Of the following individuals, who is likely to have the highest self-esteem?
    a. 16-year-old Emilio, who takes pride in his masculine qualities
    b. 16-year-old Martin, whose parents have always encouraged his androgynous behavior
    c. 43-year-old Diana, who has always tried to be as "feminine" as possible
    d. 23-year-old Tricia, who is attempting to raise her infant in an "androgynous" environment

Key Terms

Using your own words, write a brief definition or explanation of each of the following terms on a separate piece of paper.

1. initiative versus guilt
2. mastery motivation
3. authoritarian parenting
4. permissive parenting
5. authoritative parenting
6. democratic-indulgent parenting
7. rejecting-neglecting parenting
8. traditional parenting
9. instrumental aggression
10. hostile aggression
11. phobia
12. phallic stage
13. Oedipus complex
14. identification
15. Electra complex
16. penis envy
17. gender schemas
18. androgyny

ANSWERS

CHAPTER REVIEW

1. competency; self-awareness
2. Erikson; initiative versus guilt; self; society
3. theory of mind
4. learning; more
5. competency; achievement; innate; mastery motivation
6. unconditional positive regard; self-actualization
7. self-concept; positive; overestimate; in all
8. more; more
9. social skills; roles; social; social roles
10. all; survival; nurturant; in animals of both sexes
11. reciprocity; nurturance; cooperation
12. dramatic; personal concerns
13. siblings; model; social comparison
14. are; more; nurturance; cooperation; ambivalence
15. quite different from; genetic

One of the most important factors is parents' differential treatment of children, which fuels feelings of jealousy, anger, dominance, or inferiority. Sibling relationships are also a factor, since siblings guide, challenge, and encourage a child's social interactions.

16. as well or better; intellectually; verbal; creative; social

17. parents
18. is not; Baumrind; nurturance; control; communicate; maturity demands
19. authoritarian; low; high; low
20. permissive; are; well; few
21. authoritative; high; well; are
22. authoritarian; permissive; authoritative
23. democratic-indulgent; rejecting-neglecting; traditional
24. authoritative; authoritarian; rejecting-neglecting
25. temperament; less
26. size; age; gender; more
27. democratic-indulgent; math; verbal
28. effective; increasingly; boys; others
29. authoritative; authoritarian; rejecting-neglecting; stress
30. cultural; community
31. rarely; increases
32. preschool; instrumental; object, territory, or privilege
33. hostile aggression; less; is not
34. more; is; has
35. do; is
36. do; are; can
37. increased; more
38. do; differentiating reality from fantasy; desensitize

Some critics feel that television robs children of play time and tends to cut off social communication, which is essential for enhancing the social skills that children must develop.

39. emotional

Parents of very aggressive preschoolers either overuse physical aggression themselves, or have given up trying to control their children's aggression.

40. are; social problem-solving; delinquency and adult criminality
41. phobia; fairly common
42. 2; 3; 6; does
43. phallic stage; mothers; fathers; Oedipus complex
44. identification
45. Electra complex; penis envy
46. reinforced; punished; are
47. observing other people; more; self-concept
48. gender; male-female
49. cognitive-developmental; 4 or 5; gender constancy; do
50. gender-schema
51. androgyny
52. more; competent; self-esteem
53. foster; child-centered
54. do not; penis envy

PROGRESS TEST 1

Multiple-Choice Questions

1. **b.** is the answer. (p. 259)
2. **c.** is the answer. (p. 274)

   a. & b. In Freud's theory, the oral and anal stages are associated with infant and early childhood development, respectively.

   d. In Freud's theory, the latent stage is associated with development during the school years.
3. **a.** is the answer. (p. 260)

   b. & c. These are not types of play discussed in the text.

   d. Most developmentalists believe that TV does more harm than good because it robs children of the opportunity to play.
4. **b.** is the answer. (p. 264)

   d. These are variations of the basic styles uncovered by later research.
5. **a.** is the answer. (p. 264)

   b. & c. Authoritative parents communicate very well and are quite affectionate.

   d. This is not typical of authoritative parents.
6. **d.** is the answer. (p. 272)
7. **b.** is the answer. (p. 269)

   a. Instrumental aggression involves quarreling over an object, territory, or privilege.

   c. & d. These are not types of aggression identified in the text.
8. **a.** is the answer. (p. 269)

   c. Phobias are irrational fears.

   d. Antisocial behavior is characterized by unusual aggressiveness.
9. **b.** is the answer. (p. 257)

   a. This is the focus of humanist theorists.

   c. This is the focus of Erikson's psychoanalytic theory.

   d. This is the focus of cognitive theorists.
10. **a.** is the answer. (p. 273)
11. **d.** is the answer. (pp. 277–278)

    a. Through modeling children learn by observing others.

b. & c. Freud's theory and gender stereotyping tend to perpetuate, rather than counter, this idea.

12. **c.** is the answer. (p. 277)

    a. According to this theory, preschoolers' understanding of gender is limited by their belief that sex differences depend on differences in appearance or behavior.

    b. This is not a theory of gender-role development.

    d. According to this theory, children learn much of their gender behavior by observing other people.

13. **b.** is the answer. (p. 263)

    a. & d. Only-children often benefit intellectually, becoming more verbal and more creative.

    c. Because only-children may miss out on the benefits of social play, they may be weaker in their social skills.

14. **d.** is the answer. (pp. 266–268)

15. **b.** is the answer. (pp. 265–266)

    a. Traditional parents tend to be *more* child-centered than androgynous parents.

    c. & d. In fact, just the opposite is true.

True or False Items

1. F All parents make some maturity demands on their children; maturity demands are high in both the authoritarian and authoritative parenting styles. (pp. 264–265)
2. T (p. 265)
3. F Siblings are more likely to help each other than to help an unrelated child; of course, siblings are also more likely to fight with each other than with other children. (p. 262)
4. T (p. 269)
5. F Preschoolers' phobias tend to disappear over time, with or without specific treatment. (p. 272)
6. F Children from feminist or nontraditional homes often surprise their parents by expressing stereotypic ideas about feminine and masculine roles. (p. 273)
7. T (pp. 277–278)
8. T (p. 273)
9. T (p. 274)
10. F Although dramatic play appears creative and fluid, it actually involves complex rules and structures. (p. 261)

PROGRESS TEST 2

Multiple-Choice Questions

1. **b.** is the answer. (p. 265)
2. **c.** is the answer. (p. 260)

    a. & b. Siblings often provide better instruction than adults, since they are likely to guide, challenge, and encourage a child's social interactions more frequently and intimately.

    d. The text does not indicate that same-sex friends are more important in learning these than friends of the other sex.

3. **b.** is the answer. (p. 270)
4. **b.** is the answer. (pp. 266–268)
5. **b.** is the answer. (p. 278) Although androgynous college students have higher self-esteem, this is not the case at certain other stages of life, such as during the early years.
6. **b.** is the answer. (p. 274)

    a. & d. These are Freud's versions of phallic-stage development in little girls.

    c. There is no such thing as the "phallic complex."

7. **c.** is the answer. (p. 265)

    a. & b. Both authoritarian and authoritative parents make high demands on their children.

    d. Rejecting-neglecting parents are quite cold and unengaged.

8. **d.** is the answer. (pp. 261–262)
9. **d.** is the answer. (p. 267)
10. **c.** is the answer. (p. 277)

    a. Gender constancy is the realization that one is permanently male or female.

    b. Gender identity is one's personal sense of being male or female.

    d. Androgyny refers to a person's having a balance of what are commonly regarded as "male" and "female" psychological characteristics.

11. **b.** is the answer. (p. 272)

    a. Instrumental aggression involves quarreling over an object, territory, or privilege.

    c. These are a reflection of the preschool child's flights of fantasy.

    d. The text does not link phobias with physical abuse.

12. **a.** is the answer. (p. 256)

    b. This viewpoint is associated only with cognitive theory.

c. This viewpoint is associated only with humanist theory.

d. Identification is a Freudian defense mechanism.

13. c. is the answer. (p. 264)

a. Permissive parents make few demands on their children.

b. Authoritative parents rule democratically rather than dictatorially.

d. Rejecting-neglecting is a subcategory of the permissive style of parenting. Such parents are quite cold and unengaged.

14. c. is the answer. (p. 258)

15. b. is the answer. (pp. 256–257)

a. & c. According to Erikson, these are the crises of adolescence and infancy, respectively.

d. This is not a crisis described by Erikson.

Matching Items

1. d (p. 269)
2. g (p. 269)
3. i (p. 257)
4. a (p. 265)
5. h (p. 265)
6. b (p. 274)
7. e (p. 274)
8. f (p. 264)
9. c (p. 264)
10. j (p. 274)

CHALLENGE TEST

1. b. is the answer. (p. 277)

a. Identification is the defense mechanism through which children were believed by Freud to resolve the guilt of their phallic-stage urges.

c. & d. These are Freudian descriptions of phallic-stage development in girls.

2. b. is the answer. (p. 274)

a. According to Freud, the Oedipus complex refers to the male's sexual feelings toward his mother and resentment toward his father.

c. & d. These are concepts introduced by cognitive theorists and Erik Erikson, respectively.

3. a. is the answer. (pp. 256–257)

b. Erikson did not equate gender constancy with the emergence of guilt.

c. & d. These reflect the viewpoints of learning theory and Freud, respectively.

4. b. is the answer. (p. 265)

5. a. is the answer. (p. 274)

b. Cognitive theorists focus on children's understanding of gender and male-female differences, and on how their changing perceptions of gender motivate their efforts to behave consistently with their gender role.

c. The text does not discuss a humanist theory of gender-role development.

d. Learning theorists believe that role patterns are learned through reinforcement, punishment, and modeling.

6. b. is the answer. (p. 274)

7. d. is the answer. (p. 257)

8. b. is the answer. (p. 258)

a. & c. The text does not link self-understanding with verbal reasoning or deception.

9. a. is the answer. (p. 263)

10. a. is the answer. (p. 273)

b. Not until about age 3 can children consistently apply gender labels.

c. By age 2, children prefer gender-typed toys.

11. d. is the answer. (p. 264)

12. b. is the answer. (pp. 265–266)

a. Democratic-indulgent parents are warm and responsive, yet make fewer demands on their children than authoritarian parents.

c. Androgynous parents are more flexible in their gender roles than Jan's parents evidently were.

d. Authoritative parents are more democratic than Jan's father evidently was.

13. d. is the answer. The negative impact of TV violence is now accepted as a fact by social scientists. (p. 270)

14. c. is the answer. (p. 276)

a. According to psychoanalytic theory, children copy the behaviors and moral standards of their same-sex parents as they resolve the guilt associated with the sexual urges of the phallic stage.

b. Learning theorists believe that role patterns are acquired through reinforcement, punishment, and modeling.

d. According to gender-schema theory, young children's motivation to behave in gender-appropriate ways derives from the ways they organize their knowledge about people in terms of gender-based categories.

15. a. is the answer. (p. 278)

b. & d. During adolescence, and when raising young children, those who consider themselves relatively traditional for their gender tend to have high self-esteem.

c. Some of the first studies on androgyny showed that androgynous individuals generally have a higher sense of self-esteem than people who follow traditional gender-role behavior (like Diana in this example).

KEY TERMS

1. According to Erikson, the crisis of the preschool years is **initiative versus guilt**. In this crisis, preschoolers eagerly take on new tasks and play activities and feel guilty when their efforts result in failure or criticism. (p. 256)
2. In humanist theory, **mastery motivation** refers to the preschooler's drive to seek to develop all his or her skills and competencies, whether or not adults provide incentives.(p. 257)
3. **Authoritarian parents** show little affection or nurturance for their children, and have high maturity demands and low parent-child communication. (p. 264)

   Memory aid: Someone who is an *authoritarian* demands unquestioning obedience and acts in a dictatorial way.
4. **Permissive parents** make few demands on their children, yet are nurturant and accepting, and communicate well with their children. (p. 264)
5. **Authoritative parents** set limits and enforce rules, but do so more democratically than do authoritarian parents. (p. 264)

   Memory aid: **Authoritative parents** act as *authorities* do on a subject—by discussing and explaining why certain family rules are in place.
6. **Democratic-indulgent parents** adopt the undemanding, uncoercive style of permissive parents, yet are warm and responsive toward their children. (p. 265)
7. **Rejecting-neglecting parents** adopt the undemanding, uncoercive style of permissive parents, yet are cold, unengaged, and even ignorant about what their children actually do. (p. 265)
8. **Traditional parents** take somewhat old-fashioned male and female roles, the mother being quite nurturant and permissive, while the father is more authoritarian. (p. 265)
9. **Instrumental aggression** involves quarreling over an object, territory, or privilege. (p. 269)

   Memory aid: In this type of encounter, aggression serves as an *instrument* for obtaining some thing.
10. **Hostile aggression** is an attack against someone rather than a fight about some thing. (p. 269)
11. A **phobia** is an irrational fear that becomes so powerful and overwhelming that it interferes with the person's normal life. (p. 272)
12. Freud called the period from about age 3 to 7 the **phallic stage** because he believed its center of focus is the penis. (p. 274)
13. According to Freud, boys in the phallic stage develop a collection of feelings, known as the **Oedipus complex**, that center on sexual attraction to the mother and resentment of the father. (p. 274)
14. In Freud's theory, **identification** is the defense mechanism through which people imagine themselves to be like a person more powerful than themselves. (p. 274)
15. According to Freud, girls in the phallic stage may develop a collection of feelings, known as the **Electra complex**, that center on sexual attraction to the father and resentment of the mother. (p. 274)
16. An alternative Freudian description of the phallic stage as it occurs in little girls is **penis envy**, or jealousy of boys because they have a penis. This jealousy supposedly causes a little girl to resent her mother and to make herself sexually attractive so that someone with a penis, preferably her father, will love her. (p. 274)
17. **Gender schemas** refer to the ways children organize their knowledge about people in terms of gender-based categories and evaluations. (p. 277)
18. **Androgyny** refers to a person's having a balance of what are commonly regarded as "male" and "female" psychological characteristics. (pp. 277–278)

CHAPTER 11

The School Years: Biosocial Development

Chapter Overview

This chapter introduces middle childhood, the years from 7 to 11. Changes in physical size are described and the problem of obesity is addressed. The discussion then turns to the continuing development of motor skills during the school years. A final section examines the experiences of children with learning disabilities (such as dyslexia) and those diagnosed as having attention-deficit hyperactivity disorder, including the causes of and treatments for these problems.

NOTE: Answer guidelines for all Chapter 11 questions begin on page 166.

Guided Study

The text chapter should be studied one section at a time. Before you read, preview each section by skimming it, noting headings and boldface items. Then read the appropriate section objectives from the following outline. Keep these objectives in mind and, as you read the chapter section, search for the information that will enable you to meet each objective. Once you have finished a section, write out answers for its objectives.

Size and Shape (pp. 286–290)

1. Describe normal physical growth and development during middle childhood and account for the usual variations among children.

2. Discuss the problems of obese children in middle childhood and outline the best approaches to treating obesity.

3. (A Life-Span Perspective) Identify the major causes of obesity.

Motor Skills (pp. 291–292)

4. Describe the development of motor skills during the school years and discuss the reasons for limited abilities during this period.

Learning Disabilities (pp. 292–300)

5. Discuss the symptoms and possible causes of learning disabilities.

6. (A Closer Look) Explain how achievement and aptitude tests are used in identifying learning disabilities and discuss why use of such tests is controversial.

7. Describe the symptoms and possible causes of attention-deficit disorder and attention-deficit hyperactivity disorder.

8. Discuss the types of treatment available for attention-deficit hyperactivity disorder.

Chapter Review

When you have finished reading the chapter, work through the material that follows to review it. Complete the sentences and answer the questions. As you proceed, evaluate your performance for each section by consulting the answers on page 166. Do not continue with the next section until you understand each answer. If you need to, review or reread the appropriate section in the textbook before continuing.

1. Compared to that of other periods of the life span, physical development during middle childhood is ________________ (relatively smooth/often fraught with problems). For example, disease and death during these years are ________________ (more common/rarer) than during any other period. For another, sex differences in physical development and ability are ________________ (very great/minimal).

Size and Shape (pp. 286–290)

2. Children grow ________________ (faster/more slowly) during middle childhood than they did earlier or than they will in adolescence. The typical child gains about ________________ pounds and ________________ inches per year.

Describe several other features of physical development during the school years.

3. In some undeveloped countries, most of the variation in children's height and weight is caused by ________________. In developed countries, most children grow as tall as their ________________ allow. These factors affect not only size but rate of ________________ as well.

4. Among Americans, those of African descent tend to mature more ________________ (quickly/slowly) than those of European descent, who tend to mature more ________________ (quickly/slowly) than those of Asian descent.

5. Most experts define obesity as body weight that is more than ________________ percent greater than average for one's age, sex, and body size. By this criterion, at least ________________ percent of American children are obese.

6. Two physical problems associated with childhood obesity are ________________ and ________________ problems.

Identify several psychological problems commonly associated with childhood obesity.

7. Obesity is usually fostered by ____________ ____________ that promote a fattening diet and sedentary lifestyle.

8. Strenuous dieting during childhood ____________ (is/is not) potentially dangerous. A diet that is deficient in protein or calcium can hinder ____________ and ____________ growth.

9. In the case of extremely obese children, a(n) ____________-____________ process may be necessary, for excessive overfeeding of a child is often a sign of family ____________ and ____________.

10. The best way to get children to lose weight is to increase their ____________ ____________. Developmentalists agree that treating obesity early in life ____________ (is/is not) very important in ensuring the child's overall health later in life.

11. (A Life-Span Perspective) Obesity is usually caused by ____________ (a single factor/the interaction of several factors).

(A Life-Span Perspective) Identify several inherited characteristics that might contribute to obesity.

12. (A Life-Span Perspective) Inactive people burn ____________ (more/fewer) calories and are ____________ (no more/more) likely to be obese than active people.

13. (A Life-Span Perspective) American children whose parents were immigrants from developing countries are ____________ (more/less) likely to be overweight. This demonstrates the importance of another factor in obesity: the ____________.

14. (A Life-Span Perspective) Diets that emphasize ____________ do not lead to excess weight gain, whereas diets that are high in ____________ obviously do.

15. (A Life-Span Perspective) The diet of North American families who are below the poverty line tends to be high in ____________. The types of food eaten also vary with ____________ food preferences.

(A Life-Span Perspective) Give an example of how parents' attitude toward food might contribute to obesity in their children.

16. (A Life-Span Perspective) Throughout life, the number of fat cells in a person's body ____________ (remains relatively constant/increases). Overfeeding during ____________ is likely to increase the number of fat cells in a person's body and ____________ (speed up/slow down) the rate of cell multiplication. Underfeeding or malnutrition decreases the number of fat cells in a person's body and tends to ____________ (speed up/slow down) the rate of cell multiplication.

17. (A Life-Span Perspective) Excessive television-watching by children ____________ (is/is not) directly correlated with being overweight. When children watch TV their metabolism ____________ (slows down/speeds up).

(A Life-Span Perspective) Identify three factors that make television-watching fattening.

18. (A Life-Span Perspective) Fasting and/or repeated dieting ________________ (lowers/raises) the rate of metabolism. For this reason, after a certain amount of weight loss, additional pounds become ________________ (more/less) difficult to lose. In addition, dieting helps the body become ________________ (more/less) efficient at storing fat.

19. (A Life-Span Perspective) The onset of childhood obesity ________________ (is/is not) commonly associated with a traumatic experience.

20. (A Life-Span Perspective) Less than 1 percent of all cases of childhood obesity are caused by ________________ problems.

Motor Skills (pp. 291–292)

21. Children become more skilled at controlling their bodies during the school years, in part because they ________________.

22. Because boys have greater ________________ strength during childhood than girls, they tend to have an advantage in sports like ________________, whereas girls have an advantage in sports like ________________.

23. The length of time it takes a person to respond to a particular stimulus is called ________________ ________________; a key factor in this motor skill is ________________ ________________.

24. Most of the sports that adults value ________________ (are/are not) well-suited for children.

Learning Disabilities (pp. 292–300)

25. A child who has difficulty with a specific school-related skill may have a(n) ________________ ________________, if that difficulty ________________ (is/is not) attributable to an overall intellectual slowness, a physical handicap, or a lack of basic education. Part of the diagnosis of this type of difficulty is that the child scores ________________ grades below his or her intellectual potential. Using this criterion, about ________________ percent of all American schoolchildren are so designated.

26. A disability in reading is called ________________; in math, it is called ________________. Other specific academic subjects that may show learning disability are ________________ and ________________.

27. Learning disabilities ________________ (are/are not) caused by a lack of effort on the child's part. Many professionals believe that the origin of learning disabilities is ________________, perhaps caused by ________________ ________________ that have a detrimental effect on brain functioning.

28. Learning disabilities ________________ (do/do not) tend to run in families. Teratogens such as ________________ may also be a precipitating factor.

29. If a learning disability is of proven organic origin, it ________________ (is/is not) impossible to correct.

30. Help for children with learning disabilities should focus on the specific problem, and on the child's ________________ skills, which are often affected by the underlying problem.

31. (A Closer Look) Teachers and psychologists who suspect that a child may have a learning disability look for two elements: ________________ ________________.

32. (A Closer Look) Tests that are designed to measure what a child has learned are called ________________ tests. Tests that are designed to measure learning potential are called ________________ tests. In the original version of the latter tests, a person's score was translated into a(n) ________________

_______________ and that was divided by the person's _______________ _______________ to determine his or her _______________ _______________. On current tests, two-thirds of all children score within a year or two of their age-mates, somewhere between _______________ and _______________.

33. (A Closer Look) Achievement and aptitude testing is controversial, in part because a child's test performance can be affected by nonintellectual factors, such as _______________ _______________.

34. (A Closer Look) Many educators believe that labeling children as "retarded," "gifted," or "disabled," and segregating them in different classrooms, which is called _______________ _______________, is destructive.

35. A learning disability that manifests itself in a difficulty in concentrating for more than a few moments is called _______________-_______________ _______________.

When this difficulty is accompanied by excitability, impulsivity, and a need to be active, the child may suffer from _______________-_______________ _______________ _______________. The crucial problem in the latter condition seems to be a neurological difficulty in _______________.

36. For every girl diagnosed with ADD or ADHD, _______________ boys are so diagnosed.

37. Twin studies have shown that the concordance rate for ADHD is significantly higher for _______________ twins than for _______________ twins. Only the _______________ (biological/adoptive) parents of hyperactive children are likely themselves to have attentional difficulties similar to those of their children. These studies indicate that hereditary differences _______________ (do/do not) contribute to ADHD.

38. Brain metabolism tends to be _______________ (higher/lower) in ADHD individuals than in control subjects, especially in areas of the brain associated with _______________ _______________.

39. ADHD also may result from prenatal damage due to _______________. Poisoning due to exposure to _______________ can also lead to impaired concentration and hyperactivity, as can dietary factors, such as deficiency of the _______________ vitamins, exposure to chemical additives, or ingestion of certain foods.

Identify several family and environmental influences on ADHD.

40. More than half of all children with ADHD _______________ (do/do not) have continuing problems as adults.

41. The most frequent therapy for children with ADHD is _______________. Certain drugs that stimulate adults, such as _______________ and _______________, have a reverse effect on hyperactive children.

42. The most effective types of therapy for ADHD have generally been those developed from _______________ theory, such as teaching parents how to use _______________-_______________ techniques with their child.

43. Some classroom environments, called _______________ _______________, tend to increase ADHD problems. Others, called _______________ _______________, tend to reduce ADHD problems.

Describe these two types of classroom environments.

Progress Test 1

Multiple-Choice Questions

Circle your answers to the following questions and check them with the answers on page 167. If your answer is incorrect, read the explanation for why it is incorrect and then consult the appropriate pages of the text (in parentheses following the correct answer).

1. As children move into middle childhood:
   a. the rate of accidental death increases.
   b. sexual urges intensify.
   c. the rate of weight gain increases.
   d. biological growth slows and steadies.

2. During middle childhood:
   a. girls are usually stronger than boys.
   b. boys have greater physical flexibility than girls.
   c. boys have greater forearm strength than girls.
   d. the development of motor skills slows drastically.

3. To help obese children, nutritionists usually recommend:
   a. strenuous dieting to counteract early overfeeding.
   b. the use of amphetamines and other drugs.
   c. more exercise, stabilization of weight, and time to "grow out" of the fat.
   d. no specific actions.

4. A factor that is *not* primary in the development of motor skills during middle childhood is:
   a. practice.
   b. gender.
   c. brain maturation.
   d. age.

5. Dyslexia is a learning disability that affects the ability to:
   a. do math.
   b. read.
   c. write.
   d. speak.

6. In relation to weight in later life, childhood obesity:
   a. is not an accurate predictor of adolescent or adult weight.
   b. is predictive of adolescent but not adult weight.
   c. is predictive of adult but not adolescent weight.
   d. is predictive of both adolescent and adult weight.

7. (A Closer Look) Aptitude and achievement testing are controversial because:
   a. most tests are unreliable in the individual scores they yield.
   b. test performance can be affected by many factors other than the child's intellectual potential or academic achievement.
   c. they often fail to identify serious learning problems.
   d. of all the above reasons.

8. The time—usually measured in fractions of a second—it takes for a person to respond to a particular stimulus is called:
   a. the interstimulus interval.
   b. reaction time.
   c. the stimulus-response interval.
   d. response latency.

9. (A Life-Span Perspective) Researchers have suggested that excessive television-watching is a possible cause of childhood obesity because:
   a. TV bombards children with persuasive junk food commercials.
   b. children often snack while watching TV.
   c. body metabolism slows while watching TV.
   d. of all the above reasons.

10. A specific learning disability that becomes apparent when a child experiences unusual difficulty in learning to read is:
    a. dyslexia.
    b. dyscalcula.
    c. ADD.
    d. ADHD.

11. Classroom environments that seem to aggravate or increase problems in children with attention-deficit hyperactivity disorder are sometimes labeled:
    a. provocation ecologies.
    b. rarefaction ecologies.
    c. open classrooms.
    d. homogeneous groupings.

12. In developed countries, most of the variation in children' size and shape can be attributed to:
    a. the amount of daily exercise.
    b. nutrition.
    c. genes.
    d. the interaction of the above factors.

13. (A Closer Look) Tests that measure a child's potential to learn a new subject are called ______ tests.
    a. aptitude
    b. achievement
    c. vocational
    d. intelligence

14. Homogeneous grouping refers to the practice of:
    a. placing normal, gifted, and learning-disabled children in separate classrooms.
    b. integrating special children in classrooms with normal children.
    c. labeling each child according to his or her disability.
    d. maintaining a flexible, yet structured classroom environment.

15. Psychoactive drugs are most effective in treating attention-deficit hyperactivity disorder when they are administered:
    a. before the diagnosis becomes certain.
    b. for several years after the basic problem has abated.
    c. as part of the labeling process.
    d. with psychological support or therapy.

True or False Items

Write *true* or *false* on the line in front of each statement.

______ 1. Physical variations in North American children are usually caused by diet rather than heredity.

______ 2. Childhood obesity usually does not correlate with adult obesity.

______ 3. (A Life-Span Perspective) Research shows a direct correlation between excessive television-watching and obesity in children.

______ 4. The quick reaction time that is crucial in some sports can be readily achieved with practice.

______ 5. Despite the efforts of teachers and parents, most children with learning disabilities can expect their disabilities to persist and even worsen as they enter adulthood.

______ 6. Children are usually not diagnosed as having attention-deficit hyperactivity disorder until they enter school and are expected to sit still.

______ 7. Most of the children who have attention-deficit hyperactivity disorder are girls.

______ 8. (A Closer Look) Virtually all educators agree that separate education for special children is beneficial.

______ 9. Most learning disabilities are caused by a difficult birth or other early trauma to the child.

______ 10. The drugs sometimes given to children to reduce hyperactive behaviors have a reverse effect on adults.

Progress Test 2

Progress Test 2 should be completed during a final chapter review. Answer the following questions after you thoroughly understand the correct answers for the Chapter Review and Progress Test 1.

Multiple-Choice Questions

1. During the years from 7 to 11, the average child:
    a. becomes slimmer.
    b. gains about 12 pounds a year.
    c. has decreased lung capacity.
    d. is more likely to become obese than at any other period in the life span.

2. (A Life-Span Perspective) Among the factors that are known to contribute to obesity are activity level, quantity and types of food eaten, and:
    a. repeated dieting.
    b. television-watching.
    c. attitude toward food.
    d. all of the above.

3. The underlying problem in attention-deficit hyperactivity disorder appears to be:
    a. low overall intelligence.
    b. a neurological difficulty in screening out distracting stimuli.
    c. a learning disability in a specific academic skill.
    d. the existence of a conduct disorder.

4. Problems in learning to write, read, and do math are collectively referred to as:
    a. learning disabilities.
    b. attention-deficit hyperactivity disorder.
    c. hyperactivity.
    d. dyscalcula.

5. A classroom environment that seems to decrease the problems of the child with attention-deficit hyperactivity disorder is called a(n):
   a. provocation ecology.
   b. rarefaction ecology.
   c. ecological niche.
   d. therapeutic classroom.

6. (A Life-Span Perspective) Diets that emphasize ______________________ are unlikely to promote obesity.
   a. fat
   b. protein
   c. fruits, vegetables, and grains
   d. simple carbohydrates

7. The *most frequent* therapy for children with attention-deficit hyperactivity disorder is:
   a. behavior modification.
   b. medication with drugs such as amphetamines.
   c. family counseling.
   d. medication with tranquilizers.

8. A key factor in reaction time is:
   a. whether the child is male or female.
   b. brain maturation.
   c. whether the stimulus to be reacted to is an auditory or visual one.
   d. all of the above.

9. (A Closer Look) In the earliest aptitude tests, a person's score was translated into a(n) ______________________ age that was divided by the person's ______________________ age to find the ______________________ quotient.
   a. mental; chronological; intelligence
   b. chronological; mental; intelligence
   c. intelligence; chronological; mental
   d. intelligence; mental; chronological

10. Which of the following is true of children with a diagnosed learning disability?
    a. They are average or above average in intelligence.
    b. They often have a specific physical handicap, such as hearing loss.
    c. They often lack basic educational experiences.
    d. All of the above are true.

11. During the school years:
    a. boys are, on the average, at least a year ahead of girls in the development of physical abilities.
    b. girls are, on the average, at least a year ahead of boys in the development of physical abilities.
    c. boys and girls are about equal in physical abilities.
    d. motor-skill development proceeds at a slower pace, since children grow more rapidly at this age than at any other time.

12. Dietary deficiencies in ______________________ have been linked to impaired concentration.
    a. fat
    b. B vitamins
    c. calcium
    d. protein

13. Compared with other children, children with attention-deficit hyperactivity disorder come from families who:
    a. tend to stress academic performance.
    b. move infrequently.
    c. have many children.
    d. are especially concerned with controlling their children's behavior.

14. Most experts contend that at least ______________________ percent of American children need to lose weight.
    a. 10
    b. 15
    c. 20
    d. 25

15. (A Closer Look) Tests that measure what a child has already learned are called ______________________ tests.
    a. aptitude
    b. vocational
    c. achievement
    d. intelligence

Matching Items

Match each term or concept with its corresponding description or definition.

Terms or Concepts

_______ 1. dyslexia
_______ 2. dyscalcula
_______ 3. attention-deficit disorder
_______ 4. attention-deficit hyperactivity disorder
_______ 5. provocation ecologies
_______ 6. rarefaction ecologies
_______ 7. achievement tests
_______ 8. aptitude tests
_______ 9. homogeneous grouping
_______ 10. learning disability

Descriptions or Definitions

a. an unexpected difficulty with one or more academic skills
b. tests that measure learning potential
c. flexible, yet structured classroom environment
d. learning disability involving difficulty in concentrating
e. tests that measure existing knowledge
f. placing children with special needs and abilities in separate classrooms
g. difficulty in reading
h. unusually rigid or freewheeling classroom environment
i. learning disability involving difficulty in concentrating, as well as excitability and impulsivity
j. difficulty in math

Challenge Test

Answer these questions the day before an exam as a final check on your understanding of the chapter's terms and concepts.

1. According to developmentalists, the best game for a typical group of 8-year-olds would be:
   a. football or baseball.
   b. basketball.
   c. one in which reaction time is not crucial.
   d. games involving one-on-one competition.

2. Excessive overfeeding of a child is often a sign of:
   a. an overbearing mother.
   b. parental discord.
   c. family depression.
   d. all of the above.

3. Nine-year-old Jack has difficulty concentrating on his classwork for more than a few moments, repeatedly asks his teacher irrelevant questions, and is distracted by thoughts of playing outside. If his difficulties persist, Jack is likely to be diagnosed as suffering from:
   a. dyslexia.
   b. dyscalcula.
   c. attention-deficit disorder.
   d. attention-deficit hyperactivity disorder.

4. Of the following 9-year-olds, who is likely to mature physically at the youngest age?
   a. Britta, who is of European descent
   b. Michael, who is of European descent
   c. Malcolm, who is of African descent
   d. Lee, who is of Asian descent

5. Ten-year-old Clarence is quick-tempered, easily frustrated, and is often disruptive in the classroom. Clarence may be suffering from:
   a. dyslexia.
   b. dyscalcula.
   c. attention-deficit disorder
   d. attention-deficit hyperactivity disorder

6. Because 11-year-old Wayne is obese, he runs a greater risk of developing:
   a. orthopedic problems.
   b. respiratory problems.
   c. psychological problems.
   d. all of the above.

7. Of the following individuals, who is likely to have the fastest reaction time?
   a. a 7-year-old
   b. a 9-year-old
   c. an 11-year-old
   d. an adult

8. Harold weighs about 20 pounds more than his friend Jay. During school recess, Jay can usually be found playing soccer with his classmates, while Harold sits on the sidelines by himself. Harold's rejection is due to:
   a. his being physically different.
   b. his being dyslexic.
   c. his intimidating his schoolmates.
   d. his being hyperactive.

9. (A Closer Look) In determining whether an 8-year-old has a learning disability, a psychologist looks primarily for:
   a. discrepant performance in a subject area.
   b. the exclusion of other explanations.
   c. a family history of the learning disability.
   d. both a. and b.

10. (A Life-Span Perspective) Which of the following American children is more likely to be overweight?
    a. Caledonia, whose diet is high in fiber
    b. Sperry, who comes from an affluent family
    c. David, whose parents were immigrants from a developing country
    d. It is impossible to predict from the information given.

11. (A Closer Look) Angela was born in 1984. In 1992, she scored 125 on an intelligence test. What was Angela's mental age when she took the test?
    a. 6
    b. 8
    c. 10
    d. 12

12. Because Brenda's weight is more than ________________ greater than the average weight for her height, build, and sex, she is classified as obese.
    a. 5 percent
    b. 10 percent
    c. 20 percent
    d. 10 pounds

13. Danny has been diagnosed as suffering from attention-deficit hyperactivity disorder. A scan of his brain is likely to reveal:
    a. nothing out of the ordinary.
    b. an abnormally high overall rate of brain metabolism.
    c. abnormally low brain metabolism in the areas of the brain associated with the control of attention and motor activity.
    d. an unusually thin cortical layer in the frontal lobe.

14. (A Life-Span Perspective) In concluding her presentation entitled "Facts and falsehoods regarding childhood obesity," Cheryl states that despite popular belief ____________________ is *not a common cause* of childhood obesity.
    a. television-watching
    b. repeated dieting
    c. overeating of high-fat foods
    d. abnormal physiology

15. (A Life-Span Perspective) Debbie, who was overfed as a child and has dieted most of her life, wants to know the effect of overeating and dieting on the body. You tell her that the number of fat cells in a person's body:
    a. is fixed at the moment of conception.
    b. increases in response to overeating and decreases in response to dieting.
    c. increases in response to overeating but does not decrease in response to dieting.
    d. is fixed by age 1.

Key Terms

Using your own words, write a brief definition or explanation of each of the following terms on a separate piece of paper.

1. obesity
2. reaction time
3. learning disability
4. dyslexia
5. dyscalcula
6. achievement tests
7. aptitude tests
8. homogeneous grouping
9. attention-deficit disorder (ADD)
10. attention-deficit hyperactivity disorder (ADHD)
11. provocation ecologies
12. rarefaction ecologies

ANSWERS

CHAPTER REVIEW

1. relatively smooth; rarer; minimal
2. more slowly; 5; $2\frac{1}{2}$

During the school years, children become slimmer, muscles become stronger, and lung capacity increases.

3. malnutrition; genes; maturation
4. quickly; quickly
5. 20; 10
6. orthopedic; respiratory

Obese children are teased, picked on, and rejected, and so tend to have fewer friends than other children and are more likely to experience diminished self-esteem, depression, and behavior problems.

7. family attitudes and habits
8. is; brain; bone
9. family-intervention; depression; disorganization
10. physical activity; is
11. the interaction of several factors

Body type, including the amount and distribution of fat, as well as height and bone structure; individual differences in metabolic rate; and activity level are all influenced by heredity.

12. fewer; more
13. more; types of food eaten
14. fruits, vegetables, and grains; fat and sugar
15. fat; ethnic and subcultural

Parents who consider food a symbol of love and comfort may feed their babies whenever they cry, rather than first figuring out if the baby is lonely or uncomfortable rather than hungry.

16. remains relatively constant; the prenatal period, the first two years of life, and during early adolescence; speed up; slow down
17. is; slows down

While watching television, children (a) are bombarded with commercials for junk food, (b) consume many snacks, and (c) burn fewer calories than they would if they were actively playing.

18. lowers; more; more
19. is
20. physiological
21. grow more slowly
22. forearm; baseball; gymnastics
23. reaction time; brain maturation
24. are not
25. learning disability; is not; two or more; 5
26. dyslexia; dyscalcula; spelling; handwriting
27. are not; organic; prenatal factors
28. do; prenatal exposure to illegal drugs or to other toxins, such as mercury and PCBs, and postnatal exposure to lead
29. is not
30. social
31. discrepant performance and exclusion of other explanations
32. achievement; aptitude; mental age; chronological age; intelligence quotient (IQ); 85; 115
33. emotional stress, visual or hearing problems, language difficulties, and educational background, or when scores are compared to those of children from a different culture or socioeconomic status
34. homogeneous grouping
35. attention-deficit disorder; attention-deficit hyperactivity disorder; screening out irrelevant and distracting stimuli
36. four
37. identical; fraternal; biological; do
38. lower; the control of attention and motor activity
39. drug use during pregnancy or pregnancy complications; lead; B

Compared with other children, children with ADHD come from families who move often, are stressed, have fewer children, and are less concerned about the child's academic performance than about controlling the child's behavior. ADHD may also be exacerbated by being in an exciting but unstructured situation or in a situation with many behavioral demands. Similarly, children with no place to play or who watch too much television may be affected.

40. do
41. medication; amphetamines; methylphenidate (Ritalin)
42. learning; behavior-modification
43. provocation ecologies; rarefaction ecologies

In provocation ecologies, classroom structure is either unusually rigid or completely absent, and noise is either completely forbidden or tolerated to a distracting degree. In rarefaction ecologies, teachers tend to be more flexible in their reactions to minor disruptions, but also provide sufficient structure so that children know what they should be doing and when. Rarefaction ecologies also alternate short periods of concentrated schoolwork with opportunities for physical activity.

PROGRESS TEST 1

Multiple-Choice Questions

1. **d.** is the answer. (p. 286)
2. **c.** is the answer. (p. 291)

   a. Especially in forearm strength, boys are usually stronger than girls during middle childhood.

   b. During middle childhood, girls usually have greater flexibility than boys.

   d. Motor-skill development improves greatly during middle childhood.

3. **c.** is the answer. (p. 287)
   a. Strenuous dieting can be physically harmful and often makes children irritable, listless, and even sick—adding to the psychological problems of the obese child.
   b. The use of amphetamines to control weight is not recommended at any age.
4. **b.** Boys and girls are just about equal in physical abilities during the school years. (p. 291)
5. **b.** is the answer. (p. 293)
   a. This is dyscalcula.
   c. & d. The text does not give labels for learning disabilities in writing or speaking.
6. **d.** is the answer. (pp. 287–288)
7. **b.** is the answer. (p. 295)
8. **b.** is the answer. (p. 291)
9. **d.** is the answer. (p. 290)
10. **a.** is the answer. (p. 293)
    b. This learning disability involves math, rather than reading.
    c. & d. These disabilities do not manifest themselves in a particular academic skill but instead appear in psychological processes that affect learning in general.
11. **a.** is the answer. (p. 300)
    b. These are classroom environments that often reduce ADHD behaviors.
    c. Open classrooms were not discussed in the text.
    d. Homogeneous groupings are classrooms that segregate slow learners in one class, gifted in another, and learning disabled in still another.
12. **c.** is the answer. (p. 286)
    a. The amount of daily exercise a child receives is an important factor in his or her tendency toward obesity; exercise does not, however, explain most of the variation in childhood physique.
    b. In some parts of the world malnutrition accounts for most of the variation in physique; this is not true of developed countries, where most children get enough food to grow as tall as their genes allow.
13. **a.** is the answer. (p. 294)
    b. Achievement tests measure existing knowledge.
    c. Vocational tests were not discussed.
    d. Intelligence tests are a type of aptitude test.
14. **a.** is the answer. (p. 295)
15. **d.** is the answer. (p. 299)

True or False Items

1. F Physical variations in children from developed countries are caused primarily by heredity. (p. 286)
2. F If obesity is established in middle childhood, it tends to continue into adulthood. (p. 288)
3. T (p. 290)
4. F Reaction time depends on brain maturation and is not readily affected by practice. (p. 291)
5. F With the proper assistance, many learning-disabled children develop into adults who are virtually indistinguishable from other adults in their educational and occupational achievements. (pp. 295–296)
6. T (p. 296)
7. F Most children who suffer from attention-deficit hyperactivity disorder are boys. (p. 297)
8. F Many educators feel that homogeneous grouping is destructive. (p. 295)
9. F The causes of learning disabilities are difficult to pinpoint, and cannot be specified with certainty. (pp. 293–295)
10. T (p. 299)

PROGRESS TEST 2

Multiple-Choice Questions

1. **a.** is the answer. (p. 286)
   b. & c. During this period children gain about 5 pounds per year and experience increased lung capacity.
   d. Although childhood obesity is a common problem, the text does not indicate that a person is more likely to become obese at this age than at any other.
2. **d.** is the answer. (pp. 288–290)
3. **b.** is the answer. (p. 297)
4. **a.** is the answer. (p. 292)
   b. & c. ADHD and ADD are general learning disabilities that usually do not manifest themselves in specific subject areas.
   d. Dyscalcula is a learning disability in math only.
5. **b.** is the answer. (p. 300)
   a. This classroom environment tends to increase the problems of children with ADHD.
   c. & d. These are not classroom environments discussed in the text.
6. **c.** is the answer. (p. 289)

a. & d. Diets high in fat and sugar are likely to promote obesity.

b. Diets that emphasize protein are more likely to promote obesity than diets that emphasize fruits, vegetables, and grains.

7. b. is the answer. (p. 299)
8. b. is the answer. (p. 291)
9. a. is the answer. (pp. 294–295)
10. a. is the answer. (pp. 292–293)
11. c. is the answer. (p. 291)
12. b. is the answer. (p. 297)
13. d. is the answer. (p. 298)

    a., b., & c. The families of children with ADHD typically place less stress on academic performance than on controlling their children's behavior, move frequently, and have few children.
14. a. is the answer. (p. 286)
15. c. is the answer. (p. 294)

    a. Aptitude tests measure a child's potential for learning a new skill or subject.

    b. Vocational tests were not discussed.

    d. Intelligence tests are a type of aptitude test.

Matching Items

1. g (p. 293)
2. j (p. 293)
3. d (p. 296)
4. i (p. 296)
5. h (p. 300)
6. c (p. 300)
7. e (p. 294)
8. b (p. 294)
9. f (p. 295)
10. a (p. 292)

CHALLENGE TEST

1. c. is the answer. (p. 291)

   a. & b. Each of these games involves skills that are the hardest for schoolchildren to master.

   d. Because one-on-one sports are likely to accentuate individual differences in ability, they may be especially discouraging to some children.
2. c. is the answer. (p. 287)
3. c. is the answer. (p. 296)

   a. & b. Jack's difficulty is in concentrating, not in reading (dyslexia) or math (dyscalcula).

   d. ADHD is characterized by excitability and disruptive behavior, neither of which describes Jack.
4. c. is the answer. (p. 286)

   a., b., & d. Among Americans, those of African descent tend to mature more quickly than those of European descent, who, in turn, tend to be maturationally ahead of those with Asian ancestors.
5. d. is the answer. (p. 296)
6. d. is the answer. (p. 287)
7. d. is the answer. (p. 291)
8. a. is the answer. (p. 287)

   b., c., & d. Obese children are no more likely to be dyslexic, physically intimidating, or hyperactive than other children.
9. d. is the answer. (p. 294)
10. c. is the answer. (p. 289)

    a. This type of diet is less likely to promote obesity than one that is high in fat.

    b. The diet of families who are *below* the poverty line tends to be high in fat, and therefore more likely to promote obesity.
11. c. is the answer. At the time she took the test, Angela's chronological age was 8. Knowing that her IQ was 125, solving the equation for mental age yields a value of 10. (pp. 294–295)
12. c. is the answer. (p. 286)
13. c. is the answer. (p. 297)
14. d. is the answer. Physiological problems account for less than 1 percent of all cases of childhood obesity. (p. 290)
15. c. is the answer. (pp. 289–290)

KEY TERMS

1. Experts define **obesity** as body weight that is more than 20 percent greater than average for one's age, sex, and body size. (p. 286)
2. **Reaction time** is the length of time it takes a person to respond to a particular stimulus. (p. 291)
3. A **learning disability** is a difficulty in a particular subject that is not attributable to an overall intellectual slowness, a physical handicap, or a lack of basic education. (p. 292)
4. **Dyslexia** is a learning disability in reading. (p. 293)
5. **Dyscalcula** is a learning disability in math. (p. 293)
6. **Achievement tests** are tests that measure what a child has already learned in a particular academic subject or subjects. (p. 294)
7. **Aptitude tests** are designed to measure how well and how quickly a person could learn a new subject if given the chance. (p. 294)

8. **Homogeneous grouping** is the grouping of children with various learning abilities, or disabilities, into separate classrooms. (p. 295)
9. The **attention-deficit disorder (ADD)** is a general learning disability that is not manifest in a particular academic skill but instead makes it difficult for the individual to concentrate for more than a few moments. (p. 296)
10. The **attention-deficit hyperactivity disorder (ADHD)** is a general learning disability in which the individual has great difficulty concentrating and is excessively excitable, easily frustrated, impulsive, and quick-tempered. (p. 296)
11. **Provocation ecologies** are unusually rigid or freewheeling classroom environments that tend to increase ADHD behaviors. (p. 300)
12. **Rarefaction ecologies** are classroom environments that are more flexible than provocation ecologies, yet provide enough structure to reduce ADHD behaviors. (p. 300)

CHAPTER 12 The School Years: Cognitive Development

Chapter Overview

Chapter 12 looks at the development of cognitive abilities in children from age 7 to 11. The first section discusses the Piagetian approach, which describes the growth of logical and reasoning abilities during middle childhood. The second section explores the information-processing perspective, which focuses on changes in the child's selective attention, memory skills, processing capacity, knowledge base, and problem-solving strategies.

The following section looks at language learning in the school years. During this time, children develop a more analytic understanding of words and show a marked improvement in pragmatic skills, such as changing from one form of speech to another when the situation so demands. The educational and social challenges facing children who use nonstandard English, as well as those who are taught in a language other than their native tongue, are discussed. A Research Report examines educational and environmental conditions that are conducive to fluency in a second language.

The final section describes innovative new teaching methods, which emphasize active rather than passive learning and are derived from the developmental theories of Piaget, Vygotsky, and others. Studies that contrast these methods with more traditional methods have shown their effectiveness in reading and math education. The chapter concludes with a cross-cultural comparison of education in the United States, Japan, and the Republic of China.

NOTE: Answer guidelines for all Chapter 12 questions begin on page 182.

Guided Study

The text chapter should be studied one section at a time. Before you read, preview each section by skimming it, noting headings and boldface items. Then read the appropriate section objectives from the following outline. Keep these objectives in mind and, as you read the chapter section, search for the information that will enable you to meet each objective. Once you have finished a section, write out answers for its objectives.

Concrete Operational Thought (pp. 304–308)

1. Identify and discuss the logical operations of concrete operational thought and give examples of how these operations are demonstrated by schoolchildren.

2. Discuss two recent modifications of Piaget's theory and three of his ideas that continue to provide valuable insight into the thinking of children during the school years.

The Information-Processing Perspective (pp. 308–313)

3. Discuss the information-processing perspective on cognitive development during the school years, focusing on children's advances in selective attention, memory skills, and processing capacity.

4. Discuss the contributions of advances in knowledge and metacognition to cognitive development during the school years.

Language (pp. 313–321)

5. Describe language development during the school years, noting changing abilities in vocabulary, grammar, and pragmatics.

6. Explain code-switching and discuss the academic and social challenges facing children whose primary language is a nonstandard form.

7. (Research Report) Identify several conditions that foster the learning of a second language and describe the best approaches to bilingual education.

Thinking, Learning, and Schooling (pp. 322–328)

8. Discuss historical and cultural variations in the schooling of children and explain why such variations have recently become troubling.

9. Discuss the influences of Piaget, the information-processing perspective, and Vygotsky on classroom education.

10. Compare the academic performance of children in Japan, the Republic of China, and the United States and identify differences in school and home life that may account for differences in academic performance.

Chapter Review

When you have finished reading the chapter, work through the material that follows to review it. Complete the sentences and answer the questions. As you proceed, evaluate your performance for each section by consulting the answers on page 182. Do not continue with the next section until you understand each answer. If you need to, review or reread the appropriate section in the textbook before continuing.

Concrete Operational Thought (pp. 304–308)

1. According to Piaget, between ages 7 and 11 children are in the stage of ____________________ ____________________. One reason children develop the ability to understand logical principles is that they become increasingly able to ____________________, that is, to move away from a perceptual focusing on one aspect of a problem.

2. During this stage children ____________________ (are/are not) able to reverse their thinking while solving problems. A limitation of thinking during this stage is that reasoning about ____________________ is not yet possible.

3. True concrete operational thinking is preceded by a transitional period called the ____________________-____________________-____________________ ____________________.

4. The logical operation ____________________ is the idea that an object's content remains the same despite changes in its appearance. ____________________ is the idea that a transformation process can be reversed to restore the original condition. ____________________ is the idea that a transformation in one dimension is compensated for by one in another.

5. According to Piaget, once these operations are mastered they ____________________ (can/cannot) be generalized to other contexts.

6. The concept that objects can be organized in terms of categories is called ____________________. The idea that a particular object may belong to more than one class is called ____________________ ____________________.

7. The arrangement of items in a series, as from shortest to longest, is referred to as ____________________.

8. Many concrete operations underlie the basic ideas of elementary-school ____________________ and ____________________.

9. Many recent studies have found that cognitive development is ____________________ (less/more) heterogeneous than Piaget's descriptions would suggest. Two of the factors that may account for this are ____________________ differences among individuals in their abilities and aptitudes, and ____________________ differences in cultural, educational, and experiential background.

10. Many researchers believe that children begin to demonstrate concrete operational thought ____________________ (earlier/later) than Piaget predicted.

11. In most aspects, Piaget's view of children's cognitive development is considered ____________________ (correct/incorrect).

Identify three Piagetian ideas regarding cognitive development during the school years that are widely accepted.

12. Piaget's theories provided the theoretical framework for the classroom format called ____________________ ____________________, which encourages individualized learning by discovery, discussion, and deduction.

The Information-Processing Perspective (pp. 308–313)

13. Developmental researchers who apply the ____________________-____________________ perspective think of the mind as being like a computer which analyzes, stores, and retrieves information.

14. The ability to use ____________________ ____________________—to screen out distractors and concentrate on relevant information—improves steadily during the school years.

15. During middle childhood, children's use of ____________________ ____________________ for retaining new information broadens significantly. For example, they begin to use ____________________ to repeat information to be remembered and ____________________ to improve the memorability of material through regrouping. Children's use of ____________________ ____________________ to access previously learned information also improves.

16. Taken together, storage strategies and retrieval strategies are called ____________________.

17. Children in the school years are better learners and problem-solvers than younger children because they have a broader range of ____________________, and they have a larger ____________________ ____________________.

18. Most theorists attribute the expansion of processing capacity to children's more efficient use of their ____________________ memory. Processing capacity also becomes more efficient through ____________________, as familiar mental activities become routine.

19. With enhanced processing capacity in middle childhood, the preschool cognitive tendencies of ____________________ and ____________________ diminish because children can keep in mind multiple viewpoints at one time.

20. Research suggests that adults ____________________ (are/are not) always more cognitively competent than children, and that many differences between schoolchildren's and adult's memory and reasoning may be due to the children's limited ____________________ about topics.

21. The ability to evaluate a cognitive task to determine what to do—and to monitor one's performance—is called ____________________.

List some indicators of this developmental change during the school years.

22. Children benefit from educational practices that not only impart knowledge but also foster ____________________ ____________________.

23. One shortcoming of the information-processing perspective is that it has failed to show how children ____________________.

Language (pp. 313–321)

24. During middle childhood language development is much more ____________________ (subtle/obvious) than in the preschool years. Children become more ____________________ and ____________________ in their processing of vocabulary and are better able to define words by analyzing their ____________________ to other words.

25. Although most grammatical constructions of the child's native language are mastered before age ____________________, knowledge of ____________________ continues to develop throughout elementary school.

26. Children younger than 6 often have trouble understanding the ____________________ voice in grammar. In addition to improved understanding of this voice, school-age children begin to understand other grammatical constructions, such as the correct use of ____________________, the ____________________, and ____________________.

27. Children's use of pragmatics ____________________ (improves/does not improve) significantly during the school years. A clear demonstration is

found in schoolchildren's ________________-________________, which is beyond the ability of most preschool children. Other examples are found in their developing ability to ask a(n) ________________ and to learn various forms of ________________ ________________.

28. Changing from one form of speech to another is called ________________-________________. The ________________ ________________, which children use in situations such as the classroom, is characterized by extensive ________________, complex ________________, and lengthy ________________. With their friends, children tend to use the ________________ ________________, which has a more limited use of vocabulary and syntax and relies more on ________________ and ________________ to convey meaning.

29. Compared with the elaborated code, which is context-________________ (free/bound), the restricted code is context-________________ (free/bound). While adults often stress the importance of mastery of the elaborated code, the restricted code is also important in helping the child develop ________________ skills.

30. Language differences are likely to form a distinct code in groups that are ________________, ________________ ________________, and ________________ distinct. In the United States, the distinctive pattern most frequently studied is called ________________ ________________, which has linguistic roots from ________________ and the antebellum South. Dialects such as this are most properly considered ________________ (ungrammatical/a legitimate grammatical variation).

31. The best path for a child whose primary language is a nonstandard form is to ________________ (learn standard English as a distinct code/suppress the use of nonstandard English).

Describe some of the academic and social difficulties facing a child whose primary language is a nonstandard form.

32. Most of the citizens of the world ________________ (are/are not) bilingual. Cognitively and linguistically, it is a(n) ________________ (advantage/disadvantage) for children to learn more than one language. Specifically, it may enhance children's grasp of ________________ ________________ and ________________.

33. The approach to bilingual education in which the child's instruction occurs entirely in the second language is called ________________. These programs seem to work best with ________________ (younger/older) children.

34. (Research Report) One critical difference between success and failure of these programs was whether or not the children had ample opportunity to ________________ in the new language. Research has found that ________________ (one-on-one/large-group) instruction is most effective in promoting fluency in a second language.

Identify several conditions that promote the learning of a second language.

35. (Research Report) In the United States, most non-English-speaking children are placed in ____________ (standard English classes/special language immersion classes).

36. (Research Report) One reason non-English-speaking children often repeat grades and fail to graduate from high school is ____________ ____________.

Thinking, Learning, and Schooling (pp. 322–328)

37. There ____________ (is/is not) universal agreement on how best to educate schoolchildren.

38. Historically, ____________ (boys/girls) and wealthier children have been most likely to be formally taught, and to have the greatest educational demands placed upon them.

39. Schools vary extensively in the ____________ offered and the ____________ ____________ used.

40. Achievement scores show that American children are ____________ (ahead of/behind) their counterparts in other industrialized countries, especially in the subjects of ____________ and ____________.

41. Passive learning ____________ (is/is not) the most appropriate form of instruction for most schoolchildren.

42. The information-processing perspective has led to a reemphasis on ____________ ____________ and the realization that there ____________ (is/is not) a standard curriculum that should be taught to everyone in a given grade.

43. Teaching that is based on Vygotsky's perspective emphasizes the importance of ____________ ____________ in learning. A recent study found that children taught according to this model had ____________ (higher/lower) reading achievement scores than those taught by more traditional methods.

44. A new approach in math replaces rote learning with ____________-____________ materials, active discussion, and a problem-solving approach. The traditional approach to math education focuses on teaching ____________ ____________ rather than the ____________ ____________.

45. Achievement tests today demonstrate that children from three countries, ____________ ____________, have the highest scores. An early explanation of this superiority was ____________. Later research attributes this superiority to ____________ ____________.

Give several examples of how schooling in the United States differs from that in Japan and the Republic of China.

46. Compared to American parents, parents in Japan and China tend to be ____________ (more/less) involved in their children's education.

47. Values in the macrosystem are highly influential as well. As compared to ____________ (American/Japanese) teachers, ____________ (American/Japanese) teachers are greatly esteemed and receive a proportionately ____________ (higher/lower) salary.

Progress Test 1

Multiple-Choice Questions

Circle your answers to the following questions and check them with the answers on page 183. If your answer is incorrect, read the explanation for why it is incorrect and then consult the appropriate pages of the text (in parentheses following the correct answer).

1. According to Piaget, the stage of cognitive development in which a person understands specific logical ideas and can apply them to concrete problems is called:
   a. preoperational thought.
   b. operational thought.
   c. concrete operational thought.
   d. formal operational thought.

2. During the school years, children overcome the tendency to think about one idea at a time to the exclusion of other ideas; that is, they increasingly are able to:
   a. decenter.
   b. center their thinking.
   c. selectively attend to stimuli.
   d. use pragmatics in their reasoning.

3. The idea that an object that has been transformed in some way can be restored to its original form is:
   a. identity.
   b. reversibility.
   c. seriation.
   d. classification.

4. Regarding cognitive development in the school years, the most important idea contributed by information-processing theory is that:
   a. the child's mind becomes more like a computer as he or she matures.
   b. children learn to think more strategically and efficiently during the school years.
   c. most mental activities become automatic by the time a child is about 13 years old.
   d. the major improvements in reasoning that occur during the school years involve increased long-term memory capacity.

5. The ability to filter out distractions and concentrate on relevant details is called:
   a. metacognition.
   b. information processing.
   c. selective attention.
   d. decentering.

6. The best example of a retrieval strategy is:
   a. reconstructing a lecture from notes.
   b. organizing terms to be learned in categories.
   c. studying in an environment that is free of distractions.
   d. repeating a multiplication table until it is automatic.

7. A term that refers to the ability to monitor one's cognitive performance—to think about thinking—is:
   a. pragmatics.
   b. information processing.
   c. selective attention.
   d. metacognition.

8. During middle childhood, children become more analytic and logical in their understanding of words. This means that they:
   a. learn more words per year than they did during the play years.
   b. can first learn Black English or a second language.
   c. are less bound by context, appearance, and personal experience.
   d. no longer engage in verbal play.

9. Black English, which has its roots in African linguistic patterns, is:
   a. not a valid means of communication.
   b. best learned after the 5-to-7 shift.
   c. consistent in its grammatical rules.
   d. frequently employed in diplomatic communications.

10. A form of speech used in formal situations—for example, when speaking to teachers—that is characterized by complex vocabulary and lengthy sentences is the:
    a. restricted code.
    b. elaborated code.
    c. pragmatic code.
    d. grammatical code.

11. To encourage competence in standard English without damaging a child's self-esteem, teachers should:
    a. accept Black English and other nonstandard speech as legitimate in all school contexts.
    b. reinforce the idea that all nonstandard English is incorrect.
    c. allow children to select their own form of expression.
    d. help children with the pragmatics of code-switching between standard and nonstandard English.

12. The educational emphasis on the importance of social interaction in the classroom is most directly derived from the developmental theory of:
    a. Vygotsky.
    b. Piaget.
    c. information processing.
    d. those who advocate immersion learning.

13. Critics of Piaget contend that:
    a. cognitive development is more homogeneous than Piaget predicted.
    b. children's progress through the cognitive stages is more even than Piaget thought.
    c. children demonstrate partial entrance into concrete operational thought earlier than Piaget predicted.
    d. individual differences in progress through the cognitive stages are minimal.

14. Historically, boys and wealthier children were much more likely to be formally taught and to have greater educational demands placed upon them than girls or poor children. Today, this inequality:
    a. can be found only in developing countries.
    b. has largely disappeared.
    c. persists, even in developed countries.
    d. has been eliminated for girls, but not for poor children.

15. To what do cross-cultural researchers attribute the superior achievement test scores of Pacific-rim students?
    a. genetics
    b. the high quality of home and classroom educational experiences
    c. a shorter school day and year
    d. classroom environments that emphasize passive learning

True or False Items

Write *true* or *false* on the line in front of each statement.

_______ 1. One major objection to Piagetian theory is that it describes the schoolchild as an active learner, a term appropriate only for preschoolers.

_______ 2. Some cognitive researchers find that many children begin to master concrete operational thought earlier than Piaget predicted.

_______ 3. In general, the findings of information-processing theorists refute Piaget's observations of cognitive growth and development in the school years.

_______ 4. Most common grammatical constructions cannot be mastered by children until they have made the 5-to-7 shift.

_______ 5. The process of asking a riddle or telling a joke involves pragmatic language skills usually not mastered before age 7.

_______ 6. Code-switching, especially the occasional use of slang, is a behavior characteristic primarily of children in the lower social strata.

_______ 7. American parents are more likely than Japanese parents to be dissatisfied with their children's academic performance.

_______ 8. (Research Report) During the early school years, children learn a second language best if they have not already achieved proficiency in their native language.

_______ 9. Most developmentalists agree that there should be a standard curriculum for all children in a given grade.

_______ 10. New standards of math education in many nations emphasize problem-solving skills rather than simple memorization of formulas.

Progress Test 2

Progress Test 2 should be completed during a final chapter review. Answer the following questions after you thoroughly understand the correct answers for the Chapter Review and Progress Test 1.

Multiple-Choice Questions

1. According to Piaget, 8- and 9-year-olds can reason only about concrete things in their lives. "Concrete" means:
    a. logical.
    b. abstract.
    c. tangible or specific.
    d. mathematical or classifiable.

2. The transitional period during which the young child begins to master concrete operational thought is sometimes referred to as:
    a. the age of reason.
    b. the 5-to-7 shift.
    c. code-switching.
    d. metacognitive transition.

3. The concept that objects can be arranged in a series, for example, from shortest to tallest, is:
    a. classification.
    b. reversibility.
    c. seriation.
    d. identity.

4. According to Piaget, when the logical operations of identity, seriation, and reversibility have been mastered:
    a. they can be generalized to new contexts.
    b. children begin to think abstractly.
    c. centered thinking becomes possible for the first time.
    d. all of the above occur.

5. Class inclusion refers to the idea that:
   a. the identity of objects remains constant, despite changes in appearance.
   b. objects can be organized in terms of categories.
   c. a particular object or person may belong to more than one category.
   d. objects can be classified in nonhierarchical ways.

6. The logical operations of concrete operational thought are particularly important to an understanding of the basic ideas of elementary-school:
   a. spelling.
   b. reading.
   c. math and science.
   d. social studies.

7. One mnemonic technique that develops toward the end of middle childhood is the regrouping of items to be remembered into categories. This technique is called:
   a. metacognition.
   b. selective attention.
   c. rehearsal.
   d. organization.

8. Which of the following is *not* a Piagetian idea that is widely accepted by contemporary developmentalists?
   a. The thinking of school-age children is characterized by a more comprehensive logic than that of preschoolers.
   b. Children are active learners.
   c. How children think is as important as what they know.
   d. Once a certain type of reasoning ability emerges in children, it is evenly apparent in all domains of thinking.

9. Processing capacity refers to:
   a. the ability to selectively attend to more than one thought.
   b. the amount of information that a person is able to hold in working memory.
   c. the size of the child's knowledge base.
   d. all of the above.

10. Procedures for retaining new information are called:
    a. retrieval strategies.
    b. storage strategies.
    c. mnemonics.
    d. metacognition.

11. A form of speech children use among themselves in informal situations that includes slang, shared understandings, and meaningful gestures is the:
    a. elaborated code.
    b. grammatical code.
    c. restricted code.
    d. open code.

12. (Research Report) When a new language is simultaneously used for instruction in reading, writing, and math, second-language learning is fostered by:
    a. instruction based on bilingual-bicultural education.
    b. instruction that completely immerses the student in the new language.
    c. instruction that focuses on rote memorization of grammatical rules.
    d. group instruction.

13. Research on metacognition shows that school-age children learn problem-solving best when they are:
    a. shown the correct answer to the problem.
    b. shown the specific shortcomings in their strategies.
    c. criticized for an incorrect answer, then told to try again.
    d. left to work the problem on their own.

14. A new approach to math education focuses on:
    a. rote memorization of formulas before problems are introduced.
    b. "hands-on" materials and active discussion of concepts.
    c. one-on-one tutorials.
    d. pretesting children and grouping them by ability.

15. Regarding bilingual education, many contemporary developmentalists believe that:
    a. the attempted learning of two languages is confusing to children and delays proficiency in either individual language.
    b. bilingual education is linguistically, culturally, and cognitively advantageous to children.
    c. second-language education is most effective when the child has not yet mastered the native language.
    d. bilingual education programs are too expensive to justify the few developmental advantages they confer.

Matching Items

Match each term or concept with its corresponding description or definition.

Terms or Concepts

_______ 1. decenter
_______ 2. reversibility
_______ 3. reciprocity
_______ 4. classification
_______ 5. information processing
_______ 6. selective attention
_______ 7. retrieval strategies
_______ 8. mnemonics
_______ 9. metacognition
_______ 10. immersion

Descriptions or Definitions

a. the ability to screen out distractors and concentrate on relevant information
b. the idea that a transformation process can be undone to restore the original conditions
c. reasoning that moves away from an intuitive, perceptual focusing on one aspect of a problem
d. developmental perspective that conceives of the mind as being like a computer
e. the idea that a transformation in one dimension is compensated for by a transformation in another
f. educational technique in which instruction occurs entirely in the second language
g. procedures to access previously learned information
h. memory aids
i. the concept that objects can be organized in terms of categories
j. the ability to evaluate a cognitive task and to monitor one's performance on it

Challenge Test

Answer these questions the day before an exam as a final check on your understanding of the chapter's terms and concepts.

1. When a child understands that her cousin is also her grandmother's grandchild, she has probably mastered the concept of:
   a. reciprocity.
   b. class inclusion.
   c. seriation.
   d. conservation.

2. A child's game that involves the arrangement of a group of figures from shortest to tallest requires the child to have mastered the concept of:
   a. identity.
   b. reciprocity.
   c. seriation.
   d. classification.

3. A 3-year-old can recite the numbers from 1 to 7. This probably demonstrates something about his:
   a. memory capacity.
   b. mastery of the concept of seriation.
   c. mastery of the concept of classification.
   d. mastery of the concept of reciprocity.

4. A grasp of the concept of classification is most necessary for understanding:
   a. place value in mathematics.
   b. conservation.
   c. mnemonic techniques.
   d. decentering.

5. When psychologists look at the ability of children to receive, store, and organize information, they are examining cognitive development from a view based on:
   a. the observations of Piaget.
   b. information processing.
   c. learning theory.
   d. the idea that the key to thinking is the sensory register.

6. A child's ability to tell a joke that will amuse his or her audience always depends on:
   a. the child's mastery of seriation and reversibility.
   b. code-switching.
   c. the child's ability to consider another's perspective.
   d. an expansion of the child's processing capacity.

7. For a 10-year-old, some mental activities have become so familiar or routine as to require little mental work. This development is called:
   a. selective attention.
   b. mnemonics.
   c. metacognition.
   d. automatization.

8. A child who sings "i before e except after c" is using a memory-aiding device called:
   a. rehearsal.
   b. automatization.
   c. a mnemonic.
   d. class inclusion.

9. (Research Report) The existence or effectiveness of bilingual education may be limited because:
   a. it is expensive.
   b. trained teachers are scarce.
   c. parents and the community do not always support it.
   d. of all of the above reasons.

10. A 9-year-old is typically less stubborn in clinging to grammatical mistakes than a 4-year-old because the 9-year-old:
    a. has mastered the concept of conservation.
    b. is less egocentric in making and applying rules.
    c. has more experience in humor and joke-telling.
    d. understands the subjunctive.

11. Russian-speaking children do not master the subjunctive very much earlier than English-speaking children, even though the subjunctive is less complicated in Russian. The reason for this is that:
    a. cultural patterns make the subjunctive more difficult for Russian children to grasp.
    b. mastery of the subjunctive requires a particular level of cognitive development.
    c. the use of the subjunctive in Russian is very rare.
    d. Russian children score lower on language aptitude tests.

12. A second-grader says, "I don't know nothing about nothing." The teacher corrects the child because his double negative is:
    a. unacceptable in a school with primarily middle-class students.
    b. illogical and confused.
    c. incorrect in standard English.
    d. incorrect in Black English.

13. Compared with her mother, who attended elementary school in the 1950s, Bettina, who is now in the third grade, is likely to be in a class that places greater emphasis on:
    a. individualized learning.
    b. active learning.
    c. learning by discovery, discussion, and deduction.
    d. all of the above.

14. Piaget would be most likely to *disagree* with which of the following statements?
    a. "How children think is as important as what they know."
    b. "Children learn best through discovery, discussion, and deduction."
    c. "Decentered thinking is a prerequisite for logical reasoning."
    d. "Individualized learning slows both cognitive and social development."

15. Concluding her class presentation on differences between the educational experiences of Japanese and American children, Nogumi states that:
    a. Japanese children devote more time to nonacademic activities than American children.
    b. American children spend less time in school than Japanese children.
    c. Japanese children appear to be less happy and less responsive in the classroom than American children.
    d. Japanese teachers are more likely to employ individual, as opposed to group, instruction.

Key Terms

Using your own words, write a brief definition or explanation of each of the following terms on a separate piece of paper.

1. concrete operational thought
2. decenter
3. 5-to-7 shift
4. identity
5. reversibility
6. reciprocity
7. classification
8. class inclusion
9. seriation
10. information-processing
11. selective attention

12. storage strategies
13. rehearsal
14. organization
15. retrieval strategies
16. mnemonics
17. processing capacity
18. metacognition
19. code-switching
20. elaborated code
21. restricted code
22. Black English
23. immersion

ANSWERS

CHAPTER REVIEW

1. concrete operations; decenter
2. are; abstractions
3. 5-to-7 shift
4. identity; Reversibility; Reciprocity
5. can
6. classification; class inclusion
7. seriation
8. math; science
9. more; hereditary; environmental
10. earlier
11. correct

(a) Compared with the thinking of the preschool child, that of the school-age child is characterized by a more comprehensive logic and broader grasp of the underlying principles of rational thought; (b) children are active learners; and (c) how children think is as important as what they know.

12. open education
13. information-processing
14. selective attention
15. storage strategies; rehearsal; organization; retrieval strategies
16. mnemonics
17. mnemonics; processing capacity
18. working; automatization
19. centration; egocentrism
20. are not; knowledge
21. metacognition

School-age children's better use of selective attention, mnemonics, and other cognitive strategies all derive from metacognitive growth. Furthermore, they know how to identify challenging tasks and devote greater effort to them; are more likely to spontaneously monitor and evaluate their progress than are preschoolers; and are more likely to use external aids to enhance memorization and problem-solving.

22. cognitive strategies
23. develop as coherent, integrated thinkers
24. subtle; analytic; logical; relationships
25. 6; syntax
26. passive; comparatives; subjunctive; metaphors
27. improves; joke-telling; riddle; polite speech
28. code-switching; elaborated code; vocabulary; syntax; sentences; restricted code; gestures; intonation
29. free; bound; pragmatic
30. cohesive; geographically isolated; culturally; Black English; Africa; a legitimate grammatical variation
31. learn standard English as a distinct code

Such children may be teased by classmates for their unusual speech and have greater difficulty learning to read and write standard English. If the teacher and school take the stance that nonstandard English is illegitimate, children may experience a loss of self-esteem and be troubled by this attack on their cultural identity.

32. are; advantage; linguistic rules; concepts
33. immersion; younger
34. converse; one-on-one

Bilingual programs tend to work best (a) if they are specifically designed for language learning, with skilled bilingual teachers; (b) when the child already has a mastery of the native language and wants to learn the new language; (c) when the language to be learned and the native language are both valued by the child's culture; and (d) when the parents and the community are supportive of the program.

35. standard English classes
36. poor language instruction and the limited expectations parents, teachers, and the children themselves hold for their achievement
37. is not
38. boys
39. curriculum; pedagogical techniques
40. behind; math; science
41. is not

42. explicit instruction; is not
43. social interaction; higher
44. hands-on; specific formulas; underlying concepts
45. Japan, Korea, the Republic of China; genetic; educational experiences in the school and home

Japanese and Chinese children are in school more hours weekly than American children are. They also are more likely to attend supplemental classes at private schools and to have more of their classroom time devoted to academic activities. Teachers in Japan and the Republic of China tend to emphasize group instruction, while American teachers emphasize individual or small-group instruction.

46. more
47. American; Japanese; higher

PROGRESS TEST 1

Multiple-Choice Questions

1. **c.** is the answer. (p. 304)

   a. Preoperational thought is "pre-logical" thinking.

   b. There is no such stage in Piaget's theory.

   d. Formal operational thought extends logical reasoning to abstractions.

2. **a.** is the answer. (p. 304)

   b. Centered thinking *is* the tendency to think about one idea at a time.

   c. & d. Although selective attention and pragmatic skills improve during the school years, this question describes decentering.

3. **b.** is the answer. (p. 305)

   a. This is the concept that an object remains the same despite changes in its appearance.

   c. This refers to the arrangement of items in a series, as from shortest to longest.

   d. This is the concept that objects can be organized in terms of categories.

4. **b.** is the answer. (p. 308)

   a. Information-processing theorists use the mind-computer metaphor at every age.

   c. Although increasing automatization is an important aspect of development, the information-processing perspective does not suggest that most mental activities become automatic by age 13.

   d. Most of the important changes in reasoning that occur during the school years are due to the improved processing capacity of the person's *working memory.*

5. **c.** is the answer. (p. 309)

   a. This is the ability to evaluate a cognitive task and to monitor one's performance on it.

   b. Information processing is a perspective on cognitive development that focuses on how the mind analyzes, stores, retrieves, and reasons about information.

   d. Decentering refers to the school-age child's ability to consider more than one aspect of a problem simultaneously.

6. **a.** is the answer. (p. 310)

   b. & d. These are examples of storage strategies.

   c. This is a good idea, but it is not a retrieval strategy.

7. **d.** is the answer. (p. 312)

   a. Pragmatics refers to the practical use of language to communicate with others.

   b. The information-processing perspective views the mind as being like a computer.

   c. This is the ability to screen out distractors in order to focus on important information.

8. **c.** is the answer. (p. 313)

   a. Vocabulary development is more subtle during the school years than the preschool years.

   b. The learning of a second language does *not* depend on these linguistic advances.

   d. Verbal play, such as joke-telling and riddle-asking, most certainly does *not* decrease during the school years.

9. **c.** is the answer. (p. 318)

   a. Black English is used as an effective method of communication by many young African-Americans.

   b. Like all languages, most grammatical constructions in Black English are mastered before age 6.

   d. It is likely that the more formal elaborated code would be used in diplomatic communications.

10. **b.** is the answer. (p. 317)

    a. This less formal type of speech is more often used with friends.

    c. & d. No such codes were discussed.

11. **d.** is the answer. (p. 318)

    a. & c. These would be impractical; furthermore, children need to learn standard English in order to further their own academic development.

    b. This would be a blow to the child's cultural identity and self-esteem.

12. **a.** is the answer. (p. 324)

13. **c.** is the answer. (p. 307)

    a., b., & d. Just the opposite is true.

14. c. is the answer. (p. 322)
15. b. is the answer. (p. 326)

True or False Items

1. F Most educators agree that the school-age child, like the preschooler, is an active learner. (p. 308)
2. T (p. 307)
3. F The findings of information-processing theorists help explain some of the changes Piaget observed. For example, their findings on the expansion of working memory shed light on the growing ability of the school-age child to take multiple perspectives, and consequently to be less egocentric in his or her thinking. (p. 308)
4. F Most grammatical constructions are mastered before age 6. (p. 314)
5. T (pp. 315–316)
6. F Code-switching (including occasional use of slang) is a behavior demonstrated by all children. (pp. 316–317)
7. F Although the academic performance of American children lags behind that of Japanese children, American parents are more likely than Japanese (or Chinese) parents to express satisfaction with their children's academic performance. (p. 327)
8. F Children seem to learn a second language best when they have already achieved proficiency in their native language. (p. 320)
9. F The complexity of the learning process, as described by information-processing researchers, indicates that there is no basic curriculum that teachers of a given grade should be able to transmit wholesale to everyone. (p. 327)
10. T (pp. 324–325)

PROGRESS TEST 2

Multiple-Choice Questions

1. c. is the answer. (p. 304)
2. b. is the answer. (p. 304)
3. c. is the answer. (p. 306)
   a. Classification is the concept that objects can be organized in terms of categories, or classes.
   b. Reversibility is the idea that a transformation process can be reversed to restore the original conditions.
   d. Identity is the logical concept that an object's content remains the same despite changes in its appearance.
4. a. is the answer. (p. 305)
   b. Abstract thinking depends on cognitive developments that go beyond the child's ability to apply these operations to concrete circumstances.
   c. The emergence of *de*centered thinking makes an understanding of these logical operations possible.
5. c. is the answer. (p. 305)
   a. This describes identity.
   b. This describes classification.
   d. This is true, but does not define class inclusion.
6. c. is the answer. (p. 306)
7. d. is the answer. (p. 309)
   a. This is the ability to evaluate a cognitive task and to monitor one's performance on it.
   b. This is the ability to screen out distractors and focus on important information.
   c. This is the repeating of information in order to remember it.
8. d. is the answer. (p. 307)
9. b. is the answer. (p. 310)
10. b. is the answer. (p. 309)
    a. These are strategies for *accessing* already learned information.
    c. Mnemonics include both storage and retrieval strategies.
    d. This is the ability to evaluate a task and to monitor one's performance on it.
11. c. is the answer. (p. 317)
    a. This is a type of speech used in the classroom and other more formal situations.
    b. & d. No such codes were discussed.
12. a. is the answer. (p. 320)
13. b. is the answer. (p. 312)
14. b. is the answer. (p. 324)
15. b. is the answer. (p. 319)

Matching Items

1. c (p. 304)	5. d (p. 308)	8. h (p. 310)
2. b (p. 305)	6. a (p. 309)	9. j (p. 312)
3. e (p. 305)	7. g (p. 310)	10. f (p. 319)
4. i (p. 305)		

CHALLENGE TEST

1. b. is the answer. Class inclusion is the concept that an object or person can belong to more than one category—in this case, the categories "cousin" and "grandchild." (p. 305)

2. **c.** is the answer. (p. 306)

   a. This is the concept that the content of an object does not change with changes in its appearance.

   b. This is the understanding that changes in one dimension of an object are compensated for by changes in another dimension.

   d. This is the concept that objects can be grouped by categories.

3. **a.** is the answer. (pp. 309–310)

   b., c., & d. These logical operations are not understood until after the 5-to-7 shift.

4. **a.** is the answer. Mathematical place values, such as "ones," "tens," and so forth, correspond to distinct numerical classes. (p. 306)

5. **b.** is the answer. (p. 308)

6. **c.** is the answer. Joke-telling is one of the clearest demonstrations of schoolchildren's improved pragmatic skills, including the ability to know what someone else will think is funny. (p. 315)

7. **d.** is the answer. (p. 310)

   a. Selective attention is the ability to focus on important information and screen out distractors.

   b. Mnemonics are memory aids.

   c. Metacognition is the ability to evaluate a task and to monitor one's performance on it.

8. **c.** is the answer. (p. 310)

   a. Rehearsal is the repetition of to-be-learned information.

   b. Automatization refers to the tendency of well-rehearsed mental activities to become routine and automatic.

   d. Class inclusion is the idea that a particular object may belong to more than one class.

9. **d.** is the answer. (p. 320)

10. **b.** is the answer. (p. 315)

11. **b.** is the answer. (pp. 314–315)

12. **c.** is the answer. (pp. 317–318)

13. **d.** is the answer. (p. 324)

14. **d.** is the answer. Educational programs derived from Piaget's theory *encourage* individualized learning. (p. 308)

15. **b.** is the answer. (p. 326)

    a. & d. In fact, just the opposite is true.

    c. This is untrue.

KEY TERMS

1. During the stage of **concrete operational thought**, lasting from ages 7 to 11, children can think logically about events and objects but are not able to reason abstractly. (p. 304)

2. Schoolchildren are increasingly able to **decenter**, which means they are able to think more objectively and consider more than a single feature of an object or situation. (p. 304)

3. In Piaget's theory, the **5-to-7 shift** is a transitional period in which children have outgrown preoperational thinking but have not yet attained concrete operational thought. (p. 304)

4. **Identity** is the logical principle that an object's content remains the same despite changes in its appearance. (p. 305)

5. **Reversibility** is the principle that a transformation process can be reversed to restore the original conditions. (p. 305)

6. **Reciprocity** is the idea that a transformation in one dimension of an object is compensated for by a transformation in another. (p. 305)

   Example: A child who understands **reciprocity** realizes that rolling a ball of clay into a thin rope makes it longer, but also skinnier, than its original shape.

7. **Classification** is the logical concept that objects can be organized in terms of categories, or classes. (p. 305)

8. **Class inclusion** is the concept that a particular object or person may belong to more than one class. (p. 305)

9. **Seriation** refers to the arrangement of items in a series, such as from shortest to longest, or lightest to darkest. (p. 306)

10. **Information-processing** theorists think of the mind as being like a computer and are interested in the processes through which the mind analyzes, stores, and retrieves information. (p. 308)

11. **Selective attention** is the ability to screen out distractors and concentrate on relevant information. (p. 309)

12. **Storage strategies** are procedures for retaining new information. (p. 309)

13. **Rehearsal** is the repeating of information to be remembered. (p. 309)

14. **Organization** is the regrouping of information to make it easier to remember. (p. 309)

15. **Retrieval strategies** are procedures to access previously learned information. (p. 310)

16. **Mnemonics** are storage and retrieval strategies used to aid memory. (p. 310)

17. **Processing capacity** refers to the amount of information that can be held in working memory, where reasoning and thinking occur. (p. 310)
18. **Metacognition** is the ability to evaluate a cognitive task to determine what to do, and to monitor one's performance on that task. (p. 312)
19. **Code-switching** is changing from one form of speech to another. (p. 316)
20. The **elaborated code**, which is characterized by extensive vocabulary, complex syntax, and lengthy sentences, is the formal speech children use in situations such as the classroom. (p. 317)
21. The **restricted code**, which has a limited vocabulary and syntax, relies more on gestures and intonation, and is context-specific, is the informal speech children use with their friends. (p. 317)
22. **Black English**, which has its linguistic roots in Africa and the antebellum South, is a contemporary grammatical variation of standard English used by many young African-Americans. (p. 318)
23. **Immersion** is an approach to bilingual education in which the child's instruction occurs entirely in the new language. (p. 319)

CHAPTER 13 The School Years: Psychosocial Development

Chapter Overview

This chapter brings to a close the unit on the school years. We have seen that from ages 7 to 11, the child becomes stronger and more competent, mastering the biosocial and cognitive abilities that are important in his or her culture. Psychosocial accomplishments are equally impressive.

The first section of the chapter begins by reviewing the contributions of Freud and Erikson, as well as learning, cognitive, and humanist theories to our understanding of the school years; all emphasize the growing social competence of children, as well as the growing independence of children from their parents. The section continues with a description of the growth of social cognition and self-understanding. Children's interaction with peers and others in their ever-widening social world is the subject of the next section.

The following two sections discuss the problems and challenges that are often experienced by school-age children in our society, including the experience of parental divorce and remarriage, living in single-parent and blended families, as well as that of poverty, The chapter closes with a discussion of the ways children cope with stressful situations.

NOTE: Answer guidelines for all Chapter 13 questions begin on page 198.

Guided Study

The text chapter should be studied one section at a time. Before you read, preview each section by skimming it, noting headings and boldface items. Then read the appropriate section objectives from the following outline. Keep these objectives in mind and, as you read the chapter section, search for the information that will enable you to meet each objective. Once you have finished a section, write out answers for its objectives.

An Expanding Social World (pp. 332–337)

1. Identify the common themes or emphasis of three theoretical views of the psychosocial development of school-age children.

2. Define social cognition and summarize how children's theory of mind evolves during middle childhood.

3. Describe the development of self-understanding during middle childhood and its implications for children's self-esteem and vulnerability to learned helplessness.

The Peer Group (pp. 337–344)

4. Discuss the importance of peer groups, providing examples of how school-age children develop their own subculture and explaining the importance of this development.

5. Discuss the ways in which children's friendship circles and social problem-solving skills change during the school years.

6. (A Closer Look) Identify three groups of unpopular children who merit special concern; discuss the reasons for such unpopularity, noting whether anything can be done to help such children.

Family Structure and Child Development (pp. 344–355)

7. Describe how American family structures have changed in recent decades, and discuss the benefits of children living with both biological parents.

8. Discuss the impact of divorce and single-parent households on the psychosocial development of the school-age child.

9. Discuss the impact of blended families and grandparent households on the psychosocial development of the school-age child.

Poverty in Middle Childhood (pp. 356–359)

10. Discuss the effect of socioeconomic status on the biosocial, cognitive, and psychosocial development of school-age children.

Coping with Life (pp. 360–363)

11. Identify the variables that influence the impact of stresses on schoolchildren and discuss those factors that seem especially important in helping children cope with stress.

Chapter Review

When you have finished reading the chapter, work through the material that follows to review it. Complete the sentences and answer the questions. As you proceed, evaluate your performance for each section by consulting the answers on page 198. Do not continue with the next section until you understand each answer. If you need to, review or reread the appropriate section in the textbook before continuing.

An Expanding Social World (pp. 332–337)

1. Freud describes middle childhood as the period of ______________, when emotional drives are ______________, sexual needs are ______________, and unconscious conflicts are ______________.
2. According to Erikson, the crisis of middle childhood is ______________ ______________ ______________.
3. Developmentalists influenced by behaviorism, social learning theory, or by the cognitive or humanist perspectives are more concerned with children's ______________ of new knowledge. Middle childhood is seen as a time when many distinct competencies ______________.
4. School-age children advance in their understanding of other people and groups; that is, they advance in ______________ ______________. At this time, the preschooler's one-step theory of mind begins to evolve into a complex, ______________ view of others.
5. In experiments on children's social cognition, older children are more likely to focus on ______________ (observable behaviors/underlying motives) when asked to explain another person's behavior in a situation.
6. Another example of children's advancing social cognition is that, as compared to younger children, older children are more likely to focus on ______________ (physical characteristics/personality traits) when asked to describe other children.
7. During the school years children's emotional sensitivity to others ______________ (increases/does not increase).

Give several examples of how the expansion of emotional understanding influences children's social interaction.

8. In the beginning of the school years children often explain their actions by referring to the events of the immediate ______________; a few years later they more readily relate their actions to their ______________ ______________ and ______________.
9. Along with greater self-understanding during the school years comes greater self-______________, as children learn to control their reactions for strategic purposes.

Give an example of this advance in self-control.

10. As their self-understanding sharpens, children gradually become ______________ (more/less) self-critical, and their self-esteem ______________ (rises/dips). As they mature, children are also ______________ (more/less) likely to feel personally to blame for their shortcomings. This is especially true for ______________ (girls/boys).
11. During the school years children's perceptions of their intellectual competencies ______________ (decline steadily/remain optimistic).
12. Compared to preschoolers, schoolchildren are better able to distinguish between ______________ and ______________, and they regard abilities as relatively enduring traits.
13. Compared with younger children, older children are more vulnerable to ______________ ______________; that is, their past fail-

ures in a particular area have taught them to believe that they are unable to do anything to improve their performance. Many such children attribute their ________________ (failures/successes/failures and successes) to their ability rather than to things beyond their control.

The Peer Group (pp. 337–344)

14. A peer group is defined as ________________ ________________.

15. Some social scientists call the peer group's subculture the ________________ ________________ ________________, highlighting the distinctions between children's groups and the general culture.

Identify several distinguishing features of this subculture.

16. A certain amount of ________________, ________________, and ________________ is expected in every children's society. Variation in the norms for such behaviors ________________ (has/has not) been found to occur by ethnic and economic group.

17. School-age children ________________ (can/cannot) distinguish between social conventions and ethical principles.

18. As children's social awareness increases they become ________________ (more/less) selective in their interactions, and assisting or sharing with others, referred to as ________________ behavior, is increasingly seen as a sign and obligation of friendship.

19. When asked what makes their best friends different from other acquaintances, older children are more likely to cite ________________ ________________. Older children also increasingly regard friendship as a forum for ________________-________________.

20. Friendship groups typically become ________________ (larger/smaller) and ________________ (more/less) rigid during the school years.

21. Peer conflict during the school years, as compared to the preschool years, is ________________ (more/less) likely to result in retaliation, an appeal to an adult authority, or distress. This demonstrates that social problem-solving skills ________________ (advance/do not advance) during the school years.

22. Children who can predict which strategies will best resolve disagreements tend to be ________________ (more/less) popular.

23. (A Closer Look) An estimated ________________ percent of schoolchildren are unpopular and friendless most of the time. Researchers have identified several categories of such children, including ________________ children who are actively disliked by others, ________________ children who are ignored by peers because they are shy and withdrawn, and ________________ children toward whom others are ambivalent.

24. (A Closer Look) Children who are rejected by their peers often are immature in their ________________ ________________.

Give a specific example of this immaturity.

25. (A Closer Look) One study found that children who improved their ________________ skills were most likely to improve in their self-esteem as well.

Family Structure and Child Development (pp. 344–355)

26. Family structures are defined as ________________ ________________.

27. At mid-twentieth century the preferred family structure in most industrialized nations consisted of ______________________________ ______________________________.

At the same time, the preferred family structure in most developing countries in Asia and Latin America consisted of ______________________________ ______________________________, while in ______________ and ______________ nations a variety of family structures flourished.

28. The "traditional" family structure that predominated during most of America's history is becoming ______________ (more/less) common.

29. If current trends continue, only about ______________ percent of American children born in the 1990s will live with both biological parents from birth to age 18.

30. Longitudinal research studies demonstrate that children can thrive ______________ (only in certain family structures/in almost any family structure).

31. In terms of developmental effects on children, specifics of family function, such as ______________ ______________________________, are more crucial than specifics of family structure.

32. Children who have fewer physical, emotional, or learning difficulties are those who live with ______________ ______________ ______________.

Describe how children reared in this family structure fare at adolescence and early adulthood.

33. Give two reasons for the benefits of this family structure.

a. ______________________________

b. ______________________________

34. The advantages of traditional families are often ______________ (overstated/understated). Contributing to this is the fact that many studies do not take sufficient account of other factors that affect child development, the most obvious being ______________. Other factors that correlate with family structure and functioning include ______________________________ ______________________________.

35. In acknowledging that two-parent homes are generally best, the text author notes two important qualifications.

a. ______________________________

b. ______________________________

36. Children raised in families with persistently high levels of conflict usually ______________ (do/do not) become impervious to the stress and tension.

37. The disruption surrounding divorce almost always adversely affects children for at least ______________. Whether this distress is short-lived or long-lasting depends primarily on three postdivorce factors:

a. ______________________________;

b. ______________________________;

c. ______________________________.

38. The aspect of the parents' relationship that seems most critical for the development of children is the ______________________________.

Cite several sources of instability that make it more difficult for children to adjust to divorce.

39. The immediate disruptions of family life are generally harder on ______________ (older/younger) children and children who themselves are in ______________.

40. As they enter their teens, children often view divorce with a form of adolescent ______________ that causes them to over-personalize their parents' divorce.

41. Until recently, custody of children in a divorce was based almost exclusively on ______________. In the nineteenth century, for example, custody nearly always went to the ______________ (father/mother), and for most of this century, it nearly always went to the ______________ (father/mother).

42. Children who are in joint custody generally develop ______________ (better/no better) than those who rarely see their noncustodial parent.

Give several reasons for this being so.

43. The number of single-parent households has increased markedly over the past two decades in virtually every major industrialized nation except ______________.

44. When compared to others of the same ethnicity and socioeconomic status, children who live with one biological parent develop ______________ (just as well/more poorly) than those who live with two. This has been demonstrated in three areas of development: ______________ ______________, ______________ ______________, and ______________ ______________ ______________.

This generality ______________ (holds/does not hold) equally for preschoolers, school-age children, and adolescents.

45. One source of stress for single parents is that they often suffer from ______________ ______________. Another is that the ______________ of such households is substantially lower than that of two-parent households. One factor that is important in helping single parents cope is the presence of ______________ ______________.

46. Children develop quite ______________ (similarly/differently) in father-only homes as in mother-only homes.

Give several reasons that children in father-only homes may fare better than children in mother-only homes.

47. Most divorced parents ______________ (do/do not) remarry within a few years. The divorce rate for second marriages is ______________ (higher than/lower than/the same as) that for first marriages.

48. One study comparing young children in various family structures found that those living with both grandparents had poorer ______________ skills and more ______________ problems than children in any other kind of home. This effect was not seen for ______________ (European-American/African-American) children, for whom the grandparent-headed household is traditionally less unusual. This indicates that ______________ context is an important variable in the functioning of a family.

Poverty in Middle Childhood (pp. 356–359)

49. As SES decreases, the risk of health hazards—including ______________ ______________—increases. The toll of poverty on the biosocial domain is blunted for two reasons:

a. ______________

b. ______________

50. The U.S. method of supporting education makes poverty a particularly devastating liability because ______________ ______________.

51. Poverty during middle childhood may take the greatest toll on development in the ______ domain. One reason this is so is that school-age children are preoccupied with the status conveyed by ______ ______. School-age children also are compelled to engage in ______ ______ as they check each other out on everything from allowance to grades.

52. Compared with their peers of equal SES, homeless children have ______ ______.

53. Homeless children typically are about ______ behind academically.

54. Today, poverty affects ______ (fewer/more) children than adults.

Coping with Life (pp. 360–363)

55. Between ages 6 and 11 the overall frequency of various psychological problems ______ (increases/decreases), while the number of evident competencies ______ (increases/decreases).

56. Two factors that combine to buffer school-age children against the stresses they encounter are the development of ______ ______ and an expanding ______ ______.

57. The impact of a given stress on a child depends on ______ ______ and the degree to which they affect ______ ______.

58. One reason competence can compensate for life stress is that if children feel confident, their ______ benefits and they are better able to put the rest of their life in perspective. This explains why older children tend to be ______ (more/less) vulnerable to life stresses than are children who are just beginning middle childhood.

59. In promoting competence in children, the ______ ______ ______ of a school is even more important than the academic quality of its curriculum.

List several specific characteristics of schools that are more successful in promoting student competence.

60. Another element that helps children deal with problems is the ______ ______ they receive. This can be obtained from grandparents, siblings, or from ______ ______ and ______.

61. Most children ______ (do/do not) have an idyllic childhood. Such a childhood ______ (is/is not) necessary for healthy development.

62. The best strategy for helping children who are faced with multiple problems that affect their daily routines is to ______ ______.

Progress Test 1

Multiple-Choice Questions

Circle your answers to the following questions and check them with the answers on page 199. If your answer is incorrect, read the explanation for why it is incorrect and then consult the appropriate pages of the text (in parentheses following the correct answer).

1. In describing development in middle childhood, each of the major theories stresses:
   a. latency.
   b. the society of children.
   c. learned helplessness.
   d. the learning of academic and social skills.

2. Erikson sees the crisis of the school years as that of:
   a. industry versus inferiority.
   b. acceptance versus rejection.
   c. initiative versus guilt.
   d. male versus female.

3. The best strategy for helping children who are at risk of developing serious psychological problems because of multiple stresses generally seems to be:
   a. reducing the number of stresses.
   b. changing the household situation.
   c. reducing the peer group's influence.
   d. increasing competencies within the child or social supports surrounding him or her.

4. Compared to preschoolers, school-age children are:
   a. more self-centered.
   b. less egocentric.
   c. more likely to focus on the observable behaviors of others rather than on underlying motives.
   d. more emotional.

5. Compared to preschoolers, older children who disagree with each other are more likely to:
   a. experience emotional distress.
   b. seek retaliation or respond aggressively.
   c. appeal to adult authority.
   d. use humor to resolve the conflict.

6. In promoting the development of student competence, the overall ______________ of a particular school is an especially important factor.
   a. competitiveness
   b. academic quality
   c. emotional tone
   d. size

7. (A Closer Look) Compared with average or popular children, rejected children tend to be:
   a. brighter and more competitive.
   b. affluent and "stuck-up."
   c. economically disadvantaged.
   d. socially immature.

8. Studies support the general conclusion that children function well in single-parent households when:
   a. feelings of "role overload" are minimal.
   b. the father is the head of the home and major wage-earner.
   c. a network of social support reduces stress on the single parent.
   d. all of the above are true.

9. Divorce and parental remarriage typically prove beneficial to children when they result in less financial stress and:
   a. less loneliness for the parent.
   b. greater role overload.
   c. significant changes in lifestyle.
   d. the inclusion of stepsiblings.

10. Older schoolchildren tend to be ______________ vulnerable to the stresses of life than children who are just beginning middle childhood because they ______________.
    a. more; tend to overpersonalize their problems
    b. less; have better developed skills for coping with problems
    c. more; are more likely to compare their well-being with that of their peers
    d. less; are less egocentric

11. Between the ages of 6 and 11, the overall frequency of various psychological problems:
    a. increases in both boys and girls.
    b. decreases in both boys and girls.
    c. increases in boys and decreases in girls.
    d. decreases in boys and increases in girls.

12. Studies of single-parent homes demonstrate that when compared to others of the same ethnicity and SES, children:
    a. fare better in mother-only homes.
    b. fare better in father-only homes, especially if the children are girls.
    c. develop quite similarly in both mother-only and father-only homes.
    d. fare better than children in two-parent homes.

13. During the school years, children become ______________ selective about their friends and their friendship groups become ______________.
    a. less; larger
    b. less; smaller
    c. more; larger
    d. more; smaller

14. At mid-twentieth century, the "ideal" family structure:
    a. in most industrialized nations consisted of two biological parents living with their own two or three dependent children.
    b. in Asia and Latin America was the large extended family with grandparents, cousins, aunts, and uncles living within the same household.
    c. in many African and Arab nations included a greater variety of family structures, including the polygamous household.
    d. was all of the above.

15. Large-scale surveys that compare various family structures have found that children inevitably fare best when they live:
    a. with both biological parents.
    b. in any two-caregiver household.
    c. in a two-caregiver household that includes their biological mother.
    d. in none of the above situations.

True or False Items

Write *true* or *false* on the line in front of each statement.

_______ 1. As they interpret themselves according to increasingly complex self-theories, school-age children typically experience a rise in self-esteem.

_______ 2. Research suggests that children tend to be more sensitive to others, and less happy with themselves, as they grow older.

_______ 3. Children in middle childhood develop and transmit their own subculture, complete with vocabulary, dress codes, and rules of behavior.

_______ 4. (A Closer Look) Nearly one-fourth of all school-age children can be described as "rejected," "neglected," or "controversial."

_______ 5. In the United States, one child in five lives below the poverty line.

_______ 6. Socioeconomic status is less important to children in middle childhood than it is to preschool children.

_______ 7. Households headed by single fathers tend to be better off financially than households headed by single mothers.

_______ 8. The negative impact of divorce on children usually declines after the first two years.

_______ 9. The quality of family interaction seems to be a more powerful predictor of children's development than the actual structure of the family.

_______ 10. Child custody laws in the fifty states are clear in preferring joint custody over other custody arrangements.

Progress Test 2

Progress Test 2 should be completed during a final chapter review. Answer the following questions after you thoroughly understand the correct answers for the Chapter Review and Progress Test 1.

Multiple-Choice Questions

1. According to Freud, the period between ages 7 and 11 when a child's sexual drives are relatively quiet is the:
   a. phallic stage.
   b. genital stage.
   c. period of latency.
   d. period of industry versus inferiority.

2. The main reason for the special vocabulary, dress codes, and behaviors that flourish within the society of children is that they:
   a. lead to clubs and gang behavior.
   b. are unknown or unapproved by adults.
   c. imitate adult-organized society.
   d. provide an alternative to useful work in society.

3. In the area of social cognition, developmentalists are impressed by the school-age child's increasing ability to:
   a. identify and take into account other people's viewpoints.
   d. develop an increasingly wide network of friends.
   c. relate to the opposite sex.
   d. resist social models.

4. The school-age child's greater understanding of emotions is best illustrated by:
   a. an increased tendency to take everything personally.
   b. more widespread generosity and sharing.
   c. the ability to see through the insincere behavior of others.
   d. a refusal to express unfelt emotions.

5. Typically, children in middle childhood experience a decrease in self-esteem as a result of:
   a. a wavering self-theory.
   b. increased awareness of personal shortcomings and failures.
   c. rejection by peers.
   d. difficulties with members of the opposite sex.

6. A 10-year-old's sense of self-competence is most strongly influenced by his or her:
   a. peers. c. mother.
   b. siblings. d. father.

7. Research by Elliot Turiel reveals that school-age children become increasingly able to distinguish ethical principles and:
   a. social conventions.
   b. cultural values.
   c. the values of the "society of children."
   d. all of the above.

8. Social competence with peers increases during the school years because:
   a. the ability to evaluate the potential outcomes of social problem-solving strategies improves.
   b. the ability to generate alternative strategies to resolve conflicts improves.

c. children become increasingly able to redirect conflict, for example, through humor.
d. of all of the above reasons.

9. If current trends continue, it is estimated that ________________ of American children born in the 1990s will live with both biological parents from birth to age 18.
   a. less than 10 percent
   b. about 40 percent
   c. 50 percent
   d. 75 percent

10. Which of the following is true of children who live with both biological parents?
    a. They tend to have fewer physical and emotional problems.
    b. They tend to have fewer learning difficulties.
    c. They are less likely to abuse drugs.
    d. All of the above are true.

11. Two factors that most often help the child cope well with multiple stresses are social support and:
    a. learned helplessness.
    b. competence in a specific area.
    c. remedial education.
    d. referral to mental health professionals.

12. Some developmentalists believe that the advantage that traditional families confer on the psychosocial development of children is overstated because:
    a. many studies do not take sufficient account of other factors that affect child development, such as income.
    b. very little reliable research has been conducted on this issue.
    c. parents often are not honest in reporting their children's problems.
    d. of all of the above reasons.

13. Family ____________ is more crucial to children's well-being than family ____________ is.
    a. structure; SES
    b. SES; stability
    c. stability; SES
    d. functioning; structure

14. (A Closer Look) One study of socially rejected, low-achieving boys found that extra training in ____________ skills resulted in the greatest overall improvement in their social acceptance.
    a. social
    b. problem-solving
    c. academic
    d. grooming

15. (A Closer Look) What percentage of schoolchildren are unpopular and friendless most of the time?
    a. 1 to 2
    b. 5 to 10
    c. 10 to 12
    d. 12 to 15

True or False Items

Write *true* or *false* on the line in front of each statement.

______ 1. Erikson sees the task of middle childhood as that of mastering the skills valued by the culture.
______ 2. Social cognition refers to a specialized area of study within learning theory.
______ 3. Children become better able to understand the motives, beliefs, and personality traits of others at about age 8.
______ 4. Children of low socioeconomic status in middle childhood are more likely than other children to have difficulty mastering basic academic skills.
______ 5. The income of single-parent households is about the same as that of two-parent households in which only one parent works.
______ 6. In the majority of divorce cases in which the mother is the custodial parent, the father maintains a close, long-term relationship with the children.
______ 7. A blended family is one that includes a stepparent and perhaps stepsiblings.
______ 8. Serious problems between parents and children, as well as severe emotional disturbances, are more common in middle childhood than in early childhood.
______ 9. (A Closer Look) The problems of most "rejected" children nearly always disappear by adolescence.
______ 10. Friendships become more selective and exclusive as children grow older.

Challenge Test

Answer these questions the day before an exam as a final check on your understanding of the chapter's terms and concepts.

1. A child's feelings that numerous failures in a particular area are proof that he or she can do nothing to improve the situation describes:
   a. initiative versus inferiority.
   b. learned helplessness.
   c. peer rejection.
   d. positive self-esteem.

2. Ten-year-old Jahmad is a full grade behind his peers in math. Erik Erikson would probably say that Jahmad is at risk for developing a sense of:
   a. insecurity.
   b. learned helplessness.
   c. inferiority.
   d. rejection.

3. (A Closer Look) Bonnie, who is low-achieving, shy, and withdrawn, is rejected by most of her peers. Her teacher, who wants to help Bonnie increase her self-esteem and social acceptance, encourages her parents to:
   a. transfer Bonnie to a different school.
   b. help their daughter improve her social skills.
   c. help their daughter learn to accept more responsibility for her academic failures.
   d. help their daughter improve her academic skills.

4. Jorge, who has no children of his own, is worried about his 12-year-old niece because she wears unusual clothes and uses a strange vocabulary in her speech. What should Jorge do?
   a. Tell his niece's parents they need to discipline their daughter more strictly.
   b. Convince his niece to find a new group of friends.
   c. Recommend that his niece's parents seek professional counseling for their daughter since such behaviors often are the first signs of a life-long pattern of antisocial behavior.
   d. Jorge need not necessarily be worried since children typically develop their own subculture in their speech, dress, and behavior.

5. Compared to her 7-year-old brother Walter, 10-year-old Felicity is more likely to describe their cousin:
   a. in terms of physical attributes.
   b. as feeling exactly the same way she does when they are in the same social situation.
   c. in terms of personality traits.
   d. in terms of their cousin's behaviors in the immediate situation.

6. Seven-year-old Chantal fumes after a friend compliments her new dress, thinking that the comment was intended to be sarcastic. Chantal's reaction is an example of:
   a. egocentrism.
   b. learned helplessness.
   c. the distorted thought processes of children with low self-esteem.
   d. immature social cognition.

7. In discussing friendship, 9-year-old children, in contrast to younger children, will:
   a. deny that friends are important.
   b. state that they prefer same-sex playmates.
   c. stress the importance of help and emotional support in friendship.
   d. be less choosy about who they call a friend.

8. (A Closer Look) Children who have serious difficulty in peer relationships in elementary school:
   a. are at a greater risk of having emotional problems later in life.
   b. usually overcome their difficulty in a year or two.
   c. later tend to form a more intense friendship with one person than children who did not have difficulty earlier.
   d. b and c are both true.

9. After years of unhappiness in a marriage characterized by excessive conflict, Brad and Diane file for divorce and move 500 miles apart. In ruling on custody for their 7-year-old daughter, the wise judge decides:
   a. joint custody should be awarded, since this arrangement is nearly always the most beneficial for children.
   b. the mother should have custody, since this arrangement is nearly always the most beneficial for children in single-parent homes.
   c. the father should have custody, since this arrangement is nearly always the most beneficial for children in single-parent homes.
   d. to more fully investigate the competency of each parent, since whoever was the most competent and most involved parent before the divorce should continue to be the primary caregiver.

10. Of the following children, who is likely to have the lowest overall self-esteem?
    a. Karen, age 7
    b. David, age 9
    c. Carl, age 10
    d. Cindy, age 12

11. Ten-year-old Benjamin is less optimistic and self-confident than his 5-year-old sister. This may be partly explained by the tendency of older children to:
    a. evaluate their abilities by comparing them with their own competencies a year or two earlier.
    b. evaluate their competencies by comparing them with others'.
    c. be less realistic about their own abilities.
    d. do both b and c.

12. Based on research on the norms for childhood aggression, which of the following schoolchildren is likely to be viewed most favorably by his or her peers?
   a. Eddie, the class bully
   b. Luwanda, who is not arrogant but doesn't shy away from defending herself when necessary
   c. Daniel, who often suffers attacks from his peers yet refuses to retaliate
   d. Hilary, who often suffers attacks from her peers yet refuses to retaliate

13. In one study 6- and 10-year-old children were asked whether it is a more serious transgression for a child to steal an eraser than to wear pajamas to school. Which of the following summarizes the findings of this study?
   a. Both groups of children saw the theft of the eraser as being more serious.
   b. Both groups of children saw wearing pajamas to school as being more serious.
   c. The 10-year-olds, but not the 6-year-olds, were convinced that the theft was the more serious transgression.
   d. The 6-year-olds, but not the 10-year-olds, were convinced that the theft was the more serious transgression.

14. Each of the following children lives in an impoverished family. Which child is likely to have the greatest difficulty coping with this source of stress?
   a. twelve-year-old Darren, who has an emotionally disturbed father
   b. six-year-old Simone, who lives in a single-parent household
   c. ten-year-old Brenda, who is an accomplished dancer
   d. It is impossible to predict from the information provided.

15. In which of the following ethnic groups are the children of grandparent-headed households *least* likely to have behavioral problems?
   a. European-American
   b. African-American
   c. Native American
   d. Asian-American

Key Terms

Using your own words, write a brief definition or explanation of each of the following terms.

1. latency
2. industry versus inferiority
3. social cognition
4. learned helplessness
5. peer group
6. society of children
7. prosocial behaviors
8. family structures
9. social comparison

ANSWERS

CHAPTER REVIEW

1. latency; quieter; repressed; suppressed
2. industry versus inferiority
3. acquisition; coalesce
4. social cognition; multistep
5. underlying motives
6. personality traits
7. increases

Children are likely to become more sensitive to, and empathize with, the emotional experiences of others. They are also able to recognize and rephrase or avoid potentially offensive statements. In general, it helps them to get along better with other people.

8. situation; personality traits; feelings
9. regulation

Children in the school years might decide that a teacher's crankiness isn't to be taken personally or they might decide to read a book while parents are arguing.

10. more; dips; more; girls
11. decline steadily
12. ability; effort
13. learned helplessness; failures
14. a group of individuals of similar age and social status who play, work, and learn together
15. society of children

The society of children typically has a special vocabulary, dress codes, and rules of behavior.

16. aggression; counteraggression; retaliation; has
17. can
18. more; prosocial
19. mutual help; self-disclosure
20. smaller; more
21. less; advance
22. more
23. 5 to 10; rejected; neglected; controversial

24. social cognition

Rejected children often misinterpret social situations, considering a compliment as sarcastic, for example.

25. academic
26. households composed of people connected to each other in various legal and biosocial ways
27. two biological parents living with their own two or three dependent children; a large extended family often with grandparents, cousins, aunts and uncles; African; Arab
28. less
29. 40
30. in almost any family structure
31. excessive conflict, overly authoritarian parenting, and coldness
32. both biological parents

At adolescence, they are less likely to abuse drugs or be arrested and more likely to graduate from high school; in adulthood, they are more likely to graduate from college and to continue to develop with self-confidence, social acceptance, and career success.

33. a. Two adults generally provide more complete caregiving than one.
    b. Two-parent homes usually have a financial advantage over other forms.
34. overstated income; race, ethnic background, and religion
35. a. Not every biological parent is a fit parent.
    b. Not every marriage creates a nurturant household.
36. do not
37. a year or two
    a. the harmony of the parents' ongoing relationship
    b. the stability of the child's life
    c. the adequacy of the caregiving arrangement
38. degree of harmony or discord

One source of instability is the child's being separated from a caregiver to whom he or she is highly attached. Another is a reduction in the household income. Still another is the disorientation of the parents.

39. younger; transition
40. egocentrism
41. gender; father; mother
42. no better

The logistics of joint custody arrangements are often difficult for parents and disorienting for children who shuttle between homes with different rules, expectations, and emotional settings.

43. Japan
44. just as well; school achievement; emotional stability; protection from injury; holds
45. role overload; income; social support
46. similarly

Growing boys, particularly, sometimes respond better to a man's authority than to a woman's. In addition, fathers who choose custody are those who are likely to be suited for it, whereas mothers typically have custody whether they prefer it or not. Father-only homes are, on average, more secure financially.

47. do; higher than
48. language; behavior; African-American; social
49. malnutrition, disease, accidents, abuse, and neglect
    a. Schoolchildren's natural immunities, physical strengths, and growth patterns make them relatively unlikely to suffer the most devastating consequences of malnutrition and disease.
    b. Their developing independence and reasoning ability make schoolchildren better able to protect themselves against dangers.
50. public school funding depends primarily on local property taxes
51. psychosocial; material possessions; social comparison
52. fewer friends and more fears, fights, chronic illnesses, and changes in schools
53. 14 months
54. more
55. decreases; increases
56. social cognition; social world
57. the number of stresses the child is experiencing concurrently; the overall pattern of the child's daily life
58. self-esteem; less
59. overall emotional tone

Such schools care about students, and have high expectations of both students and teachers.

60. social support; religious faith; practice
61. do not; is not
62. increase competencies within the child or the social supports surrounding him or her

PROGRESS TEST 1

Multiple-Choice Questions

1. **d.** is the answer. (pp. 332–333)

   a. This is Freud's term for psychosexual development during middle childhood.

b. This refers to the schoolchild's subculture of vocabulary, dress codes, and rules of behavior.

c. This refers to the perception that one can do nothing to improve performance in a specific area.

2. **a.** is the answer. (p. 332)
3. **d.** is the answer. (p. 363)
4. **b.** is the answer. (p. 333)

   a. Just the opposite is true.

   c. Younger children are more likely to focus on the observable behaviors of others.

   d. The text does not discuss this issue.
5. **d.** is the answer. (p. 342)

   a., b., & c. As social awareness expands, schoolchildren develop a larger repertoire of social problem-solving skills.
6. **c.** is the answer. (p. 362)
7. **d.** is the answer. (p. 343)
8. **d.** is the answer. (p. 353)
9. **a.** is the answer. (p. 354)

   b., c., & d. These factors are likely to increase, rather than decrease, stress, and therefore have an adverse effect on children.
10. **b.** is the answer. (p. 360)
11. **b.** is the answer. (p. 360)
12. **c.** is the answer. (p. 353)
13. **d.** is the answer. (p. 341)
14. **d.** is the answer. (p. 344)
15. **d.** is the answer. (p. 345)

    a., b., & c. Although children who live in two-parent households *tend* to fare best, far more important to their well-being than family structure is family *functioning*.

True or False Items

1. F As they develop increasingly complex self-theories, children typically become more self-critical, and their self-esteem drops. (p. 336)
2. T (pp. 334–335)
3. T (p. 338)
4. F Only 5 to 10 percent of school-age children would fall in these categories. (p. 343)
5. T (p. 359)
6. F Socioeconomic status is more important to older children, who can compare themselves with others in terms of possessions and lifestyle. (p. 358)
7. T (p. 354)
8. T (p. 348)
9. T (p. 348)
10. F The state legislatures have been cautious in their stand on joint custody, in light of experiences that suggest that joint custody is not the best arrangement for some families—for example, families in which there is continuing hostility between parents. (pp. 350–351)

PROGRESS TEST 2

Multiple-Choice Questions

1. **c.** is the answer. (p. 332)

   a. & b. These Freudian stages precede and follow, respectively, the latency stage.

   d. This is a crisis in Erikson's theory.
2. **b.** is the answer. (p. 338)
3. **a.** is the answer. (p. 333)

   b. Friendship circles typically become smaller during middle childhood, as children become more choosy about their friends.

   c. & d. These issues are not discussed in the chapter.
4. **c.** is the answer. (pp. 334–335)
5. **b.** is the answer. (p. 336)

   a. This tends to promote, rather than reduce, self-esteem.

   c. Only 5 to 10 percent of schoolchildren experience this.

   d. This issue becomes more important during adolescence.
6. **a.** is the answer. (p. 337)
7. **a.** is the answer. (pp. 339–340)
8. **d.** is the answer. (p. 342)
9. **b.** is the answer. (p. 345)
10. **d.** is the answer. (p. 345)
11. **b.** is the answer. (p. 361)
12. **a.** is the answer. (p. 346)

    b. In fact, a great deal of research has been conducted on this issue.

    c. There is no evidence that this is so.
13. **d.** is the answer. (p. 345)
14. **c.** is the answer. (p. 344)
15. **b.** is the answer. (p. 343)

True or False Items

1. T (pp. 332–333)
2. F Social cognition refers to a person's understanding of people and the dynamics of human interaction. (p. 333)

3. T (pp. 333–334)
4. T (p. 356)
5. F The income of single-parent households is substantially lower than that of two-parent households in which only one parent works. (p. 353)
6. F Only a minority of fathers who do not have custody continue to maintain a close relationship with their children. (p. 349)
7. T (p. 354)
8. F Serious problems between parents and children, and severe emotional disturbances, are less common in middle childhood than earlier or later. (p. 360)
9. F The problems of rejected children may get worse as they get older. (p. 343)
10. T (p. 341)

CHALLENGE TEST

1. **b.** is the answer. (p. 337)

   a. This answer refers to the crisis of middle childhood as described in Erikson's theory.

   c. There is no indication that the child described in this situation is being rejected by his or her peers.

   d. This situation more accurately describes *low* self-esteem.
2. **c.** is the answer. (p. 332)
3. **d.** is the answer. (p. 344)

   a. Because it would seem to involve "running away" from her problems, this approach would likely be more harmful than helpful.

   b. Research shows that improving social skills helps improve reading comprehension only; it does not increase self-esteem.

   c. If Bonnie is like most school-age children, she is quite self-critical and already accepts responsibility for her failures.
4. **d.** is the answer. (p. 338)
5. **c.** is the answer. (p. 334)

   a., b., & d. These are more typical of preschoolers.
6. **d.** is the answer. (pp. 333–334)

   a. Egocentrism is self-centered thinking. In this example, Chantal is misinterpreting her friend's comment.

   b. & c. There is no reason to believe that Chantal is suffering from learned helplessness or low self-esteem.
7. **c.** is the answer. (p. 341)
8. **a.** is the answer. (p. 343)
9. **d.** is the answer. (p. 350)
10. **d.** is the answer. Self-esteem decreases throughout middle childhood, reaching a low at about age 12. (p. 336)
11. **b.** is the answer. (p. 336)

    a. & c. These are more typical of preschoolers than school-age children.
12. **b.** is the answer. (p. 339)

    a. Although a certain amount of aggressiveness is the norm during childhood, children who are perceived as overly arrogant or aggressive are not viewed very favorably.

    c. & d. Both girls and boys are expected to defend themselves when appropriate, and are viewed as weak if they do not.
13. **c.** is the answer. (p. 340)
14. **a.** is the answer. All other things being equal, poverty is likely to have a more adverse effect on children during middle childhood, for whom material possessions are important measures of self-worth, than earlier in life. Furthermore, family functioning is more important to children's well-being than is family structure. Thus living with an emotionally disturbed father is likely to be more damaging than living in a single-parent household. (p. 361)

    c. Brenda's success as a dancer is likely to boost her self- esteem, an important buffer to childhood stress.
15. **b.** is the answer. Extended family structures are more common, and more accepted, by African-Americans, with established patterns of interaction to ease tensions between generations. (p. 355)

KEY TERMS

1. Freud describes middle childhood as the period of **latency**, when children's emotional drives are quieter, their sexual needs are repressed, and their unconscious conflicts are submerged. (p. 332)

   Memory aid: Something that is *latent* exists but is not manifesting itself.
2. According to Erikson, the crisis of middle childhood is that of **industry versus inferiority** as children develop views of themselves as either competent or incompetent. (p. 332)
3. **Social cognition** refers to a person's understanding of other people and groups. (p. 333)
4. **Learned helplessness** develops when children's past failures in a particular area have taught them to believe that they are unable to do anything to improve their performance. (p. 337)

5. A **peer group** is defined as a group of individuals of roughly the same age and social status who play, work, and learn together. (p. 337)
6. Children in middle childhood develop and transmit their own subculture, called the **society of children**, that has its own vocabulary, dress codes, and rules of behavior. (p. 338)
7. **Prosocial behaviors** are acts of sharing and caring that benefit others more than the individual who performs them. (p. 340)
8. **Family structures** refer to households composed of people connected to each other in various legal and biosocial ways. (p. 344)
9. **Social comparison** refers to the practice of assessing one's self-worth by judging oneself relative to peers. (p. 358)

CHAPTER 14 Adolescence: Biosocial Development

Chapter Overview

Between the ages of 10 and 20, young people cross the great divide between childhood and adulthood. This crossing encompasses all three domains of development—biosocial, cognitive, and psychosocial. Chapter 14 focuses on the dramatic changes that occur in the biosocial domain, beginning with puberty and the growth spurt. The biosocial metamorphosis of the adolescent is discussed in detail, with emphasis on nutrition, sexual maturation, and the effects of the timing of puberty, including possible problems arising from early or late maturation.

NOTE: Answer guidelines for all Chapter 14 questions begin on page 213.

Guided Study

The text chapter should be studied one section at a time. Before you read, preview each section by skimming it, noting headings and boldface items. Then read the appropriate section objectives from the following outline. Keep these objectives in mind and, as you read the chapter section, search for the information that will enable you to meet each objective. Once you have finished a section, write out answers for its objectives.

Puberty (pp. 370–379)

1. Describe physical growth in both the male and the female adolescent.

2. Discuss the nutritional needs and problems of adolescents.

3. Discuss the development of the sex organs and secondary sex characteristics in males and females during puberty.

4. (A Closer Look) Discuss the adolescent's preoccupation with body image and the problems that sometimes arise in the development of a healthy body image.

The Timing of Puberty (pp. 380–384)

5. Discuss the factors that influence the onset of puberty.

6. (A Life-Span Perspective) Discuss adjustment problems of boys and girls who develop earlier or later than their peers, noting any significant short- and long-term consequences.

Chapter Review

When you have finished reading the chapter, work through the material that follows to review it. Complete the sentences and answer the questions. As you proceed, evaluate your performance for each section by consulting the answers on page 213. Do not continue with the next section until you understand each answer. If you need to, review or reread the appropriate section in the textbook before continuing.

Puberty (pp. 370–379)

1. The period of rapid physical growth and sexual maturation that ends childhood and brings the young person to adult size, shape, and sexual potential is called ________________.

   List, in order, the major physical changes of puberty in:

   girls: ________________

   ____

   boys: ________________

   ____

2. Normal children begin to notice pubertal changes between the ages of ________________ and ________________.

3. Once puberty begins, the sequence of physical changes ________________ (varies from child to child/is usually the same in all children). These changes are usually complete approximately ________________ years after the first visible signs appear.

4. Puberty begins when hormones from the ________________ trigger hormone production in the ________________ ________________, which in turn triggers increased hormone production by the ________________ ________________ and by the ________________, which include the ________________ in males and the ________________ in females.

5. The most important hormones of puberty are ________________, which increases steadily in both sexes; ________________, which increases dramatically in boys and slightly in girls; and the ________________, which increase markedly in girls and slightly in boys. These hormones begin increasing at least ________________ year(s) before the first visible signs of puberty.

6. Pubertal changes can affect personality traits, but the emotional impact of puberty depends more on other factors, such as ________________ ________________.

7. The observable changes in appearance at puberty are grouped into two categories: the ________________ ________________, and the emergence of ________________ ________________.

8. The first sign of the growth spurt is increased bone ________________ and ________________, beginning in the ends of the extremities and working toward the center. At the same time, children begin to ________________ (gain/lose) weight at a relatively rapid rate.

9. The change in weight that typically occurs between 10 and 12 years of age is due primarily to the accumulation of ________________.

The amount of weight gain an individual experiences depends on several factors, including ______, ______, ______, and ______.

10. During the spurt in height, a greater percentage of fat is retained by ______ (males/females), who naturally have a higher proportion of body fat in adulthood.

11. About a year after these height and weight changes occur, a period of ______ increase occurs, causing the pudginess and clumsiness of an earlier age to disappear. In boys, this increase is particularly notable in the ______ body.

12. Overall, the typical girl gains in weight about ______ and ______ in height between the ages of 10 and 14, while the typical boy gains the same number of inches and about ______ in weight between the ages of 12 and 16.

13. The chronological age for the growth spurt ______ (varies/does not vary) from child to child.

14. One of the last parts of the body to grow into final form is the ______.

15. The two halves of the body ______ (always/do not always) grow at the same rate.

16. Internal organs also grow during puberty. The ______ increase in size and capacity, the ______ doubles in size, heart rate ______ (increases/decreases), and blood volume ______ (increases/decreases). These changes increase the adolescent's physical ______.

Explain why the physical demands placed on a teenager, as in athletic training, should not be the same as those for a young adult of similar height and weight.

17. During puberty, one organ system, the ______ system, decreases in size, making teenagers ______ (more/less) susceptible to respiratory ailments.

18. The hormones of puberty also cause many relatively minor physical changes that can have significant emotional impact. These include increased activity in ______, ______, and ______ glands.

19. Due to rapid physical growth, the adolescent needs a higher daily intake of ______, ______, and ______. Specifically, the typical adolescent needs about 50 percent more of the minerals ______, ______, and ______ and vitamin ______ during the growth spurt. Because of menstruation, adolescent females also need additional ______ in their diets and are more likely to suffer ______- ______ ______ than any other subgroup of the population.

20. Although most adolescents in developed nations are well nourished most of the time, most also experience periods of ______, ______, or ______ ______.

21. Adolescent nutrition can also be adversely affected by ______ use, which alters the appetite and digestive processes. Another problem, particularly for adolescent girls, is ______, which can lead to serious undernourishment.

22. Research studies demonstrate that ______ (most/a minority of) adolescent girls wish they were thinner. This finding ______ (varied/did not vary) with the girls' physical maturation status.

23. Changes in ______ ______ ______ involve the sex organs that are directly involved in reproduction. By the end of puberty, reproduc-

tion _______________ (is/is still not) possible.

Describe the major changes in primary sex characteristics that occur in both sexes during puberty.

24. The first menstrual period is called _______________. For boys, the comparable indicator of reproductive potential is the first ejaculation of seminal fluid containing sperm, which is called _______________. In both sexes, full reproductive maturity occurs _______________ (at this time/several years later).

25. The first menstrual cycles are usually _______________, that is, they occur without ovulation. When pregnancy occurs before a girl's body is fully developed, the combined nutritional demands of her own growth and her fetus's increase the risk of giving birth to a(n) _______________ infant.

26. Attitudes toward menarche, menstruation, and spermarche _______________ (have/have not) changed over the past two decades, so that most young people _______________ (do/do not) face these events with anxiety, embarrassment, or guilt. In particular, _______________ is now commonly accepted by adolescents.

27. Two possible problems associated with menstruation are _______________ and _______________ in the days before menstruation begins.

28. Sexual features other than the reproductive organs are referred to as _______________ _______________ _______________.

Describe the major pubertal changes in the secondary sex characteristics of both sexes.

29. Two secondary sex characteristics that are mistakenly considered signs of womanhood and manliness, respectively, are _______________ _______________ and _______________ _______________.

30. (A Closer Look) Adolescents' mental conception of, and attitude toward, their physical appearance is referred to as their _______________ _______________.

Identify some common behaviors related to adolescents' preoccupation with their body image.

31. (A Closer Look) Partly because cigarettes are believed to decrease _______________, teenage _______________ (boys/girls) are more likely than those of the opposite sex to smoke. For other drugs, the relationship between sex and drug use is _______________ (the same/reversed).

32. (A Closer Look) When asked what traits they look for in the other sex, adolescents list _______________ _______________.

33. (A Closer Look) Media images reinforce the cultural ideal that American men should be _______________ and women should be _______________.

34. (A Closer Look) Overall, _______________ (boys/girls) tend to be more dissatisfied with

their body image than the other sex. In adolescence, feelings of ____________ correlate strongly with a negative body image.

The Timing of Puberty (pp. 380–384)

35. Although the ____________ of pubertal events is very similar for all young people, there is great variation in its ____________. Healthy children begin puberty any time between ages ____________ and ____________. Some of the factors that affect the age of onset include the child's ____________.

36. The average American girl reaches menarche at about age ____________, while the average boy first ejaculates at age ____________. The average boy is about ____________ years behind the average girl in the appearance of the growth spurt.

37. Genes are an important factor in the age of menarche, as demonstrated by the fact that ____________ and ____________ reach menarche at very similar ages.

38. The average age of onset of puberty ____________ (does/does not) vary from nation to nation and/or from ethnic group to ethnic group.

39. Stocky individuals tend to experience puberty ____________ (earlier/later) than those with taller, thinner builds.

40. Menarche seems to be related to the accumulation of a certain amount of ____________. Consequently, female dancers, runners, and other athletes menstruate ____________ (earlier/later) than the average girl, while females who are relatively inactive menstruate ____________ (earlier/later).

41. Longitudinal research suggests that family emotional distance and stress may ____________ (accelerate/delay) the onset of puberty.

42. (A Life-Span Perspective) Young people who experience puberty at the same time as their friends tend to view the experience more ____________ (positively/negatively) than those who experience it early or late. Timing is particularly important for ____________ (girls/boys).

43. (A Life-Span Perspective) For girls, ____________ (early/late) maturation may be especially troublesome.

Describe several common problems and developmental hazards experienced by early-maturing girls.

44. (A Life-Span Perspective) For most girls, the problems associated with early maturation ____________ (have/have not) subsided by seventh or eighth grade. At this time, they generally have ____________ (more/fewer) close friends than those who have not yet begun to mature. In the long run, girls who are late to mature may have ____________ (more/fewer) problems than girls who are early.

45. (A Life-Span Perspective) For boys, ____________ (early/late) maturation is usually more difficult.

Describe several characteristics and/or problems of late-maturing boys.

46. (A Life-Span Perspective) Research on the timing of puberty in boys has found that the effects of early puberty are generally ______________ (positive/negative/mixed), while the effects of late puberty are ______________ (positive/negative/ mixed).

Briefly describe the findings of follow-up studies of late-maturing boys as adults.

47. (A Life-Span Perspective) For boys, late maturation today may be ______________ (more/less) difficult than in the past.

48. (A Life-Span Perspective) In general, the more social changes adolescents go through, the ______________ (more/less) likely they are to experience problems such as a drop in grades, lowered self-esteem, and difficulties with teachers.

49. (A Life-Span Perspective) The events of puberty typically ______________ (increase/ decrease/do not affect) the distance between parents and their adolescent children.

50. (A Life-Span Perspective) The effects of early or late maturation are ______________ (more/less) apparent among adolescents of lower socioeconomic status than among middle- or upper-class teenagers.

50. (A Life-Span Perspective) The effects of early or late maturation ______________ (vary from culture to culture/are universal).

Progress Test 1

Multiple-Choice Questions

Circle your answers to the following questions and check them with the answers on page 214. If your answer is incorrect, read the explanation for why it is incorrect and then consult the appropriate pages of the text (in parentheses following the correct answer).

1. Which of the following most accurately describes the sequence of pubertal development in girls?
   a. breast buds and pubic hair; growth spurt in which fat is deposited on hips and buttocks; first menstrual period; ovulation
   b. growth spurt; breast buds and pubic hair; first menstrual period; ovulation
   c. first menstrual period; breast buds and pubic hair; growth spurt; ovulation
   d. breast buds and pubic hair; growth spurt; ovulation; first menstrual period

2. Although both sexes grow rapidly during adolescence, boys typically begin their accelerated growth about:
   a. two years later than girls.
   b. a year earlier than girls.
   c. the time they reach sexual maturity.
   d. the time their facial hair appears.

3. The first readily observable sign of the onset of puberty is:
   a. the growth spurt.
   b. the appearance of facial, body, and pubic hair.
   c. a change in the shape of the eyes.
   d. the lengthening of the torso.

4. More than any other group in the population, adolescent girls are likely to have:
   a. asthma.
   b. acne.
   c. iron-deficiency anemia.
   d. testosterone deficiency.

5. For most young women, even a year after menarche, ovulation:
   a. cannot result in pregnancy.
   b. occurs regularly.
   c. is irregular.
   d. is in remission.

6. For males, the secondary sex characteristic that usually occurs last is:
   a. breast enlargement.
   b. the appearance of facial hair.
   c. growth of the testes.
   d. the appearance of pubic hair.

7. For girls, the specific event that is taken to indicate fertility is ______________; for boys, it is ______________.
   a. the growth of breast buds; voice deepening
   b. menarche; spermarche
   c. anovulation; the testosterone surge
   d. the growth spurt; pubic hair

8. The most significant hormonal changes of puberty include an increase of ______________ in ______________ and an increase of ______________ in ______________.
   a. progesterone; boys; estrogens; girls
   b. estrogens; boys; testosterone; girls
   c. progesterone; girls; estrogens; boys
   d. estrogens; girls; testosterone; boys

9. (A Closer Look) In general, most adolescents are:
   a. overweight.
   b. satisfied with their appearance.
   c. dissatisfied with their appearance.
   d. unaffected by cultural attitudes about beauty.

10. (A Closer Look) In adolescence, as at other times in the life span, negative body image is most likely to be accompanied by:
   a. feelings of depression.
   b. loss of appetite.
   c. delayed maturation.
   d. overeating.

11. The average American girl reaches menarche at age ______________, while the average boy reaches spermarche at age ______________.
   a. 11; 12
   b. 12; 11
   c. $12\frac{1}{2}$; 13
   d. 13; 15

12. (A Life-Span Perspective) Early physical maturation:
   a. tends to be equally difficult for girls and boys.
   b. tends to be more difficult for boys than for girls.
   c. tends to be more difficult for girls than for boys.
   d. is easier for both girls and boys to cope with than late maturation.

13. (A Closer Look) After puberty, most adolescents:
   a. have a more positive body image.
   b. have a more negative body image.
   c. have the same body image they had prior to puberty.
   d. have a body image that will not change significantly for the rest of their lives.

14. (A Life-Span Perspective) Adolescents who experience many social changes, such as changing schools, moving to a new neighborhood, etc.:
   a. often experience a delay in physical maturation.
   b. are no more likely to have a difficult adolescence than are teenagers who experience few social changes.
   c. are likely to score higher in measures of social competence than teenagers who experience few social changes.
   d. are more likely to experience difficulties, such as a decrease in self-esteem.

15. (A Life-Span Perspective) Late maturity has been shown to correlate with:
   a. less parent-adolescent strife for both boys and girls.
   b. more parent-adolescent strife for boys only.
   c. increased self-esteem in both sexes.
   d. decreased self-esteem in both sexes.

True or False Items

Write *true* or *false* on the line in front of each statement.

______ 1. More calories are necessary during adolescence than at any other period during the life span.

______ 2. A girl's first menstrual cycles are usually anovulatory; that is, ovulation does not occur.

______ 3. The first indicator of reproductive potential in males is menarche.

______ 4. Lung capacity, heart size, and total volume of blood increase significantly during adolescence.

______ 5. Puberty generally begins sometime between ages 8 and 14.

______ 6. (A Closer Look) Girls who mature late and are thinner than average tend to be satisfied with their weight.

______ 7. (A Closer Look) The strong emphasis on physical appearance is unique to adolescents and finds little support from teachers, parents, and the larger culture.

______ 8. (A Closer Look) Girls are more dissatisfied than boys with their appearance, their weight, and specific body parts.

______ 9. (A Life-Span Perspective) The problems of the early-maturing girl tend to be temporary.

______ 10. (A Life-Span Perspective) Late maturation is more likely to cause lasting psychological problems for girls than for boys.

Progress Test 2

Progress Test 2 should be completed during a final chapter review. Answer the following questions after you thoroughly understand the correct answers for the Chapter Review and Progress Test 1.

Multiple-Choice Questions

1. Which of the following is the correct sequence of pubertal events in boys?
   a. growth spurt; pubic hair; first ejaculation; lowering of voice
   b. pubic hair; first ejaculation; growth spurt; lowering of voice
   c. lowering of voice; pubic hair; growth spurt; first ejaculation
   d. growth spurt; lowering of voice; pubic hair; first ejaculation

2. Which of the following statements about adolescent physical development is *not* true?
   a. Hands and feet generally lengthen before arms and legs.
   b. Facial features usually grow before the head itself reaches adult size and shape.
   c. Oil, sweat, and odor glands become more active.
   d. The lymphoid system increases slightly in size, and the heart increases by nearly half.

3. In puberty, a hormone that increases markedly in girls (and only somewhat in boys) is:
   a. estrogen. c. androgen.
   b. testosterone. d. menarche.

4. Nutritional deficiencies in adolescence are frequently the result of:
   a. eating pizza.
   b. exotic diets or food fads.
   c. anovulatory menstruation.
   d. excessive exercise.

5. In females, puberty is typically marked by a(n):
   a. significant widening of the shoulders.
   b. significant widening of the hips.
   c. enlargement of the torso and upper chest.
   d. decrease in the size of the eyes and nose.

6. Nonreproductive sexual characteristics, such as the deepening of the voice and development of breasts, are called:
   a. gender-typed traits.
   b. primary sex characteristics.
   c. secondary sex characteristics.
   d. pubertal prototypes.

7. Puberty is initiated when hormones are released from the ________, then from the ________, and then from the ________.
   a. hypothalamus; pituitary; gonads
   b. pituitary; gonads; hypothalamus
   c. gonads; pituitary; hypothalamus
   d. pituitary; hypothalamus; gonads

8. (A Closer Look) In forming their own body image, adolescents are *most* strongly influenced by:
   a. their own potential. c. cultural ideals.
   b. their parents. d. heredity.

9. (A Closer Look) With regard to appearance, adolescent girls are *most* commonly dissatisfied with:
   a. timing of maturation. c. weight.
   b. eyes and other facial features. d. legs.

10. (A Life-Span Perspective) Statistically speaking, to predict the age at which a girl first has sexual intercourse, it would be *most* useful to know her:
    a. socioeconomic level. c. religion.
    b. race or ethnic group. d. age at menarche.

11. Although the ________ of puberty is quite variable, its ________ is largely fixed.
    a. sequence; timing c. timing; sequence
    b. duration; onset d. onset; duration

12. (A Life-Span Perspective) Late physical maturation is:
    a. equally difficult for girls and boys.
    b. more difficult for boys than for girls.
    c. more difficult for girls than for boys.
    d. easier for girls and boys to cope with than early maturation.

13. Puberty is most accurately defined as:
    a. the period of rapid physical growth that occurs during adolescence.
    b. the period during which sexual maturation is attained.
    c. the period of rapid physical growth and sexual maturation that ends childhood.
    d. the period during which adolescents establish identities separate from their parents.

14. Which of the following does *not* typically occur during puberty?
    a. The lungs increase in size and capacity.
    b. The heart's size and rate of beating increase.
    c. Blood volume increases.
    d. The lymphoid system decreases in size.

15. Teenagers' susceptibility to respiratory ailments typically ________ during adolescence, due to a(n) ________ in the size of the lymphoid system.
    a. increases; increase
    b. increases; decrease
    c. decreases; increase
    d. decreases; decrease

Matching Items

Match each term or concept with its corresponding description or definition.

Terms or Concepts

_____ 1. puberty
_____ 2. GH
_____ 3. testosterone
_____ 4. estrogen
_____ 5. growth spurt
_____ 6. primary sex characteristics
_____ 7. menarche
_____ 8. spermarche
_____ 9. secondary sex characteristics
_____ 10. body image

Descriptions or Definitions

a. onset of menstruation
b. period of rapid growth and sexual maturation that ends childhood
c. hormone that increases dramatically in boys during puberty
d. hormone that increases steadily during puberty in both sexes
e. hormone that increases dramatically in girls during puberty
f. first sign is increased bone length and density
g. attitude toward one's physical appearance
h. physical characteristics not involved in reproduction
i. characteristics of sex organs involved in reproduction
j. first ejaculation containing sperm

Challenge Test

Answer these questions the day before an exam as a final check on your understanding of the chapter's terms and concepts.

1. (A Closer Look) Fifteen-year-old Janice is preoccupied with her "disgusting appearance" and seems depressed most of the time. The best thing her parents could do to help her through this difficult time would be to:

a. ignore her self-preoccupation since their attention would only reinforce it.
b. encourage her to "shape up" and not give in to self-pity.
c. kid her about her appearance in the hope that she will see how silly she is acting.
d. offer practical advice, such as clothing suggestions, to improve her body image.

2. Thirteen-year-old Rosa, an avid runner and dancer, is worried because most of her friends have begun to menstruate regularly. Her doctor tells her:

a. that she should have a complete physical exam, since female athletes usually menstruate earlier than the average girl.
b. not to worry, since female athletes usually menstruate later than the average girl.
c. that she must stop running immediately, since the absence of menstruation is a sign of a serious health problem.
d. that the likely cause of her delayed menarche is her poor diet.

3. Twelve-year-old Bradley is worried because his twin sister has suddenly grown taller and more physically mature than he. His parents should:

a. reassure him that the average boy is two years behind the average girl in the onset of the growth spurt.
b. tell him that within a year or less he will grow taller than his sister.
c. tell him that one member of each fraternal twin pair is always shorter.
d. encourage him to exercise more to accelerate the onset of his growth spurt.

4. Calvin, the class braggart, boasts that because his beard has begun to grow, he is more virile than his male classmates. Jacob informs him that:

a. the tendency to grow facial and body hair has nothing to do with virility.
b. beard growth is determined by heredity.
c. facial hair is usually the last secondary sex characteristic to develop, sometimes occurring long after males have become sexually active.
d. all of the above are true.

5. (A Life-Span Perspective) The most likely source of status for a late-maturing, middle-class boy would be:
   a. academic achievement or special talents.
   b. physical build.
   c. athletic leadership.
   d. success with the opposite sex.

6. (A Life-Span Perspective) Which of the following students is likely to be the most popular in a seventh-grade class?
   a. Vicki, the most sexually mature girl in the class
   b. Sandra, the tallest girl in the class
   c. Brad, who is at the top of the class scholastically
   d. Dan, the tallest boy in the class

7. (A Life-Span Perspective) Regarding the effects of early and late maturation on boys and girls, which of the following is *not* true?
   a. Early maturation is usually easier for boys to manage than it is for girls.
   b. Late maturation is usually easier for girls to manage than it is for boys.
   c. Late-maturing girls may be drawn into older peer groups and may become involved in problem behaviors such as early sexual activity.
   d. Late-maturing boys do not "catch up" physically, or in terms of their self-images, for many years.

8. (A Life-Span Perspective) Eleven-year-old Clarice, who matured early, is depressed because she often is teased about her well-developed figure. Her wise mother tells her that early-maturing girls:
   a. eventually have more close friends than those who are slower to mature.
   b. have fewer emotional problems in the long run than late-maturing girls.
   c. often become more popular by seventh or eighth grade.
   d. receive all of the above benefits.

9. (A Life-Span Perspective) Knowing that you are studying developmental psychology, your older brother and sister-in-law ask for your advice regarding their 14-year-old daughter, who wants to start dating. You tell them:
   a. not to worry, since girls who start dating early actually face fewer developmental hazards than the average adolescent.
   b. early dating always leads to early sexuality, and usually to pregnancy.
   c. that, because early sexual activity is more likely, girls who date early are more likely to have intercourse before high school is over, and also more likely to become pregnant.
   d. that most girls who date early are not capable of reproduction.

10. (A Closer Look) Thirteen-year-old Darren spends hours examining himself in front of the mirror. His worried parents consult the school psychologist, who tells them that Darren's behavior:
   a. is a warning sign of possible emotional trauma.
   b. is perfectly normal, since few adolescents are satisfied with their appearance.
   c. should be discouraged, since such self-absorption is often followed by depression.
   d. is puzzling, since such preoccupation with appearance is usually more typical of adolescent girls.

11. Which of the following adolescents is likely to begin puberty at the earliest age?
   a. Aretha, an African-American teenager who hates exercise
   b. Todd, a football player of European ancestry
   c. Kyu, an Asian-American honors student
   d. There is too little information to make a prediction.

12. (A Life-Span Perspective) Of the following teenagers, those most likely to be distressed about their physical development are:
   a. late-maturing girls.
   b. late-maturing boys.
   c. early-maturing boys.
   d. girls or boys who masturbate.

13. Thirteen-year-old Kristin seems apathetic and lazy to her parents. You tell them:
   a. that Kristin is showing signs of chronic depression.
   b. that Kristin may be experiencing psychosocial difficulties.
   c. that Kristin has a poor attitude and needs more discipline.
   d. to have Kristin's iron level checked.

14. I am a hormone that rises steadily during puberty in both males and females. What am I?
   a. estrogen
   b. testosterone
   c. GH
   d. menarche

15. Eleven-year-old Linda, who has just begun to experience the first signs of puberty laments, "When will the agony of puberty be over?" You

tell her that the major events of puberty typically end about ________ after the first visible signs appear.

a. 6 years
b. 3 or 4 years
c. 2 years
d. 1 year

Key Terms

Using your own words, write a brief definition or explanation of each of the following terms on a separate piece of paper.

1. puberty
2. GH (growth hormone)
3. testosterone
4. estrogens
5. growth spurt
6. primary sex characteristics
7. menarche
8. spermarche
9. secondary sex characteristics
10. body image

ANSWERS

CHAPTER REVIEW

1. puberty

Girls: emergence of breast buds, initial appearance of pubic hair, widening of the hips, peak growth spurt, first menstrual period, final breast development, completion of pubic hair growth

Boys: growth of the testes, growth of the penis, initial appearance of pubic hair, first ejaculation, peak growth spurt, voice changes, and then beard development and completion of pubic hair growth

2. 8; 14
3. is usually the same in all children; 3 or 4
4. hypothalamus; pituitary gland; adrenal glands; gonads (sex glands); testes; ovaries
5. GH (growth hormone); testosterone; estrogens; 1
6. the reaction of others to the visible signs of puberty
7. growth spurt; sexual characteristics
8. length; density; gain
9. fat; gender; heredity; diet; exercise
10. females
11. muscle; upper
12. 38 pounds (17 kilograms); 9 $\frac{5}{8}$ inches (24 centimeters); 42 pounds (19 kilograms)
13. varies
14. head
15. do not always
16. lungs; heart; decreases; increases; endurance

The fact that the more visible spurts of weight and height precede the less visible ones of the muscles and organs means that athletic training and weightlifting should match the young person's size of a year or so earlier.

17. lymphoid; less
18. oil; sweat; odor
19. calories; vitamins; minerals; calcium; iron; zinc; D; iron; iron-deficiency anemia
20. overeating; undereating; nutritional imbalance
21. drug; a preoccupation with being thin
22. most; did not vary
23. primary sex characteristics; is

Girls: growth of uterus; thickening of the vaginal lining

Boys: growth of testes; lengthening of penis; scrotal sac enlarges and become pendulous

24. menarche; spermarche; several years later
25. anovulatory; low-birth-weight
26. have; do not; masturbation
27. cramping; moodiness
28. secondary sex characteristics

Males grow taller than females and become wider at the shoulders than at the hips. Females become wider at the hips and their breasts begin to develop. About 65 percent of boys experience some temporary breast enlargement. As the larynx grows, the adolescent's voice (especially in boys) becomes lower. Head and body hair become coarser and darker in both sexes. Facial hair (especially in boys) begins to grow.

29. breast development; facial and body hair
30. body image

Many adolescents spend hours examining themselves in front of the mirror; some exercise or diet with obsessive intensity.

31. appetite; girls; reversed
32. good looks, intelligence, a good body, friendliness, conversational ability
33. tall and muscular; thin and shapely
34. girls; depression
35. sequence; timing; 8; 14; sex, genes, body type, nourishment, metabolism, and emotional and physical health

36. $12\frac{1}{2}$; 13; 2
37. sisters; monozygotic twins
38. does
39. earlier
40. fat; later; earlier
41. accelerate
42. positively; girls
43. early

Early-maturing girls may be teased about their big feet or developing breasts. Those who date early may suffer a decrease in self-esteem associated with being scrutinized by parents and criticized by friends. They are also likely to have sexual intercourse before high school is over, less likely to use contraception, and thus more likely to become pregnant and to find their educational and career accomplishments deflected.

44. have; more; fewer
45. late

Late-maturing boys tend to be less poised, less relaxed, more restless, and more talkative than early-maturing boys. Late-maturing boys are more playful, more creative, and more flexible, qualities that are not usually admired by other adolescents. They also tend to have more conflicts with parents.

46. positive; mixed

Men who had matured late tended to be less controlled, less responsible, and less dominant, and they were less likely to hold positions of leadership. Some still had feelings of inferiority and rejection. They were, however, likely to have a better sense of humor and to be more egalitarian and more perceptive than their early-maturing peers.

47. less
48. more
49. increase
50. more
51. vary from culture to culture

PROGRESS TEST 1

Multiple-Choice Questions

1. **a.** is the answer. (p. 371)
2. **a.** is the answer. (p. 380)
3. **a.** is the answer. (p. 372)
4. **c.** is the answer. This is because each menstrual period deletes some iron from the body. (p. 374)
5. **c.** is the answer. (p. 376)

   a. & b. Even a year after menarche, when ovulation is irregular, pregnancy is possible.

   d. Remission means a disappearance of symptoms, such as those of a particular disease; although at first ovulation is irregular, it certainly does not disappear.
6. **b.** is the answer. (p. 377)
7. **b.** is the answer. (pp. 375–376)
8. **d.** is the answer. (p. 371)
9. **c.** is the answer. (p. 378)

   a. Although some adolescents become overweight, many diet and lose weight in an effort to attain a desired body image.

   d. On the contrary, cultural attitudes about beauty are an extremely influential factor in the formation of a teenager's body image.
10. **a.** is the answer. (p. 379)
11. **c.** is the answer. (p. 380)
12. **c.** is the answer. (p. 382)
13. **a.** is the answer. (p. 379)
14. **d.** is the answer. (p. 383)
15. **b.** is the answer. (p. 382)

    c. & d. Maturation that occurs at a different time than one's peers' may have an impact on both sexes, but the effects of early puberty are generally positive for boys and negative for girls.

True or False Items

1. T (p. 374)
2. T (p. 376)
3. F The first indication of reproductive potential in males is ejaculation (spermarche). Menarche is the first indication of reproductive potential in females. (p. 376)
4. T (p. 373)
5. T (p. 370)
6. F Studies show that the majority of adolescent girls, even those in the thinnest group, want to lose weight. (p. 378)
7. F The strong emphasis on appearance is reflected in the culture as a whole; for example, teachers (and no doubt prospective employers) tend to judge people who are physically attractive as being more competent than those who are less attractive. (p. 378)
8. T (p. 378)
9. T (p. 382)
10. F Late maturation is more likely to cause lasting psychological problems for boys than for girls. (p. 382)

PROGRESS TEST 2

Multiple-Choice Questions

1. **b.** is the answer. (p. 370)
2. **d.** is the answer. During adolescence, the lymphoid system *decreases* in size and the heart *doubles* in size. (pp. 373–374)
3. **a.** is the answer. (p. 371)
   b. Testosterone increases markedly in boys.
   c. Androgen is another name for testosterone.
   d. Menarche is the first menstrual period.
4. **b.** is the answer. (p. 374)
5. **b.** is the answer. (p. 372)
   a. The shoulders of males tend to widen during puberty.
   c. The torso typically lengthens during puberty.
   d. The eyes and nose *increase* in size during puberty.
6. **c.** is the answer. (pp. 376–377)
   a. Although not a term used in the textbook, a gender-typed trait is one that is typical of one sex but not the other.
   b. Primary sex characteristics are those involving the reproductive organs.
   d. This is not a term used by developmental psychologists.
7. **a.** is the answer. (p. 371)
8. **c.** is the answer. (p. 378)
   a., b., & d. These certainly are factors that influence physical characteristics as well as body image; cultural ideals, however, exert an even stronger influence.
9. **c.** is the answer. (p. 378)
   a. If the timing of maturation differs substantially from that of the peer group, dissatisfaction is likely; however, this is not the most common source of dissatisfaction in teenage girls.
   b. & d. Although teenage girls are more likely than boys to be dissatisfied with certain features, which body parts are troubling varies from girl to girl.
10. **d.** is the answer. (p. 381)
11. **c.** is the answer. (p. 380)
    b. & d. The onset of puberty is quite variable; the text does not suggest that the duration of puberty varies significantly.
12. **b.** is the answer. (p. 382)
    c. & d. Girls typically have more difficulty coping with early maturation.
13. **c.** is the answer. (p. 370)
14. **b.** is the answer. Although the size of the heart increases during puberty, heart rate *decreases*. (p. 373)
15. **d.** is the answer. (p. 374)

Matching Items

1. b (p. 370)	**5.** f (p. 372)	**8.** j (p. 376)
2. d (p. 371)	**6.** i (p. 375)	**9.** h (pp. 376–377)
3. c (p. 371)	**7.** a (pp. 375–376)	**10.** g (p. 378)
4. e (p. 371)		

CHALLENGE TEST

1. **d.** is the answer. (p. 379)
   a., b., & c. These would likely make matters worse.
2. **b.** is the answer. (p. 380)
   a. Because they typically have little body fat, female dancers and athletes menstruate *later* than the average girl.
   c. Delayed maturation in a young dancer or athlete is usually quite normal.
   d. The text does not indicate that the age of menarche varies with diet.
3. **a.** is the answer. (p. 380)
   b. It usually takes longer than one year for a prepubescent male to catch up with females who have begun puberty.
   c. This is not true.
   d. The text does not suggest that exercise has an effect on the timing of the growth spurt.
4. **d.** is the answer. (p. 377)
5. **a.** is the answer. (p. 384)
   b., c., & d. These are more typically sources of status for early-maturing boys.
6. **d.** is the answer. (pp. 381–383)
   a. & b. Early-maturing girls often are teased and criticized by their friends.
   c. During adolescence, physical stature is typically a more prized attribute among peers than is scholastic achievement.
7. **c.** is the answer. It is *early*-maturing girls who often are drawn into older peer groups. (p. 381)
8. **d.** is the answer. (p. 382)
9. **c.** is the answer. (p. 381)
   a. Girls who date early face *more* developmental hazards than the average teenage girl.
   b. Early dating does not always lead to sexuality.
   d. Although ovulation is irregular at first, reproduction is possible once menarche has occurred.

10. **b.** is the answer. (p. 378)
    a. & c. These are untrue.
    d. Preoccupation with appearance is typical of both teenage boys and girls.
11. **a.** is the answer. African-Americans often begin puberty earlier than Asian-Americans or Americans of European ancestry. Furthermore, females who are inactive menstruate earlier than those who are more active. (p. 380)
12. **b.** is the answer. (p. 382)
    a. Late maturation is typically more difficult for boys than for girls.
    c. Early maturation is generally a positive experience for boys.
    d. Adolescent masturbation is no longer the source of guilt or shame that it once was.
13. **d.** Kristin's symptoms are typical of iron-deficiency anemia, which is more common in teenage girls than in any other age group. (p. 374)
14. **c.** is the answer. (p. 371)
    a. Only in girls do estrogen levels rise markedly during puberty.
    b. Only in boys do testosterone levels rise markedly during puberty.
    d. Menarche is the first menstrual period.
15. **b.** is the answer. (pp. 370–371)

KEY TERMS

1. **Puberty** is the period of rapid physical growth and sexual maturation that ends childhood and brings the young person to adult size, shape, and sexual potential. (p. 370)
2. **GH (growth hormone),** which is one of about a dozen hormones involved in puberty, rises steadily in both sexes during this period of development. (p. 371)
3. **Testosterone** is a hormone of puberty that increases dramatically in boys and slightly in girls. (p. 371)
4. The **estrogens** are hormones of puberty that increase markedly in girls and slightly in boys. (p. 371)
   Example: Levels of *testosterone* in boys, and the *estrogens* in girls, begin to increase at least a year before the first perceptible signs of puberty.
5. The **growth spurt,** which begins with an increase in bone length and density and includes rapid weight gain and organ growth, is one of the many observable signs of puberty. (p. 372)
6. During puberty, changes in **primary sex characteristics** involve those sex organs that are directly involved in reproduction. (p. 375)
7. **Menarche,** which refers to the first menstrual period, is the specific event that is taken to indicate fertility in adolescent girls. (pp. 375–376)
8. **Spermarche,** which refers to the first ejaculation of seminal fluid containing sperm, is the specific event that is taken to indicate fertility in adolescent boys. (p. 376)
9. During puberty, changes in **secondary sex characteristics** involve parts of the body other than the sex organs. (pp. 376–377)
10. **Body image** refers to adolescents' mental concept of, and attitude toward, their physical appearance. (p. 378)

CHAPTER 15 Adolescence: Cognitive Development

Chapter Overview

Chapter 15 begins with an explanation of Piaget's final stage of cognitive development: formal operational thought. With the attainment of formal operational thought, the developing person becomes able to think in an adult way, that is, to be logical, to think in terms of possibilities, to reason scientifically and abstractly.

Not everyone reaches the stage of formal operational thought, and even those who do spend much of their time thinking at less advanced levels. The second section of the chapter, on adolescent egocentrism, supports this generalization in showing that adolescents have difficulty thinking rationally about themselves and their immediate experiences. Adolescent egocentrism makes them see themselves as psychologically unique and more socially significant than they really are.

The third section addresses the question, "What kind of school best fosters adolescent intellectual growth?" Many adolescents enter secondary school feeling less motivated and more vulnerable to self-doubt than they were in elementary school. The rigid behavioral demands and intensified competition of most secondary schools do not, however, provide a supportive learning environment for adolescents. Schools can be more effectively organized by setting clear, attainable educational goals that are supported by the entire staff.

The fourth section deals with one particular area of cognitive development: moral reasoning. Kohlberg's stage theory is discussed, as well as current reevaluations of his stages. The section raises a crucial and practical question: What is the relationship between moral thinking and moral behavior?

The chapter concludes with an example of adolescent cognition at work: decision making in the area of sexual behavior. The discussion relates choices made by adolescents to their cognitive abilities and typical shortcomings, and it suggests ways in which adolescents may be helped to make healthy choices.

NOTE: Answer guidelines for all Chapter 15 questions begin on page 228.

Guided Study

The text chapter should be studied one section at a time. Before you read, preview each section by skimming it, noting headings and boldface items. Then read the appropriate section objectives from the following outline. Keep these objectives in mind and, as you read the chapter section, search for the information that will enable you to meet each objective. Once you have finished a section, write out answers for its objectives.

Adolescent Thought (pp. 388–391)

1. Describe evidence of formal operational thinking during adolescence and discuss current reevaluations of Piaget's views.

Adolescent Egocentrism (pp. 391–393)

2. Discuss adolescent egocentrism and give two examples of egocentric fantasies or fables.

Schools, Learning, and the Adolescent Mind (pp. 393–398)

3. Discuss whether the typical secondary school meets the cognitive needs of the typical adolescent.

4. Discuss the impact of ego- and task-involvement learning on the typical adolescent and explain how schools can be organized to more effectively meet adolescents' cognitive needs.

5. (A Closer Look) Discuss the impact of academic tracking on students.

Moral Development (pp. 398–402)

6. (A Life-Span Perspective) Outline Kohlberg's stage theory of moral development.

7. (A Life-Span Perspective) Identify and evaluate four criticisms of Kohlberg's theory.

8. Discuss the relationship between moral reasoning and moral behavior.

Sexual Decision Making: A Study in Adolescent Cognition (pp. 402–408)

9. Explain how adolescent thinking contributes to the high incidence of adolescent pregnancy and sexually transmitted disease.

10. Discuss and evaluate the new approach to sex education.

Chapter Review

When you have finished reading the chapter, work through the material that follows to review it. Complete the sentences and answer the questions. As you proceed, evaluate your performance for each section by consulting the answers on page 228. Do not continue with the next section until you understand each answer. If you need to, review or reread the appropriate section in the textbook before continuing.

Adolescent Thought (pp. 388–391)

1. The distinguishing feature of adolescent thought is the capacity to think in terms of ____________________ rather than merely concrete reality.
2. This last stage of cognitive development, called ____________________ ____________________ ____________________ by Piaget, is attained at about age ____________________. One specific example of this type of thinking is the development of ____________________ reasoning.
3. The adolescent's ability to suspend knowledge of reality and think creatively and playfully about hypothetical possibilities is demonstrated in what Flavell calls the ____________________ ____________________ ____________________.
4. Compared to formal operational adolescents, concrete operational children have ____________________ (more/less) difficulty arguing against their personal beliefs and self-interest.
5. Many adolescents arrive at formal operational thinking ____________________ (earlier/later) than Piaget predicted. Formal operational thinking ____________________ (is/is not) eventually demonstrated by all adults.
6. Piaget acknowledged that ____________________ and ____________________ are crucial factors in enabling an individual to attain formal operational thought.
7. Once formal operational thinking is demonstrated in one domain, it ____________________ (is/is not) necessarily demonstrated in all others.

Adolescent Egocentrism (pp. 391–393)

8. The adolescent's belief that he or she is uniquely significant and that the social world revolves around him or her is a psychological phenomenon called ____________________ ____________________. David Elkind has argued that this form of thinking occurs because adolescents fail to differentiate between the ____________________ and the ____________________.

Give an example of this flawed thinking in adolescents.

9. An adolescent's tendency to feel that he or she is somehow immune to the laws of mortality and probability is expressed in the ____________________ ____________________.
10. An adolescent's tendency to imagine that her or his own life is heroic or even mythical, and that she or he is destined for great accomplishments, is expressed in the ____________________ ____________________.
11. Adolescents, believing that they are under constant scrutiny from nearly everyone, create for themselves a(n) ____________________ ____________________.
12. Generally, egocentrism peaks from ____________________ to ____________________ adolescence and thereafter declines ____________________ (gradually/suddenly).

13. Preoccupation with the imaginary audience can be taken as an indication that the young person is not at ease with his or her ______________ world. A high degree of egocentrism is usually an indication that an adolescent ______________ (has/has not) mastered formal operational thought.

Cite several variations in the intensity of adolescent egocentrism (for example, variations by sex, socioeconomic status, etc.)

Schools, Learning, and the Adolescent Mind (pp. 393–398)

14. The best setting for personal growth, called the optimum ______________-______________ ______________, depends on several factors, including ______________ ______________ ______________.

15. The goals of the American education system ______________ (have/have not) changed significantly over the generations.

16. Adolescents are ______________ (more/less) vulnerable to criticism than their behaviors imply. At the same time, the emergence of formal operational thought makes them ______________ (more/less) interested in the opinions of others.

17. Adolescents' increasing ability to imagine and theorize often takes a(n) ______________-______________ tone. One outcome of this is a widespread dip in academic ______________-______________ as young people enter secondary school.

Cite several ways in which educational settings tend not to be supportive of adolescents' self-confidence.

18. Many teachers have ______________ (lower/higher) expectations of adolescent students than they do of younger students. As a result, most students experience a(n) ______________ (increase/drop) in motivation and achievement as they move from the sixth to the seventh grade.

19. Developmentalists generally agree that ______________ (cooperation/competition) in the classroom is healthy for adolescents.

20. In ______________-______________ learning, academic grades are based solely on individual test performance, and students are ranked against each other. In such situations, many students, especially ______________, find it psychologically safer not to work very hard. Curricular areas in which girls suddenly score lower in high school than in elementary school are those areas in which ______________ achievement scores are widely used—for example, ______________ and ______________.

21. The tendency to avoid advanced math and science is also followed by many ______________ students, especially from cultures that stress ______________ and ______________.

22. In ______________-______________ learning, grades are based on cooperatively acquiring certain competencies and knowledge that everyone is expected to attain.

23. Cooperative learning is ______________ (more/less) likely to lead to rivalry between various ethnic, religious, and racial groups.

24. (A Closer Look) The separation of students into distinct groups based on standardized tests of ability and achievement is called ____________________. This practice is often instituted for the first time at about age ____________________.

25. (A Closer Look) The impact of tracking on student motivation, pace of learning, and achievement is most deleterious for ____________________ (lower/middle/upper) track students.

Explain why this is so.

26. (A Closer Look) Studies have found that the precipitating reason for dropping out is usually ____________________.

27. Schools that are most effective in educating students share the central characteristic of ____________________.

Moral Development (pp. 398–402)

28. The development of moral actions, attitudes, and arguments is ____________________ (mostly complete by adolescence/lifelong).

Give examples of how biosocial, cognitive, and social development accelerate the pace of adolescent moral development.

29. (A Life-Span Perspective) The theorist who has extensively studied moral development by presenting children, adolescents, and adults with stories that pose ethical dilemmas is ____________________. According to his theory, the three levels of moral reasoning are ____________________, ____________________, and ____________________.

30. (A Life-Span Perspective) In preconventional reasoning, emphasis is on ____________________. "Might makes right" describes stage ____________________ (1/2), while "look out for number one" describes stage ____________________ (1/2).

31. (A Life-Span Perspective) In conventional reasoning, emphasis is on ____________________, such as being a dutiful citizen in stage ____________________ (3/4), or winning approval from others in stage ____________________ (3/4).

32. (A Life-Span Perspective) In postconventional reasoning, emphasis is on ____________________, such as ____________________ (stage 5) and ____________________ (stage 6).

33. (A Life-Span Perspective) In Kohlberg's theory, the moral conclusions people reach when reacting to ethical dilemmas are ____________________ (more/less) important than how they reason.

34. (A Life-Span Perspective) One criticism of Kohlberg's theory is that the stages reflect values associated with ____________________, ____________________ cultures. A second is that moral thinking is less ____________________ than Kohlberg implied. A third is that the theory overemphasized ____________________ thought and underestimated ____________________. A fourth is that the theory was validated only on ____________________ (males/females).

35. (A Life-Span Perspective) The criticism that Kohlberg's theory is biased against females has been most compellingly expressed by ____________________. Research studies ____________________ (have/have not) consistently supported this criticism. Some studies do find that, compared with males, females tend to focus more on ____________________ than on ____________________.

36. Most children, adolescents, and adults ______________ (do/do not) cheat, or bend rules, when their own self-interest is at stake.

37. Most studies have shown that moral reasoning ______________ (does/does not) significantly influence moral behavior. Juvenile delinquents generally ______________ (do/do not) score lower on tests of moral reasoning than do other adolescents their age.

Sexual Decision Making: A Study in Adolescent Cognition (pp. 402–408)

38. Generally, research reveals that adolescent beliefs, values, and reasoning processes ______________ (do/do not) significantly affect their sexual behavior.

39. Teenage pregnancy ______________ (is/is not) a worldwide problem. The country with the highest teenage pregnancy rate in the industrialized world is the ______________.

Describe the likely consequences to the mother and the child of an American adolescent giving birth.

40. Diseases that are spread by sexual contact are called ______________ ______________ ______________.

41. The highest rates of the most prevalent STDs occur in sexually active people between the ages of ______________ and ______________.

42. The most common transmission of the ______________ ______________, which causes AIDS, is through ______________ contact. It is presently estimated that one in every ______________ teenagers is at high risk for AIDS because of unsafe practices, such as ______________.

43. Ignorance about sex and the unavailability of contraception ______________ (do/do not) explain the high rates of adolescent pregnancy and STD.

44. Knowing sexual facts has so little effect on adolescent sexual behavior because ______________ ______________; ______________; and, because their thinking tends to be ______________, they reason in terms of their own immediate needs, rather than considering the consequences of their behavior for their sexual partner or for a possible child.

45. Because of their sense of personal ______________, many adolescents seriously underestimate the chances of pregnancy or of contracting a disease.

46. The first step in encouraging adolescents to make more rational decisions about their sexuality requires adults to be more ______________ in their thinking about adolescent sexuality.

47. Some research suggests that ______________ (sons/daughters) listen more to their parents on the topic of sex because the underlying message is somewhat more accepting of sexuality.

Briefly explain why traditional sex education is often irrelevant or ineffective.

48. A new form of sex education attempts not only to teach facts but to encourage ______________ of those facts. One program involved a(n) ______________ ______________ procedure in which, through role-playing and discussions, adolescents were taught reasoning skills for dealing with sexual pressures.

49. Collectively, research indicates that effective sex education must ______________ ______________.

Progress Test 1

Multiple-Choice Questions

Circle your answers to the following questions and check them with the answers on page 229. If your answer is incorrect, read the explanation for why it is incorrect and then consult the appropriate pages of the text (in parentheses following the correct answer).

1. Many psychologists consider the distinguishing feature of adolescent thought to be the ability to think in terms of:
   a. moral issues.
   b. concrete operations.
   c. possibility rather than reality.
   d. logical principles.

2. Piaget's last stage of cognitive development is:
   a. formal operational thought.
   b. concrete operational thought.
   c. universal ethical principles.
   d. symbolic thought.

3. Flavell's term for the adolescent's ability to suspend knowledge of reality and think creatively about possibilities is:
   a. concrete operational thought.
   b. the game of thinking.
   c. the personal fable.
   d. the scientific method.

4. The adolescent who takes risks and feels immune to the laws of mortality is a victim of the:
   a. invincibility fable.
   c. imaginary audience.
   b. personal fable.
   d. death instinct.

5. Imaginary audiences, invincibility fables, and personal fables are expressions of adolescent:
   a. morality.
   c. decision making.
   b. thinking games.
   d. egocentrism.

6. The typical adolescent is:
   a. tough-minded.
   b. indifferent to public opinion.
   c. self-absorbed and hypersensitive to criticism.
   d. all of the above.

7. When adolescents enter secondary school, many:
   a. experience a drop in academic self-confidence.
   b. are less motivated than they were in elementary school.
   c. are less conscientious than they were in elementary school.
   d. experience all of the above.

8. In ______________________, academic grades are based solely on individual test performance, and students are ranked against each other.
   a. task-involvement learning
   b. ego-involvement learning
   c. academic tracking
   d. preconventional classroom environments

9. (A Life-Span Perspective) According to Kohlberg, the highest level of moral reasoning attained by many adolescents is that in which the individual:
   a. seeks the approval of others.
   b. considers punishment and other personal consequences of behavior.
   c. believes that the right behavior means obeying the laws.
   d. recognizes that the laws one obeys ought to reflect the needs of society.

10. (A Life-Span Perspective) In making moral choices, according to Gilligan, females are more likely than males to:
    a. score at a higher level in Kohlberg's system.
    b. emphasize the needs of others.
    c. judge right and wrong in absolute terms.
    d. formulate abstract principles.

11. The main reason for high rates of STD and pregnancy during adolescence is cognitive immaturity, as evidenced by:
    a. the decline of the conventional "good girl" morality.
    b. increased sexual activity.
    c. the inability to think logically about the consequences of sexual activity.
    d. a lack of information about sexual matters.

12. Many adolescents seem to believe that *their* lovemaking will not lead to pregnancy. This belief is an expression of the:
    a. personal fable.
    c. imaginary audience.
    b. invincibility fable.
    d. game of thinking.

13. One reason that AIDS statistics do not show a high rate of infection among today's adolescents is that:
    a. adolescents are less likely than others to be infected by exposure to the human immunodeficiency virus.
    b. most adolescents use condoms.
    c. adolescents are more likely to receive medical care for STDs in general.
    d. AIDS takes about 10 years to develop in an infected individual.

14. In the social inoculation method of sex education, adolescents:
    a. develop reasoning skills to build up a "cognitive immunity" to sexual pressures.
    b. are exposed to scare tactics designed to discourage sexual activity.
    c. are taught by teenagers who have contracted a sexually transmitted disease.
    d. experience all of the above.

15. To estimate the risk of a behavior, such as unprotected sexual intercourse, it is most important that the adolescent be able to think clearly about:
    a. universal ethical principles.
    b. personal beliefs and self-interest.
    c. probability.
    d. peer pressure.

True or False Items

Write *true* or *false* on the line in front of each statement.

_______ 1. By the time they reach adolescence, most children have outgrown "the game of thinking."

_______ 2. Adolescents are generally better able than 8-year-olds to recognize the validity of arguments that clash with their own beliefs.

_______ 3. Everyone attains the stage of formal operational thought by adulthood.

_______ 4. Adolescent egocentrism tends to peak at about age 18.

_______ 5. Adolescents often create an imaginary audience as they envision how others will react to their appearance and behavior.

_______ 6. Most developmentalists feel that competitive classroom environments are a healthy cognitive influence on adolescents.

_______ 7. (A Closer Look) The separation of students into different groups based on standardized tests of ability and achievement is especially beneficial for low-achieving students.

_______ 8. (A Life-Span Perspective) Some critics of Kohlberg feel that he overrated religious faith in moral reasoning.

_______ 9. Adolescents are the group with the highest rates of all sexually transmitted diseases (STDs).

_______ 10. The new wave of sex education tries to take into account adolescent thinking patterns and often involves role-playing, discussions, and specific exercises designed to help adolescents weigh alternatives and analyze risks.

Progress Test 2

Progress Test 2 should be completed during a final chapter review. Answer the following questions after you thoroughly understand the correct answers for the Chapter Review and Progress Test 1.

Multiple-Choice Questions

1. Inhelder and Piaget's classic research found that scientific reasoning abilities:
    a. develop gradually and increase until about age 14.
    b. develop more rapidly in boys than girls.
    b. develop more rapidly in girls than boys.
    d. seem to emerge abruptly at about age 12.

2. In one experiment, the investigator held a red chip so it could be seen and said, "Either the chip in my hand is green or it is not yellow." By age 15, _______________ of the children tested were able to accurately evaluate the logic of this kind of statement.
    a. only about 15 percent
    b. about half
    c. most of the girls, but few of the boys
    d. virtually all

3. Critics of Piaget's theory contend that:
    a. many adolescents arrive at formal operational thinking later than Piaget predicted.
    b. formal operational thinking is more likely to be demonstrated in certain domains than in others.
    c. whether formal operational thinking is demonstrated depends in part on an individual's experiences, talents, and interests.
    d. all of the above are true.

4. When young people overestimate their significance to others, they are displaying:
    a. concrete operational thought.
    b. adolescent egocentrism.
    c. a lack of cognitive growth.
    d. immoral development.

5. The personal fable refers to adolescents imagining that:
   a. they are immune to the dangers of risky behaviors.
   b. they are constantly being scrutinized by others.
   c. their own lives are heroic or even mythical.
   d. the world revolves around their actions.

6. The typical secondary school environment:
   a. has more rigid behavioral demands than the average elementary school.
   b. does not meet the cognitive needs of the typical adolescent.
   c. emphasizes ego-involvement learning.
   d. does all of the above.

7. The most likely reason high school girls suddenly tend to score lower on standardized math and science tests is that:
   a. girls are socialized to be nurturant and uncompetitive.
   b. they have weaker elementary school backgrounds in these subjects.
   c. they too often have been the victims of task-involvement learning.
   d. they simply dislike these subjects.

8. In ______________________, grades are not assigned competitively, but are based on acquiring competencies that *everyone* is expected to attain.
   a. ego-involvement learning
   b. task-involvement learning
   c. academic tracking
   d. preconventional classroom environments

9. (A Closer Look) The precipitating reason for adolescents dropping out of school is usually:
   a. lack of ability.
   b. irrelevance of curriculum.
   c. lack of achievement.
   d. lack of encouragement, acceptance, and intellectual excitement from their teachers and classmates.

10. Educational settings that emphasize individual competition and tracking:
    a. are usually destructive.
    b. tend to be the most effective in educating students.
    c. are more effective in large schools than small schools.
    d. have proven very effective in educating minority students.

11. (A Life-Span Perspective) Kohlberg's stage theory of moral development is based on his research on a group of boys, on the writings of various philosophers, and on:
    a. psychoanalytic ideas.
    b. Piaget's theory of cognitive development.
    c. Carol Gilligan's research on moral dilemmas.
    d. questionnaires distributed to a nationwide sample of high school seniors.

12. (A Life-Span Perspective) A child who emphasizes social rules and obeying the laws is demonstrating ______________________ moral reasoning.
    a. preconventional
    b. conventional
    c. postconventional
    d. ideological

13. Compared to their peers, adolescents who score highest on tests that measure knowledge of sexual matters are:
    a. more likely to be sexually active.
    b. less likely to be sexually active.
    c. more likely to use contraception.
    d. not significantly different.

14. In the social inoculation method of sex education, the group or class leaders are:
    a. eighth graders.
    b. older teenagers.
    c. teachers and medical authorities.
    d. attractive celebrities.

15. (A Life-Span Perspective) Which of the following is *not* a common criticism of Kohlberg's stages of moral reasoning?
    a. They are biased in reflecting liberal, Western values.
    b. They were validated only on males.
    c. They overemphasize religious faith.
    d. Moral thinking is less stagelike than Kohlberg believes.

Matching Items

Match each term or concept with its corresponding description or definition.

Terms or Concepts

_______ 1. invincibility fable
_______ 2. imaginary audience
_______ 3. person-environment fit
_______ 4. preconventional moral reasoning
_______ 5. conventional moral reasoning
_______ 6. postconventional moral reasoning
_______ 7. tracking
_______ 8. ego-involvement learning
_______ 9. task-involvement learning
_______ 10. game of thinking

Descriptions or Definitions

a. the ability to suspend knowledge of reality and think about possibilities
b. feeling immune to the laws of mortality and probability
c. grading is based solely on individual test performance
d. a creation of adolescents who are preoccupied with how others react to their appearance and behavior
e. the match or mismatch between an adolescent's needs and the educational setting
f. grading that does not foster competition among students
g. reasoning that emphasizes avoiding punishment and gaining rewards
h. the separation of students into groups based on standardized tests of ability and achievement
i. reasoning that emphasizes moral principles
j. reasoning that emphasizes social rules

Challenge Test

Answer these questions the day before an exam as a final check on your understanding of the chapter's terms and concepts.

1. A 13-year-old can create and solve logical problems on the computer but is not usually reasonable, mature, or consistent in his or her thinking when it comes to people and social relationships. This supports the finding that:
   a. some children reach the stage of formal operational thought earlier than others.
   b. the stage of formal operational thought is not attained by age 13.
   c. formal operational thinking may be demonstrated in certain domains and not in other domains.
   d. older adolescents and adults often do poorly on standard tests of formal operational thought.

2. An experimenter hides a ball in her hand and says, "Either the ball in my hand is red or it is not red." Most preadolescent children say:
   a. the statement is true.
   b. the statement is false.
   c. they cannot tell if the statement is true or false.
   d. they do not understand what the experimenter means.

3. Fourteen-year-old Monica is very idealistic, and often develops crushes on people she doesn't even know. This reflects her newly developed cognitive ability to:
   a. deal simultaneously with two sides of an issue.
   b. take another person's viewpoint.
   c. imagine possible worlds and people.
   d. see herself as others see her.

4. Which of the following is the *best* example of a personal fable?
   a. Adriana imagines that she is destined for a life of fame and fortune.
   b. Ben makes up stories about his experiences to impress his friends.
   c. Kalil questions his religious beliefs when they seem to offer little help for a problem he faces.
   d. Julio believes that every girl he meets is attracted to him.

5. Which of the following is the *best* example of the game of thinking?
   a. Twelve-year-old Stanley feels that people are always watching him.
   b. Fourteen-year-old Mindy engages in many risky behaviors, reasoning that, "Nothing bad will happen to me."
   c. Fifteen-year-old Philip feels that no one understands his problems.
   d. Thirteen-year-old Josh delights in finding logical flaws in virtually everything his teachers and parents say.

6. Frustrated because of the dating curfew her parents have set, Melinda exclaims, "You just don't know how it feels to be in love!" Melinda's thinking demonstrates:
   a. the invincibility fable.
   b. the personal fable.
   c. the imaginary audience.
   d. adolescent egocentrism.

7. Compared to her thirteen-year-old brother, seventeen-year-old Yolanda is likely to:
   a. be more positive in thinking about herself.
   b. be more egocentric.
   c. have less confidence in her abilities.
   d. be more self-absorbed in her thinking.

8. Nathan's fear that his friends will ridicule him because of a pimple that has appeared on his nose reflects a preoccupation with:
   a. his personal fable.
   b. the invincibility fable.
   c. the imaginary audience.
   d. preconventional reasoning.

9. Thirteen-year-old Malcolm, who lately is very sensitive to the criticism of others, feels significantly less motivated and capable than when he was in elementary school. Malcolm is probably:
   a. experiencing a sense of vulnerability that is common in adolescents.
   b. a lower-track student.
   c. a student in a task-involvement classroom.
   d. all of the above.

10. A high school principal who wished to increase the interest level and achievement of minority and female students in math and science would be well advised to:
   a. create classroom environments in these subjects that are not based on competitive grading procedures.
   b. encourage greater use of standardized testing in the elementary schools that feed students to the high school.
   c. separate students into academic tracks based on achievement.
   d. do all of the above.

11. (A Closer Look) A new high school principal states that remedial math classes will be eliminated because, "Students will perform as well as they are expected to perform." Research reveals that the principal's attitude is:
   a. contradicted by evidence that setting high academic goals usually *lowers* the academic performance of lower-track students.
   b. supported by evidence that lower-track teachers are more likely to provide repetitive and uninteresting classwork, leading to low morale and a slower rate of student achievement.
   c. contradicted by evidence that the precipitating reason for truancy and dropping out of school is usually fear of failure when academic expectations are set too high.
   d. both b. and c.

12. (A Life-Span Perspective) Brad believes that morality means being a dutiful citizen and obeying the laws set down by those in power. Kohlberg would say that Brad's thinking is an example of ________________ reasoning.
   a. preconventional
   b. conventional
   c. postconventional
   d. reciprocal

13. (A Life-Span Perspective) In concluding her presentation on Kohlberg's theory of moral reasoning, Clarice states that:
   a. "Recent research reveals such large cultural differences in moral reasoning that Kohlberg's stages cannot be considered universal."
   b. "Kohlberg's description of moral reasoning applies only to males."
   c. "Few contemporary developmentalists take Kohlberg's theory seriously."
   d. "Compared to males, females focus on interpersonal issues more than on moral absolutes —but the sex difference is not very large."

14. Cindy, a sexually active teenager who does not practice contraception, is likely to think that:
   a. having a child might not be so bad.
   b. she will be perceived as being "easy" if she carries a contraceptive with her on a date.
   c. she is less likely to become pregnant, or contract a STD, than others.
   d. all of the above are true.

15. Dr. Malone, who wants to improve the effectiveness of her adolescent sex education class, would be well advised to:
    a. focus on the biological facts of reproduction and disease, since teenage misinformation is largely responsible for the high rates of unwanted pregnancy and STD.
    b. personalize the instruction, in order to make the possible consequences of sexual activity more immediate to students.
    c. teach boys and girls in separate classes, so that discussion can be more frank and open.
    d. use all of the above strategies.

Key Terms

Using your own words, write a brief definition or explanation of each of the following terms on a separate piece of paper.

1. formal operational thought
2. scientific reasoning
3. game of thinking
4. adolescent egocentrism
5. invincibility fable
6. personal fable
7. imaginary audience
8. person-environment fit
9. ego-involvement learning
10. task-involvement learning
11. tracking
12. preconventional moral reasoning
13. conventional moral reasoning
14. postconventional moral reasoning
15. sexually transmitted disease (STD)
16. social inoculation

ANSWERS

CHAPTER REVIEW

1. possibility
2. formal operational thought; 15; scientific
3. game of thinking
4. less
5. later; is not
6. society; education
7. is not
8. adolescent egocentrism; unique; universal

One example of adolescent egocentrism is a young person who believes that no one else has ever had the particular emotional experiences he or she is having (feeling sad and lonely or being in love, for example).

9. invincibility fable
10. personal fable
11. imaginary audience
12. early; middle; gradually
13. social; has not

Girls are generally more concerned with the imagined opinions of onlookers than boys. Among middle-class teens, younger teens are more self-conscious than older ones. Delinquent boys think more about the imaginary audience than do nondelinquents of either sex. Concern about the imaginary audience, rather than decreasing, increases from early to late adolescence in rural, low-SES whites and Native Americans.

14. person-environment fit; the individual's developmental stage, cognitive strengths and weaknesses, and learning style, and the traditions, educational objectives, and future needs of society
15. have
16. more; more
17. self-defeating; self-confidence

Compared to elementary schools, most secondary schools have more rigid behavioral demands, intensified competition, tougher grading standards, as well as less individualized attention and procedures.

18. lower; drop
19. cooperation
20. ego-involvement; girls; standardized; math; science
21. minority; cooperation; collaboration
22. task-involvement
23. less
24. tracking; 12
25. lower

Lower-track teachers are likely to provide repetitive, uninteresting classwork, leading to more boredom, distraction, and disturbances and, consequently, to disciplinarian instruction rather than to creative attempts to foster intellectual growth.

26. the overall lack of encouragement, acceptance, and intellectual excitement from their teachers and classmates

27. having educational goals that are high, clear, and attainable, and supported by the entire staff
28. lifelong

Biosocial development awakens drives and permits actions that previously were impossible; cognitive development fosters deeper, more abstract, and more questioning thinking; social development exposes young people to a variety of conflicting values.

29. Kohlberg; preconventional; conventional; post-conventional
30. avoiding punishments and getting rewards; 1; 2
31. social rules; 4; 3
32. moral principles; social contracts; universal ethical principles
33. less
34. liberal; Western; rigid; rational; religious faith; males
35. Gilligan; have not; interpersonal issues; moral absolutes
36. do
37. does; do
38. do
39. is; United States

For the mother, the consequences include interference with education and social and vocational growth; for the child, they include greater risk of prenatal and birth complications, of lower academic achievement, and, at adolescence, of drug abuse, arrest, and early parenthood.

40. sexually transmitted diseases
41. 10; 19
42. HIV virus; sexual; 5; having several sexual partners and failing to use condoms
43. do not
44. young people have difficulty envisioning and evaluating alternatives; they tend to focus on immediate considerations rather than on future ones; egocentric
45. invincibility
46. rational
47. sons

Adolescents are often put off by traditional sex education courses that focus on biological facts, rather than dealing with their actual sexual dilemmas and pressures.

48. personalization; social inoculation
49. begin early and have curricula geared to the cognitive abilities of the participants

PROGRESS TEST 1

Multiple-Choice Questions

1. **c.** is the answer. (p. 388)

   a. Although moral reasoning becomes much deeper during adolescence, it is not limited to this stage of development.

   b. & d. Concrete operational thought, which *is* logical, is the distinguishing feature of childhood thinking.

2. **a.** is the answer. (p. 388)

   b. In Piaget's theory, this stage precedes formal operational thought.

   c. & d. These are not stages in Piaget's theory.

3. **b.** is the answer. (p. 389)
4. **a.** is the answer. (p. 391)

   b. This refers to adolescents' tendency to imagine their own lives as heroic or even mythical.

   c. This refers to adolescents' tendency to fantasize about how others will react to their appearance and behavior.

   d. This is a concept in Freud's theory.

5. **d.** is the answer. These thought processes are manifestations of adolescents' tendency to see themselves as being much more central and important to the social scene than they really are. (pp. 391–393)
6. **c.** is the answer. (p. 394)
7. **d.** is the answer. (p. 394)
8. **b.** is the answer. (p. 395)

   a. In task-involvement learning, grades are based on acquiring certain competencies and knowledge that everyone, with enough time and effort, is expected to attain.

   c. Tracking refers to the separation of students into distinct groups based on standardized tests of ability and achievement.

   d. This is not a type of classroom environment discussed in the text.

9. **d.** is the answer. (p. 399)

   a. & c. These are examples of conventional morality.

   b. This is an example of preconventional morality.

10. **b.** is the answer. (p. 401)

    a. Gilligan maintains that Kohlberg's scoring system tends to devalue the female perspective.

    c. & d. According to Gilligan, males are more likely to reason from absolute, or abstract, moral principles.

11. **c.** is the answer. (p. 404)

    a. The text does not suggest that declining moral standards are responsible for the increased rate of STD.

    b. Although this may be true, in itself it is not necessarily a result of adolescent cognitive immaturity.

    d. Various studies have found that merely understanding the facts of sexuality does not correlate with more responsible and cautious sexual behavior.

12. **b.** is the answer. (p. 405)

    a. This refers to adolescents' tendency to imagine their own lives as heroic or even mythical.

    c. This refers to adolescents' tendency to fantasize about how others will react to their appearance and behavior.

    d. This is the adolescent ability to suspend knowledge of reality in order to think playfully about possibilities.

13. **d.** is the answer. (p. 403)
14. **a.** is the answer. (p. 407)
15. **c.** is the answer. (p. 405)

True or False Items

1. F Children do not engage in the game of thinking until they are about age 15. (p. 389)
2. T (p. 389)
3. F Some people never reach the stage of formal operational thought. (p. 390)
4. F Adolescent egocentrism tends to peak from early to middle adolescence. (p. 392)
5. T (p. 392)
6. F In such competitive situations, many students find it easier and psychologically safer not to try, thereby avoiding the potential pains of both success and failure. (p. 397)
7. F Lower-track students' pace of learning actually slows, as the curriculum generally repeats basic skills that should have been mastered years before. (p. 396)
8. F Some critics feel that Kohlberg underrated religious faith. (p. 400)
9. T (p. 403)
10. T (p. 407)

PROGRESS TEST 2

Multiple-Choice Questions

1. **a.** is the answer. (p. 388)
2. **b.** is the answer. (p. 389)
3. **d.** is the answer. (p. 390)
4. **b.** is the answer. (p. 391)
5. **c.** is the answer. (p. 392)

   a. This describes the invincibility fable.

   b. This describes the imaginary audience.

   d. This describes adolescent egocentrism.

6. **d.** is the answer. (p. 394)
7. **a.** is the answer. (p. 395)

   b. The elementary school backgrounds of boys and girls in math and science are usually very similar.

   c. Both girls and boys are usually exposed to ego- rather than task-involvement learning. Furthermore, task-involvement learning is *more* likely than ego-involvement learning to promote cognitive growth and learning for all students.

   d. There is no evidence that this is so.

8. **b.** is the answer. (p. 395)

   a. In ego-involvement learning, grades *are* assigned competitively.

   c. Tracking refers to the separation of students into distinct groups based on standardized tests of ability and achievement.

   d. This is not a type of classroom environment discussed in the text.

9. **d.** is the answer. (p. 396)
10. **a.** is the answer. (p. 395)
11. **b.** is the answer. (p. 400)
12. **b.** is the answer. (p. 399)

    a. In this type of moral reasoning, the emphasis is on avoiding punishments and gaining rewards.

    c. In this type of moral reasoning, the emphasis is on moral principles.

    d. This is not one of Kohlberg's stages of moral reasoning.

13. **d.** is the answer. (p. 404)
14. **b.** is the answer. (p. 407)
15. **c.** is the answer. In fact, just the opposite is true. (p. 400)

Matching Items

1. b (p. 391)
2. d (p. 392)
3. e (p. 393)
4. g (p. 399)
5. j (p. 399)
6. i (p. 399)
7. h (p. 396)
8. c (p. 395)
9. f (p. 395)
10. a (p. 389)

CHALLENGE TEST

1. **c.** is the answer. (p. 390)
2. **c.** is the answer. Although this statement is logically verifiable, preadolescents who lack formal operational thought cannot prove or disprove it. (p. 389)
3. **c.** is the answer. (p. 392)
4. **a.** is the answer. (p. 392)

   b. & d. Ben's and Julio's behaviors are more indicative of a preoccupation with the imaginary audience.

   c. Kalil's questioning attitude is a normal adolescent tendency that helps foster moral reasoning.
5. **d.** is the answer. (p. 389)

   a. This is an example of the imaginary audience.

   b. This is an example of the invincibility fable.

   c. This is an example of adolescent egocentrism.
6. **d.** is the answer. (p. 391)
7. **a.** is the answer. (p. 393)
8. **c.** is the answer. (p. 392)

   a. In this fable adolescents see themselves destined for fame and fortune.

   b. In this fable young people feel that they are somehow immune to the laws of mortality and probability.

   d. This is a stage of moral reasoning in Kohlberg's theory.
9. **a.** is the answer. (p. 394)
10. **a.** is the answer. (p. 395)
11. **b.** is the answer. (p. 396)
12. **b.** is the answer. (p. 399)

    a. In preconventional reasoning moral behavior involves avoiding punishments and gaining rewards.

    c. In postconventional reasoning emphasis is on moral principles established by society.

    d. This is not a type of moral reasoning identified by Kohlberg.
13. **d.** is the answer. (p. 401)
14. **d.** is the answer. (pp. 404–405)
15. **b.** is the answer. (p. 407)

KEY TERMS

1. In Piaget's theory, the last stage of cognitive development—called **formal operational thought**—is usually attained at about age 15. The hallmark of formal operational thinking is the capacity to reason in terms of possibility rather than merely concrete reality. (p. 388)
2. One specific example of formal operational thought is **scientific reasoning,** in which adolescents become able to hypothesize a general law or principle and reason logically about it. (p. 388)
3. The **game of thinking,** a concept introduced by Flavell, refers to the adolescents' ability to suspend their knowledge of reality and to think playfully about possibilities. (p. 389)
4. **Adolescent egocentrism** refers to the tendency of adolescents to see themselves as much more central and significant on the social stage than they actually are. (p. 391)
5. Adolescents who experience the **invincibility fable** feel that they are immune to the laws of probability and the dangers of risky behaviors. (p. 391)
6. One example of adolescent egocentrism is the **personal fable,** through which adolescents imagine their own lives as heroic or even mythical. (p. 392)

   Memory aid: A *fable* is a mythical story.
7. Adolescents often create an **imaginary audience** for themselves, as they fantasize about how others will react to their appearance and behavior. (p. 392)
8. The term **person-environment fit** refers to the best setting for an individual's development, as in the optimum educational setting. (p. 393)
9. In **ego-involvement learning,** academic grading is based solely on individual test performance, and students are ranked against each other. (p. 395)

   Memory aid: In **ego-involvement learning,** one's ego is on the line as one is placed in competition with other students.

10. In **task-involvement learning**, grades are based on mastery of knowledge that everyone is expected to attain. (p. 395)
11. **Tracking** is the separation of students into academic groups based on standardized tests of ability and achievement. (p. 396)
12. The first of Kohlberg's stages of moral reasoning, **preconventional moral reasoning** emphasizes obedience to authority in order to avoid punishment (stage 1), and being nice to other people so they will be nice to you (stage 2). (p. 399)
13. The second of Kohlberg's stages, **conventional moral reasoning** emphasizes winning the approval of others (stage 3), and obeying the laws set down by those in power (stage 4). (p. 399)
14. The last of Kohlberg's stages, **postconventional moral reasoning** emphasizes the social and contractual nature of moral principles (stage 5), and the existence of universal ethical principles (stage 6). (p. 399)
15. **Sexually transmitted disease (STD)** includes all diseases that are spread by sexual contact. (p. 403)
16. **Social inoculation** is a new form of sex education in which role-playing and discussion is used to help adolescents develop a cognitive immunity to the various kinds of sexual pressures they might face in the future. (p. 407)

    Memory aid: An *inoculation* is an injection of a disease agent into a person, usually to cause a mild form of the disease in order to help a person develop an immunity to it.

CHAPTER 16 Adolescence: Psychosocial Development

Chapter Overview

Chapter 16 focuses on the psychosocial development, particularly the formation of identity, that is required for the attainment of adult status and maturity. The influences of family, friends, and society on this development are examined in some detail. The special problems posed by drug use, delinquency, and abuse of adolescents are discussed, and suggestions for alleviating or treating these problems are given. Suicide—one of the most perplexing problems of adolescence—is then explored. The chapter concludes with the message that, while no other period of life is characterized by so many changes in the three domains of development, for most young people the teenage years are happy ones. Furthermore, in almost every case serious problems in adolescence stem from earlier developmental events.

NOTE: Answer guidelines for all Chapter 16 questions begin on page 244.

Guided Study

The text chapter should be studied one section at a time. Before you read, preview each section by skimming it, noting headings and boldface items. Then read the appropriate section objectives from the following outline. Keep these objectives in mind and, as you read the chapter section, search for the information that will enable you to meet each objective. Once you have finished a section, write out answers for its objectives.

Identity (pp. 412–415)

1. Describe Erikson's view of the development of identity during adolescence, including the importance of social influences on identity formation.

2. Describe and give examples of each of the four major identity statuses and the characteristics associated with each.

3. (A Closer Look) Discuss the problems of identity formation encountered by minority adolescents.

Family and Friends (pp. 415–425)

4. Discuss parental influence on identity formation, including the effect of parent-child conflict and the factors that affect its frequency and severity.

5. Discuss the role of friends and peer groups in identity formation, including their role in developing male-female relationships.

6. Examine the sometimes complementary, sometimes conflicting influences of parents and peers on adolescents.

Special Problems (pp. 425–436)

7. Discuss drug use and delinquency among adolescents today, noting their prevalence, significance for later development, and best approaches for prevention or treatment.

8. Discuss adolescent maltreatment and sexual abuse, noting its prevalence, long-term consequences, and best approaches for prevention or treatment.

9. (Text and A Closer Look) Discuss adolescent suicide, noting its prevalence, contributing factors, and warning signs.

Chapter Review

When you have finished reading the chapter, work through the material that follows to review it. Complete the sentences and answer the questions. As you proceed, evaluate your performance for each section by consulting the answers on page 244. Do not continue with the next section until you understand each answer. If you need to, review or reread the appropriate section in the textbook before continuing.

Identity (pp. 412–415)

1. The individual's attempt to define himself or herself as a unique individual is what Erikson calls the quest for ______________.

2. The ultimate goal of adolescence is to establish a new identity that involves both repudiation and assimilation of childhood values; this is called ______________ ______________.

3. The young person who prematurely accepts earlier roles and parental values without exploring alternatives or truly forging a unique identity is experiencing identity ______________.

4. An adolescent who adopts an identity that is the opposite of the one he or she is expected to adopt

has taken on a(n) ________________
________________.

5. The young person who has few commitments to goals or values and is apathetic about defining his or her identity is experiencing ________________ ________________.

6. A "time-out" period during which a young person experiments with different identities, postponing important choices, is called a(n) ________________.

7. A developmentalist who has extensively compared adolescents' identity statuses with various measures of their cognitive and psychological development is ________________.

8. In terms of their attitudes toward parents, the diffused adolescent is often ________________, the moratorium adolescent is more ________________, the forecloser shows more ________________ and ________________, and the achiever treats parents with more ________________.

9. Adolescents who have ________________ ________________ and those who have ________________ ________________ tend to have a strong sense of ethnic identification. Those who have ________________ tend to be high in prejudice, while those who are ________________ ________________ tend to be relatively low in prejudice.

10. The process of identity formation can take ________________ or longer.

11. Societies aid the identity formation of adolescents in two ways: by providing ________________, and by providing ________________ and ________________ that ease the transition from childhood to adulthood.

12. In a culture where most people hold the same religious, moral, political, and sexual values, identity is ________________ (easier/more difficult) to achieve.

13. (A Closer Look) For members of minority ethnic groups, identity achievement is often ________________ (more/less) difficult than it is for other adolescents. This may cause them to embrace a(n) ________________ identity or, as is more often the case, to experience identity ________________ prematurely.

14. (A Closer Look) School staff and curricula typically ________________ (are/are not) very helpful to the minority adolescent in finding the right balance between his or her heritage and the majority culture.

15. (A Closer Look) Relationships with parents and other relatives ________________ (are/are not) particularly stressful for minority adolescents in the United States. Members of minority groups are often criticized by their ________________ if they make an effort to join the majority culture.

16. (A Closer Look) Over the past forty years in America, the emphasis on the individual's racial and ethnic heritage has ________________ (increased/decreased).

Family and Friends (pp. 415–425)

17. People who focus on differences between the younger and older generations speak of a(n) ________________ ________________.

Numerous studies have shown that parents and adolescents substantially ________________ (agree/disagree) in their political, religious, educational, and vocational opinions. One notable exception concerns attitudes about ________________. Parents tend to estimate the size of the generation gap as ________________ (smaller/larger) than adolescents do.

18. The idea that family members in different developmental stages have a natural tendency to see the family in different ways is called the ________________ ________________.

19. Conflict between parents and adolescents ________________ (occurs/does not occur) in every culture that has been studied.

20. In terms of the adolescent's achievement and self-esteem, ________________ parenting is bet-

ter than either ____________ or ____________ parenting.

21. Parent-child conflict is most common in ____________ (early/late) adolescence, and is more likely to involve ____________ (mothers/fathers) and their ____________- (early/late) maturing offspring.

22. Parent-child conflict is ____________ (more/less) frequent in stable, single-parent homes than in families where the parents are married, newly ____________, ____________, or ____________.

23. First-born children tend to have ____________ (more/fewer) conflicts with parents than later-borns do.

24. Factors in the macrosystem that influence parents' expectations include family ____________, ____________, ____________, and ____________.

Briefly describe the relationship between the likelihood of adolescent rebellion and family socioeconomic status.

25. Parental watchfulness about where one's child is and what he or she is doing and with whom is called parental ____________. The higher a family's SES, the ____________ (greater/less) the need for stringent curfews, restrictions on friends, and other seemingly authoritarian measures.

26. By late adolescence, parent-child relations in all family types and nations, and among children of both sexes, tend to be ____________ (more/less) harmonious.

27. If there is a "generation gap," it is more likely to occur in ____________ (early/late) adolescence, and to center on issues of ____________, and ____________. Approximately ____________ percent of all families find that conflict continues throughout adolescence.

28. According to John Coleman, during adolescence the peer group serves three important functions.

a. ____________

b. ____________

c. ____________

29. Usually, the first sign of heterosexual attraction is a seeming ____________ of members of the other sex. The pattern by which adolescents "warm up" to the other sex ____________ (is similar/varies greatly) from nation to nation.

30. The typical adolescent friendship circle is ____________ (large/small) and ____________ (stable/fluid).

31. Generally, feeling at ease with one's sexual identity takes ____________ (less time/longer) if one's preferences are for one's own sex.

32. Anthropological research reveals ____________ (very little variation/wide variations) in the pace and character of the emergence of true intimacy. Peers ____________ (do/do not) play an important role in this process in most cultures.

33. Despite the ____________ influences of parents and peers, there are distinct differences between them as sources of social support.

34. In conversations, ____________ (parents/peers) are more likely to offer and justify their own thoughts than to try to understand an adolescent's ideas. This is one reason that adolescents are more likely to share personal information with ____________ (parents/peers).

35. Generally speaking, parent and peer influences are usually ____________ (complementary/opposing). Adolescents who experience extreme or overpowering influences in either their parent or peer relationships ____________ (are/are not) more vul-

nerable to problems, such as drug use or delinquency.

Special Problems (pp. 425–436)

36. When serious adolescent problems occur, they usually are a consequence of long-standing problems in the ______________ and persistent vulnerabilities in the adolescent's ______________, as well as the special strains of adolescence.

37. Confidential surveys reveal that most high school seniors today ______________ (have/have not) tried alcohol and tobacco. Approximately ______________ percent have tried at least one illegal drug, most commonly ______________. Drug usage ______________ (does/does not) vary significantly from one geographical region or ethnic group to another.

38. Generally, ______________ (males/females) use more drugs than the other sex. This difference is ______________ (increasing/decreasing).

39. Compared to the late 1970s, drug use during the 1980s gradually ______________ (increased/decreased) among high school students.

40. Both one-time experimentation and regular use of crack-cocaine have ______________ (increased/decreased) among high school seniors.

41. Regular users of alcohol are more vulnerable to virtually every serious problem of adolescence, including ______________ ______________, which is the leading cause of adolescent mortality.

42. Frequent use of psychoactive drugs impairs normal learning and ______________ growth.

43. Those individuals who use more drugs, more often, at younger ages, than their classmates are ______________ (more/no more) likely to have multiple drug- and alcohol-abuse problems later.

44. The rise and fall in adolescent use of ______________, ______________, ______________, and ______________ indicates that this group is continually vulnerable to drugs that are new, and potentially more devastating.

45. Researchers have found that patterns of drug use—whether one is a frequent user, abstainer, or experimenter—reflect preexisting ______________ ______________.

Describe the typical adolescent who is a frequent user of illegal drugs.

46. The findings of the fifteen-year longitudinal study of adolescent drug use indicate that, for adolescents who are ______________ vulnerable, abstinence from drugs is the best choice.

Identify the two problems of adolescent drug abuse.

47. Arrests are far more likely to occur during the decade of ______________ than in any other decade of life.

Briefly describe data on gender, class, and ethnic differences in adolescent arrests.

48. Arrest statistics have been questioned because, at least in some jurisdictions, police are more inclined to arrest ______________ teenagers than others.

49. If all illegal acts—including minor infractions—are included, most adolescents ______ (do at one time or another/do not) engage in law-breaking that could lead to arrest.

50. The period of greatest increase in criminal activity appears to be age ______. By age 20, the rate of criminal activity is about ______ the rate at age 17.

51. Adolescents whose law-breaking ends as adulthood approaches usually cite ______, rather than ______, as their reason for stopping their criminal behavior.

52. A number of studies have revealed that children who by age 10 have ______ ______, and significant ______ at home are more likely to become delinquent. This is especially true if, as early as age 6, they show signs of ______-______ ______ and ______ behavior.

53. Most experts agree that those adolescents whose crimes include ______ acts need intensive intervention.

54. The best response to adolescent crime is to encourage the teenager to understand the ______ ______ of his or her offense.

Identify several promising approaches to preventing adolescent delinquency.

55. Family difficulties, such as divorce and child maltreatment, tend to ______ (increase/decrease) when the oldest child reaches age 11 or 12. The seriousness of adolescent maltreatment is often ______ (overestimated/underestimated).

56. Adolescents react to maltreatment in ways that younger children rarely do, with ______, or by ______.

57. Adolescent problems, such as pregnancy, often are tied to ______.

58. Sexual abuse usually is a ______ (single event/series of episodes). At about age 11, the rate of sexual abuse begins to ______ (rise/fall).

59. Two important issues, in terms of the developmental consequences of sexual abuse, are whether the abuse is ______, and whether it ______.

60. Although ______ (boys/girls) are the most common victims of sexual abuse, increasingly it is recognized that the other sex is also often sexually abused.

61. Sexual molestation of ______ (girls/boys) occurs more often outside the home and is committed by someone, most often a ______ (male/female), who is not a family member.

62. Mothers and other female relatives seem to be ______ (more/less) often the perpetrators of obvious sexual abuse.

63. Parents who are ______, ______ ______, ______, or ______-______ are much more likely to be sexually abusive. Income and education level ______ (do/do not) predict who is likely to be sexually abusive.

64. The psychological effects of sexual abuse depend on the ______ and ______ of the abuse, and on the ______ once the abuse is known.

65. One of the most troubling consequences of incest is that the young person may ______ ______.

66. Adolescent victims of abuse tend to become involved again in ______ ______.

Explain one way in which the effects of sexual abuse may be transmitted from generation to generation.

67. Prevention of sexual abuse requires recognizing factors that begin in the ________________, such as cultural values about sex and about children.

68. Another recommended preventive measure is to ________________ (begin/avoid) sex education at younger ages.

69. The suicide rate between ages 15 and 19 is ________________ (higher/lower) than half that for any subsequent age group. The rate of adolescent suicide has ________________ (increased/decreased) over the past 25 years.

70. Suicidal adolescents tend to be more ________________ than normal adolescents, and show a greater tendency to be ________________, ________________, and ________________.

71. An attempted suicide by an adolescent usually ________________ (is/is not) triggered by a single event. One of the most prominent problems associated with adolescent suicide attempts is long-standing ________________ ________________.

72. (A Closer Look) List five warning signs of suicide.

a. ________________

b. ________________

c. ________________

d. ________________

e. ________________

Conclusion (p. 437)

73. For most young people, the teenage years overall are ________________ (happy/unhappy) ones.

74. Adolescents who have one serious problem usually ________________ (do/do not) have other problems as well. In most cases, serious adolescent problems ________________ (do/do not) stem from earlier developmental events.

Progress Test 1

Multiple-Choice Questions

Circle your answers to the following questions and check them with the answers on page 246. If your answer is incorrect, read the explanation for why it is incorrect and then consult the appropriate pages of the text (in parentheses following the correct answer).

1. According to Erikson, the primary task of adolescence is that of establishing:
   a. basic trust.
   b. identity.
   c. intimacy.
   d. integrity.

2. According to developmentalists who study identity formation, foreclosure involves:
   a. accepting an identity prematurely, without exploration.
   b. taking time off from school, work, and other commitments.
   c. opposing parental values.
   d. failing to commit oneself to a vocational goal.

3. When adolescents adopt an identity that is the opposite of the one they are expected to adopt, they are considered to be taking on a:
   a. foreclosed identity.
   b. diffused identity.
   c. negative identity.
   d. reverse identity.

4. The main sources of emotional support for most young people who are establishing independence from their parents are:
   a. older adolescents of the opposite sex.
   b. older siblings.
   c. teachers.
   d. peer groups.

5. (A Closer Look) For members of minority ethnic groups, identity achievement may be particularly complicated because:
   a. school staff are often ignorant of very real differences among members of minority groups.
   b. democratic ideology espouses a color-blind, multiethnic society in which background is irrelevant.

c. parents and other relatives are often unsure about how much to encourage their children to adapt to the majority culture and how much to preserve past tradition.
d. of all of the above reasons.

6. In a crime-ridden neighborhood, parents can protect their adolescents by keeping close watch over activities, friends, and so on, a practice called:
   a. generational stake.
   b. foreclosure.
   c. peer screening.
   d. parental monitoring.

7. Use of cocaine among high school students seems to have peaked:
   a. in the 1960s.
   b. in 1975.
   c. in the mid 1980s.
   d. last year.

8. If there is a "generation gap," it is likely to occur in ____________________ adolescence and to center on issues of ____________________ .
   a. early; morality
   b. late; self-discipline
   c. early; self-control
   d. late; politics

9. (A Closer Look) Because of the conflict between their ethnic background and the larger culture, minority adolescents will *most often*:
   a. reject the traditional values of both their ethnic culture and the majority culture.
   b. foreclose on identity prematurely.
   c. declare a moratorium.
   d. experience identity diffusion.

10. The incidence of sexual abuse is difficult to estimate because:
    a. the occurrence of sexual abuse is so rare.
    b. people tend to exaggerate.
    c. typically the child complies.
    d. the offense is underreported.

11. Although the sexual abuse of boys is in some ways less devastating that that of girls, abused boys:
    a. feel shame at the idea of being weak.
    b. have fewer sources of social support.
    c. are more likely to be abused by fathers.
    d. have all of the above problems.

12. Compared with normal adolescents, suicidal adolescents are:
    a. more concerned about the future.
    b. less accomplished academically.
    c. more solitary, self-destructive, and depressed.
    d. less likely to have attempted suicide.

13. Most experts feel that the adolescent law-breaker who is most in need of intensive intervention is the one who:
    a. has attention-deficit disorder and other learning problems.
    b. comes from a low-income or single-parent family.
    c. engages in antisocial crimes, such as muggings.
    d. has been arrested more than once for playing hookey and disorderly conduct.

14. When a young girl is a victim of long-standing sexual abuse, the most likely perpetrator is a:
    a. mentally disturbed stranger.
    b. boyfriend.
    c. father or close family friend.
    d. brother or younger male relative.

15. Conflict between parents and adolescent offspring:
    a. is most likely to involve fathers and their early-maturing offspring.
    b. is more frequent in single-parent homes.
    c. is more likely between first-borns and their parents than between later-borns and their parents.
    d. is likely in all of the above situations.

True or False Items

Write *true* or *false* on the line in front of each statement.

_______ 1. In cultures where everyone's values are similar and social change is slight, identity is relatively easy to achieve.

_______ 2. Most adolescents have political views and educational values that are markedly different from those of their parents.

_______ 3. Peer pressure is inherently destructive to the adolescent seeking an identity.

_______ 4. For most adolescents, group socializing and dating precede the establishment of true intimacy with one member of the opposite sex.

_______ 5. The drug most likely to have been tried by a high school senior is alcohol.

_______ 6. A study cited in the text found that, among adolescents, frequent drug users did not differ psychologically from infrequent users, or experimenters.

_______ 7. The vast majority of adolescent boys report that they have at some time engaged in law-breaking that might have led to arrest.

_______ 8. A common long-term consequence of incest is that the young person has a disturbed understanding of parent-child relationships and may make an inadequate parent.

_______ 9. Females who have been sexually abused are more likely than other young women to marry an abusive man.

_______ 10. (A Closer Look) Warning signs of suicide include a sudden decline in school attendance and achievement, and withdrawal from social relationships.

Progress Test 2

Progress Test 2 should be completed during a final chapter review. Answer the following questions after you thoroughly understand the correct answers for the Chapter Review and Progress Test 1.

Multiple-Choice Questions

1. The best way to limit adolescent law-breaking in general would be to:
   a. strengthen the family, school, and community fabric.
   b. increase the number of police officers in the community.
   c. improve the criminal justice system.
   d. establish rehabilitative facilities for law-breakers.

2. (A Closer Look) Which of the following was *not* identified as a warning sign of suicide in an adolescent?
   a. a sudden decline in school achievement
   b. an attempted suicide
   c. a break in a love relationship
   d. a sudden interest in friends and family

3. Research has found that one of the best predictors of later delinquent behavior is when an adolescent:
   a. quarrels with brothers and sisters.
   b. questions parental values.
   c. experiences difficulty in school.
   d. is considered a leader in his or her peer group.

4. Adolescents who get along well with peers probably:
   a. are experiencing unusually severe conflict with their parents.
   b. are simply "caving in" to peer pressure and not thinking for themselves.
   c. also have good relationships with their parents.
   d. are first-borns.

5. Which style of parenting do most psychologists recommend?
   a. authoritarian c. very strict
   b. permissive d. authoritative

6. Which of the following is the *most* accurate description of the typical friendship circle of young adolescents?
   a. a small and stable group of friends
   b. a small and fluid group of friends
   c. a large and stable group of friends
   d. a large and fluid group of friends

7. The adolescent experiencing identity diffusion is typically:
   a. very apathetic.
   b. a risk-taker anxious to experiment with alternative identities.
   c. willing to accept parental values wholesale, without exploring alternatives.
   d. one who rebels against all forms of authority.

8. Adolescents help each other in many ways, including:
   a. identity formation. c. social skills.
   b. independence. d. all of the above.

9. Crime statistics show that during adolescence:
   a. males and females are equally likely to be arrested.
   b. males are more likely to be arrested than females.
   c. females are more likely to be arrested than males.
   d. males commit more crimes than females, but are less likely to be arrested.

10. Which of the following is the most common problem behavior among adolescents?
    a. pregnancy
    b. daily use of illegal drugs
    c. minor law-breaking
    d. attempts at suicide

11. A "time-out" period during which a young person experiments with different identities, postponing important choices, is called a(n):
    a. identity foreclosure.
    b. negative identity.
    c. identity diffusion.
    d. moratorium.

12. When adolescents' political, religious, educational, and vocational opinions are compared with their parents, the so-called "generation gap":
    a. is much smaller than when the younger and older generations are compared overall.
    b. is much wider than when the younger and older generations are compared overall.
    c. is wider between parents and sons than between parents and daughters.
    d. is wider between parents and daughters than between parents and sons.

13. Compared to the late 1970s, during the 1980s drug use among high school students:
    a. increased among most minority groups.
    b. remained unchanged among most groups.
    c. decreased among virtually every group.
    d. decreased for alcohol and tobacco, but increased for marijuana and crack.

14. Individuals who experiment with drugs early are:
    a. typically affluent teenagers who are experiencing an identity moratorium.
    b. more likely to have multiple drug problems later on.
    c. less likely to have alcohol-abuse problems later on.
    d. usually able to resist later peer pressure leading to long-term addiction.

15. Parents who are ________________ are much more likely to abuse or neglect their adolescent children.
    a. immature
    b. socially isolated
    c. alcoholic
    d. all of the above

Matching Items

Match each term or concept with its corresponding description or definition.

Terms or Concepts

________ 1. identity
________ 2. identity achievement
________ 3. foreclosure
________ 4. negative identity
________ 5. identity diffusion
________ 6. moratorium
________ 7. generation gap
________ 8. generational stake
________ 9. parental monitoring

Descriptions or Definitions

a. premature identity formation
b. family members in different developmental stages see the family in different ways
c. an adolescent state in which the individual has few commitments to goals or values
d. differences between the younger and older generations
e. an identity opposite of the one an adolescent is expected to adopt
f. awareness of where children are and what they are doing
g. an individual's self-definition
h. a time-out period during which adolescents experiment with alternative identities
i. the adolescent establishes his or her own goals and values

Challenge Test

Answer these questions the day before an exam as a final check on your understanding of the chapter's terms and concepts

1. From childhood, Sharon thought she wanted to follow in her mother's footsteps and be a homemaker. Now, at age 40 with a home and family, she admits to herself that what she really wanted to be was a medical researcher. Erik Erikson would probably say that Sharon:
   a. adopted a negative identity when she was a child.
   b. experienced identity foreclosure at an early age.
   c. never progressed beyond the obvious identity diffusion she experienced as a child.
   d. took a moratorium from identity formation.

2. Fifteen-year-old David is rebelling against his devoutly religious parents by taking drugs, stealing, and engaging in other antisocial behaviors. Evidently, David has:
   a. foreclosed his identity.
   b. decided to take an identity moratorium.
   c. adopted a negative identity.
   d. experienced identity diffusion.

3. Fourteen-year-old Sean, who is fiercely proud of his Irish heritage, is prejudiced against members of several other ethnic groups. It is likely that, in forming his identity, Sean:
   a. attained identity achievement.
   b. foreclosed his identity prematurely.
   c. experienced a lengthy moratorium.
   d. experienced identity diffusion.

4. In 1957, 6-year-old Raisel and her parents emigrated from Poland to the United States. Compared to her parents, who grew up in a culture in which virtually everyone held the same religious, moral, political, and sexual values, Raisel is likely to have:
   a. an easier time achieving her own unique identity.
   b. a more difficult time forging her identity.
   c. a greater span of time in which to forge her own identity.
   d. a shorter span of time in which to forge her identity.

5. An adolescent tends to exaggerate the importance of differences in her values and those of her parents. Her parents see these differences as smaller and less important. This phenomenon is called the:
   a. generation gap.
   b. generational stake.
   c. family enigma.
   d. parental imperative.

6. In our society, the most obvious examples of institutionalized moratoria on identity formation are:
   a. the Boy Scouts and the Girl Scouts.
   b. college and the peacetime military.
   c. marriage and divorce.
   d. Bar Mitzvahs and baptisms.

7. First-time parents Norma and Norman are worried that, during adolescence, their healthy parental influence will be undone as their children are encouraged by peers to become sexually promiscuous, drug-addicted, or delinquent. Their wise neighbor, who is a developmental psychologist, tells them that:
   a. during adolescence, peers are generally more likely to complement the influence of parents than they are to pull their friends in the opposite direction.
   b. research suggests that peers provide a negative influence in every major task of adolescence.
   c. only through authoritarian parenting can parents give children the skills they need to resist peer pressure.
   d. unless their children show early signs of learning difficulties or antisocial behavior, parental monitoring is unnecessary.

8. Regarding experimentation with psychoactive drugs, the *best* choice for the young adolescent who tends to be emotionally vulnerable or unstable is:
   a. avoiding drugs that are socially disinhibiting, such as alcohol.
   b. occasional experimentation with marijuana and no more than one other drug.
   c. occasional use of mood-elevating drugs, such as cocaine.
   d. complete abstinence from psychoactive drugs.

9. In forming an identity, the young person seeks to make meaningful connections with his or her past. This seeking is described by Erikson as an unconscious striving for:
   a. individual uniqueness.
   b. peer group membership.
   c. continuity of experience.
   d. vocational identity.

10. (A Closer Look) A friend tells you that he doesn't want to live any more because his girlfriend has left him. The most helpful response would be:
    a. "Don't be ridiculous. You have plenty to live for."
    b. "Everyone has these experiences; you'll get over it."
    c. "She wasn't right for you. You're certain to find someone else."
    d. "When did this happen? Let's talk about it."

11. Statistically, the person least likely to commit a crime is a(n):
    a. African-American or Latino adolescent.
    b. middle-class white boy.
    c. white adolescent of any socioeconomic background.
    d. Asian-American.

12. In longitudinal studies, many adults report lawbreaking that ended in adulthood. The reason they most often give for having stopped their criminal behavior is:
    a. incarceration or other severe punishment.
    b. peer influence.
    c. intervention, such as psychotherapy.
    d. maturity, or simply growing up.

13. Adolescents who lack confidence or who rebel by leaving home, taking drugs, or becoming sexually active before age 16 are more likely to come from:
    a. authoritative low-income families.
    b. authoritative high-income families.
    c. very strict, or very permissive, lower-income families.
    d. average-income families in which disciplinary measures are moderate.

14. When he was a teenager, Dwayne used various psychoactive drugs regularly. As a result, it is *most* likely that at age 30 Dwayne is:
    a. an avid activist against drug use.
    b. a more mature and happier individual.
    c. not very good at relating to people.
    d. all of the above.

15. Twenty-four-year-old Connie, who has a distorted view of sexuality, has gone from one abusive relationship with a man to another. It is likely that Connie:
    a. has been abusing drugs all her life.
    b. was sexually abused as a child.
    c. will eventually become a normal, nurturing mother.
    d. had attention-deficit disorder as a child.

Key Terms

Using your own words, write a brief definition or explanation of each of the following terms on a separate piece of paper.

1. identity
2. identity achievement
3. foreclosure
4. negative identity
5. identity diffusion
6. moratorium
7. generation gap
8. generational stake
9. parental monitoring

ANSWERS

CHAPTER REVIEW

1. identity
2. identity achievement
3. foreclosure
4. negative identity
5. identity diffusion
6. moratorium
7. James Marcia
8. withdrawn; independent; respect; deference; concern
9. achieved identity; prematurely foreclosed; foreclosed; identity achievers
10. ten years
11. values; social structures; customs
12. easier
13. more; negative; foreclosure

14. are not

15. are; peers

16. increased

17. generation gap; agree; sex; smaller

18. generational stake

19. occurs

20. authoritative; authoritarian; permissive

21. early; mothers; early

22. less; divorced; cohabiting; remarried

23. more

24. income; education; culture; traditions

Adolescents who lack confidence or who rebel by leaving home, taking drugs, or becoming sexually active before age 16 are more likely to come from very strict, or very permissive, lower-income families than from homes that are more moderate in discipline and average in SES.

25. monitoring; less

26. more

27. early; self-discipline; self-control; 20

28. **a.** as a self-help group, a sounding board of contemporaries

b. as a source of support for the adolescent who is questioning the validity of adult standards and authority

c. as a vehicle for experimenting and discovering which of their personality characteristics and possible behaviors will be accepted and admired

29. dislike; is similar

30. large; fluid

31. longer

32. wide variations; do

33. complementary

34. parents; peers

35. complementary; are

36. home; temperament

37. have; 50; marijuana; does

38. males; decreasing

39. decreased

40. decreased

41. violent death

42. social

43. more

44. LSD; PCP; cocaine; crack

45. personality characteristics

The typical user is a "troubled adolescent" who is interpersonally alienated, emotionally withdrawn, and manifestly unhappy, and who expresses his or her maladjustment through undercontrolled, overly antisocial behavior.

46. emotionally

One problem applies to all adolescents, whose poor judgment about when and how to experiment with drugs, and whose behavior when "under the influence," might lead to fatal accidents or other serious consequences. The second applies to those adolescents who use drugs as an attempt to solve or forget long-standing problems.

47. adolescence

Boys are four times as likely to be arrested as girls, lower-SES adolescents are almost twice as likely to be arrested as middle-class adolescents, and African-American and Latino youths are close to twice as likely to be arrested as European-Americans, who, themselves, are more than twice as likely to be arrested as Asian-Americans.

48. lower-SES or dark-skinned

49. do at one time or another

50. 15 or 16; half

51. maturity; contact with the criminal justice system

52. learning difficulties; stresses; attention-deficit disorder; antisocial

53. antisocial

54. social consequences

Programs that help parents discipline their children authoritatively, strengthening schools so that fewer young people have learning problems, and shoring up neighborhood networks so that community institutions provide constructive challenges for youths are all promising ways of preventing delinquency.

55. increase; underestimated

56. self-destruction; counterattack

57. maltreatment

58. series of episodes; rise

59. ongoing; interferes with normal development

60. girls

61. boys; male

62. less

63. immature; socially isolated; alcoholic; drug-abusing; do not

64. extent; duration; reaction of other people

65. never learn what a normal adult-child or man-woman relationship should be

66. violent relationships

Female victims of sexual abuse may have a distorted view of sexuality, and thus are more likely to marry abusive men. If these men begin to abuse their daughters, the mother is less alert to the problem or feels trapped and unable to help.

67. macrosystem; rare
68. begin
69. lower; increased
70. solitary; depressed; self-punishing; emotional
71. is not; family conflict
72. a. a sudden decline in school attendance and achievement
    b. a break in a love relationship
    c. withdrawal from social relationships
    d. an attempted suicide
    e. cluster suicides
73. happy
74. do; do

PROGRESS TEST 1

Multiple-Choice Questions

1. **b.** is the answer. (p. 412)
   a. According to Erikson, this is the crisis of infancy.
   c. & d. In Erikson's theory, these crises occur later in life.
2. **a.** is the answer. (p. 412)
   b. This describes an identity moratorium.
   c. This describes negative identity.
   d. This describes identity diffusion.
3. **c.** is the answer. (p. 412)
4. **d.** is the answer. (p. 421)
5. **d.** is the answer. (p. 416)
6. **d.** is the answer. (p. 420)
   a. The generational stake refers to differences in how family members from different generations view the family.
   b. Foreclosure refers to the premature establishment of identity.
   c. Peer screening is an aspect of parental monitoring, but was not specifically discussed in the text.
7. **c.** is the answer. (p. 426)
8. **c.** is the answer. (p. 421)
9. **b.** is the answer. (p. 416)
   a. This occurs in some cases, but not in *most* cases.
   c. Moratorium is a "time-out" in identity formation in order to allow the adolescent to try out alternative identities. It is generally not a solution in such cases.
   d. Young people who experience identity diffusion are often apathetic, which is not the case here.
10. **d.** is the answer. (p. 432)
11. **a.** is the answer. (p. 433)
    b. This was not discussed in the text.
    c. This is true of girls.
12. **c.** is the answer. (p. 435)
13. **c.** is the answer. (pp. 430–431)
14. **c.** is the answer. (p. 433)
15. **c.** is the answer. (pp. 419–420)
    a. In fact, parent-child conflict is more likely to involve mothers and their early-maturing offspring.
    b. Conflicts are less frequent in stable, single-parent homes than in homes where parents are married, newly divorced, cohabiting, or remarried.

True or False Items

1. T (p. 415)
2. F Numerous studies have shown substantial agreement between parents and their adolescent children on political opinions and educational values. (p. 418)
3. F (p. 423)
4. T (p. 422)
5. T (p. 425)
6. F Frequent drug users were more troubled, alienated, and likely to have unsatisfactory interpersonal relationships than experimenters, who were outgoing and cheerful. (p. 428)
7. T (pp. 429–430)
8. T (p. 434)
9. T (p. 434)
10. T (p. 436)

PROGRESS TEST 2

Multiple-Choice Questions

1. **a.** is the answer. (p. 431)
2. **d.** is the answer. In fact, just the opposite is true: a sudden disinterest in friends and family may be a warning sign of suicide. (p. 436)
3. **c.** is the answer. (p. 430)

4. **c.** is the answer. (p. 424)

   d. The text does not discuss the relationship between birth order and peer relationships.

5. **d.** is the answer. (p. 419)
6. **d.** is the answer. (p. 422)
7. **a.** is the answer. (p. 413)

   b. This describes an adolescent undergoing an identity moratorium.

   c. This describes identity foreclosure.

   d. This describes an adolescent who is adopting a negative identity.

8. **d.** is the answer. (p. 421)
9. **b.** is the answer. (p. 429)
10. **c.** is the answer. (p. 430)
11. **d.** is the answer. (p. 413)

    a. Identity foreclosure occurs when the adolescent prematurely adopts an identity, without fully exploring alternatives.

    b. Adolescents who adopt an identity that is opposite to the one they are expected to develop have taken on a negative identity.

    c. Identity diffusion occurs when the adolescent is apathetic and has few commitments to goals or values.

12. **a.** is the answer. (p. 418)

    c. & d. The text does not suggest that the size of the generation gap varies with the offspring's sex.

13. **c.** is the answer. (p. 426)
14. **b.** is the answer. (p. 427)
15. **d.** is the answer. (p. 433)

Matching Items

1. g (p. 412)	**4.** e (p. 412)	**7.** d (p. 415)
2. i (p. 412)	**5.** c (p. 413)	**8.** b (p. 418)
3. a (p. 412)	**6.** h (p. 413)	**9.** f (p. 420)

CHALLENGE TEST

1. **b.** is the answer. Apparently, Sharon never explored alternatives or truly forged a unique personal identity. (p. 412)

   a. Individuals who rebel by adopting an identity that is the opposite of the one they are expected to adopt have taken on a negative identity.

   c. Individuals who experience identity diffusion have few commitments to goals or values. This was not Sharon's problem.

   d. Had she taken a moratorium on identity formation, Sharon would have experimented with alternative identities and perhaps would have chosen that of a medical researcher.

2. **c.** is the answer. (pp. 412–414)
3. **b.** is the answer. (p. 412)

   a. Identity achievers often have a strong sense of ethnic identification, but usually are low in prejudice.

   c. & d. The text does not present research that links ethnic pride and prejudice with either identity diffusion or moratorium.

4. **b.** is the answer. Minority adolescents struggle with finding the right balance between transcending their background and becoming immersed in it. (p. 415)

   c. & d. The text does not suggest that the amount of time adolescents have to forge their identities varies from one ethnic group to another, or has changed over historical time.

5. **b.** is the answer. (p. 418)

   a. The generation gap refers to actual differences in attitudes and values between the younger and older generations. This example is concerned with how large these differences are perceived to be.

   c. & d. These terms are not used in the text in discussing family conflict.

6. **b.** is the answer. (p. 413)
7. **a.** is the answer. (p. 423)

   b. In fact, just the opposite is true.

   c. Developmentalists recommend authoritative, rather than authoritarian, parenting.

   d. Parental monitoring is important for all adolescents.

8. **d.** is the answer. (p. 428)
9. **c.** is the answer. (p. 412)
10. **d.** is the answer. Adolescents give high praise to those who are good listeners, as opposed to those who are more likely to offer and justify their own thoughts. (pp. 424, 436)
11. **d.** is the answer. (p. 436)
12. **d.** is the answer. (p. 430)
13. **c.** is the answer. (p. 420)

    a., b., & d. Adolescents from authoritative families (in which disciplinary measures typically are moderate), regardless of SES, tend to be better adjusted and more confident than those from very strict or very permissive families.

14. **c.** is the answer. (p. 427)
15. **b.** is the answer. (p. 434)

KEY TERMS

1. According to Erikson, the search for **identity** is the primary task and crisis of adolescence, a crisis in which the young person attempts to define himself or herself as a unique person. (p. 412)
2. In Erikson's theory, **identity achievement** occurs when adolescents attain their new identity by establishing their own goals and values, and abandoning some of those set by parents and society. (p. 412)
3. In identity **foreclosure,** the adolescent forms an identity prematurely, by accepting earlier roles and parental values wholesale, without truly forging a unique personal identity. (p. 412)
4. Adolescents who take on a **negative identity** adopt an identity that is the opposite of the one they are expected to adopt. (p. 412)
5. Adolescents who experience **identity diffusion** have few commitments to goals or values and are often apathetic about trying to find an identity. (p. 413)
6. In the process of finding a mature identity, many young people seem to declare a **moratorium,** a kind of time-out during which they experiment with alternative identities without trying to settle on any one. (p. 413)
7. The **generation gap** consists of the perceived differences in attitudes and values between the younger generation and the older one. (p. 415)
8. The **generational stake** refers to the tendency of each family member, because of that person's different developmental stage, to see the family in a certain way. (p. 418)
9. **Parental monitoring** is parental watchfulness about where one's child is and what he or she is doing, and with whom. (p. 420)

CHAPTER 17 Early Adulthood: Biosocial Development

Chapter Overview

In this chapter we encounter the developing person in the prime of life. Early adulthood is the best time for hard physical labor—because strength is at a peak—and for reproduction—because overall health is good and fertility is high. However, with the attainment of full maturity, a new aspect of physical development comes into play—that is, decline. Chapter 17 takes a look at how people perceive changes that occur as the body ages as well as how decisions they make regarding lifestyle affect the course of their overall development.

The chapter begins with a description of the growth, strength, and health of the individual during adulthood. The following section reviews both visible age-related changes, such as wrinkling, and less obvious changes, such as declines in the efficiency of the body's systems. Sexual-reproductive health, a matter of great concern to young adults, is discussed in the next section, with particular attention paid to trends in sexual responsiveness during adulthood and fertility problems that may develop. The final section looks at three problems that are more prevalent during young adulthood than at any other period of the life span: drug and alcohol abuse, compulsive eating and destructive dieting, and violent death.

NOTE: Answer guidelines for all Chapter 17 questions begin on page 260.

Guided Study

The text chapter should be studied one section at a time. Before you read, preview each section by skimming it, noting headings and boldface items. Then read the appropriate section objectives from the following outline. Keep these objectives in mind and, as you read the chapter section, search for the information that will enable you to meet each objective. Once you have finished a section, write out answers for its objectives.

Growth, Strength, and Health (p. 444)

1. Describe changes in growth, strength, and overall health that occur during early adulthood.

Age-Related Changes (pp. 445–447)

2. Describe age-related changes in physical appearance that become noticeable by the late 20s.

3. Discuss changes in the efficiency of various body functions, focusing on the significance of these changes for the individual.

The Sexual-Reproductive System (pp. 447–451)

4. Identify age-related trends in the sexual responsiveness of both men and women during the decades from 20 to 40.

5. Describe the main causes of infertility in men and women, and list several techniques used to treat this problem, noting some of the issues raised by the techniques.

Three Troubling Problems (pp. 452–460)

6. (A Life-Span Perspective) Identify several factors that promote alcoholism and state five possible reasons for the high rate of drug use and abuse during early adulthood.

7. Identify the potentially harmful effects of repeated dieting.

8. Describe the typical victims of anorexia nervosa and bulimia nervosa and discuss possible explanations for these disorders.

9. Explain how restrictive stereotypes of "masculine" and "feminine" behavior may be related to the self-destructive behaviors of many young Americans.

10. (Text and Research Report) Discuss the factors that may determine whether a young male adult will suffer a violent death.

Chapter Review

When you have finished reading the chapter, work through the material that follows to review it. Complete the sentences and answer the questions. As you proceed, evaluate your performance for each section by consulting the answers on page 260. Do not continue with the next section until you understand each answer. If you need to, review or reread the appropriate section in the textbook before continuing.

1. With the attainment of full maturity, human development is released from the constraints of ____________ programmed maturation. At the same time, ____________, or age-related decline, may begin.

Growth, Strength, and Health (p. 444)

2. In general, noticeable increases in height have stopped by about age ________ in females and ________ in males.
3. Growth in ________ and increases in ________ continue into the 20s. Before middle age, the average man adds ________ pounds, and the average woman ________ pounds, to their weight at age 20.
4. Women typically have a higher percentage of ________ and a lower ________ than men do, a sex difference that ________ (increases/decreases) throughout life.
5. Physical strength reaches a peak at about age ________, and then decreases.
6. Medical attention in early adulthood is more often necessitated by ________ than by illness.
7. Of the fatal diseases, ________ is the leading killer of young adults.

Age-Related Changes (pp. 445–447)

8. By the ________, most people notice the first signs of aging in their physical appearance. The earliest signs of aging include wrinkles, caused by loss of ________ in facial skin, and the first ________ ________, caused by a loss of pigment-producing cells.
9. In general, the body systems of the typical 40-year-old are ________ percent less efficient than they were at age 20. The rate of decline in body systems is influenced by both ________ ________ and ________, however.
10. Many of the body's functions serve to maintain ________; that is, they keep physiological functioning in a state of balance. The older a person is, the ________ (less time/longer) it takes for these adjustments to occur. This makes it more difficult for older bodies to adapt to, and recover from, ________.
11. For most of us, our bodies, if adequately maintained, are capable of functioning quite well until we are at least age ________. The declines of aging primarily affect our ________ ________, which is defined as ________ ________.
12. The muscles of the body ________ (do/do not) have the equivalent of an organ reserve.
13. The average maximum heart rate ________ (declines/remains stable/increases) with age. Resting heart rate ________ (declines/remains stable/increases) with age.

Briefly explain why most of the age-related biological changes that occur during the first decades of adulthood are of little consequence to the individual.

14. Age-related biological changes *are* noticeable in two areas: those that influence ________ performance, and those that influence the ________-________ system.

The Sexual-Reproductive System (pp. 447–451)

15. In both sexes, sexual responsiveness, sexual preference, and sexual orientation vary for many reasons, including ________ ________, ________ ________, and ________ ________ and ________.
16. During the early years of manhood, sexual excitement, which includes ________ ________ ________ and ________ ________, can occur very quickly. As men grow older, they often need stimulation that is more

_______________ to initiate sexual excitement.

17. Age-related trends in sexual responsiveness _______________ (are/are not) as clear-cut for women. As they mature from adolescence toward middle adulthood, women become more likely to experience _______________.

State three possible reasons for this age-related trend in women.

18. Most women can still bear a first child as late as age _______________, and most men can father a child throughout _______________ _______________.

19. About _______________ percent of all married couples discover they are infertile, which is defined as _______________ _______________.

Age is _______________ (often/rarely) a contributing factor to this problem. Until middle age, _______________ (men contribute/women contribute/both sexes contribute equally) to most fertility problems.

20. The most common fertility problem in men lies in the _______________ _______________ of sperm, or in the sperm's poor _______________, which is defined as their ability to _______________ _______________.

About _______________ percent of young American adult males are infertile.

21. Sperm grow in the _______________ over a period of _______________.

List several factors that can alter normal sperm development.

22. A common fertility problem in women is difficulty with _______________. Approximately _______________ percent of women do not ovulate naturally, no matter what their age. Most women find that ovulation becomes _______________ (more/less) regular as middle age approaches. Older women take _______________ (longer/less time) to conceive, and they are more likely to give birth to _______________ when they do.

23. The other common fertility problem for women is blocked _______________ _______________, often caused by _______________ _______________ _______________ that was not treated promptly. Sexually transmitted diseases, such as _______________, can cause such infections.

24. A woman who has trouble conceiving may have _______________, a condition in which fragments of the _______________ _______________ block the reproductive tract. This disorder is most common between the ages of _______________ and _______________.

25. Most physicians recommend that women begin their childbearing before age _______________.

26. Minor genital abnormalities that cause infertility in the male are often correctable through _______________.

27. Many infertility problems can also be overcome by _______________ _______________ _______________, in which ova are fertilized outside the ovaries. The success rate of this technique is about one baby in _______________ attempts. Two variations

of this technique, ______ and ______, involve inserting either ______ or ______ into a Fallopian tube.

28. These alternative paths to reproduction raise profound ______ and ______ questions.

29. About ______ of all infertile couples who remain untreated eventually have a baby, and about ______ of the couples who are treated never do.

Three Troubling Problems (pp. 452–460)

30. Three problems that are more prevalent in early adulthood than at any other age are ______ ______, ______ ______, and ______ ______.

31. (A Life-Span Perspective) Drug abuse is defined as ______.

32. (A Life-Span Perspective) The role of heredity in drug abuse has been most clearly demonstrated in connection with ______.

Briefly explain why, biochemically, some people are more likely than other people to abuse alcohol.

33. (A Life-Span Perspective) Other aspects of alcoholism are related to heritable personality traits, including ______, ______, and ______.

The likelihood of drug abuse is also affected by ______, ______, ______, and ______ ______.

34. (A Life-Span Perspective) Substance abuse, which peaks at about age ______, generally ______ (increases/decreases) from early adolescence through early adulthood.

35. (A Life-Span Perspective) State five reasons for the high rate of drug use and abuse in the first years of adulthood.

a. ______

b. ______

c. ______

d. ______

e. ______

36. (A Life-Span Perspective) Drug abuse in early adulthood usually ______ (does/does not) signal a lifetime of addiction.

37. Many scientists believe that each person has a certain ______ point for his or her weight.

List the factors that determine this point.

38. The tendency to maintain body weight at this homeostatic level can be undermined by ______ ______ and ______ ______.

39. Most women who lose weight by dieting ______ (do/do not) eventually regain it.

40. Repeated and extensive weight loss alters body ______ so that the body begins to maintain its weight on ______ (fewer/a greater number of) calories.

41. Gradual weight gain over the decades of adulthood ______ (is/is not) unhealthy for most women. Insufficient body fat halts natural ______ ______, making menstruation irregular and reproduction difficult or impossible.

42. Another problem with crash dieting is that it can result in ______________________ ______________________, put strain on the ______________________, and sometimes even lead to death.

43. Young women are particularly likely to abuse ______________________ in order to suppress appetite. Dieting may also trigger physiological changes that lead to an eating disorder such as ______________________ ______________________, an affliction characterized by ______________________, or the ______________________ (more/less) common disorder ______________________ ______________________, which involves successive bouts of binge eating followed by purging through vomiting or massive doses of laxatives.

44. Binge-purge eating can cause a wide range of health problems, including damage to the ______________________ ______________________ and ______________________ ______________________ from the strain of electrolyte imbalance. A group that is at particular risk for eating disorders is ______________________ ______________________.

45. The psychological consequences of excessive dieting often include ______________________ ______________________-______________________ and ______________________, which can trigger an eating disorder and behaviors that act as immediate ______________________ in relieving emotional distress.

46. Recovery from an eating disorder usually ______________________ (requires/does not require) outside intervention.

State the psychoanalytic and sociological explanations for eating disorders.

47. Stereotypes about "manly" behavior may lead to a problem that afflicts mostly young men—that is, behavior that leads to ______________________ ______________________.

List the biosocial factors that have been suggested as causes of masculine violence.

List cultural and familial factors that may promote masculine violence.

48. Researchers agree that ______________________ ______________________ are at the root of masculine violence.

49. (Research Report) The extent of masculine violence, as reflected in rates of ______________________, ______________________ (varies/does not vary) from culture to culture.

50. (Research Report) A contextual factor frequently cited for the high rates of homicide among young American men is the availability of ______________________. Research ______________________ (confirms/does not confirm) that the presence of a gun often transforms nonlethal aggressive impulses into deadly ones. Cities that have more stringent gun laws also tend to have lower rates of ______________________.

51. (Research Report) Within nations, violent death varies by subgroup, largely because of ______________________, ______________________, and ______________________ forces. Overall, suicide rates are ______________________ (higher/lower) among African-Americans than European-Americans.

State a possible reason for the differences in suicide rates between African- and European-Americans, and between Hispanic-Americans and Native Americans.

52. (Research Report) The leading cause of death for young African-American men is ________________, while among European-American men, ________________ are the number one cause.

Progress Test 1

Multiple-Choice Questions

Circle your answers to the following questions and check them with the answers on page 261. If your answer is incorrect, read the explanation for why it is incorrect and then consult the appropriate pages of the text (in parentheses following the correct answer).

1. Senescence refers to:
   a. a loss of efficiency in the body's regulatory systems.
   b. age-related decline.
   c. decreased physical strength.
   d. vulnerability to disease.

2. When do noticeable increases in height stop?
   a. at about the same age in men and women
   b. at an earlier age in women than in men
   c. at an earlier age in men than in women
   d. There is such diversity in physiological development that it is impossible to generalize regarding this issue.

3. A difference between men and women during early adulthood is that men have:
   a. a higher percentage of body fat.
   b. lower metabolism.
   c. proportionately more muscle.
   d. greater organ reserve.

4. The majority of young adults rate their own health as:
   a. very good or excellent.
   b. average or fair.
   c. poor.
   d. worse than it was during adolescence.

5. The automatic adjustment of the body's systems to keep physiological functions in a state of equilibrium, even during heavy exertion, is called:
   a. organ reserve.
   b. homeostasis.
   c. stress.
   d. muscle capacity.

6. The average 50-year-old can expect to retain ________________ of the strength he or she had at age 20.
   a. less than 50 percent
   b. about 50 percent
   c. as much as 90 percent
   d. 100 percent, with proper exercise and other healthy lifestyle habits

7. As men grow older:
   a. they often need more direct stimulation to initiate sexual excitement.
   b. a longer time elapses between the beginning of sexual excitement and full erection.
   c. a longer time elapses between orgasm and the end of the refractory period.
   d. all of the above occur.

8. It is estimated that infertility affects:
   a. at least half of all married couples in which the woman is in her early 30s.
   b. men more than women.
   c. about one-third of all married couples.
   d. about 15 percent of all married couples.

9. Sperm develop in the testes over a period of:
   a. one month.
   b. four days.
   c. seventy-four days.
   d. one year.

10. Endometriosis is:
    a. a sexually transmitted disease.
    b. lack of ovulation or irregular ovulation in an older woman.
    c. a disease characterized by the presence of uterine tissue on the surface of the ovaries or the Fallopian tubes.
    d. a condition that invariably results from pelvic inflammatory disease.

11. Artificial insemination is a solution for infertility that is caused by:
    a. ovulatory problems in the woman.
    b. endometriosis.
    c. low sperm count.
    d. PID.

12. A woman is far more likely than a man to abuse:
    a. alcohol.
    b. cocaine.
    c. diet pills.
    d. heavy drugs of all kinds.

13. Eating disorders such as anorexia nervosa and bulimia nervosa are most often associated with:
    a. depression.
    b. alcohol abuse.
    c. obesity.
    d. suicide.

14. (Research Report) The leading cause of death among young adult African-American men is:
    a. cancer.
    b. homicide.
    c. fatal accidents.
    d. suicide.

15. (A Life-Span Perspective) Which of the following was not suggested as a reason for the high rate of drug use and abuse in the first years of adulthood?
    a. Young adults typically have not yet made major life decisions regarding career, mate, and so forth.
    b. The social surroundings of young adults encourage drug use.
    c. Young adults may use drugs as a way of striving for independence from their families.
    d. Young adults often fear social rejection.

True or False Items

Write *true* or *false* on the line in front of each statement.

_______ 1. Conditioned older athletes can perform much better than younger persons.

_______ 2. Few adults actually use all the muscle capacity that they could develop during young adulthood.

_______ 3. The older a person is, the longer it takes for his or her blood glucose level to return to normal after heavy exertion.

_______ 4. Age-related trends in sexual responsiveness are similar for men and women.

_______ 5. (A Life-Span Perspective) One reason that young people are attracted to alcohol and other drugs is that these substances are known to be effective in enhancing sexual responsiveness and performance.

_______ 6. Compared with a woman in her 20s, a 40-year-old woman is more likely to have cycles with no ovulation and cycles in which several ova are released.

_______ 7. Most physicians recommend that women who want to have children begin childbearing before age 35.

_______ 8. (A Life-Span Perspective) Research suggests that there may be a genetic basis to alcoholism.

_______ 9. An adult woman who is 10 pounds overweight is probably healthier than one who is very thin.

_______ 10. (Research Report) The rate of suicide is lower for Native Americans than for Hispanic-Americans.

Progress Test 2

Progress Test 2 should be completed during a final chapter review. Answer the following questions after you thoroughly understand the correct answers for the Chapter Review and Progress Test 1.

Multiple-Choice Questions

1. The early 20s are the peak years for:
    a. hard physical work.
    b. problem-free reproduction.
    c. athletic performance.
    d. all of the above.

2. Of the fatal diseases, _______________ is the leading cause of death in young adults.
    a. heart disease
    b. cancer
    c. diabetes
    d. multiple sclerosis

3. The first sign of aging that is likely to be noticed by a man during his late 20s is:
    a. reduced organ reserve.
    b. diminishing physical strength.
    c. failure of homeostatic mechanisms during heavy exertion.
    d. graying or thinning of the hair.

4. The efficiency of most body systems:
    a. remains stable throughout the 20s.
    b. begins to decline during the 20s.
    c. begins to decline during the 30s.
    d. declines significantly at about age 30.

5. Normally, the average resting heart rate for both men and women:
   a. declines noticeably during the 30s.
   b. declines much faster than does the average maximum heart rate.
   c. reaches a peak at about age 30.
   d. remains stable until late adulthood.

6. As they mature from adolescence through early adulthood, women become more likely to experience orgasm during love-making because:
   a. the slowing of the man's responses makes the sex act likely to last longer.
   b. with experience, both partners are more likely to focus on aspects of love-making that intensify the woman's sexual responses.
   c. the current generation of women between young and middle adulthood feel freer to explore their own sexuality.
   d. of all of the above reasons.

7. The most common fertility problem in men lies in:
   a. the low number of their sperm.
   b. the sperm's poor motility.
   c. the condition called endometriosis.
   d. both a. and b.

8. PID refers to:
   a. a drug taken to stimulate ovulation.
   b. a sexually transmitted disease.
   c. pelvic inflammatory disease.
   d. fertilization outside the uterus.

9. A technique that involves fertilization of the ovum outside the uterus is referred to as:
   a. endometriosis.
   b. artificial insemination.
   c. in vitro fertilization.
   d. surrogate fertilization.

10. In most cases of infertility, age is:
   a. a relatively unimportant factor.
   b. one factor among many.
   c. the primary factor.
   d. not a factor at all.

11. The typical bulimic patient is a:
   a. college-age woman.
   b. woman who starves herself to the point of emaciation.
   c. woman in her late 40s.
   d. woman who suffers from life-threatening obesity.

12. Repeated or extensive weight loss may result in:
   a. altered metabolism such that the body begins to maintain its weight on fewer calories.
   b. unusual stress on the heart.
   c. low self-esteem.
   d. all of the above.

13. Relative to all other age groups, young adult males are at increased risk for virtually every kind of:
   a. eating disorder.
   b. violent death.
   c. acute disease.
   d. chronic disease.

14. (A Life-Span Perspective) According to a large longitudinal study, the use of legal and illegal drugs in the United States peaks:
   a. during adolescence.
   b. at about age 23.
   c. during the 30s.
   d. during late adulthood.

15. (Research Report) Compared to communities with strict gun control laws, those with no restrictions on gun ownership:
   a. have slightly lower rates of homicide and suicide.
   b. have significantly lower rates of homicide and suicide.
   c. have about the same rates of homicide and suicide.
   d. have higher rates of homicide and suicide.

Matching Items

Match each definition or description with its corresponding term.

Terms

_______ 1. senescence
_______ 2. homeostasis
_______ 3. organ reserve
_______ 4. infertile
_______ 5. motility
_______ 6. pelvic inflammatory disease (PID)
_______ 7. endometriosis
_______ 8. in vitro fertilization (IVF)
_______ 9. anorexia nervosa
_______ 10. bulimia nervosa

Definitions or Descriptions

a. fertilization of ova outside the body
b. a condition characterizing about 15 percent of all married couples
c. often caused by sexually transmitted diseases
d. extra capacity for responding to stressful events
e. a state of physiological equilibrium
f. an affliction characterized by binge-purge eating
g. age-related decline
h. condition in which fragments of the uterus block the reproductive tract
i. an affliction characterized by self-starvation
j. with age, declines in male sperm

Challenge Test

Answer these questions the day before an exam as a final check on your understanding of the chapter's terms and concepts.

1. Your instructor asks you to summarize, in one sentence, the extent and cause of biosocial decline during early adulthood. You wisely respond:
   a. "Any difficulties experienced by young adults in biosocial development are usually related to factors other than aging."
   b. "Significant declines in all aspects of physical well-being become apparent by the mid 20s."
   c. "With the attainment of full maturity, development is released from the constraints of heredity."
   d. "The first signs of aging are usually not apparent until middle adulthood."

2. When we are hot, we perspire in order to give off body heat. This is an example of the way our body functions maintain:
   a. senescence.
   b. homeostasis.
   c. endometriosis.
   d. motility.

3. Due to a decline in organ reserve, 28-year-old Brenda:
   a. has a higher resting heart rate than she did when she was younger.
   b. needs longer to recover from strenuous exercise than she did when she was younger.
   c. has a higher maximum heart rate than her younger sister.
   d. has all of the above.

4. Summarizing the results of cross-sectional research, the lecturer states that "Women's sexual responses are heightened by maturity." The most likely explanation for the lecturer's statement is that:
   a. in women, sexual sensitivity increases with age.
   b. cohort differences are operating.
   c. the sample is unrepresentative of the population.
   d. cross-sectional research tends to exaggerate age differences.

5. If Benny is like most men, as he grows older, he will require:
   a. less direct stimulation to become sexually excited.
   b. a shorter refractory period following each orgasm.
   c. a longer time between erection and ejaculation.
   d. all of the above.

6. Corretta and Vernon Castle have been trying to conceive a baby for over a year. Because they are both in their thirties, their physician suspects that:
   a. Vernon is infertile.
   b. Corretta is infertile.
   c. neither Vernon nor Corretta is infertile.
   d. Vernon and Corretta are equally likely to be infertile.

7. Twenty-five-year-old Michelle believes that she is infertile. Because she has been sexually active with a number of partners and once had gonorrhea, her doctor suspects she may have:
   a. endometriosis.
   b. low motility.
   c. irregular ovulation.
   d. pelvic inflammatory disease.

8. Sheila dieted for several weeks until she lost ten pounds. Upon returning to a normal diet, she is horrified to find that she has gained some of the weight back. It is likely that Sheila's weight gain was caused by:
   a. overconsumption of high fat foods.
   b. too little exercise in her daily routine.
   c. her former diet, which altered her body metabolism.
   d. a low body set point.

9. Of the following, who is most likely to suffer from anorexia nervosa?
   a. Bill, a 23-year-old professional football player
   b. Florence, a 30-year-old account executive
   c. Lynn, a 20-year-old college student
   d. Carl, a professional dancer

10. Twenty-year-old Gwynn, who is 9 pounds heavier than the national average for her height and build, should probably:
    a. go on a crash diet, since every additional pound of fat is hazardous to her health.
    b. gradually reduce her weight to slightly below the national average.
    c. realize that because of her high body set point she will be unable to have children.
    d. not worry, since this is probably a healthy weight for her body.

11. As a psychoanalyst, Dr. Mendoza is most likely to believe that eating disorders are caused by:
    a. the reinforcing effects of fasting, binging, and purging.
    b. low self-esteem and depression, which act as a stimulus for destructive patterns of eating.
    c. unresolved conflicts with parents.
    d. the desire of working women to project a strong, self-controlled image.

12. (Research Report) Kim and Delbert want to move with their young son to a community that discourages violence. They should look for a community with:
    a. strict gun control laws.
    b. strong religious values.
    c. considerable ethnic diversity.
    d. all of the above.

13. (Research Report) In my subgroup suicide rates are relatively low, probably because we tend to have more extensive family and friendship networks than other subgroups. Who am I?
    a. a European-American
    b. an Hispanic-American
    c. an African-American
    d. a Native American

14. (A Life-Span Perspective) Naveed becomes flushed and nauseated after a single drink of alcohol. Fearing something is wrong, he consults his doctor who tells him:
    a. he probably has an inherited predisposition toward alcoholism.
    b. he has an inherited enzyme reaction that makes his body intolerant of alcohol.
    c. he has a chromosomal abnormality.
    d. he is genetically vulnerable to both drug abuse and depression.

15. (A Life-Span Perspective) Nathan has a powerful attraction to excitement, a low tolerance for frustration, and a vulnerability to depression. He also may be vulnerable to:
    a. alcoholism.
    b. cocaine abuse.
    c. most psychoactive drugs.
    d. none of the above.

Key Terms

Using your own words, write a brief definition or explanation of each of the following terms on a separate piece of paper.

1. senescence
2. homeostasis
3. organ reserve
4. infertile
5. motility
6. pelvic inflammatory disease (PID)
7. endometriosis
8. in vitro fertilization (IVF)
9. drug abuse
10. anorexia nervosa
11. bulimia nervosa
12. violent death

ANSWERS

CHAPTER REVIEW

1. genetically; senescence
2. 18; 21
3. muscle; fat; 15; 14
4. fat; metabolism; increases
5. 30
6. injuries
7. cancer
8. late 20s; elasticity; gray hairs
9. 20; genetic makeup; lifestyle
10. homeostasis; longer; stress
11. 70; organ reserve; the extra capacity that each organ has for responding to unusually stressful events or conditions that demand intense or prolonged effort
12. do
13. declines; remains stable

The declines of aging primarily affect our organ reserve. In the course of normal daily life, adults seldom have to call upon this capacity, so the deficits in organ reserve generally go unnoticed.

14. athletic; sexual-reproductive
15. innate predispositions; childhood experiences; cultural norms; taboos
16. faster heart beat; penile erection; direct (or explicit)
17. are not; orgasm
    - a. The slowing of the man's responses lengthens the sex act, providing the more prolonged stimulation that many women need to reach orgasm.
    - b. With experience, both partners may be more likely to recognize and focus on those aspects of love-making that intensify the woman's sexual responses.
    - c. The current generation of women between young and middle adulthood came of age in an era of increasing sexual awareness and openness.
18. 40; late adulthood
19. 15; being unable to conceive a child after a year or more of trying; often; both sexes contribute equally
20. low number; motility; swim quickly and far enough to reach an ovum; 5
21. testes; 74 days

Anything that impairs normal body functioning, such as illness with a high fever, medical therapy involving radiation or prescription drugs, exposure to environmental toxins, unusual stress, or an episode of drug abuse.

22. ovulation; 2; less; longer; twins
23. Fallopian tubes; pelvic inflammatory disease (PID); gonorrhea or chlamydia
24. endometriosis; uterine lining; 25; 35
25. 35
26. surgery
27. in vitro fertilization (IVF); seven; GIFT; ZIFT; gametes; zygotes
28. legal; ethical
29. one-third; one-half
30. drug abuse; destructive dieting; violent death
31. any drug use that impairs one's physical, cognitive, or social well-being
32. alcohol

Some people are unlikely to misuse alcohol because an inherited enzyme reaction makes their bodies so intolerant of alcohol that a single drink renders them flushed and nauseated. Others inherit a metabolism that makes alcohol more pleasurable.

33. an attraction to excitement; a low tolerance for frustration; a vulnerability to depression; gender; family upbringing; cultural context
34. 23; decreases
35.
    - a. For some young adults, drug abuse is a way of striving for independence from parents.
    - b. Many abuse drugs in an effort to escape the life stresses that cluster during the 20s.
    - c. Many young adults use alcohol and other drugs because they fear social rejection and sexual unresponsiveness.
    - d. Young adults are the group least likely to be regularly exposed to religious faith and practice.
    - e. The social surroundings of many young adults encourage drug use.
36. does not
37. set

Heredity, age, gender, childhood eating habits, and exercise levels help determine one's set point.

38. cultural pressures; personality patterns
39. do
40. metabolism; fewer
41. is not; hormonal rhythms

42. nutritional imbalance; heart
43. illegal or prescribed stimulants; anorexia nervosa; self-starvation; more; bulimia nervosa
44. gastrointestinal system; cardiac arrest; college women
45. low self-esteem; depression; reinforcers
46. requires

According to psychoanalytic theory, women with eating disorders have a conflict with their parents, who provided their first nourishment. A more sociological explanation is that as women enter the work place they try to project a strong, self-controlled, "masculine" image.

47. violent death

Biosocial factors include higher testosterone levels, dyslexia, attention-deficit disorder with hyperactivity, and certain genetic abnormalities.

Cultural and familial factors include child maltreatment, divorce, movie and television violence, the glorification of war, and the lure of drug abuse.

48. social values
49. homicide; varies
50. firearms; confirms; suicide
51. cohort; ethnic; socioeconomic; lower

In comparison to European-Americans, African-Americans tend to have more extensive family and friendship networks, which helps protect against the sense of isolation that is typically a precondition to suicide. The Catholic tradition of most Hispanic-Americans holds suicide to be a moral sin, whereas in some Native American traditions, suicide is considered a noble sacrifice.

52. homicide; accidents

PROGRESS TEST 1

Multiple-Choice Questions

1. **b.** is the answer. (p. 443)

   a., c., & d. Each of these is a specific example of the more general process of senescence.
2. **b.** is the answer. (p. 444)
3. **c.** is the answer. (p. 444)

   a. & b. These are true of women.

   d. Men and women do not differ in this characteristic.
4. **a.** is the answer. (p. 444)
5. **b.** is the answer. (p. 446)

   a. This is the extra capacity that each organ of the body has for responding to unusually stressful events or conditions that demand intense or prolonged effort.

   c. Stress, which is not defined in this chapter, refers to events or situations that tax the body's resources.

   d. This simply refers to a muscle's potential for work.
6. **c.** is the answer. (p. 446)
7. **d.** is the answer. (p. 448)
8. **d.** is the answer. (p. 449)

   b. Until middle age, infertility is equally likely in women and men.
9. **c.** is the answer. (p. 449)
10. **c.** is the answer. (p. 450)

    a. Sexually transmitted diseases can cause infertility by contributing to pelvic inflammatory disease (PID).

    b. This is another common fertility problem in women.

    d. PID often is a cause of infertility; it is not, however, the same as endometriosis.
11. **c.** is the answer. (p. 450)

    a., b., & d. Artificial insemination requires normal ovulation and a healthy reproductive tract. These conditions can be overcome by other techniques, such as in vitro fertilization.
12. **c.** is the answer. (p. 456)
13. **a.** is the answer. Depression and low self-esteem often serve as stimulus triggers for fasting, binging, and purging, which may temporarily relieve these states of emotional distress. (p. 457)
14. **b.** is the answer. (p. 459)

    a. Although this is the most common fatal disease in early adulthood, it certainly is not the most common cause of death.

    c. This is the leading cause of death for young European-American men.

    d. Suicide is much less frequently a cause of death for African-American men, partly because they tend to have extensive family and friendship networks that provide social support.
15. **a.** is the answer. In fact, just the opposite is true. Many of these major decisions are made during the 20s. (p. 453)

True or False Items

1. T (p. 447)
2. T (p. 446)

3. T (p. 446)
4. F Age seems to affect men and women differently with respect to sexual responsiveness—with men becoming less responsive and women, more responsive. (p. 448)
5. F Although many young people think that alcohol and other drugs enhance sexuality, this is largely a myth; in fact, heavy drug use is known to diminish rather than enhance sexual responsiveness. (p. 454)
6. T (p. 450)
7. T (p. 450)
8. T (p. 452)
9. T (p. 456)
10. F In part because suicide is considered a mortal sin in Catholicism, the most common religion among Hispanic-Americans, its rate is very low in this ethnic group. (p. 459)

PROGRESS TEST 2

Multiple-Choice Questions

1. **d.** is the answer. (p. 444)
2. **b.** is the answer. (p. 444)
3. **d.** is the answer. (p. 445)
   a., b., & c. These often remain unnoticed until middle age.
4. **b.** is the answer. (p. 445)
5. **d.** is the answer. (p. 447)
6. **d.** is the answer. (p. 448)
7. **d.** is the answer. (p. 449)
   c. This is a common fertility problem in women.
8. **c.** is the answer. (p. 450)
   b. Sexually transmitted diseases can cause PID.
   d. This describes in vitro fertilization.
9. **c.** is the answer. (p. 450)
   a. Endometriosis is a condition in which fragments of the uterine lining become implanted and grow on the surface of the ovaries or the Fallopian tubes, blocking the reproductive tract.
   b. In this technique sperm collected from a male donor are artificially inserted into the uterus.
   d. This technique is not discussed in the text.
10. **b.** is the answer. (p. 450)
11. **a.** is the answer. (p. 457)
    b. This describes a woman suffering from anorexia nervosa.
    c. Eating disorders are much more common in younger women.
    d. Most women with bulimia nervosa are usually close to normal in weight.
12. **d.** is the answer. (p. 456)
13. **b.** is the answer. (p. 458)
    a. Eating disorders are more common in women than men.
    c. & d. Disease is relatively rare at this age.
14. **b.** is the answer. (p. 453)
15. **d.** is the answer. (p. 459)

Matching Items

1. g (p. 443)
2. e (p. 446)
3. d (p. 446)
4. b (p. 449)
5. j (p. 449)
6. c (p. 450)
7. h (p. 450)
8. a (p. 450)
9. i (p. 457)
10. f (p. 457)

CHALLENGE TEST

1. **a.** is the answer. (p. 444)
   b. Physical declines during the 20s are usually of little consequence.
   c. Although this is true, it does not address the instructor's request.
   d. The first signs of aging become apparent at an earlier age.
2. **b.** is the answer. (p. 446)
   a. This is age-related decline.
   c. This is a common fertility problem for women.
   d. This is a characteristic of sperm.
3. **b.** is the answer. (p. 446)
   a. Resting heart rate remains stable throughout adulthood.
   c. Maximum heart rate declines with age.
4. **b.** is the answer. This is true because the current generation of women between young and middle adulthood came of age in an era of increasing sexual awareness and openness. (p. 448)
5. **c.** is the answer. (p. 448)
6. **d.** is the answer. Before middle age, men and women are equally likely to be infertile. (p. 449)
7. **d.** is the answer. (p. 450)
   a. In this condition, fragments of the uterine lining become implanted and grow on the surface of the ovaries or the Fallopian tubes, blocking the reproductive tract.
   b. This is a common fertility problem in men.

c. Although this may contribute to infertility, Michelle's age and the fact that sexually transmitted diseases can cause PID makes d. the best answer.

8. c. is the answer. (p. 456)
9. c. is the answer. (p. 457)

   a. & d. Eating disorders are more common in women than men.

   b. Eating disorders are more common in younger women.
10. d. is the answer. (p. 456)
11. c. is the answer. (p. 457)

    a. & b. These explanations would more likely be offered by those who emphasize learning theory, cognitive theory, or humanistic theory.

    d. This is a sociological explanation of eating disorders.
12. a. is the answer. Communities with strict gun control laws have lower rates of homicide and suicide. (p. 459)

    b. & c. The text does not make a generalization about the relationship of either religious values or ethnic diversity to violence.
13. c. is the answer. (p. 459)

    a. The rate of suicide is higher among European-Americans than African-Americans.

    b. The rate of suicide is relatively low among Hispanic-Americans, but for a different reason.

    d. Native Americans have a relatively high rate of suicide.
14. b. is the answer. (p. 452)

    a. & d. In fact, just the opposite is probably true. Because of his intolerance to alcohol, Naveed is unlikely to misuse this drug.

    c. There is no evidence that this is so.
15. c. is the answer. (p. 452)

    a. & b. Although these are also correct, they are both psychoactive drugs, making c. the best answer.

KEY TERMS

1. **Senescence** is age-related decline throughout the body. (p. 443)
2. **Homeostasis** refers to the process by which body functions are automatically adjusted to keep our physiological functioning in a state of balance. (p. 446)
3. **Organ reserve** is the extra capacity of each body organ for responding to unusually stressful events or conditions that demand intense or prolonged effort. (p. 446)
4. A couple is said to be **infertile** if they have been unable to conceive a child after a year or more of trying. (p. 449)
5. One of the most common fertility problems in men is poor **motility**, meaning that the sperm are unable to swim quickly and far enough to reach an ovum. (p. 449)
6. **Pelvic inflammatory disease (PID)** is a common fertility problem for women, in which pelvic infections lead to blocked Fallopian tubes. (p. 450)
7. If a woman has trouble conceiving, it may be that she has **endometriosis**, a condition in which fragments of the uterine lining become implanted and grow on the surface of the ovaries or the Fallopian tubes, blocking the reproductive tract. (p. 450)
8. **In vitro fertilization (IVF)** is a technique in which ova are surgically removed from the ovaries and fertilized by sperm in the laboratory. (p. 450)
9. **Drug abuse** is defined as any drug use that impairs one's physical, cognitive, or social well-being. (p. 452)
10. **Anorexia nervosa** is an affliction characterized by self-starvation that is most common in high-achieving college-age women. (p. 457)
11. **Bulimia nervosa** is an eating disorder that involves compulsive binge eating followed by purging through vomiting or taking massive doses of laxatives. (p. 457)

12 Stereotypes about "manly" behavior may lead to a problem that afflicts mostly young men—**violent death** from accident, homicide, or suicide. (p. 458)

CHAPTER 18 Early Adulthood: Cognitive Development

Chapter Overview

During the course of adulthood, there are many shifts in cognitive development—in the speed and efficiency with which we process information, in the focus and depth of our cognitive processes, perhaps in the quality, or wisdom, of our thinking. Developmental psychologists use three different approaches in explaining these shifts, with each approach providing insights into the nature of adult cognition. This chapter takes a Piagetian approach, describing age-related changes in an attempt to uncover patterns or predictable stages.

The chapter begins with the stages of cognitive development proposed by K. Warner Schaie. The cognitive challenges described by Schaie result in a new, postformal thought, evidenced by dialectical and adaptive thinking—the dynamic, in-the-world cognitive style that adults typically use to solve the problems of daily life—and by problem finding.

The next section examines the effect of the college experience on cognitive growth; findings here indicate that years of education correlate with virtually every measure of cognition as thinking becomes progressively more flexible and tolerant. A final section discusses the importance of life events, such as parenthood, job promotion, or illness, in triggering cognitive growth during young adulthood.

NOTE: Answer guidelines for all Chapter 18 questions begin on page 272.

Guided Study

The text chapter should be studied one section at a time. Before you read, preview each section by skimming it, noting headings and boldface items. Then read the appropriate section objectives from the following outline. Keep these objectives in mind and, as you read the chapter section, search for the information that will enable you to meet each objective. Once you have finished a section, write out answers for its objectives.

Adult Thinking (pp. 464–466)

1. Describe the Piagetian approach to the study of adult cognition and identify two other approaches.

2. List and briefly describe the five stages of cognition proposed by K. Warner Schaie.

Beyond Formal Operations: Postformal Thought (pp. 466–471)

3. Identify the main characteristics of postformal thought and tell how it differs from formal operational thought.

4. Explain how adaptive thought and problem finding contribute to cognitive growth.

5. Define dialectical thought and give examples of its usefulness.

6. Evaluate or draw a conclusion about our current understanding of postformal thought.

Adult Moral Reasoning (pp. 471–474)

7. Explain Carol Gilligan's view of how moral reasoning changes during adulthood.

8. (A Closer Look) Briefly describe the six stages of faith outlined by James Fowler.

Cognitive Growth and Higher Education (pp. 475–478)

9. Discuss the relationship between cognitive growth and higher education.

Cognitive Growth and Life Events (pp. 478–480)

10. Discuss how life events may trigger new patterns of thinking and result in cognitive growth.

Chapter Review

When you have finished reading the chapter, work through the material that follows to review it. Complete the sentences and answer the questions. As you proceed, evaluate your performance for each section by consulting the answers on page 272. Do not continue with the next section until you understand each answer. If you need to, review or reread the appropriate section in the textbook before continuing.

1. Unlike the relatively "straightforward" cognitive growth of earlier ages, cognitive development during adulthood is ____________________. Developmentalists have used three approaches to explain this development: the ____________________ approach, the ____________________ approach, and the ____________________-____________________ approach. These approaches focus on changes in ____________________, ____________________, and ____________________ during adulthood.

Adult Thinking (pp. 464–466)

2. Compared to adolescent thinking, adult thinking is more ____________________, ____________________, and ____________________.

Adults are also less inclined toward the "________________ ________________" as their thinking becomes more specialized and job-oriented.

3. Gisela Labouvie-Vief has noted that one hallmark of mature adult thinking is the realization that most of life's answers are ________________ rather than ________________.

4. One reason for the cognitive changes of adulthood is commitment to the responsibilities of ________________ and ________________.
This idea has been stressed by ________________, who has proposed four stages of adult cognition that correspond to the ________________ emphases of adult life.

5. According to this theorist, childhood and adolescence constitute a period of indiscriminate ________________ of information.
Beginning in the ________________, young people enter the ________________ stage as their thinking becomes more goal-directed.

6. As ________________ adulthood approaches, many people enter a(n) ________________ stage, as thinking shifts to integrate long-range personal and family goals with career goals.

7. Some adults reach the ________________ stage of cognition as the middle years bring a deep concern about social responsibility. Finally, in late adulthood a(n) ________________ stage appears, when thoughts turn to making sense of life as a whole.

Beyond Formal Operations: Postformal Thought
(pp. 466–471)

8. The final stage of cognitive development in Piaget's theory is the stage of ________________ ________________ ________________, which ________________ (is/is not) reached by all individuals.

9. Other researchers have argued that the cognitive challenges of adulthood result in a new stage of ________________ thought that is less abstract, more integrative, and better adapted to life's inconsistencies.

10. Deidre Kramer has identified three basic characteristics of this type of thinking: ________________, ________________ ________________ ________________, and ________________.

11. Labouvie-Vief has pointed out that traditional models of cognition stress ________________ thinking and devalue the importance of ________________ ________________ and ________________ ________________.
In her view, the former kind of thinking is ________________ (more/less) adaptive for schoolchildren, adolescents, and young adults than for mature adults.

12. In her research, Labouvie-Vief found that although older adults recognize logical premises in solving real-life problems, they also explore the real-life possibilities and ________________ ________________ that might bear on an issue.

13. Perhaps the most distinctive feature of adult cognition is ________________ ________________, which refers to the capacity to ________________ ________________.
According to Patricia Arlin, this capacity is based on ________________ ________________, which recognizes that different perspectives have a significant impact on problem solving.

14. Problem finding is a central ingredient to ________________ and ________________ creativity.

15. Some theorists consider ________________ ________________ the most advanced form of cognition. This thinking recognizes that every idea, or ________________, implies an opposing idea, or ________________; these are then forged into a(n) ________________ of the two. This type of thinking fosters a world view that recognizes that most of life's important questions ________________ (have/do not have) single, unchangeable, correct answers.

16. Developmentalists ________________ (do/do not all) agree that postformal thought represents a distinct stage of cognitive development.

Cite several criticisms of the theory that postformal thought represents a distinct stage of cognitive development.

Adult Moral Reasoning (pp. 471–474)

17. The theorist who maintains that the concerns of adulthood also affect moral reasoning is ________________.

18. Carol Gilligan believes that in matters of moral reasoning ________________ (males/females) tend to be more concerned with the question of rights and justice, whereas ________________ (males/females) are more concerned with personal relationships. Gilligan also maintains that as people become responsible for the needs of others they begin to construct principles that are ________________ and ________________, because they see that moral reasoning based chiefly on justice principles is inadequate to solve real-life moral dilemmas.

19. (A Closer Look) The theorist who has outlined six stages in the development of faith is ________________. In the space below, identify and briefly describe each stage.

    Stage One: ________________

    Stage Two: ________________

    Stage Three: ________________

    Stage Four: ________________

    Stage Five: ________________

    Stage Six: ________________

Cognitive Growth and Higher Education (pp. 475–478)

20. Years of education ________________ (are/are not) strongly correlated with most measures of adult cognition. This relationship is ________________ (stronger/weaker) than that between socioeconomic status and adult cognition.

21. College education leads people to become more ________________ of other viewpoints.

Briefly outline the year-by-year progression in how the thinking of college students becomes more flexible and tolerant.

22. William Perry found that the thinking of students, over the course of their college careers, progressed through ________________ levels of complexity.

23. College seems to make people more accepting of other viewpoints because it makes people less ________________ by them.

24. Research has shown that the more years of higher education a person has, the deeper and more ________________ that person's reasoning is likely to become.

25. Collegiate populations have become ________________ (more/less) diverse and heterogeneous in recent years.

26. While enrollment at four-year residential colleges has ________________ (held steady/increased), enrollment at nonresidential, public, and/or two-year colleges has ________________ (held steady/increased). In this regard, the type of college one attends ________________ (does/does not) seem to make a significant difference in the cognitive growth of students.

List several educational factors that *do* seem to have an impact on cognitive growth in college students.

27. A college education seems to succeed in accomplishing perhaps its most important goal: preparing students to become ______________-______________ ______________.

Cognitive Growth and Life Events (pp. 478–480)

28. It has been suggested that significant life events, such as ______________ ______________, can trigger new patterns of thinking.

Progress Test 1

Multiple-Choice Questions

Circle your answers to the following questions and check them with the answers on page 273. If your answer is incorrect, read the explanation for why it is incorrect and then consult the appropriate pages of the text (in parentheses following the correct answer).

1. A central idea of Schaie's theory is that prior to adulthood, cognitive development is:
   a. based on indiscriminate learning.
   b. closely related to the experiences of the individual.
   c. especially diverse.
   d. largely the product of the school system.

2. Which of the following is *not* one of the major approaches to the study of adult cognition described in the text?
   a. the information-processing approach
   b. the Piagetian approach
   c. the systems approach
   d. the psychometric approach

3. Compared to adolescent thinking, adult thinking tends to be:
   a. more personal.
   b. more practical.
   c. more integrative.
   d. all of the above.

4. According to Labouvie-Vief, an important catalyst for the cognitive changes of adulthood is:
   a. higher education.
   b. commitment to the responsibilities of career and family.
   c. religious faith.
   d. all of the above.

5. Schaie's name for the form of adult cognition typically attained during early adulthood is the:
   a. reintegrative stage.
   b. acquisition stage.
   c. achieving stage.
   d. responsible and executive stages.

6. According to Schaie, around middle adulthood some adults experience two new cognitive stages, the first of which is the:
   a. achieving stage.
   b. acquisition stage.
   c. responsible stage.
   d. executive stage.

7. Postformal thinking is most useful for solving ______________ problems.
   a. science
   b. mathematics
   c. everyday
   d. abstract, logical

8. The term for the kind of thinking that involves the consideration of both poles of an idea and their reconciliation, or synthesis, in a new idea is:
   a. subjective thinking.
   b. postformal thought.
   c. adaptive reasoning.
   d. dialectical reasoning.

9. Thesis is to antithesis as ______________ is to ______________
   a. a new idea; an opposing idea
   b. abstract; concrete
   c. concrete; abstract
   d. provisional; absolute

10. The concept of "relativistic logic" emphasizes that adult thinking:
    a. is marked by a growing ability to see multiple perspectives on issues.
    b. is more abstract than adolescent thinking.
    c. is more self-centered than adolescent thinking.
    d. is more rational than adolescent thinking.

11. According to the text, whether a person achieves postformal thought depends *mainly* on his or her:
    a. religion.
    b. life experiences and education.
    c. age.
    d. his or her cultural background.

12. Critics of the idea that postformal thinking represents a fifth stage of cognitive development point out that:
    a. the characteristics of postformal thought are not universal.
    b. the characteristics of postformal thought do not build on the prior accomplishments of formal operations.
    c. there is relatively little information about the maintenance of postformal thought into late adulthood.
    d. all of the above are true.

13. According to Carol Gilligan:
    a. in matters of moral reasoning, females tend to be more concerned with the question of rights and justice.
    b. in matters of moral reasoning, males tend to put human needs above principles of justice.
    c. moral reasoning advances during adulthood in response to the more complex moral dilemmas that life poses.
    d. all of the above are true.

14. An important factor in determining whether college students learn to think deeply is:
    a. the amount of contact between students and faculty.
    b. the degree of emphasis on individualized instruction.
    c. the educational background of the faculty.
    d. all of the above.

15. Research has revealed that a typical outcome of college education is that students become:
    a. very liberal politically.
    b. less committed to any particular ideology.
    c. less tolerant of others' views.
    d. more tolerant of others' views.

True or False Items

Write *true* or *false* on the line in front of each statement.

_______ 1. Recent research shows that the main reason most young adults today attend college is to improve their thinking and reasoning skills.

_______ 2. While Schaie's stages of adult cognition are not universal, they have been found to apply to everyone in our culture.

_______ 3. Objective, logical thinking is "adaptive" for the school-age child and adolescent who is in the process of categorizing and organizing his or her experiences.

_______ 4. Because they recognize the changing and subjective nature of beliefs and values, dialectical thinkers avoid making personal or intellectual commitments.

_______ 5. Certain kinds of experiences during adulthood—especially those that entail assuming responsibility for others—can propel an individual from one level of moral reasoning to another.

_______ 6. In recent years, the number of college students has risen dramatically, both in residential four-year colleges and in nonresidential two-year schools.

_______ 7. Postformal thought is less absolute and less abstract than formal thought.

_______ 8. (A Closer Look) Mythic-literal faith, like other "lower" stages in the development of faith, is not generally found past adolescence.

_______ 9. In predicting an individual's level of cognitive development, it would be more helpful to know that person's educational background than his or her age.

_______ 10. The college student of today is more likely to live at home and attend school on a part-time basis than were the students of the previous generation.

Progress Test 2

Progress Test 2 should be completed during a final chapter review. Answer the following questions after you thoroughly understand the correct answers for the Chapter Review and Progress Test 1.

Multiple-Choice Questions

1. Which approach to adult cognitive development emphasizes the analysis of components of intelligence?
    a. Piagetian
    b. psychometric
    c. information-processing
    d. all of the above

2. Which approach to adult cognitive development studies encoding, storage, and retrieval?
    a. Piagetian
    b. psychometric
    c. information-processing
    d. all of the above

3. As adult thinking becomes more focused on occupational and interpersonal demands, it also becomes less inclined toward:
    a. the game of thinking.
    b. dialectical thought.
    c. adaptive thought.
    d. all of the above.

4. According to Schaie, childhood and adolescence constitute the ______________ in cognitive development.
   a. period of acquisition
   b. achieving stage
   c. executive stage
   d. reintegrative stage

5. According to Schaie, in late adulthood the ______________ stage appears, when thoughts turn to ______________.
   a. achieving; making sure one's family is taken care of
   b. executive; consolidating career gains
   c. reintegrative; making sense of life as a whole
   d. acquisition; contributing to the welfare of humanity

6. Formal operational thinking is most useful for solving problems that:
   a. involve logical relationships or theoretical possibilities.
   b. require integrative skills.
   c. involve the synthesis of diverse issues.
   d. require seeing perspectives other than one's own.

7. Which of the following is *not* a characteristic of postformal thought as identified by Deidre Kramer?
   a. abstraction
   b. relativism
   c. acceptance of contradiction
   d. integration

8. The goal of dialectical thinking is forging a(n) ______________ from opposing poles of an idea.
   a. thesis
   b. antithesis
   c. synthesis
   d. hypothesis

9. Formal operational thinking is to postformal thinking as ______________ is to ______________.
   a. problem finding; problem solving
   b. problem solving; problem finding
   c. thesis; antithesis
   d. antithesis; thesis

10. Carol Gilligan suggests that during adulthood:
    a. men and women come to recognize the limitations of basing moral reasoning solely on principles of justice.
    b. men and women come to recognize the limitations of basing moral reasoning solely on individual needs.
    c. men and women develop a more reflective, less absolute moral awareness.
    d. all of the above are true.

11. (A Closer Look) According to James Fowler, individual-reflective faith is marked by:
    a. a willingness to accept contradictions.
    b. a burning need to enunciate universal values.
    c. a literal, wholehearted belief in myths and symbols.
    d. the beginnings of independent questioning of teachers and other figures of authority.

12. Conclusions of research showing clear development of dialectical reasoning among college students are complicated by:
    a. the increasing diversity and heterogeneity of today's student population.
    b. the exclusion from the sample of the brightest and most able students.
    c. the fact that the development of dialectical reasoning and other high-level intellectual skills is no longer an avowed goal of most colleges.
    d. the fact that attendance at college has not been shown to correlate in any meaningful way with measures of adult cognition.

13. (A Closer Look) According to James Fowler, the simplest stage of faith is the stage of:
    a. universalizing faith.
    b. intuitive-projective faith.
    c. mythic-literal faith.
    d. conventional faith.

14. Many of the problems of adult life are characterized by ambiguity, partial truths, and extenuating circumstances, and therefore are often best solved using ______________ thinking.
    a. formal
    b. reintegrative
    c. adaptive, or postformal
    d. executive

15. In contrast to the systematic problem-______________ abilities of the formal operational thinker, sometimes the most distinctive feature of adult thought is problem ______________.
    a. finding; solving
    b. solving; finding
    c. finding; restructuring
    d. restructuring; finding

Matching Items

Match each definition or description with its corresponding term.

Terms

_______ 1. period of acquisition
_______ 2. achieving stage
_______ 3. responsible stage
_______ 4. executive stage
_______ 5. reintegrative stage
_______ 6. postformal thought
_______ 7. dialectical thought
_______ 8. problem finding

Definitions or Descriptions

a. thinking that is integrative and synthetic
b. cognitive stage characterized by goal-directed thinking
c. the capacity to formulate new questions from ambiguous situations
d. cognitive stage characterized by indiscriminate learning
e. considered by some to be the most advanced form of cognition
f. cognitive stage characterized by concern about larger social systems
g. cognitive stage in which personal and family goals are integrated with career goals
h. cognitive stage characterized by inward reflection

Challenge Test

Answer these questions the day before an exam as a final check on your understanding of the chapter's terms and concepts.

1. Kerry, a middle-aged psychologist and a parent, has become a spokesperson for the mentally disable. He is probably functioning in Schaie's:
   a. reintegrative stage.
   b. achieving stage.
   c. stage of universalizing faith.
   d. executive stage.

2. Carol Gilligan's research suggests that the individual who is most likely to allow the context of personal relationships to wholly determine moral decisions is a:
   a. 20-year-old man.
   b. 20-year-old woman.
   c. 40-year-old woman.
   d. 50-year-old person of either sex.

3. Longitudinal research suggests that a college sophomore or junior is most likely to have reached a phase in which he or she:
   a. believes that there are clear and perfect truths to be discovered.
   b. questions personal and social values, and even the idea of *truth* itself.
   c. rejects opposing ideas in the interest of finding one right answer.
   d. accepts a simplistic either/or dualism.

4. In his scheme of cognitive and ethical development, Perry describes a position in which the college student says, "I see I am going to have to make my own decisions in an uncertain world with no one to tell me I'm right." This position marks the beginning of a phase of:
   a. either/or dualism.
   b. modified dualism.
   c. relativism.
   d. commitments in relativism.

5. After suffering a heart attack in his 30s, Rob begins to think differently about life and its deeper meaning. This is an example of:
   a. the effect of a mentor on cognitive development.
   b. having reached the reintegrative stage of adult cognition.
   c. a life event that results in cognitive growth.
   d. a biological or age-related change in intelligence.

6. Dr. Polaski studies how thinking during adulthood builds on the earlier formal thinking skills of adolescence. Evidently, Dr. Polaski follows the _______________ approach to the study of development.
   a. Piagetian
   b. psychometric
   c. cognitive
   d. information-processing

7. Who would be the most likely to agree with the statement, "Personal commitment guides the development of adult thought"?
   a. Schaie
   b. Gilligan
   c. Kohlberg
   d. Perry

8. When she was younger, May-Ling believed that "Honesty is always the best policy." She now realizes that although honesty is desirable, it is not *always* the best policy. May-Ling's current thinking is an example of:
   a. formal thought.
   b. dialectical thinking.
   c. mythic-literal thinking.
   d. conjunctive thinking.

9. Who would be the most likely to agree with the statement, "To be truly ethical a person must have the experience of sustained responsibility for the welfare of others"?
   a. Schaie
   b. Kohlberg
   c. Piaget
   d. Fowler

10. Spike is in his third year at a residential liberal arts college, while his brother Lee is in his third year at a nonresidential community college. In terms of their cognitive growth, what is the most likely outcome?
    a. Spike will more rapidly develop complex critical thinking skills.
    b. Lee will develop greater self-confidence in his abilities since he is studying from the secure base of his home and family.
    c. All other things being equal, Spike and Lee will develop quite similarly.
    d. It is impossible to predict.

11. In concluding her presentation on "The College Student of Today," Coretta states that:
    a. "The number of students in higher education has increased significantly in virtually every country worldwide."
    b. "There are more low-income and ethnic-minority students today than ever before."
    c. "More students choose specific career-based majors rather than a liberal arts education."
    d. all of the above are true.

12. The story of "Dorothy" in the text demonstrates that ______________ may trigger cognitive development.
    a. deep religious faith
    b. higher education, even at an advanced age
    c. significant life events
    d. commitment to a career

13. In concluding his paper on postformal thinking, Stanley notes that:
    a. postformal thinking is not the same kind of universal, age-related stage that Piaget described for earlier cognitive growth.
    b. very few adults attain this highest stage of reasoning.
    c. most everyday problems require sensitivity to subjective feelings and therefore do not foster postformal thinking.
    d. all of the above are true.

14. In predicting an individual's level of cognitive development, it would be most helpful to know that person's:
    a. age.
    b. socioeconomic status.
    c. educational background.
    d. history of life challenges.

15. (A Closer Look) In Fowler's theory, at the highest stages of faith development, people incorporate a powerful vision of compassion for others into their lives. This stage is called:
    a. conjunctive faith.
    b. individual-reflective faith.
    c. synthetic-conventional faith.
    d. universalizing faith.

Key Terms

Using your own words, write a brief definition or explanation of each of the following terms on a separate piece of paper.

1. period of acquisition
2. achieving stage
3. responsible stage
4. executive stage
5. reintegrative stage
6. postformal thought
7. problem finding
8. dialectical thought

ANSWERS

CHAPTER REVIEW

1. multidirectional; Piagetian; psychometric; information-processing; thinking; knowing; processing

2. personal; practical; integrative; game of thinking
3. provisional; enduring
4. career; family; K. Warner Schaie; social
5. acquisition; late teens or early 20s; achieving
6. middle; responsible
7. executive; reintegrative
8. formal operational thought; is not
9. postformal
10. relativism; acceptance of contradiction; integration
11. objective or logical; subjective feelings; personal experience; more
12. extenuating circumstances
13. problem finding; formulate new questions from ambiguous problems or situations; relativistic logic
14. artistic; scientific
15. dialectical thought; thesis; antithesis; synthesis; do not have
16. do not

Critics point out that research on postformal thought has not kept pace with theories about it. They also contend that postformal thought is not universally experienced and does not necessarily build on the prior accomplishments of formal operations.

17. Kohlberg
18. males; females; relative; changeable
19. James Fowler

Intuitive-projective faith is magical, illogical, filled with fantasy, and typical of children ages 3 to 7.

Mythic-literal faith, which is typical of middle childhood, is characterized by taking the myths and stories of religion literally.

Synthetic-conventional faith is a nonintellectual acceptance of cultural or religious values in the context of interpersonal relationships.

Individual-reflective faith is characterized by intellectual detachment from the values of culture and the approval of significant others.

Conjunctive faith incorporates both powerful unconscious ideas and conscious values.

Universalizing faith is characterized by a powerful vision of universal compassion, justice, and love that leads people to put their own personal welfare aside in an effort to serve these values.

20. are; stronger
21. tolerant

First-year students often believe that there are clear and perfect truths to be found. This phase is followed by a wholesale questioning of values. Finally, after considering opposite ideas, students become committed to certain values, at the same time realizing the need to remain open-minded.

22. nine
23. threatened
24. dialectical
25. more
26. held steady; increased; does not

The factors include the amount of contact between students and faculty; the degree of emphasis on individualized instruction and hands-on learning; the educational background of the faculty; and the students' involvement in the intellectual and cultural life of the university.

27. life-long learners
28. the birth of a child, the loss of a loved one, a new intimate relationship or the end of an old one, a job promotion or dismissal, being the victim of an attack

PROGRESS TEST 1

Multiple-Choice Questions

1. **a.** is the answer. According to Schaie, children and adolescents are in a period of acquisition, during which information is absorbed and problem-solving techniques are learned with little regard for their usefulness. (p. 465)

   b. & c. According to Schaie, these become increasingly true during adulthood as cognition reflects personal, career, and family goals.

   d. Schaie's theory does not discuss the impact of the school system on cognitive development.
2. **c.** is the answer. (p. 464)
3. **d.** is the answer (p. 464)
4. **b.** is the answer. (p. 464)
5. **c.** is the answer. (p. 465)

   a. In Schaie's theory, this stage appears in late adulthood.

   b. This stage appears in childhood and adolescence.

   d. These stages appear during middle adulthood.
6. **c.** is the answer. (p. 465)
7. **c.** is the answer. (p. 467)

   a., b., & d. Because of its more analytical nature, formal thinking is most useful for solving these types of problems.

8. **d.** is the answer. (pp. 468–469)

   a. Thinking that is subjective relies on personal reflection rather than objective observation.

   b. Although dialectical reasoning *is* characteristic of postformal thought, this question refers specifically to dialectical thinking.

   c. Adaptive reasoning, which also is characteristic of postformal thought, goes beyond mere logic in solving problems to also explore real-life complexities and extenuating circumstances.

9. **a.** is the answer (p. 469)
10. **a.** is the answer. (p. 468)
11. **b.** is the answer. (pp. 470–471)
12. **d.** is the answer. (p. 470)
13. **c.** is the answer. (p. 474)

    a. In Gilligan's theory, this is more true of males than females.

    b. In Gilligan's theory, this is more true of females than males.

14. **d.** is the answer. (p. 477)
15. **d.** is the answer. (p. 475)

True or False Items

1. F Most people today attend college primarily to secure better jobs. (p. 475)
2. F Schaie's stages are neither universal nor applicable to everyone in our culture. (p. 466)
3. T (p. 467)
4. F Dialectical thinkers recognize the need to make commitments to values even though these values will change over time. (p. 470)
5. T (p. 471)
6. F Enrollment in residential four-year schools has remained stable, while enrollment in nonresidential and two-year schools has risen dramatically. (p. 476)
7. T (p. 467)
8. F Many adults remain in the "lower" stages of faith, which, like "higher" stages, allow for attaining strength and wholeness. (p. 472)
9. T (p. 475)
10. T (p. 477)

PROGRESS TEST 2

Multiple-Choice Questions

1. **b.** is the answer. (p. 464)

   a. This approach emphasizes the possible emergence in adulthood of new stages of thinking that build on the skills of earlier stages.

   c. This approach studies the encoding, storage, and retrieval of information throughout life.

2. **c.** is the answer. (p. 464)
3. **a.** is the answer. (p. 464)

   b. & c. During adulthood, thinking typically becomes more dialectical and adaptive.

4. **a.** is the answer. (p. 465)

   b. In Schaie's theory, this stage appears during the late teens or early 20s.

   c. This stage may appear during middle adulthood.

   d. This stage appears during late adulthood.

5. **c.** is the answer. (p. 466)

   a. The achieving stage appears during the late teens or early 20s. Furthermore, during this stage thinking is goal-directed.

   b. This stage appears during middle adulthood and is characterized by a deepening sense of social responsibility.

   d. This stage appears during childhood and adolescence and is characterized by the indiscriminate acquisition of knowledge.

6. a. is the answer. (p. 467)

   b., c., & d. Postformal thought is most useful for solving problems such as these.

7. **a.** is the answer. (p. 467)
8. **c.** is the answer. (p. 469)

   a. A thesis is a new idea.

   b. An antithesis is an idea that opposes a particular thesis.

   d. Hypotheses, which are testable predictions about behavior, are not an aspect of dialectical thinking.

9. **b.** is the answer. The logical, analytical nature of formal thinking is focused on problem solving. Adults often excel at problem finding, which refers to the capacity to formulate new questions from ambiguous situations. (p. 468)
10. **d.** is the answer. (p. 471)
11. **d.** is the answer. (p. 472)

    a. This describes conjunctive faith.

    b. This describes universalizing faith.

    c. This describes mythic-literal faith.

12. **a.** is the answer. (p. 477)

    b. & c. These are untrue.

    d. In fact, number of years of education correlates *strongly* with virtually every measure of adult cognition.

13. **b.** is the answer. (p. 472)

14. **c.** is the answer. (p. 467)

   a. Formal thinking is best suited to solving problems that require logic and analytical thinking.

   b. This is the ultimate stage of cognition in Schaie's theory, during which thinking turns to making sense out of life as a whole.

   d. This is a middle adulthood stage of cognition in Schaie's theory, during which people develop a deeper sense of social responsibility.

15. **b.** is the answer. (p. 468)

Matching Items

1. d (p. 465)	5. h (p. 466)
2. b (p. 465)	6. a (p. 467)
3. g (p. 465)	7. e (pp. 468–469)
4. f (p. 466)	8. c (p. 468)

CHALLENGE TEST

1. **d.** is the answer. (p. 466)

   a. This stage typically appears during late adulthood.

   b. This stage typically appears during the teens or early 20s.

   c. This is a stage in Fowler's theory of faith.

2. **b.** is the answer. (p. 471)

   a. According to Gilligan, males tend to be more concerned with human rights and justice than with human needs and personal relationships, which are more the concern of females.

   c. & d. These answers are incorrect because, according to Gilligan, as people mature and their experience of life expands, they begin to realize that moral reasoning based chiefly on justice principles or on individual needs is inadequate to resolve real-life moral dilemmas.

3. **b.** is the answer. (p. 475)

   a. First-year college students are more likely to believe this is so.

   c. & d. Over the course of their college careers, students become *less* likely to do either of these.

4. **d.** is the answer. (p. 476)

5. **c.** is the answer. (p. 478)

6. **a.** is the answer. (p. 464)

   b. This approach analyzes components of intelligence such as those measured by IQ tests.

   c. Each of these approaches is cognitive in nature.

   d. This approach studies the encoding, storage, and retrieval of information throughout life.

7. **a.** is the answer. (p. 465)

   b. & c. These theorists are concerned specifically with moral development.

   d. Perry's research is concerned with how college influences ethical reasoning.

8. **b.** is the answer. May-Ling has formed a synthesis between the thesis that honesty is the best policy and its antithesis. (p. 469)

   a. This is an example of postformal rather than formal thinking.

   c. & d. These are stages in the development of faith as proposed by James Fowler.

9. **b.** is the answer. (p. 471)

   a. & c. Neither Schaie nor Piaget focus on ethics in their theories.

   d. Fowler's theory, which identifies stages in the development of faith, does not emphasize this experience.

10. **c.** is the answer. (p. 477)

11. **d.** is the answer. (p. 477)

12. **c.** is the answer. (p. 480)

13. **a.** is the answer. (p. 467)

   b. Because postformal thinking is typical of adult thought, this is untrue.

   c. It is exactly this sort of problem that *fosters* postformal thinking.

14. **c.** is the answer. (p. 475)

   a. & b. Years of education are more strongly correlated with cognitive development than are age and socioeconomic status.

   d. Although significant life events can trigger cognitive development, the text does not suggest that the relationship between life events and measures of cognition is predictable.

15. **d.** is the answer. (p. 473)

KEY TERMS

1. K. Warner Schaie believes that childhood and adolescence constitute a **period of acquisition,** during which information is absorbed indiscriminately. (p. 465)

2. According to Schaie, beginning in the late teens or early 20s, young people enter the **achieving stage,** in which thinking becomes more goal-directed than it was during earlier periods of life. (p. 465)

3. In Schaie's theory, as middle adulthood approaches, people enter the **responsible stage** as personal and family goals are integrated with career goals. (p. 466)

4. According to Schaie, middle adulthood brings an unusually broad and deep sense of social responsibility which leads to the **executive stage** of cognition. (p. 466)
5. In Schaie's theory, during late adulthood a **reintegrative stage** appears, when thoughts turn to making sense of life as a whole. (p. 466)
6. Proposed by some developmentalists as a fifth stage of cognitive development, **postformal thought** is less abstract, less absolute, and more integrative and synthetic than formal thought. (p. 467)
7. **Problem finding** refers to the distinctive capacity of adult thought that enables the formulation of new questions from ambiguous problems or situations. (p. 468)
8. **Dialectical thought** is thinking that involves considering both poles of an idea (thesis and antithesis) simultaneously and then forging them into a synthesis. (p. 468)

CHAPTER 19 Early Adulthood: Psychosocial Development

Chapter Overview

Biologically mature and no longer bound by parental authority, the young adult typically is now free to choose a particular path of development. In the twentieth century, the options are incredibly varied. Not surprisingly, then, the hallmark of psychosocial development during early adulthood is diversity. Nevertheless, developmentalists have identified several themes or patterns that help us understand the course of development between the ages of 20 and 40.

The chapter begins with a discussion of the two basic psychosocial needs of adulthood, love and work. No matter what terminology is used, these two needs are recognized by almost all developmentalists.

The next section addresses the need for intimacy in adulthood, focusing on the development of friendship, love, and marriage. A Life-Span Perspective considers the impact of divorce on families.

The final section of the chapter is concerned with generativity, or the motivation to achieve during adulthood, highlighting the importance of work and parenthood and addressing the special challenges facing stepparents, adoptive parents, and foster parents.

NOTE: Answer guidelines for all Chapter 19 questions begin on page 288.

Guided Study

The text chapter should be studied one section at a time. Before you read, preview each section by skimming it, noting headings and boldface items. Then read the appropriate section objectives from the following outline. Keep these objectives in mind and, as you read the chapter section, search for the information that will enable you to meet each objective. Once you have finished a section, write out answers for its objectives.

The Two Tasks of Adulthood (pp. 484–487)

1. Identify the two basic tasks, or crises, of adulthood, and describe common developmental patterns that emerge during the 20s and 30s.

2. Explain how the social clock influences the timing of important events during early adulthood.

Intimacy (pp. 487–502)

3. Review the developmental course of friendship during adulthood, noting gender differences in friendship patterns and the impact of marriage on friendships.

4. Explain how American relationship patterns have shifted in recent years.

5. Identify Sternberg's three components of love and discuss the pattern by which they develop in relationships.

6. Discuss the impact of cohabitation on relationships and identify three factors that influence marital success.

7. (A Life-Span Perspective) Discuss the impact of social systems on divorce, the reasons for today's rising divorce rate, and the usual impact of divorce on families.

8. Discuss the benefits of remarriage, as well as its most common problems or challenges.

Generativity (pp. 503–513)

9. Discuss the importance of work to the individual and describe the usual first job and subsequent career developments of early adulthood.

10. (A Life-Span Perspective) Focusing on broad themes, describe the stages of the family life cycle, noting the rewards and challenges of each stage.

11. Discuss the special challenges facing stepparents, adoptive parents, and foster parents.

12. (A Closer Look) Discuss the advantages and disadvantages of family life when the mother is exclusively a homemaker and when she is employed outside the home.

Chapter Review

When you have finished reading the chapter, work through the material that follows to review it. Complete the sentences and answer the questions. As you proceed, evaluate your performance for each section by consulting the answers on page 288. Do not continue with the next section until you understand each answer. If you need to, review or reread the appropriate section in the textbook before continuing.

The Two Tasks of Adulthood (pp. 484–487)

1. Developmentalists generally agree that two psychosocial needs must be met during adulthood. According to Maslow, the need for ________ and ________ is followed by a need for ________ and ________. Other psychologists have described these needs in terms of ________ ________.

2. According to Freud, the healthy adult was one who could ________ and ________.

3. In Erikson's theory, the identity crisis of adolescence is followed in early adulthood by the crisis of ________ ________ ________, and then later by the crisis of ________ ________ ________.

4. Within the broad framework of love and work, several researchers have suggested that adults typically shift back and forth between periods of ________ and ________ and periods of ________ and ________.

Briefly describe the most common pattern of development during the early and middle 20s.

Explain why age 30 is particularly meaningful for many women.

5. For American women, age ________ is the peak age for having a last child. By age 35, more than ________ of married American women are surgically sterilized.

6. For men, age 30 represents a period of questioning that is more focused on ________ than on parenthood. At this age, men enter a stage Daniel Levinson calls ________.

7. Because development is no longer chiefly propelled by ________, the stages of adulthood are determined in large measure by the ________ ________, which is defined as ________ ________.

8. A prime influence on the social clock is ________ ________.

   The lower a person's SES, the ________ (younger/older) the age at which he or she is expected to leave school, begin work, marry, have children, and so forth.

9. The influence of SES is particularly apparent with regard to the age at which women become ________.

   Women from low-SES backgrounds may feel pressure to marry at age ________, and most stop childbearing by age ________, while wealthy women may not feel pressure to marry until age ________ or to stop childbearing until age ________.

10. Internationally, the social clock ________ (varies/does not vary) significantly.

11. In the United States, the settings of the social clock for marriage and career ________ (have/have not) varied historically.

12. Contemporary American culture allows for ________ (more/less) diversity in the settings of the social clock.

Intimacy (pp. 487–502)

13. Two main sources of intimacy in early adulthood are ________ ________ and ________ ________.

14. As a buffer against stress and a source of positive feelings, ________________ are particularly important.

Briefly state why this is so.

15. Because at the start of adulthood most individuals are ________________ and free of overriding ________________, they find it relatively ________________ (easy/difficult) to form friendship networks.

16. During early adulthood ________________ (men/women/both men and women) tend to be more satisfied with their ________________ ________________ than with almost any other part of their lives.

17. Sex differences in friendship ________________ (are/are not) especially apparent during adulthood. In general, men's friendships are based on ________________, while friendships between women tend to be more ________________.

Briefly contrast the types of conversations men and women are likely to have with their friends.

18. Research has shown that ________________ (women/men) are more likely to reveal their weaknesses to friends, whereas ________________ (women/men) are more likely to reveal their strengths.

19. Another gender difference is that men's friendships are more clearly tinged with open ________________. Thus, men may view friendship as a means of maintaining a positive ________________, while women regard it as a means of coping with ________________ ________________.

20. List three reasons that men's friendships seem so much less intimate than women's.

a. ________________

b. ________________

c. ________________

Describe some of the opportunities and problems of cross-sex friendships.

21. A woman's tendency to seek mutual loyalty among confidantes may handicap her ________________. Men who cannot share problems with friends may be handicapped ________________.

22. For most young adults, marriage is followed by a(n) ________________ (shrinking/ enlarging) of the friendship circle.

23. Typically, as a marriage lasts over a period of years, both partners become ________________ (more/less) jealous of outsiders.

24. In the United States today, the proportion of adults who are unmarried is ________________ (higher/lower) than at any other time in this century; only ________________ percent of brides are virgins; ________________ percent of all births are to unmarried mothers; and the divorce rate is ________________ percent of the marriage rate.

25. The majority of American adults spend about ________________ of the years between 20 and 40 single.

26. Most adults ________________ (do/do not) seek sexual fulfillment and commitment to one partner.

27. Increasingly common among young adults is the relationship pattern called ________________

______________, in which an individual forms a series of intimate and committed relationships with only one person at a time. This pattern ______________ (does/does not) hold for homosexual relationships.

28. Over the life span, love is affected by numerous factors, including ______________ ______________.

29. Individual love styles are affected by the person's ______________ and history of ______________ ______________.

30. Robert Sternberg has argued that love has three distinct components: ______________, ______________, and ______________. Sternberg also believes that the emergence and prominence of each component tends to follow a pattern that is ______________ (unpredictable/predictable).

31. Early in a relationship ______________ intimacy tends to be high, while ______________ intimacy is much lower.

32. Relationships grow because ______________ intensifies, leading to the gradual establishment and strengthening of ______________.

33. When commitment is added to passion and intimacy, the result is ______________ love.

34. With time, ______________ tends to fade and ______________ tends to stabilize, even as ______________ develops.

35. Whereas ______________ (men/women) are more likely to be "romantics," ______________ (men/women) are more likely to be "pragmatists" in the development of intimate relationships.

36. Once they commit themselves to a relationship, ______________ (men/women) tend to be less willing than the other sex to give it up.

37. Increasingly common among young adults in many countries is the living pattern called ______________, in which two unrelated adults of the opposite sex live together.

38. Most cohabiting adults see living together as ______________ (an economic arrangement/a tryout for marriage). Cohabitation ______________ (does/does not) seem to strengthen marriage.

39. Couples who decide to cohabit are at a ______________ (higher/lower) risk of divorce, since they tend to be ______________ ______________.

40. The younger marriage partners are when they first wed, the ______________ (more/less) likely their marriage is to succeed. According to Erikson, this may be because intimacy is hard to establish until ______________ is reached.

41. Marriage between people who are similar in age, SES, ethnicity, and the like, called ______________, is ______________ (more/less) likely to succeed than marriage that is outside the group, called ______________.

42. A third factor affecting marriage is ______________, the extent to which the partners perceive equality in the relationship. According to ______________ theory, marriage is an arrangement in which each person contributes something useful to the other.

43. (A Life-Span Perspective) In the United States almost one out of every ______________ marriages ends in divorce. This rate ______________ (varies/does not vary significantly) from country to country. Worldwide, divorce has ______________ (increased/decreased/remained stable) over most of the past fifty years.

44. (A Life-Span Perspective) One reason for the increased divorce rate in the United States was passage of ______________ laws that granted divorce simply on the assertion of incompatibility.

45. (A Life-Span Perspective) Compared to earlier cohorts, married couples today are ______________ (more/less) likely to consider their marriages very happy. Many developmentalists believe that spouses today expect ______________ (more/less) from each other than spouses in the past did.

Contrast the typical reasons cited for divorce by women in the 1940s and those in the 1970s.

46. (A Life-Span Perspective) Marriages that fail usually do so within the first ________________ years. Most people find the initial impact of divorce to be quite ________________ (negative/positive), and adjustment to divorce ________________ (more/less) difficult than they expected.

47. (A Life-Span Perspective) Newly divorced people are more prone to ________________ ________________. In most cases, such effects ________________ (do/do not) eventually dissipate with time.

48. (A Life-Span Perspective) Compared to others, single divorced adults are ________________ (most/least) likely to be very happy with their lives. The presence of ________________ is a key factor that makes adjustment to divorce more difficult, particularly for custodial ________________ (mothers/fathers).

49. Nearly ________________ percent of divorced people remarry, on average, within ________________ years of being divorced. In the United States, nearly ________________ of all marriages are remarriages for at least one of the spouses.

50. Remarried people generally ________________ (do/do not) report higher rates of happiness than people in first marriages. The divorce rate in remarriages is ________________ (higher/lower) than that for first marriages.

Generativity (pp. 503–513)

51. When people have been asked what they would do if they were to become sudden millionaires, most reported that they would ________________ (keep working/quit working).

52. By age 30, the average American worker has had ________________ distinct occupations. Satisfaction with work is less related to variations in ________________ and ________________ than to workers' feelings that their work is ________________.

53. For many workers, the opportunity to choose one's own work hours, called ________________, increases satisfaction.

54. One aspect of the organizational culture that is crucial to the success of new workers is the availability of a(n) ________________. Difficulty of finding a suitable mentor may be one reason many women and minorities bump up against a(n) ________________ ________________, an invisible barrier to job advancement.

55. (A Life-Span Perspective) The stages of the family life cycle are based on the age of the ________________ ________________. In the first stage, called the ________________ period, most couples make decisions related to the timing of childbearing. With the arrival of the first child, parents enter the ________________ period, in which the chief joy is getting to know the new human being they have created and the chief difficulty is ________________ ________________.

56. (A Life-Span Perspective) When the oldest child is between the ages of ________________ and ________________, parents enter the ________________ period of parenthood. This is often the period of greatest ________________ (happiness/direct confrontation) between husband and wife and between parent and child. During the next stage, called the ________________ period, parenting grows ________________ (easier/more difficult) as parents encourage and guide children toward adolescence.

57. (A Life-Span Perspective) Adolescence, which is known as the ________________ period of parenthood, brings new challenges as teenagers begin to demand the privileges of adulthood before accepting the responsibilities that go with them. The remaining stages are the

_______________ stage, in which grown children set out on their own, and the _______________-_______________ stage, in which the last of the children have done so. This last stage of the family cycle is generally _______________ (more/less) satisfying than any of the previous stages since the honeymoon.

58. Proportionately, about _______________ of all North American adults will become stepparents, adoptive parents, or foster parents at some point in their lives.

59. Strong bonds between parent and child are particularly hard to create when a child has already formed _______________ to other caregivers.

60. Because they are legally connected to their children for life, _______________ (adoptive/step/foster) parents have an advantage in establishing bonds with their children.

61. Stepchildren, foster children, and adoptive children tend to leave home _______________ (at the same age as/earlier than/later than) children living with one or both biological parents.

62. (A Closer Look) Until the _______________ _______________, most married couples worked _______________ (apart/together). Unlike women of earlier generations, the typical pattern for today's young women is to _______________ (leave work when their children are small/continue working throughout motherhood).

63. (A Closer Look) If a new mother quits her job, she gives up an external source of _______________, _______________, and _______________. Most mothers who have left the work force completely _______________ (do/do not) feel the career disruption was worth it.

64. (A Closer Look) Unsatisfied workers are more likely to be _______________ (rejecting/accepting) toward their families and therefore tend to have the _______________ (happiest/least happy) children. Women who are exclusively homemakers are _______________ (less/more) likely to be depressed than women who combine parenthood and work.

65. (A Closer Look) When women work as many hours outside the home as their husbands, they tend to do _______________ (about the same amount/more) of the housework and child care than their husbands. The more children a couple has, the _______________ (more/less) likely they are to share equally in household tasks.

Progress Test 1

Multiple-Choice Questions

Circle your answers to the following questions and check them with the answers on page 290. If your answer is incorrect, read the explanation for why it is incorrect and then consult the appropriate pages of the text (in parentheses following the correct answer).

1. According to Erik Erikson, the first basic task of adulthood is to establish:
   a. a residence apart from parents.
   b. intimacy with others.
   c. generativity through work or parenthood.
   d. a career commitment.

2. According to many developmentalists, the years of adulthood are marked by shifts that are *best* characterized as involving:
   a. becoming one's own person.
   b. consolidation.
   c. periods of change and constancy.
   d. questioning and change.

3. The choices most adults make in their early 20s regarding marriage, parenthood, employment specialization, and so forth:
   a. are usually lifetime decisions.
   b. almost always reflect rebellion from parental influences.
   c. are usually provisional in nature.
   d. are very different for women and men.

4. The BOOM stage, during which a man seeks greater responsibility and independence at work, was named and described by:
   a. Abraham Maslow.
   b. Bernice Neugarten.
   c. Daniel Levinson.
   d. Erik Erikson.

5. In the United States and other Western countries, the lower a person's socioeconomic status:
   a. the younger the age at which the social clock is "set" for many life events.
   b. the older the age at which the social clock is "set" for many life events.
   c. the more variable are the settings for the social clock.
   d. the less likely it is that divorce will occur.

6. According to Erikson, the failure to achieve intimacy during early adulthood is most likely to result in:
   a. generativity.
   b. stagnation.
   c. role diffusion.
   d. self-absorption.

7. Regarding friendships, most young adults tend to:
   a. be very satisfied.
   b. be very dissatisfied.
   c. find it difficult to form social networks.
   d. be without close friends.

8. Between ages 20 and 30:
   a. many adults participate in a series of relationships characterized by serial monogamy.
   b. 3 to 5 percent of men and women are already divorced.
   c. the unmarried are in the majority.
   d. all of the above are true.

9. According to Robert Sternberg, consummate love emerges:
   a. as a direct response to passion.
   b. as a direct response to physical intimacy.
   c. when commitment is added to passion and intimacy.
   d. during the honeymoon period of parenthood.

10. An arrangement in which two unrelated, unmarried adults of the opposite sex live together is called:
    a. cross-sex friendship.
    b. a passive-congenial pattern.
    c. cohabitation.
    d. affiliation.

11. Differences in religious customs or rituals are *most* likely to arise in a:
    a. homogamous couple.
    b. heterogamous couple.
    c. cohabiting couple.
    d. very young married couple.

12. The divorce rate for second marriages is:
    a. higher than that for first marriages.
    b. lower than that for first marriages.
    c. about the same as that for first marriages.
    d. highest for childless marriages.

13. A career-oriented woman or minority-group member is most likely to experience difficulties in finding a(n):
    a. first job.
    b. dream or vision of life.
    c. older person to serve as mentor.
    d. career that utilizes his or her abilities and interests.

14. (A Closer Look) Adults who combine the roles of spouse, parent, and employee tend to report:
    a. less overall happiness than other adults.
    b. more overall happiness than other adults.
    c. regrets over parental roles.
    d. problems in career advancement.

15. Compared to adolescents who live with their biological parents, stepchildren, foster children, and adoptive children:
    a. leave home at an older age.
    b. leave home at a younger age.
    c. have fewer developmental problems.
    d. have the same developmental problems.

True or False Items

Write *true* or *false* on the line in front of each statement.

_______ 1. According to Erikson, the adult experiences a crisis of intimacy versus isolation, and, after that, a crisis of generativity versus stagnation.

_______ 2. In the United States, most women who become mothers decide to have their first child at about age 30.

_______ 3. Because in the United States today the social clock allows for diversity in the assumption of adult roles, early adulthood is no longer a period of psychosocial stress for most people.

_______ 4. Most adults find that their friendship circle becomes larger after marriage.

_______ 5. Single adults who live alone typically experience profound loneliness.

_______ 6. Men are more likely than women to believe in love at first sight, and to believe that each person is destined to find his or her one true love.

_______ 7. (A Life-Span Perspective) Most divorced fathers manage to fulfill the emotional and financial needs of their children after divorce, even if they do not have custody.

_______ 8. (A Life-Span Perspective) During the nurturing period of the family life cycle, most parents are overwhelmed—at least occasionally—by the demands of caring for an infant.

_______ 9. (A Closer Look) Fathers are more likely to share in child-care and housework responsibilities when the family is large and the mother holds a full-time job.

_______ 10. Many stepchildren are fiercely loyal to the absent parent.

Progress Test 2

Progress Test 2 should be completed during a final chapter review. Answer the following questions after you thoroughly understand the correct answers for the Chapter Review and Progress Test 1.

Multiple-Choice Questions

1. Erikson theorizes that if generativity is not attained, the adult is most likely to experience:
   a. lack of advancement in his or her career.
   b. infertility or childlessness.
   c. feelings of emptiness and stagnation.
   d. feelings of profound aloneness or isolation.

2. During the early 20s, most adults make some decisions about social-group and church membership. This is primarily an example of the attempt to satisfy:
   a. competence needs.
   b. achievement needs.
   c. intimacy needs.
   d. the social clock.

3. Which of the following was *not* cited in the text as a reason for men's friendships tending to be much less intimate than women's?
   a. The tendency of boys to be more active and girls more verbal during childhood lays the groundwork for interaction patterns in adulthood.
   b. Intimacy is grounded in mutual vulnerability, a characteristic discouraged in men.
   c. Many men fear their friendships will be associated with homosexuality.
   d. Men tend to be more focused on achievement needs than women.

4. The prime effect of the social clock is to make an individual aware of:
   a. his or her socioeconomic status.
   b. the diversity of psychosocial paths during early adulthood.
   c. the means of fulfilling affiliation and achievement needs.
   d. the "right" or "best" time for assuming adult roles.

5. In modern American culture, the social clock:
   a. establishes prescribed ages for many adult roles that tend to cluster in the early and mid-20s.
   b. creates pressure on young adults to take on new responsibilities.
   c. allows for more diversity than it once did.
   d. does all of the above.

6. Researchers reviewing developmental trends in friendship have found that the number of cross-sex friendships an individual has:
   a. remains about the same throughout adulthood.
   b. decreases after marriage.
   c. increases during later adulthood.
   d. varies according to the individual's socioeconomic status.

7. Whereas men's friendships tend to be based on ________________, friendships between women tend to be based on ________________.
   a. shared confidences; shared interests
   b. cooperation; competition
   c. shared interests; shared confidences
   d. finding support for personal problems; discussion of practical issues

8. According to Robert Sternberg, the three dimensions of love are:
   a. passion, intimacy, and consummate love.
   b. physical intimacy, emotional intimacy, and consummate love.
   c. passion, commitment, and consummate love.
   d. passion, intimacy, and commitment.

9. Research on cohabitation in the United States suggests that:
   a. relatively few young adults ever live with an unrelated partner of the other sex.
   b. most cohabiting young adults see their arrangement as primarily economic in nature.
   c. marriages that are preceded by cohabitation typically are less durable.
   d. all of the above are true.

10. A homogamous marriage is best defined as a marriage between:
    a. people who resemble each other physically.
    b. people of similar social backgrounds.
    c. people of dissimilar socioeconomic backgrounds.
    d. two caring people of the same sex.

11. (A Life-Span Perspective) The text suggests that the main reason for the rising divorce rate is that today's couples experience:
    a. greater rigidity of sex roles in marriage.
    b. higher expectations about marriage and the marriage partner.
    c. deterioration in their overall communication skills.
    d. increased incidence of drug- and alcohol-related abuse.

12. In the beginning, most young people choose the job that:
    a. happens to be available.
    b. represents a break with parental values.
    c. reflects a life dream.
    d. is consistent with their abilities and interests.

13. (A Life-Span Perspective) Research suggests that for most couples, closeness and satisfaction in marriage are highest during the honeymoon and ______________ periods.
    a. nurturing
    b. interpretive
    c. interdependent
    d. empty-nest

14. Stepparents, adoptive parents, and foster parents:
    a. experience rewards that go beyond the immediate household.
    b. have basically the same parenting problems as biological parents.
    c. tend to have fewer problems as parents, since they typically begin parenthood when the children are older.
    d. typically develop equally secure attachments to their children as do biological parents.

15. (A Closer Look) A national survey suggests that the majority of employed mothers would prefer:
    a. not to have to work outside the home.
    b. to spend more time pursuing career goals.
    c. to spend more time with their husbands and children.
    d. to work longer hours and earn more money.

Matching Items

Match each definition or description with its corresponding term.

Terms

______ 1. social clock
______ 2. serial monogamy
______ 3. cohabitation
______ 4. homogamy
______ 5. heterogamy
______ 6. marital equity
______ 7. exchange theory
______ 8. flextime
______ 9. mentor
______ 10. glass ceiling

Definitions or Descriptions

a. the opportunity to choose one's own work hours
b. a marriage between people with similar interests and backgrounds
c. an invisible barrier to career advancement
d. a more experienced worker who serves as a teacher, confidant, and role model
e. a marriage between people with dissimilar interests and backgrounds
f. the culturally set timetable at which key life events are deemed appropriate
g. predicts success in marriages in which each partner contributes something useful to the other
h. arrangement in which two unrelated adults of the opposite sex live together
i. the extent to which partners perceive equality in their relationship
j. relationship pattern in which an individual forms a series of intimate, committed relationships with only one person at a time

Challenge Test

Answer these questions the day before an exam as a final check on your understanding of the chapter's terms and concepts.

1. Jack is in his mid-20s. Compared to his father, who was 25 during the late 1950s, Jack is:
   a. more likely to have settled on a career.
   b. less likely to have settled on a career.
   c. likely to feel more social pressure to make decisions regarding career, marriage, and so forth.
   d. more likely to be concerned with satisfying his need for achievement at a younger age.

2. Concluding her presentation on gender differences in friendship, Marie states that:
   a. "Friendships among women are more clearly influenced by competition."
   b. "Partly because of homophobia, many men and women avoid any expression of affection toward others of the same sex."
   c. "Whereas friendship for women may be important as a way of coping with problems, for men, friendship serves primarily as a way of maintaining a favorable self-concept."
   d. All of the above are true.

3. Jill married at age 25. If she is like most women, several years later she will probably have:
   a. a smaller circle of friends.
   b. a larger circle of friends.
   c. fewer friends than her husband.
   d. the same number of friends as she did before marriage.

4. Dr. Wilson is preparing a lecture on relationship patterns in heterosexual and homosexual couples. One point she should make is that:
   a. the basic needs underlying both types of relationship have shifted dramatically in recent years.
   b. serial monogamy has emerged as a common pattern in heterosexual relationships.
   c. serial monogamy has emerged as a common pattern in homosexual relationships.
   d. serial monogamy has emerged as a common pattern in both heterosexual and homosexual relationships.

5. Rwanda and Rodney have been dating for about a month. Their relationship is most likely characterized by:
   a. strong feelings of commitment.
   b. consummate love.
   c. physical intimacy and feelings of closeness without true emotional intimacy.
   d. all of the above.

6. As a pragmatist, I believe that economic and ethnic differences can be major barriers in the development of love. Who am I?
   a. a man in his 30s
   b. a woman
   c. a man in his 20s
   d. a divorced woman

7. If asked to explain the high failure rate of marriages between young adults, Erik Erikson would most likely say that:
   a. achievement goals are often more important than intimacy in early adulthood.
   b. intimacy is difficult to establish until identity is formed.
   c. divorce has almost become an expected stage in development.
   d. today's cohort of young adults has higher expectations of marriage than did previous cohorts.

8. (A Life-Span Perspective) Of the following people, who is *least* likely to report being "very happy" with his or her present life?
   a. Drew, who has never married
   b. Leah, who became a widow five years ago
   c. Malcolm, who has been married ten years
   d. Sharice, a single, divorced adult

9. Which of the following employer initiatives would be most likely to increase employee job satisfaction?
   a. offering higher wages
   b. offering improved worker benefits
   c. offering employees flextime
   d. All of the above have about the same impact on employee satisfaction.

10. Which of the following descriptions *best* describes a mentor?
    a. a loving parent who helps a child
    b. a good friend who helps a friend
    c. a technical consultant who helps clients
    d. an older, experienced worker who helps a younger one

11. Of the following people, who is the most likely to encounter a glass ceiling in his or her career?
    a. Ben, a middle-aged white social worker
    b. Simone, an African-American engineer
    c. Don, an Asian-American attorney
    d. Paul, a white banker in his mid-20s

12. The parents of a 1-year-old child are in the _______________ stage of the family life cycle.
   a. authority
   b. nurturing
   c. interpretive
   d. interdependent

13. Your sister, who has a 3-year-old child, complains to you that she and her husband are arguing more now than at any other time in their marriage. You tell her that:
   a. because of mounting pressures, the authority period of parenthood is often the period of the greatest direct confrontation between wives and husbands.
   b. the nurturing period of parenthood presents parents with the greatest challenges and pressures.
   c. she is probably unhappy because fathers usually become less involved parents when children move beyond infancy.
   d. having a second child would probably restore marital harmony.

14. Your brother, who became a stepparent when he married, complains that he can't seem to develop a strong bond with his 9-year-old stepchild. You tell him:
   a. strong bonds between parent and child are particularly hard to create once a child is old enough to have formed attachments to other caregivers.
   b. the child is simply immature emotionally and will, with time, warm up considerably.
   c. most stepparents find that they eventually develop a deeper, more satisfying relationship with stepchildren than they had ever imagined.
   d. he should encourage the child to think of him as the child's biological father.

15. (A Closer Look) Diane and Vincente, who both work, have five children between 1 and 8 years of age. It is most likely that:
   a. they share responsibility for the tasks at home.
   b. Vincente does everything except cook dinner.
   c. Diane does most of the domestic work.
   d. Diane and Vincente alternate taking responsibility for domestic work each week.

Key Terms

Using your own words, write a brief definition or explanation of each of the following terms on a separate piece of paper.

1. intimacy versus isolation
2. generativity versus stagnation
3. social clock
4. serial monogamy
5. cohabitation
6. homogamy
7. heterogamy
8. marital equity
9. exchange theory
10. flextime
11. mentor
12. glass ceiling

ANSWERS

CHAPTER REVIEW

1. love; belonging; success; esteem; affiliation and achievement, or affection and instrumentality, or acceptance and competence
2. love; work
3. intimacy versus isolation; generativity versus stagnation
4. openness; change; commitment; constancy

During the early 20s, the individual breaks away from parents to become self-supporting, establishing his or her own residence and making choices about education, employment, marriage, and social-group membership. These choices are provisional in nature. By the mid-20s, however, most adults have made some important commitments and decisions, and in doing so have become recognizably adult.

Women who have no children must confront the fact that their childbearing years will soon be running out. This often leads to a reexamination of life goals. Women who have children begin to realize how quickly their children are becoming more independent; many decide at this age not to have more.

5. 30; one-third
6. vocation (or work); BOOM (Becoming One's Own Man)
7. biology; social clock; a culturally set timetable that establishes when various events and behaviors in life are appropriate and called for
8. socioeconomic status; younger

9. wives and mothers; 18; 25; 30; 40
10. varies
11. have
12. more
13. close friendship; sexual partnership
14. friends

Friends choose each other, often for the very qualities that make them good sources of emotional support. They are also a source of self-esteem.

15. mobile; commitments; easy
16. both men and women; friendship networks
17. are; shared activities and interests; intimate and emotional

Women talk more often about their intimate concerns and delve deeper into personal and family issues; men typically talk about practical matters or personal opinions about sports, politics, or people in general.

18. women; men
19. competition; self-concept; problems via shared fears, sorrows, and disappointments
20. a. Intimacy is grounded in mutual vulnerability, a characteristic discouraged in men.
    b. From childhood, boys are inclined to be more active and girls more verbal.
    c. Many men avoid any expression of affection toward other men because they fear its association with homosexuality.

Cross-sex friendships offer men and women an opportunity to explore their commonalities and to expand their perspectives on key social and ethical issues. Because each sex tends to have its own expectations for friendship, misunderstandings can occur in cross-sex friendships. Another hazard is that men are often inclined to try to sexualize friendships.

21. vocationally; psychologically
22. shrinking
23. less
24. higher; 10; 30; 48
25. half
26. do
27. serial monogamy; does
28. personal preferences, developmental stages, gender differences, socioeconomic forces, and historical and cultural context
29. temperament; childhood attachments
30. passion; intimacy; commitment; predictable
31. physical; emotional
32. intimacy; commitment
33. consummate
34. passion; intimacy; commitment
35. men; women
36. women
37. cohabitation
38. a tryout for marriage; does not
39. higher; less conventional, less religious, and lower in SES
40. less; identity
41. homogamy; more; heterogamy
42. equity; exchange
43. two; varies; increased
44. no-fault
45. less; more

In 1948, cruelty, excessive drinking, and nonsupport were among the most common reasons cited for divorce by women. In the 1970s, lack of communication and poor understanding were the most common reasons.

46. five; negative; more
47. loneliness, disequilibrium, irrational sexual behavior, and erratic patterns of eating, sleeping, working, and drug and alcohol use; do
48. least; children; mothers
49. 80; three; half
50. do not; higher
51. keep working
52. three; wages; benefits; meaningful
53. flextime
54. mentor; glass ceiling
55. oldest child; honeymoon; nurturing; the overwhelming necessity of meeting the infant's need for twenty-four-hour care
56. 2; 5; authority; direct confrontation; interpretive; easier
57. interdependent; launching; empty-nest; more
58. one-third
59. attachments
60. adoptive
61. earlier than
62. Industrial Revolution; together; continue working throughout motherhood
63. self-esteem; social support; status; do
64. rejecting; least happy; more
65. more; less

PROGRESS TEST 1

Multiple-Choice Questions

1. **b.** is the answer. (p. 484)
2. **c.** is the answer. (p. 484)
3. **c.** is the answer. (p. 485)
   b. Although rebellion is sometimes an aspect of establishing independence, most of the choices of early adulthood reflect more mature decision-making.
   d. The tasks of early adulthood are basically the same for both sexes.
4. **c.** is the answer. (p. 485)
5. **a.** is the answer. (p. 486)
   d. Low SES is actually a risk factor for divorce.
6. **d.** is the answer. (p. 487)
   a. Generativity is a characteristic of the crisis following the intimacy crisis.
   b. Stagnation occurs when generativity needs are not met.
   c. Erikson's theory does not address this issue.
7. **a.** is the answer. (p. 488)
   c. Because they are mobile and tend to have fewer commitments, young adults find it relatively easy to form friendships.
   d. Almost never do young adults feel bereft of friendship.
8. **d.** is the answer. (p. 491)
9. **c.** is the answer. (p. 493)
   d. Sternberg's theory is not concerned with the stages of parenthood.
10. **c.** is the answer. (p. 494)
11. **b.** is the answer. (p. 496)
    a. By definition, homogamous couples share values, background, and the like.
    c. & d. These may or may not be true, depending on the extent to which such a couple is homogamous.
12. **a.** is the answer. (p. 502)
    d. The text does not discuss whether the rate of divorce varies with the presence or absence of children.
13. **c.** is the answer. (p. 505)
14. **b.** is the answer. (p. 509)
    c. Most parents report that they are pleased that they have had children.
15. **b.** is the answer. (p. 513)
    c. & d. The text does not discuss variations in the incidence of developmental problems in the various family structures.

True or False Items

1. T (p. 484)
2. F In the United States, a mother is more likely to decide to have her *last* child at age 30. (p. 485)
3. F Although the social clock allows for diversity, prescribed ages for many adult roles still cluster in the early and mid-20s. If an individual has not yet begun to assume adult roles during these years, he or she may experience considerable pressure from family members as well as from society. (p. 487)
4. F Most adults find that their friendship circle *shrinks* after marriage. (p. 490)
5. F Most single adults have a network of supportive friends, and most enjoy their independence. (p. 491)
6. T (p. 493)
7. F Most fathers gradually become alienated from their children, and few offer adequate support. (p. 501)
8. T (p. 507)
9. F The more children a couple has, the *less* likely it is that the husband will share equally in child care and housework. (p. 509)
10. T (p. 510)

PROGRESS TEST 2

Multiple-Choice Questions

1. **c.** is the answer. (p. 484)
   a. Lack of career advancement may prevent generativity.
   b. Erikson's theory does not address these issues.
   d. Such feelings are related to the need for intimacy rather than generativity.
2. **c.** is the answer. (p. 485)
   a. & b. These needs are related to generativity.
   d. The social clock refers to the culturally set timetable for beginning a career, finding a mate, and so forth.
3. **d.** is the answer. (pp. 488–489)
4. **d.** is the answer. (p. 486)
5. **d.** is the answer. (pp. 486–487)
6. **b.** is the answer. (p. 490)
   d. The text does not indicate that friendship circles vary with SES.
7. **c.** is the answer. (p. 488)
8. **d.** is the answer. (p. 492)

a., b., & c. According to Sternberg, consummate love emerges when commitment is added to passion and intimacy.

9. **c.** is the answer. (p. 495)

   a. Approximately one-half of all young adult North Americans cohabit for at least a few months.

   b. For most cohabitating young adults, living together is *seen* less as an economic arrangement than as a tryout for marriage.

10. **b.** is the answer. (p. 496)

    a. & d. These characteristics do not pertain to homogamy.

    c. This describes a heterogamous marriage.

11. **b.** is the answer. (p. 498)
12. **a.** is the answer. (p. 503)
13. **d.** is the answer. (p. 511)

    a., b., & c. Because of child-rearing demands, these periods are typically less satisfying for parents.

14. **a.** is the answer. (p. 513)

    d. Without the emotional pull of both early contact and genetic connections, close attachments may be difficult to establish.

15. **c.** is the answer. (p. 509)

Matching Items

1. f (p. 486)	5. e (p. 496)	8. a (p. 504)
2. j (p. 491)	6. i (p. 496)	9. d (pp. 504–505)
3. h (p. 494)	7. g (p. 496)	10. c (p. 505)
4. b (p. 496)		

CHALLENGE TEST

1. **b.** is the answer. (p. 504)

   c. & d. The text does not indicate that there are cohort effects in these areas.

2. **c.** is the answer. (p. 489)

   a. & b. These are more characteristic of friendships among men than women.

3. **a.** is the answer. (p. 490)
4. **d.** is the answer. (p. 491)

   a. The basic needs underlying relationships have not changed.

5. **c.** is the answer. (p. 492)

   a. & b. These feelings emerge more gradually in relationships.

6. **b.** is the answer. (p. 494)

   a. & c. Men tend to be less pragmatic than women in their relationships.

   d. The text does not equate divorce with such beliefs.

7. **b.** is the answer. (pp. 495–496)

   a. In Erikson's theory, the crisis of intimacy *precedes* the need to be productive through work.

   c. & d. Although these items are true, Erikson's theory does not address these issues.

8. **d.** is the answer. (p. 500)
9. **c.** is the answer. (p. 504)
10. **d.** is the answer. (pp. 504–505)
11. **b.** is the answer. (p. 505)

    a., c., & d. Women and members of minority groups are more likely to encounter glass ceilings in their careers.

12. **b.** is the answer. (p. 507)

    a. The authority period is from age 2 to 5.

    c. The interpretive period is from age 5 to 12.

    d. The interdependent period occurs during adolescence.

13. **a.** is the answer. (p. 510)

    c. Fathers often become *more* involved when children move beyond infancy.

    d. If anything, having a second child might increase family pressure and further disrupt marital harmony.

14. **a.** is the answer. (pp. 511–513)

    b. Many stepchildren remain fiercely loyal to the absent parent.

    c. Most stepparents actually have unrealistically high expectations of the relationship they will establish with their stepchildren.

    d. Doing so would only confuse the child and, quite possibly, cause resentment and further alienation.

15. **c.** is the answer. The more children a couple has, the less likely they are to share household tasks. Generally, the woman carries the major burden. (p. 509)

KEY TERMS

1. According to Erik Erikson, the first crisis of adulthood is **intimacy versus isolation,** which involves the need to share one's personal life with someone else or risk profound loneliness. (p. 484)
2. In Erikson's theory, the second crisis of adulthood is **generativity versus stagnation,** which involves the need to be productive in some mean-

ingful way, usually through work or parenthood. (p. 484)

3. The **social clock** represents the culturally set timetable that establishes when various events and behaviors in life are appropriate and called for. (p. 486)
4. **Serial monogamy** is the increasingly common relationship pattern in which the individual forms a series of intimate, committed relationships, with only one person at a time, inside or outside of the marriage contract. (p. 491)
5. Increasingly common among young adults in all industrialized countries is the living pattern called **cohabitation,** in which two unrelated adults of the opposite sex live together. (p. 494)
6. **Homogamy** refers to marriage between people who are similar in age, socioeconomic background, interests, ethnicity, religion, and the like. (p. 496)
7. **Heterogamy** refers to marriage between people who are dissimilar in age, interests, and goals, as well as in background. (p. 496)
8. **Marital equity** refers to the extent to which partners perceive equality in their relationship. (p. 496)
9. According to **exchange theory,** a successful marriage is an arrangement in which each partner contributes something useful to the other, such that both consider the exchange a fair one. (p. 496)
10. For many workers, the opportunity to choose their own work hours, called **flextime,** generally increases their job satisfaction. (p. 504)
11. A key development for many young workers is a relationship with an older, more experienced worker, or **mentor,** who serves as a teacher, confidant, and role model. (p. 504)
12. A **glass ceiling** is an invisible barrier to career advancement that is most often encountered by women and minority workers. (p. 505)

CHAPTER 20 Middle Adulthood: Biosocial Development

Chapter Overview

This chapter deals with biosocial development during the years from 40 to 60. The first section describes changes in appearance and in the functioning of the sense organs and vital body systems, noting the potential impact of these changes. The next section identifies variations in health related to lifestyle factors and stress, pointing out that, overall, middle-aged persons are healthier today than in earlier cohorts. The chapter concludes with a discussion of the changes in the sexual-reproductive system that occur during middle adulthood and shows why most individuals find these changes less troubling than they were led to expect them to be.

NOTE: Answer guidelines for all Chapter 20 questions begin on page 303.

Guided Study

The text chapter should be studied one section at a time. Before you read, preview each section by skimming it, noting headings and boldface items. Then read the appropriate section objectives from the following outline. Keep these objectives in mind and, as you read the chapter section, search for the information that will enable you to meet each objective. Once you have finished a section, write out answers for its objectives.

Normal Changes in Middle Adulthood (pp. 520–523)

1. Identify the typical physical changes of middle adulthood and discuss their impact.

2. Describe how the functions of the sense organs and vital body systems change during middle adulthood.

Variations in Health (pp. 523–532)

3. Identify and differentiate four measures of health.

4. Explain how variations in health are related to ethnicity.

5. Cite sex differences in mortality and morbidity rates and several ways in which these differences have been exacerbated by the medical community.

6. (Research Report) Describe the relationship between certain lifestyle factors—smoking, alcohol use, nutrition, body weight, and exercise—and health.

7. Discuss the relationship between stress and health and describe developmental changes in how people cope with stress.

The Sexual-Reproductive System (pp. 532–536)

8. Identify the typical changes that occur in the sexual-reproductive system during middle adulthood.

9. Discuss historical changes in the psychological impact of menopause and identify age-related changes in sexual expression.

Chapter Review

When you have finished reading the chapter, work through the material that follows to review it. Complete the sentences and answer the questions. As you proceed, evaluate your performance for each section by consulting the answers on page 303. Do not continue with the next section until you understand each answer. If you need to, review or reread the appropriate section in the textbook before continuing.

Normal Changes in Middle Adulthood (pp. 520–523)

1. Some of the normal changes in appearance that occur during middle adulthood include ________
____
____
____

2. The physical changes that typically occur during middle adulthood usually __________________ (do/do not) have significant health consequences.

3. The physical changes of middle adulthood may have a substantial impact on a person's ____________________; this is particularly true for __________________ (men/women).

4. The overall impact that aging has on the individual depends in large measure on the individual's ____________________ toward growing old.

5. Age-related deficits in the sense organs are most obvious in __________________ and __________________.

6. Hearing losses in middle age are more evident in ____________________ (men/women), especially for __________________- (high/low) frequency sounds.

7. After puberty, ______ affects focusing much more than age does. Young people tend simply to be ______ (nearsighted/farsighted/astigmatic), whereas older adults are more likely to suffer from all of these disorders.

8. Other aspects of vision that decline steadily with age are ______ ______, ______-______ ______, and ______ ______. These changes are particularly likely to become apparent after age ______.

9. A more serious vision problem is the disease ______, caused by an increase of ______ within the eyeball. By age ______, this disease is the leading cause of ______. The incidence of this disease is especially high among ______-______.

10. Systemic declines in the efficiency and the organ reserve of the ______, ______, and ______ ______ make middle-aged people ______ (more/less) vulnerable to disease.

11. Thanks to better ______ ______ and ______ ______, the overall death rate among the middle-aged is ______ what it was fifty years ago, especially for the two leading causes of death in this age group: ______ ______ and ______.

Variations in Health (pp. 523–532)

12. Individuals who are relatively well educated, financially secure, and living in or near cities tend to live ______ (shorter/longer) lives and have ______ (more/fewer) chronic illnesses or disabilities.

13. In the United States, people living in the ______ and ______ are healthier than those in the ______ and ______. The reasons for such differences include variations in ______ ______.

14. Perhaps the most solid indicator of health of given age groups is the death rate, or ______.

15. A more comprehensive measure of health is ______, defined as ______ of all kinds; it can be sudden, or ______, or it can be ______, extending over a long time period.

16. To be a true index of health, morbidity must be defined in terms of ______, which refers to a person's inability to perform normal activities, and ______, which refers to how healthy and energetic a person feels.

17. In terms of quality of life, ______ is probably the most important measure of health.

18. Between the ages of 40 and 60, the chance of dying is twice as high for ______-______, and only half as high for ______-______, as it is for Americans of European descent. In between are the mortality rates for ______ ______ and ______-______.

Self-reported health status, morbidity, and disability ______ (do/do not) follow the same ethnic patterns.

19. Rates of heart disease, stroke, and cancer are particularly high for ______-______, who tend to have high ______ ______ and poor health habits.

20. The major reason for ethnic variations in health and illness during middle age is ______ ______.

When middle-aged and older people of the same income and education are compared,

_______________-Americans actually have _______________ (higher/lower) death rates than _______________-Americans.

21. Compared to middle-aged women, middle-aged men are _______________ as likely to die of any cause and three times as likely to die of _______________ _______________.

Not until age _______________ are the rates equivalent.

22. Beginning in middle age, women have higher _______________ rates than men, particularly after _______________. Contributing to this gender difference is the tendency of the medical community to focus on treating _______________ _______________ rather than _______________ _______________, and on preventing _______________ rather than avoiding _______________. This has meant that more research money is dedicated to studying diseases that are more common in _______________ (men/women). Consequently, _______________ and _______________ of heart disease in women has been based on an opposite-sex model.

23. (Research Report) Cigarette-smoking is a known risk factor for most serious diseases, including _______________ _______________.

24. (Research Report) The third leading preventable cause of death, after _______________ _______________ and _______________, is _______________-_______________ _______________.

25. (Research Report) Some studies find that adults who drink moderately may live longer, possibly because alcohol increases the blood's supply of _______________, a protein that helps rid the body of excess _______________ and _______________. Another possible explanation of the relationship between moderate drinking and longevity is that moderate drinking is more common among people of high _______________.

26. (Research Report) Alcohol dependence and abuse are most common at about age _______________.

List some of the damaging effects of heavy drinking on the body.

27. (Research Report) During middle adulthood, _______________ plays an important role with regard to the onset of cancer and heart disease. Adults in industrialized countries typically consume _______________ percent of their calories as fat. The National Cancer Institute recommends that adults increase their consumption of _______________, and reduce their consumption of fat to no more than _______________ percent.

28. (Research Report) Obesity, defined as _______________ _______________, is present in _______________ (what ratio?) of all middle-aged people. Obesity is a risk factor for _______________ _______________, _______________, and _______________, and a contributing factor for _______________, the most common disability in older adults.

29. (Research Report) Physicians _______________ (do/do not) agree on whether being underweight is healthy.

30. (Research Report) Between age 20 and 50, a person's metabolism _______________ (slows/increases) by about a third, which means that middle-aged people need to eat _______________ (more/less) simply to maintain their weight.

31. (Research Report) People who are active _______________ (do/do not) have lower rates of serious illness and death than inactive people. Exercise that is sufficiently strenuous to raise the pulse to about _______________ percent of its maximum capacity three or more

times a week for at least ______ minutes per workout is especially healthful.

List some of the health benefits of regular exercise.

32. Most individuals exercise ______ (more/less) as they grow older. The crucial factor in improving health habits is ______.

33. Stress is defined as ______ ______.

34. Unsettling conditions that trigger stress are called ______.

35. What makes something stressful is the individual's ______ to it.

List several factors that influence a person's reaction to a potential stressor.

36. Stress ______ (does/does not) increase the risk of physical disease.

37. Stress increases ______ ______ and elevates ______ ______. It also produces changes in the concentration of ______ and other chemicals in the body. In addition, stress reduces the effectiveness of the ______ system.

38. People who have a network of social support are ______ (better/no better) able to cope with the effects of stress.

39. People who maintain a(n) ______ view of life tend to cope with stress more effectively.

40. Physiological adjustments to stress take ______ (more/less) time as people grow older.

41. Several studies have found that as people grow older, they often become ______ (better/worse) at handling stressors.

42. Stress ______ (is/is not) a major contributor to most forms of mental illness.

43. Disorders such as drug abuse, schizophrenia, and depression become ______ (more/less) common as people grow older.

44. Give four possible explanations for the apparent developmental changes that may occur in the way stress is experienced and dealt with.

    a. ______
    b. ______
    c. ______
    d. ______

The Sexual-Reproductive System (pp. 532–536)

45. After about age ______, many women find that the time between their menstrual periods becomes ______ (shorter/longer).

46. At an average age of ______, a woman reaches ______, as ovulation and menstruation stop and the production of the hormone ______ drops considerably. Strictly speaking, this event is dated ______ year(s) after a woman's last menstrual cycle.

47. All the various biological and psychological changes that accompany menopause are referred to as the ______. Symptoms such as hot flashes and flushes and cold sweats are caused by ______ ______, that is, a temporary disruption in the body mechanisms that maintain body temperature.

48. The prevalent conception of menopause as a time of difficulty and depression ______ (is/is not) largely a myth.

49. Women who have had their ovaries surgically removed are most likely to need ______ ______ ______, or HRT, in order to

experience relief from menopausal symptoms.

50. HRT is also recommended for women who are at risk for ______________, a condition of thin and brittle bones. Women who are at high risk for this condition include those who are ______________, ______________, and ______________. For most women, a childhood diet high in ______________, regular ______________-______________ ______________, and avoiding ______________ and ______________ significantly lessen the likelihood of developing this condition.

Briefly explain why menopause is more often welcomed by women today than in the past.

51. Physiologically, men ______________ (do/do not) experience anything like the female climacteric. Although the average levels of testosterone decline gradually, if at all, with age, they can dip if a man becomes ______________ ______________ or unusually worried.

52. During middle adulthood, sexual stimulation takes ______________ (longer/less time) and needs to be ______________ (more/less) direct than earlier in life.

53. Frequency of intercourse and orgasm usually ______________ (declines/increases/remains unchanged) during middle age.

54. For middle-aged adults, enjoyment of sex is more closely related to ______________ ______________ ______________ than to income, education, or life satisfaction.

Progress Test 1

Multiple-Choice Questions

Circle your answers to the following questions and check them with the answers on page 304. If your answer is incorrect, read the explanation for why it is incorrect and then consult the appropriate pages of the text (in parentheses following the correct answer).

1. During the years from 40 to 60, the average adult:
   a. becomes proportionally slimmer.
   b. gains about 5 pounds per year.
   c. gains about 1 pound per year.
   d. is more likely to be noticeably overweight.

2. The overall impact of aging depends *largely* on the individual's:
   a. general physical health.
   b. genetic predisposition toward disease.
   c. attitudes about aging.
   d. health habits and lifestyle.

3. Age-related deficits in hearing are most noticeable for:
   a. high-frequency sounds.
   b. low-frequency sounds.
   c. mid-range-frequency sounds.
   d. normal conversation.

4. Compared to the acuity problems of younger adults, which tend to be confined to ______________, those of older adults also tend to include ______________.
   a. farsightedness; nearsightedness
   b. farsightedness; nearsightedness and astigmatism
   c. astigmatism; farsightedness
   d. nearsightedness; farsightedness and astigmatism

5. Characterized by an increase in fluid within the eyeball, this eye disease is the leading cause of blindness by age 70. It is called:
   a. myopia.
   b. astigmatism.
   c. cataracts.
   d. glaucoma.

6. At midlife, individuals who ______________ tend to live longer and have fewer chronic illnesses or disabilities.
   a. are relatively well educated
   b. are financially secure
   c. live in or near cities
   d. are/do all of the above

7. The health statistic that measures disease of all kinds is:
   a. mortality.
   b. morbidity.
   c. disability.
   d. vitality.

8. On average, women reach menopause at age:
   a. 39.
   b. 42.
   c. 46.
   d. 51.

9. The major reason for ethnic variations in health and illness during middle age is:
   a. heredity.
   b. cultural factors.
   c. SES.
   d. stress.

10. In middle age, ____________ rates are higher for men than women, while ____________ rates are higher for women than men.
    a. mortality; morbidity
    b. morbidity; mortality
    c. vitality; disability
    d. disability; vitality

11. The leading cause of mortality in both sexes is:
    a. lung cancer.
    b. accidents.
    c. heart disease.
    d. stroke.

12. (Research Report) In order, the three leading preventable causes of death are:
    a. active smoking, excessive alcohol consumption, and second-hand smoke.
    b. active smoking, stress, and excessive alcohol consumption.
    c. poor nutrition, active smoking, and stress.
    d. obesity, active smoking, and stress.

13. (Research Report) Individuals are considered obese when their body weight exceeds the average for their height by:
    a. 10 percent.
    b. 20 percent.
    c. 25 percent.
    d. 50 percent.

14. Stress is defined in the text as the:
    a. adverse psychological reactions to an unpleasant life event.
    b. adverse physical and emotional reactions brought on by a stressor.
    c. specific physiological changes experienced by all persons in response to unpleasant events.
    d. psychological impact on a person when his or her attempt to reach some goal is blocked.

15. Research on patterns of coping with stress indicates that:
    a. active coping strategies, in which problems are met head-on, usually are best.
    b. passive coping strategies, such as downplaying problems, usually are best.
    c. active strategies are best when young; passive strategies are best when older.
    d. it is best to have several strategies, both active and passive, in order to effectively cope with stress.

True or False Items

Write *true* or *false* on the line in front of each statement.

______ 1. The mortality rate of middle-aged European-Americans is higher than that of middle-aged African-Americans.

______ 2. During middle age, people become more likely to use adaptive means of coping with stress.

______ 3. (Research Report) Approximately half of all middle-aged Americans are obese.

______ 4. (Research Report) Moderate users of alcohol are more likely than teetotalers to have heart attackss.

______ 5. (Research Report) Those who exercise regularly have lower rates of serious illness than do sedentary people.

______ 6. Middle-aged adults are less likely to improve their health habits than are members of any other age group.

______ 7. During middle adulthood, sexual responses slow down, particularly in men.

______ 8. The climacteric refers specifically to the psychological changes that accompany menopause.

______ 9. Despite popular reference to it, there is no "male menopause."

______ 10. Culture, expectations, and attitude, more than biology, determine the psychological reaction to menopause.

Progress Test 2

Progress Test 2 should be completed during a final chapter review. Answer the following questions after you thoroughly understand the correct answers for the Chapter Review and Progress Test 1.

Multiple-Choice Questions

1. For most people, the normal changes in appearance that occur during middle age have the greatest impact on their:
   a. physical strength.
   b. flexibility.
   c. cardiovascular reserve.
   d. self-image.

2. Age-related deficits in the sense organs are most obvious in:
   a. taste and touch.
   b. vision and hearing.
   c. smell and balance.
   d. balance and hearing.

3. After puberty, visual acuity is influenced more by ______________ than by ______________.
   a. heredity; age
   b. age; heredity
   c. overall health; heredity
   d. heredity; overall health

4. People are more vulnerable to disease during middle adulthood because:
   a. they are exposed to more sources of stress than when they were younger.
   b. they tend to have poorer health habits.
   c. the efficiency of their vital body systems declines.
   d. of all of the above reasons.

5. Overall, the death rate of people between ages 40 and 60 is about ______________ what it was fifty years ago.
   a. one-and-a-half times
   b. twice
   c. one-third
   d. one-half

6. Thin, Caucasian, postmenopausal women are at increased risk of:
   a. postmenopausal depression.
   b. vasomotor instability.
   c. osteoporosis.
   d. "hot flashes."

7. To be a true index of health, morbidity must be refined in terms of which of the following health measure(s)?
   a. mortality
   b. disability and mortality
   c. vitality
   d. disability and vitality

8. The best predictor of sexual interest and activity during middle adulthood is an individual's:
   a. age.
   b. sex.
   c. overall health.
   d. past sexual interest and experiences.

9. The mortality rates of women and men become equivalent at age:
   a. 65.
   b. 70.
   c. 80.
   d. 85.

10. What is one reason that middle-aged women have higher morbidity rates than men in the same age group?
    a. Traditionally, less research money has been dedicated to problems more likely to affect women than men, but unlikely to lead to sudden death.
    b. They tend to have fewer strategies for actively coping with stress.
    c. There simply are more middle-aged women than men living.
    d. All of the above are true.

11. In any given individual, what causes stress, and how he or she responds to it, depend most on:
    a. temperament.
    b. past experiences.
    c. resources and strategies for coping with stress.
    d. a combination of these and other factors in influencing the way an individual interprets a potential stressor.

12. (Research Report) Which of the following is *not* true regarding alcohol consumption?
    a. Alcohol decreases the blood's supply of high-density lipoprotein.
    b. Although binge drinking is more common in early adulthood, alcohol dependence is more common in middle adulthood.
    c. Alcohol is implicated in about half of all accidents, suicides, and homicides.
    d. Alcohol abuse is considered the most expensive health problem in the United States today.

13. (Research Report) Which of the following diets has been associated with increased risk of certain cancers?
    a. low-fat diet
    b. low-fat, high-protein diet
    c. high-fat, high-fiber diet
    d. high-fat, low-fiber diet

14. Which of the following may be responsible for the sharp drop in the incidence of mental disorders during middle age?
    a. Middle-aged people have fewer psychosocial demands, and therefore less stress, than younger people.
    b. Middle-aged people may have more social buffers against stress than younger adults.
    c. Middle-aged people are more likely to seek professional help for stress-related problems.
    d. All of the above may contribute to the decreased incidence of mental disorders during middle age.

15. (Research Report) The third leading preventable cause of death is:
    a. cigarette-smoking.
    b. alcohol abuse.
    c. second-hand smoke.
    d. a high-fat, low-fiber diet.

Matching Items

Match each definition or description with its corresponding term.

Terms

_______ 1. mortality
_______ 2. morbidity
_______ 3. vitality
_______ 4. stress
_______ 5. glaucoma
_______ 6. menopause
_______ 7. climacteric
_______ 8. vasomotor instability
_______ 9. HRT
_______ 10. osteoporosis

Definitions or Descriptions

a. the adverse reaction to demands put on an individual
b. disease of all kinds
c. the cause of hot flashes and flushes and cold sweats
d. the leading cause of blindness by age 70
e. often prescribed following a hysterectomy
f. a condition of thin and brittle bones
g. measured by the number of deaths each year per thousand individuals
h. the cessation of ovulation and menstruation
i. more important to quality of life than any other measure of health
j. the various biological and psychological changes that accompany menopause

Challenge Test

Answer these questions the day before an exam as a final check on your understanding of the chapter's terms and concepts.

1. (Research Report) Which of the following types of exercise would be most beneficial in promoting general health and reducing risk of disease?
    a. sprinting 100 yards in 12 seconds
    b. lifting weights three times a week
    c. playing three sets of tennis twice a week
    d. cycling regularly at an intensity that raises the heart rate to 75 percent of its maximum

2. Mr. Johnson has experienced more frequent colds and bouts of flu since he lost his job last year. His increased susceptibility to illness is likely due to:
    a. a reduction in the effectiveness of his immune system due to stress.
    b. an increase in immune-system activity brought on by the stress of losing his job.
    c. a decrease in the level of testosterone circulating in his bloodstream.
    d. an increase in the level of testosterone circulating in his bloodstream.

3. Fifty-five-year-old Dewey is concerned because sexual stimulation seems to take longer and needs to be more direct than earlier. As a friend, you should tell him:
   a. "You should see a therapist. It is not normal."
   b. "See a doctor if your 'sexual prowess' doesn't improve soon. You may have some underlying physical problem."
   c. "Don't worry. This is normal for middle-aged men."
   d. "You're too old to have sex, so just give it up."

4. The mortality rates of the following ethnic groups, in order from highest to lowest, are:
   a. Asian-Americans; African-Americans; Americans of European descent.
   b. African-Americans; Asian-Americans; Americans of European descent.
   c. African-Americans; Americans of European descent; Asian-Americans.
   d. Americans of European descent; African-Americans; Asian-Americans.

5. Which of the following is true regarding changes in vision during middle age?
   a. They lead to serious accidents such as falls.
   b. They lead to night-time car accidents due to the blindness caused by oncoming headlights.
   c. They make it harder to focus on small print for several hours.
   d. They do both a. and b.

6. In the United States, people who live in the _______________ tend to be healthier than those who live in the _______________.
   a. East; West
   b. West and Midwest; South and Middle Atlantic
   c. South; North
   d. Northeast; Northwest

7. African-Americans are particularly susceptible to illnesses and disabilities that are related to:
   a. high blood pressure.
   b. poor diet.
   c. cigarette-smoking.
   d. all of the above.

8. One hundred years ago, the psychological impact of menopause on women was probably:
   a. about the same as it is today.
   b. less than it is today.
   c. greater than it is today.
   d. determined more by expectations and culture than it is today.

9. Which of the following *most* accurately describes research findings regarding psychological adjustment to menopause?
   a. Older women tend to have very negative attitudes about menopause.
   b. Both younger and older women tend to have very negative attitudes about menopause.
   c. Menopause tends to be a more negative experience in countries other than the United States.
   d. Most women find menopause more welcome than regretted.

10. Rodney, a 45-year-old African-American store manager, has been experiencing some problems with his vision lately. His optometrist should probably:
    a. reassure Rodney that everyone's vision begins to deteriorate rapidly after age 40.
    b. give Rodney a glaucoma test.
    c. reduce the strength of Rodney's lenses so that his eye muscles will be strengthened.
    d. do all of the above.

11. Fifty-year-old Beth has a college degree, a good job, and lives near Seattle, Washington. Compared to her sister, who dropped out of high school and is struggling to make ends meet on a dairy farm in rural Wisconsin, Beth is most likely to:
    a. live longer.
    b. have fewer chronic illnesses.
    c. have fewer disabilities.
    d. do/have all of the above.

12. Morbidity is to mortality as _______________ is to _______________.
    a. disease; death rate
    b. death rate; disease
    c. inability to perform normal daily activities; disease
    d. disease; subjective feeling of being healthy

13. (Research Report) Critics of researchers who believe that moderate alcohol consumption leads to a longer life point out that:
    a. alcohol lowers the blood's supply of high-density lipoprotein, thereby increasing the chance of blood clots.
    b. drinking itself is not a health benefit but rather reflects the link between good health and economic well-being.
    c. alcohol stimulates calcium retention, thereby increasing the risk of cancer.
    d. all of the above are true.

14. (Research Report) Concluding her presentation on body weight and health, Lynn states that:
    a. "Research consistently shows that 'you can't be too thin.'"
    b. "Animal research demonstrates that it is better to be a little overweight than underweight."
    c. "As long as a person is not obese, physicians disagree about how thin he or she should be."
    d. "As long as metabolism remains normal, being overweight is not a health problem."

15. (Research Report) Compared to his identical twin brother, 48-year-old Andy has lower blood pressure, better circulation, a lower ratio of body fat to body weight, and higher HDL in his blood. The most probable explanation for these differences is that Andy:
    a. doesn't smoke.
    b. eats a high-fiber diet.
    c. engages in regular aerobic exercise.
    d. does all of the above.

Key Terms

Using your own words, write a brief definition or explanation of each of the following terms on a separate piece of paper.

1. glaucoma
2. mortality
3. morbidity
4. disability
5. vitality
6. stress
7. stressor
8. menopause
9. climacteric
10. vasomotor instability
11. hormone replacement therapy (HRT)
12. osteoporosis

ANSWERS

CHAPTER REVIEW

1. hair turns gray and thins; skin becomes drier and more wrinkled; pockets of fat settle on the upper arms, buttocks, and eyelids; back muscles, connecting tissues, and bones lose strength, causing some individuals to become shorter; many become noticeably overweight
2. do not
3. self-image; women
4. attitude
5. hearing; vision
6. men; high
7. heredity; nearsighted
8. depth perception; eye-muscle resilience; dark adaptation; 50
9. glaucoma; fluid; 70; blindness; African-Americans
10. lungs; heart; digestive system; more
11. health habits; disease prevention; half; heart disease; cancer
12. longer; fewer
13. West; Midwest; South; Middle Atlantic; the quality of the environment and health care, as well as genetic, dietary, religious, and cultural patterns
14. mortality
15. morbidity; disease; acute; chronic
16. disability; vitality
17. vitality
18. African-Americans; Asian-Americans; Native Americans; Hispanic-Americans; do
19. African-Americans; blood pressure
20. socioeconomic status; European; higher; African
21. twice; heart disease; 85
22. morbidity; menopause; acute illnesses; chronic conditions; death; disability; men; diagnosis; treatment
23. cancer of the lung, bladder, kidney, mouth, and stomach, as well as heart disease, stroke, and emphysema
24. active smoking; alcohol; second-hand smoke
25. HDL (high-density lipoprotein); fat; cholesterol; SES
26. 40

Heavy drinking is the main cause of cirrhosis of the liver; it also stresses the heart and stomach, destroys brain cells, hastens calcium loss, and is a risk factor for many forms of cancer.

27. nutrition; 40; fiber; 30
28. weight that is 20 percent or more above the average for a given height; one-third; heart disease; diabetes; stroke; arthritis
29. do not
30. slows; less

31. do; 75; 30

Regular aerobic exercise increases heart and lung capacity, lowers blood pressure, increases HDL in the blood, reduces the ratio of body fat to body weight, and enhances cognitive functioning. It also sometimes helps reduce depression and hostility.

32. less; attitude

33. the adverse physical and emotional reaction to demands put on the individual by stressors

34. stressors

35. reaction

Factors include the individual's temperament, past experiences, physical vulnerabilities, resources and strategies for coping, the overall context, and how these factors influence the way the individual interprets a potential stressor.

36. does

37. heart rate; blood pressure; hormones; immune

38. better

39. optimistic

40. more

41. better

42. is

43. less

44. Middle-aged people:

- **a.** tend to have fewer psychosocial demands than young adults;
- **b.** may be better buffered by their social networks against stress;
- **c.** may be more likely to seek, and better able to afford, professional help for their problems;
- **d.** may evidence a more flexible cognitive approach to the appraisal of potential stressors.

45. 35; shorter

46. 51; menopause; estrogen; one

47. climacteric; vasomotor instability

48. is

49. hormone replacement therapy

50. osteoporosis; thin; Caucasian; postmenopausal; calcium; weight-bearing exercise; cigarettes; alcohol

Traditionally, the more children a couple had, the more fortunate they were considered to be. The impact of the loss of fertility was therefore much more significant. Today, the end of childbearing is determined less by age than by personal factors such as financial situation. Thus, as the time when sexual activity is no longer accompanied by fear of pregnancy, menopause is more often welcomed than regretted.

51. do not; sexually inactive

52. longer; more

53. declines

54. past sexual interests

PROGRESS TEST 1

Multiple-Choice Questions

1. **d.** is the answer. (p. 520)
b. & **c.** Weight gain varies substantially from person to person.

2. **c.** is the answer. (p. 521)

3. **a.** is the answer. (pp. 521–522)

4. **d.** is the answer. (p. 522)

5. **d.** is the answer. (p. 522)
a. This is the technical name for nearsightedness.
b. & **c.** These are serious, but usually correctable, eye conditions.

6. **d.** is the answer. (p. 523)

7. **b.** is the answer. (p. 524)
a. This is the overall death rate.
c. This refers to a person's inability to perform activities that most others can.
d. This refers to how physically, intellectually, and socially healthy an individual feels.

8. **d.** is the answer. (p. 533)

9. **c.** is the answer. (p. 525)

10. **a.** is the answer. (p. 525)

11. **c.** is the answer. (p. 526)

12. **a.** is the answer. (p. 527)

13. **b.** is the answer. (p. 527)

14. **b.** is the answer. (p. 529)

15. **d.** is the answer. (p. 531)
a., b., & **c.** Both active and passive coping strategies are adaptive in certain situations (regardless of one's age) and maladaptive in others.

True or False Items

1. F The death rate for African-Americans is twice that of Americans of European descent. (p. 525)

2. T (p. 531)

3. F Approximately one-third are obese. (p. 527)

4. F Moderate use of alcohol is associated with reduced risk of heart attacks. (p. 527)

5. T (p. 528)

6. F Middle-aged adults are much more likely to improve their health habits than younger adults. (p. 526)

7. T (p. 535)
8. F The climacteric refers to both the physiological and the psychological changes that accompany menopause. (p. 533)
9. T (p. 534)
10. T (p. 533)

PROGRESS TEST 2

Multiple-Choice Questions

1. **d.** is the answer. (p. 520)

   a., b., & c. For the most part, the normal physical changes of middle adulthood have no significant health consequences.

2. **b.** is the answer. (p. 521)
3. **a.** is the answer. (p. 522)

   c. & d. Although overall health is an important factor in all aspects of aging, the text does not compare the relative influences of overall health and heredity on visual acuity.

4. **c.** is the answer. (pp. 522–523)

   a. Although this may be true, it is a person's *reaction*, rather than stress per se, that determines the impact of a potential source of stress.

   b. In fact, the middle-aged often have better health habits.

5. **d.** is the answer. (p. 523)
6. **c.** is the answer. (p. 533)

   a., b., & d. The incidence rates of the phenomena listed in the question do not vary with weight, ethnicity, or fertility.

7. **d.** is the answer. (p. 524)
8. **d.** is the answer. (p. 535)
9. **d.** is the answer. (p. 525)
10. **a.** is the answer. (p. 525)
11. **d.** is the answer. (p. 530)
12. **a.** is the answer. Alcohol *increases* the blood's supply of HDL, which is one possible reason that adults who drink in moderation may live longer than "teetotalers." (p. 527)
13. **d.** is the answer. (p. 527)
14. **d.** is the answer. (p. 532)
15. **c.** is the answer. (p. 527)

Matching Items

1. g (p. 524)
2. b (p. 524)
3. i (p. 524)
4. a (p. 529)
5. d (p. 522)
6. h (p. 533)
7. j (p. 533)
8. c (p. 533)
9. e (p. 533)
10. f (p. 533)

CHALLENGE TEST

1. **d.** is the answer. (p. 528)

   a., b., & c. These forms of exercise will not produce the beneficial effects of regular aerobic exercise.

2. **a.** is the answer. (p. 530)

   b. Stress *decreases* immune system activity.

   c. & d. The text does not discuss the impact of stress on testosterone. Furthermore, changes in testosterone level would not necessarily lead to the types of health problems Mr. Johnson is experiencing.

3. **c.** is the answer. (p. 535)
4. **c.** is the answer. (p. 525)
5. **c.** is the answer. (p. 522)

   a. & b. These are more common in early or late adulthood. Although middle-aged people do have trouble with blindness from oncoming headlights, they cope quite well with this problem.

6. **b.** is the answer. (p. 524)
7. **d.** is the answer. (p. 525)
8. **c.** is the answer. At that point in history, the more children a couple had, the more fortunate they were considered to be. (p. 534)
9. **d.** is the answer. (p. 534)

   a., b., & c. The text does not indicate that attitudes toward menopause vary with age, or that its experience varies from country to country.

10. **b.** is the answer. The incidence of glaucoma is especially high among African-Americans. (p. 522)

    a. Age-related changes in vision are particularly likely to become apparent after age *50*.

    c. This probably would not help Rodney at all.

11. **d.** is the answer. People who are relatively well educated, financially secure, and live in or near cities tend to receive all of these benefits. (p. 523)
12. **a.** is the answer. (p. 524)

    b. This answer would be correct if the statement were "Mortality is to morbidity."

    c. This answer would be correct if the statement were "Disability is to morbidity."

    d. This answer would be correct if the statement were "Morbidity is to vitality."

13. **b.** is the answer. Moderate drinking is more common among people of high SES than among people of low SES, who tend more to be either abstinent or heavy drinkers. (p. 527)

a. Alcohol actually *increases* HDL.

c. Alcohol actually hastens calcium loss.

14. c. is the answer. (p. 527)

    a. At least one longitudinal study found that death was as likely to occur among those who were 10 percent underweight as among those who were 30 percent overweight.

    b. Animal research demonstrates just the opposite.

    d. Metabolic rate influences the likelihood of being overweight, but does not counteract its health consequences.

15. c. is the answer. (p. 528)

    a. & b. Although both of these behaviors promote health, only regular aerobic exercise produces *all* the health benefits that Andy is experiencing.

KEY TERMS

1. **Glaucoma,** an eye disease characterized by an increase of fluid within the eyeball, becomes increasingly common after age 40, and is the leading cause of blindness by age 70. (p. 522)
2. **Mortality,** or death rate, is measured by the number of deaths each year per thousand individuals. (p. 524)
3. **Morbidity,** defined as disease of all kinds, can be sudden and severe (acute), or extend over a long time period (chronic). (p. 524)
4. **Disability** refers to a person's inability to perform activities that most others can. (p. 524)
5. **Vitality** refers to how healthy and energetic, physically, intellectually, and socially, an individual actually feels. (p. 524)
6. **Stress** is the adverse physical and emotional reaction to demands put on the individual by stressors. (p. 529)
7. A **stressor** is an unsettling condition or experience that triggers the stress reaction in an individual. (p. 529)
8. At **menopause,** ovulation and menstruation stop and the production of the hormone estrogen drops considerably. (p. 533)
9. The **climacteric** refers to all the various biological and psychological changes that accompany menopause. (p. 533)
10. **Vasomotor instability** is a temporary disruption in the body mechanisms that constrict or dilate the blood vessels to maintain body temperature. (p. 533)
11. **Hormone replacement therapy (HRT)** is intended to help relieve menopausal symptoms, especially in women who experience an abrupt drop in hormone level because their ovaries are surgically removed. (p. 533)
12. **Osteoporosis** is a condition of thin and brittle bones leading to increased fractures and frailty in old age for which women who are thin, Caucasian, and postmenopausal are at increased risk. (p. 533)

CHAPTER 21 Middle Adulthood: Cognitive Development

Chapter Overview

The way psychologists conceptualize intelligence has changed considerably in recent years. Chapter 21 begins with a discussion of the debate over whether cognitive abilities inevitably decline during adulthood, or may possibly remain stable or even increase.

The chapter then examines the contemporary view of intelligence, which emphasizes that it is multidimensional, multidirectional, plastic, and characterized more by interindividual variation than by consistency from person to person.

Following a section devoted to the relatively new study of practical intelligence, a final section discusses the cognitive expertise that often comes with experience, pointing out the ways in which expert thinking differs from that of the novice. Expert thinking is more specialized, flexible, and intuitive, and is guided by more and better problem-solving strategies.

The chapter concludes with the message that during middle adulthood individual differences are much more critical in determining the course of cognitive development than is chronological age alone.

NOTE: Answer guidelines for all Chapter 21 questions begin on page 317.

Guided Study

The text chapter should be studied one section at a time. Before you read, preview each section by skimming it, noting headings and boldface items. Then read the appropriate section objectives from the following outline. Keep these objectives in mind and, as you read the chapter section, search for the information that will enable you to meet each objective. Once you have finished a section, write out answers for its objectives.

Decline in Adult Intelligence? (pp. 540–543)

1. Briefly trace the history of the controversy regarding adult intelligence, including the findings of cross-sectional and longitudinal research.

2. Explain the sequential research technique, how it corrects for some of the problems of cross-sectional and longitudinal research, and its findings regarding adult intelligence.

3. State three general conclusions about intellectual changes during adulthood.

Fluid and Crystallized Intelligence (pp. 543–547)

4. Distinguish between fluid and crystallized intelligence and explain how each is affected by age.

5. Discuss the controversy surrounding the issue of whether faster thinking is better thinking, and explain why some researchers believe that intelligence tests are biased against older adults.

Intelligence Reconsidered (pp. 547–552)

6. Describe the contemporary view of intelligence, which places emphasis on the multidimensional and multidirectional nature of intellectual abilities.

7. Discuss the impact of interindividual variation and plasticity on intelligence.

Practical Intelligence (pp. 552–554)

8. Explain the practical intelligence approach to the study of adult intelligence, its rationale, and how it differs from traditional measures of adult intelligence.

Expertise (pp. 554–556)

9. Describe how the cognitive processes of experts differ from those of novices.

Chapter Review

When you have finished reading the chapter, work through the material that follows to review it. Complete the sentences and answer the questions. As you proceed, evaluate your performance for each section by consulting the answers on page 317. Do not continue with the next section until you understand each answer. If you need to, review or reread the appropriate section in the textbook before continuing.

1. Researchers such as ____________________ assert that intellectual decline during adulthood is inevitable. On the other hand, researchers such as ____________________ contend that intelligence is more dependent on the impact of other factors, including ____________________ ____________________.

Decline in Adult Intelligence? (pp. 540–543)

2. For most of this century, psychologists were convinced that intelligence peaks during ____________________, and then gradually declines. This belief was based on evidence from soldiers given an intelligence test, called ____________________, during World War I.

3. During the 1950s, Nancy Bayley and Melita Oden found that on several tests of concept mastery, the scores of gifted individuals ________________ (increased/decreased/remained unchanged) between ages 20 and 50.

4. Follow-up research by Bayley demonstrated a general ________________ (increase/decrease) in intellectual functioning from childhood through adulthood. This developmental trend was true for ________________ (most/a few) of the subtests of the Wechsler Adult Intelligence Scale. Performance on two of the ten subtests, ________________ and ________________ ________________, violated this trend by showing a(n) ________________ (increase/decline) in test scores.

5. Bayley's study is an example of a ________________ (cross-sectional/longitudinal) research design. Earlier studies relied on ________________ (cross-sectional/longitudinal) research designs.

Briefly explain why cross-sectional research can sometimes yield a misleading picture of adult development.

6. One of the first researchers to recognize the importance of ________________ effects on cross-sectional research was ________________. This researcher found that on five "primary mental abilities," including ________________ ________________, ________________ ________________, ________________, ________________ ________________, and ________________ ________________, most people improved throughout most of adulthood.

7. Cite two reasons that longitudinal findings may be misleading.

   a. ________________

   b. ________________

8. While cross-sectional studies may ________________ (overestimate/underestimate) intellectual decline, longitudinal designs may ________________ (overestimate/underestimate) it.

9. Schaie developed a new research technique combining cross-sectional and longitudinal approaches, called ________________ research.

Briefly explain this type of research design.

10. Schaie's research on adult changes in intelligence reveals the following sequence (write an age period on each line): gain until the ________________ are reached; stability until the ________________ are reached; average decline may begin for some as early as the ________________; but this decline is typically of small magnitude until the ________________ are reached.

11. Schaie also found that more recently born cohorts ________________ (did/did not) outperform earlier cohorts when they were the same age.

12. Schaie also found that recent cohorts were better than earlier cohorts at ________________ skills, but worse at ________________ skills. This was especially true when adults born at midcentury, when ________________ ________________ was on the rise, were compared with those born at the beginning of the century, when ________________ ________________ was stressed.

13. Cite the three general conclusions about intellectual changes during adulthood that have emerged from the work of Schaie and others.

   a. ________________

   b. ________________

   c. ________________

Fluid and Crystallized Intelligence (pp. 543–547)

14. According to Cattell and, later, Horn, ______________ intelligence is flexible reasoning used to draw inferences and understand relations between concepts. This type of intelligence is also made up of basic mental abilities, including ______________ ______________, ______________ ______________, and ______________ ______________.

15. The accumulation of facts, information, and knowledge that comes with education and experience with a particular culture is referred to as ______________ intelligence.

16. Originally, Cattell and Horn thought ______________ intelligence was primarily genetic, and ______________ intelligence, primarily learned.

17. According to Horn's research, during adulthood ______________ intelligence declines markedly, although this decline is temporarily disguised by a(n) ______________ (increase/decrease) in ______________ intelligence.

18. Horn's research also reveals that ______________ intelligence continues to expand throughout most of adulthood.

19. Horn believes that ______________ intelligence declines during adulthood because of the accumulation of damage to ______________ ______________ that results from ______________, ______________, and the biological changes associated with age. Because its underlying knowledge structures are overlapping and interconnected, ______________ intelligence is less affected by these changes.

20. Researchers have also found that whereas individual differences in ______________ intelligence remain fairly constant over time, individual differences in ______________ intelligence increase with age.

21. Speed of thinking is a critical element of ______________ intelligence. Some specialists in adult development consider this an inappropriate aspect of intelligence testing because ______________ ______________.

22. Although some researchers argue that slower thinking is less ______________ and results in ______________ thinking, others argue that speed of thinking should not be confused with the quality of thought.

23. List two points of agreement between Horn and Schaie regarding adult intellectual change.

    a. ______________

    b. ______________

Intelligence Reconsidered (pp. 547–552)

24. Historically, psychologists have thought of intelligence as ______________ (a single entity/several distinct abilities).

25. A leading theoretician, ______________, argued that there is such a thing as general intelligence, which he called ______________.

26. Recent research reveals that adult intellectual competence is ______________. A leading proponent of this view is ______________.

27. Horn has suggested that intelligence may consist of as many as ______________ distinct elements, while ______________ believes that there are seven autonomous intelligences. Evidence from brain-damaged people ______________ (supports/does not support) the multidimensional view of intelligence.

28. The value placed on different dimensions of intellectual ability ______________ (varies/does not vary) from culture to culture.

29. The theorist who has proposed that intelligence is composed of three distinct parts is ______________. The ______________

part consists of mental processes fostering efficient learning, remembering, and thinking. The ________________ part enables the person to adapt his or her abilities to environmental demands. The ________________ part concerns the extent to which intellectual functions are applied to situations that are familiar or novel in the person's personal history.

30. Some theorists, such as Gardner, Sternberg, Schaie, and Horn, believe that the multiple dimensions of intelligence are ________________ organized. Others believe that one's ________________, ________________, and ________________-________________ lead an adult to develop intellectual competencies in specific types of thinking and not in others.

31. The multiple dimensions of intelligence can follow different trajectories with age; that is, they are ________________. Some, such as ________________-________________, generally fall steadily, while others, such as ________________, generally rise. Other abilities, such as ________________ ________________, might rise, fall, and rise again, depending on how much they are used in daily life.

32. Genetic makeup, individual experiences, and differences in physical and mental health contribute to the ________________ variation that is the basis for the variety of patterns of adult cognitive development.

33. Intellectual abilities are characterized by their ________________, which means that abilities can become enhanced or diminished, depending on how, when, and why a person uses them.

34. Intellectual plasticity ________________ (declines/does not decline) with increasing age.

Practical Intelligence (pp. 552–554)

35. Contextual theorists of adult development, such as ________________ and ________________, believe that assessments of adult intelligence should encompass the intellectual skills used in everyday problem solving. This new approach is called the study of ________________ intelligence.

36. Some measures of practical intelligence focus on behaviors involved in ________________ ________________.

Cite three ways in which practical problems differ from traditional adult intelligence measures.

a. ________________

b. ________________

c. ________________

37. Practical intelligence ________________ (increases/decreases/is stable) throughout most of the adult years. This type of intelligence ________________ (does/does not) draw upon the skills of fluid and crystallized intelligence.

Expertise (pp. 554–556)

38. Some developmentalists believe that as we age, we develop specialized competencies, or ________________, in activities that are important to us.

39. There are several differences between experts and novices. First, novices tend to rely more on ________________ (formal/informal) procedures and rules to guide them, whereas experts are more ________________ and less ________________ in their performance.

40. Second, many elements of expert performance become ________________, almost instinctive, which enables experts to process information more quickly and efficiently.

41. A third difference is that ________________ ________________.

42. A final difference is that experts are more ________________.

43. A conclusion of this chapter is that in middle adulthood ________________

______________ are more critical in determining the course of cognitive development than is age alone.

Progress Test 1

Multiple-Choice Questions

Circle your answers to the following questions and check them with the answers on page 318. If your answer is incorrect, read the explanation for why it is incorrect and then consult the appropriate pages of the text (in parentheses following the correct answer).

1. Most of the evidence for an age-related decline in intelligence came from:
   a. cross-sectional research.
   b. longitudinal research.
   c. sequential research.
   d. random sampling.

2. The major flaw in cross-sectional research is the virtual impossibility of:
   a. selecting subjects who are similar in every aspect except age.
   b. tracking all subjects over a number of years.
   c. finding volunteers with high IQs.
   d. testing concept mastery.

3. Because of the limitations of other research methods, K. Warner Schaie developed a new research design based on:
   a. observer-participant methods.
   b. in-depth questionnaires.
   c. personal interviews.
   d. both cross-sectional and longitudinal methods.

4. Differences in cognitive development attributable to historical or generational circumstances are called:
   a. plasticity.
   b. fluid intelligence.
   c. cohort effects.
   d. crystallized intelligence.

5. Which of the following is most likely to *decrease* with age?
   a. vocabulary
   b. accumulated facts
   c. speed of thinking
   d. practical intelligence

6. The basic mental abilities that go into learning and understanding any subject have been classified as:
   a. crystallized intelligence.
   b. plastic intelligence.
   c. fluid intelligence.
   d. rote memory.

7. Raymond Cattell and John Horn believe that intelligence is made up of fluid intelligence, which ______________ during adulthood, and crystallized intelligence, which ______________.
   a. remains stable; declines
   b. declines; remains stable
   c. increases; declines
   d. declines; increases

8. Charles Spearman argued for the existence of a single general intelligence factor, which he referred to as:
   a. "g."
   b. practical intelligence.
   c. componential intelligence.
   d. contextual intelligence.

9. The plasticity of adult intellectual abilities refers primarily to the effects of:
   a. fluid intelligence.
   b. experience.
   c. genetic inheritance.
   d. crystallized intelligence.

10. The shift from conscious, deliberate processing of information to a more unconscious, effortless performance is referred to as:
    a. automaticity.
    b. subliminal execution.
    c. plasticity.
    d. encoding.

11. Concerning expertise, which of the following is true?
    a. In performing tasks, experts tend to be more set in their ways, preferring to use strategies that have worked in the past.
    b. The reasoning of experts is usually more formal, disciplined, and stereotyped than that of the novice.
    c. In performing tasks, experts tend to be more flexible and to enjoy experimentation more than novices do.
    d. Experts often have difficulty adjusting to situations that are exceptions to the rule.

12. Because each person is genetically unique and has unique life experiences, ______ during middle adulthood is(are) more important in determining intellectual development than ______.
   a. cohort differences; interindividual variation
   b. interindividual variation; cohort differences
   c. nature; nurture
   d. interindividual variation; age

13. Which of the following describes the results of Nancy Bayley's follow-up study of members of the Berkeley Growth Study?
   a. Most subjects reached a plateau in intellectual functioning at age 21.
   b. The typical person at age 36 improved on two of ten subtests of the Wechsler Adult Intelligence Scale: Picture Completion and Arithmetic.
   c. The typical person at age 36 was still improving on the most important subtests of the intelligence scale.
   d. No conclusions could be reached because the sample of subjects was not representative.

14. Which of the following is *not* one of the general conclusions of research about intellectual changes during adulthood?
   a. In general, most intellectual abilities increase or remain stable throughout early and middle adulthood until the 60s.
   b. Cohort differences have a powerful influence on intellectual differences in adulthood.
   c. Intellectual functioning is affected by educational background, health, and mental well-being.
   d. Intelligence becomes less specialized with increasing age.

15. The psychologist who has proposed that intelligence is composed of componential, contextual, and experiential components is:
   a. Charles Spearman.
   b. Howard Gardner.
   c. Robert Sternberg.
   d. K. Warner Schaie.

True or False Items

Write *true* or *false* on the line in front of each statement.

______ 1. K. Warner Schaie believes that, throughout life, intelligence is molded by life experiences, health, education, and other factors.

______ 2. John Horn maintains that intellectual decline with age is inevitable.

______ 3. To date, cross-sectional research has shown a gradual increase in intellectual ability.

______ 4. Longitudinal research usually shows that intelligence in most abilities increases throughout early and middle adulthood.

______ 5. By age 60, most people decline in even the most basic cognitive abilities.

______ 6. Experts agree that speed of thinking is the single best measure of cognitive ability.

______ 7. All people reach an intellectual peak in adolescence.

______ 8. Historically, most psychologists have considered intelligence to be comprised of several distinct abilities.

______ 9. Today, most researchers studying cognitive abilities believe that intelligence is multidimensional.

______ 10. Compared to novices, experts tend to be more intuitive and less stereotyped in their work performance.

Progress Test 2

Progress Test 2 should be completed during a final chapter review. Answer the following questions after you thoroughly understand the correct answers for the Chapter Review and Progress Test 1.

Multiple-Choice Questions

1. The debate over the status of adult intelligence focuses on the question of its inevitable decline and on:
   a. pharmacological deterrents to that decline.
   b. the accompanying decline in moral reasoning.
   c. its possible continuing growth.
   d. the validity of longitudinal versus personal-observation research.

2. Which of the following generational differences emerged in Schaie's studies of intelligence?
   a. Recent cohorts of young adults were better at math than those who were young in previous decades.
   b. Recent cohorts of young adults were better at reasoning ability, but worse at math, than those who were young in previous decades.

c. Recent cohorts of young adults were better at all intellectual abilities than those who were young in previous decades.
d. Recent cohorts of young adults were worse at all intellectual abilities than those who were young in previous decades.

3. The accumulation of facts that comes about with education and experience has been classified as:
a. crystallized intelligence.
b. plastic intelligence.
c. fluid intelligence.
d. rote memory.

4. According to the text, the current view of intelligence recognizes all of the following characteristics *except*:
a. multidimensionality.
b. plasticity.
c. interindividual variation.
d. "g."

5. Thinking that is more intuitive, flexible, specialized, and automatic is characteristic of:
a. fluid intelligence.
b. crystallized intelligence.
c. expertise.
d. plasticity.

6. The ________________ nature of intelligence was attested to by Howard Gardner, who proposed the existence of seven different intelligences.
a. multidirectional c. plastic
b. multidimensional d. practical

7. The ________________ nature of intelligence refers to the fact that each intellectual ability may rise, fall, or remain stable, according to its own unique developmental trajectory.
a. multidirectional c. plastic
b. multidimensional d. practical

8. At the present stage of research into adult cognition, which of the following statements has the most research support?
a. Intellectual abilities inevitably decline from adolescence onward.
b. Moderate increases in adult intelligence occur through middle adulthood.
c. Some 90 percent of adults tested in cross-sectional studies show no decline in intellectual abilities until age 40.
d. Intelligence becomes crystallized for most adults between ages 32 and 41.

9. Research on expertise indicates that during adulthood, intelligence:
a. increases in most primary mental abilities.
b. increases in specific areas of interest to the person.
c. increases only in those areas associated with the individual's career.
d. shows a uniform decline in all areas.

10. Horn's research indicates that during adulthood, declines occur in:
a. crystallized intelligence.
b. fluid intelligence.
c. both crystallized and fluid intelligence.
d. neither crystallized nor fluid intelligence.

11. Fluid intelligence is based on all of the following *except*:
a. short-term memory. c. speed of thinking.
b. abstract thinking. d. general knowledge.

12. In recent years, researchers are more likely than before to consider intelligence as:
a. a single entity.
b. primarily determined by heredity.
c. entirely the product of learning.
d. made up of several abilities.

13. One of the drawbacks of longitudinal studies of intelligence is that:
a. they are especially prone to the distortion of cohort effects.
b. people who are retested may show improved performance as a result of practice.
c. the biases of the experimenter are more likely to distort the results than is true of other research methods.
d. all of the above are true.

14. To a developmentalist, an *expert* is a person who:
a. is extraordinarily gifted at a particular task.
b. is significantly better at a task than people who have not put time and effort into performing that task.
c. scores at the ninetieth percentile or better on a test of achievement.
d. is none of the above.

15. One reason for the variety in patterns in adult intelligence is that during adulthood:
a. intelligence is fairly stable in some areas.
b. intelligence increases in some areas.
c. intelligence decreases in some areas.
d. people develop specialized competencies in activities that are personally meaningful.

Matching Items

Match each definition or description with its corresponding term.

Terms

_______ 1. fluid intelligence
_______ 2. crystallized intelligence
_______ 3. multidimensional
_______ 4. multidirectional
_______ 5. interindividual variation
_______ 6. plasticity
_______ 7. practical intelligence
_______ 8. expertise

Definitions or Descriptions

a. intellectual skills used in everyday problem solving
b. individual differences caused by heredity and experience
c. intelligence is made up of several different abilities
d. specialized competence
e. flexible reasoning used to draw inferences
f. intellectual flexibility
g. cognitive abilities can follow different trajectories with age
h. the accumulation of facts, information, and knowledge

Challenge Test

Answer these questions the day before an exam as a final check on your understanding of the chapter's terms and concepts.

1. Why do many experts believe that the most commonly used IQ tests are biased against older adults?

a. Most tests emphasize speed of thinking, and adults tend to be slower at almost everything.
b. Many adults are at a disadvantage on tests simply because they rarely use the skills such tests measure.
c. The cognitive abilities of adults often grow in areas that IQ tests do not measure.
d. For all of the above reasons, IQ tests are biased against older adults.

2. In Sternberg's theory, which part of intelligence is most similar to the abilities comprising fluid intelligence?

a. componential
b. contextual
c. experiential
d. none of the above are part of Sternberg's theory.

3. Concerning the acquisition of fluid and crystallized intelligence, most experts agree that:

a. both fluid and crystallized intelligence are primarily determined by heredity.
b. both fluid and crystallized intelligence are primarily acquired through learning.
c. fluid intelligence is primarily genetic, whereas crystallized intelligence is primarily learned.
d. the nature-nurture distinction is invalid.

4. Regarding the multidimensionality of intelligence, which of the following statements has the most empirical support?

a. Most intellectual abilities remain stable with age.
b. Most intellectual abilities decline with age.
c. Each intellectual ability may increase, decrease, or remain stable with age.
d. There is a single mental capacity underlying all intellectual skills, and this capacity may rise or fall with age.

5. Compared to novice chess players, chess experts:

a. have superior long-term memory.
b. have superior memory for all types of material.
c. make less of an attempt to memorize the positions of chess pieces.
d. are characterized by all of the above.

6. A psychologist has found that the mathematical ability of adults born in the 1920s is significantly different from that of those born in the 1950s. She suspects that this difference is a reflection of the different educational emphases of the two historical periods. This is an example of:

a. longitudinal research. **c.** a cohort effect.
b. sequential research. **d.** all of the above.

7. Sharetta knows more about her field of specialization now at age 45 than she did at age 35. This increase is most likely due to:
   a. an increase in crystallized intelligence.
   b. an increase in fluid intelligence.
   c. increases in both fluid and crystallized intelligence.
   d. a cohort difference.

8. A contemporary developmental psychologist is most likely to *disagree* with the statement that:
   a. many people show increases in intelligence during middle adulthood.
   b. for many behaviors, the responses of older adults are slower than those of younger adults.
   c. intelligence peaks during adolescence and declines thereafter.
   d. intelligence is multidimensional and multidirectional.

9. Regarding their accuracy in measuring adult intellectual decline, cross-sectional research is to longitudinal research as ________________ is to ________________.
   a. underestimate; overestimate
   b. overestimate; underestimate
   c. accurate; inaccurate
   d. inaccurate; accurate

10. Dr. Hatfield wants to analyze the possible effects of retesting, cohort differences, and aging on adult changes in intelligence. Which research method should she use?
    a. cross-sectional
    b. longitudinal
    c. sequential
    d. case study

11. Which researcher would most likely agree with the following statement? "Fluid intelligence declines during adulthood because of the gradual accumulation of irreversible damage to brain structures that results from disease, injury, and aging."
    a. K. Warner Schaie
    b. Raymond Cattell
    c. John Horn
    d. Howard Gardner

12. When Merle retired from teaching, he had great difficulty adjusting to the changes in his lifestyle. Robert Sternberg would probably say that Merle was somewhat lacking in which aspect of his intelligence?
    a. componential
    b. contextual
    c. experiential
    d. plasticity

13. Following her presentation on "Contemporary Thinking About Adult Intelligence," Sonia is asked to summarize the current state of the debate over the course of intelligence throughout adulthood. Her response is:
    a. "Intelligence increases throughout most of adulthood."
    b. "Following its peak in adolescence, intelligence declines throughout adulthood."
    c. "The recognition of adult cognition as multidimensional, multidirectional, variable, and plastic has defused this debate."
    d. "The issue remains controversial; some researchers maintain that intelligence increases during adulthood, while others contend that it decreases."

14. Compared to her 20-year-old daughter, 40-year-old Lynda is likely to perform better on measures of what type of intelligence?
    a. fluid
    b. practical
    c. componential
    d. none of the above

15. Most developmentalists would agree with which of the following statements?
    a. Faster thinking is deeper thinking.
    b. Slower thinking is deeper thinking.
    c. Speed of thinking is a critical element of fluid intelligence.
    d. Speed of thinking is a critical element of crystallized intelligence.

Key Terms

Using your own words, write a brief definition or explanation of each of the following terms on a separate piece of paper.

1. fluid intelligence
2. crystallized intelligence
3. multidimensional
4. multidirectional
5. interindividual variation
6. plasticity
7. practical intelligence
8. expertise

ANSWERS

CHAPTER REVIEW

1. John Horn; K. Warner Schaie; health, education, and life experiences
2. adolescence; Alpha
3. increased
4. increase; most; Arithmetic; Picture Completion; decline
5. longitudinal; cross-sectional

Cross-sectional research may be misleading not only because it is impossible to select adults who are similar to each other in every important aspect except age, but also because each age group has its own unique history of life experiences.

6. cohort; Schaie; verbal comprehension; spatial visualization; reasoning; mathematical ability; word fluency
7. a. People who are retested several times may improve their performance simply as a result of practice.
   b. It is difficult to retain adults in a large sample over long periods of time.
8. overestimate; underestimate
9. sequential

In this approach, each time the original group of subjects is retested a new group is added and tested at each age interval.

10. late 30s or early 40s; mid 50s or early 60s; mid 50s; 70s
11. did
12. reasoning; number; progressive education; rote learning
13. a. In general, most intellectual abilities increase or remain stable throughout early and middle adulthood until the decade of the 60s.
    b. Cohort differences have a powerful influence on intellectual differences in adulthood.
    c. Intellectual functioning is affected by educational background, current health status, and mental well-being.
14. fluid; inductive reasoning; abstract thinking; speed of processing
15. crystallized
16. fluid; crystallized
17. fluid; increase; crystallized
18. crystallized
19. fluid; brain structures; disease; injury; crystallized
20. fluid; crystallized
21. fluid; older adults are slower than younger adults at almost everything
22. efficient; simpler (or shallower)
23. a. Intelligence does not peak in adolescence and then declines.
    b. Intelligence becomes more individualized with increasing age, reflecting each person's unique background and current experiences.
24. a single entity
25. Charles Spearman; "g"
26. multidimensional; Paul Baltes
27. ten; Howard Gardner; supports
28. varies
29. Robert Sternberg; componential; contextual; experiential
30. innately; interests; experiences; work-related skills
31. multidirectional; short-term memory; vocabulary; mathematical reasoning
32. interindividual
33. plasticity
34. declines
35. Roger Dixon; Stephen Cici; practical
36. domestic problem solving, career decision making, consumer behavior, and conflict resolution
    a. Because these challenges entail everyday reasoning, adults are often more intrinsically motivated to master them.
    b. They are more likely to involve skills that have been strengthened and improved through regular use.
    c. Unlike conventional intelligence problems, which allow for a single correct answer, solutions to these problems can be evaluated in a number of different ways.
37. increases; does
38. expertise
39. formal; intuitive; stereotyped
40. automatic
41. experts have better strategies, and more of them, for accomplishing a particular task
42. flexible (or creative)
43. individual differences

PROGRESS TEST 1

Multiple-Choice Questions

1. **a.** is the answer. (p. 541)
   b. Although results from this type of research may also be misleading, longitudinal studies often demonstrate age-related *increases* in intelligence.
   c. Sequential research is the technique devised by K. Warner Schaie that combines the strengths of the cross-sectional and longitudinal methods.
   d. Random sampling refers to the selection of subjects for a research study.
2. **a.** is the answer. (p. 541)
   b. This is a problem in longitudinal research.
   c. & d. Neither of these are particularly troublesome in cross-sectional research.
3. **d.** is the answer. (p. 542)
   a., b., & c. Sequential research as described in this chapter is based on *objective* intelligence testing.
4. **c.** is the answer. (p. 541)
   a. Plasticity refers to the flexible nature of intelligence.
   b. Fluid intelligence is made up of those basic mental abilities required for understanding any subject matter.
   d. Crystallized intelligence is the accumulation of facts and knowledge that comes with education and experience.
5. **c.** is the answer. (p. 545)
   a., b., & d. These often increase with age.
6. **c.** is the answer. (p. 543)
   a. Crystallized intelligence is the accumulation of facts and knowledge that comes with education and experience.
   b. Although intelligence is characterized by plasticity, "plastic intelligence" is not discussed as a specific type of intelligence.
   d. Rote memory is memory that is based on the conscious repetition of to-be-remembered information.
7. **d.** is the answer. (pp. 543–544)
8. **a.** is the answer. (p. 547)
   b. Practical intelligence refers to the intellectual skills used in everyday problem solving.
   c. & d. These are two aspects of intelligence identified in Robert Sternberg's theory.
9. **b.** is the answer. Life experiences give intelligence its flexibility and account for the variety of patterns of adult cognitive development. (p. 550)
10. **a.** is the answer. (p. 555)
    b. This was not discussed in the chapter.
    c. Plasticity refers to the flexible nature of intelligence.
    d. Encoding refers to the placing of information into memory.
11. **c.** is the answer. (p. 555)
    a., b., & d. These are more typical of *novices* than experts.
12. **d.** is the answer. (pp. 549–550)
    a. & b. Cohort differences are a source of interindividual variation.
    c. The text does not discuss the relative impact of nature and nurture on intelligence during adulthood.
13. **c.** is the answer. (p. 541)
    b. In fact, these were the only two subtests on which performance did *not* improve.
    d. No such criticism was made of Bayley's study.
14. **d.** is the answer. In fact, intelligence often becomes *more specialized* with age. (p. 543)
15. **c.** is the answer. (p. 548)
    a. Charles Spearman proposed the existence of an underlying general intelligence, which he called "g."
    b. Howard Gardner proposed that intelligence consists of seven autonomous abilities.
    d. K. Warner Schaie was one of the first researchers to recognize the potentially distorting cohort effects on cross-sectional research.

True or False Items

1. T (p. 540)
2. T (p. 544)
3. F Cross-sectional research shows a decline in intellectual ability. (p. 541)
4. T (p. 542)
5. F Many adults show intellectual improvement over most of adulthood, with no decline, even by age 60. (p. 547)
6. F No such agreement exists. Some experts argue that speed of thinking should not be confused with quality of thinking. Others feel that speed of thinking affects the efficiency of cognitive processing and, therefore, the quality of thinking. (p. 545)
7. F There is agreement that intelligence does *not* peak in adolescence and decline thereafter. (p. 547)

8. F Historically, psychologists have conceived of intelligence as a single entity. (p. 547)
9. T (p. 548)
10. T (p. 555)

PROGRESS TEST 2

Multiple-Choice Questions

1. **c.** is the answer. (p. 543)
2. **b.** is the answer. (p. 542)
3. **a.** is the answer. (p. 544)
   b. Although intelligence is characterized by plasticity, "plastic intelligence" is not discussed as a specific type of intelligence.
   c. Fluid intelligence consists of the basic abilities that go into the understanding of any subject.
   d. Rote memory is based on the conscious repetition of to-be-remembered information.
4. **d.** is the answer. This is Charles Spearman's term for his idea of a general intelligence, in which intelligence is a single entity. (p. 547)
5. **c.** is the answer. (p. 554)
6. **b.** is the answer. (p. 548)
7. **a.** is the answer. (p. 549)
   b. This refers to the fact that intelligence consists of multiple abilities.
   c. This characteristic suggests that intelligence can be molded in many ways.
   d. Practical intelligence refers to the skills used in everyday problem solving.
8. **b.** is the answer. This is especially true for specialized skills that are personally relevant and meaningful. (p. 547)
   a. There is agreement that intelligence does *not* peak during adolescence.
   c. Cross-sectional research usually provides evidence of *declining* ability throughout adulthood.
   d. Crystallized intelligence refers to the accumulation of knowledge with experience; intelligence does not "crystallize" at any specific age.
9. **b.** is the answer. (p. 554)
10. **b.** is the answer. (p. 544)
    a., c., & d. Crystallized intelligence typically *increases* during adulthood.
11. **d.** is the answer. This is an aspect of crystallized intelligence. (p. 544)
12. **d.** is the answer. (p. 548)
    a. Contemporary researchers emphasize the multidimensional nature of intelligence.
    b. & c. Contemporary researchers see intelligence as the product of both heredity and learning.
13. **b.** is the answer. (p. 542)
    a. This is a drawback of cross-sectional research.
    c. Longitudinal studies are no more sensitive to experimenter bias than other research methods.
14. **b.** is the answer. (p. 554)
15. **d.** is the answer. (p. 554)

Matching Items

1. e (p. 543)	5. b (p. 549)
2. h (p. 544)	6. f (p. 550)
3. c (p. 548)	7. a (p. 552)
4. g (p. 549)	8. d (p. 554)

CHALLENGE TEST

1. **d.** is the answer. (pp. 545, 552–553)
2. **a.** is the answer. This part consists of mental processes fostering efficient learning, remembering, and thinking. (p. 548)
   b. This part enables the person to accommodate successfully to changes in the environment.
   c. This part concerns the extent to which intellectual functions are applied to situations that are familiar or novel in a person's history.
3. **d.** is the answer. This is so in part because the acquisition of crystallized intelligence is affected by the quality of fluid intelligence. (p. 544)
4. **c.** is the answer. (p. 549)
5. **c.** is the answer. (p. 555)
6. **c.** is the answer. (p. 541)
   a. & b. From the information given, it is impossible to determine which research method the psychologist used.
7. **a.** is the answer. (p. 544)
   b. & c. According to Horn's research, fluid intelligence declines markedly during adulthood.
   d. Cohort effects refer to generational differences in life experiences.
8. **c.** is the answer. (p. 547)
9. **b.** is the answer. (p. 542)
   c. & d. Both cross-sectional and longitudinal research are potentially misleading.
10. **c.** is the answer. (p. 542)
    a. & b. Schaie developed the sequential research method to overcome the drawbacks of the cross-sectional and longitudinal methods, which were

susceptible to cohort and retesting effects, respectively.

d. A case study focuses on a single subject and therefore could provide no information on cohort effects.

11. c. is the answer. (p. 544)

a. Schaie disagrees with the view that intelligence inevitably declines during adulthood.

b. & d. Cattell and Gardner were early proponents of the view that intelligence is multidimensional in nature. The text does not discuss their viewpoints on age-related changes in intelligence.

12. b. is the answer. Contextual intelligence enables the person to accommodate successfully to changes in the environment, such as those accompanying retirement. (p. 548)

a. This part of intelligence consists of mental processes that foster efficient learning, remembering, and thinking.

c. This part of intelligence concerns the extent to which intellectual functions are applied to situations that are familiar or novel in a person's history.

d. Plasticity refers to the flexible nature of intelligence; it is not an aspect of Sternberg's theory.

13. c. is the answer. (pp. 548–550)

14. b. is the answer. (p. 553)

15. c. is the answer. (pp. 544–545)

KEY TERMS

1. **Fluid intelligence** is made up of those basic mental abilities—inductive reasoning, abstract thinking, speed of processing, and the like—required for understanding any subject matter. (p. 543)
2. **Crystallized intelligence** is the accumulation of facts, information, and knowledge that comes with education and experience within a particular culture. (p. 544)
3. Contemporary developmentalists recognize that adult intelligence is **multidimensional**, that is, it involves several distinct dimensions. (p. 548)
4. Intellectual abilities are **multidirectional** in that they can rise, fall, or rise, fall, and rise again as the individual gets older. (p. 549)
5. **Interindividual variation** refers to individual differences in heredity, experience, and health that influence intelligence. (p. 549)
6. Intelligence is characterized by **plasticity**, meaning that abilities can become enhanced or diminished, depending on how, when, and why a person uses them. (p. 550)
7. A new approach to adult intelligence—the study of **practical intelligence**—focuses on the intellectual skills used in everyday problem solving. (p. 552)
8. A hallmark of adulthood is the development of **expertise**, or specialized competencies, in activities that are personally meaningful to us. (p. 554)

CHAPTER 22

Middle Adulthood: Psychosocial Development

Chapter Overview

Chapter 22 is concerned with midlife, commonly believed to be a time of crisis and transition, when self-doubt, reevaluation of career goals, changes in family responsibilities, and a growing awareness of one's mortality lead to turmoil. The chapter first examines the research on this "midlife crisis," showing that although middle adulthood may have its share of pressures and stress, a crisis is not inevitable.

The next section depicts the changing dynamics between middle-aged adults and their adult children and aging parents, showing why the various demands of the younger and older generations have led the middle-aged to be called the "sandwich generation." Changes in the marital relationship are also examined.

The chapter next explores the changing dynamics of the career path in middle age, focusing on the typical shifts of interest that occur during the career plateau and describing two common worker problems, burn-out and alienation.

The last section of the chapter examines the question of whether there is stability of personality throughout adulthood, identifying five basic clusters of personality traits that remain fairly stable throughout adulthood. One personality trend that does occur during middle age, as gender roles become less rigid, is the tendency of both sexes to move toward androgyny.

NOTE: Answer guidelines for all Chapter 22 questions begin on page 332.

Guided Study

The text chapter should be studied one section at a time. Before you read, preview each section by skimming it, noting headings and boldface items. Then read the appropriate section objectives from the following outline. Keep these objectives in mind and, as you read the chapter section, search for the information that will enable you to meet each objective. Once you have finished a section, write out answers for its objectives.

Midlife: Crisis, Shift, or Transition? (pp. 560–565)

1. Discuss the concept of the midlife crisis and evaluate research evidence concerning its occurrence.

2. Discuss the impact of gender, cohort, and context on the experience of the midlife crisis.

Family Dynamics in Middle Adulthood (pp. 565–571)

3. Characterize the relationship between middle-aged adults and the younger and older generations and explain why middle-aged adults are considered the "sandwich generation."

4. Discuss how and why marital relationships tend to change during middle adulthood.

Career Dynamics in Middle Adulthood (pp. 571–575)

5. Discuss the shift in career dynamics that typically occurs during middle age.

6. Explain why the current cohort of workers has several adjustment problems not experienced by earlier cohorts.

7. (A Closer Look) Describe two job-related problems that may occur during midlife, who is most likely to experience them, and how they can be prevented.

Personality Throughout Adulthood (pp. 576–579)

8. Describe the "Big Five" personality-trait clusters and discuss reasons for their relative stability during adulthood.

9. Identify two age-related trends in personality, explaining the tendency of both men and women to become more androgynous during middle age.

Chapter Review

When you have finished reading the chapter, work through the material that follows to review it. Complete the sentences and answer the questions. As you proceed, evaluate your performance for each section by consulting the answers on page 332. Do not continue with the next section until you understand each answer. If you need to, review or reread the appropriate section in the textbook before continuing.

Midlife: Crisis, Shift, or Transition? (pp. 560–565)

1. At about age ________________, people reach a point called ________________, which ushers in ________________

_______________, which lasts until about age _______________.

2. Midlife is popularly thought of as a period of _______________ and _______________ _______________.

List several sources of upheaval that may make middle age a troubling time.

3. At this time, many adults reassess the balance between _______________ and _______________.

4. The notion of a midlife crisis, which is _______________ (well accepted/controversial) in developmental psychology, receives the strongest evidence from researcher _______________.

5. Levinson found that at midlife, many of the men he studied made major changes in their lives, including _______________ _______________.

6. Other studies have found that many people, especially _______________ (women/men), experience some form of midlife distress, such as increased _______________ problems, greater life _______________, or specific complaints such as _______________ _______________ _______________.

7. Research studies have found that responses to midlife depended largely on the individual's _______________.

Those who were relatively _______________ and _______________ _______________ were more likely either to have a crisis or to cope effectively than those who were not. Those with _______________ _______________ were more likely either to blame others for their problems or to "punish" themselves _______________.

8. The notion that women inevitably experience a crisis in middle age _______________ (is fairly recent/has been around for a long time). Research on adult women has found _______________ (relatively little/significant) age-related stress in middle age.

9. Contextual factors, such as socioeconomic status and cohort differences, _______________ (are/are not) important in the incidence of midlife crisis.

10. A survey of American women in the 1950s found that, as women grew older, self-esteem _______________ (increased/decreased) and the incidence of psychological problems _______________ (increased/decreased). Twenty years later, women responding to the same questions _______________ (continued to feel/no longer felt) lower self-esteem with age.

Give one possible reason that the earlier survey yielded this pattern of results.

11. Beginning about _______________, American women started to enter or reenter colleges and the labor market in greater numbers. Today, women in middle age _______________ (have/do not have) work opportunities and therefore _______________ (do/do not) suffer a loss of self-esteem.

12. Most middle-aged women who have both career and family believe that their _______________ (career/family) roles are the more important ones. If midlife difficulties occur in contemporary women, they are more likely to be experienced by _______________ or _______________.

13. In the case of American men, historical changes may have worked to make their midlife years ________________ (more difficult/easier).

Briefly explain why this is so.

14. The notion of a universal midlife crisis was derived from research on a particular cohort: ________________________________.

15. In traditional societies, where aging brings increased ________________ and ________________, the midlife crisis is very ________________ (common/rare).

State the circumstances under which a midlife crisis is likely to occur.

Family Dynamics in Middle Adulthood (pp. 565–571)

16. American families today are ________________ (more/less) likely to consist of several generations living under the same roof.

17. The relationship between most middle-aged adults and their parents tends to ________________ (improve/worsen) with time.

Briefly explain why this is especially true today.

18. The relationship between middle-aged parents and their children tends to improve with age, especially if the children ________________ ________________________________.

19. Fathers are particularly likely to find fault with their young adult ________________ (daughters/sons), especially about their lack of ________________. When parents complain about their adult daughters, it often relates to their ________________ ________________.

20. Because they provide information about new developments in the culture, young adult children often serve as a(n) ________________ ________________.

21. For many middle-aged adults, a new intergenerational tie is formed when their adult children ________________________________.

22. Throughout adulthood, ________________ (men/women) tend to focus more on family; that is, they tend to be ________________.

23. In recent years, the demands placed on middle-aged adults by the younger and older generations have ________________ (increased/decreased), so that this group is referred to as the ________________ ________________.

24. The number of young adults living with their parents has ________________ (increased/decreased) over the past twenty years. The circumstances of the younger cohort that contribute to this phenomenon include ________________ ________________________________.

Even when young adults have households of their own, the middle-aged generation is called on to provide support, particularly in ________________ aid and ________________ ________________.

25. Almost everyone, sometime before age ________________, is called on to provide care for a frail, elderly relative; ________________ (men/women) are more likely to be cast in this caregiver role.

26. Throughout adulthood, the family relationship most closely linked to personal happiness is ________________.

27. Serious trouble in a long-term marriage may lead to greater ________________, low ________________, and ________________.

28. After the first ________________ years or so, the longer a couple has been married, the ________________ (happier/unhappier) they tend to be.

List several possible reasons for this finding.

29. This does not mean that all marriages improve in middle age. Some relationships survived to middle age because ______________________________ ______________________________.
If middle age means that such a couple must spend more time together, their marriage may be sorely tested.

Career Dynamics in Middle Adulthood (pp. 571–575)

30. Job satisfaction generally ______________ (increases/decreases) during middle adulthood, especially if ______________ and ______________ continue to rise.

31. Compared to younger adults, middle-aged adults are ______________ (more/less) likely to experience role overload.

32. One possible source of stress for middle-aged workers is coming to grips with the ______________ phase of their work lives as they reach a career plateau. When they reach this phase, many workers feel pressure to ______________ their work goals.
Because such workers often begin to feel more satisfied with the balance between work and family, they become more helpful as ______________ to younger fellow workers.

33. A longitudinal study of managers at AT&T found that those workers who became more nurturant and communal during middle-age were those who ______________ (did/did not) advance in their careers at this time.

34. The average American worker spends ______________ (more/less/about the same amount of) time on the job than twenty years ago, and is earning ______________ (more/less) than expected. An additional source of stress for the current cohort of workers is the fear that they will be ______________ ______________ before they are ready.

35. In general, the longer one has a particular job, the ______________ (more/less) one tends to like it.

36. A worker who is experiencing ______________-______________ feels disillusioned and exhausted by the demands of working the same job for a long period of time.

37. Service and factory workers may experience ______________ if they begin to feel distant from the product being produced or service being offered.

38. Job-related stresses during middle age are most often experienced by those who have invested ______________ (a great deal/relatively little) of themselves in their work life. This pattern is typical of middle-aged men, and of those middle-aged women who do not have ______________ or a(n) ______________.

39. Because they manage a daily "mosaic of activities," the current cohort of married mothers may have a(n) ______________ (advantage/disadvantage) in resistance to job-related stress.

40. (A Closer Look) Although it can occur in almost any occupation, burn-out is particularly prevalent in ______________ professions such as ______________________________.

41. (A Closer Look) At the individual level, there are two remedies to burn-out.
a. ______________________________
b. ______________________________
A more encompassing remedy is to change the overall ______________ and ______________ patterns in an institution in which burn-out is likely.

42. (A Closer Look) Alienation is particularly likely to occur in ______________ ______________ or ______________ and when the relationship between management and worker is ______________.

43. (A Closer Look) Alienation makes many middle-aged men vulnerable to a variety of problems, including _______________ _______________.

List several techniques that may remedy alienation.

Personality Throughout Adulthood (pp. 576–579)

44. Perhaps the most crucial factor in determining whether middle adulthood is a time of continuity or crisis is the stability of the individual's _______________.

45. People tend to _______________ (overestimate/underestimate) the extent of their own personality changes in life.

46. Research has revealed five basic clusters of personality traits that remain quite stable throughout adulthood: _______________, _______________, _______________, _______________, and _______________.

47. These trait clusters are determined by many factors, including _______________, _______________, early _______________-_______________, and _______________.

48. By about age _______________, the five trait clusters are usually quite stable in an individual.

Explain why personality tends to stabilize at this age.

49. People who are high in _______________ tend to enact behaviors that alienate people around them.

50. List two age-related trends in personality.

a. _______________

b. _______________

51. A biosocial explanation for the trend toward androgyny at midlife is that it is the result of reduced levels of _______________ _______________. Another explanation comes from the psychoanalyst _______________, who believed that everyone has both a masculine and a feminine side; young people adhere to their prescribed gender roles, while middle-aged adults have time to explore their _______________ side.

52. According to David _______________, as adults get older the urgency of child-rearing—which he calls the _______________ _______________—lessens, allowing adults to develop broader gender roles.

Progress Test 1

Multiple-Choice Questions

Circle your answers to the following questions and check them with the answers on page 333. If your answer is incorrect, read the explanation for why it is incorrect and then consult the appropriate pages of the text (in parentheses following the correct answer).

1. For some people at about age 40, dissatisfaction with self, career, or family develops into a:
   a. basic personality change.
   b. midlife crisis.
   c. withdrawal from society.
   d. fear of success.

2. Which of the following midlife changes may explain why some individuals experience midlife distress?
   a. During midlife, people become more aware of their own mortality.
   b. Adults may have trouble adjusting to shifting parental roles during middle adulthood.
   c. Many adults reach a career plateau during middle age.
   d. All of the above changes are common during middle age and may lead to midlife distress.

3. Concerning the prevalence of midlife crises, which of the following statements has the *greatest* empirical support?
   a. Virtually all men, and most women, experience a midlife crisis.
   b. Virtually all men, and about 50 percent of women, experience a midlife crisis.

c. Women are more likely to experience a midlife crisis than are men.
d. Cohort and context effects, as well as the individual's personal style of coping with problems, are important factors in determining whether or not a midlife crisis occurs.

4. Which of the following groups is likely to experience the *greatest* difficulty adjusting to midlife?
   a. married women who have careers
   b. unmarried women who have careers
   c. working women who are married and have children
   d. unmarried women without children and married women who do not have jobs

5. The notion of a universal "midlife crisis" was derived from research on a:
   a. diverse group consisting of both men and women.
   b. cohort of mostly white, middle-class males.
   c. cohort consisting of mostly white, middle-class females.
   d. random sample of men of various ages and socioeconomic classes.

6. Middle-aged adults who are pressed on one side by adult children and on the other by aging parents are:
   a. said to be in the sandwich generation.
   b. especially likely to suffer burn-out.
   c. especially likely to suffer alienation.
   d. all of the above.

7. Which of the following statements *best* describes the relationship of most middle-aged adults to their aging parents?
   a. The relationship tends to improve with time.
   b. During middle adulthood, the relationship tends to deteriorate.
   c. For women, but not men, the relationship tends to improve with time.
   d. The relationship usually remains as good or as bad as it was in the past.

8. In families, women tend to function as the ______________, celebrating family achievements, keeping the family together, and staying in touch with distant relatives.
   a. sandwich generation
   b. nuclear bond
   c. intergenerational gatekeepers
   d. kinkeepers

9. When middle-aged parents complain about their adult children, fathers are especially likely to complain about their sons' ______________, and both complain about their daughters' ______________.
   a. love life; lack of achievement
   b. lack of achievement; love life
   c. appearance; family planning goals
   d. career goals; appearance

10. The number of young adults living with their parents has risen sharply over the past two decades because of which of the following circumstances?
   a. longer education
   b. lower salaries
   c. more single parenthood
   d. all of the above

11. When workers feel themselves to be "cogs in a machine" rather than contributing individuals, they often experience a state called:
   a. maintenance phase syndrome.
   b. burn-out.
   c. alienation.
   d. midlife crisis.

12. Concerning the degree of stability of personality traits, which of the following statements has the greatest research support?
   a. There is little evidence that personality traits remain stable during adulthood.
   b. In women, but less so in men, there is notable continuity in many personality characteristics.
   c. In men, but less so in women, there is notable continuity in many personality characteristics.
   d. In both men and women, there is notable continuity in many personality characteristics.

13. People who exhibit the personality dimension of ______________ tend to be outgoing, active, and assertive.
   a. extroversion
   b. agreeableness
   c. conscientiousness
   d. neuroticism

14. According to Jung's theory of personality:
   a. as men and women get older, gender roles become more distinct.
   b. to some extent, everyone has both a masculine and a feminine side to his or her character.
   c. the recent blurring of gender roles is making adjustment to midlife more difficult for both men and women.
   d. gender roles are most distinct during childhood.

15. Which of the following personality traits was *not* identified in the text as tending to remain stable throughout adulthood?
    a. neuroticism
    b. introversion
    c. openness
    d. conscientiousness

True or False Items

Write *true* or *false* on the line in front of each statement.

_______ 1. At least 75 percent of American men experience a significant midlife crisis between ages 38 and 43.

_______ 2. Better than age as a predictor of whether a midlife crisis will occur is an individual's personal style of coping with problems.

_______ 3. Less educated men who are also lower in socioeconomic status are more likely to manifest midlife stress psychosomatically than men higher in socioeconomic status.

_______ 4. In general, the historical changes of the past thirty years have made adjustment to midlife more difficult for women.

_______ 5. The extended family is typical of modern societies, such as those of twentieth-century North America.

_______ 6. During middle adulthood, workers are more likely to change jobs than was the case earlier in their careers.

_______ 7. (A Closer Look) Worker alienation is most likely to occur in helping professions such as medicine, teaching, and social work.

_______ 8. (A Closer Look) Worker burn-out is most common in assembly-line workers.

_______ 9. As adults mature, personality tends to improve.

_______ 10. There is no evidence that the stability of personality traits is influenced by heredity.

Progress Test 2

Progress Test 2 should be completed during a final chapter review. Answer the following questions after you thoroughly understand the correct answers for the Chapter Review and Progress Test 1.

Multiple-Choice Questions

1. Society recognizes *midlife* as occurring at about age ____________, and *middle age* as lasting until about age ____________.
    a. 45; 60
    b. 40; 60
    c. 45; 65
    d. 40; 65

2. The researcher offering the greatest evidence for a midlife crisis is:
    a. David Gutmann.
    b. Carl Jung.
    c. Daniel Levinson.
    d. Walter Mischel.

3. Which of the following statements *most* accurately describes the typical experiences of women during midlife?
    a. In response to the biological changes accompanying menopause, *most* women become depressed during midlife.
    b. Compared to previous generations, recent cohorts of women have experienced greater difficulty adjusting to midlife.
    c. Recent cohorts of women have tended to find midlife a more liberating experience than those of previous generations.
    d. Women's adjustment to midlife has not significantly changed over the past thirty years.

4. Which of the following statements *most* accurately summarizes the impact of recent cohort experiences on adjustment to middle age?
    a. Changed expectations of the male role have made men more susceptible to midlife stress.
    b. Changed expectations of the female role have made women more susceptible to midlife stress.
    c. The blurring of gender roles has made adjustment to midlife easier on men.
    d. Adjustment to midlife today is no different for men, but much different for women, than it was in previous generations.

5. Midlife crises are very rare in:
    a. traditional societies where aging brings increased power and respect.
    b. people living in fluid societies who reach middle-age at a time when sociocultural values shift.
    c. Western societies.
    d. relatively well-educated individuals.

6. Regarding the strength of the contemporary family bond, most developmentalists believe that:
    a. family links are considerably weaker in the typical contemporary American family than in earlier decades.
    b. family links are considerably weaker in the typical contemporary American family than in other cultures.
    c. both a. and b. are true.
    d. despite the fact that extended families are less common, family links are not weaker today.

7. Which of the following statements *best* describes the relationship of most middle-aged adults to their adult children?
   a. The relationship tends to improve with time.
   b. During middle adulthood, the relationship tends to deteriorate.
   c. For women, but not men, the relationship tends to improve with time.
   d. The relationship usually remains as good or as bad as it was in the past.

8. Which of the following statements explains why women are particularly likely to report an increase in marital satisfaction during middle adulthood?
   a. Marital satisfaction is closely tied to financial security, which tends to improve during middle adulthood.
   b. The successful launching of children is a source of great pride and happiness.
   c. There often is improvement in marital equity during this period.
   d. For all of the above reasons, women are likely to report improvement in their marriages during middle adulthood.

9. During middle age, most workers reach the ________________ phase of career development.
   a. burn-out
   b. alienation
   c. agency
   d. maintenance

10. One reason that many workers remain stuck in unsatisfying jobs is that:
    a. in our culture, the "one life, one career" imperative remains strong.
    b. employers prefer to hire older workers who already possess job-related skills.
    c. they are afraid of switching jobs.
    d. as retirement approaches, self-esteem is no longer tied to job-achievement in middle-aged workers.

11. (A Closer Look) When the pace and conditions of work totally deplete the worker of energy and enthusiasm, workers may experience a state called:
    a. maintenance phase syndrome.
    b. burn-out.
    c. alienation.
    d. midlife crisis.

12. Which of the following personality traits tends to remain stable throughout adulthood?
    a. agreeableness
    b. neuroticism
    c. openness
    d. all of the above

13. Concerning gender roles in later life, David Gutmann believes that:
    a. during middle and late adulthood, each sex moves toward a middle ground between the traditional gender roles.
    b. once the demands of the "parental imperative" are removed, traditional gender roles are quickly reestablished.
    c. gender roles are unrelated to life experiences.
    d. all of the above are true.

14. Of the following, which is a biosocial explanation offered in the text for the tendency of both men and women to move toward androgyny during middle age?
    a. Sex hormones decline during this period.
    b. Life experiences lead to a loosening of traditional gender roles.
    c. Both sexes have a "shadow side" to their personality that emerges at midlife.
    d. The physical changes of this time, including decreased functioning of most vital systems, lead to a reassessment of the purpose of life.

15. Concerning developmental changes in personality traits, the text notes that:
    a. there are no significant changes in personality as people move through middle adulthood.
    b. because women are more likely than men to experience an abrupt transition in their roles, their personalities are more likely to change.
    c. many people become less defensively neurotic, more open, and more androgynous during middle adulthood.
    d. b. and c. are true.

Matching Items

Match each definition or description with its corresponding term.

Terms

_______ 1. midlife crisis
_______ 2. kinkeepers
_______ 3. sandwich generation
_______ 4. burn-out
_______ 5. alienation
_______ 6. extroversion
_______ 7. agreeableness
_______ 8. conscientiousness
_______ 9. neuroticism
_______ 10. openness

Definitions or Descriptions

a. tendency to be outgoing
b. job-related disillusionment and exhaustion
c. tendency to be imaginative
d. provokes a radical reexamination of one's life
e. tendency to be organized
f. those who focus more on the family
g. tendency to be helpful
h. job-related feeling of being unconnected to the product being produced or service being rendered
i. those pressured by the needs of the older and younger generations
j. tendency to be moody

Challenge Test

Answer these questions the day before an exam as a final check on your understanding of the chapter's terms and concepts.

1. Forty-five-year-old Ken, who has been single-mindedly climbing the career ladder, suddenly feels that he has no more opportunity for advancement. He also feels that he has neglected his family and made many wrong decisions in charting his life's course. Ken's feelings are probably signs of:
   a. normal development during middle age.
   b. an unsuccessful passage through early adulthood.
   c. neuroticism.
   d. androgyny.

2. Compared to his more affluent and better-educated identical twin, 50-year-old Carl is more likely to:
   a. blame others for his midlife troubles.
   b. develop a psychosomatic reaction to his midlife troubles.
   c. cope effectively with his midlife troubles.
   d. do both a. and b.

3. It has long been assumed that, for biological reasons, I will inevitably experience a midlife crisis. Who am I?
   a. a middle-aged man
   b. a middle-aged woman
   c. a worker experiencing burn-out
   d. a worker experiencing alienation

4. Middle-aged Sonya is well educated, and has both a career and adult children. Compared to her mother, who was a homemaker exclusively, Sonya is likely to:
   a. experience greater midlife stress due to "role overload."
   b. have about the same reaction to middle age.
   c. feel lower self-esteem as she gets older.
   d. feel higher self-esteem as she gets older.

5. Recent decades have seen several sociocultural changes. Compare 40-year-old John's ability to cope with middle age with that of his father, who reached middle age in the 1950s.
   a. He will have more difficulty coping.
   b. He will have less difficulty coping.
   c. He will have about the same amount of difficulty coping.
   d. It is impossible to predict their respective abilities to cope.

6. The parents of Rebecca and her middle-aged twin, Josh, have become frail and unable to care for themselves. It is likely that:
   a. Rebecca and Josh will play equal roles as caregivers for their parents.
   b. Rebecca will play a larger role in caring for their parents.
   c. Josh will play a larger role in caring for their parents.
   d. If Rebecca and Josh are well educated, their parents will be placed in a professional caregiving facility.

7. Forty-year-old Rachel has never married. Compared to how her aunt, who also never married, felt at this age, how is Rachel likely to feel?
   a. more satisfied with her life
   b. less satisfied with her life
   c. about equally satisfied with life
   d. It is impossible to predict how she feels.

8. Ben and Nancy have been married for ten years. Although they are very happy, Nancy worries that with time this happiness will decrease. Research would suggest that Nancy's fear:
   a. may or may not be reasonable, depending on whether she and her husband are experiencing a midlife crisis.
   b. is reasonable, since marital discord is most common in couples who have been married ten years or more.
   c. is unfounded, since after the first ten years or so, the longer a couple has been married, the happier they tend to be.
   d. is probably a sign of neuroticism.

9. Fifty-year-old Jake and his wife Melinda have been married for twenty-five years and have three children. Except for discussions about the children, they have had minimal contact. What does this mean for their marriage in middle age?
   a. It will not change, because they are accustomed to this pattern of noncommunication.
   b. It will be sorely tested, since they must now spend more time together.
   c. It will improve, because their time alone will allow them to renew their relationship.
   d. It will automatically end in divorce.

10. Fifty-year-old Sarah has a successful career. Compared to her 25-year-old newly married daughter, who is employed in the same field, Sarah is more likely to:
    a. find both family and career roles to be less burdensome.
    b. find that satisfaction with family life tends to mitigate stress at work, and vice versa.
    c. see her career in a more balanced perspective.
    d. experience all of the above.

11. (A Closer Look) Sandy is a social worker who, after twenty years of work, has lost the enthusiasm she once held for her job. Sandy, like many in the helping professions, is experiencing:
    a. alienation.
    b. burn-out.
    c. maintenance phase syndrome.
    d. professional anxiety.

12. (A Closer Look) Sandy's boss is concerned about her employee's recent loss of enthusiasm as a social worker. To "reignite" Sandy's enthusiasm, she would be well advised to:
    a. shift Sandy's responsibilities to other areas, such as to more administrative duties.
    b. increase Sandy's case load, so she will see how much people need her.
    c. help Sandy develop more realistic expectations about her work and what can be accomplished.
    d. discourage Sandy from sharing her woes with other social workers, since doing so would only make her situation seem more hopeless.

13. "The very fact that, biologically and culturally, women have been the primary caregivers and kinkeepers now gives them an adaptive advantage in their midlife careers." The basis for this statement is evidence that, at midlife:
    a. many men are hitting a work plateau.
    b. many men are feeling burn-out and alienation.
    c. many women, free from consuming family responsibilities, increase their personal involvement in a career.
    d. all of the above are true.

14. All his life, Bill has been a worrier, often suffering from bouts of anxiety and depression. Which personality cluster best describes these traits?
    a. neuroticism
    b. extroversion
    c. openness
    d. conscientiousness

15. Jan and her sister Sue have experienced similar frequent changes in careers, residences, and spouses. Jan has found these upheavals much less stressful than Sue and so is probably characterized by which of the following personality traits?
    a. agreeableness
    b. conscientiousness
    c. openness
    d. extroversion

Key Terms

Using your own words, write a brief definition or explanation of each of the following terms on a separate piece of paper.

1. midlife
2. middle age
3. midlife crisis
4. kinkeepers

5. sandwich generation
6. burn-out
7. alienation
8. the Big Five
9. extroversion
10. agreeableness
11. conscientiousness
12. neuroticism
13. openness

ANSWERS

CHAPTER REVIEW

1. 40; midlife; middle age; 60
2. crisis; dramatic change

People become aware that they are beginning to grow old, and often must make adjustments in their parental roles and achievement goals.

3. work; family
4. controversial; Daniel Levinson
5. divorce, remarriage, or a shift in occupation or lifestyle
6. men; psychological; dissatisfaction; feeling that their intellect was fading, that their children needed authoritarian control, that their enjoyment of food had diminished, and that their sex lives were unsatisfying
7. personal style of coping with problems; affluent; well educated; less education; psychosomatically
8. has been around for a long time; relatively little
9. are
10. decreased; increased; no longer felt

The reason seems to lie in social conditions. Most women who reached middle age several decades ago had been homemakers exclusively, and for most, their chief sources of self-esteem were their roles as mother and wife and their physical attractiveness. With middle age came the leaving of children, an inevitable change in appearance, and, consequently, a loss of self-esteem.

11. 1970; have; do not
12. family; unmarried women without children; married women without jobs
13. more difficult

Many men reaching midlife in recent years have had to cope with shifting social values that questioned traditional gender roles and, what were for many, fundamental assumptions about authority.

14. mostly white, middle-class males
15. power; respect; rare

A midlife crisis is likely to occur in people who reach middle age just when a sociocultural shift and the particulars of their own lives undercut the values and goals they have pursued throughout early adulthood.

16. less
17. improve

Most of today's elderly are healthy, active, and independent, giving them and their grown children a measure of freedom and privacy that enhances the relationship between them.

18. have emerged from adolescence successfully
19. sons; achievement; love life
20. cohort bridge
21. have children themselves
22. women; kinkeepers
23. increased; sandwich generation
24. increased; longer education, lower salaries, higher unemployment, fewer marriages, and more single parenthood; material; child care
25. 60; women
26. marriage
27. loneliness; self-esteem; depression
28. 10; happier

Families at this stage typically have greater financial security and have met the goal of raising a family. Shared activities, the growing accumulation of experiences, and a tendency toward greater marital equity at this time also contribute to greater marital satisfaction.

29. they learned to do things apart, in effect, becoming "emotionally divorced"
30. increases; status; salary
31. less
32. maintenance; redefine; mentors
33. did not
34. more; less; laid off or retired
35. less
36. burn-out
37. alienation
38. a great deal; children; spouse
39. advantage

40. helping; teaching, nursing, medicine, and social work
41. a. Reduce one's expectations of what can be accomplished.
    b. Share responsibilities.
    structure; communication
42. large factories; corporations; hostile
43. drinking too much, sleeping too little, depression, and marital or family problems

Techniques that make workers more involved in the total production and decision-making process, or that allow workers more say in their own activities, can help alleviate alienation.

44. personality
45. overestimate
46. extroversion; agreeableness; conscientiousness; neuroticism; openness
47. genes; culture; child-rearing; the experiences and choices made earlier in life
48. 30

By age 30, most people have settled into an ecological niche that evokes and reinforces their particular personality needs and interests.

49. neuroticism
50. **a.** Personality tends to improve with age.
    b. Both men and women tend to move toward androgyny.
51. sex hormones; Carl Jung; shadow
52. Gutmann; parental imperative

PROGRESS TEST 1

Multiple-Choice Questions

1. **b.** is the answer. (p. 560)
   a. By age 30, personality becomes quite stable.
   c. & d. Neither of these are common occurrences at midlife.
2. **d.** is the answer. (p. 560)
3. **d.** is the answer. (pp. 563–564)
   a. & b. Recent studies have shown that the prevalence of the midlife crisis has been greatly exaggerated.
   c. In fact, men are more likely to experience a midlife crisis than are women.
4. **d.** is the answer. (p. 564)
   a. & c. When women have both work and family roles, each role provides a buffer against whatever stress may arise in the other.
   b. For such women, career satisfaction provides a buffer against midlife stress.
5. **b.** is the answer. (p. 565)
6. **a.** is the answer. (p. 568)
   b. & c. These are job-related problems.
7. **a.** is the answer. (p. 566)
   c. The relationship improves for both men and women.
   d. Because most of today's elderly are healthy, active, and independent, this gives them and their grown children a measure of freedom and privacy that enhances the relationship between them.
8. **d.** is the answer. (p. 568)
   a. This term describes middle-aged women *and* men, who are pressured by the needs of both the younger and older generations.
   b. & c. These terms are not used in the text.
9. **b.** is the answer. (p. 567)
10. **d.** is the answer. (p. 568)
11. **c.** is the answer. (p. 573)
    a. This is the career phase in which workers have reached a plateau in advancement.
    b. This is the feeling of exhaustion and disillusionment that may occur when a worker has been in the same job for a long time.
    d. This is the broad term for the events that provoke radical reexamination and sudden change during middle age.
12. **d.** is the answer. (p. 576)
13. **a.** is the answer. (p. 576)
    b. This is the tendency to be kind and helpful.
    c. This is the tendency to be organized, deliberate, and conforming.
    d. This is the tendency to be anxious, moody, and self-punishing.
14. **b.** is the answer. (p. 578)
    a. Jung's theory states just the opposite.
    c. If anything, the loosening of gender roles would make adjustment easier.
    d. According to Jung, gender roles are most distinct during adolescence and early adulthood, when pressures to attract the other sex and the "parental imperative" are highest.
15. **b.** is the answer. (pp. 576–577)

True or False Items

1. F Although the men in Daniel Levinson's study virtually all experienced midlife crises, other studies have found that crises at midlife are not inevitable. (pp. 561–562)

2. T (p. 562)
3. T (p. 562)
4. F This seems to be true of men who reached midlife during the 1960s and 1970s, but for women, the historical changes have, if anything, made midlife somewhat easier. (pp. 564–565)
5. F The extended family is typical of traditional societies, but not those in North America. (p. 566)
6. F Workers are less likely to switch jobs during middle age. (p. 573)
7. F Alienation is typical of workers in large factories and corporations. (p. 575)
8. F Burn-out is most common in the helping professions, such as medicine, teaching, and social work. (p. 574)
9. T (p. 578)
10. F The stability of personality is at least partly attributable to heredity. (p. 576)

PROGRESS TEST 2

Multiple-Choice Questions

1. **b.** is the answer. (p. 559)
2. **c.** is the answer. (p. 561)

   a. & b. The contributions of these theorists are discussed in the context of the middle-age trend toward androgyny that occurs in both men and women.

   d. Mischel conducted research on personality development.
3. **c.** is the answer. (pp. 563–564)
4. **a.** is the answer. (pp. 564–565)
5. **a.** is the answer. (p. 565)

   b. Midlife crises are *most* common in these people.

   c. & d. Depending on gender, cohort, context, and personal coping style, midlife crises may or may not occur in such societies and groups. However, midlife crises are certainly not uncommon.
6. **d.** is the answer. (p. 566)
7. **a.** is the answer. (p. 567)

   c. The relationship improves for both men and women.

   d. It generally improves, especially if the children have emerged from adolescence successfully. Because most of today's elderly are healthy, active, and independent, this gives them and their grown children a measure of freedom and privacy that enhances the relationship between them.
8. **d.** is the answer. (pp. 570–571)
9. **d.** is the answer. (p. 571)

   a. & b. These job-related problems are not inevitable phases in career development.

   c. This is not a career phase identified in the text.
10. **c.** is the answer. (p. 573)

    a. In fact, just the opposite is true.

    b. Employers generally prefer to hire younger workers.

    d. Although many middle-aged workers achieve a greater balance in their perspective on work and family, achievement needs remain strong during this period.
11. **b.** is the answer. (p. 574)

    a. This refers to the career phase in which workers have reached a plateau in advancement.

    c. This occurs when a factory or service worker feels distant from the actual product being produced or service being offered.

    d. This is the broad term for the events that provoke radical reexamination and sudden change during middle age.
12. **d.** is the answer. (p. 576)
13. **a.** is the answer. (p. 578)

    b. According to Gutmann, when these demands have been removed, traditional gender roles *loosen.*

    c. Gutmann believes just the opposite to be true.
14. **a.** is the answer. (p. 578)

    b. This explanation, offered by David Gutmann, is *not* biosocial.

    c. This explanation, offered by Carl Jung, is also *not* biosocial.

    d. This explanation, although biosocial, was not offered in the text.
15. **c.** is the answer. (p. 578)

Matching Items

1. d (p. 560)	5. h (p. 573)	8. e (p. 576)
2. f (p. 568)	6. a (p. 576)	9. j (p. 576)
3. i (p. 568)	7. g (p. 576)	10. c (p. 576)
4. b (p. 573)		

CHALLENGE TEST

1. **a.** is the answer. (p. 560)

   b. & c. Ken's feelings are common in middle-aged male workers, and not necessarily indicative of neuroticism.

   d. This is the loosening of rigid gender roles that occurs in many men and women during middle age.

2. **d.** is the answer. (p. 562)
3. **b.** is the answer. (p. 562)

   c. & d. These are specifically job-related problems.
4. **d.** is the answer. (p. 564)

   a. Younger adults are more likely than middle-aged adults to experience role overload. Furthermore, satisfaction with a work role can help buffer difficulties in other roles, and vice versa.
5. **a.** is the answer. Many men reaching midlife in recent years have had to cope with shifting social values that questioned traditional gender roles and, what were for many, fundamental assumptions about authority. (pp. 564–565)
6. **b.** is the answer. Because women tend to be kinkeepers, Rebecca is likely to play a larger role than her brother. (p. 569)

   d. The relationship of education to care of frail parents is not discussed in the text.
7. **a.** is the answer. Rachel is less likely than women in earlier cohorts to define herself in terms of marriage and motherhood. (p. 564)
8. **c.** is the answer. (p. 570)

   a. Marital satisfaction can be an important buffer against midlife stress.

   d. There is no reason to believe Nancy's concern is abnormal, or neurotic.
9. **b.** is the answer. (p. 570)

   d. This may occur, but it is not an automatic result of years of emotional separation.
10. **d.** is the answer. (p. 564)
11. **b.** is the answer. (p. 574)

    a. Alienation tends to occur in factory and service workers.

    c. This describes the career phase in which workers have reached a plateau in advancement.

    d. This term is not used in the text.
12. **c.** is the answer. (p. 574)

    a., b., & d. These strategies would be likely to make Sandy's situation worse.
13. **d.** is the answer. (p. 573)
14. **a.** is the answer. (p. 576)

    b. This is the tendency to be outgoing.

    c. This is the tendency to be imaginative and curious.

    d. This is the tendency to be organized, deliberate, and conforming.
15. **c.** is the answer. Openness to new experiences might make these life experiences less threatening. (p. 576)

KEY TERMS

1. Our society recognizes a point called **midlife** at about age 40, when the average adult has about as many years of life ahead as have already passed. (p. 559)
2. Midlife ushers in **middle age**, which lasts until about age 60. (p. 559)
3. The **midlife crisis** is a troubling shift in a person's sense of the purpose of life, most often experienced in those who reach middle age when a sociocultural shift and the particulars of their own lives undercut the values and goals they have pursued throughout early adulthood. (p. 560)
4. Because women tend to focus more on family than men do, they are the **kinkeepers**, the people who celebrate family achievements, gather the family together, and keep in touch with family members who have moved away. (p. 568)
5. Middle-aged adults are commonly referred to as the **sandwich generation** because they are often squeezed by the needs of the younger and older generations. (p. 568)
6. **Burn-out** is a job-related problem experienced by workers who have been in the same job for years and feel disillusioned and exhausted by the demands of trying to help others. (p. 573)

   Memory Aid: **Burn-out** was so named because workers who experience this problem "fizzle out," similar to the way a fire does once its fuel supply has been exhausted.
7. **Alienation** is a job-related problem experienced by factory or service workers who feel distant from the actual product being produced or service being offered. (p. 573)
8. **The Big Five** are clusters of personality traits that remain quite stable after about age 30. (p. 576)
9. **Extroversion** is the tendency to be outgoing, assertive, and active. (p. 576)
10. **Agreeableness** is the tendency to be kind and helpful. (p. 576)
11. **Conscientiousness** is the tendency to be organized, deliberate, and conforming. (p. 576)
12. **Neuroticism** is the tendency to be anxious, moody, and self-punishing. (p. 576)
13. **Openness** is the tendency to be imaginative, curious, and artistic, willing to welcome new experiences when they arise. (p. 576)

CHAPTER 23

Late Adulthood: Biosocial Development

Chapter Overview

Chapter 23 covers biosocial development during late adulthood, discussing the myths and reality of this final stage of the life span. In a society such as ours, which glorifies youth, there is a tendency to exaggerate the physical decline brought on by aging. In fact, the changes that occur during the later years are largely a continuation of those that began earlier in adulthood, and the vast majority of the elderly consider themselves to be in good health.

Nonetheless, the aging process is characterized by various changes in appearance, by an increased incidence of impaired vision and hearing, by declines in the major body systems, and by a slowing of brain activity. These are all changes to which the individual must adjust. In addition, the incidence of chronic diseases increases significantly with age.

Several theories have been advanced to explain the aging process. The most useful of these focus in some way on our genetic makeup. However, environment and lifestyle factors also play a role, as is apparent from studies of those who live a long life.

NOTE: Answer guidelines for all Chapter 23 questions begin on page 347.

Guided Study

The text chapter should be studied one section at a time. Before you read, preview each section by skimming it, noting headings and boldface items. Then read the appropriate section objectives from the following outline. Keep these objectives in mind and, as you read the chapter section, search for the information that will enable you to meet each objective. Once you have finished a section, write out answers for its objectives.

Ageism (pp. 586–588)

1. Define ageism and discuss some of the factors that contribute to ageism in our society.

2. (A Closer Look) Describe ongoing changes in the age distribution of the American population.

The Aging Process (pp. 588–595)

3. List several effects that aging characteristically has on the individual's appearance and on the functioning of the sense organs.

4. Discuss adjustments older adults may have to make in various areas of life, including diet and exercise.

5. Assess what ongoing research has and has not shown regarding changes in the aging brain, including age-related changes in sleep patterns.

Aging and Disease (pp. 595–599)

6. List three reasons that the incidence of chronic disease increases significantly with age and give one possible explanation for gender differences in chronic disease.

7. Explain how the immune system functions and describe age-related changes in its efficiency.

Causes of the Aging Process (pp. 599–603)

8. Outline the wear-and-tear, cellular, and programmed senescence theories of aging.

9. Explain what the Hayflick limit is and how it supports the idea of a genetic clock.

Life Extension (pp. 603–607)

10. Identify lifestyle characteristics associated with the healthy, long-lived adult.

11. (A Closer Look) Discuss nutritional needs during late adulthood and suggest how these might best be met.

Chapter Review

When you have finished reading the chapter, work through the material that follows to review it. Complete the sentences and answer the questions. As you proceed, evaluate your performance for each section by consulting the answers on page 347. Do not continue with the next section until you understand each answer. If you need to, review or reread the appropriate section in the textbook before continuing.

1. In a recent survey, most older adults reported that their health limited their activities ______ (very little/a great deal) and that they were very ______ (satisfied/unsatisfied) with their lives.
2. In the United States, one older adult in every ______ is a nursing home resident. This proportion is higher in some countries, such as ______ and ______, and lower in others, such as ______ and ______.
3. No nation in the world has more than ______ percent of its older population in nursing homes.

Ageism (pp. 586–588)

4. The prejudice that people tend to feel about older people is called ______.
5. The main reason for the strength of ageism is our culture's emphasis on ______, ______, and progress. Other reasons include the increasing age ______ of society and the tendency to ______ about any group on the basis of its most noticeable members.
6. Older adults who are healthy, relatively well-off financially, and integrated into the lives of their families and society are classified as ______-______; they make up the ______ (majority/minority) of the elderly.
7. Older adults who suffer major physical, mental, or social losses are classified as ______-______.
8. Ageist stereotypes are based on the ______-______ group of older adults.
9. Many professionals who work with the elderly, such as those who specialize in ______, have inadvertently ______ (strengthened/weakened) ageist prejudices.
10. The cultural bias that associates youth with health and vigor, and age with disease and fragility, ______ (is/is not) weakening.
11. (A Closer Look) The study of population is called ______. In the past, when populations were sorted according to age, the resulting picture was a(n) ______ ______, with the youngest and ______ (smallest/largest) group at the bottom and the oldest and ______ (smallest/largest) group at the top.

    List two reasons for this picture.

    a. ______

    b. ______
12. (A Closer Look) Today, because of ______ ______ and increased ______, the shape of the population is becoming closer to a(n) ______.
13. (A Closer Look) The fastest-growing segment of the population are people age ______ and older.

List several possible benefits and problems that will result from the increasing number of older people.

The Aging Process (pp. 588–595)

14. The weakening and decline of the body is called ______. As in earlier periods ______, ______, and other aspects of lifestyle have an important impact on aging.
15. As people age, the skin becomes ______, ______,

and ___ (more/less) elastic, which produces wrinkling and makes blood vessels and pockets of fat more visible. Dark patches of skin known as ___ ___ also become visible.

16. Most older people are about ___ shorter than they were in early adulthood, because their ___ have settled closer together.

17. With age, body fat tends to collect more in the ___ and ___ ___ than in the arms, legs, and upper face.

18. Body weight is often ___ (higher/lower) in late adulthood, particularly in ___ (men/women), who have more ___ and less body ___ than the other sex.

19. Another reason for the change in body weight is ___, the loss of bone ___ that causes bones to become more porous and fragile.

20. Approximately ___ percent of Americans over age 65 have some visual impairment. Approximately ___ report that inadequate hearing hampers living. Most of the visual and auditory losses of the aged ___ (can/cannot) be corrected.

21. Because hearing aids are regarded as a symbol of agedness, less than ___ percent of the elderly use them.

22. At some point in old age, the slowdown of body functioning and depletion of ___ ___ make it necessary to adjust daily routines.

23. For the very old, regular exercise ___ (is/is not) beneficial.

Describe the most beneficial type and frequency of exercise for older adults.

24. Physiologically, the brain loses at least ___ percent of its weight and ___ percent of its size, and is ___ in functioning by late adulthood. One reason for these changes is the increased rate of death of ___ after about age ___. The amount of cell death ___ (varies/is uniform) across different areas of the brain.

25. The most obvious measure of the slowing of brain function is ___ ___. Slowed neural processes are also reflected in ___-___ patterns, such as the slowing of ___-wave activity.

26. The slowing of neural processes may be related to reduced production of brain chemicals called ___ during old age. It also may be related to reduced ___ ___ to the brain.

27. Brain activity ___ (is/is not) directly related to the brain's size or weight or number of cells.

28. When brain cells die, existing cells ___ (do/do not) take over their function. The branching ___ reaching out from remaining neurons continue to develop throughout adulthood.

29. Most studies of cognition and aging are ___-___, which leads to ___ (overestimates/underestimates) of decline.

30. Research has found that, in animals, aging is most likely to result in a loss of brain cells when animals are ___, ___, and ___. For animals living in ___ environments, aging does not reduce the number of cells significantly.

31. Although older adults get about as much ___ and ___ sleep as younger adults, they get significantly less

______________________________________ .

The sleep problems of older adults often create

______________________________________ ,

as well as psychological difficulties, particularly

__________________ and __________________ .

Describe one promising approach to treating insomnia in older adults.

Aging and Disease (pp. 595–599)

32. It __________________ (is/is not) inevitable that aging brings on disease.

33. The incidence of chronic diseases __________________ (increases/does not increase) with age. However, whether a person becomes ill depends less on age than on __________________ factors, past and current __________________ , and __________________ factors such as social support.

Give two reasons for this being so.

a. ______________________________________

b. ______________________________________

34. Older people take __________________ (less/more) time to recover from illnesses, and are __________________ (less/more) likely to die of them.

35. Although the elderly see doctors more often than younger adults, they are not more likely to be __________________ .

36. Worldwide, variation in the rates of cancer are quite __________________ (small/large).

37. The rates of various chronic illness __________________ (do/do not) vary with gender.

38. Although men die at a higher rate than women, women are more likely to be __________________ .

Give several possible explanations for this gender difference.

39. In terms of life expectancy, women have about a(n) __________________-year advantage over men.

40. Normal aging reduces the __________________ of the heart muscle and lengthens the time the heart needs to relax between __________________ . It also reduces the __________________ of the cardiovascular system. Aging in itself __________________ (does/does not) cause heart disease.

41. Many older adults show a number of risk factors related to heart disease, including __________________ .

42. Heart disease causes about __________________ percent of all deaths over age 65. Cancer is the cause of about __________________ percent of all deaths in the aged.

43. The predisposing factors that may lead to cancer include __________________ __________________ and __________________ __________________ .

44. Among those over age 85, the rate of cancer death has __________________ (increased/decreased) over the past twenty years.

Explain why this is so.

45. Another reason that the aged are more vulnerable to diseases such as cancer is diminished __________________ .

46. The "attack" cells of the immune system include the __________________ from the bone marrow, which create __________________ that

attack invading ______ and ______, and the ______ from the ______ gland.

47. The first notable change in the immune system involves the ______ ______, which begins to shrink during ______ and by age 50 weighs between 5 and 10 percent of what it did in its prime.

Causes of the Aging Process (pp. 599–603)

48. A goal of many researchers is a limiting of the time any person spends ill, that is, a(n) ______ ______ ______.

49. The oldest theory of aging is the ______-______-______ theory, which compares the human body to a(n) ______. Overall this analogy ______ (is a good one/doesn't hold up).

50. A more promising theory suggests that some occurrence in the ______ themselves, such as the accumulation of accidents that occur during ______ ______, causes aging. According to this theory, toxic environmental agents cause mutations in the structure of ______ and ______ and damage the instructions for creating new cells.

51. Another aspect of the cellular theory of aging is that metabolic processes can cause electrons to separate from their atoms, resulting in atoms called ______ ______, and produce errors in cell maintenance and repair. The potential for damage from these atoms is one reason that scientists are concerned about the loss of the earth's protective ______ layer.

52. According to another theory, as the immune system declines, cellular errors and damage may accumulate to the point that the body can no longer hold them in check, leading to what has been called a(n) ______ ______. This theory may explain why the disease ______, in which cell reproduction goes awry, is much more common in older adults.

53. Some scientists believe in the concept of ______ ______; that is, they believe that we are genetically programmed to die after a fixed number of years, called ______ ______ ______ for a given species.

54. The time span, which in humans is 115 years, is quite different from ______ ______ ______, which is defined as ______ ______.

55. Life expectancy varies according to ______, ______, and ______ factors that affect frequency of ______ in childhood, adolescence, or middle age. In the United States in 1990, average life expectancy at birth was about ______ for men and ______ for women.

56. According to one theory of programmed senescence, DNA acts as a(n) ______ ______, switching on genes that promote aging at a genetically predetermined age. Support for this theory comes from several diseases that involve premature signs of aging and early death, including ______ ______ and the rare disease ______.

57. When human cells are allowed to replicate outside the body, the cells stop replicating at a certain point, referred to as a(n) ______ ______. Cells from people with diseases characterized by accelerated aging replicate ______ (more/ fewer) times before dying.

58. How close a person comes to reaching maximum life span ______ (is/is not) genetically influenced. Compared with dizygotic twins, monozygotic twins ______

(are/are not) much closer in rate of aging and age at death.

Life Extension (pp. 603–607)

59. Many gerontologists believe that research may soon increase the average ______________, that is, the period of vital and vigorous years.

60. The places famous for long-lived people are in ______________, ______________ regions where pollution is minimized. Furthermore, in these places, tradition ensures that the elderly are ______________ and play an important social role. Because of the absence of ______________, some researchers believe the people in these regions are lying about their true age.

List four characteristics shared by long-lived people in these regions.

a. ______________

b. ______________

c. ______________

d. ______________

61. (A Closer Look) Vitamin and mineral needs do not ______________ (increase/decrease) with age. However, calorie requirements ______________ (increase/decrease) by about ______________ percent from those of early and middle adulthood. During late adulthood, a diet that is ______________ and healthy is even more important than earlier.

62. (A Closer Look) Getting enough nutrients is more problematic for the aged than for younger adults primarily because the efficiency of the ______________ ______________ is reduced. Another reason is that the senses of ______________ and ______________ diminish with age.

List three external factors that make getting enough nutrients more difficult for some older adults.

a. ______________

b. ______________

c. ______________

63. (A Closer Look) Many of the elderly also take ______________ that affect nutritional requirements. Advocates of life extension ______________ (do/do not) recommend that the aged take vitamin and mineral supplements. Some believe that vitamin C and other ______________, which reduce the number of ______________ ______________ of oxygen, might slow down the disease and aging process.

64. (A Closer Look) Most of the elderly ______________ (are/are not) relatively well nourished and are more likely to ______________ (overdose on/be deficient in) vitamins than the reverse. Some vitamins, such as ______________, are toxic in large doses.

Progress Test 1

Multiple-Choice Questions

Circle your answers to the following questions and check them with the answers on page 349. If your answer is incorrect, read the explanation for why it is incorrect and then consult the appropriate pages of the text (in parentheses following the correct answer).

1. Ageism is:
   a. the study of aging and the aged.
   b. prejudice or discrimination against older people.
   c. the genetic disease that causes children to age prematurely.
   d. the view of aging that the body and its parts deteriorate with use.

2. (A Closer Look) The U.S. demographic pyramid is becoming a square because of:
   a. increasing birth rates and life spans.
   b. decreasing birth rates and life spans.
   c. decreasing birth rates and increasing life spans.
   d. rapid population growth.

3. Careful diet and regular exercise:
   a. have little, if any, effect on the process of senescence.
   b. accelerate the normally gradual process of senescence.

c. can soften the impact of senescence.
d. can make it possible for the individual to avoid the effects of senescence altogether.

4. Auditory losses with age are more serious than visual losses because:
   a. they affect a far larger segment of America's elderly population.
   b. they are more difficult for doctors to diagnose than are visual losses.
   c. hearing aids, in contrast to glasses, are ineffective as a corrective measure.
   d. those who suffer from them are less likely to take the necessary corrective steps.

5. As the individual ages, the amounts of some neurotransmitters in the brain:
   a. increase, compensating for the reduced number of cells.
   b. decrease, contributing to slower reaction time.
   c. increase, compensating for reduced blood flow to the brain.
   d. decrease, making the aged brain somewhat feeble.

6. Factors that explain the increased incidence of chronic diseases during late adulthood include all of the following *except:*
   a. increased hypochondria.
   b. accumulated risk factors.
   c. decreased efficiency of body systems.
   d. diminished immunity.

7. A direct result of damage to cellular DNA is:
   a. errors in the reproduction of cells.
   b. an increase in the formation of free radicals.
   c. decreased efficiency of the immune system.
   d. the occurrence of a disease called progeria.

8. Explanations of aging that focus on causes at the cellular level include the theories of:
   a. wear and tear and cellular accidents.
   b. wear and tear and error catastrophe.
   c. cellular accidents and error catastrophe.
   d. error catastrophe and a genetic clock.

9. According to the theory of a genetic clock, aging:
   a. is actually directed by the genes.
   b. occurs as a result of damage to the genes.
   c. occurs as a result of hormonal abnormalities.
   d. can be reversed through environmental changes.

10. Laboratory research on the reproduction of cells cultured from humans and animals has found that:
    a. cell division cannot occur outside the organism.
    b. the number of cell divisions was the same regardless of the species of the donor.
    c. the number of cell divisions was different depending on the age of the donor.
    d. under the ideal conditions of the laboratory, cell division can continue indefinitely.

11. Extension of the life span by genetic engineering:
    a. is now known to be impossible.
    b. might be possible in the future.
    c. has already been achieved in several parts of the world.
    d. is clearly undesirable for both the individual and the larger society.

12. Highly unstable atoms that have unpaired electrons and cause damage to other molecules in body cells are called:
    a. B-cells.
    b. T-cells.
    c. free radicals.
    d. both a. and b.

13. In triggering our first maturational changes and then the aging process, our genetic makeup is in effect acting as a(n):
    a. immune system.
    b. error catastrophe.
    c. demographic pyramid.
    d. genetic clock.

14. Researcher Marion Diamond has found that laboratory rats:
    a. inevitably lose brain cells with age.
    b. lose brain cells if they are overfed and overstressed.
    c. do not lose brain cells to any significant degree if they live in enriched environments.
    d. actually gain brain cells if they are raised in an enriched environment.

15. Compared to men, women are more likely to:
    a. notice disease symptoms.
    b. avoid drug use (including tobacco and alcohol).
    c. have less hostile and less impatient behavior patterns.
    d. do all of the above.

True or False Items

Write *true* or *false* on the line in front of each statement.

_______ 1. Younger adults tend to underestimate the range of problems associated with aging.

_______ 2. As a result of cell death, by late adulthood the brain loses about 5 percent of its weight and shrinks in size by about 15 percent.

_______ 3. Because of demographic changes, the majority of America's elderly population is now predominantly "old-old" rather than "young-old."

_______ 4. Professionals in the field of aging have in the past contributed to negative stereotypes about the aged.

_______ 5. Although the thymus gland shrinks with age, the efficiency of the immune system is not affected.

_______ 6. The immune system helps to control the effects of cellular damage.

_______ 7. A decline in the number of free radicals may accelerate the aging process.

_______ 8. Although average life expectancy has increased during the course of the twentieth century, maximum life span has remained unchanged.

_______ 9. (A Closer Look) In view of changed nutritional needs during late adulthood, nutritionists generally recommend that the elderly supplement their diet with large doses of vitamins.

_______ 10. The importance of lifestyle factors in contributing to longevity is underscored by studies of the long-lived.

Progress Test 2

Progress Test 2 should be completed during a final chapter review. Answer the following questions after you thoroughly understand the correct answers for the Chapter Review and Progress Test 1.

Multiple-Choice Questions

1. The main factors that contribute to ageism in our society include all of the following except:
   a. a tendency to value youth.
   b. rapid developments in medical science.
   c. increasing age segregation in work and other activities.
   d. a tendency to stereotype the elderly in a negative way.

2. (A Closer Look) An important demographic change in America is that:
   a. ageism is beginning to diminish.
   b. population growth has virtually ceased.
   c. the median age is falling.
   d. the number of older people in the population is increasing.

3. Changes in appearance during late adulthood include all of the following *except*:
   a. a slight reduction in height.
   b. a significant increase in weight.
   c. a redistribution of body fat.
   d. a marked wrinkling of the skin.

4. The incidence of visual and auditory impairments during late adulthood:
   a. increases with each decade of life.
   b. is primarily confined to individuals who had problems during earlier adulthood.
   c. can be significantly reduced by proper diet and exercise.
   d. inevitably causes psychological and social problems in affected individuals.

5. A primary difference in sleep patterns between younger and older adults is that older adults:
   a. wake up far more frequently during the night.
   b. have far less REM (dreaming) sleep.
   c. require far more sleep in order to avoid fatigue.
   d. have far fewer problems falling asleep.

6. The weakening of the heart that occurs during the course of normal aging:
   a. makes the older person more susceptible to heart disease.
   b. once in progress, leads inevitably to heart disease.
   c. leads to a gradual breakdown of the immune system.
   d. raises blood pressure and cholesterol levels.

7. According to one theory, when error catastrophe occurs:
   a. molecules of different kinds become linked.
   b. other cells take over the functions of cells that are damaged.
   c. the genetic clock switches on the aging process.
   d. normal aging gives way to disease.

8. The oldest age to which a human can live is ultimately limited by:
   a. error catastrophe.
   b. the maximum life span.
   c. the average life expectancy.
   d. the Hayflick limit.

9. The disease called progeria, in which aging occurs prematurely in children, provides support for explanations of aging that focus on:
   a. wear and tear.
   b. error catastrophe.
   c. cross-linkage.
   d. a genetic clock.

10. (A Closer Look) Nutritionists have found that most of America's elderly tend to:
    a. have serious vitamin and mineral deficiencies.
    b. consume far too many calories.
    c. consume far too few calories.
    d. be relatively well nourished.

11. In studies of three regions of the world known for the longevity of their inhabitants, the long-lived showed all of the following characteristics *except*:
    a. their diets were moderate.
    b. they were spared from doing any kind of work.
    c. they interacted frequently with family members, friends, and neighbors.
    d. they engaged in some form of exercise on a daily basis.

12. In defending itself against internal and external invaders, the immune system relies on two kinds of "attack" cells: __________, manufactured in the bone marrow, and __________, manufactured by the thymus gland.
    a. B-cells; T-cells
    b. T-cells; B-cells
    c. free radicals; T-cells
    d. B-cells; free radicals

13. The view of aging that the body and its parts deteriorate with use and with accumulated exposure to environmental stresses is known as the __________ theory.
    a. programmed senescence
    b. genetic clock
    c. error catastrophe
    d. wear-and-tear

14. (A Closer Look) The statistical study of population and population trends is called:
    a. gerontology.
    b. demography.
    c. ageism.
    d. senescence.

15. In humans, average life expectancy varies according to all of the following *except*:
    a. historical factors.
    b. ethnic factors.
    c. cultural factors.
    d. socioeconomic factors.

Matching Items

Match each definition or description with its corresponding term.

Terms

_______ 1. young-old
_______ 2. old-old
_______ 3. senescence
_______ 4. neurotransmitters
_______ 5. B-cells
_______ 6. T-cells
_______ 7. compression of morbidity
_______ 8. free radicals
_______ 9. Hayflick limit
_______ 10. healthspan

Definitions or Descriptions

a. brain chemicals involved in nerve impulse communication
b. limiting the time a person is ill
c. the number of times a cell replicates before dying
d. unstable atoms that damage cells
e. attack infected cells and strengthen other aspects of the immune system's functioning
f. the majority of the elderly
g. the period of vital and vigorous years
h. the minority of the elderly
i. create antibodies that attack bacteria and viruses
j. the weakening and decline of the body

Challenge Test

Answer these questions the day before an exam as a final check on your understanding of the chapter's terms and concepts.

1. Which of the following is *most* likely to be a result of ageism?
   a. the participation of the elderly in community activities
   b. laws requiring workers to retire by a certain age
   c. an increase in multigenerational families
   d. greater interest in the study of gerontology

2. Until recently, professionals who worked with the elderly tended to paint a negative picture because:
   a. the elderly they dealt with were not a representative sample of the nation's elderly.
   b. they wanted to bring the problems of the elderly to society's attention.
   c. they disagreed with the attitudes and beliefs many Americans held toward the elderly.
   d. gerontology was not yet an area of scientific study.

3. An 85-year-old man enjoys good health and actively participates in family and community activities. This person is best described as being:
   a. ageist.
   b. young-old.
   c. old-old.
   d. a gerontologist.

4. (A Closer Look) Concluding her presentation on demographic trends in the United States, Marisa states that, "By the year 2025:
   a. there will be more people aged 60 and older than below age 30."
   b. there will be more people aged 30 to 59 than below age 30."
   c. there will be more people below age 30 than above age 60."
   d. the American population will be divided roughly into thirds—one-third below age 30, one-third aged 30 to 59, and one-third aged 60 and older."

5. In her lecture on aging, Dr. Fraser notes that most studies of cognition and aging have been ____________ in nature, and have tended to ____________ age-related declines.
   a. cross-sectional; overestimate
   b. cross-sectional; underestimate
   c. longitudinal; overestimate
   d. longitudinal; underestimate

6. Given the changes and needs of late adulthood, an older person should probably:
   a. avoid most forms of exercise.
   b. follow a regular but slower-paced program of exercise.
   c. exercise for longer periods than younger adults.
   d. focus on swimming and water exercises.

7. Developmentalists who study the aging brain emphasize the:
   a. importance of brain size in determining brain function.
   b. serious consequences of the cell death that occurs with aging.
   c. marked improvement in reaction time that occurs with aging.
   d. adaptive potential of the aging brain.

8. A flu that younger adults readily recover from can prove fatal to older adults. The main reason for this is that older adults:
   a. are often reluctant to consult doctors.
   b. have a greater genetic predisposition to the flu.
   c. have diminished immunity.
   d. are often weakened by inadequate nutrition.

9. The wear-and-tear theory might be best suited to explain:
   a. the overall process of aging.
   b. the wrinkling of the skin that is characteristic of older adults.
   c. the arm and shoulder problems of a veteran baseball pitcher.
   d. the process of cell replacement by which minor cuts are healed.

10. (A Closer Look) With regard to nutrition, most elderly should probably be advised to:
    a. take large doses of vitamins and, especially, antioxidants.
    b. eat foods that are high in calories.
    c. consume a varied and healthy diet.
    d. eat large meals but eat less often.

11. Charlotte wants to make sure her elderly grandmother has every environmental advantage to keep her mind healthy. Based on neural studies of aging in animals, she concludes that:
    a. the age-related loss of brain tissue means that her grandmother's mind will inevitably become feeble.
    b. her grandmother should not be overstressed or overstimulated by sensory stimuli.

c. as long as her grandmother receives the proper nutrition, her mind will remain healthy.
d. her grandmother should have a healthy diet and continue to lead an active life filled with stimulating experiences.

12. Ruben, who is 70, is worried that his broken sleep pattern is a sign of a serious illness. His doctor tells him:
 a. neurological tests are needed, since most older people sleep more than younger people.
 b. he is probably under too much stress.
 c. his symptoms are not necessarily a sign of a serious illness, since many older adults tend to wake up numerous times each night.
 d. he should stop worrying and take a sleeping pill each night.

13. Mary and Charlie are both 65. As they advance through late adulthood, it is likely that:
 a. Mary will seek earlier preventive care for her health complaints than Charlie.
 b. Charlie will be more well than Mary.
 c. if all other risk factors are equal, Mary will live about six years longer than Charlie.
 d. all of the above are true.

14. Eddie is preparing a report on gender differences in morbidity and mortality as people age. His report should include information on:
 a. immune responses in men and women.
 b. risk factors such as smoking, drinking, and the use of other drugs.
 c. behavior patterns that contribute to disease.
 d. all of the above.

15. In concluding her presentation on human longevity, Katrina states that:
 a. current average life expectancy is about twice what it was at the turn of the century.
 b. current maximum life span is about twice what it was at the turn of the century.
 c. both average life expectancy and maximum life span have increased since the turn of the century.
 d. although maximum life span has not increased, average life expectancy has, because infants are less likely to die.

Key Terms

Using your own words, write a brief definition or explanation of each of the following terms on a separate piece of paper.

1. ageism
2. young-old
3. old-old
4. gerontology
5. senescence
6. demography
7. demographic pyramid
8. neurotransmitters
9. B-cells
10. T-cells
11. compression of morbidity
12. wear-and-tear theory
13. free radicals
14. error catastrophe
15. programmed senescence
16. maximum life span
17. average life expectancy
18. genetic clock
19. progeria
20. Hayflick limit
21. healthspan

ANSWERS

CHAPTER REVIEW

1. very little; satisfied
2. 20; Canada; Australia; Japan; Hong Kong
3. 8
4. ageism
5. growth; strength; segregation; generalize
6. young-old; majority
7. old-old
8. old-old
9. gerontology; strengthened
10. is
11. demography; demographic pyramid; largest; smallest
 a. Each generation of young adults gave birth to more than enough children to replace themselves.

b. A sizable number of each cohort died before advancing to the next higher section of the pyramid.

12. falling birth rates; longevity; square
13. 75

Some experts warn of new social problems, such as increased expense for medical care and decreased concern for the quality of education for children. Others envision social benefits, such as lower crime rates and more civic involvement.

14. senescence; diet, exercise
15. dryer, thinner; less; age spots
16. one inch; vertebrae
17. torso; lower face
18. lower; men; muscle; fat
19. osteoporosis; calcium
20. 90; one-third; can
21. 10
22. organ reserve
23. is

Activities that involve continuous rhythmic movements three or more times a week for half an hour are more beneficial than those that require sudden, strenuous effort.

24. 5; 15; slower; neurons; 60; varies
25. reaction time; brain-wave; alpha
26. neurotransmitters; blood flow
27. is not
28. do; dendrites
29. cross-sectional; overestimates
30. underfed; understimulated; overstressed; enriched
31. light; REM; deep sleep; chronic fatigue; anxiety; depression

Instead of treating insomnia as a disorder that requires medication, a more promising strategy is to help older people understand that changes in their sleep patterns are normal and can be successfully adapted to.

32. is not
33. increases; genetic, lifestyle; psychological
    a. Older people are more likely to have accumulated several risk factors for chronic diseases.
    b. Many of the biological changes that occur with aging reduce the efficiency of the body's systems, making the older person more susceptible to disease.
34. more; more
35. hypochondriacs
36. large
37. do
38. disabled

Women are more likely to notice disease symptoms and go to a doctor, thus getting earlier treatment or preventive care. Men are more likely to use drugs (including tobacco and alcohol) and to have impatient and hostile behavior patterns.

39. six
40. functioning; contractions; elasticity; does not
41. elevated blood pressure, high cholesterol level, obesity, lack of exercise, a history of smoking
42. 40; 20
43. genetic vulnerability; environmental insults
44. increased

This is because the cohort that currently makes up the old-old was the first group to enthusiastically take up cigarette-smoking. They also ate more animal fat and were exposed to more pollution.

45. immunity
46. B-cells; antibodies; bacteria; viruses; T-cells; thymus
47. thymus gland; adolescence
48. compression of morbidity
49. wear-and-tear; machine; doesn't hold up
50. cells; cell reproduction; DNA; RNA
51. free radicals; ozone
52. error catastrophe; cancer
53. programmed senescence; maximum life span
54. average life expectancy; the number of years the average newborn of a particular population of a given species is likely to live
55. historical; cultural; socioeconomic; death; 72; 79
56. biological clock; Down syndrome; progeria
57. Hayflick limit; fewer
58. is; are
59. healthspan
60. rural; mountainous; respected; verifiable birth or marriage records
    a. Diet is moderate, consisting mostly of fresh vegetables.
    b. Work continues throughout life.
    c. Families and community are important.
    d. Exercise and relaxation are part of the daily routine.

61. decrease; decrease; 20; varied
62. digestive system; smell; taste
    a. poverty
    b. living alone
    c. dental problems
63. drugs; do; antioxidants; free radicals
64. are; overdose on; A

PROGRESS TEST 1

Multiple-Choice Questions

1. **b.** is the answer. (pp. 586–587)
   a. This is gerontology.
   c. This is progeria.
   d. This is the wear-and-tear theory.
2. **c.** is the answer. (p. 589)
3. **c.** is the answer. (p. 588)
4. **d.** is the answer. (p. 591)
   a. Visual and auditory losses affect about the same number of aged persons.
   b. & c. Hearing losses are no more difficult to detect, or to correct, than vision losses.
5. **b.** is the answer. (p. 593)
   d. Although the decrease in neurotransmitters slows reaction time, in most ways older adults think as well as they did when they were younger.
6. **a.** is the answer. (pp. 595–596)
7. **a.** is the answer. (p. 600)
   b. In fact, free radicals damage DNA, rather than vice versa.
   c. The immune system compensates for, but is not directly affected by, damage to cellular DNA.
   d. This genetic disease occurs too infrequently to be considered a *direct* result of damage to cellular DNA.
8. **c.** is the answer. (pp. 600–601)
9. **a.** is the answer. (p. 602)
   b. & c. According to the genetic clock theory, time, rather than genetic damage or hormonal abnormalities, regulates the aging process.
   d. The genetic clock theory makes no provision for environmental alteration of the genetic mechanisms of aging.
10. **c.** is the answer. (p. 603)
11. **b.** is the answer. Genetic engineering may one day be able to reprogram aging genes to extend human life. (p. 603)
    d. Although this point is certainly debatable, the text does not reach this conclusion.
12. **c.** is the answer. (p. 601)
    a., b., & d. These are the "attack" cells of the immune system.
13. **d.** is the answer. (p. 602)
    a. This is the body's system for defending itself against bacteria and other "invaders."
    b. This is the theory that aging is caused by accumulating cellular errors.
    c. This is a metaphor for the distribution of age groups, with the largest and youngest group at the bottom, and the smallest and oldest group at the top.
14. **c.** is the answer. (p. 594)
    b. Actually, the rats were most likely to lose brain cells with age if they were *underfed* and overstressed.
    d. Although an enriched environment seemed to mitigate the loss of brain cells, it did not lead to an increase in their number.
15. **d.** is the answer. (pp. 596–597)

True or False Items

1. F The problems associated with aging tend to be overestimated, not underestimated. (p. 584)
2. T (p. 592)
3. F Although our population is aging, the terms "old-old" and "young-old" refer to degree of physical and social well-being, not to age. (pp. 587–588)
4. T (p. 588)
5. F The shrinking of the thymus gland contributes to diminished immunity. (p. 598)
6. T (p. 598)
7. F Inasmuch as free radicals damage DNA and other molecules, it is their *presence* that may contribute to aging. (p. 601)
8. T (p. 602)
9. F Research has shown that large doses of vitamins may be harmful. (p. 606)
10. T (pp. 604, 607)

PROGRESS TEST 2

Multiple-Choice Questions

1. **b.** is the answer. If anything, because medical advances have prolonged vitality in the aged, they would tend to decrease ageism. (p. 587)

2. **d.** is the answer. (p. 589)
   a. Ageism is prejudice, not a demographic change.
   b. Although birth rates have fallen, population growth has not ceased.
   c. Actually, with the "squaring of the pyramid," the median age is rising.
3. **b.** is the answer. Weight often decreases during late adulthood. (p. 590)
4. **a.** is the answer. (p. 591)
   b. Most elderly adults eventually have some problems with hearing and vision.
   c. Diet and exercise have little, if any, impact on age-related changes in the sense organs.
   d. Such problems are certainly *not* inevitable, particularly if sensory difficulties are corrected.
5. **a.** is the answer. (p. 594)
   b. Older adults get about as much REM sleep as younger adults.
   c. In fact, older adults generally require less sleep than younger adults.
   d. This was not mentioned in the chapter as a difference in the sleep patterns of older adults.
6. **a.** is the answer. (p. 597)
   b. Aging in itself does not cause heart disease.
   c. The weakening of the heart itself does not weaken the immune system.
   d. These are risk factors that predispose one to heart disease, but they are not caused by the weakening of the heart muscle.
7. **d.** is the answer. (p. 601)
   a. This was not discussed in the text.
   b. This kind of compensation may occur in the brain, as some cells are lost due to aging.
   c. According to the genetic clock theory, the genes themselves regulate aging.
8. **b.** is the answer. (p. 602)
   a. This is a theory of aging.
   c. This statistic refers to the number of years the average newborn of a particular population of a given species is likely to live.
   d. This is the number of times a cultured cell replicates before dying.
9. **d.** is the answer. (p. 602)
   a. & b. Progeria is a genetic disease; it is not caused by the wearing out of the body or by accumulating cellular errors.
   c. This explanation for aging was not discussed.
10. **d.** is the answer. (p. 606)
11. **b.** is the answer. In fact, just the opposite is true. (p. 604)
12. **a.** is the answer. (p. 598)
    c. & d. Free radicals are unstable atoms that may cause cellular damage and aging.
13. **d.** is the answer. (p. 599)
    a. & b. According to these theories, aging is genetically predetermined.
    c. This theory attributes aging and disease to the accumulation of cellular errors.
14. **b.** is the answer. (p. 589)
    a. This is the study of old age.
    c. This is prejudice against the elderly.
    d. This is the weakening and decline of the body that occurs with age.
15. **b.** is the answer. (p. 602)

Matching Items

1. f (p. 587)
2. h (p. 587)
3. j (p. 588)
4. a (p. 593)
5. i (p. 598)
6. e (p. 598)
7. b (p. 599)
8. d (p. 601)
9. c (p. 603)
10. g (p. 604)

CHALLENGE TEST

1. **b.** is the answer. (p. 587)
2. **a.** is the answer. Most research was based on the aged who were in nursing homes or retirement communities. (p. 588)
3. **b.** is the answer. (p. 588)
   a. An ageist is a person who is prejudiced against the elderly.
   c. People who are "old-old" have social, physical, and mental problems that hamper their successful aging.
   d. A gerontologist is a person who studies aging.
4. **d.** is the answer. (p. 589)
5. **a.** is the answer. (p. 594)
6. **b.** is the answer. (p. 592)
   c. & d. Older adults need not exercise longer, nor should their exercise be limited to water activities.
7. **d.** is the answer. (p. 594)
   a. & b. Brain functioning is not directly related to brain size or cell death.
   c. Reaction time slows with age.
8. **c.** is the answer. (p. 598)
   a. In fact, older adults are more likely to consult doctors.
   b. There is no evidence this is true.
   d. Most older adults are adequately nourished.
9. **c.** is the answer. In this example, excessive use of the muscles of the arm and shoulder has contributed to their "wearing out." (p. 600)

10. **c.** is the answer. (p. 606)
    a. Large doses of vitamins can be harmful.
    b. Older adults need fewer calories to maintain body weight.
    d. This is an unhealthy dietary regimen.
11. **d.** is the answer. (p. 594)
    a. This is untrue.
    b. Although being overstressed is undesirable, sensory stimulation helps maintain the efficiency of neural functioning.
    c. Although diet is important, other lifestyle factors also influence the aging brain.
12. **c.** is the answer. (p. 594)
    a. Most older people sleep *less* than younger people.
    b. There is no reason to believe this is true.
    d. Regular use of sleeping pills is an unhealthy practice.
13. **d.** is the answer. (pp. 596–597)
14. **d.** is the answer. (p. 597)
15. **d.** is the answer. (p. 602)
    a. Current average life expectancy is twenty-eight years more than it was at the turn of the century.
    b. & c. Maximum life span has not changed since the turn of the century.

KEY TERMS

1. **Ageism** is prejudice against older people. (p. 586)
2. Most of America's elderly can be classified as **young-old**, meaning that they are "healthy and vigorous, relatively well-off financially, well integrated into the lives of their families and communities, and politically active." (p. 587)
3. Older people who are classified as **old-old** are those who suffer major physical, mental, or social problems in later life. (p. 587)
4. **Gerontology** is the study of old age. (p. 587)
5. **Senescence** is the weakening and decline of the body that accompanies aging. (p. 588)
6. **Demography** is the study of population. (p. 589)
7. In previous years, when populations were sorted by age, the resulting picture was a **demographic pyramid**, with the youngest and largest group at the bottom and the oldest and smallest at the top. (p. 589)
8. **Neurotransmitters** are chemicals in the brain that allow a nerve impulse to be communicated from one cell to another. (p. 593)
9. **B-cells** are immune system cells that are manufactured in the bone marrow and create antibodies that attack specific invading bacteria and viruses. (p. 598)

    Memory aid: The *B*-cells come from the *b*one marrow and attack *b*acteria.
10. **T-cells** are immune system cells that are manufactured in the thymus and produce substances that attack infected cells of the body. (p. 598)
11. Researchers who are interested in improving the health of the elderly focus on a **compression of morbidity**, that is, a limiting of the time any person spends ill. (p. 599)
12. According to the **wear-and-tear theory** of aging, the parts of the human body deteriorate with use, as well as with accumulated exposure to pollution, radiation, inadequate nutrition, disease, and various other stresses. (p. 599)
13. **Free radicals** are highly unstable atoms with unpaired electrons that are capable of reacting with other molecules in the cell, tearing them apart, and possibly accelerating aging. (p. 601)
14. According to some theories, unhealthy aging, disease, and death are caused by an **error catastrophe**, that is, by an accumulation of errors in cell reproduction so extensive that the immune system cannot compensate. (p. 601)
15. **Programmed senescence** refers to the theory that people are genetically programmed to die after a fixed number of years. (p. 601)
16. The **maximum life span** is the maximum number of years that a particular species is genetically programmed to live. For humans, the maximum life span is 115 years. (p. 602)
17. **Average life expectancy** is the number of years the average newborn of a particular population of a given species is likely to live. (p. 602)
18. According to one theory, our genetic makeup acts, in effect, as a **genetic clock**, triggering hormonal changes in the brain, regulating cellular processes, and "timing" aging and the moment of death. (p. 602)
19. **Progeria** is a rare genetic disease in which children have a normal infancy but by age 5 stop growing, begin to age prematurely, and die by their teens. (p. 602)
20. The **Hayflick limit** is the maximum number of times that cells cultured from humans and animals divide before dying. (p. 603)
21. The **healthspan** is the period of vital and vigorous years before an older person becomes frail and ill. (p. 604)

CHAPTER 24 Late Adulthood: Cognitive Development

Chapter Overview

This chapter describes the changes in cognitive functioning associated with late adulthood. The first section reviews experimental evidence that suggests declines in both the information-processing and problem-solving abilities of older adults, as well as the reasons for those declines.

Nonetheless, as the second section points out, real-life conditions provide older adults with ample opportunity to compensate for the pattern of decline observed in the laboratory. It appears that, for most people, cognitive functioning in daily life remains essentially unimpaired.

The main exception to the generally positive picture of cognitive functioning during late adulthood is dementia, the subject of the third section. This pathological loss of intellectual ability can be caused by a variety of diseases and circumstances; risk factors, treatment, and prognosis differ accordingly.

The final section of the chapter makes it clear that cognitive changes during late adulthood are by no means restricted to declines in intellectual functioning. For many individuals, late adulthood is a time of great aesthetic, creative, philosophical, and spiritual growth.

NOTE: Answer guidelines for all Chapter 24 questions begin on page 363.

Guided Study

The text chapter should be studied one section at a time. Before you read, preview each section by skimming it, noting headings and boldface items. Then read the appropriate section objectives from the following outline. Keep these objectives in mind and, as you read the chapter section, search for the information that will enable you to meet each objective. Once you have finished a section, write out answers for its objectives.

Intellectual Changes in Information Processing (pp. 612–622)

1. Summarize the laboratory findings regarding changes in the sensitivity of the sensory register and the capacity of working memory during late adulthood.

2. Summarize the laboratory findings regarding changes in the older adult's ability to access the knowledge base and to use control processes efficiently.

3. Suggest three factors, other than the aging process itself, that might contribute to age-related declines in cognitive functioning.

4. Summarize and critique the findings of studies showing that special training can reduce the intellectual decrements associated with aging.

5. (Research Report) Discuss the treatment of elderly people who have been institutionalized in terms of its effect on cognitive ability.

Cognitive Functioning in the Real World (pp. 622–625)

6. Characterize and explain discrepancies between how the elderly perform on memory and problem-solving tasks in the laboratory, on the one hand, and in daily life, on the other.

Dementia (pp. 625–633)

7. Define dementia and describe its stages.

8. Identify the two most common forms of dementia and discuss the differences between them.

9. Identify and describe several other organic and nonorganic causes of dementia.

New Cognitive Development in Later Life (pp. 633–637)

10. Discuss the claims of developmentalists regarding the possibility of positive cognitive development during late adulthood and cite several areas of life in which such development may occur.

Chapter Review

When you have finished reading the chapter, work through the material that follows to review it. Complete the sentences and answer the questions. As you proceed, evaluate your performance for each section by consulting the answers on page 363. Do not continue with the next section until you understand each answer. If you need to, review or reread the appropriate section in the textbook before continuing.

1. Adult cognitive development is ________________, meaning that some abilities increase, others wane, and some remain stable.

2. By late adulthood, the cumulative effects of increasing ________________ and declining ________________ capacities push cognitive development in opposite directions.

Intellectual Changes in Information Processing (pp. 612–622)

3. In Schaie's longitudinal study, older adults began to show significant declines on the five "primary mental abilities": ________________ ________________, ________________ ________________, ________________,

________________ ________________,
and ________________ ________________.

4. The ________________ ________________ stores incoming sensory information for a split second after it is received. Research suggests that the effects of aging ________________ (have no impact on/create small decrements in) the sensitivity of the sensory register.

5. As a result of aging, it may take ________________ (more/less) time for information to register via the senses and ________________ (more/less) time for it to fade.

6. Research demonstrates that the speed with which the brain registers new information ________________ (declines/does not decline) with age.

7. Age-related changes in the sensory register ________________ (can/cannot) easily be compensated for. Most researchers attribute the overall decline in information processing associated with age to ________________ (memory deficits/sensory difficulties).

8. With age, the sensory receptors, especially the ________________ and ________________, become less adept at picking up stimuli that are ________________.

9. Once information is perceived, it must be placed in ________________ ________________.

10. Working memory has two interrelated functions: to temporarily ________________ information and then to ________________ it. Compared to younger adults, older adults seem to have ________________ (smaller/larger/about the same) working-memory capacity. One way to compensate for this change is to provide ________________ (younger/older) adults with ________________ (more/less) time to analyze information.

11. The ________________ ________________ consists of one's long-term storehouse of information and memories and is organized into two subcomponents: ________________ memory and ________________ memory.

12. With increasing age, adults experience greater difficulty accessing information from ________________ ________________.

Many researchers believe that this difficulty is due in part to the older adult's inability to use efficient ________________ ________________.

13. Retrieval of information from ________________ memory may be quite good in older adults.

List two possible reasons why this type of retrieval remains efficient.

14. The ________________ ________________ of human information processing function in an executive role and include ________________ strategies, ________________ strategies, and ________________ that aid problem solving. Older adults tend to use ________________ (simpler and less efficient/more complex but less efficient/about the same) control processes as younger adults.

15. When approaching a task involving memory, older adults are more likely to ________________ (underestimate/overestimate) the difficulty of the task than younger adults.

16. Compared to younger adults, older adults have ________________ (very inaccurate/comparable) knowledge of how their own memory works. Thus older adults' deficits in control processes are ________________ (global/specific).

17. In solving abstract problems, older adults tend to ________________ (outperform/do worse than) younger adults.

18. To an older adult, one of the most salient changes associated with aging is ________________ ________________. Older adults may ________________ (overestimate/underestimate) their memory skills when they were younger; consequently, they tend to ________________ (overestimate/underesti-

mate) their current memory losses. As a result of this misperception, older adults may lose their memory ______________—that is, their confidence in their memory and related cognitive skills.

Briefly describe the impact of this growing belief on cognitive functioning during late adulthood.

19. Adults who have low memory ______________ also perform poorly on memory and reasoning tasks.

20. According to ______________, many of the cognitive changes of late adulthood can be explained by decrements in the processing resources that enable cognition, such as ______________, ______________, or the ______________.

21. Research consistently demonstrates that good cognitive functioning is positively correlated with ______________ ______________, particularly that involving the ______________ system. People who have ______________ ______________ or untreated ______________ tend to show reduced intellectual ability, perhaps because these conditions affect ______________ ______________ to the brain.

22. Degenerative physical conditions like ______________, and mental-health problems like ______________, also reduce intellectual capacity.

23. One of the best-known training programs intended to improve the cognitive skills of older adults is ______________, which focuses on skills related to ______________ intelligence. Adults who have participated in this training ______________ (have/have not) demonstrated significant cognitive gains.

The conclusions drawn from research on the remediation of age-related declines in cognition require some qualifications. List two of these.

24. (Research Report) Because many nursing homes reinforce ______________, ______________, and ______________ behaviors in residents, they may not foster the kinds of practical competencies that are experienced by older adults who live independently. Research has shown that active social-learning training can improve the ______________-______________ skills of nursing-home residents and reduce their ______________ on Piagetian tasks.

Cognitive Functioning in the Real World
(pp. 622–625)

25. Most older adults ______________ (do/do not) acknowledge that their memory has declined with age and ______________ (do/do not) consider memory loss a significant handicap in daily life. Most older adults report that their skill at solving everyday problems has ______________ (declined/improved) with age.

Give several reasons that laboratory tests of memory may put older persons at a disadvantage.

26. In general, memory tests are constructed to minimize spontaneous ______________, or the use of one item to recall another. In many cases, the cumulative effect of ______________, ______________, and enhanced ______________ can offset

the memory loss that laboratory research has so often found in older adults.

27. Research has shown that problem solving in daily life ________________ (is/is not) less impaired with age than problem solving in a laboratory setting.

28. In a study comparing young, middle-aged, and older adults on answers to complex real-life problems, the oldest were the most ________________ and least ________________ in their solutions. Other research has shown that when ________________ ________________ ________________ are taken into account, older and young adults ________________ (do/do not) differ significantly in their moral reasoning.

29. Research ________________ (does/does not) support the popular stereotype of the elderly as rigid, stubborn thinkers.

Briefly summarize the evidence regarding age-related changes in information processing.

Dementia (pp. 625–633)

30. Although pathological loss of intellectual ability in elderly people is often referred to as ________________, a more precise term for this loss is ________________, which is defined as ________________. This condition, which ________________ (is/is not) an inevitable occurrence of old age, has several general symptoms, including ________________ ________________ ________________.

31. Traditionally, when dementia occurred before age ________________, it was called ________________ ________________; when it occurred after this age, it was called ________________ ________________. This age-based distinction is arbitrary, however, because the ________________, ________________, and ________________ are the same no matter what the person's age.

32. Dementia is usually ________________ (stable/progressive) and ________________ (does/does not) have identifiable stages.

33. The first stage of dementia is a general ________________ that is often indistinguishable from the ________________ ________________ that many older people experience. In the second stage, there are noticeable deficits in ________________ and ________________-________________. The third stage begins when memory loss becomes ________________ and people are no longer able to take care of their ________________.

34. Approximately 70 percent of all people who suffer from dementia are afflicted with ________________ ________________. This disorder is characterized by abnormalities in the ________________ ________________, called ________________ and ________________, that destroy normal brain functioning. The brain damage that accompanies this disease ________________ (does/does not) vary with the age of the victim.

35. When Alzheimer's disease appears in ________________ (middle/late) adulthood, it usually progresses ________________ (less/more) quickly, reaching the last phase within ________________ years. By late adulthood, this disease affects one in every ________________ adults, most of whom are over age ________________.

36. One form of Alzheimer's disease is caused by a dominant gene located on chromosome ________________ that synthesizes ________________, which gradually accumulate. Other forms of the disease are multifactorial, caused by the combination of a(n) ________________ vulnerability and other

_______________ _______________.

One possible cause is a slow _______________, perhaps contracted in childhood but kept at bay by the _______________ system until old age. Another possible cause is the cumulative effect of toxins derived from the victim's _______________ or from the _______________.

37. The two ways to definitively diagnose Alzheimer's disease are by _______________ or, after death, by _______________.

38. Today, there _______________ (are/are not) effective treatments for preventing Alzheimer's disease and slowing its progress.

39. The second major type of dementia is _______________-_______________ _______________. This condition occurs because a temporary obstruction of the _______________ _______________, called a(n) _______________, prevents a sufficient supply of blood from reaching the brain. This causes destruction of brain tissue, commonly called a(n) _______________.

40. The underlying cause of MID is _______________, which is common in people who have problems with their _______________ systems, including those with _______________ _______________, _______________, tingling or _______________ in their extremities, and _______________. Measures to improve circulation, such as _______________, or to control hypertension and diabetes through _______________ and _______________, can help to prevent or control the progress of MID.

41. Unlike the person with Alzheimer's disease, the person with MID shows a _______________ (gradual/sudden) drop in intellectual functioning. The prognosis for a person with MID is generally quite _______________ (good/poor).

42. Another cause of dementia is _______________ _______________, which produces muscle tremors or rigidity. This disease is related to the degeneration of neurons that produce the neurotransmitter _______________. Among the factors implicated as contributors to this disease are _______________ _______________ and certain _______________.

43. Other diseases that can result in dementia are _______________.

44. Dementia can also result from _______________ _______________, which usually involves an extra chromosome at the same location where the genetic defect for _______________ disease is located.

45. Oftentimes the elderly are thought to be suffering from brain disease when, in fact, their symptoms are caused by some other factor such as _______________, _______________, _______________ _______________, or _______________.

Give three reasons that drug-related changes in intellectual functioning are common in the elderly.

46. Malnutrition, especially deficiencies of _______________ and _______________ _______________, can cause confusion and loss of memory.

47. The rate of alcoholism is lower among elderly _______________ (men/women) than among younger members of this sex; the same _______________ (is/is not necessarily) true of older members of the other sex.

48. In general, psychological illnesses such as schizophrenia are _______________ (more/less) common in the elderly than in younger adults. Approximately _______________ percent of the elderly who are diagnosed as demented are actually experiencing psychological illness.

49. At some time during their later years, __________ (most/a small percentage of) older adults experience symptoms of depression. The cognitive declines associated with depression are sometimes called __________. Generally speaking, depression __________ (is/is not) very treatable in late adulthood.

50. One consequence of untreated depression among the elderly is that the rate of __________ is higher for those over age __________ than for any other group.

51. In most cases, the precipitating event for suicide is a(n) __________, with __________ and __________ being the most common such events. A related cause is __________, particularly __________ or diseases that affect the __________.

New Cognitive Development in Later Life
(pp. 633–637)

52. Most of the major theorists __________ (do/do not) believe that positive changes can occur in the intellectual functioning of older adults.

53. According to Erik Erikson, older adults are more interested in __________ __________ than younger adults and, as the "social witnesses" to life, are more aware of the __________ of the generations.

54. According to Abraham Maslow, older adults are more likely to achieve __________.

55. Many people become more appreciative of __________ and __________ as they get older.

56. Many people also become more __________ and __________ than when they were younger. Neugarten refers to this turn of the mind as __________, by which she means a heightening of the older person's propensity for __________.

57. Another formulation of this attempt to put life into perspective is called the __________ __________, in which the older person connects his or her own life with the future.

58. The reflectivity of old age may explain why professional productivity in the fields of __________ and __________ peaks in the 60s and 70s.

59. One of the most positive attributes commonly associated with older people is __________, which Baltes defines as expert knowledge in the __________ __________ of life.

List five features that distinguish wisdom from other forms of human understanding.

60. Closely related to the idea that the elderly are more wise and philosophical than the young is the idea that the old are more __________.

Progress Test 1

Multiple-Choice Questions

Circle your answers to the following questions and check them with the answers on page 364. If your answer is incorrect, read the explanation for why it is incorrect and then consult the appropriate pages of the text (in parentheses following the correct answer).

1. The information-processing component that is concerned with the temporary storage of incoming sensory information is:
   a. working memory.
   b. long-term memory.
   c. the knowledge base.
   d. the sensory register.

2. Older adults tend to have the greatest difficulty picking up sensory stimuli that are:
   a. very loud or bright.
   b. ambiguous or of low intensity.
   c. abstract or meaningless.
   d. all of the above.

3. The two basic functions of working memory are:
   a. storage that enables conscious processing and processing of information.
   b. temporary storage and processing of sensory stimuli.
   c. retrieval of information stored for several minutes.
   d. retrieval of information stored for years or decades.

4. Aging seems to have the greatest impact on which aspect of the knowledge base?
   a. secondary memory
   b. tertiary memory
   c. remote memory
   d. working memory

5. Strategies to retain and retrieve information in the knowledge base are part of which basic component of information processing?
   a. sensory register
   b. working memory
   c. control processes
   d. tertiary memory

6. According to Timothy Salthouse, many of the cognitive changes of late adulthood are caused by:
   a. slower cognitive processing.
   b. decreased capacity in working memory.
   c. attention deficits.
   d. all of the above.

7. The relationship between good cognitive functioning and good health is most accurately described as:
   a. a weak, positive correlation.
   b. a strong, positive correlation.
   c. no correlation.
   d. a weak, negative correlation.

8. (Research Report) Research showing that special training can remediate age-related cognitive declines must be interpreted cautiously because:
   a. it generally has involved relatively healthy and independent adults rather than those who are in poor health.
   b. there is evidence that intellectual plasticity increases with age.
   c. the studies are few in number and are based on very small sample sizes.
   d. of all of the above reasons.

9. Which of the following is a characteristic of laboratory experiments that inhibits the older adult's memory abilities?
   a. practice
   b. priming
   c. motivation
   d. time limitations

10. Dementia refers to:
    a. pathological loss of intellectual functioning.
    b. the increasing forgetfulness that sometimes accompanies the aging process.
    c. abnormal behavior associated with mental illness and with advanced stages of alcoholism.
    d. a genetic disorder that doesn't become overtly manifested until late adulthood.

11. The various types of dementia differ from one another in all of the following ways *except*:
    a. underlying causes.
    b. associated risk factors.
    c. general symptoms.
    d. possibilities for, and methods of, treatment.

12. Alzheimer's disease is characterized by:
    a. a proliferation of plaques and tangles in the cerebral cortex.
    b. a destruction of brain tissue as a result of strokes.
    c. rigidity and tremor of the muscles.
    d. an excess of fluid pressing on the brain.

13. The progression of multi-infarct dementia and Alzheimer's disease differs in that:
    a. multi-infarct dementia never progresses beyond the first stage.
    b. multi-infarct dementia is marked by sudden drops and temporary improvements, whereas decline in Alzheimer's disease is steady.
    c. multi-infarct dementia leads to rapid deterioration and death, whereas Alzheimer's disease may progress over a period of years.
    d. the progression of Alzheimer's disease may be halted or slowed, whereas the progression of multi-infarct dementia is irreversible.

14. Medication has been associated with symptoms of dementia in the elderly for all of the following reasons *except*:
    a. standard drug dosages are often too strong for the elderly.
    b. the elderly tend to become psychologically dependent upon drugs.
    c. drugs sometimes have the side effect of slowing mental processes.
    d. the intermixing of drugs can sometimes have detrimental effects on cognitive functioning.

15. The primary purpose of the life review is to:
    a. enhance one's spirituality.
    b. produce an autobiography.
    c. give advice to younger generations.
    d. put one's life into perspective.

True or False Items

Write *true* or *false* on the line in front of each statement.

_______ 1. As long as their vision and hearing remain unimpaired, older adults are no less efficient than younger adults at inputting information.

_______ 2. Changes in the sensory register are a major contributor to declines in information processing.

_______ 3. Compared with other aspects of memory, tertiary memory actually improves a great deal as the individual ages.

_______ 4. A majority of the elderly feel frustrated and hampered by memory loss in their daily lives.

_______ 5. In studies of problem solving in real-life contexts, the scores of older adults were similar to those of younger adults.

_______ 6. The majority of cases of dementia are organically caused.

_______ 7. Alzheimer's disease is in some cases inherited.

_______ 8. Dementia is usually progressive, with three main stages.

_______ 9. Late adulthood is often associated with a narrowing of interests and an exclusive focus on the self.

_______ 10. According to Maslow, self-actualization is actually more likely to be reached during late adulthood.

Progress Test 2

Progress Test 2 should be completed during a final chapter review. Answer the following questions after you thoroughly understand the correct answers for the Chapter Review and Progress Test 1.

Multiple-Choice Questions

1. Research suggests that aging results in:
   a. increased sensitivity of the sensory register.
   b. a significant decrease in the sensitivity of the sensory register that cannot usually be compensated for.
   c. a small decrease in the sensory register's sensitivity that can usually be compensated for.
   d. no noticeable changes in the sensory register.

2. Which of the following most accurately characterizes age-related changes in working memory?
   a. Both storage capacity and processing efficiency decline.
   b. Storage capacity declines while processing efficiency remains stable.
   c. Storage capacity remains stable while processing efficiency declines.
   d. Both storage capacity and processing efficiency remain stable.

3. Information remembered for years or decades is stored in:
   a. sensory register.
   b. working memory.
   c. tertiary memory.
   d. secondary memory.

4. Why might retrieval of information from remote memory often be quite good in older adults?
   a. It was stored at an early age.
   b. It has been frequently retrieved.
   c. Both a. and b. are true.
   d. There is no way of verifying the accuracy of such retrieval.

5. In general, with increasing age the control processes used to remember new information:
   a. become more efficient.
   b. become more complex.
   c. become more intertwined.
   d. become simpler and less efficient.

6. A health problem that seems to be especially damaging to cognitive functioning is:
   a. respiratory disease.
   b. heart disease.
   c. visual impairment.
   d. a disease affecting the endocrine system.

7. (Research Report) Research indicates that older adults in nursing homes tend to:
   a. develop better perspective-taking skills due to constant contact with others.
   b. take more control over their daily activities.
   c. become egocentric, losing their perspective-taking skills.
   d. improve their communication skills.

8. One study tested memory in different age groups by requiring younger and older adults to remember to make telephone calls at a certain time. It was found that:
   a. older adults did worse than younger adults because their memories were not as good.
   b. older adults did better than younger adults because they were able to trust their memories.
   c. older adults did better than younger adults because they didn't trust their memories and therefore used various reminders.
   d. older adults did worse than younger adults because they were less accustomed to having to do things at a certain time.

9. In research studies on problem solving, older adults generally perform at least as well as younger adults in all of the following tasks *except*:
   a. solving problems presented in real-life contexts.
   b. solving abstract problems.
   c. solving hypothetical problems that involve older persons.
   d. solving problems in their own lives.

10. Dementia:
   a. is more likely to occur among the aged.
   b. has no relationship to age.
   c. cannot occur before the age of 60.
   d. is an inevitable occurrence during late adulthood.

11. The most common cause of dementia is:
   a. Alzheimer's disease.
   b. multi-infarct dementia.
   c. Parkinson's disease.
   d. alcoholism and depression.

12. Organic causes of dementia include all of the following *except*:
   a. Parkinson's disease. c. brain tumors.
   b. Down syndrome. d. leukemia.

13. The psychological illness most likely to be misdiagnosed as dementia is:
   a. schizophrenia. c. personality disorder.
   b. depression. d. phobic disorders.

14. On balance, it can be concluded that positive cognitive development during late adulthood:
   a. occurs only for a small minority of individuals.
   b. leads to thought processes that are more appropriate to the final stage of life.
   c. makes older adults far less pragmatic than younger adults.
   d. is impossible in view of increasing deficits in cognitive functioning.

15. A key factor underlying the older adult's cognitive developments in the realms of aesthetics, philosophy, and spiritualism may be:
   a. the realization that one's life is drawing to a close.
   b. the despair associated with a sense of isolation from the community.
   c. the need to leave one's mark on history.
   d. a growing indifference to the outside world.

Matching Items

Match each definition or description with its corresponding term.

Terms

_______ 1. sensory register
_______ 2. working memory
_______ 3. knowledge base
_______ 4. control processes
_______ 5. memory self-efficacy
_______ 6. dementia
_______ 7. Alzheimer's disease
_______ 8. multi-infarct dementia (MID)
_______ 9. Parkinson's disease
_______ 10. interiority
_______ 11. life review

Definitions or Descriptions

a. the tendency of people to become more philosophical and introspective as they age
b. temporarily stores information for conscious processing
c. strategies for retaining and retrieving information
d. severely impaired thinking, memory, or problem-solving ability
e. stores incoming sensory information for a split second
f. caused by a temporary obstruction of the blood vessels
g. stores information for several minutes to several decades
h. caused by a degeneration of neurons that produce dopamine
i. putting one's life into perspective
j. characterized by plaques and tangles in the cerebral cortex
k. confidence in one's memory and related cognitive skills

Challenge Test

Answer these questions the day before an exam as a final check on your understanding of the chapter's terms and concepts.

1. An experiment in which older people fail to see the second of two slides presented in rapid succession primarily documents a problem in:
   a. sensory register.
   b. long-term memory.
   c. short-term memory.
   d. spontaneous priming.

2. An example of priming is:
   a. trying to remember an author's name by remembering the titles of various books he or she has written.
   b. trying to solve a problem more efficiently by thinking of how to shorten the number of steps involved.
   c. writing down a telephone number to be sure you won't forget it.
   d. asking a friend to call and remind you about the time of a meeting that you'll both be attending.

3. One reason that alcoholism among the elderly may be even more serious than alcoholism earlier in life is that:
   a. rates of alcoholism are significantly higher among the elderly.
   b. older alcoholics are more likely to engage in "binge" drinking.
   c. at the same blood alcohol levels, older adults show greater cognitive impairment than younger adults.
   d. older adults have a far greater tolerance for alcohol.

4. Depression among the elderly is a serious problem because:
   a. rates of depression are far higher for the elderly than for younger adults.
   b. in late adulthood depression becomes extremely difficult to treat.
   c. depression in the elderly often goes untreated, contributing to a higher rate of suicide than for any other age group.
   d. organic forms of dementia cause depression.

5. Given the nature of cognitive development, a profession in which an individual's greatest achievements are particularly likely to occur during late adulthood is:
   a. medicine.
   c. mathematics.
   b. philosophy.
   d. administration.

6. Developmentalists believe that older people's tendency to reminisce:
   a. represents an unhealthy preoccupation with the self and the past.
   b. is an underlying cause of age segregation.
   c. is a necessary and healthy process.
   d. is a result of a heightened aesthetic sense.

7. Studies indicate that the *greatest* age-related difference between young and older adults with regard to religion is that older adults are far more inclined to:
   a. perceive other areas of life as being more important than religion.
   b. attend church on a regular basis.
   c. insist on obeying all the particular rites and rules of their religion.
   d. feel that religion plays a central role in their lives.

8. Because of deficits in the sensory register, older people may tend to:
   a. forget the names of people and places.
   b. be distracted by irrelevant stimuli.
   c. miss details in a dimly lit room.
   d. reminisce at length about the past.

9. Holding material in your mind for a minute or two requires which type of memory?
   a. secondary memory
   c. tertiary memory
   b. working memory
   d. sensory register

10. Seventy-five-year-old Lena has vivid memories of her childhood experiences on the family farm. This type of memory is called:
    a. sensory register.
    c. tertiary memory.
    b. working memory.
    d. secondary memory.

11. Which type of material would 72-year-old Jessica probably have the greatest difficulty remembering?
    a. the dates of birth of family members
    b. a short series of numbers she has just heard
    c. the first house she lived in
    d. technical terms from her field of expertise prior to retirement

12. Sixty-five-year-old Lena is becoming more reflective and philosophical as she grows older. Bernice Neugarten would probably say that Lena:
    a. had unhappy experiences as a younger adult.
    b. is demonstrating a normal, age-related tendency toward interiority.
    c. will probably become introverted and reclusive as she gets older.
    d. feels that her life has been a failure.

13. Concerning the public's fear of Alzheimer's disease, which of the following is true?
    a. A serious loss of memory, such as that occurring in people with Alzheimer's disease, can be expected by most people once they reach their 60s.
    b. Of people 65 to 75, at most 5 percent of the population is affected by conditions such as Alzheimer's disease.
    c. Alzheimer's disease is much more common today than it was 50 years ago.
    d. Alzheimer's disease is less common today than it was 50 years ago.

14. At the present stage of research into cognitive development during late adulthood, which of the following statements has the greatest support?
    a. There is uniform decline in all stages of memory during late adulthood.
    b. Tertiary memory shows the greatest decline with age.
    c. Working memory shows the greatest decline with age.
    d. The decline in memory may be the result of the failure to use effective encoding and retrieval strategies.

15. Lately, Wayne's father, who is 73, doesn't seem to care about such basic needs as eating and dressing, moves and speaks slowly, and often ignores or becomes distracted during conversation. The family doctor diagnoses Wayne's father as:
    a. being in the early stages of Alzheimer's disease.
    b. being in the later stages of Alzheimer's disease.
    c. suffering from senile dementia.
    d. possibly suffering from depression.

Key Terms

1. sensory register
2. working memory
3. knowledge base
4. control processes
5. memory self-efficacy
6. dementia
7. Alzheimer's disease
8. multi-infarct dementia (MID)
9. Parkinson's disease
10. interiority
11. life review

ANSWERS

CHAPTER REVIEW

1. multidirectional
2. experience; biological
3. verbal comprehension; spatial visualization; reasoning; mathematical ability; word fluency
4. sensory register; create small decrements in
5. more; more
6. declines
7. can; memory deficits
8. eyes; ears; ambiguous or of low intensity
9. working memory
10. store; process; smaller; older; more
11. knowledge base; secondary (or long-term); tertiary (or remote)
12. secondary memory; memory strategies
13. remote (or tertiary)

This type of retrieval remains efficient possibly because information from tertiary memory was stored at an early age and because it has been frequently retrieved.

14. control processes; memory; retrieval; rules-of-thumb; simpler and less efficient
15. underestimate
16. comparable; specific
17. do worse than
18. memory decline; overestimate; overestimate; self-efficacy

The idea that one is declining in memory and cognitive skills can diminish motivation, self-confidence, and the effort to succeed in situations requiring such skills.

19. self-efficacy
20. Timothy Salthouse; the speed of behavior and thought; a large capacity in working memory; the efficient deployment of attention
21. good health; circulatory; heart disease; hypertension; blood flow
22. alcoholism; depression
23. ADEPT; fluid; have

First, because such studies typically enlist relatively healthy, independent adults, we do not know if their findings are equally true of all older adults. Second, because plasticity declines with increasing age, the gains that older adults might derive from training are unlikely to match the gains that younger adults would receive from such training.

24. passive; dependent; predictable; perspective-taking; egocentrism

25. do; do not; improved

The typical experiment on memory consists of items that are fairly meaningless, which reduces motivation in older adults. It also imposes time limits and prevents spontaneous priming.

26. priming; practice; priming; motivation
27. is
28. dialectical; mechanistic; years of education; do not
29. does not

Although information processing slows down in late adulthood and memory and abstract problem-solving ability probably decline in other ways as well, an older adult's ability to cope with the cognitive demands of daily life may not be significantly impaired by these changes.

30. senility; dementia; severely impaired thinking, memory, or problem-solving ability; is not; severe memory loss, rambling conversation and language lapses, confusion about place and time, inability to function socially or professionally, and changes in personality
31. 60; presenile dementia; senile dementia (or senile psychosis); symptoms; causes; treatments
32. progressive; does
33. forgetfulness; benign forgetfulness; concentration; short-term memory; dangerous; basic needs
34. Alzheimer's disease; cerebral cortex; plaques; tangles; does not
35. middle; more; three to five; 20; 75
36. 21; toxins; genetic; life circumstances; virus; immune; diet; environment
37. biopsy; autopsy
38. are not
39. multi-infarct dementia; blood vessels; infarct; stroke (or ministroke)
40. arteriosclerosis; circulatory; heart disease; hypertension; numbness; diabetes; exercise; diet; drugs
41. sudden; poor
42. Parkinson's disease; dopamine; genetic vulnerability; viruses
43. Huntington's disease, Pick's disease, and AIDS
44. Down syndrome; Alzheimer's
45. medication; alcohol; mental illness; depression

Older adults use a proportionately higher amount of prescription drugs than any other age group, often in amounts that may be an overdose for someone their age. They also are more likely to take several drugs, the intermixing of which can have a deleterious effect, and to suffer from malnutrition.

46. B-vitamins; folic acid
47. men; is not necessarily
48. less; 10
49. most; pseudodementia; is
50. suicide; 60
51. social loss; retirement; widowhood; illness; cancer; brain
52. do
53. arts, children, and the whole of human experience; interdependence
54. self-actualization
55. nature; art
56. reflective; philosophical; interiority; introspection
57. life review
58. history; philosophy
59. wisdom; fundamental pragmatics

Wisdom is unspecialized and concerns all of human experience; entails practical and factual knowledge; defines a contextual approach to life problems; accepts uncertainty in defining and solving life's problems; and recognizes individual differences in values, goals, and priorities.

60. spiritual

PROGRESS TEST 1

Multiple-Choice Questions

1. **d.** is the answer. (p. 612)

   a. Working memory deals with mental, rather than sensory, activity.

   b. & c. Long-term memory, which is a subcomponent of the knowledge base, includes information that is stored for several minutes to several years.

2. **b.** is the answer. (p. 613)
3. **a.** is the answer. (pp. 613–614)

   b. These are the functions of the sensory register.

   c. This is the function of secondary memory.

   d. This is the function of tertiary memory.

4. **a.** is the answer. (p. 615)

   b. & c. Tertiary memory, which is also called remote memory, frequently remains quite efficient in older adults.

   d. This is not a subcomponent of the knowledge base.

5. **c.** is the answer. (p. 616)
6. **d.** is the answer. (p. 618)
7. **b.** is the answer. (p. 619)
8. **a.** is the answer. (p. 620)

b. Plasticity tends to *decrease* with age.

c. The text did not mention this as a limitation of such studies.

9. d. is the answer. (p. 622)
10. a. is the answer. (p. 625)
11. b. is the answer. (pp. 626–633)
12. a. is the answer. (p. 627)

b. This describes multi-infarct dementia.

c. This describes Parkinson's disease.

d. This was not given in the text as a cause of dementia.

13. b. is the answer. (pp. 628–629)

a. Because multiple infarcts typically occur, the disease *is* progressive in nature.

c. The text does not suggest that MID necessarily leads to quick death.

d. At present, Alzheimer's disease is untreatable.

14. b. is the answer. (p. 630)
15. d. is the answer. (p. 635)

True or False Items

1. F The slowing of perceptual processes and decreases in attention associated with aging are also likely to affect efficiency of input. (p. 614)
2. F If they do in fact occur, changes in the sensory register are too insignificant to seriously affect information processing. (p. 613)
3. F Although tertiary memory does not decline significantly, there is no evidence that it improves. (p. 615)
4. F Most older adults perceive some memory loss but do not feel that it affects their daily functioning. (p. 622)
5. T (p. 624)
6. T (pp. 627–630)
7. T (p. 628)
8. T (p. 626)
9. F Interests often broaden during late adulthood, and there is by no means exclusive focus on the self. (p. 633)
10. T (p. 633)

PROGRESS TEST 2

Multiple-Choice Questions

1. c. is the answer. (p. 613)
2. a. is the answer. (p. 614)
3. c. is the answer. (p. 615)

a. The sensory register stores information for a split second.

b. Working memory stores information briefly.

d. Secondary memory stores information for several minutes to several years.

4. c. is the answer. (p. 615)
5. d. is the answer. (p. 616)
6. b. is the answer. Heart disease decreases blood flow to the brain and may impair cognitive functioning. (p. 619)
7. c. is the answer. (p. 621)
8. c. is the answer. (p. 623)
9. b. is the answer. (p. 624)
10. a. is the answer. (p. 625)
11. a. is the answer. (p. 627)

b. MID is responsible for about 15 percent of all dementia.

c. & d. Compared to Alzheimer's disease, which accounts for about 70 percent of all dementia, these account for a much lower percentage.

12. d. is the answer. (pp. 629–630)
13. b. is the answer. (p. 631)

a. & c. These psychological illnesses are less common in the elderly than in younger adults, *and* less common than depression among the elderly.

d. This disorder was not discussed in association with dementia.

14. b. is the answer. (p. 638)

a. & d. Positive cognitive development is *typical* of older adults.

c. Pragmatism is one characteristic of wisdom, an attribute commonly associated with older people.

15. a. is the answer. (p. 634)

b. & c. Although these may be true of some older adults, they are not necessarily a *key* factor in cognitive development during late adulthood.

d. In fact, older adults are typically *more* concerned with the whole of human experience.

Matching Items

1. e (p. 612)	5. k (p. 618)	9. h (p. 629)
2. b (p. 613)	6. d (p. 625)	10. a (p. 634)
3. g (p. 615)	7. j (p. 627)	11. i (p. 635)
4. c (p. 616)	8. f (p. 629)	

CHALLENGE TEST

1. a. is the answer. (pp. 612–613)

b. & c. Long- and short-term memory store information for further processing; in this example, the difficulty pertains to sensory input.

d. Spontaneous priming involves using a word to facilitate retrieval of other information.

2. **a.** is the answer. (p. 616)
b., c., & d. These are examples of control processes that facilitate problem solving (b.) and retrieval (c. & d.).

3. **c.** is the answer. (p. 631)
a. The rate of alcoholism is lower among elderly men than among younger men.
b. Alcoholism among the elderly is more likely to take the form of steady, measured drinking.
d. Older adults probably have less tolerance for alcohol.

4. **c.** is the answer. (p. 632)
a. In general, psychological illnesses are less common in the elderly than in younger adults.
b. Depression is quite treatable at any age.
d. Symptoms of *depression* are often mistaken as signs of *dementia*.

5. **b.** is the answer. (p. 634)

6. **c.** is the answer. (p. 635)
d. This would lead to a greater appreciation of nature and art, but not necessarily to a tendency to reminisce.

7. **d.** is the answer. (p. 637)

8. **c.** is the answer. (p. 613)
a. & d. The sensory register is concerned with noticing sensory events rather than with memory.
b. Age-related deficits in the sensory register are most likely for ambiguous or weak stimuli.

9. **a.** is the answer. (p. 615)
b. Working memory stores information temporarily, for less than a minute.
c. Tertiary, or remote, memory includes information remembered for years or decades.
d. The sensory register stores information for a split second.

10. **c.** is the answer. (p. 615)
a. The sensory register stores incoming sensory information for a split second.
b. Working memory temporarily stores information for further processing.
d. Secondary, or long-term, memory stores information for several minutes to several years.

11. **b.** is the answer. Older individuals are particularly likely to experience difficulty holding new information in mind, particularly when it is essentially meaningless. (p. 614)
a., c., & d. These are examples of tertiary memory, which declines very little with age.

12. **b.** is the answer. (p. 634)

13. **b.** is the answer. (p. 625)
c. & d. The text does not indicate the existence of cohort effects in the incidence of Alzheimer's disease.

14. **d.** is the answer. (p. 616)
a. Some aspects of information processing, such as tertiary memory, show less decline with age than others, such as working memory.
b. & c. The text does not indicate that one particular subcomponent of memory shows the *greatest* decline.

15. **d.** is the answer. (p. 631)
a., b., & c. The symptoms Wayne's father is experiencing are those of depression, which is often misdiagnosed as dementia in the elderly.

KEY TERMS

1. The **sensory register,** which stores incoming sensory information for a split second after it is received, becomes less sensitive in older adults. (p. 612)
2. **Working memory,** which temporarily stores information for conscious processing, declines in capacity and efficiency of function with advancing age. (p. 613)
3. The **knowledge base** has two components: secondary, or long-term, memory stores information for several minutes to several years; tertiary, or remote, memory stores information for years or decades. Retrieval from secondary memory becomes more difficult with age, while that from remote memory remains quite good. (p. 615)
4. Memory **control processes,** which include strategies for retaining information in the knowledge base, retrieval strategies for reaccessing information, and rules-of-thumb that aid problem solving, tend to become simpler and less efficient with age. (p. 616)
5. Loss of **memory self-efficacy** is a loss of confidence in one's memory and related cognitive skills. (p. 618)
6. **Dementia** is severely impaired thinking, memory, or problem-solving ability. (p. 625)
7. **Alzheimer's disease,** a progressive disorder that accounts for about 70 percent of all dementia, is characterized by plaques and tangles in the cerebral cortex that destroy normal brain functioning. (p. 627)
8. **Multi-infarct dementia (MID),** which accounts for about 15 percent of all dementia, occurs

because an infarct, or temporary obstruction of the blood vessels (often called a stroke), prevents a sufficient supply of blood from reaching an area of the brain. (p. 629)

9. **Parkinson's disease,** which produces dementia as well as muscle rigidity or tremors, is related to the degeneration of neurons that produce dopamine. (p. 629)

10. **Interiority** refers to the tendency of people to become more philosophical and introspective as they age. (p. 634)

11. In the **life review,** an older person attempts to put his or her life into perspective by recalling and recounting various aspects of life to members of the younger generations. (p. 635)

CHAPTER 25

Late Adulthood: Psychosocial Development

Chapter Overview

Ageism distorts popular perceptions of the later years with negative stereotypes. Certain psychosocial changes are common during this stage of the life span—retirement, the death of a spouse, and failing health—yet people respond to these experiences in vastly different ways.

Individual experiences may help to explain the fact that theories of psychosocial aging, discussed in the first section of the chapter, are often diametrically opposed. The second section of the chapter focuses on the challenges to generativity that accompany late adulthood, such as finding new sources of achievement once derived from work. In the third section, the importance of friends, neighbors, and family in providing social support is discussed, as are the different experiences of married and single older adults. The fourth section focuses on the frail elderly—the minority of older adults, often poor and/or ill, who require extensive care. The chapter closes with a discussion of Erikson's stage of integrity versus despair, in which the individual who achieves integrity becomes self-actualized and has a strong sense of self-worth.

NOTE: Answer guidelines for all Chapter 25 questions begin on page 379.

Guided Study

The text chapter should be studied one section at a time. Before you read, preview each section by skimming it, noting headings and boldface items. Then read the appropriate section objectives from the following outline. Keep these objectives in mind and, as you read the chapter section, search for the information that will enable you to meet each objective. Once you have finished a section, write out answers for its objectives.

Theories of Psychosocial Aging (pp. 642–645)

1. Compare and contrast the disengagement, activity, and continuity theories of psychosocial development during late adulthood.

2. Discuss the increasing diversity of older adults and how it complicates the study of psychosocial development.

Generativity in Late Adulthood (pp. 645–656)

3. Discuss the impact of retirement on the individual and the factors that influence adjustment to this event.

4. (A Closer Look) Explain how the economic circumstances of the elderly have changed in recent years and discuss the issue of generational equity.

5. List and discuss several alternative sources of achievement during late adulthood.

6. (Text and A Closer Look) Discuss the relationship between the generations as it exists today and identify several reasons for the current pattern of detachment.

Affiliation: The Social Convoy (pp. 657–665)

7. Describe the components of the social convoy and explain this convoy's increasing importance during late adulthood, including its impact on preferences for living arrangements in retirement.

8. Discuss how, and why, marriage relationships tend to change as people grow old.

9. Discuss the impact of being old and single (never-married, divorced, or widowed) on both women and men.

The Frail Elderly (pp. 665–673)

10. Describe the frail elderly and explain why their number is growing.

11. (Closer Looks) Identify and discuss four factors that may protect the elderly from frailty and describe the typical case of elder maltreatment.

12. (Text and A Closer Look) Discuss alternative care arrangements for the frail elderly, identifying some of the potential advantages and disadvantages of each.

Integrity and Community (pp. 673–674)

13. Discuss Erikson's stage of integrity versus despair and the process of achieving integrity in old age.

Chapter Review

When you have finished reading the chapter, work through the material that follows to review it. Complete the sentences and answer the questions. As you proceed, evaluate your performance for each section by consulting the answers on page 379. Do not continue with the next section until you understand each answer. If you need to, review or reread the appropriate section in the textbook before continuing.

Theories of Psychosocial Aging (pp. 642–645)

1. According to ________________ theory, in old age the individual and society mutually withdraw from each other.

   List the four steps of disengagement.

   a. ________________________________

   b. ________________________________

   c. ________________________________

   d. ________________________________

2. According to disengagement theory, the elderly's participation in the disengagement process ________________ (is/is not) voluntary. This theory is ________________ (controversial among/almost universally accepted by) gerontologists.

3. The most unfortunate aspect of disengagement theory is that it seems to justify ________________ of the elderly.

4. Many critics of disengagement theory endorse ________________ theory, which proposes that older people need and want to substitute new involvements for the roles they lose with aging.

5. Activity theory ________________ (has/does not have) unequivocal support from research.

6. The best sign of satisfaction among the elderly is how close their level of activity is to ________________.

7. Remaining highly active socially ________________ (does/does not) necessarily extend longevity.

8. Social isolation ________________ (at any age/in old age) diminishes ________________, impairs ________________, and shortens ________________.

9. According to ________________ theory, people cope with late adulthood in much the same way that they did earlier in life. Thus, the so-called ________________ personality traits are maintained throughout old age. This theory has recently received strong support from research in the field of ________________, which has shown that various life events seem to be at least as much affected by ________________ as by life circumstances.

10. Demographically, the elderly are a group that is quite ________________ (diverse/homogeneous). As a common denominator, age becomes increasingly ________________ (relevant/irrelevant) as life goes on.

11. Where and with whom an elderly individual lives is determined less by age than by ________________ and ________________. Within a given nation, the living arrangements of older adults are strongly influenced by ________________, ________________, and ________________.

12. In the United States, diversity among the elderly appears to be ________________ (increasing/decreasing).

Generativity in Late Adulthood (pp. 645–656)

13. Today, most adults ________________ (do/do not) retire while they are still physically able to work.

14. The trend toward earlier retirement is occurring primarily because of ________________ (choice/compulsion/incapacity).

15. Except in certain professions, mandatory retirement is ________________ (legal/illegal) in the United States.

16. Approximately ________________ percent of all retirees leave work because of failing health.

17. Poverty in old age is ______________ (more/less) common today than in the past, primarily because ______________ are almost universal.

18. (A Closer Look) Ironically, while the financial circumstances of the American elderly have improved in recent years, other age groups, notably ______________, have grown poorer. More than one American child in five now lives below the poverty line. This has led to calls for ______________ ______________, defined as ______________ ______________.

19. (A Closer Look) For most of the nonpoor elderly, extra savings serve as a bulwark against two dreaded circumstances: ______________ ______________ and ______________ ______________. Because ______________ is at the heart of intergenerational relationships, it is unfair and counterproductive to blame the elderly for the financial plight of the younger generations.

20. Most retirees ______________ (do/do not) adjust well to retirement.

21. Those most likely to experience difficulty adjusting to retirement are those who retired ______________ and ______________.

22. Given the choice, most employees prefer to retire ______________ (abruptly/gradually).

23. Many of the elderly use the time they once spent earning a living to develop ______________ and interests that had already been part of their life.

24. The eagerness of the elderly to pursue educational interests is exemplified by the rapid growth of ______________, a program in which older people live on college campuses and take special classes.

25. Compared to younger adults, older adults are ______________ (more/less) likely to feel a strong obligation to serve their community. Informal volunteer help is performed by about ______________ of all the elderly.

26. The major United States organization affecting the elderly is the ______________.

27. Most children feel substantial ______________ ______________, that is, the sense of duty and need to protect and care for their aging parents.

28. Most families evidence three signs of intergenerational closeness: ______________ ______________, ______________ ______________, and ______________ ______________.

29. The most complex aspect of the relationship between the generations involves the exchange of ______________ and ______________.

30. (A Closer Look) As people age, relationships with younger family members become more ______________ and enjoyable. In general, the older a grandparent is, the ______________ (more/less) likely he or she is to see the grandparent role as central.

31. Today's pattern of detachment between grandparents and grandchildren is ______________ (much the same as/quite different from) that typical in the first half of this century.

Give several reasons for this pattern.

32. Styles of grandparenting vary by ______________, ______________, and ______________ ______________. In general, ______________ (grandmothers/grandfathers) are more active in the grandparenting role.

33. Compared to other ethnic groups in the United States, the groups that are likely to be more involved in the lives of their children and grandchildren are ______________ ______________.

Give several reasons that older African-Americans are more often extensively involved in the care of their grandchildren.

34. Grandparent care among African-Americans increases as ________________ falls.

35. According to many researchers, the more remote grandparenting that is increasingly common in today's ________________ families diminishes the sense of ________________ ________________ and interdependence.

Affiliation: The Social Convoy (pp. 657–665)

36. The phrase ________________ ________________ highlights the fact that the life course is travelled in the company of others.

37. Older people's satisfaction with life is more strongly correlated to contact with ________________ than to contact with younger members of their own family.

38. Compared to younger adults, older adults are ________________ (more/less) likely to want more friends.

39. Compared to men, women tend to have ________________ (larger/smaller) social circles and ________________ (more/less) intimate relationships with their friends. The strength of late-life friendships correlates with feelings of ________________ and ________________.

40. Bonds between siblings often ________________ (intensify/weaken) in late adulthood.

41. The older an adult is, the ________________ (more/less) likely he or she is to move to a new residence. One reason is the need of the current cohort of older Americans, about ________________ of whom are immigrants or first-generation Americans, to be near ________________ people.

42. Only about 10 percent of the elderly move into publicly subsidized ________________ ________________, where all residents must be over a certain age.

43. A larger percentage live in ________________ ________________ retirement communities, or environments where more than half the residents are elderly.

44. Most elderly Americans ________________ (are/are not) married, and they tend to be ________________, ________________, and ________________ than those who never married, or who are divorced or widowed.

45. The best predictor of the nature of a marriage in its later stages is ________________.
Most older married couples believe their marriage ________________ (has/has not) improved over the years.

Give two possible reasons for this trend.

46. The longer a couple is married, the more likely both are to believe that their relationship is ________________ and ________________.
Poor health generally has a ________________ (major/minor) impact on the marital relationship.

47. Being old and single is ________________ (more/less) acceptable than it was a generation or two ago. Those who never married tend to be particularly ________________ (content/unhappy) with their state of affairs.

48. Divorce is very ________________ (rare/common) in late life. As a group, older divorced ________________ (men/women) tend to fare better.

Briefly explain this gender difference.

49. The death of a mate usually means not only the loss of a close friend and lover but also a lower ________________, less ________________, a(n) ________________ social circle, and disrupted ________________ ________________.

50. In general, living without a spouse is somewhat easier for ________________ (widows/widowers).

State several reasons for this being so.

51. Remarriage in late adulthood tends to be ________________ (happier/unhappier) than remarriage in earlier adulthood.

The Frail Elderly (pp. 665–673)

52. Elderly people who are physically infirm, very ill, or cognitively impaired are called the ________________ ________________.

53. The crucial sign of frailty is an inability to perform the ________________, which comprise five tasks: ________________, ________________, ________________, ________________, ________________.

54. Actions that require some intellectual competence and forethought are classified as ________________ ________________. These include such things as ________________ ________________.

55. The number of frail elderly is ________________ (increasing/decreasing) for reasons that are ________________, ________________, and ________________.

56. The fastest-growing segment of the American population is people aged ________________ and older.

57. As more people reach old age, the absolute numbers of frail individuals will ________________ (increase/decrease).

58. The medical establishment is still more geared toward ________________ ________________ rather than treatment of ________________ ________________. The result has been an increasing ________________ (morbidity/mortality) rate, even as ________________ (morbidity/mortality) rates fall.

59. In 1965, Congress passed the ________________ ________________ ________________, providing every older person a wealth of benefits.

Briefly explain why passage of this act did not solve the problems of all the frail elderly.

60. The likelihood of disability depends less on ________________ ________________ than on factors such as ________________ ________________.

61. The main goal of the frail elderly is to keep on living as ________________ as possible.

62. (A Closer Look) Many elderly persons never become frail because of four protective factors: ________________, ________________, ________________, ________________, ________________, and ________________ ________________.

63. Care of most of the frail elderly usually ________________ (falls on one person/is shared by several family members).

64. If a frail elder is spouseless, the caregiver is usually a(n) ______________. Although caregivers are most often ______________ (women/men), this pattern is changing because of ______________ ______________.

State three reasons that caregivers may feel unfairly burdened and resentful.

a. ______________

b. ______________

c. ______________

65. The amount of stress, resentment, and ill health experienced by caregivers correlates most strongly with their ______________ ______________ of the support they experience.

66. In many cases, a good alternative to a frail elder living with a relative is some form of ______________ ______________, in which a group of older people live together with outside help.

67. (A Closer Look) Abuse or neglect of older adults is called ______________ ______________.

68. The worst nursing homes tend to be those profit-making ventures where most patients are subsidized entirely by ______________. Too often nursing homes reinforce ______________ in patients, who become less active and lose self-esteem.

Integrity and Community (pp. 673–674)

Identify three themes of development that are strongly apparent in late adulthood.

a. ______________

b. ______________

c. ______________

69. In Erikson's theory, the final crisis of development is that of ______________ versus ______________, in which older adults attempt to integrate their personal experiences with their vision of the future of their ______________.

70. Instead of comparing themselves with others, those who achieve integrity become ______________ and ______________.

Progress Test 1

Multiple-Choice Questions

Circle your answers to the following questions and check them with the answers on page 381. If your answer is incorrect, read the explanation for why it is incorrect and then consult the appropriate pages of the text (in parentheses following the correct answer).

1. According to disengagement theory, during late adulthood people tend to:
   a. become less role-centered and more passive.
   b. have regrets about how they have lived their lives.
   c. become involved in a range of new activities.
   d. exaggerate lifelong personality traits.

2. According to activity theory:
   a. the more roles and activities older people have, the greater their life satisfaction becomes.
   b. physical exercise is the key to psychological health during old age.
   c. activities should gradually be reduced as the individual ages.
   d. activities undertaken during late adulthood should be consistent with those the individual has engaged in earlier in life.

3. Social isolation:
   a. diminishes happiness.
   b. impairs health.
   c. shortens life.
   d. does all of the above.

4. Longitudinal studies of monozygotic and dizygotic twins have recently found evidence that:
   a. genetic influences weaken as life experiences accumulate.
   b. strongly supports disengagement theory.
   c. some traits seem even more apparent in late adulthood than earlier.
   d. all of the above are true.

5. Diversity among individuals during late adulthood:
   a. is less than at earlier stages in life.
   b. stems from differences in temperament and personal experiences.
   c. is more evident for females than for males.
   d. tends to disrupt long-standing social bonds.

6. Compared with workers in the past, workers today are:
   a. more likely to retire at a later age.
   b. more likely to retire for health-related reasons.
   c. more likely to retire at their employers' request.
   d. less likely to have the financial means to retire.

7. (A Closer Look) Regarding the issue of generational equity, most gerontologists today maintain that:
   a. limits must be put on public money that flows to elders at the expense of children.
   b. those who feel that "we soak the young to enrich the old" fail to take into consideration the tremendous diversity of income among the elderly.
   c. by the year 2025, Social Security will be unable to meet the retirement needs of aging baby boomers.
   d. the economic needs of the elderly are more legitimate than those of younger adults.

8. After retirement, the need for achievement:
   a. declines for most people.
   b. is often met by expanding leisure activities.
   c. is most commonly fulfilled by increased involvement in grandparenting.
   d. often becomes a source of stress because appropriate outlets are absent.

9. By and large, grandparents today:
   a. assume a relatively remote grandparenting role and are reasonably satisfied with it.
   b. tend to take on a more active role than did grandparents in the past because they have more leisure time.
   c. assume a relatively remote grandparenting role but would like to be much more involved with their grandchildren.
   d. rarely see their grandchildren as a result of geographical distance.

10. African-American children are more likely to live with their grandparents than children from other ethnic groups because:
   a. the multigenerational family is more traditional in this ethnic group.
   b. African-Americans tend to begin and end their childbearing earlier than other groups.
   c. of current economic and social conditions, especially in crowded and dangerous cities.
   d. of all the above reasons.

11. The importance of long-standing friendships is reflected in which of the following?
   a. the intensification of friendly bonds between in-laws
   b. the mother-daughter relationship becomes more like one between two friends
   c. the intensification of friendly bonds between siblings
   d. a change in the husband-wife relationship to one of friendship

12. In general, during late adulthood the *fewest* problems are experienced by individuals who:
   a. are married.
   b. have always been single.
   c. have long been divorced.
   d. are widowed.

13. Adjustment to the death of a spouse tends to be:
   a. easier for men in all respects.
   b. initially easier for men but over the long term easier for women.
   c. emotionally easier for women but financially easier for men.
   d. determined primarily by individual personality traits, and therefore shows very few sex differences.

14. Compared with remarriage in earlier adulthood, remarriage in late adulthood is more likely to:
   a. fail because the spouses have become more set in their ways and thus have difficulty making the adjustment.
   b. fail because the stepparent role is all the more difficult when the children are grown.
   c. succeed because the spouses have usually had a positive previous experience, which helps them in building a new relationship.
   d. succeed because the spouses bring fewer needs and expectations to the new marriage.

15. A common problem in nursing homes is:
   a. inadequate standards of hygiene and safety.
   b. a failure to adequately supervise residents.
   c. a neglect of chronic medical problems.
   d. insufficient attention to residents' psychological needs.

True or False Items

Write *true* or *false* on the line in front of each statement.

_______ 1. The various theories of psychosocial aging ask different questions but come to similar conclusions.

_______ 2. As one of the most disruptive experiences in the life span, widowhood tends to have similar effects on most older adults.

_______ 3. As life goes on, age becomes less relevant as an index to developmental patterns.

_______ 4. Until recently, failing health was the main cause of retirement.

_______ 5. How well the individual adjusts to retirement will depend largely on his or her prior attitudes toward retirement.

_______ 6. Grandparenting patterns today tend to provide members of each generation with more independence but less continuity.

_______ 7. As many as one-third of the elderly are involved in structured volunteer work.

_______ 8. Most older people suffer significantly from a lack of close friendships.

_______ 9. Nearly one in two older adults makes a long-distance move after retirement.

_______ 10. Loneliness during late adulthood is greater for individuals who were never married than for any other group.

Progress Test 2

Progress Test 2 should be completed during a final chapter review. Answer the following questions after you thoroughly understand the correct answers for the Chapter Review and Progress Test 1.

Multiple-Choice Questions

1. A claim commonly made by those who object to disengagement theory is that:
   a. people generally become more active during late adulthood.
   b. disengagement may not be voluntary on the part of the individual.
   c. disengagement often leads to greater life satisfaction for older adults.
   d. disengagement is more common at earlier stages in the life cycle.

2. Which of the following is a criticism of activity theory?
   a. It may promote ageism.
   b. It may create a kind of reverse ageism.
   c. It focuses on the continuity of the later years.
   d. It pays too much attention to the diversity of older adults.

3. According to continuity theory, during late adulthood people:
   a. become less role-centered.
   b. become more passive.
   c. become involved in a range of new activities.
   d. cope with challenges in much the same way they did earlier in life.

4. One reason for inconsistencies among the various theories of psychosocial aging is the fact that:
   a. the theories are not based on empirical data.
   b. late adulthood encompasses a large age span.
   c. older adults are very diverse as a group.
   d. psychosocial needs during late adulthood are very different from those at earlier stages of life.

5. (A Closer Look) The "war on poverty" in the United States during the 1960s:
   a. extended Social Security.
   b. provided a range of medical and social benefits to the aged.
   c. reduced the proportion of the elderly below the poverty line.
   d. accomplished all of the above.

6. Adjustment to retirement tends to be most difficult for individuals who:
   a. spent relatively few years in the work force.
   b. entered retirement involuntarily and abruptly.
   c. thought retirement would be a change they would welcome.
   d. had relatively uninteresting jobs.

7. The major United States organization affecting the elderly is:
   a. Elderhostel.
   b. the American Association of Retired Persons.
   c. Foster Grandparents.
   d. Service Corps of Retired Executives.

8. (A Closer Look) In general, relationships between older adults and younger family members over time:
   a. become increasingly close.
   b. become increasingly remote.
   c. become more selective and enjoyable.
   d. remain as they have always been.

9. Which of the following was *not* suggested as a reason for today's pattern of detachment between grandparents and grandchildren?

a. increased geographical mobility of offspring
b. greater financial independence of older adults
c. the rising divorce rate
d. longer life expectancy

10. One of the most important factors contributing to life satisfaction for older adults appears to be:
a. contact with friends.
b. contact with younger family members.
c. the number of new experiences to which they are exposed.
d. continuity in the daily routine.

11. Formal age-segregated retirement communities tend to:
a. isolate the individual from family and friends.
b. offer security at the cost of independence.
c. provide the individual with a social network.
d. ignore residents' needs for privacy and time alone.

12. In general, the longer a couple has been married, the more likely they are to:
a. be happier with each other.
b. have frequent, minor disagreements.
c. feel the relationship is not equitable.
d. do all of the above.

13. Adjustment to divorce in late adulthood tends to be:
a. equally easy for men and women.
b. easier for women.
c. easier for men.
d. initially easier for women, but over the long term easier for men.

14. Which of the following is *not* a major factor contributing to an increase in the number of frail elderly?
a. an increase in average life expectancy
b. a research focus on acute, rather than chronic, illnesses
c. inadequate expenditures on social services
d. a lack of facilities in many areas to care for the elderly

15. According to Erikson, achieving integrity during late adulthood above all involves:
a. the ability to perceive one's own life as worthwhile.
b. being open to new influences and experiences.
c. treating other people with respect.
d. developing a consistent and yet varied daily routine.

Matching Items

Match each definition or description with its corresponding term.

Terms

_______ 1. disengagement theory
_______ 2. activity theory
_______ 3. continuity theory
_______ 4. generational equity
_______ 5. filial obligation
_______ 6. congregate care
_______ 7. activities of daily life (ADLs)
_______ 8. instrumental activities of daily life (IADLs)
_______ 9. naturally occurring retirement communities (NORCs)
_______ 10. Elderhostel

Definitions or Descriptions

a. a group of older people live together with outside help
b. an educational program for the elderly
c. eating, bathing, toileting, walking, and dressing
d. neighborhood where more than half the residents are elderly
e. theory that people become less role-centered as they age
f. actions that require intellectual competence and forethought
g. equal contributions from, and fair benefits for, each age cohort
h. theory that older people need to substitute new involvements for the roles that they lose with retirement
i. a sense of duty and need to care for aging parents
j. theory that each person copes with late adulthood in the same way he or she did earlier in life

Challenge Test

Answer these questions the day before an exam as a final check on your understanding of the chapter's terms and concepts.

1. Which of the following statements *most* accurately describes psychosocial development in late adulthood?
   a. Many leading gerontologists believe that people become more alike as they get older.
   b. Older adults generally fit into one of two distinct personality types.
   c. Many gerontologists believe that the diversity of personalities and patterns is especially pronounced among the elderly.
   d. Few changes in psychosocial development occur after middle adulthood.

2. An advocate of which of the following theories would be most likely to agree with the statement, "Because of their more passive style of interaction, older people are less likely to be chosen for new roles"?
   a. disengagement c. activity
   b. continuity d. discontinuity

3. Activity theory could best be used to make an argument *against*:
   a. increases in Medicare coverage.
   b. mandatory retirement age.
   c. home health care for the frail elderly.
   d. age-segregated housing.

4. A high-level, "workaholic" executive retires. Suddenly finding himself with lots of time on his hands, he establishes and runs an organization to help place inner-city teenagers in jobs. This individual's situation exemplifies aspects of all the following psychosocial theories of aging *except*:
   a. disengagement theory.
   b. activity theory.
   c. continuity theory.
   d. discontinuity theory.

5. When they retire, most older adults:
   a. immediately feel more satisfied with their new way of life.
   b. adjust well to retirement and even improve in health and happiness.
   c. have serious, long-term difficulties adjusting to retirement.
   d. disengage from other roles and activities as well.

6. The one *most* likely to agree with the statement, "Older adults have an obligation to help others and serve the community," is:
   a. a middle-aged adult. c. an older man.
   b. an older woman. d. an older adult.

7. Lately, Claude feels a strong filial obligation. This means that he:
   a. feels committed to "giving something back" to his community.
   b. wishes to leave a legacy for the next generation.
   c. has a sense of duty and need to protect and care for his aging parents.
   d. has a desire to make sure his wife and children are well cared for.

8. The most striking historical shift in the lifestyle of the unmarried elderly is the:
   a. increasing numbers preferring to live alone.
   b. decreasing numbers who are frail.
   c. increasing numbers still working.
   d. growing "volunteer spirit" among this group.

9. When asked why the current cohort of older Americans find it particularly important to live near familiar people, a gerontologist would probably say that:
   a. this is true only of ethnic minorities who fear being exposed to prejudice if they move to an unfamiliar neighborhood.
   b. fear of loneliness is greater among the elderly today than ever before.
   c. this is because about a fourth of this cohort are immigrants or first-generation Americans.
   d. this widely held belief is unsupported by empirical research.

10. Of the following older adults, who is most likely to be involved in a large network of intimate friendships?
    a. William, a 65-year-old who never married
    b. Darrel, a 60-year-old widower
    c. Florence, a 63-year-old widow
    d. Kay, a 66-year-old married woman

11. Florence, who is African-American, became a grandmother at age 39. Compared to her mother, who became a grandmother at age 61, Florence is likely to:
    a. be more satisfied with her role as a grandmother.
    b. be less satisfied with her role as a grandmother.

c. have a larger network of social support as a grandmother.
d. have a smaller network of social support as a grandmother.

12. Claudine is the primary caregiver for her elderly parents. The amount of stress she feels in this role depends above all on:
a. how frail her parents are.
b. her subjective interpretation of the support she receives from others.
c. her relationship to her parents prior to their becoming frail.
d. her overall financial situation.

13. Although not frail, Wilma's elderly mother can no longer live independently. In selecting appropriate housing for her mother, Wilma would be best advised to choose:
a. a profit-making nursing home.
b. a nursing home where most patients are subsidized entirely by Medicaid.
c. some form of congregate care.
d. an Elderhostel.

14. In concluding her presentation on the frail elderly, Janet notes that "the number of frail elderly is currently ______________ than the number who are active, financially stable, and capable; however, the frail elderly are ______________ in absolute number."
a. greater; decreasing
b. less; increasing
c. greater; increasing
d. less; decreasing

15. Jack, who is 73, looks back on his life with a sense of pride and contentment; Eleanor feels unhappy with her life and that it is "too late to start over." In Erikson's terminology, Jack is experiencing ______________, while Eleanor is experiencing ______________.
a. generativity; stagnation
b. identity; emptiness
c. integrity; despair
d. completion; termination

Key Terms

Using your own words, write a brief definition or explanation of each of the following terms on a separate piece of paper.

1. disengagement theory
2. activity theory
3. continuity theory
4. generational equity
5. Elderhostel
6. American Association of Retired Persons (AARP)
7. filial obligation
8. social convoy
9. planned retirement communities
10. naturally occurring retirement communities (NORCs)
11. frail elderly
12. activities of daily life (ADLs)
13. instrumental activities of daily life (IADLs)
14. Older Americans Act
15. congregate care
16. elder maltreatment
17. integrity versus despair

ANSWERS

CHAPTER REVIEW

1. disengagement
   a. Beginning in late middle age, a person's social sphere becomes increasingly narrow.
   b. People adjust to this narrowing of the social sphere by relinquishing many of the roles they have played and accepting the gradual closing of their social circle.
   c. As people become less role-centered, their style of interaction changes from an active to a passive one.
   d. Because they are less likely to be chosen for new roles, older people disengage even more.
2. is; controversial among
3. ageist stereotypes
4. activity
5. does not have
6. the level they desire
7. does not
8. at any age; happiness; health; life
9. continuity; Big Five; behavioral genetics; genetics
10. diverse; irrelevant

11. culture; economics; cohort; income; ethnicity
12. increasing
13. do
14. choice
15. illegal
16. 25
17. less; pensions
18. children; generational equity; equal contributions from, and fair benefits for, each generation
19. lingering helplessness; abject poverty; interdependence
20. do
21. prematurely; involuntarily
22. gradually
23. hobbies
24. Elderhostel
25. more; two-thirds
26. American Association of Retired Persons (AARP)
27. filial obligation
28. mutual assistance; frequent contact; shared affection
29. advice; respect
30. selective; less
31. quite different than

The reasons for this pattern include increased geographical mobility of offspring, greater financial independence of grandparents today, more working grandmothers, the rising divorce rate, and the tendency for relationships between parents and children to become more egalitarian in recent decades.

32. sex; age; ethnic group; grandmothers
33. African-Americans, Asian-Americans, Italian-Americans, and Hispanic-Americans

The multigenerational family is traditional for this group. African-Americans also begin and end childbearing earlier, which means that grandparents often are younger. Finally, socioeconomic conditions have meant that having young children live with their grandparents aids economic survival for the family, as well as healthier development for the children.

34. income
35. affluent; generational continuity
36. social convoy
37. friends
38. less
39. larger; more; well-being; self-esteem
40. intensify
41. less; one-fourth; familiar
42. planned retirement communities
43. naturally occurring
44. are; healthier; wealthier; happier
45. its nature early on; has

One reason is that the accumulation of shared life experiences makes husbands and wives more compatible. Another is that the frequency of disagreements tends to decline as the length of time a couple has been married increases.

46. fair; equitable; minor
47. more; content
48. rare; women

For divorced older women life is likely to improve with age, especially if they have successfully raised children or succeeded in a career against all odds. Because women are usually the kinkeepers, many former husbands find themselves isolated from children, grandchildren, and old friends.

49. income; status; broken; daily routines
50. widows

One reason is that elderly women often expect to outlive their husbands, and have anticipated this event. Another is that in most communities widows can get help from support groups. A third is that many elderly men were dependent on their wives to perform the basic tasks of daily living.

51. happier
52. frail elderly
53. activities of daily life (ADLs); eating; bathing; toileting; walking; dressing
54. instrumental activities of daily life (IADLs); shopping, paying bills, making phone calls
55. increasing; demographic; medical; political
56. 85
57. increase
58. death prevention; chronic illness; morbidity; mortality
59. Older Americans Act

The benefits provided by this act are neither comprehensive nor free and are relatively scarce in rural areas, where a disproportionate share of the elderly reside.

60. chronological age; social support, attitudes, and the physical setting
61. independently
62. attitude; social network; physical setting; financial resources
63. falls on one person
64. daughter or daughter-in-law; women; low birth

rates, high divorce rates, and more women being employed

a. If one relative is doing the caregiving, other family members tend to feel relief rather than an obligation to help.

b. Care-receivers and caregivers often disagree about the nature and extent of care that is needed.

c. Services designed for caregivers are difficult to obtain from social agencies.

65. subjective interpretation
66. congregate care
67. elder maltreatment
68. Medicaid; dependence

a. There is interplay among the domains of development.

b. Developmental diversity is the norm.

c. Cohort effects abound.

69. integrity; despair; community
70. self-affirming; self-actualizing

PROGRESS TEST 1

Multiple-Choice Questions

1. **a.** is the answer. (p. 642)

   b. This answer depicts a person struggling with Erikson's crisis of integrity versus despair.

   c. This answer describes activity theory.

   d. Disengagement theory does not address this issue.

2. **a.** is the answer. (p. 643)

   b. Activity theory does not address the issue of exercise per se.

   c. In fact, activity theory would imply just the opposite.

   d. This answer has more to do with continuity theory than activity theory.

3. **d.** is the answer. (p. 643)
4. **c.** is the answer. (p. 644)

   a. Such studies have found that genetic influences do not weaken with age.

   b. This research provides support for continuity theory rather than disengagement theory.

5. **b.** is the answer. (p. 644)

   a. During late adulthood diversity continues to be the rule.

   c. Diversity is equally extensive for men and women.

   d. Diversity has to do with differences from one person to another; it has no bearing on *individual* social bonds.

6. **c.** is the answer. (p. 646)

   a. & b. Workers are retiring earlier than in the past, and not usually for health-related reasons.

   d. Because pensions are nearly universal, this answer is incorrect.

7. **b.** is the answer. (p. 648)

   a. This is the position of those who advocate generational equity, a position not supported by most gerontologists.

   c. No such prediction was made in the text.

   d. Gerontologists emphasize the special, legitimate needs of every age group.

8. **b.** is the answer. (pp. 647, 650)

   a. The need for achievement remains strong after retirement.

   c. This is true only for some older adults.

   d. Most older adults adjust quite well to retirement.

9. **a.** is the answer. (p. 654)

   b. Grandparents in the past tended to take a more active role than those today.

   c. Most grandparents are satisfied with the relationship they have with their grandchildren.

   d. This is true for some, but certainly not most, grandparents.

10. **d.** is the answer. (pp. 655–656)
11. **c.** is the answer. (p. 658)

    a. , b., & d. These may occur in some cases, but they are not discussed in the text.

12. **a.** is the answer. (p. 660)
13. **c.** is the answer. (pp. 663–664)
14. **c.** is the answer. This is true because both partners are usually widowed rather than divorced. (p. 664)

    a. & b. Remarriage during late adulthood tends to be more successful than remarriage at an earlier age.

    d. There is no evidence that this is true.

15. **d.** is the answer. (p. 672)

    a., b., & c. These are true only of the worst nursing homes.

True or False Items

1. F The various theories of psychosocial aging start with essentially the same questions and arrive at very different answers. (pp. 642–643)

2. F As a result of diversity of personality and life circumstances, people's responses to widowhood, as to other events, will vary greatly. (pp. 663–664)
3. T (p. 644)
4. T (p. 645)
5. F Many factors combine to determine how the individual adjusts to retirement, and the individual's experience of retirement is often very different from his or her preconceptions. (p. 647)
6. T (p. 656)
7. T (p. 651)
8. F Most older adults have at least one close friend and, as compared with younger adults, are less likely to feel a need for more friendships. (p. 657)
9. F Only one in six older adults moves to another state. (p. 658)
10. F If anything, loneliness tends to be less in never-married older adults. (p. 662)

PROGRESS TEST 2

Multiple-Choice Questions

1. **b.** is the answer. (p. 642)

   a. Activity theory proposes that the more active the elderly are, the greater their life satisfaction; it does not maintain that people generally become more active during late adulthood.

   c. & d. Neither of these answers is true, nor a criticism of disengagement theory.
2. **b.** is the answer. (p. 643)

   a. This is a criticism of disengagement theory.

   c. Activity theorists emphasize the discontinuity of later life.

   d. By saying that all older people should be active, activity theorists ignore the diversity of late adulthood.
3. **d.** is the answer. (p. 643)

   a. & b. These answers describe disengagement theory.

   c. This answer pertains to activity theory.
4. **c.** is the answer. (p. 644)

   a. In fact, the theories are based on extensive empirical research.

   b. & d. The text does not indicate that this period of life is as fundamentally different from other periods as these answers suggest.
5. **d.** is the answer. (p. 648)
6. **b.** is the answer. (p. 647)
7. **b.** is the answer. (p. 652)

   a. Elderhostel is an educational program for older adults.

   c. & d. These service organizations affect a much smaller percentage of the elderly.
8. **c.** is the answer. (p. 655)
9. **d.** is the answer. (p. 654)
10. **a.** is the answer. (p. 657)

    b., c., & d. The importance of these factors varies from one older adult to another.
11. **c.** is the answer. (p. 659)

    a. In fact, such communities tend to *surround* the older adult with friends.

    b. & d. Age-segregated communities are *not* nursing homes, in which these issues might arise.
12. **a.** is the answer. (p. 660)

    b. & c. The longer a couple has been married, the *less* likely they are to have frequent disagreements or feel that the relationship is not equitable.
13. **b.** is the answer. (p. 663)
14. **c.** is the answer. Many nations spend substantial money on services for the elderly. (pp. 665–666)

    a. As more people reach old age, the absolute numbers of frail individuals will increase.

    b. Such research neglects the study of diseases that are nonfatal, yet disabling.

    d. Services are relatively scarce in rural areas, where a large number of elderly people reside.
15. **a.** is the answer. (p. 674)

Matching Items

1. e (p. 642)	5. i (p. 652)	8. f (p. 665)
2. h (p. 643)	6. a (p. 671)	9. d (p. 659)
3. j (p. 643)	7. c (p. 665)	10. b (p. 650)
4. g (p. 648)		

CHALLENGE TEST

1. **c.** is the answer. (p. 645)
2. **a.** is the answer. (p. 642)

   b. Continuity theorists maintain that older adults cope with aging in much the same ways as when they were younger.

   c. Activity theorists stress the need for older adults to find new involvements to replace roles lost with retirement.

   d. This theory was not discussed.
3. **b.** is the answer. This is because activity theory equates well-being in late adulthood with remaining active. (p. 643)

4. **a.** is the answer. According to disengagement theory, older adults become more passive and uninvolved as they grow older. (p. 642)

   d. This theory of aging was not discussed.

5. **b.** is the answer. (p. 647)

   a. Retirement almost always requires some period of adjustment.

   d. There is much evidence that *conflicts* with disengagement theory.

6. **d.** is the answer. (p. 651)

   a. Middle-aged adults tend to be more focused on individual and family needs.

   b. & c. The text does not suggest that there is a gender difference in older adults' sense of obligation to serve others.

7. **c.** is the answer. (p. 652)

8. **a.** is the answer. (p. 662)

   b. In fact, the number of frail elderly is increasing.

   c. People are retiring earlier today than ever before.

   d. Older adults have always had a strong volunteer spirit.

9. **c.** is the answer. (p. 658)

   a. Although this is particularly true for ethnic minorities, it is certainly not limited to them.

   b. There is no evidence that this is so.

   d. On the contrary, there is substantial empirical support for this finding.

10. **c.** is the answer. (p. 663)

    a. & b. At every age, women have larger social circles, and more intimate relationships with their friends, than men.

    d. Widows tend to be more involved in friendship networks than married women.

11. **b.** is the answer. African-American grandmothers who are under age 40 or so often feel pressured to provide care for a new grandchild they were not eager for in the first place. (p. 656)

    c. & d. There is no reason to believe there would be a cohort effect in their networks of social support.

12. **b.** is the answer. (p. 670)

13. **c.** is the answer. (p. 671)

    a. Although many profit-making nursing homes are quite good, congregate care is often a better choice since it is less likely to promote dependence in residents.

    b. This is often the *worst* type of facility.

    d. This is an educational program for the elderly.

14. **b.** is the answer. (p. 665)

15. **c.** is the answer. (p. 674)

    a. This is not the crisis of late adulthood in Erikson's theory.

    b. & d. These are not crises in Erikson's theory.

KEY TERMS

1. The **disengagement theory** of aging maintains that, in old age, the individual and society mutually withdraw from each other. (p. 642)
2. The **activity theory** of aging maintains that older people need to substitute new involvements and new friends for the roles that they lose with retirement, relocation, and so forth. (p. 643)
3. According to the **continuity theory** of aging, each person copes with late adulthood in much the same way that he or she coped with earlier periods of life. (p. 643)
4. **Generational equity** refers to equal contributions from, and fair benefits for, each generation. (p. 648)
5. **Elderhostel** is a rapidly growing program in which older people live on college campuses and take special classes, usually during college vacation periods. (p. 650)
6. The **American Association of Retired Persons (AARP)** is the major United States organization affecting the elderly and the largest organized interest group in America. (p. 652)
7. **Filial obligation** is the sense of duty people feel to protect and care for their aging parents. (p. 652)
8. The **social convoy** is the network of people with whom we establish meaningful relationships as we travel through life. (p. 657)
9. Approximately ten percent of the elderly move into **planned retirement communities** where all residents must be over a certain age. (p. 658)
10. Approximately 27 percent of elderly Americans live in **naturally occurring retirement communities (NORCs)**, which are neighborhoods or apartment complexes where more than half the residents are elderly. (p. 659)
11. The **frail elderly** are the minority of older adults who are physically infirm, very ill, or cognitively impaired. (p. 665)
12. In determining frailty, gerontologists often refer to the **activities of daily life (ADLs)**, which comprise five tasks: eating, bathing, toileting, walking, and dressing. (p. 665)

13. The **instrumental activities of daily life (IADLs)** are actions that require some intellectual competence and forethought, such as shopping for food, paying bills, and taking medication. (p. 665)
14. The **Older Americans Act**, which was passed by the American Congress in 1965, provides every older person, regardless of income, a wealth of benefits and social services. (p. 666)
15. In **congregate care** a group of older people live together with some help from outside personnel. (p. 671)
16. **Elder maltreatment**, or mistreatment of the frail elderly, ranges from direct physical attacks to ongoing emotional neglect. (p. 671)
17. In Erikson's theory, the crisis of late adulthood is that of **integrity versus despair**, in which people look upon their lives with pride and contentment (integrity), or feel that they have failed (despair). (p. 674)

EPILOGUE

Death and Dying

Chapter Overview

Death marks the close of the life span—a close individuals must come to terms with both for themselves and their loved ones. Indeed, an understanding and acceptance of death is crucial if life is to be lived to the fullest.

The first section provides an historical perspective on death and dying, noting that the meanings of death, and the reactions that death prompts, vary from individual to individual, and according to their historical and cultural context. In twentieth-century Western culture, for example, death has largely been removed from everyday life and transferred to the professional sphere.

The second section presents various research findings on death and dying, with particular emphasis on the pioneering work of Elizabeth Kübler-Ross. In addition to underscoring the problems created by our culture's denial of death, this research describes the emotions experienced by those who are actually on the brink of death. Also discussed are several developments that, as part of a recent shift from denial to greater acceptance, may help the terminally ill patient to die "a good death." The process of recovery for those who have lost a loved one is the subject of the final section.

NOTE: Answer guidelines for all Epilogue questions begin on page 394.

Guided Study

The text chapter should be studied one section at a time. Before you read, preview each section by skimming it, noting headings and boldface items. Then read the appropriate section objectives from the following outline. Keep these objectives in mind and, as you read the chapter section, search for the information that will enable you to meet each objective. Once you have finished a section, write out answers for its objectives.

Death in Context (pp. 679–680)

1. Describe some cultural variations in how death is viewed and treated.

2. Explain how the treatment of death in twentieth-century North America and Western Europe differs from the treatment of death throughout most of history.

Research on Death and Dying (pp. 681–687)

3. Describe the development of the field of thanatology.

4. Briefly describe the emotions typical of each of Kübler-Ross's stages of dying.

5. Evaluate Kübler-Ross's stages of dying in light of more recent research and discuss age-related differences in the conceptualization of death.

6. Explain what is meant by a "good death" and why such a death is difficult to ensure today.

7. Suggest some measures the individual and his or her family can take to ensure that he or she dies a good death.

8. (A Closer Look) Explain what a hospice is and identify both the advantages and disadvantages of hospices.

Bereavement (pp. 688–691)

9. Describe the functions of mourning and list the various stages of the mourning process.

10. Discuss the ways in which the emotional impact of an expected death might differ from that of an unexpected death; suggest steps that can be taken in helping someone to recover from bereavement.

Chapter Review

When you have finished reading the chapter, work through the material that follows to review it. Complete the sentences and answer the questions. As you proceed, evaluate your performance for each section by consulting the answers on page 394. Do not continue with the next section until you understand each answer. If you need to, review or reread the appropriate section in the textbook before continuing.

Death in Context (pp. 679–680)

1. The specific meanings that are attached to death vary from individual to individual and according to their ________________ and ________________ context.

2. In most ________________ traditions, elders take on an important new status through death.
3. In many ________________ nations, death affirms faith in Allah and caring for the dying is a holy reminder of mortality.
4. In ________________, helping the dying to relinquish their ties to this world and prepare for the next is considered an obligation for the immediate family.
5. Throughout most of Western history, death ________________ (was accepted as a familiar event/was withdrawn from everyday life.)
6. During the twentieth century, in ________________ ________________ and ________________ ________________, the denial of death became commonplace, even permeating the ________________ profession. Consequently, before the end of biological life the dying, in effect, experience a(n) ________________ death.

Research on Death and Dying (pp. 681–687)

7. A major factor in the recent shift to a more accepting view of death was the pioneering work of ________________.
8. In her interviews with the dying, Kübler-Ross quickly discovered the importance of ________________ (concealing/not concealing) information about their condition.
9. The study of death is called ________________.
10. Kübler-Ross's research led her to propose that the dying go through ________________ (how many?) emotional stages. The first is ________________, in which the dying refuse to believe that their condition is terminal.
11. The second stage of dying is ________________ directed toward others. The third stage is ________________, in which a person tries to negotiate away death.
12. The fourth stage is ________________, during which the person mourns his or her impending death. The final stage is ________________, in which death is understood as the last stage of this life.
13. Other researchers typically ________________ (have/have not) found the same five stages of dying occurring in sequence. More typically, the reaction depends on the ________________ of the death.
14. The age of the dying person ________________ (does/does not) significantly affect his or her emotional response to death.

Briefly describe the typical reactions of the following individuals to their own impending death:

a young child: ________________

an adolescent: ________________

a young adult: ________________

a middle-aged adult: ________________

an older adult: ________________

15. Kübler-Ross's stages make feelings about death much more ________________ and ________________ than they actually are.

Describe a "good death."

16. Because of modern medical techniques, a swift and peaceful death is ________________ (more/less) difficult to ensure.
17. The medical profession and the general public are becoming increasingly aware of the ________________ (desirability/undesirability) of using extraordinary measures that pro-

long life. An alternative to hospital care for the terminally ill is the ______________.

18. (A Closer Look) The hospice was conceived in response to the ______________ of the typical hospital death.

19. (A Closer Look) Hospice patients are assigned a(n) ______________ ______________ ______________, who is present much of the time and is responsible for some of the routine care.

20. (A Closer Look) The hospice concept ______________ (is/is not) universally accepted.

State several criticisms of hospice care.

21. There is a growing consensus that the ultimate authority regarding what measures are to be used in terminal cases should be the ______________.

22. Today, many people make a(n) ______________ ______________, a document that indicates what kind of medical intervention they want should they become terminally ill.

23. Mercifully allowing a person to die by not doing something that might extend life is called ______________ ______________.

Doctors and nurses ______________ (agree/disagree) on the distinction between ordinary *and* extraordinary measures to prolong death.

24. Especially controversial are issues concerning ______________ ______________, in which someone provides the means for a person to end his or her life, and ______________ ______________, in which someone intentionally acts to terminate the life of a suffering person.

25. In 1993, the legislature in the ______________ passed a law guaranteeing that doctors would not be prosecuted for assisting suicide if they followed several guidelines. A major problem with such an orderly approach is that doctors can ______________ (usually/rarely) predict, with complete accuracy, the course of any illness or the consequences of measures to prevent, postpone, or hasten death.

26. In countries such as the ______________ ______________, where the cost of medical interventions on the terminally ill is usually borne by ______________ insurance, greater emphasis is placed on procedures that often prolong suffering in the dying.

Bereavement (pp. 688–691)

27. The various ways of expressing grief at the death of a loved one are collectively known as ______________.

28. Before the mid-twentieth century, American mourners were encouraged to ______________ (express their emotions openly and fully/"bear up" and hold their grief back).

29. In recent times, the bereft receive less ______________ than ______________.

Explain how many psychologists and psychiatrists feel about the trend toward the stifling of mourning.

30. In instances of ______________, the bereaved leave intact the belongings of the dead.

31. The mourning process typically begins with ______________, when some people seem calm and rational and others seem dazed and distant.

32. The second phase is an intense ______________ to be with the deceased.

33. The third phase of mourning is ______________ and ______________, often characterized by irrational anger and confused thinking.

34. In the final phase of mourning, called ________________, the death is put into perspective.

List several cultural practices that aid recovery from mourning.

35. The phases of mourning ________________ (do/do not) follow a predictable schedule.

36. Even after recovery, the bereft may experience ________________ ________________ and suddenly be overwhelmed once more with grief.

37. Deaths that change the ________________ ________________ are particularly likely to be grievous.

38. Because this age group is likely to experience the loss of a number of friends and relatives in a fairly short span of time, the ________________ are particularly vulnerable to ________________ ________________.

39. Generally speaking, death that is expected ________________ (is/is not) easier to cope with.

40. Sometimes the diagnosis of terminal illness allows a period of ________________ ________________, when the dying person and loved ones share their affection for each other.

41. Generally speaking, deaths that are unexpected, violent, and sudden are ________________ (more/no more) difficult to bear.

42. List two steps that others can follow to help a bereaved person.

a. ________________

b. ________________

43. A frequent theme of those who work with the bereaved is the value of a(n) ________________ ________________.

Progress Test 1

Circle your answers to the following questions and check them with the answers on page 395. If your answer is incorrect, read the explanation for why it is incorrect and then consult the appropriate pages of the text (in parentheses following the correct answer).

Multiple-Choice Questions

1. Throughout most of Western history:
   a. death was withdrawn from daily life and therefore more feared.
   b. death was more accepted as a natural event than it is today.
   c. the bereaved were discouraged from expressing their emotions openly.
   d. a. and c. are both true.

2. Kübler-Ross found that doctors often chose not to inform terminally ill patients of their condition and sometimes concealed the information from families as well. Such an approach would tend to:
   a. minimize possibilities for anticipatory grief.
   b. increase bereavement overload.
   c. discourage anniversary reactions.
   d. maximize possibilities for passive euthanasia.

3. Kübler-Ross's primary contribution was to:
   a. open the first hospice, thus initiating the hospice movement.
   b. show how the emotions of the dying occur in a series of clear-cut stages.
   c. initiate a shift away from the denial of death toward a more accepting view.
   d. show the correlation between people's conceptualization of death and their developmental stage.

4. Kübler-Ross's stages of dying are, in order:
   a. anger, denial, bargaining, depression, acceptance.
   b. depression, anger, denial, bargaining, acceptance.
   c. denial, anger, bargaining, depression, acceptance.
   d. bargaining, denial, anger, acceptance, depression.

5. Recent research regarding the emotions of terminally ill patients has found that:
   a. all patients reach the stage of acceptance.
   b. emotional stages generally follow one another in an orderly sequence.
   c. age has an important effect on emotions.
   d. most experience depression.

6. A "good death" is one in which:
   a. the individual has put his or her affairs in order.
   b. the individual has reached some acceptance of death.
   c. death is swift and peaceful.
   d. all of the above occur.

7. *Hospice* is best defined as:
   a. a document that indicates what kind of medical intervention a terminally ill person wants.
   b. mercifully allowing a person to die by not doing something that might extend life.
   c. an alternative to hospital care for the terminally ill.
   d. any assisted suicide.

8. The problems associated with passive euthanasia include all of the following *except*:
   a. most health professionals object to the concept of passive euthanasia.
   b. predictions regarding the course of an illness are inexact.
   c. the quality of life of the dying individual is impossible to measure objectively.
   d. dying patients are often not in any condition to make a rational decision.

9. When a person intentionally acts to terminate the life of a suffering person, ________ has occurred.
   a. passive euthanasia
   b. active euthanasia
   c. an assisted suicide
   d. mummification

10. All of the following may be considered normal responses in the bereavement process *except*:
    a. mummification.
    b. anniversary reactions.
    c. bereavement overload.
    d. anticipatory grief.

11. An important factor in how long it takes a mourner to recover is:
    a. how well the particular culture provides for his or her needs.
    b. the presence of traditional practices that keep the bereaved from feeling isolated.
    c. memorial customs that ease the transition back to normal life.
    d. all of the above.

12. Which of the following is true of the phases of mourning?
    a. They occur in a more predictable sequence than the stages of dying.
    b. They are no more predictable than the stages of dying.
    c. They are more predictable in people who are deeply religious.
    d. a. and c. are both true.

13. Sudden surges of sadness felt by the bereaved on holidays, birthdays, or the date of the death are referred to as:
    a. anticipatory grief.
    b. anniversary reactions.
    c. bereavement overload.
    d. mummification.

14. The elderly are particularly vulnerable to bereavement overload because:
    a. they are likely to experience the loss of a number of friends and relatives in a fairly short span of time.
    b. cognitive decline often distorts their thinking.
    c. they also are more susceptible to anniversary reactions.
    d. of all of the above reasons.

15. (A Closer Look) Criticisms made against hospices include all of the following *except*:
    a. the number of patients served is limited.
    b. in some cases a life is being ended that could have been prolonged.
    c. burn-out and the rapid growth of hospices might limit the number of competent hospice workers.
    d. the patient is needlessly isolated from family and friends.

True or False Items

Write *true* or *false* on the line in front of each statement.

________ 1. The terminally ill generally want to know about and discuss their condition.

________ 2. Subsequent research has confirmed the accuracy of Kübler-Ross's findings regarding the five stages of dying.

________ 3. Modern life-prolonging medical technologies have tended to make dying a "good death" more difficult and less likely to occur.

________ 4. Following the death of a loved one, the bereaved can best ensure their psychological health and well-being by increasing their social contacts and the number of activities in which they are involved.

________ 5. Mourning is generally characterized by an initial period of shock.

________ 6. Anniversary reactions are a sign that the bereaved person has not yet recovered from his or her grief.

_______ 7. Bereavement overload occurs when an individual has not openly expressed his or her grief and as a result becomes overwhelmed by it.

_______ 8. (A Closer Look) Hospices administer pain-killing medication but do not make use of artificial life-support systems.

_______ 9. In the long run, the bereavement process may have a beneficial effect on the individual.

_______ 10. (A Closer Look) There is general consensus that hospice care is a good alternative to hospital care for the dying.

Progress Test 2

Progress Test 2 should be completed during a final chapter review. Answer the following questions after you thoroughly understand the correct answers for the Chapter Review and Progress Test 1.

Multiple-Choice Questions

1. In our society, death has generally become:
   a. far less painful for the dying individual.
   b. emotionally far less painful for the bereaved.
   c. withdrawn from daily life and so more feared.
   d. more accepted as a natural end of the life span.

2. According to the text, a major factor in the recent shift to a more accepting view of death was the:
   a. hospice movement.
   b. work of Kübler-Ross.
   c. legalization of passive euthanasia.
   d. legalization of thanatology.

3. Thanatology is best defined as the:
   a. study of death.
   b. movement toward ensuring a "good death" for the terminally ill.
   c. tendency of Western cultures to deny death.
   d. final stage of bereavement.

4. What often appears to be depression in the dying, in many cases, may be:
   a. resignation to one's fate.
   b. a side effect of pain killers or other drugs.
   c. an indication that the person is denying his or her condition.
   d. any of the above.

5. Recent research reveals that Kübler-Ross's stages of dying:
   a. occur in sequence in virtually all terminally ill patients.
   b. do not occur in hospice residents.
   c. are typical only in Western cultures.
   d. make feelings about death seem much more predictable and universal than they actually are.

6. Today, a "good death" is difficult to ensure because:
   a. modern medicine can sustain life beyond its time.
   b. many doctors view death as an enemy to be fended off at all costs.
   c. the dying often are in discomfort or outright pain because analgesic medications are underprescribed.
   d. of all of the above reasons.

7. Living wills are an attempt to:
   a. make sure that passive euthanasia will not be used in individual cases.
   b. specify the extent of medical treatment desired in the event of terminal illness.
   c. specify conditions for the use of active euthanasia.
   d. ensure that death will occur at home rather than in a hospital.

8. The decisions involved in both passive and active euthanasia are almost always difficult because:
   a. it is impossible for most people to make a living will so specific that it can fully guide actions to be taken by others in the future.
   b. even when a living will exists, it is difficult for people to know what procedures will be the most humane for the dying person.
   c. some people are reluctant to sign a living will because they are suspicious that they will receive no care when they become ill.
   d. of all of the above reasons.

9. In the modern Western world:
   a. open mourning is encouraged.
   b. psychologists have discovered that the best thing the bereaved can do is to keep busy and quickly get on with life.
   c. mourning seems to have gone out of fashion.
   d. mummification has become an accepted form of mourning.

10. The phenomenon in which a bereaved person leaves intact the belongings of the person mourned is known as:
    a. passive euthanasia.
    b. mummification.
    c. bereavement overload.
    d. anticipatory grief.

11. Mummification is most likely to occur when:
   a. the bereaved person has not openly expressed his or her grief.
   b. the dying process was long and difficult.
   c. the mourner has deep feelings of guilt about the dead person.
   d. societies have a formal mourning period.

12. In order, the typical stages of the mourning process are:
   a. despair, depression, longing, recovery.
   b. depression, recovery, longing.
   c. longing, depression, recovery.
   d. shock, longing, depression and despair, recovery.

13. The period during which the dying person and the mourners can cry together and share their affection for each other is referred to as:
   a. bereavement overload.
   b. an anniversary reaction.
   c. anticipatory grief.
   d. mummification.

14. When subsequent deaths occur before the individual has finished mourning a first death, there is a possibility of:
   a. an anniversary reaction.
   b. anticipatory grief.
   c. bereavement overload.
   d. all of the above.

15. Death of a loved one is most difficult to bear when:
   a. the death is a long, protracted one.
   b. it is sudden and violent.
   c. a period of anticipatory grief has already elapsed.
   d. there are no other mourners.

Matching Items

Match each term or concept with its corresponding description or definition.

Terms or Concepts

_______ 1. thanatology
_______ 2. hospice
_______ 3. living will
_______ 4. passive euthanasia
_______ 5. active euthanasia
_______ 6. assisted suicide
_______ 7. mummification
_______ 8. anniversary reactions
_______ 9. bereavement overload
_______ 10. anticipatory grief

Definitions or Descriptions

a. leaving the belongings of deceased person intact
b. an alternative to hospital care for the terminally ill
c. mourning with a terminally ill patient before his or her death
d. mercifully not doing something that will extend the life of a terminally ill patient
e. a document expressing a person's wishes for treatment should he or she become terminally ill and incapable of making such decisions
f. providing the means for a terminally ill patient to end his or her life
g. the study of death
h. experiencing the loss of a loved one before recovery from the mourning of another
i. intentionally taking an action to end the life of a terminally ill patient
j. a bereaved person's tendency to reexperience depression and longing on birthdays or other important dates related to the deceased person

Challenge Test

Answer these questions the day before an exam as a final check on your understanding of the chapter's terms and concepts.

1. Among my people, elders take on an important new status through death as they join the ancestors who watch over our entire village. I am:
   a. African.
   b. Muslim.
   c. Hindu.
   d. Native American.

2. Among my people, family members have an obligation to help the dying to relinquish their ties to this world and prepare for the next. I am:
   a. African.
   b. Muslim.
   c. Hindu.
   d. Native American.

3. The terminally ill patient who promises to live a better life if spared from dying is probably in which of Kübler-Ross's stages?
   a. denial
   b. anger
   c. depression
   d. bargaining

4. The terminally ill patient who is convinced his laboratory tests must be wrong is probably in which of Kübler-Ross's stages?
   a. denial
   b. anger
   c. depression
   d. bargaining

5. A terminally ill school-age child is likely to:
   a. fear death primarily because it means being separated from family members.
   b. become upset about his or her appearance.
   c. become absorbed with learning the facts about his or her illness.
   d. be angry at the idea that, just as life is about to begin, it must end.

6. A terminally ill adolescent is likely to:
   a. fear death primarily because it means being separated from family members.
   b. become upset about his or her appearance.
   c. become absorbed with learning the facts about his or her illness.
   d. be angry at the idea that, just as life is about to begin, it must end.

7. Roger, who is middle-aged, is terminally ill. He is most likely to need:
   a. constant companionship.
   b. detailed information about the "mechanics" of dying.
   c. counseling to help overcome his anger at having his life cut short.
   d. reassurance that others will take over his obligations and responsibilities.

8. Dr. Welby writes the orders DNR (do not resuscitate) on her patient's chart. Evidently the patient has requested:
   a. a living will.
   b. passive euthanasia.
   c. active euthanasia.
   d. an assisted suicide.

9. Seeing his terminally ill father without hope and in excruciating pain, Carl provided the means for him to end his life. This is an example of:
   a. passive euthanasia.
   b. active euthanasia.
   c. an assisted suicide.
   d. an act that became legal in most countries in 1993.

10. The doctor who injects a terminally ill patient with a lethal drug is practicing:
    a. passive euthanasia.
    b. active euthanasia.
    c. an assisted suicide.
    d. an act that became legal in most countries in 1993.

11. Summarizing her presentation on the process of mourning, Rita states that most developmentalists view mourning as:
    a. an unnecessary and emotionally crippling process.
    b. a disruptive force in development.
    c. a necessary and healthy process.
    d. important for some but, not all, individuals.

12. Which of the following statements would probably be the most helpful to a grieving person?
    a. "Why don't you get out more and get back into the swing of things?"
    b. "You're tough; bear up!"
    c. "If you need someone to talk to, call me any time."
    d. "It must have been his or her time to die."

13. Harriet's husband Fred died two years ago. Although she finally accepted Fred's death after a normal period of mourning, Harriet becomes overwhelmed with sadness on holidays. Harriet's emotional reaction probably indicates that:
    a. she is unable to let go of Fred and should seek professional counseling.
    b. she needs to force herself to stop thinking about Fred.

c. she most likely never developed a sense of identity that was independent of her husband.
d. she is experiencing normal emotions, similar to those of other people who have lost a loved one.

14. Although Mary's husband Joe died several years ago, she has left intact his possessions and even airs out his suits and burns his pipe tobacco. Mary's behavior most likely indicates that:
a. Joe died unexpectedly.
b. Joe did not experience a "good death."
c. Mary never recovered from mourning Joe.
d. she is experiencing normal emotions.

15. Dr. Robinson is about to counsel her first terminally ill patient and his family. Research suggests that her most helpful strategy would be to:
a. keep most of the facts from both the patient and his family in order not to upset them.
b. be truthful to the patient but not his family.
c. be truthful to the family only, and swear them to secrecy.
d. honestly inform both the patient and his family.

Key Terms

Using your own words, write a brief definition or explanation of each of the following terms on a separate piece of paper.

1. thanatology
2. hospice
3. living will
4. passive euthanasia
5. assisted suicide
6. active euthanasia
7. mourning
8. mummification
9. anniversary reactions
10. bereavement overload
11. anticipatory grief

ANSWERS

CHAPTER REVIEW

1. historical; cultural
2. African
3. Muslim
4. Hinduism
5. was accepted as a familiar event
6. North America; Western Europe; medical; social
7. Elizabeth Kübler-Ross
8. not concealing
9. thanatology
10. five; denial
11. anger; bargaining
12. depression; acceptance
13. have not; context
14. does

Young children, who may not understand the concept of death, are usually upset because it suggests being separated from those they love.

Because they tend to focus on the quality of present life, *adolescents* may primarily be concerned with the effect of their condition on their appearance and social relationships.

Young adults often feel rage and depression at the idea that, just as life is about to begin in earnest, it must end.

For *middle-aged adults,* death is an interruption of important obligations and responsibilities.

An *older adult*'s feelings about dying depend on the particular situation. If one's spouse has already died, for example, acceptance of death is comparatively easy.

15. predictable; universal

A "good death" is one that is swift, peaceful, and occurs after a person has put his or her affairs in order, reached some spiritual understanding of life and an acceptance of death, and said goodbye to loved ones.

16. more
17. undesirability; hospice
18. dehumanization
19. lay primary caregiver
20. is not

The fact that hospice patients must be diagnosed as terminally ill and give up all hope of recovery severely limits the number of participants. Some critics fear that those who enter hospices may be giving in to death prematurely. Rapid growth of hospice care might outstrip the number of qualified health-care workers available. Many parts of the world have no hospices available.

21. patient
22. living will

23. passive euthanasia; disagree
24. assisted suicide; active euthanasia
25. Netherlands; rarely
26. United States; private
27. mourning
28. express their emotions openly and fully
29. consoling; advising

Many warn that if grief is not expressed openly, its indirect manifestations may cripple a person's life.

30. mummification
31. shock
22. longing
33. depression; despair
34. recovery

Among these practices are meaningful rituals that keep the bereaved from feeling isolated; the encouragement and opportunity to grieve openly; memorial customs that ease the transition back to normal life; emotional support and companionship; and practical help to overcome problems that result from the death.

35. do not
36. anniversary reactions
37. generational line
38. elderly; bereavement overload
39. is
40. anticipatory grief
41. more
42. **a.** Be aware that powerful and complicated emotions are likely.
    b. Understand that bereavement is often a lengthy process.
43. intimate, caring relationship

PROGRESS TEST 1

Multiple-Choice Questions

1. **b.** is the answer. (p. 680)
2. **a.** is the answer. (pp. 681, 690)
   b. Bereavement overload occurs when an individual who is still mourning one death experiences the death of another loved one.
   c. In an anniversary reaction, a bereaved person who has recovered from mourning may, on birthdays, holidays, or the anniversary of the death, suddenly reexperience depression and longing.
   d. Passive euthanasia is mercifully allowing a person to die by not doing something that might extend his or her life.
3. **c.** is the answer. (p. 681)
   a. Cecily Saunders opened the first hospice.
   b. Subsequent research has shown this to be untrue.
   d. This correlation stems from research conducted by others investigating Kübler-Ross's theory.
4. **c.** is the answer. (pp. 681–682)
5. **c.** is the answer. (p. 682)
6. **d.** is the answer. (p. 683)
7. **c.** is the answer. (p. 684)
   a. This is a living will.
   b. This is passive euthanasia.
8. **a.** is the answer. Almost everyone agrees that, under appropriate circumstances, passive euthanasia is merciful. (p. 686)
9. **b.** is the answer. (p. 686)
   a. Passive euthanasia is mercifully allowing a person to die by *not* doing something that might extend his or her life.
   c. In assisted suicide, someone provides the means for a person to end his or her life.
   d. Mummification occurs when a bereaved person leaves the belongings of the deceased just as they were during the person's lifetime.
10. **a.** is the answer. (p. 688)
11. **d.** is the answer. (p. 689)
12. **b.** is the answer. (p. 689)
    c. The text does not discuss the relationship between religious belief and the phases of mourning.
13. **b.** is the answer. (p. 689)
    a. This is when a terminally ill person and his or her loved ones have a chance to share affection and mourn together before the death occurs.
    c. This is when a person loses a loved one while still mourning the death of another.
    d. This is when a bereaved person leaves the belongings of the deceased just as they were during the person's lifetime.
14. **a.** is the answer. (p. 690)
    b. & c. These issues are not implicated in bereavement overload.
15. **d.** is the answer. A central feature of hospices is that the dying are *not* isolated from loved ones, as they might be in a hospital. (p. 685)

True or False Items

1. T (p. 681)

2. F Subsequent research has not confirmed Kübler-Ross's findings that the emotions of an individual faced with death occur in orderly stages. (p. 682)
3. T (p. 683)
4. F The psychological well-being of the bereaved depends above all on their being able to openly express their grief. (p. 688)
5. T (p. 688)
6. F Anniversary reactions are normal and can be expected even among the bereaved who have recovered. (p. 689)
7. F Bereavement overload occurs when an individual who is still mourning one death experiences the death of another loved one. (p. 690)
8. T (p. 685)
9. T (p. 691)
10. F Hospice care remains a controversial subject. (p. 685)

PROGRESS TEST 2

Multiple-Choice Questions

1. **c.** is the answer. (p. 680)
2. **b.** is the answer. (p. 681)

   c. The impact of passive euthanasia on attitudes toward death was not discussed in the text. Moreover, this procedure has not been legalized.

   d. Thanatology is the study of death.
3. **a.** is the answer. (p. 681)
4. **b.** is the answer. (p. 682)
5. **d.** is the answer. (p. 682)

   b. & c. There is no evidence that hospice residents experience different emotional stages than others who are dying, or that these stages are a product of Western culture.
6. **d.** is the answer. (pp. 683–684)
7. **b.** is the answer. (p. 684)
8. **d.** is the answer. (p. 687)
9. **c.** is the answer. (p. 688)

   b. The psychological well-being of the bereaved depends above all on their being able to openly express their grief.

   d. Mummification is *not* considered a normal form of mourning.
10. **b.** is the answer. (p. 688)

    a. Passive euthanasia is mercifully allowing a person to die by not doing something that might extend his or her life.

    c. Bereavement overload occurs when an individual who is still mourning one death experiences the death of another loved one.

    d. With anticipatory grief, a terminally ill person and his or her loved ones have an opportunity to share affection and mourn together before the death actually occurs.
11. **a.** is the answer. (p. 688)

    d. Such rituals tend to *prevent* mummification and other signs of incomplete recovery.
12. **d.** is the answer. (p. 688)
13. **c.** is the answer. (p. 690)
14. **c.** is the answer. (p. 690)
15. **b.** is the answer. (p. 690)

    a. & c. In such situations, death is expected and generally easier to bear.

    d. This issue was not discussed.

Matching Items

1. g (p. 681)
2. b (p. 684)
3. e (p. 684)
4. d (p. 686)
5. i (p. 686)
6. f (p. 686)
7. a (p. 688)
8. j (p. 689)
9. h (p. 690)
10. c (p. 690)

CHALLENGE TEST

1. **a.** is the answer. (p. 679)

   b. The text notes that in many Muslim nations, death serves to affirm faith in Allah.

   d. The text does not discuss the way in which Native Americans conceptualize death.
2. **c.** is the answer. (p. 680)
3. **d.** is the answer. (pp. 681–682)

   a. People in this stage refuse to believe that their condition is terminal.

   b. In this stage the dying person directs anger at others for his or her condition.

   c. In this stage the dying person mourns his or her own impending death.
4. **a.** is the answer. (p. 681)
5. **c.** is the answer. (p. 682)

   a., b., & d. These are more typical of young children, adolescents, and young adults, respectively.
6. **b.** is the answer. (p. 682)
7. **d.** is the answer. (p. 682)
8. **b.** is the answer. (p. 686)

   a. A living will is a document expressing how a person wishes to be cared for should he or she become terminally ill.

   c. This is when a person *intentionally acts* to end another's life.

d. In this situation, a person provides the means for another to take his or her own life.

9. **c.** is the answer. (p. 686)
10. **b.** is the answer. (p. 686)
11. **c.** is the answer. (p. 688)
12. **c.** is the answer. (p. 690)
    a., b., & d. These statements discourage the bereaved person from mourning.
13. **d.** is the answer. Harriet is experiencing an anniversary reaction. (p. 689)
14. **c.** is the answer. Mary is mummifying her dead husband. (p. 688)
15. **d.** is the answer. (p. 681)

KEY TERMS

1. **Thanatology** is the study of death. (p. 681)
2. The **hospice** is a facility that allows terminally ill patients to die with dignity and without undue pain. (p. 684)
3. A **living will** is a document that indicates what kind of medical intervention a person wants should he or she become terminally ill and incapable of expressing his or her wishes. (p. 684)
4. **Passive euthanasia** is mercifully allowing a person to die by not doing something that might extend his or her life. (p. 686)
5. An **assisted suicide** is one in which someone provides the means for a person to end his or her life. (p. 686)
6. **Active euthanasia** is when someone intentionally acts to terminate the life of a suffering person. (p. 686)
7. **Mourning** refers to all the ways of expressing grief at the death of a loved one. (p. 688)
8. **Mummification** occurs when a bereaved person leaves the belongings of the deceased just as they were during the person's lifetime and even continues to perform certain accustomed daily rituals involving these belongings. (p. 688)
9. In **anniversary reactions** a bereaved person who has recovered from mourning may, on birthdays, holidays, or the anniversary of the death, suddenly reexperience depression and longing. (p. 689)
10. The elderly are particularly vulnerable to **bereavement overload,** which occurs when an individual who is still mourning one death experiences the death of another loved one. (p. 690)
11. When a death is expected, loved ones may experience a period of **anticipatory grief,** in which they can show the dying person both their sorrow and their affection. (p. 690)